Lecture Notes in Computer Science   11865

More information about this series at http://www.springer.com/series/7407

Maurice H. ter Beek · Alessandro Fantechi ·
Laura Semini (Eds.)

From Software Engineering to Formal Methods and Tools, and Back

Essays Dedicated to Stefania Gnesi
on the Occasion of Her 65th Birthday

 Springer

Editors
Maurice H. ter Beek 🄳
Consiglio Nazionale delle Ricerche
Pisa, Italy

Alessandro Fantechi 🄳
Università degli Studi di Firenze
Florence, Italy

Laura Semini 🄳
Università di Pisa
Pisa, Italy

ISSN 0302-9743   ISSN 1611-3349   (electronic)
Lecture Notes in Computer Science
ISBN 978-3-030-30984-8   ISBN 978-3-030-30985-5   (eBook)
https://doi.org/10.1007/978-3-030-30985-5

LNCS Sublibrary: SL1 – Theoretical Computer Science and General Issues

This Springer imprint is published by the registered company Springer Nature Switzerland AG
The registered company address is: Gewerbestrasse 11, 6330 Cham, Switzerland

Stefania Gnesi

Preface

This Festschrift contains 32 contributions by collaborators, colleagues, and friends of Stefania Gnesi to celebrate her 65th birthday.

The Festschrift consists of eight sections, seven of which reflect the main research areas to which Stefania has contributed. Following a survey of Stefania's legacy in research and a homage by her thesis supervisor, these seven sections are ordered according to Stefania's life cycle in research, *from software engineering to formal methods and tools, and back*:

- Software Engineering
- Formal Methods and Tools
- Requirements Engineering
- Natural Language Processing
- Software Product Lines
- Formal Verification
- Applications

Each contribution was carefully reviewed by two readers. We would like to thank these colleagues, listed on the following page, for their assistance.

The Festschrift was presented to Stefania on October 8, 2019, during a one-day colloquium held in Porto, Portugal, preceding the 23rd Symposium on Formal Methods (FM 2019), as part of the 3rd World Congress on Formal Methods. We would like to thank José N. Oliveira, general chair of FM 2019, and his team for the organization of this colloquium, internally known as secret project 'X'.

Finally, we would like to thank Springer, and in particular Alfred Hofmann, for agreeing to publish this Festschrift and we acknowledge the support from EasyChair for assisting us in managing the complete process from submissions to this volume.

21 July 2019

Maurice H. ter Beek
Alessandro Fantechi
Laura Semini

Organization

Reviewers

Davide Basile
Maurice ter Beek
Cinzia Bernardeschi
Antonia Bertolino
Tommaso Bolognesi
Antonio Bucchiarone
Silvano Chiaradonna
Vincenzo Ciancia
Rocco De Nicola
Pierpaolo Degano
Felicita Di Giandomenico
Alessandro Fantechi
Alessio Ferrari
Gian Luigi Ferrari
José Fiadeiro
John Fitzgerald
Mario Fusani
Gabriele Lenzini
Letterio Galletta
Vincenzo Gervasi
Carlo Ghezzi
Patrick Heymans
Paola Inverardi
Giuseppe Lami
Cosimo Laneve

Diego Latella
Axel Legay
Antónia Lopes
Dino Mandrioli
Tiziana Margaria
Mieke Massink
Radu Mateescu
Franco Mazzanti
Pedro Merino
Luisa Mich
Marinella Petrocchi
Andrea Polini
Rosario Pugliese
Barbara Re
Matteo Rossi
Klaus Schmid
Laura Semini
Giorgio Spagnolo
Paola Spoletini
Bernhard Steffen
Francesco Tiezzi
Gianluca Trentanni
Andrea Vandin
Erik de Vink
Martin Wirsing

Contents

Formal Verification

Applications

The Legacy of Stefania Gnesi
From Software Engineering to Formal Methods and Tools, and Back

Maurice H. ter Beek[1]([⊠]) [iD], Alessandro Fantechi[2] [iD], and Laura Semini[3] [iD]

[1] ISTI–CNR, Pisa, Italy
`maurice.terbeek@isti.cnr.it`
[2] University of Florence, Florence, Italy
`alessandro.fantechi@unifi.it`
[3] University of Pisa, Pisa, Italy
`laura.semini@unipi.it`

1 The Early Years

Stefania Gnesi was born in Livorno in 1954. She studied Computer Science at the University of Pisa, where she graduated *summa cum laude* in 1978.

During her studies at ISI, which was the University of Pisa's Institute for Computer Science, a young discipline at that time, Stefania became interested in the continuing challenge associated with the production of software, namely to demonstrate that the developed software is actually doing what is expected to do, a challenge made harder in many cases by the fact that the expectations themselves are not precisely expressed. This has kept her busy ever since.

To face this challenge her very first steps in research, towards the end of her university studies, of purely theoretical nature, proved very valuable. In a publication in the *Journal of the ACM* [63] (not bad for a first journal paper!), resulting from her thesis under the supervision of Prof. Ugo Montanari, it is shown that finding the solution of a dynamic programming problem in the form of polyadic functional equations is equivalent to searching a minimal cost path in an and/or graph with monotone cost functions. An important computational application of this result is that the solution of a system of functional equations can always be reduced to the problem of searching a minimal cost solution tree in an and/or graph.

2 Software Engineering

After short periods as consultant in industry and teaching Mathematics and Computer Science in a secondary school, Stefania joined the Distributed Systems group of Norma Lijtmaer at the *Istituto di Elaborazione dell'Informazione* (IEI), a predecessor of the *Istituto di Scienza e Tecnologia dell'Informazione* (ISTI) of the Italian National Research Council (CNR). There she first became interested

© Springer Nature Switzerland AG 2019
M. H. ter Beek et al. (Eds.): Gnesi Festschrift, LNCS 11865, pp. 1–11, 2019.
https://doi.org/10.1007/978-3-030-30985-5_1

in bridging theory and practice in Software Engineering. Her participation in the European project *The Draft Formal Definition of ANSI/MIL-STD-1815A Ada* was centered around executing the Ada language's operational semantics by means of a logic programming approach, which resulted in a publication in the very first European Software Engineering Conference (ESEC 1987) [35].

In this context, it is worthwhile to recall that for over a decade, starting from the mid-nineties, Stefania taught Software Engineering courses at the Universities of Siena and Florence.

3   Formal Methods and Tools

Towards the end of the eighties, Stefania initiated her career-long involvement in Formal Methods and Tools. By participating in the EU project LOTOSPHERE, Stefania developed an increasing interest in temporal logic, and especially in the newly developed formal verification technique of model checking, the research area to which Stefania has contributed the most. First and foremost the study of the relations between process algebras and adequate (action-based) temporal logics, resulting in publications in the 2nd International Conference on Formal Description Techniques for Distributed Systems and Communication Protocols (FORTE 1989) [37] and in the 3rd International Workshop (now a Conference) on Computer Aided Verification (CAV 1991) [29], as well as in the 4th volume of the international journal on *Formal Methods in System Design* [40].

Again, her interest in bringing together theory and practice pushed her to co-organize, at the IEI–CNR in Pisa, in December 1992, an ERCIM Workshop on Theory and Practice in Verification, gathering several prominent researchers in the field from Europe and overseas. Also the first toolkit to which Stefania contributed, namely JACK (Just Another Concurrency Kit) [22], was developed during these years, resulting in a publication in the 1st International Workshop (now a Conference) on Tools and Algorithms for Construction and Analysis of Systems (TACAS 1995) [28]. A few years later, she was involved in one of the first applications of model checking to railway control systems in the context of an industrial collaboration, resulting in a publication in the International Conference on Dependable Systems and Networks (DSN 2000) [59], succeeded by other related experiences inside the EU project GUARDS [20], and by several other projects in the railway domain as well as in other domains, for example addressing mobile and service-oriented architectures and computing in the EU projects AGILE [1,48] and SENSORIA [10,38] that ran from 2002 to 2010.

Many of these and subsequent projects led to the introduction of a number of tailored model-checking tools. In fact, JACK was followed by toolsets like HAL, resulting in a publication in the 10th International Conference on Computer Aided Verification (CAV 1998) [49], SAM, witnessed by a publication in the International Workshop on Current Trends in Applied Formal Methods (FM-Trends 1998) [39], and the KandISTI family members FMC, CMC, UMC and VMC, resulting in publications in the *ACM Transactions on Software Engineering and Methodology* [38,48] and in the international journal *Science of Computer Programming* [9], among others.

4 Requirements Engineering/Natural Language Processing

In parallel to her interest in Formal Methods and Tools, and still closely look-ing at the early stages of software development, Stefania became interested in Requirements Engineering and in particular in the formalization of software requirements written in natural language. This triggered pioneering work on the automatic translation of behavioural requirements into her favourite temporal logic ACTL, by means of Natural Language Processing (NLP) techniques, at that time still in their infancy, as well as the application of such NLP tech-niques to support the semantic analysis of requirements specified as Use Cases. This research led to publications in the 4th International Workshop (now Work-ing Conference) on Requirements Engineering: Foundation for Software Quality (REFSQ 1998) [30] and in the 10th Anniversary IEEE Joint International Con-ference on Requirements Engineering (RE 2002) [36].

In the end, this turned out to be a prolific line of research, in particular when steered in the direction of using NLP techniques to evaluate the quality of requirements documents, in terms of absence of ambiguous requirements, vague requirements, underspecification, etc., as witnessed by yearly publications in the International Requirements Engineering Conference since 2015 [46] and in the international journals *Requirements Engineering* [47], *IEEE Software* [43] and *Empirical Software Engineering* [45]. The QuARS tool developed at ISTI–CNR, first presented in a special issue on Automated Tools for Requirements Engi-neering of the international journal on *Computer Systems Science & Engineer-ing* [65] and in the 23rd IEEE/ACM International Conference on Automated Software Engineering (ASE 2008) [23], was also used for this purpose inside the EU projects MODTRAIN/MODCONTROL [24]. QuARS continues to be in use, as witnessed by recent tool demos during the 2nd Workshop on Natural Language Processing for Requirements Engineering (NLP4RE 2019) [64] and the 23rd International Systems and Software Product Line Conference (SPLC 2019) [41].

5 Software Product Lines

A more recent scientific community to which Stefania has made several impor-tant contributions is that of Software Product Line Engineering (SPLE), a field of research that she joined through her involvement in the EUREKA project CAFÉ. Also in this area, she applied her knowledge and skills on formal mod-elling and analysis, this time to so-called product families. It all started with a contribution on testing in the 5th International Workshop on Software Product-Family Engineering (PFE 2003) [21], a predecessor of the annual Software Prod-uct Line Conference (SPLC), in which Stefania has published a paper almost every year this decade. She has been a member of the Steering Committee of SPLC from 2014 to 2018.

However, her main contributions to SPLE concern Modal Transition Systems with variability constraints to serve as behavioural variability models [4], with associated action-based and variability-aware temporal logics [2] and model-checking algorithms and tools [3], which culminated in a publication in the *Journal of Logical and Algebraic Methods in Programming* [13], followed recently by a study of the model's expressiveness in the international journal *Science of Computer Programming* [12]. Curiously, one of her most cited SPLC contributions is the toy example of a family of coffee machines, published in the 12th International Software Product Line Conference (SPLC 2008) [33], which was reused in numerous subsequent papers in the field. In Fig. 1, we reproduce the coffee vending machine example.

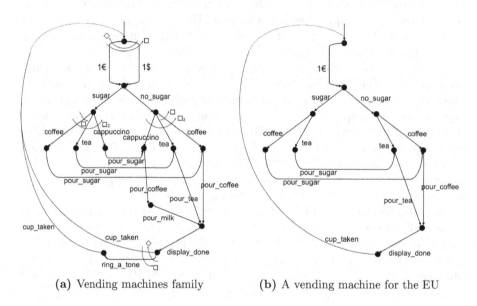

(a) Vending machines family   (b) A vending machine for the EU

Fig. 1. Classical coffee vending machine example reproduced from [33]

6   Formal Verification and Applications

As head of the Formal Methods and Tools (FMT) laboratory of ISTI–CNR for almost two decades, from December 2002 until July 2019, Stefania also touched upon other research streams that have been pursued by members of the lab. These were typically characterised by Formal Verification and analysis as well as Applications to system designs made precise by formal modelling.

Example research streams include: Stochastic modelling and analysis, resulting in publications ranging from the 5th IEEE International Symposium on High-Assurance Systems Engineering (HASE 2000) [60] to the *Journal of Rail*

Transport Planning & Management [7]; Groupware, resulting in publications in the 27th International Conference on Software Engineering (ICSE 2005) [19] and in the *Journal of Logic and Algebraic Programming* [11]; Security, witnessed by publications in the 7th International Conference on Formal Methods for Open Object-Based Distributed Systems (FMOODS 2005) [25] and in the Proceedings of the MEFISTO project on Formal Methods for Security and Time [61]; Web Services, witnessed by a publication in the 4th IEEE European Conference on Web Services (ECOWS 2006) [17]; Telecommunications, witnessed by a publication in the 10th International Conference on Feature Interactions in Telecommunications and Software Systems (ICFI 2009) [18]; Collective Adaptive Systems and Smart Cities, in particular smart transportation in the form of bike-sharing systems, resulting in various publications, even touching upon Machine Learning [5,8,16], in the context of the EU project QUANTICOL; Business Process Modelling, witnessed by publications in the Demo Track of the 15th International Conference on Business Process Modeling (BPM 2017) [51] and in the journal of *Data & Knowledge Engineering* [26] in the context of the EU project Learn PAd.

The recent participation of the FMT lab in the Shift2Rail EU project AST-Rail can be seen as a recognition of the vast experience of the lab in Formal Methods, Formal Verification and Tools, and in particular in Applications to the Railway domain. A specific workstream of ASTRail was concerned with an assessment of the suitability of formal methods in supporting the transition to the next generation of ERTMS/ETCS railway signalling systems, triggered by the fact that the Shift2Rail initiative considers formal methods to be fundamental to the provision of safe and reliable technological advances to increase the competitiveness of the railway industry. Indeed, Stefania and her colleagues from the FMT lab have co-authored numerous authoritative papers on the subject throughout the last decade [6,15,31,32,34,42,44]. Moreover, due to several strong links to railway signalling industries, Stefania was chosen as CNR representative in the Italian railway technology district DITECFER, from 2011 to date.

7   Conclusions

The international attitude of Stefania's professional activity may also be concluded, besides her participation in the above mentioned European projects, from her participation in international bodies. To begin with, we recall her long-standing activities in the ERCIM working group on Formal Methods for Industrial Critical Systems (FMICS). After the success of the aforementioned ERCIM Workshop on Theory and Practice in Verification held in Pisa in December 1992, Stefania co-founded FMICS, making it the oldest active ERCIM working group. Stefania is an FMICS board member ever since and she chaired the board from 2002 to 2005. Initiated in 1996, next year the annual FMICS conference will celebrate its 25th edition. Stefania co-edited a book that surveys over a decade of award-winning collaborative work within the FMICS working group, presenting a number of mainstream formal methods used for designing industrial critical systems [62]. Also, at FMICS 2003, she was invited to present an overview of current research on formal methods in her research group [53].

Furthermore, Stefania has been a member of the board of the association Formal Methods Europe (FME) for over 15 years now and deputy chair since 2004. Currently, she is responsible for overseeing FME's flagship conference series on Formal Methods, which this year was organised as the 3rd World Congress on Formal Methods, featuring a colloquium in honour of Stefania's 65th birthday in which many of the contributors to this Festschrift participated.

The experience of Stefania in organising workshops and conferences was exercised many times in events hosted in Pisa and in Florence under her guidance, including FM 2003, SEFM 2010, IFM & ABZ 2012, VaMoS 2013, SPLC 2014, FMICS-AVoCS 2016, and the upcoming REFSQ 2020. She also chaired the Program Committee of leading workshops and conferences in her fields of research, such as FMICS, SEFM, VaMoS, SPLC, FASE, FMSPLE, AVoCS and— of course—FM, resulting in several co-editorships of special issues of renowned journals [14,15,27,32,50,52,54–58], among which *Formal Aspects of Computing* and the *International Journal on Software Tools for Technology Transfer*, of which she is an editorial board member.

Last but not least, since 2013, Stefania co-organises the FormaliSE conference series affiliated with the International Conference on Software Engineering (ICSE). FormaliSE is an annual conference on Formal Methods in Software Engineering and as such yet another expression of Stefania's constant attention to inject formality into Software Engineering, thus returning to where she started: from Software Engineering to Formal Methods and Tools, and Back.

Acknowledgements. The three of us are very honoured to have had the opportunity to collaborate for a long time with lady Stefania (for more than 35, 20 and 15 years, respectively) and especially to be close friends.

Alessandro, Laura and Maurice

References

1. Andrade, L., et al.: AGILE: software architecture for mobility. In: Wirsing, M., Pattinson, D., Hennicker, R. (eds.) WADT 2002. LNCS, vol. 2755, pp. 1–33. Springer, Heidelberg (2003). https://doi.org/10.1007/978-3-540-40020-2_1

2. Asirelli, P., ter Beek, M.H., Fantechi, A., Gnesi, S.: A logical framework to deal with variability. In: Méry, D., Merz, S. (eds.) IFM 2010. LNCS, vol. 6396, pp. 43–58. Springer, Heidelberg (2010). https://doi.org/10.1007/978-3-642-16265-7_5

3. Asirelli, P., ter Beek, M.H., Fantechi, A., Gnesi, S.: A model-checking tool for families of services. In: Bruni, R., Dingel, J. (eds.) FMOODS/FORTE -2011. LNCS, vol. 6722, pp. 44–58. Springer, Heidelberg (2011). https://doi.org/10.1007/978-3-642-21461-5_3

4. Asirelli, P., ter Beek, M.H., Fantechi, A., Gnesi, S.: Formal description of variability in product families. In: Proceedings of the 15th International Software Product Line Conference (SPLC 2011), pp. 130–139. IEEE (2011). https://doi.org/10.1109/SPLC.2011.34

5. Bacciu, D., Carta, A., Gnesi, S., Semini, L.: An experience in using machine learning for short-term predictions in smart transportation systems. J. Logical Algebraic Methods Program. **87**, 52–66 (2017). https://doi.org/10.1016/j.jlamp.2016.11.002

6. Basile, D., et al.: On the industrial uptake of formal methods in the railway domain. In: Furia, C.A., Winter, K. (eds.) IFM 2018. LNCS, vol. 11023, pp. 20–29. Springer, Cham (2018). https://doi.org/10.1007/978-3-319-98938-9_2

7. Basile, D., Chiaradonna, S., Di Giandomenico, F., Gnesi, S.: A stochastic model-based approach to analyse reliable energy-saving rail road switch heating systems. J. Rail Transp. Plann. Manag. **6**(2), 163–181 (2016). https://doi.org/10.1016/j.jrtpm.2016.03.003

8. ter Beek, M.H., et al.: A quantitative approach to the design and analysis of collective adaptive systems for smart cities. ERCIM News **98**, 32 (2014). http://ercim-news.ercim.eu/en98/special/a-quantitative-approach-to-the-design-and-analysis-of-collective-adaptive-systems-for-smart-cities

9. ter Beek, M.H., Fantechi, A., Gnesi, S., Mazzanti, F.: A state/event-based model-checking approach for the analysis of abstract system properties. Sci. Comput. Program. **76**(2), 119–135 (2011). https://doi.org/10.1016/j.scico.2010.07.002

10. ter Beek, M.H., Gnesi, S., Koch, N., Mazzanti, F.: Formal verification of an automotive scenario in service-oriented computing. In: Proceedings of the 30th International Conference on Software Engineering (ICSE 2008), pp. 613–622. ACM (2008). https://doi.org/10.1145/1368088.1368173

11. ter Beek, M.H., Gnesi, S., Latella, D., Massink, M., Sebastianis, M., Trentanni, G.: Assisting the design of a groupware system. J. Logic Algebraic Program. **78**(4), 191–232 (2009). https://doi.org/10.1016/j.jlap.2008.11.004

12. ter Beek, M.H., Damiani, F., Gnesi, S., Mazzanti, F., Paolini, L.: On the expressiveness of modal transition systems with variability constraints. Sci. Comput. Program. **169**, 1–17 (2019). https://doi.org/10.1016/j.scico.2018.09.006

13. ter Beek, M.H., Fantechi, A., Gnesi, S., Mazzanti, F.: Modelling and analysing variability in product families: model checking of modal transition systems with variability constraints. J. Logical Algebraic Methods Program. **85**(2), 287–315 (2016). https://doi.org/10.1016/j.jlamp.2015.11.006

14. ter Beek, M.H., Gnesi, S., Knapp, A.: Formal methods and automated verification. Int. J. Softw. Tools Technol. Transfer **20**(4), 355–358 (2018). https://doi.org/10.1007/s10009-018-0494-5

15. ter Beek, M.H., Gnesi, S., Knapp, A.: Formal methods for transport systems. Int. J. Softw. Tools Technol. Transfer **20**(2), 237–241 (2018). https://doi.org/10.1007/s10009-018-0487-4

16. ter Beek, M.H., Gnesi, S., Latella, D., Massink, M.: Towards automatic decision support for bike-sharing system design. In: Bianculli, D., Calinescu, R., Rumpe, B. (eds.) SEFM 2015. LNCS, vol. 9509, pp. 266–280. Springer, Heidelberg (2015). https://doi.org/10.1007/978-3-662-49224-6_22

17. ter Beek, M.H., Gnesi, S., Mazzanti, F., Moiso, C.: Formal modelling and verification of an asynchronous extension of SOAP. In: Proceedings of the 4th IEEE European Conference on Web Services (ECOWS 2006), pp. 287–296. IEEE (2006). https://doi.org/10.1109/ECOWS.2006.22

18. ter Beek, M.H., Gnesi, S., Montangero, C., Semini, L.: Detecting policy conflicts by model checking UML state machines. In: Nakamura, M., Reiff-Marganiec, S. (eds.) Proceedings of Feature Interactions in Software and Communication Systems X (ICFI 2009), pp. 59–74. IOS Press (2009). https://doi.org/10.3233/978-1-60750-014-8-59

19. ter Beek, M.H., Massink, M., Latella, D., Gnesi, S., Forghieri, A., Sebastianis, M.: A case study on the automated verification of groupware protocols. In: Proceedings of the 27th International Conference on Software Engineering (ICSE 2005), pp. 596–603. ACM (2005). https://doi.org/10.1145/1062455.1062560

20. Bernardeschi, C., Fantechi, A., Gnesi, S.: Formal validation of fault-tolerance mechanisms inside GUARDS. Reliab. Eng. Sys. Saf. **71**(3), 261–270 (2001). https://doi.org/10.1016/S0951-8320(00)00078-8

21. Bertolino, A., Gnesi, S.: PLUTO: a test methodology for product families. In: van der Linden, F.J. (ed.) PFE 2003. LNCS, vol. 3014, pp. 181–197. Springer, Heidelberg (2004). https://doi.org/10.1007/978-3-540-24667-1_14

22. Bouali, A., Gnesi, S., Larosa, S.: JACK: just another concurrency kit - the integration project. Bull. EATCS **54**, 207–223 (1994)

23. Bucchiarone, A., Gnesi, S., Lami, G., Trentanni, G., Fantechi, A.: QuARS express - a tool demonstration. In: Proceedings of the 23rd IEEE/ACM International Conference on Automated Software Engineering (ASE 2008), pp. 473–474. IEEE (2008). https://doi.org/10.1109/ASE.2008.77

24. Bucchiarone, A., Gnesi, S., Trentanni, G., Fantechi, A.: Evaluation of natural language requirements in the MODCONTROL project. ERCIM News **75**, 52–53 (2008). http://ercim-news.ercim.eu/evaluation-of-natural-language-requirements-in-the-modcontrol-project

25. Corin, R., Di Caprio, G., Etalle, S., Gnesi, S., Lenzini, G., Moiso, C.: A formal security analysis of an OSA/Parlay authentication interface. In: Steffen, M., Zavattaro, G. (eds.) FMOODS 2005. LNCS, vol. 3535, pp. 131–146. Springer, Heidelberg (2005). https://doi.org/10.1007/11494881_9

26. Corradini, F., et al.: A guidelines framework for understandable BPMN models. Data Knowl. Eng. **113**, 129–154 (2018). https://doi.org/10.1016/j.datak.2017.11.003

27. Cuéllar, J., Gnesi, S., Latella, D.: Foreword. Sci. Comput. Program. **36**(1), 1–3 (2000). https://doi.org/10.1016/S0167-6423(99)00014-3

28. De Francesco, N., Fantechi, A., Gnesi, S., Inverardi, P.: Model checking of non-finite state processes by finite approximations. In: Brinksma, E., Cleaveland, W.R., Larsen, K.G., Margaria, T., Steffen, B. (eds.) TACAS 1995. LNCS, vol. 1019, pp. 195–215. Springer, Heidelberg (1995). https://doi.org/10.1007/3-540-60630-0_10

29. De Nicola, R., Fantechi, A., Gnesi, S., Ristori, G.: An action based framework for verifying logical and behavioural properties of concurrent systems. In: Larsen, K.G., Skou, A. (eds.) CAV 1991. LNCS, vol. 575, pp. 37–47. Springer, Heidelberg (1992). https://doi.org/10.1007/3-540-55179-4_5

30. Fabbrini, F., Fusani, M., Gervasi, V., Gnesi, S., Ruggieri, S.: On linguistic quality of natural language requirements. In: Dubois, E., Opdahl, A.L., Pohl, K. (eds.) Proceedings of the 4th International Workshop on Requirements Engineering: Foundation for Software Quality (REFSQ 1998), pp. 57–62. Presses Universitaires de Namur (1998)

31. Fantechi, A., Ferrari, A., Gnesi, S.: Formal methods and safety certification: challenges in the railways domain. In: Margaria, T., Steffen, B. (eds.) ISoLA 2016. LNCS, vol. 9953, pp. 261–265. Springer, Cham (2016). https://doi.org/10.1007/978-3-319-47169-3_18

32. Fantechi, A., Flammini, F., Gnesi, S.: Formal methods for railway control systems. Int. J. Softw. Tools Technol. Transfer **16**(6), 643–646 (2014). https://doi.org/10.1007/s10009-014-0342-1

33. Fantechi, A., Gnesi, S.: Formal modeling for product families engineering. In: Proceedings of the 12th International Software Product Line Conference (SPLC 2008), pp. 193–202. IEEE (2008). https://doi.org/10.1109/SPLC.2008.45
34. Fantechi, A., Gnesi, S.: On the adoption of model checking in safety-related software industry. In: Flammini, F., Bologna, S., Vittorini, V. (eds.) SAFECOMP 2011. LNCS, vol. 6894, pp. 383–396. Springer, Heidelberg (2011). https://doi.org/10.1007/978-3-642-24270-0_28
35. Fantechi, A., Gnesi, S., Inverardi, P., Montanari, U.: An execution environment for the formal definition of Ada. In: Nichols, H., Simpson, D. (eds.) ESEC 1987. LNCS, vol. 289, pp. 327–335. Springer, Heidelberg (1987). https://doi.org/10.1007/BFb0022125
36. Fantechi, A., Gnesi, S., Lami, G., Maccari, A.: Application of linguistic techniques for use case analysis. In: Proceedings of the 10th Anniversary IEEE Joint International Conference on Requirements Engineering (RE 2002), pp. 157–164. IEEE (2002). https://doi.org/10.1109/ICRE.2002.1048518
37. Fantechi, A., Gnesi, S., Laneve, C.: An expressive temporal logic for basic LOTOS. In: Vuong, S.T. (ed.) Proceedings of the IFIP TC/WG6.1 2nd International Conference on Formal Description Techniques for Distributed Systems and Communication Protocols (FORTE 1989), pp. 261–276. North-Holland (1989)
38. Fantechi, A., Gnesi, S., Lapadula, A., Mazzanti, F., Pugliese, R., Tiezzi, F.: A logical verification methodology for service-oriented computing. ACM Trans. Softw. Eng. Methodol. 21(3), 16:1–16:46 (2012). https://doi.org/10.1145/2211616.2211619
39. Fantechi, A., Gnesi, S., Mazzanti, F., Pugliese, R., Tronci, E.: A symbolic model checker for ACTL. In: Hutter, D., Stephan, W., Traverso, P., Ullmann, M. (eds.) FM-Trends 1998. LNCS, vol. 1641, pp. 228–242. Springer, Heidelberg (1999). https://doi.org/10.1007/3-540-48257-1_14
40. Fantechi, A., Gnesi, S., Ristori, G.: Model checking for action-based logics. Formal Methods Sys. Des. 4(2), 187–203 (1994). https://doi.org/10.1007/BF01384084
41. Fantechi, A., Gnesi, S., Semini, L.: Applying the QuARS tool to detect variability. In: Proceedings of the 23rd International Systems and Software Product Line Conference (SPLC 2019), pp. 29–32. ACM (2019). https://doi.org/10.1145/3307630.3342388
42. Ferrari, A., et al.: Survey on formal methods and tools in railways: the ASTRail approach. In: Collart-Dutilleul, S., Lecomte, T., Romanovsky, A. (eds.) RSSRail 2019. LNCS, vol. 11495, pp. 226–241. Springer, Cham (2019). https://doi.org/10.1007/978-3-030-18744-6_15
43. Ferrari, A., Dell'Orletta, F., Esuli, A., Gervasi, V., Gnesi, S.: Natural language requirements processing: a 4D vision. IEEE Softw. 34(6), 28–35 (2017). https://doi.org/10.1109/MS.2017.4121207
44. Ferrari, A., Fantechi, A., Gnesi, S., Magnani, G.: Model-based development and formal methods in the railway industry. IEEE Softw. 30(3), 28–34 (2013). https://doi.org/10.1109/MS.2013.44
45. Ferrari, A., et al.: Detecting requirements defects with NLP patterns: an industrial experience. Empirical Softw. Eng. 23(6), 3684–3733 (2018). https://doi.org/10.1007/s10664-018-9596-7
46. Ferrari, A., Spoletini, P., Gnesi, S.: Ambiguity as a resource to disclose tacit knowledge. In: Proceedings of the 23rd IEEE International Requirements Engineering Conference (RE 2015), pp. 26–35. IEEE (2015). https://doi.org/10.1109/RE.2015.7320405

47. Ferrari, A., Spoletini, P., Gnesi, S.: Ambiguity and tacit knowledge in requirements. Requirements Eng. **21**(3), 333–355 (2016). https://doi.org/10.1007/s00766-016-0249-3
48. Ferrari, G.L., Gnesi, S., Montanari, U., Pistore, M.: A model-checking verification environment for mobile processes. ACM Trans. Softw. Eng. Methodol. **12**(4), 440–473 (2003). https://doi.org/10.1145/990010.990013
49. Ferrari, G., Gnesi, S., Montanari, U., Pistore, M., Ristori, G.: Verifying mobile processes in the HAL environment. In: Hu, A.J., Vardi, M.Y. (eds.) CAV 1998. LNCS, vol. 1427, pp. 511–515. Springer, Heidelberg (1998). https://doi.org/10.1007/BFb0028772
50. Fitzgerald, J.S., Gnesi, S., Mandrioli, D.: The industrialization of formal methods. Int. J. Softw. Tools Technol. Transfer **8**(4–5), 301–302 (2006). https://doi.org/10.1007/s10009-005-0208-7
51. Fornari, F., Gnesi, S., La Rosa, M., Polini, A., Re, B., Spagnolo, G.O.: Checking business process modeling guidelines in apromore. In: Clarisó, R., et al. (eds.) Proceedings of the 15th International Conference on Business Process Modeling (BPM 2017) Demo Track. CEUR Workshop Proceedings, vol. 1920. CEUR-WS.org (2017). http://ceur-ws.org/Vol-1920/BPM_2017_paper_204.pdf
52. Garavel, H., Gnesi, S., Schieferdecker, I.: Special issue on the fifth international workshop of the ERCIM working group on formal methods for industrial critical systems. Sci. Comput. Program. **46**(3), 195–196 (2003). https://doi.org/10.1016/S0167-6423(02)00091-6
53. Gnesi, S.: Formal specification and verification of complex systems. Electron. Notes Theoret. Comput. Sci. **80**, 294–298 (2003). https://doi.org/10.1016/S1571-0661(04)80829-6
54. Gnesi, S., Cavalcanti, A., Fitzgerald, J., Heitmeyer, C.: Editorial. Formal Aspects Comput. **31**(2), 131–132 (2019). https://doi.org/10.1007/s00165-019-00481-4
55. Gnesi, S., Jarzabek, S.: Special section on the 17th international software product. Int. J. Softw. Tools Technol. Transfer **17**(5), 555–557 (2015). https://doi.org/10.1007/s10009-015-0386-x
56. Gnesi, S., Latella, D.: Editorial. Formal Aspects Comput. **10**(4), 311–312 (1998). https://doi.org/10.1007/s001650050019
57. Gnesi, S., Latella, D.: Special issue on the first international workshop of the ERCIM working group on formal methods for industrial critical systems. Formal Methods Sys. Des. **12**(2), 123–124 (1998). https://doi.org/10.1023/A:1008669025349
58. Gnesi, S., Latella, D.: Introduction: special issue on the fourth international workshop of the ERCIM working group on formal methods for industrial critical systems. Formal Methods Syst. Des. **19**(2), 119–120 (2001). https://doi.org/10.1023/A:1011279615774
59. Gnesi, S., Latella, D., Lenzini, G., Abbaneo, C., Amendola, A.M., Marmo, P.: An automatic SPIN validation of a safety critical railway control system. In: Proceedings of the International Conference on Dependable Systems and Networks (DSN 2000), pp. 119–124. IEEE (2000). https://doi.org/10.1109/ICDSN.2000.857524
60. Gnesi, S., Latella, D., Massink, M.: A stochastic extension of a behavioural subset of UML statechart diagrams. In: Proceedings of the 5th IEEE International Symposium on High-Assurance Systems Engineering (HASE 2000), pp. 55–64. IEEE (2000). https://doi.org/10.1109/HASE.2000.895442
61. Gnesi, S., Lenzini, G., Martinelli, F.: Applying generalized non deducibility on compositions (GNDC) approach in dependability. Electron. Notes Theoret. Comput. Sci. **99**, 111–126 (2004). https://doi.org/10.1016/j.entcs.2004.02.005

62. Gnesi, S., Margaria, T. (eds.): Formal Methods for Industrial Critical Systems: A Survey of Applications. Wiley, Hoboken (2013)
63. Gnesi, S., Montanari, U., Martelli, A.: Dynamic programming as graph searching: an algebraic approach. J. ACM **28**(4), 737–751 (1981). https://doi.org/10.1145/322276.322285
64. Gnesi, S., Trentanni, G.: QuARS: a NLP tool for requirements analysis. In: Spoletini, P., et al. (eds.) Proceedings of REFSQ-2019 2nd Workshop on Natural Language Processing for Requirements Engineering (NLP4RE 2019). CEUR Workshop Proceedings, vol. 2376. CEUR-WS.org (2019). http://ceur-ws.org/Vol-2376/NLP4RE19_paper07.pdf
65. Lami, G., Gnesi, S., Trentanni, G., Fabbrini, F., Fusani, M.: An automatic tool for the analysis of natural language requirements. Comput. Syst. Sci. Eng. **20**(1), 53–62 (2005)

From Dynamic Programming to Programming Science
Some Recollections in Honour of Stefania Gnesi

Ugo Montanari[✉]

Dipartimento di Informatica, University of Pisa, Pisa, Italy
ugo@di.unipi.it

Scienze dell'Informazione

Stefania Gnesi graduated *summa cum laude* in Scienze dell'Informazione at the University of Pisa in June 1978.

At the time, I had recently moved from the IEI–CNR Institute (Istituto di Elaborazione dell'Informazione of the Consiglio Nazionale delle Ricerche) to the Department (well, maybe Institute) of Scienze dell'Informazione, University of Pisa. I was teaching the only course available there about theoretical computer science: computability, automata and formal languages, program and programming language semantics.

When Stefania came and asked for a thesis, I suggested her to focus on an interesting area about algebras, algebra homomorphisms and initial algebras. The subject had been developed at the same time at IBM, by the ADJ Group, and, in Paris, by Maurice Nivat (under the name of *magmas libres*). I had heard about them at a summer school at Erice in 1976. A homomorphism relating two algebras A and B with the same signature allows to evaluate part of a (possibly infinite) term first in A and then part in B, without changing the result. The key contribution of Stefania's thesis (shared with her husband Alfonso Catalano) was to consider as a case study the functional equations of dynamic programming (algebra B) and to solve them by searching for the shortest path (tree) in a graph (algebra A). The correspondence of the two views, proved taking advantage of a result by ADJ in *Initial Algebra Semantics and Continuous Algebras*, JACM Jan. 1977, allows to take advantage of useful structural properties of the graph, which are not explicit in the equations.

The contribution was very well accepted by the community, resulting in two publications: one in a workshop at Bad Honnef (1978), which turned out to be the first of a long series on Graph Grammars and Applications, eventually evolving into the ICGT International Conference on Graph Transformations. The other in the Journal of the ACM (1981), possibly the top Journal in our area.

The Formal Definition of Ada and the PFI

Another interesting occasion of collaboration materialised about the execution environment for the formal definition of Ada. In the seventies, the US Department of Defense (DoD) supported a series of initiatives for defining and

© Springer Nature Switzerland AG 2019
M. H. ter Beek et al. (Eds.): Gnesi Festschrift, LNCS 11865, pp. 12–15, 2019.
https://doi.org/10.1007/978-3-030-30985-5_2

implementing the *ultimate* programming language, planning to replace with it the large variety of undependable programming languages DoD software was programmed into. A document, the *Steelman*, making explicit the requirements of the language, was produced, and it was concluded in 1977 that no existent programming language actually did fit them. Four proposals for the language were supported by DoD and one of them, the *Green* proposal designed by Jean Ichbiah was chosen, and it was given the name *Ada*, after Augusta Ada, Countess of Lovelace, Charles Babbage collaborator.

The EU (or its approximation existing at the time) decided instead to focus on two aspects, Ada *formal definition*, and *programming environment*. About the latter issue, EU supported a large project called *A Basis for Portable Common Tool Environments* (PCTE), the Olivetti research team working in Pisa actively collaborated to. About Ada formal definition, EU supported a project called *The Draft Formal Definition of ANSI/MIL-STD 1815A Ada*, with Danish Datamatic Center (DDC), Consorzio per la Ricerca e le Applicazioni Informatiche (CRAI) and IEI–CNR, CRAI subcontractor, as participating institutions, and consultants at the Universities of Genova, Pisa and Lyngby.

In particular, Alessandro Fantechi, Stefania Gnesi, Paola Inverardi and myself (with F. Leggio and P. Talini) worked at an execution environment for the Formal Definition of Ada, presented at ESEC 1987 and published in ACM SIGPLAN. The environment was based on a logic programming approach, that is the translation of the formal definition itself in an executable logic program. The use of novel techniques like metaprogramming and partial evaluation, aiming at improving modularity and efficiency of the system, was also explored.

As a related activity, I co-edited with Nico Habermann (Carnegie-Mellon University) a Springer LNCS book on System Development and Ada. For all these initiatives the technical and managing contribution of Stefania was essential.

The contribution of Stefania's IEI research group to Ada subsequent development was long lasting. In particular, Franco Mazzanti was very active on it. He studied, and contributed to, several aspects of Ada programming, e.g. recently about multicore programming.

In the period 1979–1985, Italian CNR supported the large and important project Progetto Finalizzato Informatica, PFI. It consisted of three parts, dedicated to: (i) national manufacturers (I was the coordinator); (ii) public administration; and (iii) industrial automation. Stefania's IEI group contributed in several forms to the project Cnet, the largest of the first part, concerning the design and prototypical implementation of (parts of) a campus net equipped with suggestive applications.

The project leader of Cnet was Norma Lijtmaer, also at IEI. She had a very significant experience in computer science research, teaching and actual system design. In particular, she designed the operating system of the Laben 70 computer built by Montedison's Laben branch for process control applications. The activity of Stefania and Norma within PFI was the beginning of a long lasting collaboration and friendship, which materialised e.g. in the workshop organised by Stefania in honour of Norma for her retirement, Dai Sistemi Distribuiti a Internet: Giornata di Incontro e Discussione in Onore di Norma Lijtmaer, July 1, 2002.

JACK and HAL

At the beginning of the nineties, Stefania started to focus her research interests on the subject she has contributed the most to, i.e. formal methods for proving properties of concurrent systems. Together with Rocco De Nicola, Alessandro Fantechi and Gioia Ristori (CAV 1991) she developed a framework consisting of an action based branching time logic called ACTL and of tools for manipulating process algebra terms and for checking validity of ACTL formulas. In particular, she developed the tool environment JACK (standing for Just Another Concurrency Kit), which turned out to be very useful, together with its expansions, for supporting experimental activity on formal methods at IEI and at the University of Pisa.

One such expansion, the HD Automata Laboratory (HAL), gave me a precious occasion for collaborating with Stefania directly. History Dependent (HD) automata, introduced in the PhD thesis of Marco Pistore at Pisa, are composed, as ordinary automata, of states and of transitions between states. However, states and transitions of HD-automata are enriched with sets of local names. In particular, each transition can refer to the names associated to its source state but can also introduce new names, which can then appear in the destination state. In addition, in a transition some names may disappear, thus resulting in a garbage collection step. Hence, names are not global and static entities but they are explicitly represented within states and transitions and can be dynamically created and deleted.

A number of history dependent models of computation (namely models where links to previous states can be stored and passed) can be conveniently mapped to HD-automata, yielding corresponding notions of bisimulation. Typical examples are process algebras (e.g. CCS) with causal dependencies or Petri nets with history preserving bisimilarity. Even more interesting is the case of pi-calculus agents (without matching) with early/late bisimilarity. Moreover, it is possible to unfold (finite) HD-automata into (finite) ordinary automata. The combination of these results allowed Stefania and collaborators (Gianluigi Ferrari, Gianluigi Ferro, Marco Pistore, Gioia Ristori and myself) to significantly extend JACK/HAL capabilities to handle nontrivial pi-calculus case studies (CAV'98, TOSEM 2003).

SENSORIA et al.

More recent occasions of collaboration with Stefania Gnesi materialised when we both were participating in national and European projects. I can mention the Italian FIRB project TOCAI.IT (Tecnologie Orientate alla Conoscenza per Aggregazioni di Imprese in Internet) and the European projects PROFUNDIS

(Proofs of Functionality for Mobile Distributed Systems) and AGILE (Software Architecture for Mobility).

In the latter project, our convergent contributions took advantage of architecture-based approaches based on graph-oriented techniques as means of controlling the complexity of system construction and evolution, where mobility aspects were particularly relevant.

Similar topics were also carried on within project SENSORIA (Software Engineering for Service-Oriented Overlay Computers, an Integrated Project of the European Union's Sixth Framework Programme). In SENSORIA, Stefania Gnesi had the important role of responsible for the work package on Case Studies, whose aim was to provide a context of realistic case studies for developing intuitions that could feed and steer the research process according to the expectations of society and its economy.

In particular, in the paper coauthored by Stefania and by several researchers in her and my group—published in the book for my 65th birthday—she outlines and compares our approaches to the themes of SENSORIA.

Programming Science

Programming science is a key component in today's world structure and evolution. To connect the mathematical foundations in theoretical computer science with the empirical components of programming methodology is to bridge a wide gap. Still, when it happens, as in the case of program typing and modularity, or of program verification via model checking or other systematic means, the progress in both theory and practice is invaluable.

Stefania Gnesi has been very successful in her role of leader in the science of programming area at Pisa, in particular about theoretical and experimental innovation activities. Very relevant are her collaborations with industry, e.g. with Alstom, Intecs Sistemi, FIAT Auto and Ansaldo Trasporti.

Furthermore, Stefania's scientific role has been widely recognised in the international community, both in terms of publications and of prestigious positions, e.g. deputy chair of the association FME (Formal Methods Europe) and member of IFIP WG 1.3 on Foundation of Systems Specification.

Software Engineering

Ten Years of Self-adaptive Systems: From Dynamic Ensembles to Collective Adaptive Systems

Antonio Bucchiarone[1(✉)] and Marina Mongiello[2]

[1] Fondazione Bruno Kessler (FBK), Via Sommarive 18, Trento, Italy
bucchiarone@fbk.eu
[2] Dipartimento di Ingegneria Elettrica e dell'Informazione, Politecnico di Bari,
Via E. Orabona n. 4, Bari, Italy
marina.mongiello@poliba.it

Abstract. Self-adaptive systems have been introduced to manage situations where software systems operate under continuous perturbations due to the unpredicted behaviors of their clients and the occurrence of exogenous changes in the environment in which they operate. Adaptation is triggered by the run-time occurrence of an extraordinary circumstance, and it is handled by an adaptation process that involves components affected by the issue, and is able to handle the run-time modification of the structure and behavior of a running system. In this paper we report our experience gained in the last 10 years on models, techniques and applications in the field of self-adaptation. We present the various steps taken by means of a formal framework introduced to characterize the different aspects of an *ensemble-based software engineering approach*. We present (i) how to model dynamic ensembles using typed graph grammars, (ii) how to specialize and re-configure ensembles and, (ii) how to manage collective adaptations in an ensemble. All these aspects have been part of our research on self-adaptation and have been used to specify and deploy concrete solutions in different application domains.

Keywords: Self-adaptive systems · Ensembles ·
Collective Adaptive Systems

1 Introduction and Paper Positioning

Contemporary and future software systems are composed of large-scale *ensembles* of widely distributed, largely autonomous and heterogeneous entities situated in both the physical world and in back-end computer systems. The term ensemble has been used for a few years in the literature to denote this class of very large scale systems of systems, which may present substantial socio-technical embedding [1,2]. The ensembles do not only denote the special complexity they present to designers, engineers and system administrators; they also suggests how much of that complexity comes from bringing together and combining in

© Springer Nature Switzerland AG 2019
M. H. ter Beek et al. (Eds.): Gnesi Festschrift, LNCS 11865, pp. 19–39, 2019.
https://doi.org/10.1007/978-3-030-30985-5_3

the same operating environment many heterogeneous and autonomous components, systems, users, with the related concerns. Those ensembles are often open-boundary and multi-ownership, resulting in the lack of a viable central point of command and control [3–5]. Moreover, human interaction via ubiquitous computing devices is often deeply embedded and must be considered an integral part of these kind of systems [6]. These systems can be effectively managed only via decentralized adaptation. Such adaptation must be itself collective, that is, multiple entities must adapt simultaneously in a way that, on the one hand, properly addresses a critical runtime condition, while, on the other hand, does not break the working consistency of the ensemble, but rather preserves the collaboration and its benefits.

There have been many recent theoretical and methodological solutions in the field of software adaptation which can deal with large-scale distributed and heterogeneous software systems [7–9]. At the same time, the study of both individual and collective adaptation mechanisms has a long history, e.g., in the area of agent-based and multi-agent systems [10] and in the area of autonomic systems [11]. For collective adaptation, the idea of dynamically adapting the behavior of a set of interacting software components in order to meet new or unexpected requirements or contingencies has been a very hot research topic over the last ten years for several research communities [12,13]. Yet, also in this case, it is widely recognized that the number of open issues in the area is still significant [14]. Most of the proposed solutions work under an architectural model in which the knowledge necessary to adapt a system is logically centralized and the control of adaptation is exerted centrally. There is still a lack of understanding on how to engineer Collective Adaptive Systems (CAS), in which a central control is not possible [15].

In our view, an *ensemble* is a specification that defines how a certain type of collaboration occurs between several entities [16]. An ensemble introduces a set of *cells*, i.e. roles that can be taken by participating entities, and a set of rules (*adaptors*) regulating the operation of participating cells in the scope of the ensemble. The life-cycle of the ensemble is depicted in Fig. 1 and can be described as follows. The ensemble is created by some cell (creator) whenever a need for collaboration emerges. The creator must have a way to specify the rules that govern that ensemble, including criteria for entering or exiting. After creation, cells may dynamically join the ensemble (entities that take specified roles). Even once they have entered the ensemble, participants remain autonomous, that is, largely preserve their freedom of action, and continue operation within the ensemble, trying to achieve their objectives. However, they must do so while respecting the ensemble rules. In particular, when any one ensemble participant needs to adapt its behaviour, the adaptation is performed collectively to remain in compliance with ensemble rules, which may trigger adaptation in multiple other participants. Cells exit the ensemble instance when their objectives are achieved or when the participation in the ensemble is not anymore beneficial; additional rules may be used to regulate such sudden withdrawals. The ensemble instance is terminated when certain conditions are achieved (e.g., all participants have exited the ensemble).

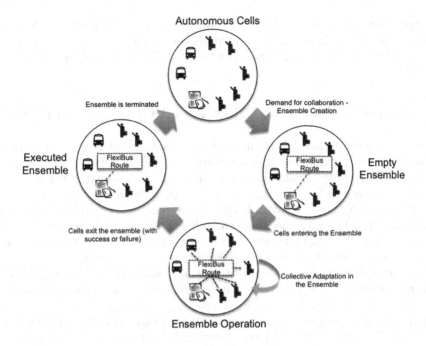

Fig. 1. Ensemble life cycle

A holistic ensemble developement life cycle (EDLC) was proposed in 2013 by Bures et al. in [17,18] inside the EU project ASCENS. The life cycle they propose is a framework which covers the full development process and addresses design and development for adaptation, self-awareness, self-optimization, and continuous system evolution. Their life cycle acts as a cycle between runtime and design development of self-adaptive systems relating the main phases of a system development both at runtime and design time. With respect to that model the life cycle we propose is the cycle of an ensemble, starting with the creation of cells till their termination.

The goal of this paper is to report our experience gained in the last 10 years in the field of collective adaptive systems that saw its birth as a result of research led by Stefania Gnesi in the years 2005–2008, where her research group at CNR-ISTI started to promote the use of graphs and graphs transformations as a framework for the modelling, execution and adaptation of self-adaptive systems [19,20].

We present the various steps taken by means of a formal framework introduced to characterize the different phases of an *ensemble-based software engineering* life-cycle, as the one depicted in Fig. 1. In the following sections, we start formalizing an ensemble as a graph grammar and we describe its different forms of adaptation (in Sect. 2). In Sect. 3, we present how each cell of an ensemble can specialize and adapt its behavior during the ensemble execution. We conclude by presenting how multiple ensembles can compose a collective adaptive system (CAS) and how adaptations can be solved involving multiple cells in an ensemble.

2 Dynamic Ensembles Using Typed Graph Grammars

To give a uniform formal presentation of an ensemble, that is abstract enough, we have been inspired by our previous works in dynamic software architectures [19–21], selecting graph grammars as a formal framework. In particular we select graph grammars as a formal framework for mapping the different elements of an ensemble because (i) they provide both a formal basis and a graphical representation that is in line with the usual way self-adaptive systems are represented, (ii) they allow for a natural way of describing models and configurations, and (iii) they have been largely used for specifying adaptive systems.

An ensemble is formed by a set of *cells* and *adaptors*, which are modelled as **hyperedges**, and the *fragments* (i.e., functionalities they provide) to which the hyperedges are attached, which are modelled as **nodes**. Figure 2 depicts an hypergraph containing two nodes **Fragment1** and **Fragment2**, the hyperedge cell (an entity that exposes two different functionalities as process fragments [22]), the hyperedge **Adaptor** (a software component that has two tentacles to the fragment **Fragment1** and one to the fragment **Fragment2**). Note that cell edges are drawn as square boxes and adaptor edges as rounded boxes. Moreover, we show the ordering of tentacles by labeling the corresponding arrows with natural numbers (in some cases we use suitable names instead of numbers as labels to make it easier to read).

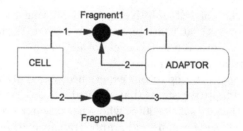

Fig. 2. A hypergraph describing an ensemble

Definition 1 (Hypergraph). *A (hyper)graph is a triple $H = (N_H, E_H, \phi_H)$, where N_H is the set of nodes, E_H is the set of (hyper)edges, and $\phi_H : E_H \rightarrow N_H^+$ describes the connections of the graph, where N_H^+ stands for the set of non-empty strings of elements of N_H. We call $|\phi_H(e)|$ the rank of e, with $|\phi_H(e)| > 0$ for any $e \in E_H$.*

The connection function ϕ_H associates each hyperedge e with the ordered, non empty sequence of nodes e is attached to. An *ensemble* is just a hypergraph T that describes only the types of fragments, adaptors, cells and the allowed connections. A configuration compliant with such ensemble is then described by the notion of a *Typed hypergraph*.

Definition 2 (Typed Hypergraph). *Given a hypergraph T (called the ensemble), a T-typed hypergraph or configuration is a pair $< |G|, \tau_G >$, where $|G|$ is the underlying graph and $\tau_G : |G| \to T$ is the total hypergraph morphism.*

The graph $|G|$ defines the configuration of an ensemble while τ_G defines the (static) *typing* of the resources. Consider the ensemble T in Fig. 2: there is one unique type `cell` of cells exposing two `fragments` of different types, and one `Adaptor` attached to two fragments of type `Fragment1` and one fragment of type `Fragment2`. Then, a possible *T-typed* hypergraph (or configuration of the ensemble T) is in Fig. 3: it has two different cells with their corresponding fragments, and one adaptor. The typing morphism is implicitly defined by the name of the elements in the configuration, which consist of the type name plus a subindex identifying the particular instance (e.g., fragment `Fragment1A` has type `Fragment1`). We remark that the typing morphism requires cells to have exactly one fragment of type `Fragment1` and one of type `Fragment2`. Similarly, the only connections valid for an adaptor are those that attach its first two tentacles to fragments of type `Fragment1` and the third one to a fragment of type `Fragment2`. All such constraints are enforced by the existence of a typing morphism.

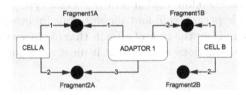

Fig. 3. A hypergraph describing a configuration for the ensemble in Fig. 2

The *adaptation* of the ensemble is described by a set of rewriting productions. A production p is a partial, injective morphism of *T-typed* graphs, i.e., it has the following shape: $p : L \to R$ where L and R are T-typed hypergraphs, called the *left-hand* and the *right-hand* side of the production, respectively. Given a T-typed Graph G and a production p, a rewriting of G using p can be informally described as follow: (1) find a (type preserving) match of the left-hand-side L in G, i.e., identify a subgraph of G that corresponds with L; (2) remove from the graph G all the items corresponding to the left-hand-side that are not in the right-hand-side; (3) add all the items of the right-hand-side that are not in the left-hand-side; (4) the elements that are both in L and R are preserved by the rewrite. Finally, an *ensemble* is described by a T-typed graph grammar.

Definition 3 (T-Typed Graph Grammar). *A T-typed graph grammar G is a tuple $< T, G_{in}, P >$ where G_{in} is the initial (T-typed) graph and P is a set of productions.*

Adaptation in an ensemble, can be managed using different approaches [23]. *Programmed Adaptation* assumes that all the adaptation types are specified at design time and triggered by the ensemble itself. For this reason we can define a *Programmed Ensemble* as a graph grammar $G_A = < T, G_{in}, P >$, where T stands for the style of the ensemble, G_{in} is the initial configuration, and the set of productions P gives the evolution of the ensemble. The grammar fixes the types of all the elements (cells, fragments, adaptors) in the ensemble and their possible connections, where the productions state the possible ways in which a configuration may change.

Self-repairing ensembles are equipped with a mechanism that monitors the ensemble behavior to determine whether it behaves within fixed parameters. If a deviation occurs, then the ensemble itself is in charge of adapting the configuration. We can define a *self-repairing ensemble* as a graph grammar $G_A = <T, G_{in}, P>$ in which the set of productions is partitioned into three different sets, i.e., $P = P_{pgm} \cup P_{env} \cup P_{rpr}$. Rules in P_{pgm} describe the normal, ideal behavior of an ensemble, and rules in P_{env} model the *environment* or, in other words, the ways in which the behavior of the ensemble may deviate from the expected one. Rules in P_{rpr} indicate the way in which an undesirable configuration can be repaired in order to become a valid one.

Open Ensembles are ensembles able to evolve freely by adding and removing cells and adaptors without any restrictions. The typed grammar corresponding to open ensembles should therefore exploit a fully general type graph that contains an infinite number of hyperarcs $cell_i$ and $adaptor_i$, one for every natural $i, j \in N$. Any hyperarc $cell_i$ stands for the type of all cells that exposes exactly i fragments. Similarly, the set of productions is infinite as it must allow for adding/removing any kind of cells.

3 Ensemble Specialization and Reconfiguration

The dynamism of the environment in which the ensembles introduced above must operate make their deployment and maintenance a hard task to accomplish in a really efficient way. The situation in which they operate may be different or may change during their life. Application end-users may change their preferences and emergent requirements can arise. In this context, the only way an ensemble can manage such changes is at run-time, since environment conditions, available functionalities and users' need are not known a priori.

In our approach (as depicted in Fig. 1), the functionalities provided by different entities are represented by *Cells*. Implementing a functionality may involve interacting with other cells through pre-defined protocols (e.g., the *adaptor* introduced in Fig. 2). Moreover, a cell is defined in terms of its behavior and its protocol (functionalities/fragments that it provides) and can be created either by instantiating cell archetypes or by other cells through the process of *specialization*. At the same time, due to the high dynamism of the environment in which each cell operates, a cell must be able to *re-configure* its behavior at run-time in order to satisfy new users' requirements and to fit new situations (i.e., unexpected context changes).

Behaviours and cell functionalities are represented by sets of tasks that have to be carried out in a certain order (i.e., process and process fragment), but while the first is used to describe how a cell evolves (i.e., behaves), the latter represent the capabilities that a cell exposes to the system and that can be used by other cells to perform their tasks. At the same time each cell provides a set of *context properties* that describe particular aspects of the system domain (i.e., current location of a user, status of the network, temperature detected, etc.) that it takes into account during its execution.

A system model for ensembles that allows to express requirements using a wide variety of logics and fitness criteria over arbitrary preorders is proposed by Holz and Wirsing in the paper [24]. Using this system model they give a precise definition of black-box adaptation and show how this naturally leads to a preorder of adaptability on ensembles, the model they propose can integrate different models, logics and objectives. With respect to that system model we model the ensembles starting from the life cycle previously described by means of cells, and considering their evolution from the creation, when the need of collaboration emerges, through other steps of collaboration till their termination. Starting from a preliminary result [25], in the following we propose a conceptual framework to characterize the ensemble life-cycle. We represent the ensemble behavior as a composition of three components: execution, context and adaptation, and we give a formal definition of all their concepts, defining their corresponding semantics and pointing out the interactions among them.

Definition 4 (Context Property). *A context property c is a triplet $c = \langle V, \nu, t \rangle$ where V is the set of possible values that the property can assume belonging to a certain domain , ν is the actual value of the property and $t : V \to V$ is the function regulating how the property value ν changes.*

Each cell is *autonomous* in the sense that it evolves according to its own behaviour. We denote by $\mathcal{P}$ the set of all possible behaviours P and by $\mathcal{F}$ the set of functionalities. We then define the semantics of a behaviour through a labelled transition system (LTS) as follows:

Definition 5 (Behaviour Evolution). *Behaviour evolution is defined via a labelled transition system $L = (\mathcal{P}, A, \hookrightarrow)$, where A is the alphabet of task labels α and $\hookrightarrow \subseteq \mathcal{P} \times A \times \mathcal{P}$ is the transition relation.*

Formally a cell is defined as:

Definition 6 (Cell). *A cell e is a triplet $e = \langle P, \rho, \phi \rangle$ where P is the cell behaviour, ρ is a set of context properties that a cell uses and ϕ is a set of functionalities provided by the cell.*

We denote by P_e, ρ_e and ϕ_e the corresponding elements of an cell e.

We define the *system context* (sometimes shortened as context) through the set of all *context properties* provided by the different cells that are part of an ensemble at a certain execution time. Formally we define a *system context* as:

Definition 7 (System Context). *Let $\mathcal{E}$ the set of all the cells part of an ensemble at a certain execution time. We then characterize the context C as the union of all context properties:*

$$C = \biguplus_{e \in \mathcal{E}} \rho_e$$

We denote by $\mathcal{C}$ the set of contexts C. The successful completion of a cell task may depend on some assumptions on the context. To this aim, we assume the existence of a set of assumptions g on (some properties of) the context, written in a suitable logic $\mathcal{G}$. We then assume the existence of a predicate $C \vdash g$ indicating the fact that the context satisfies the assumption g, and $C \nvdash g$ when C does not satisfy g.

Context evolution does not depend directly on the system execution. To this end we assume that there exists a reduction semantics regulating how the context evolves, that is:

Definition 8 (Context Evolution). *Context Evolution is defined via a reduction relation $\dashrightarrow$ over configuration, that is $\dashrightarrow \subseteq \mathcal{C} \times \mathcal{C}$.*

A cell behaviour is *context-aware* if its execution depends on a particular configuration of the context.

Assumption on the context made by a cell behaviour should be matched against the context configuration. Hence, at cell level, if the execution of a particular task implies some assumptions on the context, these have to be satisfied by the context in order to proceed with the normal execution. We now have all the ingredients to define the semantics of a cell context-aware behaviour.

Definition 9 (Context-aware Evolution). *Context-aware behaviour evolution is defined via a labelled transition system $L = (Q, A, \rightarrow)$, where Q is a set of states $\mathcal{C} \times \mathcal{P}$, A is the alphabet of task labels α and $\rightarrow \subseteq Q \times A \times Q$ is the transition relation.*

In order to support adaptation a system should be able to generate adaptation problems. To clearly distinguish an adaptation need from the other tasks of a cell behaviour we use the special symbol $\boxplus$.

Definition 10 (Adaptiveness). *A cell e is able to trigger adaptation if the alphabet A of the LTS regulating its context-aware evolution contains the adaptation need, that is $\boxplus \in A$.*

Definition 11 (Context Awareness). *A cell e is said to be context-aware if it is adaptive and the transition relation of its context-aware evolution is closed under the following rules:*

$$(\text{C.Ok}) \quad \frac{P \xrightarrow{\gamma(g)} P' \quad C \vdash g}{(C, P) \xrightarrow{\gamma} (C, P')} \qquad (\text{C.No}) \quad \frac{P \xrightarrow{\gamma(g)} P' \quad C \nvdash g \quad P'' = \Theta(P')}{(C, P) \xrightarrow{\boxplus} (C, P'')}$$

where $\gamma(g)$ indicates the fact that the task γ can be executed only if the context assumption g holds and $\Theta : \mathcal{P} \to \mathcal{P}$ is an annotation function used to annotate some information about the violation that lead P to P'.

Let us note that whenever an assumption does not hold in the current context, then the adaptation need $\boxplus$ is triggered and it is used to execute a *cell adaptation* with the goal to solve a precise adaptation problem. Moreover we have that $\to$ exploits the relation $\hookrightarrow$.

Definition 12 (System Execution). *System Execution is defined via a reduction relation $\mapsto$ over context configurations and sets of cells, that is $\mapsto : \mathcal{C} \times \mathcal{E} \to \mathcal{C} \times \mathcal{E}$.*

One property that a CAS should enjoy is *openness*: it should allow for entrance and exit of cells. This improves the dynamicity of the system, allowing for example to let cells with *better* or *new* functionalities get into the system or to let cells that have completed their tasks exit the system. For example in a P2P system openness allows new peers to join the network and to discover new neighbours.

We can now define this property formally:

Definition 13 (Openness). *A system is open if its reduction relation is closed under the following rules:*

$$(\text{In}) \quad \frac{e = \langle P_e, \rho_e, \phi_e \rangle \quad \Phi(e)}{(C, \mathcal{E}) \mapsto (C \uplus \rho_e, \mathcal{E} \uplus e)} \qquad (\text{Out}) \quad \frac{e = \langle P_e, \rho_e, \phi_e \rangle \quad e \in \mathcal{E} \quad \Omega(e)}{(C, \mathcal{E}) \mapsto (C \setminus \rho_e, \mathcal{E} \setminus e)}$$

where $\Phi(\cdot)$ and $\Omega(\cdot)$ are some predicates regulating when a cell has to enter or exit the system.

Rules for openness are straightforward: rule IN allows a new cell e to get into the system; as a side effect, the system context is enriched with its context properties. Rule OUT allows a cell to get out of the system; as a side effect, its properties are taken away from the context. When these two rules are instantiated with predicates that are always true, then entry and exit of cells becomes non deterministic.

When an adaptation need is triggered by a cell behaviour, this means that some assumptions on the context do not hold. This implies that the cell behaviour has a wrong view of the context, or that the context has changed due to some exogenous events. In such a case an *adaptable* system should be able to change the cell behaviour in order to satisfy the new context. We now formally define an adaptation problem:

Definition 14 (Adaptation Problem). *An adaptation problem a is a triplet* $a = \langle C, g, F \rangle$ *where g is the goal on some context properties that adaptation should achieve, C is the system context at the moment that the need is triggered and, F is a set of functionalities of the cells present in the system at the moment that the need is triggered. These functionalities will be used to build the adaptation solution.*

We now define the semantics of the *system adaptation* component using an LTS as follows:

Definition 15 (System Adaptation). *System Adaptation is defined via a labelled transition system* $L = (Q, A, \rightarrow)$, *where Q is a set of states in* $\mathcal{C} \times \mathcal{F} \times \mathcal{P}$, *A is the alphabet of action labels* α *and* $\rightarrow \subseteq Q \times A \times Q$. *We require that the alphabet A contains at least the symbols* ✓ *indicating that the adaptation solution has been found.*

Property 1. (ADAPTIVE SYSTEM). A system is adaptive if its reduction relation is closed under the following rule:

$$
(\text{ADAPT}) \quad \frac{(C, P) \xrightarrow{\boxplus} (C, P') \quad (C, F, P') \xrightarrow{\checkmark} (C, F, P'')}{\langle C, \mathcal{E} \uplus e \rangle \mapsto \langle C, \mathcal{E} \uplus e'' \rangle} \quad \begin{array}{c} e = (P, \rho, \phi) \quad e'' = (P'', \rho, \phi) \quad F = fun(\mathcal{E}) \end{array}
$$

where $fun(\cdot)$ is a function that selects functionalities from the available cells.

The above rule is straightforward: if a cell triggers an adaptation need, then the *system adaptation* component is asked to find a solution (indicated by the symbol ✓) and then the system adapts the cell to the new behaviour.

Given an adaptation problem a the *system adaptation* component is in charge to understand, from the behaviour P present in the problem a, what is the goal that the adaptation should achieve. Once the goal is inferred, the *system adaptation* component uses an adaptation function formally defined as follows:

Definition 16 (Adaptation Function). *An adaptation function is a function* $f : \mathcal{C} \times \mathcal{G} \times \mathcal{F} \rightarrow \mathcal{P} \cup \{\star\}$.

Let us note that the adaptation function is a total function as the co-domain of the function allows the use of the symbol $\star$ in the case that a solution to the problem does not exist. Moreover we allow the *system adaptation* component to return an empty solution, indicated with the null behaviour **0**, in order to deal with cases in which there is no more need of adaptation since the context has changed.

An adaptation mechanism can be seen as a transformation function that combines the result of the adaptation function with the original behaviour that raised the need, in order to obtain the new adapted behaviour. Formally we have:

Definition 17 (Adaptation Mechanism). *An adaptation mechanism is a function* $\mu : \mathcal{P} \to \mathcal{P}$ *that takes in input the behaviour that raised a need, and returns the new adapted behaviour.*

Naturally an adaptation mechanism should exploit the adaptation function in order to find a solution to the problem and then compose the solution with the behaviour that raised the need. When different adaptation mechanisms are combined and executed in a precise order, *adaptation strategies* are realized. They are able to deal with complex adaptation needs that cannot be addressed by applying adaptation mechanism in isolation.

4 Collective Adaptation in Ensembles

In adaptive systems with collective behavior, new approaches for adaptation are therefore needed that allow (i) multiple cells to collectively adapt with (ii) negotiations to decide which collective changes are best. Collective adaptation also raises a second important challenge: which parts of the system (cells) should be engaged in an adaptation? This is not at all trivial, since solutions for the same problem may be generated at different levels.

Service-based system (SBS) represent one example of a CAS where the cells, defined in our general framework, are represented by service providers and end-users, each specifying its behaviour through a set of tasks to be executed in a precise order (i.e., business processes) and each providing a set of functionalities (i.e., services). The context in which SBSs must operate continuously changes at run-time, starting from the change of the situation in which tasks are executed, to the availability of services, the human actors interacting with the application as well as their requirements and preferences. This means that SBSs should operate differently for different contextual situations, deal with the fact that involved services are not known a priori, and be able to dynamically react to changes to better fit the new situations.

We show hereby how it is possible to model this example of CAS by exploiting the formal framework introduced above. We use examples coming from a running scenario taken from a realistic smart city e-mobility application, where the SBS needs to deal with the variability of the actors involved, as well as of the situations in which it must operate.

Following Definition 6 a cell is a triplet of the form $e = \langle P, \rho, \phi \rangle$ with P the cell behaviour, ρ the set of context properties and F the set of functionalities that the cell exposes to the system. In our example, behaviours P (from now on processes) are specified using business processes expressed in a subset of the APFL language [26] depicted in Fig. 5, which call APFL*lite*.

For the sake of space, we do not define context properties ρ and fragments ϕ of cells, the logic $\mathcal{G}$ of assumptions g in the context, and the context evolution relation $\dashrightarrow$ (Definition 8). We just require that the logic $\mathcal{G}$ contains the formula $\top$ that always holds whatever is the context, that is $\forall C . C \vdash \top$, and that it allows for assumptions on the status of a context property.

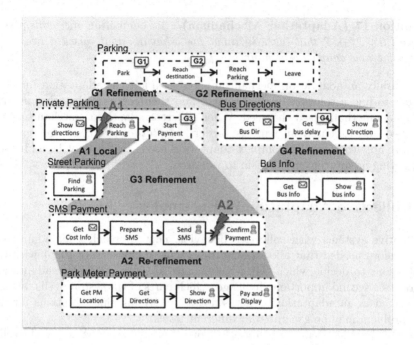

Fig. 4. Execution and Adaptation in the Smart Mobility scenario

Behaviour Evolution. The syntax of processes P is depicted in Fig. 5. A process can be the null process **0**, a task A, a compensable task $A \div g$, an abstract task (g), an adaptation need $\boxplus$, a cause $\langle g \rangle$ indicating the condition g that caused an adaptation need. Finally processes can be composed in sequence $P.Q$, where "." is the composition operator. An abstract task (g) specifies just the goal that its execution should achieve; at runtime, this goal is used by the *system adaptation*, to obtain a proper process P able to satisfy the goal g. The compensation g of a compensable task $A \div g$ indicates the fact that if the task A is executed then its compensation g has been taken into account by the system in the case in which the adaptation strategy requires to compensate the execution of the task A. Let us note that compensations takes the simple form of an assumption g.

A task can be either a basic task π or a scoped task $[g_1, \pi, g_2]$. A basic task is either an invoke $\overline{a}_{id}$, indicating the invocation of the task a located at the cell id, or a receive a. We assume the existence of the following denumerable infinite mutually disjoint sets: the set $\mathcal{N}$ of cell names and the set $\mathcal{A}$ of tasks names. We let id and its decorated version to range over $\mathcal{N}$ and a, b and their decorated version to range over $\mathcal{A}$. A scoped task is just a basic task decorated with a precondition g_1 and a postcondition g_2.

For the sake of space, and without losing generality, we let our syntax (and language) to be as small as possible without introducing all the other constructs provided by well established languages such as BPEL.

$$\pi ::= a \mid \bar{a}_{id} \qquad\qquad\qquad\qquad\qquad\qquad \text{basic tasks}$$
$$A ::= [g_1, \pi, g_2] \mid \pi \qquad\qquad\qquad\qquad\qquad \text{tasks}$$
$$P ::= 0 \mid A \mid A \div g \mid (g) \mid \boxplus \mid \langle g \rangle \mid P.P \qquad \text{processes}$$
$$g, g_1, g_2 \in \mathcal{G} \quad a \in \mathcal{A} \quad id \in \mathcal{N}$$

Fig. 5. Syntax of APFLite processes

Following Definition 5 we define the semantics of a behaviour P via a LTS $L = (Q, A, \hookrightarrow)$ where $\hookrightarrow$ obeys to the rules depicted in Fig. 6. All the rules are straightforward as they just transform a prefix into a label. Said otherwise, relation $\hookrightarrow$ tells us what a process can *potentially* do.

$$(\text{P.Act}) \ \frac{\alpha \in \{a, \bar{a}_{id}, \langle g \rangle, \boxplus\}}{\alpha.P \overset{\alpha}{\hookrightarrow} P} \qquad\qquad (\text{P.Cmp}) \ \frac{A.P \overset{\alpha}{\hookrightarrow} P}{A \div g.P \overset{\alpha \div g}{\hookrightarrow} P}$$

$$(\text{P.Sc}) \ \frac{\pi.0 \overset{\alpha}{\hookrightarrow} 0}{[g_1, \pi, g_2].P \xrightarrow{c(g_1, \alpha, g_2)} P} \qquad (\text{P.Ref}) \ (g).P \xrightarrow{r(g)} P \qquad (\text{P.Nil}) \ 0.P \overset{\tau}{\hookrightarrow} P$$

Fig. 6. Behaviour evolution

Context-Aware Behaviour Evolution. In our system, process execution is subject to context properties. Indeed the execution of scoped or abstract tasks is subject to assumptions on the context. To this end, following the Definition 9, we introduce a layer of rules that we call Context-aware Behaviour Evolution, in charge of executing processes under the context. Relation $\rightarrow$ obeys to the rules depicted in Fig. 7.

During the execution, a process needs to store several kinds of information about the its execution that are useful to implement different adaptation strategies. Information saved consist of: the compensations of all the executed tasks and abstract tasks that a particular business process has executed. Hence rules in Fig. 7 deal with elements of the form $(C, P, G, \mathcal{R})$ (instead of the simple pair (C, P) as in Definition 9), where G is a list of compensations and $\mathcal{R}$ is a list of refinements already created. To this end we indicate by ϵ the empty list and by $::$ the concatenation operator among lists. Lists are ordered and when we write $g :: G$, the element g represents the head of the list and G the tail. Moreover the operator $::$ obeys the following rules:

$$\epsilon :: G = G \qquad\qquad \top :: G = G$$

Compensation lists are built in a way that the first element is always the compensation of the last executed compensable task as shown by rule C.Cmp.

$$(\textbf{C.Cond}) \quad \frac{P \xrightarrow{c(g_1,\alpha,g_2)\div g'} P' \quad C \vdash g_1 \quad C \vdash g_2}{(C,P,G,\mathcal{R}) \xrightarrow{\alpha} (C,P',g' :: G,\mathcal{R})}$$

$$(\textsc{C.Pre}) \quad \frac{P \xrightarrow{c(g_1,\alpha,g_2)\div g'} P' \quad C \vdash g_1 \quad C \nvdash g_2 \quad P_2 = \boxplus.\langle g_2\rangle.P'}{(C,P,G,\mathcal{R}) \xrightarrow{\alpha} (C,P_2,g' :: G,\mathcal{R})}$$

$$(\textsc{C.Cmp}) \quad \frac{P \xrightarrow{\alpha \div g} P' \quad \alpha \neq c(\_,\_,\_)}{(C,P,G,\mathcal{R}) \xrightarrow{\alpha} (C,P,g :: G,\mathcal{R})} \qquad (\textbf{C.H1}) \quad \frac{P \xrightarrow{c(g_1,\alpha,g_2)} P' \quad C \nvdash g_1}{(C,P,G,\mathcal{R}) \xrightarrow{\boxplus} (C,P,G,\mathcal{R})}$$

$$(\textsc{C.H2}) \quad \frac{P \xrightarrow{\boxplus} P'}{(C,P,G,\mathcal{R}) \xrightarrow{\boxplus} (C,P',G,\mathcal{R})} \qquad (\textsc{C.V}) \quad \frac{P \xrightarrow{r(g)} P'}{(C,P,G,\mathcal{R}) \xrightarrow{\boxplus} (C,P,G,\mathcal{R})}$$

$$(\textsc{C.Basic}) \quad \frac{P \xrightarrow{\alpha} P' \quad \alpha \in \{a,\bar{a}_{id},\tau\}}{(C,P,G,\mathcal{R}) \xrightarrow{\alpha} (C,P',G,\mathcal{R})}$$

Fig. 7. Context-aware behaviour evolution

Let us briefly comment other rules. Three rules deal with a scope $[g_1,\pi,g_2]$, depending on the context configuration. Rule C.Cond allows to execute the task π when both g_1,g_2 are satisfied. Rule C.H1 is triggered when precondition g_1 is not satisfied and then adaptation is required. Rule C.Pre is triggered when postcondition g_2 is not satisfied, in this case the task π is still executed but then adaptation is required (by imposing $P_2 = \boxplus.\langle g\rangle.P'$). Rule C.V deals with abstract tasks, rule C.H2 deal with adaptation need and rule C.Basic deals with basic tasks. Let us note that rules **C.Cond** and **C.H1** are an instance of the rules of Property 11.

System Execution. Following Definition 12 we let $\mapsto$ be the smallest reduction relation that obeys the rules depicted in Fig. 8. For the sake of brevity we slightly differ from the Definition 12 by letting $\mapsto$ operate on triplets of the form $\langle C,\mathcal{E},F\rangle$ instead of simple pairs $\langle C,\mathcal{E}\rangle$. F is the set of all the functionalities present in the system at a certain execution time, and it is clear that it can be calculated each time by just inspecting the cell set $\mathcal{E}$. When indicating the structure of the cell we avoid to specify its set of context properties and fragments, while focusing just on the process and its runtime information such as the compensations list, the refinements list and the pending messages queue. This last one is used to implement an asynchronous communication mechanism among cells. Rules S.Snd and S.Rcv deals with asynchronous communication though message queues. Let us note that in the rule S.Snd $\mathcal{E}'$ is the cell set $\mathcal{E}$ in which the behaviour of the cell $id[\ldots]$ evolved from P to P'. Rule S.Ctx deal with context changes, while rule S.Int deals with internal (τ) actions of cells. Rule S.Adapt is triggered whenever a process launches an adaptation need. Note that this rules makes our

$$(\text{S.SND}) \ \frac{(C, \mathsf{P}) \xrightarrow{\overline{a}_{id}} (C, \mathsf{P}') \quad id[\mathsf{P}, \mathcal{M}] \in \mathcal{E}}{\langle C, F, \mathcal{E} \uplus id[\mathsf{Q}; \mathcal{N}] \rangle \mapsto \langle C, F, \mathcal{E} \uplus id[\mathsf{Q}; \mathcal{N} \uplus \overline{a}] \rangle}$$

$$(\text{S.RCV}) \ \frac{(C, \mathsf{P}) \xrightarrow{a} (C, \mathsf{P}')}{\langle C, F, \mathcal{E} \uplus id[\mathsf{P}; \mathcal{M} \uplus \overline{a}] \rangle \mapsto \langle C', F, \mathcal{E} \uplus id[\mathsf{P}'; \mathcal{M}] \rangle}$$

$$(\text{S.CTX}) \ \frac{C \dashrightarrow C'}{\langle C, F, \mathcal{E} \rangle \mapsto \langle C', F, \mathcal{E} \rangle} \qquad (\text{S.INT}) \ \frac{(C, \mathsf{P}) \xrightarrow{\tau} (C, \mathsf{P}')}{\langle C, F, \mathcal{E} \uplus id[\mathsf{P}; \mathcal{M}] \rangle \mapsto \langle C, F, \mathcal{E} \uplus id[\mathsf{P}'; \mathcal{M}] \rangle}$$

$$(\textbf{S.Adapt}) \ \frac{(C, \mathsf{P}) \xrightarrow{\boxplus} (C, \mathsf{P}') \quad (C, F, \mathsf{P}') \xrightarrow{\checkmark} (C, F, \mathsf{P}'')}{\langle C, F, \mathcal{E} \uplus id[\mathsf{P}; \mathcal{M}] \rangle \mapsto \langle C, F, \mathcal{E} \uplus id[\mathsf{P}''; \mathcal{M}] \rangle}$$

$$(\textbf{S.In}) \ \frac{e = id[\mathsf{P}, \rho, \phi]}{\langle C, F, \mathcal{E} \rangle \mapsto \langle C \uplus \rho, F \uplus \phi, \mathcal{E} \uplus e \rangle} \qquad (\textbf{S.Out}) \ \frac{e = id[\mathsf{P}, \rho, \phi]}{\langle C, F, \mathcal{E} \uplus e \rangle \mapsto \langle C \setminus \rho, F \setminus \phi, \mathcal{E} \rangle}$$

$$\text{with } \mathsf{P}, \mathsf{Q} = P, G, \mathcal{R}$$

Fig. 8. System execution

$$(\text{AM.R}) \ \frac{P \xrightarrow{r(g)} P' \quad Q = ad(C, F, g) \quad Q \neq \star \quad \mathcal{R}' = \{g, P', G\} :: \mathcal{R}}{(C, F, P, G, \mathcal{R}) \xrightarrow{\checkmark} (C, F, Q.P', \epsilon, \mathcal{R}')}$$

$$(\text{AM.L1}) \ \frac{P \xrightarrow{c(g_1, \alpha, g_2)} P' \quad Q = ad(C, \mathcal{F}, g_1) \quad Q \neq \star}{(C, F, P, G, \mathcal{R}) \xrightarrow{\checkmark} (C, F, Q.P, \mathcal{R}')}$$

$$(\text{AM.L2}) \ \frac{P \xrightarrow{\langle g \rangle} P' \quad Q = ad(C, F, g) \quad Q \neq \star}{(C, F, P, G, \mathcal{R}) \xrightarrow{\checkmark} (C, F, Q.P', G, \mathcal{R}')}$$

Fig. 9. Adaptation mechanisms

system *adaptive* according to Property 1. Rules S.IN and S.OUT deal with the *openness* property of a CAS. In these last two rules we assume the compensation list and the refinement lists as empty.

System Adaptation. Following Definition 16 an adaptation function f is a function $f : \mathcal{C} \times \mathcal{G} \times \mathcal{F} \to \mathcal{P}$. In our system we identify the function ad as being an adaptation function. The *system adaptation* component is called by the *system execution* component through the reduction $\xrightarrow{\checkmark}$. This kind of reduction can be generated by the adaptation mechanisms in Fig. 9 or by the re-refinement strategy implemented of Fig. 10 (rule As.RROK). When an adaptation need is caught by the *system execution* component, then it is checked whether a single mechanism is applicable, otherwise the *system adaptation* component resorts to the

$$(\text{AS.No}) \ \frac{P \xrightarrow{\alpha} P' \quad \alpha \in \{(g_1), c(g_1, \pi, g_2), \langle g_1 \rangle\} \quad ad(C, F, g_1) = \star}{(C, F, P, G, \mathcal{R}) \xrightarrow{\boxplus} (C, F, P, G, \mathcal{R})}$$

$$(\text{AS.RRNo}) \ \frac{(C, F, P, G, \mathcal{R}) \xrightarrow{\boxplus} (C, F, P_1, G_1, \mathcal{R}_1) \quad \mathcal{R}_1 = \{g, Q_2, G_2\} :: \mathcal{R}_2 \quad ad(C, F, G_1 :: g) = \star}{(C, F, P, G, \mathcal{R}) \xrightarrow{\boxplus} (C, F, P, G_1 :: G_2, \mathcal{R}_2)}$$

$$(\text{AS.RROk}) \ \frac{(C, F, P, G, \mathcal{R}) \xrightarrow{\boxplus} (C, F, P_1, G_1, \mathcal{R}_1) \quad \mathcal{R}_1 = \{g, Q_2, G_2\} :: \mathcal{R}' \quad Q = ad(C, F, G_1 :: g) \quad Q \neq \star}{(C, F, P, G, \mathcal{R}) \xrightarrow{\checkmark} (C, F, Q.Q_2, G_2, \mathcal{R}')}$$

Fig. 10. Re-refinement strategy

strategy. Rule AM.R implements the refinement mechanism in case the process P is of the form $P = (g).P'$. In this case a direct call to the adaptation function is made using as goal the g of the abstract task, and if a solution is found $Q \neq \star$, then the adapted process returned to the system will take the form $Q.P'$, that is the process P in which the abstract task (g) has been substituted with its refinement Q. Another effect of the rule AM.R is the one to save information useful for the re-refinement strategy. Rules AM.L1 and AM.L2 implement local adaptation mechanisms. When mechanisms are not directly applicable then a strategy is taken into account. The presented strategy tries to re-refine the last refined task taking into account also the compensations of the tasks that has been executed since the last refinement. If a solution is not found then recursively past refinements are tried. This is why the list $\mathcal{R}$ of refinement closures $\{g, P', G\}$ is kept. The meaning of the closure is to save the goal g of the last refined task along with the current list of compensations and the rest of the process to be executed once the refined process as been executed. Hence, each time a refinement is executed (rule AM.R) a new closure is created and put on the top of the list. Then the refined process is given an empty ϵ compensations list and a new refinements list. Rules in Fig. 10 unroll the refinements list that implement the re-refinement strategy, unrolling the refinements list until a solution is found.

5 Implementation

The life-cycle presented in this paper and its formal representation, has been used in the last years to guide the realization of a software framework for the definition and management of Collective Adaptive Systems. Other approaches are emerging in the literature. For example, Bures et al. in [27] address this issue by identifying a new class of component-based systems—Ensemble-Based Component Systems (EBCS)—specifically tailored for designing Resilient Distributed Systems (RDS). The paper also presents the Distributed Emergent Ensembles of

Components Resilient Distributed Systems (RDS) that respond to and influence activities in the real world are engineered using component model as instantiation of EBCS. With respect to the component-based approach they propose, we use a service-based approach. Our method is open to the use of new services (i.e., cells) at runtime making the approach more dynamic in terms of extension to the inclusion of new runtime features. Besides, we guarantee both intra- and inter-ensemble adaptations, i.e. adaptations inside and between the ensembles.

To realize our solution, we have applied an incremental software development approach that led to the realization of an overall framework able to support all ensemble's phases introduced in this paper. A Collective Adaptation Engine (CAE), has been first released as a standalone component[1] and subsequently used as a component, in the *DeMOCAS* framework [28][2]. It has been implemented by using *Java* as programming language (to be executed, *Java 8* is required).

DeMOCAS is a framework for the modeling and execution of service-based CASs. It includes tools to model dynamic ensembles (as described in Sect. 2), and mechanisms for ensembles specialization and adaptation (as introduced in Sects. 3 and 4). DeMOCAS is built around three main aspects: (i) dynamic settings: each CAS is a collection of autonomous agents entering and exiting the system dynamically; (ii) collaborative nature of systems: agents can collaborate in groups (i.e., ensembles) for their mutual benefit; (iii) collective adaptation: multiple agents must adapt their behavior in concert to respond to critical runtime impediments.

In this framework, collective adaptation is performed by exploiting the formal framework (partially) described in Sect. 4, and by associating a MAPE (Monitor, Analyze, Plan, Execute) loop with each agent. In Fig. 11 we show the Collective Adaptation Viewer of DeMOCAS. The viewer reports an example of an issue resolution result in the urban mobility domain (i.e., the issue Intense Traffic triggered by a Flexibus Driver, during its route execution). In the left side, all the agents involved in the issue resolution process are listed. The issue resolution tree of an agent (i.e., the Route Manager) that executes its own instance of the collective adaptation algorithm to solve the triggered issue is shown in the right side.

DeMOCAS has been used in different projects realizing collective adaptive systems in different application domains. ATLAS [29], a World-Wide travel assistant where mobility service providers need to collaborate to meet citizens' needs, CARPooL [30], where passengers with similar needs are grouped and managed in an automatic, distributed, and adaptive carpooling system, and finally Adjust Light [31] where smart devices and things (i.e., sensors and actuators) cooperate to achieve automatically the right light level in a room. All these concrete applications have demonstrated both the domain independent nature of the approach, and its feasibility for realizing adaptive applications.

---

[1] For the interested reader, the prototype is available in its entirety on a GitHub repository https://github.com/das-fbk/CollectiveAdaptationEngine.

[2] https://github.com/das-fbk/DeMOCAS.

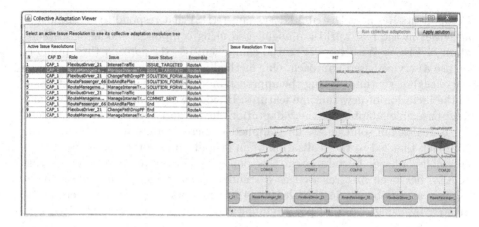

Fig. 11. Collective Adaptation Viewer.

6 Conclusion and Future Directions

The paper aims to report our research experience on self-adaptive systems, in particular adaptive systems composed by distributed and heterogeneous ensembles. Through a formal framework we have introduced a life-cycle for collective adaptive systems that we have designed, implemented and experimented in the last ten years. This research has drawn out important directions hereby summarized. While the solutions proposed in these years have as primary objective the development of techniques for runtime adaptation, we would like to extend the framework supporting CAS developers with a user-friendly modeling tool. Initial work in this direction has been proposed in [32] where we propose *CAStlE* [33], a DSL made-up of three main views: one devoted to adaptive systems design; one addressing ensembles definition; and one tackling the collective adaptation.

Managing concurrency and conflict resolution are two very important aspects of CAS and they deserve the right attention. For this we have started a new research path whose objective is to extend our framework with algorithms based on concurrent planning [34], able to manage conflicting goals between cells. Moreover, in the situation where collective adaptation solutions are not possible, our intention is to take inspiration from a preliminary work presented in [35] and extend the framework introducing game theoretic techniques. Finally, we would like to introduce quality analysis and learning techniques, to retrieve an study emerging phenomena when dealing with dynamic and open collective adaptive systems.

References

1. Hölzl, M., Rauschmayer, A., Wirsing, M.: Engineering of software-intensive systems: state of the art and research challenges. In: Wirsing, M., Banâtre, J.-P., Hölzl, M., Rauschmayer, A. (eds.) Software-Intensive Systems and New Computing Paradigms. LNCS, vol. 5380, pp. 1–44. Springer, Heidelberg (2008). https://doi.org/10.1007/978-3-540-89437-7_1

2. Zambonelli, F., Bicocchi, N., Cabri, G., Leonardi, L., Puviani, M.: On self-adaptation, self-expression, and self-awareness in autonomic service component ensembles. In: SASOW, pp. 108–113. IEEE Computer Society (2011)
3. Preda, M.D., Gabbrielli, M., Giallorenzo, S., Lanese, I., Mauro, J.: Developing correct, distributed, adaptive software. Sci. Comput. Program. **97**, 41–46 (2015)
4. Hennicker, R., Klarl, A.: Foundations for ensemble modeling–the HELENA approach. In: Iida, S., Meseguer, J., Ogata, K. (eds.) Specification, Algebra, and Software. LNCS, vol. 8373, pp. 359–381. Springer, Heidelberg (2014). https://doi.org/10.1007/978-3-642-54624-2_18
5. Bonnet, J., Gleizes, M.P., Kaddoum, E., Rainjonneau, S., Flandin, G.: Multi-satellite mission planning using a self-adaptive multi-agent system. In: 2015 IEEE 9th International Conference on Self-Adaptive and Self-Organizing Systems, Cambridge, MA, USA, 21–25 September 2015, pp. 11–20. IEEE Computer Society (2015)
6. Zambonelli, F., et al.: Self-aware pervasive service ecosystems. Procedia Comput. Sci. **7**, 197–199 (2011). Proceedings of the 2nd European Future Technologies Conference and Exhibition 2011 (FET 2011)
7. de Lemos, R., et al.: Software engineering for self-adaptive systems: a second research roadmap. In: de Lemos, R., Giese, H., Müller, H.A., Shaw, M. (eds.) Software Engineering for Self-Adaptive Systems II. LNCS, vol. 7475, pp. 1–32. Springer, Heidelberg (2013). https://doi.org/10.1007/978-3-642-35813-5_1
8. Krupitzer, C., Breitbach, M., Roth, F.M., VanSyckel, S., Schiele, G., Becker, C.: A survey on engineering approaches for self-adaptive systems (extended version) (2018)
9. Weyns, D., Andersson, J.: On the challenges of self-adaptation in systems of systems. In: Proceedings of the First International Workshop on Software Engineering for Systems-of-Systems, pp. 47–51. ACM (2013)
10. Jennings, N.R.: An agent-based approach for building complex software systems. Commun. ACM **44**(4), 35–41 (2001)
11. Kephart, J.O., Chess, D.M.: The vision of autonomic computing. Computer **36**(1), 41–50 (2003)
12. Tinnemeier, N.A.M., Dastani, M., Meyer, J.-J.C.: Roles and norms for programming agent organizations. In: 8th International Joint Conference on Autonomous Agents and Multiagent Systems (AAMAS 2009), Budapest, Hungary, 10–15 May 2009, vol. 1, pp. 121–128 (2009)
13. Andersson, J., De Lemos, R., Malek, S., Weyns, D.: Reflecting on self-adaptive software systems. In 2009 ICSE Workshop on Software Engineering for Adaptive and Self-Managing Systems, pp. 38–47. IEEE (2009)
14. Cheng, B.H.C., et al.: Software engineering for self-adaptive systems: a research roadmap. In: Cheng, B.H.C., de Lemos, R., Giese, H., Inverardi, P., Magee, J. (eds.) Software Engineering for Self-Adaptive Systems. LNCS, vol. 5525, pp. 1–26. Springer, Heidelberg (2009). https://doi.org/10.1007/978-3-642-02161-9_1
15. FOCAS Partners: FoCAS manifesto - a roadmap to the future of collective adaptive systems (2016). http://www.focas.eu/focas-manifesto.pdf
16. Bucchiarone, A., Mezzina, C.A., Pistore, M., Raik, H., Valetto, G.: Collective adaptation in process-based systems. In: SASO 2014, pp. 151–156. IEEE Computer Society (2014)
17. Bures, T., et al.: A life cycle for the development of autonomic systems: the e-mobility showcase. In: 2013 IEEE 7th International Conference on Self-Adaptation and Self-Organizing Systems Workshops, pp. 71–76. IEEE (2013)

18. Wirsing, M., Hölzl, M., Koch, N., Mayer, P. (eds.): Software Engineering for Collective Autonomic Systems. LNCS, vol. 8998. Springer, Cham (2015). https://doi.org/10.1007/978-3-319-16310-9
19. Bucchiarone, A., Dennis, G., Gnesi, S.: A graph-based design framework for global computing systems. Electr. Notes Theor. Comput. Sci. **236**, 117–130 (2009)
20. Bruni, R., Bucchiarone, A., Gnesi, S., Melgratti, H.: Modelling dynamic software architectures using typed graph grammars. Electron. Notes Theoret. Comput. Sci. **213**(1), 39–53 (2008)
21. ter Beek, M.H., Bucchiarone, A., Gnesi, S.: Dynamic software architecture development: towards an automated process. In: 35th Euromicro Conference on Software Engineering and Advanced Applications, SEAA 2009, Proceedings, Patras, Greece, 27–29 August 2009, pp. 105–108 (2009)
22. Bucchiarone, A., Marconi, A., Pistore, M., Raik, H.: A context-aware framework for dynamic composition of process fragments in the Internet of Services. J. Internet Serv. Appl. **8**(1), 601–623 (2017)
23. Bucchiarone, A., Ehrig, H., Ermel, C., Pelliccione, P., Runge, O.: Rule-based modeling and static analysis of self-adaptive systems by graph transformation. In: Software, Services, and Systems - Essays Dedicated to Martin Wirsing on the Occasion of His Retirement from the Chair of Programming and Software Engineering, pp. 582–601 (2015)
24. Hölzl, M., Wirsing, M.: Towards a system model for ensembles. In: Agha, G., Danvy, O., Meseguer, J. (eds.) Formal Modeling: Actors, Open Systems, Biological Systems. LNCS, vol. 7000, pp. 241–261. Springer, Heidelberg (2011). https://doi.org/10.1007/978-3-642-24933-4_12
25. Bucchiarone, A., Marconi, A., Mezzina, C.A., Pistore, M.: A conceptual framework for collective adaptive systems. In: Proceedings of the 28th Annual ACM Symposium on Applied Computing, SAC 2013, Coimbra, Portugal, 18–22 March 2013, pp. 1935–1936 (2013)
26. Bucchiarone, A., Lluch-Lafuente, A., Marconi, A., Pistore, M.: A formalisation of adaptable pervasive flows. In: 6th International Workshop, Web Services and Formal Methods, WS-FM 2009, Bologna, Italy, 4–5 September 2009, Revised Selected Papers, pp. 61–75 (2009)
27. Bures, T., Gerostathopoulos, I., Hnetynka, P., Keznikl, J., Kit, M., Plasil, F.: DEECO: an ensemble-based component system. In: Proceedings of the 16th International ACM SIGSOFT Symposium on Component-Based Software Engineering, pp. 81–90. ACM (2013)
28. Bucchiarone, A., De Sanctis, M., Marconi, A., Martinelli, A.: DeMOCAS: domain objects for service-based collective adaptive systems. In: Drira, K., et al. (eds.) ICSOC 2016. LNCS, vol. 10380, pp. 174–178. Springer, Cham (2017). https://doi.org/10.1007/978-3-319-68136-8_19
29. Bucchiarone, A., De Sanctis, M., Marconi, A.: ATLAS: a world-wide travel assistant exploiting service-based adaptive technologies. In: Maximilien, M., Vallecillo, A., Wang, J., Oriol, M. (eds.) ICSOC 2017. LNCS, vol. 10601, pp. 561–570. Springer, Cham (2017). https://doi.org/10.1007/978-3-319-69035-3_41
30. Furelos-Blanco, D., Bucchiarone, A., Jonsson, A.: CARPooL: collective adaptation using concurrent planning. In: Proceedings of the 17th International Conference on Autonomous Agents and MultiAgent Systems, AAMAS 2018, Stockholm, Sweden, 10–15 July 2018, pp. 1815–1817. International Foundation for Autonomous Agents and Multiagent Systems Richland, SC, USA/ACM (2018)

31. Alkhabbas, F., De Sanctis, M., Spalazzese, R., Bucchiarone, A., Davidsson, P., Marconi, A.: Enacting emergent configurations in the iot through domain objects. In: Pahl, C., Vukovic, M., Yin, J., Yu, Q. (eds.) ICSOC 2018. LNCS, vol. 11236, pp. 279–294. Springer, Cham (2018). https://doi.org/10.1007/978-3-030-03596-9_19
32. Bucchiarone, A., Cicchetti, A., De Sanctis, M.: Towards a domain specific language for engineering collective adaptive systems. In: 2nd IEEE International Workshops on Foundations and Applications of Self* Systems, FAS*W@SASO/ICCAC 2017, Tucson, AZ, USA, 18–22 September 2017, pp. 19–26. IEEE Computer Society (2017)
33. Bucchiarone, A., Cicchetti, A., De Sanctis, M.: CAStlE: a tool for collective adaptive systems engineering. In: 2nd IEEE International Workshops on Foundations and Applications of Self* Systems, FAS*W@SASO/ICCAC 2017, Tucson, AZ, USA, 18–22 September 2017, pp. 385–386. IEEE Computer Society (2017)
34. Bucchiarone, A., Furelos-Blanco, D., Jonsson, A., Khandokar, F., Mourshed, M.M.: Collective adaptation through concurrent planning: the case of sustainable urban mobility. In: Proceedings of the 17th International Conference on Autonomous Agents and MultiAgent Systems, AAMAS 2018, Stockholm, Sweden, 10–15 July 2018, pp. 1880–1882. International Foundation for Autonomous Agents and Multiagent Systems Richland, SC, USA/ACM (2018)
35. Andrikopoulos, V., et al.: A game theoretic approach for managing multi-modal urban mobility systems. In: Ahram, T., Karwowski, W., Marek, T. (eds.) Proceedings of the 5th International Conference on Applied Human Factors and Ergonomics AHFE 2014, Krakow, Poland, 19–23 July 2014, pp. 5716–5725 (2014)

Multi-modelling and Co-simulation in the Engineering of Cyber-Physical Systems: Towards the Digital Twin

John Fitzgerald[1]($\boxtimes$), Peter Gorm Larsen[2], and Ken Pierce[1]

[1] School of Computing, Newcastle University, Newcastle upon Tyne, UK
{john.fitzgerald,kenneth.pierce}@ncl.ac.uk
[2] DIGIT, Department of Engineering, Aarhus University, Aarhus, Denmark
pgl@eng.au.dk

Abstract. Ensuring the dependability of Cyber-Physical Systems (CPSs) poses challenges for model-based engineering, stemming from the semantic heterogeneity of the models of computational, physical and human processes, and from the range of stakeholders involved. We argue that delivering such dependability requires a marriage of multi-disciplinary models developed during design with models derived from real operational data. Assets developed during design thus become the basis of a learning digital twin, able to support decision making both in redesign and in responsive operation. Starting from an open integrated toolchain leveraging formal models for CPS design, we consider the extension of this concept towards digital twins. A small example inspired by agricultural robotics illustrates some of the opportunities for research and innovation in delivering digital twins that contribute to dependability.

1 Introduction

Cyber-Physical Systems (CPSs) which integrate networking, sensor and computational technology with data science and artificial intelligence, offer significant potential benefits to the quality of life and the sustainability of businesses [9]. However, their developers and operators face significant challenges in maintaining global properties such as reliability and security [8]. First, CPS development and operation involves a wide variety of stakeholders, models, analytic methods and tools. Multi-disciplinary federations of diverse design-time models, called *multi-models*, enable machine-assisted analytics to identify defects and evaluate overall properties such as security that span the cyber/physical boundary. Second, multi-models provide a basis for exploring design alternatives before commitments are made to implementation. However, such multi-models describe systems 'as designed', are not normally available in operation, and over time diverge from the system 'as built', as the latter, its environment, and its users evolve.

Dependable operation of CPSs requires both the ability to address the consequences of evolving system components, and the ability to explore and identify optimal changes that do not unduly compromise overall dependability. This combination of prediction and response alongside support for informed decision-making

© Springer Nature Switzerland AG 2019
M. H. ter Beek et al. (Eds.): Gnesi Festschrift, LNCS 11865, pp. 40–55, 2019.
https://doi.org/10.1007/978-3-030-30985-5_4

and redesign by humans requires both the data derived from operations and the models developed in design. Tackling the challenges of CPS design thus requires a marriage of both descriptive multi-models of the type that might be developed in a design process, and inductive models derived from data acquired during operation. This combination of models, cutting across formalisms as well as across design and operation, has the potential to form a *learning digital twin* for a CPS, enabling off-line and on-line decision-making. The goal of our work is to enable the well-founded engineering of such learning digital twins for dependable CPSs.

In this paper, we outline steps towards the model-based engineering of digital twins that link descriptive and inductive models. We first review aspects of the state of the art (Sect. 2), and then propose core elements of a learning digital twin (Sect. 3). We illustrate the challenges of prototyping such a twin by considering a small example inspired by agricultural robotics (Sect. 4). We finally draw conclusions regarding the future directions for this work (Sect. 5).

2   Challenges in Engineering Cyber-Physical Systems

Our goal is to enable the well-founded model-based engineering of learning digital twins for CPSs. This entails the linkage of models of both computational and physical processes, as well as the linkage of descriptive models with operational data. In this section, we first consider a small motivating scenario, and then review the capabilities of current technology.

2.1   A Future CPS at Scale

Imagine an arable farm in Denmark in 2030. More organic and diverse than a decade earlier, it needs a wide variety of efficient, reliable and high-precision processes such as weeding. To reduce the risk of soil compaction and erosion, field operations are done by fleets of small autonomous robots that are provided as a service by companies whose operators remotely monitor their fleets, dealing with their interactions with other systems provided by other suppliers, such as weather forecasting and produce storage, managing the reliability of their diverse fleets as a whole, and dealing with interactions with the few remaining machines that the farmer actually owns.

Operation adjustment: One hot day, one of the weeding robots slows down. The cause is a battery protection routine in the software that was updated three weeks earlier. Back then, an artificial intelligence monitoring the (cloud) data gathered from all the machines, noticed degrading battery life in robots that operate in extremely warm conditions. The protection routine was updated to make the robot run at a speed that avoids overheating. Such a speed was computed for each robot as a function of its wear level and temperature, through multiple simulations. A day later, the robot is weeding at full power.

Operational prediction: Back at the robot supplier's data centre, a full system simulation monitors the whole fleet, looking ahead 24 h, and taking into account the farm's requirements, weather, and other data. A problem is discovered and an alarm is raised and sent to an operator, who takes a close look. Using her VR headset, she is immersed in a 3D view of the farm. She fast-forwards 15 h and sees a robot traffic jam at the charging station. They are all expected to reach the station at the same time, resulting in a congestion. Routines at the data centre have, in the meantime, suggested changes in the energy management plan so that the charging is more organised. The operator accepts this solution and it is sent to the farmer for approval.

This scenario illustrates some of the potential of CPSs, but realising this vision requires capabilities in at least four areas. First, the ability to integrate diverse design models. Second, the capacity to correlate such models with data observed from the CPS in operation, creating an accessible 'digital twin' of the CPS as it works in its real operating environment. Third, the ability to integrate and even learn from data gathered in operation so as to discover mismatches. Fourth, the ability to use these models and data as a basis for prediction, decision-making, and adaptation. Below, we briefly consider technologies that seek to address these needs.

2.2   Multi-modelling and Co-simulation

For CPSs such as those that arise in our agricultural scenario, there will rarely be a single model developed during design that unifies the cyber and physical elements. Rather, there will be several semantically diverse models for these system elements such as Discrete-Event (DE) models of computational processes versus Continuous Time (CT) models of physical elements. Further, the details of models will often be retained by the suppliers of these elements who may not wish to compromise their Intellectual Property (IP) by sharing them. In order to analyse properties such as overall system dependability, it is necessary to analyse these ensembles of diverse (and diversely owned) models. We term such ensembles *multi-models*, and the tasks of constructing, maintaining and analysing them we describe as *multi-modelling*.

In previous work, we developed and piloted an open tool chain for multi-modelling [10,24]. A key technique here is *co-simulation* [13], in which a co-simulation orchestration engine (COE) [35] manages the passage of time and sharing of data among individual simulations in order to give a coherent whole-system simulation. Since there are many modelling and simulation tools in use, standards are emerging to enable co-simulation. The Functional Mock-up Interface (FMI) standard [3][1], supports co-simulation of models packaged as Functional Mock-up Units (FMUs), each of which is treated as a 'black box', supporting the separation of IP. The standard allows functions to set inputs, compute over simulation intervals, and get outputs from FMUs that may run in diverse simulators. The coordination of the simulators is done through an orchestration engine [35]. Such engines have not yet been standardised, and offer challenges in both research and practice [32]. Current co-simulation algorithms lack explicit

---

[1] http://fmi-standard.org/.

support for dynamic reconfiguration of simulators, limiting their value in situations where CPS reconfigurations arise as part of a maintenance intervention, for example [17].

2.3 Digital Twins

A digital twin is a virtual replica of physical assets, processes, people, places, systems or devices created and maintained in order to answer questions about its physical counterpart (the physical twin). Coupled with new sensor technology, such a replica can provide a new layer of engineering insight, which will be valuable in improving a product performance, and providing a seed for the next generation of the product, in particular, the transition towards autonomy.

Although several commercial digital twin-based solutions are on offer (e.g., see those of ANSYS[2] and Siemens[3]), there remain important challenges around the engineering of such twins. For example, there is no clear way on how to keep the digital twin calibrated under re-configurations and changes in the physical twin. Another example is how to provide intuitive representation of the abnormal behaviour of the physical twin, so that supervisory control systems (or humans) can react to it rapidly.

2.4 Machine Learning for CPSs

In the context of digital twins, prediction is commonly performed through applying simulation (e.g., [20]). While the importance of Machine Learning (ML) models has been highlighted [31], works exploiting ML for real-time predictions are few. In CPSs, standard ML approaches have been used to identify error situations, and have been exploited mainly for diagnostic purposes, e.g. [1]). In the field of built environment, approaches to speeding building performance simulation has been proposed, using co-simulation [2,28].

ML approaches can be broadly categorised as Deep (or Representation) Learning [38], or statistical ML [33]. Exploiting digital twins in the CPS setting requires ML models for the analysis of data coming from the real and virtual spaces. The adoption of such sophisticated models requires advances on defining the best network topology for each problem to be solved [36].

2.5 Decision Support and Visualisation with Digital Twins

Humans play a crucial role in CPSs, but in order to do so must be able to make sense of the information coming from the CPS, sometimes in pressured environments [14,30]. The presentation and visualisation of a CPS and the associated operational and design data is critical and, although there is research into using augmented reality to assist with CPS maintenance (e.g., [6]), more work is needed on: interfaces that adapt to the evolution of the twins, in order

---

[2] https://www.ansys.com/products/systems/digital-twin.
[3] https://community.plm.automation.siemens.com/t5/Digital-Twin/ct-p/DigitalTwin.

to avoid flooding the user with irrelevant information; intuitive representation of properties of interest for decision support [21]; and on supporting decision-making across organisations. Finally, we note that, in a CPS, 'faults' will not be unusual, given the independence of constituent systems, and decision support enabled by statistical model checking and fault injection will be crucial, though there appears to be little work to date on the interaction of these techniques.

3   Towards a Learning Digital Twin

We envision an open platform for creating *learning digital twins* that integrates multi-models with data derived from CPS operations, and with inductive models learned from such operational data, enabling decision-making. The goal of our current work is to create and evaluate such a learning digital twin, using platforms that admit, as far as possible, open integration of a wide range of tools.

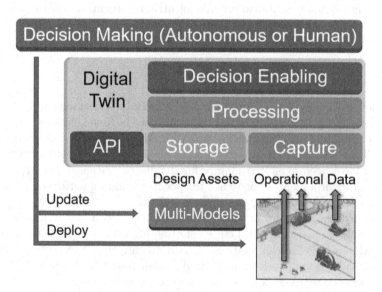

Fig. 1. Functionality of a perpetually learning digital twin.

Figure 1 shows the main features of a learning digital twin of the kind we envisage. In operation, the CPS will be interacting with the physical world and human users, generating additional data related to system commissioning, configuration or tuning from the administrator side. The twin receives data from the real CPS, and multi-models developed within design activities. It supports decision-making, whether autonomous or human, which may result in updates to both the operational CPS and consistent updates to multi-models. Within the digital twin, the following levels of functionality are delivered:

- **Multi-model and Data Storage** include the basic handling of multi-models covering the architecture and interaction between the operational CPS and the digital twin, recording and maintaining time series data acquired from sensors, correlating it to existing multi-models.
- **Model and Data Processing** turns data into information. It includes static and dynamic analysis on multi-models, via a range of tools, including co-simulation and model checking. Data Analytics includes the analysis of time series data and in particular the use of ML techniques to derive models based on the CPS 'as built', as well as incident prediction. Specific techniques can be down-selected depending application and data characteristics.
- **Decision Enabling** presents information to decision-makers based on the model and data processing analyses done on operational data and multi-models. This will include decision support through possibilities to carry out trials, visualisation and Design Space Exploration (DSE).
- **The API** enables interaction between the digital twin and externals, including (potentially) other digital twins.

To develop a learning digital twin, we can build on baseline technologies for multi-modelling and co-simulation, and for the acquisition and integration of data from operational CPSs. For example, the INTO-CPS open toolchain[4] provides a basis for multi-model development and analysis using FMI for co-simulation, and has integrated several discipline-specific model-based engineering tools, including the Vienna Development Method (VDM) tool Overture[5] and the 20-sim tool[6] [7,11,25,29]. However, this technology has not been used in a digital twin context before and so we are investigating the adjustments needed to support the reactive detection of deviations from predicted behaviour, and in decision support.

In order to manage operational data, it is necessary to utilise cloud-based platforms such as e-Science Central [15] or MindSphere[7] to enable connection of devices, data management, plug-in data analytics, and user collaboration. Within this multi-modelling framework, there is potential to exploit tools for simulation of, for example, mechatronic systems; Agent-Based Modelling for aspects of human behaviour (e.g., NetLogo[8]); visualisation (e.g., Unity[9]); and statistical model checking (e.g., [22,26]).

---

[4] http://projects.au.dk/into-cps/.
[5] http://www.overturetool.org.
[6] https://www.20sim.com/.
[7] https://new.siemens.com/global/en/products/software/mindsphere.html.
[8] https://ccl.northwestern.edu/netlogo/.
[9] https://unity.com/.

4   A Case Study: The Line-Following Robot

4.1   Introduction

In order to explore the approach that we advocate, we consider a simple example based on a general-purpose Line Following Robot (LFR), a desktop-sized version of which is shown in Fig. 2. The LFR has been used to illustrate co-simulation [16], and as a pilot study in projects developing co-simulation technology. Althgouh very simple, the LFR ha ssome features in common with agricultural robots of the kind that underpin the example in Sect. 2.1, and that have been modelled in industry [12].

The LFR can follow a line painted on the ground. The line contrasts with its background, and infra-red sensors located on the front of the robot distinguish the dark line from the lighter ground. The robot's two wheels are powered by individual motors that allow it to make controlled changes in position and orientation. The number and position of the sensors may be configured in the multi-model. A controller takes input from the sensors to make outputs to the motors.

In the INTO-CPS technology, we typically give CPS architectural descriptions in SysML [34]. A profile has been developed to support the description of multi-models. An INTO-CPS application is then able to derive the code to link FMUs and a co-simulation orchestration engine. The individual FMUs may include discrete event or continuous time executables derived from a range of tools. In this example, the discrete event formalism is VDM-RT [37], a dialect of VDM; the continuous time formalism is a bond graph notation. The VDM models are developed and simulated in Overture [23]; the bond graph models are developed and executed in 20-sim [19].

Fig. 2. Desktop-sized LFR

4.2   Architectural Structure and Functional Mock-Up Units

The SysML Connection Diagram in Fig. 3 shows connections between the *Controller*, *Body*, *Sensor1* and *Sensor2* component instances (FMUs). Broadly speaking, the *Controller* receives sensor readings from both *Sensor1* and *Sensor2* components; the *Controller* in turn sends servo commands to the *Body* component; and finally the *Body* sends the robot position to both sensor components.

The interface for each FMU is governed by a model description XML file. For the `Controller` FMU that is developed using VDM-RT, the information about its inputs and outputs is present in a special `HardwareInterface` class defined in the object-oriented VDM-RT notation:

```
class HardwareInterface

instance variables

   public leftVal : RealPort := new RealPort(0.0);
   public rightVal : RealPort := new RealPort(0.0);
   public servo_right_out : RealPort := new RealPort(0.0);
   public servo_left_out : RealPort := new RealPort(0.0);

end HardwareInterface
```

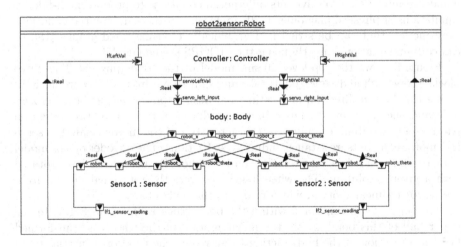

Fig. 3. LFR connections diagram

The actual control functionality takes the values of `leftVal` and `rightVal` as inputs and assigns output to the two output ports. Essentially this is defined using simple case analysis, but it can also be defined with a modal approach (for example a degraded mode when one of the sensors no longer work). In the VDM-RT model, there is a `Controller` class defined as follows:

```
class Controller

instance variables
    servoLeft: RobotServo;
    servoRight: RobotServo;
    sensorRightVal :RobotSensor;
    sensorLeftVal :RobotSensor;

operations

private control_loop : () ==> ()
control_loop() == ...

thread

periodic(10000,0,0,0)(control_loop);
end Controller
```

The `control_loop` operation reads the sensor values and determines if the robot should turn left, go straight or turn right in the next time step. The periodic thread definition at the end sets the real-time characteristics (period, jitter, delay and offset) of the control loop.

The physical elements of the robot have been modelled in 20-sim, which uses numerical integration to solve sets differential equations to produce high-fidelity simulations of physical phenomena. 20-sim generates these differential equations from models that can be structured graphically or using bond graphs [18], or can contain equations directly using the SIDOPS+ language [5].

Figure 4 shows the top-level 20-sim model of the robot physics. The **servo** blocks (**servo_left** and **servo_right**) take an input signal from the controller indicating the desired direction of rotation and desired power output between zero (off) and one (full power). These blocks produce a rotational motion based on parameters describing the physical characteristics of the motor inside the servo (i.e. motor constants, resistance, inductance, friction). The **encoder** blocks model optical rotary encoders that tell the controller how far the wheels have rotated with a given resolution. The **wheel** blocks convert the rotational motion from the servos to linear motion, which feed into the **body** block.

The bond graph contained within the body block is shown in Fig. 5. In the upper half of this bond graph, the linear motion of the wheels is transformed (**TF**) into rotation of the body, acting to overcome the rotational inertia (**I**). In the lower half, the linear motion of the wheels is transformed (**MTF**) into the translation of the body, overcoming friction (**R**) and inertia (**I**). The **theta** and **position** blocks integrate the rotation and translation over time, which become the **robot_state**: (x, y, θ).

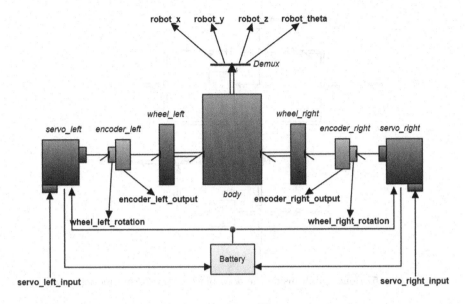

Fig. 4. 20-sim model of robot physics

4.3   Matching the Descriptive Model to Deployed Components

The architecture of a CPS as built and deployed in its operating environment may differ from its original design, either because it has been constructed using legacy components, or because it has evolved over time, or because the environment no longer meets the assumptions underpinning design. This is particularly the case in large-scale systems embedded in the physical infrastructure. It is therefore not in general trivial to map operational data gathered from the deployed CPS to the design-level multi-model. In our example, the communication shown in the design model between the body FMU and the two sensor FMUs is not directly accessible in the deployed system[10]. Thus, a first adaptation that is necessary in order to be able to use the engineered multi-model as a digital twin is to consider the body and sensor FMUs as a single blackbox FMU, by making use of nested co-simulation [35]. In addition, the LFR as built in fact uses six pins to encode the two servo inputs that are shown in the design-level architecture. Thus, it is necessary also to adapt either the existing Controller FMU or the new hierarchical FMU representing the entire physical system. Such changes could naturally also be made at the multi-model level. This illustrates the need to develop methods around the management of design models at a range of abstraction levels, including an indication of when it is beneficial to alter the composition.

---

[10] We expect that this may often be the case between FMUs that represent physical elements by means of CT models.

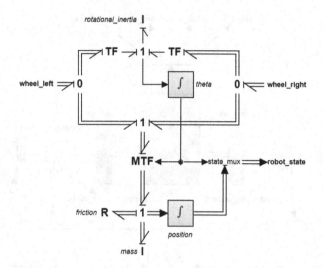

Fig. 5. Bond graph inside the *body* block of the 20-sim model

4.4   Operational Data Gathering

In order to extract data from the physical twin either the CPS needs to be able to have an edge-computing device locally, or send its logged data in real time to a cloud solution. In either case, the live data can be provided to drive a co-simulation that serves as an oracle, comparing co-simulation controller outputs with the real system's output signals. The values from the real CPS cannot be expected to be exactly the same as those predicted by the co-simulation, and so it will be necessary to consider the level of approximation that is acceptable, which can in principle be different for different variables and system contexts.

4.5   Model and Data Processing

We envision support for processing in two different ways: (1) using co-simulation with the multi-models developed during the engineering of the CPS and (2) using ML. Both forms of processing will use the live streaming of the data that is available between the FMUs in the real CPS. Whenever the example is co-simulated both the inputs and outputs are logged in a time-series form for all four FMUs. Each entry here contains the time, the step-size, and all inputs and outputs from the four CPUs (in the same order). In this way it is possible to see with different graphs how the co-simulation is progressing.

In Fig. 6 the sensor outputs are listed for respectively the real LFR and the co-simulated LFR. At the modelling level the sensors are modelled such that they are yielding a number indicating how dark the surface that the sensor is seeing. In the realised version of the LFR though a cheaper sensor is used so this simply gives a binary result. Thus, the comparison of the result in a digital twin context needs to take this into account. This illustrates the kind of differences that arise between 'as designed' and 'as built'. Essentially this means that for the two sensors there are four possible inputs.

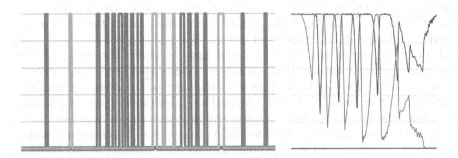

Fig. 6. Sensor outputs from real LFR and sensor outputs from the simulation.

The interesting point from the controller perspective is that there is an appropriate relationship between the sensor input and the actuator output (to the wheels). Since the controller here is a basic bang-bang controller taking simple sensor inputs it is relatively easy to see that there is a high correspondence between the four possible inputs and the outputs. In a new version of the co-simulation orchestration the live streaming of this real data will be fed into the different FMUs, but instead of sending it on to the receiving FMUs it will be compared against the data predicted from the FMUs. If the discrepancy is too large, the intention is to support decisions by human operators.

4.6 Decision Enabling

In a simple example like the LFR it is difficult to envision complex decisions, but we could imagine intelligent controllers that, for example, would enable support with degraded modes if any of the sensors would fail. Such a change could probably be conducted autonomously. However, in particular if there are many alternative solutions to choose between (and none of them are particularly advantageous) it would probably make more sense to involve a human in the final decision. As in the future scenario described in Sect. 2.1, it would be important to be able to fast-forward simulations to visualise what the consequences of different potential interventions. In this context, exploring alternative solutions using DSE will be important in managing the trade-offs between alternative solutions.

5   Looking Forward

Digital Twin technology is attracting considerable attention in a wide range of engineering domains[11] , and at a range of scales, from individual machines within a factory, up to national infrastructure [4]. In this paper, we have proposed that digital twins for future CPSs can benefit from utilisation of the often formal multi-disciplinary models developed during design alongside operational data and inductive models learned from the system 'as built'. We argue that the use of design-time formal models – which have benefitted from highly rigorous validation – may be beneficial in giving confidence on the overall system-level properties of the digital twin. We have outlined something of the functionality of such a twin, and have begun to try to realise it on a simple example.

Even the very basic robot study highlights some of the challenges in providing foundations, methods and tools for the rigorous engineering of digital twins for CPSs. In particular it has shown the need to address mismatches between models that record design intent, and the real-world realisation. As even our simple example showed, there is a need to consider structural differences as well as differences at the level of individual data.

In lifting the idea of the formal model-based digital twin to future large-scale CPSs, it is important to consider the range of abstraction levels of models. In such systems, it is impractical to analyse an infrastructure CPS at one level of abstraction only: too low a level and simulation results may not be timely; too high a level and they are not useful. A dynamic approach, where abstraction levels can be changed during co-simulation, may yield more practical results. Research questions include how to trigger level changes, and how to ensure alignment of different models of the same phenomena.

Finally, although digital twins offer the potential for adaptivity and improved maintenance, it is worth highlighting the extent to which reliance is placed on their correct functioning. A twin can be, at a certain level, a potential single point of failure, and the extensive network communication in a CPS twin leaves open the need to address issues of security and trust. Given the challenges we outline above, we would argue that there is a case for a concerted effort to develop formal foundations, methods and tools to support the digital twins as a vehicle for moving models into run-time and operational contexts. Formal model-based engineering techniques continue to have a key role to play in this promising and challenging field.

Acknowledgements. We are grateful to the Poul Due Jensen Foundation, which has supported the establishment of a new Centre for Digital Twin Technology at Aarhus University, which will take forward the principles, tools and applications of the engineering of digital twins. We gladly acknowledge the collaboration of many colleagues, including Carl Gamble, Nicholas Ainslie, John Mace, Jennifer Whyte, Martin Mayfield, Hugo Macedo, Frederik Foldager, Claudio Gomes, Casper Thule, Kenneth Lausdahl, Christian Kleijn, Mihai Neghina and Stelios Basagiannis.

---

[11] The Gartner group puts digital twins in its 10 strategically most important technologies in 2019: https://www.gartner.com/smarterwithgartner/gartner-top-10-strategic-technology-trends-for-2019/.

Dedication. It is a pleasure to offer this paper in honour of Stefania Gnesi, whose work as a leading member of the formal methods and model-based design communities internationally has enabled the collaborations that have underpinned our research. Stefania's work for the Formal Methods Europe Association – over decades – has helped shape one of the world's leading symposia in the field. In her role as chair of ERCIM-FMICS and as a co-founder of the FormaliSE conference, she has done much to bring formal methods to the wider industry and engineering communities. Indeed, FormaliSE was one of the first places in which we discussed progress in co-simulation of formal models [10]. The greatest tribute that we can pay to Stefania is to ensure that our community continues to build on the foundations that she has done so much to establish.

References

1. Akhtar, N., Mian, A.: Threat of adversarial attacks on deep learning in computer vision: a survey. CoRR abs/1801.00553 (2018). https://arxiv.org/abs/1801.00553
2. Berger, J., Mazuroski, W., Oliveria, R.C., Mendes, N.: Intelligent co-simulation: neural network vs. proper orthogonal decomposition applied to a 2D diffusive problem. J. Build. Perform. Simul. **11**(5), 568–587 (2018). https://doi.org/10.1080/19401493.2017.1414879
3. Blochwitz, T.: Functional mock-up interface for model exchange and co-simulation, July 2014. https://www.fmi-standard.org/downloads
4. Bolton, A., Enzer, M., Schooling, J., et al.: The Gemini Principles: guiding values for the national digital twin and information management framework. Centre for Digital Built Britain and Digital Framework Task Group (2018). https://doi.org/10.17863/CAM.32260
5. Breunese, A.P., Broenink, J.F.: Modeling mechatronic systems using the SIDOPS+ language. In: The Society for Computer Simulation International, pp. 301–306 (1997)
6. Controllab Products: Design of a Compensated Motion Crane using INTO-CPS. Technical report, Press Release EU, Enschede, Netherlands (2018)
7. Couto, L.D., Basagianis, S., Mady, A.E.D., Ridouane, E.H., Larsen, P.G., Hasanagic, M.: Injecting formal verification in FMI-based co-simulation of cyber-physical systems. In: The 1st Workshop on Formal Co-Simulation of Cyber-Physical Systems (CoSim-CPS). Trento, Italy, September 2017
8. ECS-SRA: Electronic Components & Systems Strategic Research Agenda. Technical report, Electronic Components & Systems (ECS) (2019)
9. Electronic Components and Systems for European Leadership (ECSEL) Private Members Board: Multi Annual Strategic Research and Innovation Agenda for ECSEL Joint Undertaking (2016)
10. Fitzgerald, J., Gamble, C., Larsen, P.G., Pierce, K., Woodcock, J.: Cyber-Physical Systems design: Formal Foundations, Methods and Integrated Tool Chains. In: FormaliSE: FME Workshop on Formal Methods in Software Engineering. ICSE 2015, Florence, Italy, May 2015
11. Fitzgerald, J., Gamble, C., Payne, R., Larsen, P.G., Basagiannis, S., Mady, A.E.D.: Collaborative model-based systems engineering for cyber-physical systems - a case study in building automation. In: Proceedings INCOSE International Symposium on Systems Engineering. Edinburgh, Scotland, July 2016
12. Foldager, F., Balling, O., Gamble, C., Larsen, P.G., Boel, M., Green, O.: Design space exploration in the development of agricultural robots. In: AgEng Conference. Wageningen, The Netherlands, July 2018

13. Gomes, C., Thule, C., Broman, D., Larsen, P.G., Vangheluwe, H.: Co-simulation: a survey. ACM Comput. Surv. **51**(3), 49:1–49:33 (2018)
14. Grieves, M., Vickers, J.: Digital twin: mitigating unpredictable, undesirable emergent behavior in complex systems. In: Kahlen, F.-J., Flumerfelt, S., Alves, A. (eds.) Transdisciplinary Perspectives on Complex Systems, pp. 85–113. Springer, Cham (2017). https://doi.org/10.1007/978-3-319-38756-7_4
15. Hiden, H., Woodman, S., Watson, P., Cala, J.: Developing cloud applications using the e-science central platform. Philos. Trans. R. Soc. A: Math. Phys. Eng. Sci. **371**(1983), 1–12 (2013)
16. Ingram, C., Pierce, K., Gamble, C., Wolff, S., Christensen, M.P., Larsen, P.G.: Examples compendium. Technical Report, The DESTECS Project (INFSO-ICT-248134), October 2012
17. Jung, T., Shah, P., Weyrich, M.: Dynamic co-simulation of internet-of-things-components using a multi- agent-system. In: 51st CIRP Conference on Manufacturing Systems, vol. 72, pp. 874–879. Procedia CIRP, Elsevier (2018)
18. Karnopp, D., Rosenberg, R.: Analysis and Simulation of Multiport Systems: The Bond Graph Approach to Physical System Dynamic. MIT Press, Cambridge (1968)
19. Kleijn, C.: Modelling and simulation of fluid power systems with 20-sim. Intl. J. Fluid Power **7**(3), 57–60 (2006)
20. Knapp, G., Mukherjee, T., Zuback, J., Wei, H., Palmer, T.A., De, T.D.: Building blocks for a digital twin of additive manufacturing. Acta Mater. **135**, 390–399 (2010)
21. Kunarth, M., Winkler, H.: Integrating the digital twin of the manufacturing system into a decision support system for improving the order management process. Procedia CIRP **72**, 225–231 (2018)
22. Larsen, K.G., Legay, A.: Statistical model checking: past, present, and future. In: Margariaand Steffen [27], pp. 3–15. https://doi.org/10.1007/978-3-319-47166-2_1
23. Larsen, P.G., Battle, N., Ferreira, M., Fitzgerald, J., Lausdahl, K., Verhoef, M.: The overture initiative - integrating tools for VDM. SIGSOFT Softw. Eng. Notes **35**(1), 1–6 (2010). https://doi.org/10.1145/1668862.1668864
24. Larsen, P.G., et al.: Integrated tool chain for model-based design of cyber-physical systems: the INTO-CPS Project. In: CPS Data Workshop. Vienna, Austria, April 2016
25. Larsen, P.G., Fitzgerald, J., Woodcock, J., Lecomte, T.: Trustworthy Cyber-Physical Systems Engineering, Chapter 8: Collaborative Modelling and Simulation for Cyber-Physical Systems. Chapman and Hall/CRC, September 2016. ISBN 9781498742450
26. Legay, A., Sedwards, S., Traonouez, L.: Plasma lab: A modular statistical model checking platform. In: Margaria and Steffen [27], pp. 77–93. https://doi.org/10.1007/978-3-319-47166-2_6
27. Margaria, T., Steffen, B. (eds.): ISoLA 2016. LNCS, vol. 9952. Springer, Cham (2016). https://doi.org/10.1007/978-3-319-47166-2
28. Mazuroski, W., Berger, J., Oliveria, R.C., Mendes, N.: An artificial intelligence-based method to efficiently bring CFD to building simulation. J. Build. Perform. Simul. **11**(5), 588–603 (2018). https://doi.org/10.1080/19401493.2017.1414880
29. Neghina, M., Zamrescu, C.B., Larsen, P.G., Lausdahl, K., Pierce, K.: Multi-paradigm discrete-event modelling and co-simulation of cyber-physical systems. Stud. Inf. Control **27**(1), 33–42 (2018)
30. Perrow, C.: Normal Accidents: Living with High Risk Technologies-Updated Edition. Princeton University Press, New Jersey (2011)

31. Qi, Q., Tao, F.: Digital twin and big data towards smart manufacturing and industry 4.0: 360 degree comparison. IEEE Access **6**, 3585–3593 (2018)
32. Schweiger, G., et al.: Functional Mock-up Interface: an empirical survey identifies research challenges and current barriers. In: The American Modelica Conference, Cambridge, MA, USA (2018)
33. Sugiyama, M.: Introduction to Statistical Machine Learning, 1st edn. Morgan Kaufmann, Boston (2015)
34. OMG Systems Modeling Language (OMG SysML™). Technical Report. Version 1.4, Object Management Group, September 2015. http://www.omg.org/spec/SysML/1.4/
35. Thule, C., Lausdahl, K., Gomes, C., Meisl, G., Larsen, P.G.: Maestro: the INTO-CPS co-simulation framework. Simul. Model. Pract. Theory **92**, 45–61 (2019). https://doi.org/10.1016/j.simpat.2018.12.005. http://www.sciencedirect.com/science/article/pii/S1569190X1830193X
36. Tran, D.T., Kiranyaz, S., Gabbouj, M., Iosifidis, A.: Heterogeneous Multilayer Generalized Operational Perceptron. arXiv:1804.05093, pp. 1–12 (2018)
37. Verhoef, M., Larsen, P.G., Hooman, J.: Modeling and validating distributed embedded real-time systems with VDM++. In: Misra, J., Nipkow, T., Sekerinski, E. (eds.) FM 2006. LNCS, vol. 4085, pp. 147–162. Springer, Heidelberg (2006). https://doi.org/10.1007/11813040_11
38. LeCun, Y., Bengio, Y., Hinton, G.: Deep learning. Nature **521**, 436–444 (2015)

Changing Software in a Changing World: How to Test in Presence of Variability, Adaptation and Evolution?

Antonia Bertolino[1](✉) and Paola Inverardi[2]

[1] ISTI–CNR, Pisa, Italy
`antonia.bertolino@isti.cnr.it`
[2] University of L'Aquila, L'Aquila, Italy
`paola.inverardi@univaq.it`

Abstract. Modern software-intensive and pervasive systems need to be able to manage different requirements of variability, adaptation and evolution. The latter are surely related properties, all bringing uncertainty, but covering different aspects and requiring different approaches. Testing of such systems introduces many challenges: variability would require the test of too many configurations and variants well beyond feasibility; adaptation should be based on context-aware testing over many predictable or even unpredictable scenarios; evolution would entail testing a system for which the reference model has become out-of-date. It is evident how current testing approaches are not adequate for such types of systems. We make a brief overview of testing challenges for changing software in a changing world, and hint at some promising approaches, arguing how these would need to be part of a holistic validation approach that can handle uncertainty.

Keywords: Adaptation and evolution · Context-aware software · Software variability · Testing changing software

1 Introduction

Nowadays software is ubiquitous and governs our lives interacting with smart objects and other software systems that increasingly pervade our surrounding environment. We got used to require that software -be it working from our portable device or in the public front office we ask or in a newly bought home appliance- reacts promptly to satisfy our requests. We even expect that it is capable to face unforeseen circumstances and events or even more that it can anticipate our future needs.

Under pressure of tackling continuous changes that can potentially occur in many ways, software systems themselves change continuously. For instance, they can be Systems-of-Systems (SoS) emerging from the on-the-fly dynamic composition of services, or they can perform self-repair after a problem, or their components can be substituted at runtime.

© Springer Nature Switzerland AG 2019
M. H. ter Beek et al. (Eds.): Gnesi Festschrift, LNCS 11865, pp. 56–66, 2019.
https://doi.org/10.1007/978-3-030-30985-5_5

Consequently, a traditional view of the software lifecycle as involving three main stages: specification, coding (even if by model-driven transformations), and testing is not adequate anymore.

In the software engineering literature, the problem of handling change has been addressed along different research threads. One thread regards software product line (PL) research. In the past two decades huge progress has been done with methodologies and tools that can model and manage variants of products within one family. By adopting a PL approach, developers can a-priori define points of variations and acceptable alternative solutions for differing instantiations of a broad software architecture. Such notion of change, which is referred to as *variability*, has been a main research focus of Stefania Gnesi for several years: in her work she has shown that variability can be formally described [2], or even extracted a posteriori from the requirements [16]. More recently, the notion of Dynamic Software Product Line (DSPL) has emerged [23], which delays the decision of variations to runtime and extends the scope of variability.

On another thread, researchers have investigated approaches to engineer software systems that can adapt to intervening events and situations. Such approaches generally adopt variations of the MAPE (Monitor, Analyze, Plan, Execute) model [24], i.e., the system needs to sense the context and be able to react accordingly. Self-*adaptation* refers to systems that autonomously can decide how to change themselves so to ensure continuous service.

Similar to adaptation is the notion of *evolution*: whereby adaptation is generally referred to as a reactive change triggered by changes in the external world, evolution is rather conceived as a proactive attitude towards change. An evolving system aims at continuously improving itself and providing enhanced services. It must be able to change its goals and behaviour so to provide a service that can satisfy novel requirements. Indeed, placing change in the center of the software process is recognized as the only way to prevent software aging [33].

Although focusing on different facets of change, the notions of variability, adaptation and evolution share several challenges and requirements. They all make it difficult for a software developer to analyse a system and take decisions on it. By stretching somehow the term, in the context of this work we will refer to this difficulty in understanding or predicting a system behaviour as *uncertainty*. We use this term to imply that we cannot know what to expect from a system, because it can take too many possible configurations (variability), or can adapt to context (adaption), or can change its goals (evolution). Indeed, following [21], uncertainty can be defined as the difference between the amount of information required to perform a task and the amount of information already possessed.

The task we are interested here is validation of systems that *change*. Systems for which at the moment of validation complete information is lacking either because it is unknown or because it is too large. In fact, we started by saying that software systems are pervasive and thus we cannot underestimate the need to ensure a reliable behaviour, notwithstanding changes. However, what does it mean to test a system that exposes variability, adaptation or evolution, and which approaches can be applied are still open research questions.

In this opinion paper, we first overview current views of variability, adaptation and evolution, including their shared definitions and most common approaches (Sect. 2). Then, we discuss the challenges descending for testing such type of systems and hint at promising approaches (Sect. 3). Conclusions and possible research directions conclude the paper (Sect. 4).

2   Many Dimensions of Change

As discussed in the introduction modern systems are subject to a number of potential changes during their life time. Those changes cannot always be anticipated or it might not be convenient to anticipate all of them. This introduces levels of uncertainty in the predictable behavior of the system. In the following we analyze the three dimensions of changes we have earlier introduced to understand what are the potential sources of uncertainty.

2.1   Changing Software

Software needs to be able to change. *Variability* is the dimension that characterizes the software that shall encompass the possibility of designing alternatives in the systems, that will be solved only before execution, either statically via a configuration step, or dynamically by providing the necessary information. No matter how variability is resolved, it introduces in the validation step of the development process the need to deal with the system's strong degree of non-deterministic behaviors. When explicitly introduced in the software life cycle [3,25], variability can help reducing the uncertainty by constraining the behavioral analysis into well defined boundaries. However such boundaries can still permit an extremely large search space of potential configurations, like it may happen in the Software Product Line context, thus retaining in practice a degree of uncertainty in the final system behavior. In the past years an extensive research thread contributed by Stefania Gnesi and co-authors has proposed different behavioral expressive models able to compactly represent such search spaces [5,6,40], however verification of such systems has not yet reached the maturity of being routinely used in a development process.

2.2   Changing World

Software needs to be sensitive to the changes that the world around it encompasses. Both adaptation and evolution respond, in different ways, to this need. *Adaptation* refers to the ability of a software system to react in presence of changes of context that may compromise the system behavior, either qualitatively or quantitatively. It is a change that the system needs to undergo not to compromise the compliance of its behavior with respect to the requirements [26]. It typically appears concerning quantitative properties, e.g., degradation of performance due to unexpected high workload. It is associated with the so called self-* properties and autonomic systems [30] and, as already mentioned, it is often implemented through possibly multiple feedback loops. Adaptation may let the system acquire completely new behaviors not foreseen at design time, which is even more evident nowadays with the increasing adoption of learning techniques. How to accomplish adaptation by maintaining system's correctness is a challenge that has received a large deal of attention in the research community and has also motivated the need to move part of the development artifacts at run time (e.g., models at run time) [31].

Evolution has been traditionally the last step in the software life cycle coupled with maintenance. Traditionally it was considered for long living systems that might need to change in order to meet new emerging requirements from users, operating system platform producers, machine changes. In such context the pace of change allowed to integrate the evolution step in the ordinary software life cycle with relatively little effort. For example, traceability issues all along the development phases were required [15] as well as regression test emerged in the validation step. Modern software systems are instead experiencing a fast twist in pace due to the speed of changes both in terms of user expectation and in terms of technological upgrades. In this respect the difficulties of evolution are exacerbated. One main issue concerns the problem of keeping the consistency among the different models of a system (i.e., co-evolution), notably requirements, architecture and code implementation [32].

It appears evident that for modern software systems, validation in the presence of variability, adaptation and evolution needs to take into account a certain degree of uncertainty as anticipated in [20]. Referring to the introduced notion of uncertainty, this means that at the moment these systems are validated, developers do not possess the (complete) information about the systems that the validation step may require. In the following we will discuss how the change dimensions impact on testing and consider some research challenges we foresee in validating software in presence of uncertainty due to changes.

3 Testing Software that Changes

In this section we reflect on the implications brought by change on the software testing discipline. We start by sketching a theoretical framework on which the aims and foundations of software testing are laid. Then we analyse the challenges posed by uncertainties deriving from each of the three kinds of change discussed in the previous section. We conclude by pointing at some promising directions emerging from the literature for addressing the challenges.

3.1 Software Testing Foundations in Light of Change

As defined by Bertolino in [7], software testing consists of the dynamic verification of the behavior of a program on a finite set of test cases, suitably selected from the usually infinite executions domain, against the specified expected behavior.

This definition highlights the main concerns in software testing, in particular that we need a strategy to select a feasible set of test inputs and that we must be able to compare the test output against an expected behaviour, *a.k.a.* the *oracle* problem [4].

In the early 80's, a framework providing a theoretical foundation of software testing was proposed by Gourlay [22]. The framework established a mathematical relation among sets of specifications S, programs P and tests T, and defined the oracle as an *ok* predicate over a test $t \in T$, a specification $s \in S$, and a program $p \in P$. More formally, Gourlay's framework defined a theoretical predicate $corr(p, s)$ over specifications and programs implying that a program p is correct with respect to a specification s, and postulated that $\forall p \in P, \forall s \in S, \forall t \in T, corr(p, s) \Rightarrow ok(t, p, s)$.

More recently, Staats and coauthors [38] revisited Gourlay's framework, and introduced a set O of test oracles (in place of the unique oracle *ok*), whereby a test oracle o is a predicate over programs and tests; they defined a new $corr_t$ predicate over tests, program and specifications that holds if and only if when running test t, specification s holds for program p.

However, neither Bertolino's definition for software testing, nor Staats and coauthors' revisited version of Gourlay's theoretical framework consider explicitly that a program, and/or its input domain and/or its expected behaviour (i.e., oracle), can change and how the derived uncertainty can impact testing validity and effectiveness.

Indeed, *variability, adaptation and evolution clearly affect the notion of testing,* and we claim that in presence of change the theoretical framework for testing should be revised to cope with the uncertainty they bring.

In presence of variability, not only we need to select a finite set of test cases, but also we need to select a set of configurations among those implied by the variation points.

In presence of adaptation, a test case should include a test input but also the context in which the test is executed, and the program itself becomes a function of the context. As a consequence, also the very concept of correctness of a program with respect to a specification may change depending on context.

In presence of evolution, again the correctness relation between a program and the specification becomes relative, in this case because specification can proactively change.

Therefore, we leave as a challenging task for future work a revision of testing theory as formulated in [22] and in [38] to take into account change and uncertainty.

3.2 Testing Challenges Ahead

In front of a rich literature addressing the design and management of changing systems, research on how such systems should be tested is still lacking. For example, focusing on adaptation, in 2009 Salehie and Tahvildari [35] affirmed that testing and assurance are probably the least focused phases, and there are only few works addressing this topic. Concerning variability, in 2014 Galster and coauthors observed that it is *"studied in all software engineering phases, but testing is underrepresented"* [19]. Fortunately today this situation seems to be changing, and several works appear addressing efficient approaches to variability testing, such as, e.g., [1,27].

The testing challenges implied by change in the three forms that we distinguish have been studied in the literature generally along separate threads. It is rarely the case that the three dimensions of change have been considered in holistic way.

Concerning variability, this has been mostly addressed in the domain of software Product Lines. The systematic survey in [12] distinguishes two main research interests, namely the PL features and the PL products. Along the first one, testing aims at verifying all feature interactions by testing all variations across all dimensions. The second one concerns the actual testing of the products members of a family. In both cases, the great challenge is to manage the huge number of potential test cases, which can increase exponentially with the PL features.

The testing challenges stemming from adaptation have been characterised by Siqueira and coauthors [37], who made a systematic survey of literature. They list several general challenges, among which: the exponential growth of the number of configurations to be tested; the difficulty of anticipating environment changes when testing on a large-scale multi-vendor system; the problem to keep traceability between the requirements and the test cases due to the changing characteristics; the arduousness of simulating realistic contexts and workloads due to unpredictability and unclear system boundaries.

Evolution is the dimension of change that has been more extensively addressed in the software testing literature, because it corresponds in a sense to the classical problem of regression testing. Strictly speaking, regression testing concerns the re-testing of previously tested software to verify that changes do not cause previously successfully passed test cases to fail. In recent work, the step of "test suite augmentation" within regression testing process is attracting more emphasis: it refers to creating new test cases specifically addressing the changed behaviour of the evolving software [36]. However, proposed test suite augmentation approaches are mostly code-based, and they do not scale up to consider the complexity of modern evolving systems. The challenges in testing evolving software include finding black-box approaches that can consider dependencies among concurrently running processes, as addressed for instance in [41], as well as dependencies from context changes, as described in [34].

Moreover, a challenge that we see as shared by all three types of change concerns the difficulty of setting an oracle, be it automated or even manual. If we accept that the software behaviour may change because of context adaptation, or evolution of requirements, how can we discern whether an observed behaviour that is not as we would have expected at a given moment is a failure, or is rather a correct deviation because of a change?

When a test is executed we need a way to decide whether a test is successful or fails. However, if we consider the testing of a changing software program P, one issue is that since the system has evolved or has assumed very different forms, we cannot have a readily available reference model to act as an oracle. Even assuming that an oracle is available, for example from a specification, we have to take into account that due to evolution the specification $Spec_t$ that was available at time t may become invalid in later time. So, if at time $t' > t$ we observe that P is not compliant with $Spec_t$, what can we deduce? Is it because the system has evolved (in good way) and hence we need to also evolve $Spec$? Or instead it is because there is a failure in P behaviour?

In other words, in presence of changing systems, when an observed behaviour is not compliant with the oracle, how can we decide whether it is for good (hence the $Spec$ we referred to is obsolete and, e.g., a new specification should be mined [18]), or for bad (the system has evolved in unacceptable way or some failure has occurred)?

3.3 Promising Testing Techniques

Based on our overview of how the foundations of testing software that changes differ from those laid down for "traditional" testing, it is clear that we need to find completely novel approaches to testing software in light of the uncertainty brought by dynamic adaptation and evolution, and of the huge number of possible configurations to test due to variability.

In this section we overview some recent techniques that could be adapted to deal with change in all its three forms.

A natural approach to address the lack or obsolescence of models that can be referred as test oracle or even for test generation is that of mining the model from the program, in particular from the traces obtained by test executions. This is the idea outlined in the *anti-model based testing* proposal by Bertolino et al. [10], even though at the time it was aimed at testing applications when a model is not available. Later on, the idea is further developed by Kanstrén et al. [28], who used the term *observation-based modeling*.

Another promising research avenue is the one to identify so-called "core relatives" [39], which are defined as *pieces of code exhibiting "similar" behavior*, even though structurally different and producing different outputs. Such techniques could be usefully adapted in testing changes.

A well established approach for software testing within some specific domain where deriving an oracle is extremely difficult is *metamorphic testing*: this approach was introduced in the late 90's [13], and has been applied in several contexts and to solve various problems [14]. Metamorphic testing is based on a set of properties that must hold between different executions of the tested system: these necessary properties are called the metamorphic relations. Therefore, even if we do not know what is the expected correct result for an execution, we can compare the outputs across different executions against the expected relations, and detect possible failures when the properties are not fulfilled.

We see several interesting ways in which metamorphic testing naturally applies to the case of testing changing software. For example, where sensible, we could define a set of necessary relations to be maintained across adaptation or evolution, and perform metamorphic testing based on such relations to verify if the software continues to keep the necessary properties. In presence of variability, metamorphic relations could be used to express common features within a family of products.

Yet another potential direction to explore could be to raise the level of abstraction at which the testing is conducted, and perform the testing of the model and not of the implementation, as proposed by Briand and coauthors [11]. The authors proposed to deal with uncertainty by associating appropriate probability distributions to the model elements. A more detailed and complex approach should be conceived to be able to consider all dimensions of variability, adaptation and evolution.

From the field of deep learning systems, we could also adopt the concept of *surprise adequacy* testing [29]: the authors propose that for testing these systems where we cannot know the exact correct outputs, we could expect that what we observe in operation can be different from what we observed during training, but not too much different: they say that the "surprise" we observe must not be too big. We could apply a similar concept for testing in operation a changing system: we establish some "surprise" distances we can admit in operation, and test accordingly.

Inspired by the Proteus framework by Fredericks and Cheng [17], a test platform for changing software should support the adaptive generation of test plans including a core set of test cases that must be satisfied even after change, and an additional set of test cases aiming at testing possible adaptations/evolutions. The former should be based on invariant properties that could be tested applying metamorphic testing between source test cases before change, and follow up test cases after change. The latter would require test suite augmentation: we could perform observation-based testing and assess the mined model against a defined degree of surprise, i.e., distance we can tolerate.

4 Perspectives for Research

As we discussed, testing software in presence of change opens a number of challenging research directions. Notwithstanding, testing remains indispensable, as for such dynamic systems we cannot assume the availability of valid reference models or test suites. On the contrary, we have to deal with uncertainty and the only fact is the behaviour we observe. Because of this, we cannot adopt traditional model-based testing techniques, and need to adapt approaches for anti-model based testing or observation-based modeling or model testing.

An appropriate approach for testing in presence of change should handle change in its three identified dimensions, which should be considered in combination, scaling up further the complexity of the task.

We have overviewed some promising research directions for testing changing software in a changing world. As we cannot rely on the availability of an oracle, we have suggested to adapt metamorphic testing principles for testing changing software but still guaranteeing a core set of invariant properties. In combination we also suggested the opportunity to adapt a notion of surprise-based testing for test suite augmentation.

We have only scraped the surface of the tackled problem, though: for example, we did not discuss when and how testing should occur. For sure monitoring software behaviour is essential, but what would be a proper trigger for moving from passive testing, to proactive? We would need to introduce proper test governance policies [9].

Moreover, we did not discuss the challenges behind reproducing the context of a changing world within which the testing should occur. As this could be too costly or even infeasible, several authors have suggested to perform the testing in production (e.g., [8]), but this poses many new challenges.

For sure many other challenges exist and many new research avenues could be identified. The aim of this paper was not that of providing an exhaustive survey of issues and opportunities, but rather that of depicting a preliminary understanding of the problem difficulties and outlining promising directions for tackling them.

Acknowledgements. This work has been partially supported by the GAUSS national research project (MIUR - PRIN 2015, Contract 2015KWREMX).

References

1. Al-Hajjaji, M., Thüm, T., Lochau, M., Meinicke, J., Saake, G.: Effective product-line testing using similarity-based product prioritization. Softw. Syst. Model. **18**(1), 499–521 (2019)
2. Asirelli, P., Ter Beek, M.H., Gnesi, S., Fantechi, A.: Formal description of variability in product families. In: 2011 15th International Software Product Line Conference, pp. 130–139. IEEE (2011)
3. Autili, M., Benedetto, P.D., Inverardi, P.: A hybrid approach for resource-based comparison of adaptable java applications. Sci. Comput. Program. **78**(8), 987–1009 (2013). https://doi.org/10.1016/j.scico.2012.01.005
4. Barr, E.T., Harman, M., McMinn, P., Shahbaz, M., Yoo, S.: The oracle problem in software testing: a survey. IEEE Trans. Softw. Eng. **41**(5), 507–525 (2014)
5. ter Beek, M.H., Damiani, F., Gnesi, S., Mazzanti, F., Paolini, L.: On the expressiveness of modal transition systems with variability constraints. Sci. Comput. Program. **169**, 1–17 (2019). https://doi.org/10.1016/j.scico.2018.09.006
6. Beohar, H., Varshosaz, M., Mousavi, M.R.: Basic behavioral models for software product lines: expressiveness and testing pre-orders. Sci. Comput. Program. **123**, 42–60 (2016). https://doi.org/10.1016/j.scico.2015.06.005
7. Bertolino, A.: Software testing. In: P. Bourque, R.D. (ed.) SWEBOK Guide to the Software Engineering Body of Knowledge Trial Version, chap. 5, pp. 69–86. IEEE CS, Los Alamitos (2001)
8. Bertolino, A., Angelis, G.D., Kellomaki, S., Polini, A.: Enhancing service federation trustworthiness through online testing. IEEE Comput. **45**(1), 66–72 (2012). https://doi.org/10.1109/MC.2011.227
9. Bertolino, A., Polini, A.: SOA test governance: enabling service integration testing across organization and technology borders. In: 2009 International Conference on Software Testing, Verification, and Validation Workshops, pp. 277–286. IEEE (2009)

10. Bertolino, A., Polini, A., Inverardi, P., Muccini, H.: Towards anti-model-based testing. In: Proceedings of DSN 2004 (Extended abstract), pp. 124–125 (2004)
11. Briand, L., Nejati, S., Sabetzadeh, M., Bianculli, D.: Testing the untestable: model testing of complex software-intensive systems. In: Proceedings of the 38th International Conference on Software Engineering Companion, ICSE 2016, pp. 789–792. ACM, New York (2016). https://doi.org/10.1145/2889160.2889212, http://doi.acm.org/10.1145/2889160.2889212
12. do Carmo Machado, I., Mcgregor, J.D., Cavalcanti, Y.C., De Almeida, E.S.: Onstrategies for testing software product lines: a systematic literature review. Inf. Softw. Technol. **56**(10), 1183–1199 (2014)
13. Chen, T.Y., Cheung, S.C., Yiu, S.M.: Metamorphic testing: a new approach for generating next test cases. Technical report, Technical Report HKUST-CS98-01, Department of Computer Science, Hong Kong (1998)
14. Chen, T.Y., et al.: Metamorphic testing: a review of challenges and opportunities. ACM Comput. Surv. **51**(1), 4:1–4:27 (2018). https://doi.org/10.1145/3143561. http://doi.acm.org/10.1145/3143561
15. Cleland-Huang, J., Gotel, O., Hayes, J.H., Mäder, P., Zisman, A.: Software traceability: trends and future directions. In: Proceedings of the on Future of Software Engineering, FOSE 2014, Hyderabad, India, May 31–June 7, 2014. pp. 55–69 (2014). https://doi.org/10.1145/2593882.2593891
16. Fantechi, A., Ferrari, A., Gnesi, S., Semini, L.: Requirement engineering of software product lines: extracting variability using NLP. In: 2018 IEEE 26th International Requirements Engineering Conference (RE), pp. 418–423. IEEE (2018)
17. Fredericks, E.M., Cheng, B.H.: Automated generation of adaptive test plans for self-adaptive systems. In: Proceedings of the 10th International Symposium on Software Engineering for Adaptive and Self-Managing Systems, pp. 157–168. IEEE Press (2015)
18. Gabel, M., Su, Z.: Testing mined specifications. In: Proceedings of the ACM SIGSOFT 20th International Symposium on the Foundations of Software Engineering, FSE 2012, pp. 4:1–4:11. ACM, New York (2012). https://doi.org/10.1145/2393596.2393598, http://doi.acm.org/10.1145/2393596.2393598
19. Galster, M., Weyns, D., Tofan, D., Michalik, B., Avgeriou, P.: Variability in software systemsa systematic literature review. IEEE Trans. Softw. Eng. **40**(3), 282–306 (2014)
20. Garlan, D.: Software engineering in an uncertain world. In: Proceedings of the FSE/SDP workshop on Future of software engineering research, pp. 125–128. ACM (2010)
21. Giese, H., et al.: Living with uncertainty in the age of runtime models. In: Bencomo, N., France, R., Cheng, B.H.C., Aßmann, U. (eds.) Models@run.time. LNCS, vol. 8378, pp. 47–100. Springer, Cham (2014). https://doi.org/10.1007/978-3-319-08915-7_3
22. Gourlay, J.S.: A mathematical framework for the investigation of testing. IEEE Trans. Softw. Eng. **6**, 686–709 (1983)
23. Hallsteinsen, S., Hinchey, M., Park, S., Schmid, K.: Dynamic software product lines. Computer **41**(4), 93–95 (2008)
24. IBM White Paper: An architectural blueprint for autonomic computing (2006)
25. Inverardi, P., Mazzanti, F.: Experimenting with dynamic linking with ada. Softw. Pract. Exper. **23**(1), 1–14 (1993). https://doi.org/10.1002/spe.4380230102

26. Inverardi, P., Tivoli, M.: The future of software: adaptation and dependability. In: Software Engineering, International Summer Schools, ISSSE 2006–2008, Salerno, Italy, Revised Tutorial Lectures, pp. 1–31 (2008). https://doi.org/10.1007/978-3-540-95888-8_1
27. Jakubovski Filho, H.L., Ferreira, T.N., Vergilio, S.R.: Preference based multi-objective algorithms applied to the variability testing of software product lines. J. Syst. Softw. **151**, 194–209 (2019)
28. Kanstrén, T., Piel, E., Gross, H.G.: Observation-based modeling for model-based testing. Technical Report Series TUD-SERG-2009-012 (2009)
29. Kim, J., Feldt, R., Yoo, S.: Guiding deep learning system testing using surprise adequacy. arXiv preprint arXiv:1808.08444 (2018)
30. Kounev, S., et al.: The notion of self-aware computing. In: Self-Aware Computing Systems, pp. 3–16 (2017). https://doi.org/10.1007/978-3-319-47474-8_1
31. de Lemos, R., et al.: Software engineering for self-adaptive systems: research challenges in the provision of assurances. In: de Lemos, R., Garlan, D., Ghezzi, C., Giese, H. (eds.) Software Engineering for Self-Adaptive Systems III. Assurances. LNCS, vol. 9640, pp. 3–30. Springer, Cham (2017). https://doi.org/10.1007/978-3-319-74183-3_1
32. Mens, T., Serebrenik, A., Cleve, A. (eds.): Evolving Software Systems. Springer, Heidelberg (2014). https://doi.org/10.1007/978-3-642-45398-4
33. Mens, T., Wermelinger, M., Ducasse, S., Demeyer, S., Hirschfeld, R., Jazayeri, M.: Challenges in software evolution. In: Proceedings of the Eighth International Workshop on Principles of Software Evolution, IWPSE 2005, pp. 13–22. IEEE Computer Society, Washington, DC (2005). https://doi.org/10.1109/IWPSE.2005.7
34. Nanda, A., Mani, S., Sinha, S., Harrold, M.J., Orso, A.: Regression testing in the presence of non-code changes. In: 2011 Fourth IEEE International Conference on Software Testing, Verification and Validation, pp. 21–30. IEEE (2011)
35. Salehie, M., Tahvildari, L.: Self-adaptive software: landscape and research challenges. ACM Trans. Auton. Adapt. Syst. (TAAS) **4**(2), 14 (2009)
36. Santelices, R., Chittimalli, P.K., Apiwattanapong, T., Orso, A., Harrold, M.J.: Test-suite augmentation for evolving software. In: 2008 23rd IEEE/ACM International Conference on Automated Software Engineering, pp. 218–227. IEEE (2008)
37. Siqueira, B.R., Ferrari, F.C., Serikawa, M.A., Menotti, R., de Camargo, V.V.: Characterisation of challenges for testing of adaptive systems. In: Proceedings of the 1st Brazilian Symposium on Systematic and Automated Software Testing, SAST 2016, Maringa, Parana, Brazil, 19–20 September, 2016, pp. 11:1–11:10 (2016). https://doi.org/10.1145/2993288.2993294
38. Staats, M., Whalen, M.W., Heimdahl, M.P.: Programs, tests, and oracles: the foundations of testing revisited. In: Proceedings of the 33rd International Conference on Software Engineering, pp. 391–400. ACM (2011)
39. Su, F.H., Bell, J., Harvey, K., Sethumadhavan, S., Kaiser, G., Jebara, T.: Code relatives: detecting similarly behaving software. In: Proceedings of the 2016 24th ACM SIGSOFT International Symposium on Foundations of Software Engineering, pp. 702–714. ACM (2016)
40. Varshosaz, M., Beohar, H., Mousavi, M.R.: Basic behavioral models for software product lines: revisited. Sci. Comput. Program. **168**, 171–185 (2018). https://doi.org/10.1016/j.scico.2018.09.001
41. Yu, T.: Simevo: Testing evolving multi-process software systems. In: 2017 IEEE International Conference on Software Maintenance and Evolution (ICSME), pp. 204–215. IEEE (2017)

Improving Software Engineering Research Through Experimentation Workbenches

Klaus Schmid[✉], Sascha El-Sharkawy[✉], and Christian Kröher[✉]

Institute of Computer Science, University of Hildesheim, Hildesheim, Germany
{schmid,elscha,kroeher}@sse.uni-hildesheim.de
https://sse.uni-hildesheim.de/en/

Abstract. Experimentation with software prototypes plays a fundamental role in software engineering research. In contrast to many other scientific disciplines, however, explicit support for this key activity in software engineering is relatively small. While some approaches to improve this situation have been proposed by the software engineering community, experiments are still very difficult and sometimes impossible to replicate.

In this paper, we propose the concept of an *experimentation workbench* as a means of explicit support for experimentation in software engineering research. In particular, we discuss core requirements that an experimentation workbench should satisfy in order to qualify as such and to offer a real benefit for researchers. Beyond their core benefits for experimentation, we stipulate that experimentation workbenches will also have benefits in regard to reproducibility and repeatability of software engineering research. Further, we illustrate this concept with a scenario and a case study, and describe relevant challenges as well as our experience with experimentation workbenches.

Keywords: Experimentation workbench ·
Empirical software engineering · Static analysis ·
Software product line analysis

1 Introduction

A significant part of software engineering is experimental in nature. This holds both for method-oriented research, which typically requires humans-in-the-loop, as well as more implementation-oriented research (related to program analysis, verification, software generation, etc.), which is the focus of this contribution.

The challenges to experimental research in software engineering are very similar to these in other experimental disciplines, like physics or psychology. Those include replicability of research results, efficient support for the experimental process, like conducting variations, or enabling others to reuse the scientific results. In some disciplines these issues have gained wide-spread attention, like in psychology due to the reproducibility crisis [2]. In large-scale physics, like the Large Hadron Collider (LHC), creating documentation solutions and supporting

© Springer Nature Switzerland AG 2019
M. H. ter Beek et al. (Eds.): Gnesi Festschrift, LNCS 11865, pp. 67–82, 2019.
https://doi.org/10.1007/978-3-030-30985-5_6

many variations of experiments is considered well before any experiments are actually built, i.e., creating the experiments are major systematic engineering activities in their own right. This inspired us to compare this situation with software engineering research, in particular experimental research based on software tools.

In software engineering, deficiencies in the systematic support of the research process are increasingly recognized as an issue. In our own experience (and that of others), even if the relevant software is provided, e.g., as open-source, it is very difficult and sometimes impossible to replicate the experiments as they may rely on (unavailable) third party tools or undocumented execution details. Thus, the replication of a single evaluation may require several days or weeks of work only for reverse engineering missing information or assets. This has also influenced organizations, like the Association for Computing Machinery (ACM), to address this need and provide guidelines to improve the situation, e.g., with assessing publications [1]. As part of these guidelines, ACM defines a terminology that distinguishes repeatability, replicability, and reproducibility. In this paper, we will follow this terminology and, hence, use these terms as follows:

- *Repeatability* means that researchers receive the same results with their own experimental setup on multiple trials.
- *Replicability* means that a different person receives the same results with the same experimental setup as reported by a researcher on multiple trials.
- *Reproducibility* means that a different person receives the same results as reported by a researcher with their own experimental setup on multiple trials.

A typical way to improve repeatability, replicability, and reproducibility is the publication of all artifacts relevant to an experiment. For instance, conferences increasingly provide the possibility to back up publications with artifacts and assess their quality [1]. Other measures include the use of docker or virtual machines to improve replicability [3]. However, these approaches are typically applied after the fact, i.e., after the experiments are finished, as opposed to practices in established experimental disciplines. This post-mortem approach may lead to threats to validity as it leads to the risk of missing important details in the documentation artifacts. These solutions do also not address other issues in the scientific process, like exploration of experimental variation.

Here, driven from our own experiences in conducting technical research experiments, we propose the concept of an *experimentation workbench* for software engineering to remedy this situation and make the scientific workflow and its requirements a central aspect in the tools we build. A key motivation for our proposal is the question:

> *"How would a support environment for software engineering research look like, if we would specifically engineer one?"*

Today, we are used to *development workbenches* like Eclipse [32], but while they are heavily used in research, they (only) aim at supporting the software development process in general. They do not address any specific research-oriented requirements. Other uses of the term workbench include artifacts, like *language workbenches* [7]. Again, this term is more directed towards (language) development, not so much towards research. We choose the term *experimentation workbench* in analogy to these uses of the term. The term experimentation workbench is also not completely new. It has already been used in networking [9], however, with slightly different semantics, namely to denote a specific form of simulation environment.

An experimentation workbench, as we envision it, is not only about replicability, but about supporting the scientific process at large (e.g., rapid variation, reuse in new research), as we will discuss in the following sections. Thus, among other things, it should also support general reproducibility. This would move software engineering more in line with other experimental sciences. The requirements we put forward for defining the concept of experimentation workbenches are our main contribution. We believe thinking in these terms from the beginning and supporting the scientific process with such environments can be a major contribution to our community. In summary, our contributions are:

- The definition of the concept of an experimentation workbench along with a description of its defining requirements.
- An illustrative scenario highlighting the benefits of experimentation workbenches.
- An example implementation (KernelHaven).
- A discussion of challenges for creating experimentation workbenches.
- A report of our experiences with realizing and using experimentation workbenches in our research on product line analysis.

Below, we will further refine the concept of experimentation workbenches in a scenario (Sect. 2), before we define the fundamental requirements in Sect. 3. We illustrate the defined concept based on KernelHaven in Sect. 4, discuss major challenges to realizing experimentation workbenches in Sect. 5, and provide our experiences in Sect. 6. Finally, we conclude in Sect. 7.

2   Usage Scenario

In this section, we describe a scenario to clarify our expectations on how experimentation workbenches support the experimentation workflow. We assume experimentation workbenches to be constructed for a specific research domain. For our scenario we use the domain of static product line analysis as a reference, which is a rather active field of research [34]. It aims at questions like detecting code that can never be part of a product, as there is no product configuration that would allow this, or detecting type inconsistencies that only arise for specific code configurations. All these analyses have a certain structure: the different inputs like a variability model, source code, etc. must be analyzed and transformed into appropriate formats for integration and analysis. We choose this domain to match it to the example experimentation workbench discussed in Sect. 4. Figure 1

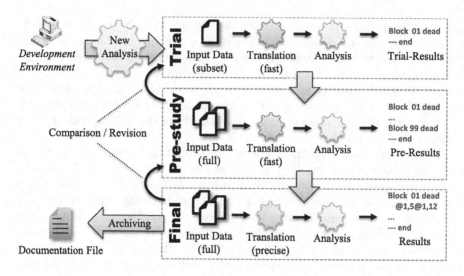

Fig. 1. Example workflow using an experimentation workbench.

shows an illustration of an example workflow in this domain as supported by an experimentation workbench. We discuss this workflow below by means of a scenario.

Preparation. Stefania wants to test her new analysis approach. She implemented it as a plugin for an experimentation workbench. This analysis works on an abstract representation of a product line and requires inputs from the variability model, the variability-enhanced build model, and C-code files. She uses Linux as a case study, which is often used in research, but huge. For translating the source code into an appropriate format for her analysis, two techniques are available: a fast, but not so precise one, and one precise, but rather slow.

Trial. First, Stefania wants to perform a trial with a small subset of the data. Thus, she defines the case study subset, the fast translation technique, and her analysis by configuration of the experimentation workbench. This is possible as data format standardization (along with necessary translations) and other services are offered by the experimentation workbench. The workbench also addresses parallelization and other technical issues regarding resource utilization allowing her to focus only on the realization of her analysis. In particular, no coding is required (except for implementing her analysis). This run gives the expected results after a few minutes.

Pre-study. Stefania changes the configuration to include all input data for her pre-study. She starts the analysis, which finishes already in a few hours. The results are again positive, but some files have not been correctly processed as she still used the fast but imprecise translation technique of her first trial.

Final. Stefania switches from the fast translation to the more precise one simply by configuration of the experimentation workbench. This technique uses a different approach and produces different outputs, but the experimentation workbench handles format translations transparently. Hence, changing the complete analysis is again as easy as simply modifying a configuration option. This helps to avoid introducing accidental changes of the experiment that could occur if more complex programming would be involved. Stefania compares the final results with her pre-study. This is easy to do as she used the documentation feature, which results in automatic archiving of all input and output data, implementation artifacts, source code, and the entire configuration of the experimentation workbench. Apart from the impact of the more detailed analysis, the results match. Hence, Stefania shares the documentation file with her fellow researchers, who can directly rerun the analysis and compare the results or do further studies.

It is exactly this kind of fast, iterative changes along with the comprehensive documentation that the concept of an experimentation workbench is about.

3   Concepts and Requirements

As illustrated in the usage scenario above, experimentation workbenches should support researchers in easily performing experiments, explore the space of possibilities, document them, and share them with others, who then can build on them, refine them, apply their own techniques or create further derived experiments. These goals partially overlap with other approaches to improve the scientific process in software engineering.

For example, benchmarking as a scientific approach can support community building and can help to accelerate scientific advancement [29]. However, it does not address aspects like replication, supporting the experimentation process itself, etc. Concepts like Jupyter notebooks [26] support experimentation and to some limited degree replication and sharing, so they already come close. We could consider them as one specific instance of an experimentation workbench for data science, but this is usually not applicable to software engineering experimentation and it is still very generic, leaving the major burden of programming to the researchers. Other concepts like using docker images or virtual machines in software engineering address replication [3], but not other experimentation-oriented capabilities. Thus, while various approaches exist that address related topics, so far no one fully addresses the problems of the software engineering researcher as we do here with the concept of experimentation workbenches.

In our vision, experimentation workbenches provide key capabilities to support typical research activities in the scientific workflow. However, we do not expect that there will be a single experimentation workbench for all kinds of software engineering research just as there is no single experimentation facility in physics. Rather, we expect that the generic requirements, we present below, will be instantiated in domain-oriented ways. For clarity, we abstract here from any activities that are already well-supported, e.g., by development environments, and focus on those, for which there is typically no automated support available. In our view these are, in particular, the following ones:

R1 Support the setup (definition) of experiments.
R2 Support the analysis of experiments.
R3 Support the fast execution of variants of the experiment, including applying
the experiment setup to different cases.
R4 Support the documentation of all relevant artefacts for replication.
R5 Support the reuse of experiments (by third parties).
R6 Support the extension and specialization of experiments by third parties.

Supporting the *setup of experiments* (*R1*) means, in particular, that technical issues that are not relevant to the study, but only required to ensure its execution, are handled by the workbench as far as possible. These could include providing initialization code, process coordination, and parallelization. Platform independence could be another aspect, which is not mandatory, but rather a design decision made by the developers and judged according to the requirements of the type of experimentation to be supported. Ideally, researchers only need to focus on the algorithmic aspects of their contributions. Thus, the front end to the researcher should provide a configuration interface or a Domain-Specific Language (DSL) or a combination of both to assist in these tasks.

After an experiment execution an *experiment analysis* (*R2*) must be done in order to determine what the results mean in relation to the initial research question. This could be provided by visualization tools, by providing certain kinds of tabularization, or simply by analysis scripts. The needs in this area are strongly domain-dependent as the analysis will depend on the types and amounts of data produced, requirements on statistics, and so forth. However, in many cases it will be possible to address these requirements using environments for data analysis like R [33]. Thus, if appropriate interfaces are available, there is no need to re-implement this for each workbench.

In experimentation it is often the case that one wants to *analyze variations in the data or in algorithms* to determine their impact on the overall outcome. This requires the possibility to set up new versions of an experiment with little effort and to easily go back to the previous analysis, if an experiment turns out to be not successful (*R3*). Sometimes such a variation can also be driven by performing a simplified version to improve turn-around time.

Finally, an experimentation workbench should support *documentation of experiments* such that automated replication is easily facilitated (*R4*). Such a replication package should at least include all inputs, outputs, code, and analysis results, if applicable. Thus, the package should directly support the inspection of any results, but also the direct replication of the experiments by any third-party.

Ideally, it should be possible to directly *reuse* not only the results, but even the experiments (*R5*). While this reusability enables repeatability by allowing researchers to always receive the same results with the same experimental setup, it also supports replicability and reproducibility by different persons. In particular, third parties should be able to easily re-conduct an experiment by reusing the experimental setup either directly, or with only slight adaptations, e.g., to fit their environment, which still conform to the initially documented experiment.

The direct reuse of an experiment (*R5*) may not always be sufficient to enable reproducibility. For example, if a third party aims at conducting a previous experiment of other researchers using a different case study. This may require variations like different algorithms to provide the necessary data from software artifacts as the new case study consists of different types of artifacts than the initial one (e.g., Java source code instead of C source code). This may require *extensions or specializations* of the initial experimentation, which ideally should be directly supported by the experimentation workbench (*R6*). Moreover, from the perspective of the overall scientific process that should be supported along the lines of the well-known adage of "standing on the shoulders of giants", this requirement is actually particularly important. Today, such an extension is extremely difficult, even if all the code is available as open source as existing experimental implementations are typically not created for reuse or even extension by third-parties. Thus, we want to emphasize this here due its importance to the scientific process.

4   An Experimentation Workbench for Static Product Line Analysis

In this section, we discuss KernelHaven[1] as an example of an open source experimentation workbench [20,21]. We do not argue that it is the ideal or perfect implementation of an experimentation workbench, but we use it here as a reference to describe some properties and technical implications of the concepts and requirements introduced in Sect. 3. KernelHaven instantiates these generic requirements for the domain of static analysis of software product lines. While we focus on this domain here, a specialized instance[2] of KernelHaven exists, which addresses metrics for software product lines [12] as a subset of static product line analysis (cf. requirement *R6* in Sect. 3).

In order to abstract from technical details and allow to rapidly set up new experiment variants (*R3*), it is necessary to take a domain-oriented perspective. The resulting workbench will only support experiments in this domain. In our case of product line analysis, Fig. 2 shows the resulting structure of that workbench. It consists of various *extractors*, which transform the *available assets* into a *common data model* that provides a good basis for *analysis*. In our domain, the relevant information is typically derived from three categories of assets: the variability model, the build system, and code assets. Hence, a *code pipeline*, a *build pipeline*, and a *variability model pipeline* further structure the workbench in Fig. 2, which perform this derivation for the respective category of assets individually.

While this workbench was initially developed for experiments on Linux, its architecture is much broader as all analysis and extractor components are implemented by a flexible plugin system. Thus, for example, the application to a proprietary variational build system only requires the development of an

---

[1] Available at GitHub: https://github.com/KernelHaven/KernelHaven.
[2] Available at GitHub: https://github.com/KernelHaven/MetricHaven.

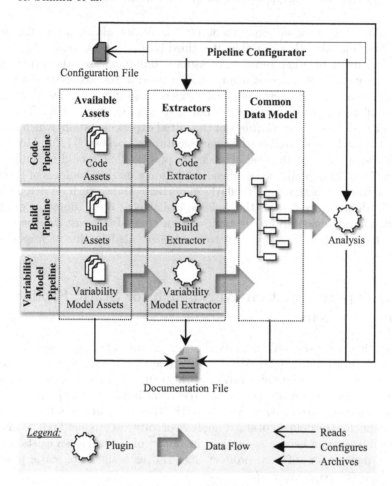

Fig. 2. KernelHaven Overview.

appropriate extraction plugin.[3] The common data model, which is used to represent the collected data of the various extractors, allows the reuse of existing analysis plugins without additional work.

Figure 2 shows that the *pipeline configurator* reads a *configuration file* to configure the whole infrastructure. It performs initialization of all subsystems (in particular the wiring, initialization and starting of the components), creates the corresponding processes, and allocates hardware resources. Also issues like parallelization of the various processes are handled by the infrastructure. Initially an adequate number of processes are created and throughout data dependencies are used to manage the parallel processing.

---

[3] In the case of minor variations, of course, also variations of existing plugins or even parameterized instances can be used. In order to support this a parametrization approach for plugins exists.

The configuration-oriented approach, which leads to an open ecosystem platform, directly addresses requirements *R1* to *R3* (cf. Sect. 3). The platform can also be configured to directly invoke documentation-related activities like archiving all relevant data, sources, implementations, configuration information, and so forth. This addresses requirement *R4* in Sect. 3. Requirements *R5* and *R6* are addressed by combining that (a) other researchers can rerun the experiments due to auto-documentation and (b) build on them by changing the configuration using either existing or self-developed plugins. The auto-documentation feature of KernelHaven therefore produces the experiment documentation in terms of an archive that contains all input, intermediate, and output data, as well as the main infrastructure, all plug-ins, and the configuration file. This feature directly supports reproducibility as a core task of research: the archive provides the original experimental setup to other researchers, enables them to rerun the same experiment on the same input data, and allows inspection of the previous results.

Initially, KernelHaven plugins were mostly derived from existing research prototypes. For example, they wrap a pre-existing tool and handle all the details of driving these tools (e.g., particular parametrization or environment needs). This has two major effects:

- The (re-)use of successful tools has been tremendously simplified: while for some tools, like TypeChef [18], people typically need several days to make it work reliably, the plugin embeds the relevant knowledge to make it reusable in minutes.
- The combination of tools is now possible simply by configuration: while combining existing tools as well as integrating with existing ones requires a lot of work and tool-knowledge, it is now a matter of defining the desired plugins as a parameter in a configuration file.

An important part of the domain design is the definition of the data structures and relevant data transformations to make extractors interchangeable. This can also be illustrated with KernelHaven. The toolset provides several extractor plugins, which can operate on C-Source code and can provide variability-tagged source-code fragments. One is derived from Undertaker [6], another one from TypeChef [18]. They differ, however, very significantly in terms of the level of detail they provide: Undertaker scans the source-file, identifies code blocks as sequences of lines and tags them with the relevant variability derived from any #ifdef-command. In the process it ignores header-files. On the other hand, TypeChef performs full variability-aware parsing, including header-files and macro expansions. As a consequence, it provides a complete AST adorned with variability information.

While the results of the two tools differ fundamentally, they share some information. Both extract the included variability information from source-files using preprocessor directives, i.e., the *presence conditions*. This commonality is sufficient for some types of analyses, like the identification of dead code [31]. In KernelHaven, all entities for representing extracted code information inherit from a class, which stores this common information. This allows to exchange

```
1  code.extractor.class = UndertakerExtractor
2  code.extractor.file_regex = .*\.c
3  build.extractor.class = KbuildMinerExtractor
4  variability.extractor.class = KconfigReaderExtractor
5  analysis.class = DeadCodeAnalysis
6  ...
```

Listing 1.1. Excerpt of a KernelHaven configuration file.

code extractors as long as the desired analysis does not require the specific output of a certain extractor. The plugin system knows about these dependencies and takes care of them. An example is illustrated in Listing 1.1, which shows the relevant part to perform a dead code analysis on Linux with the Undertaker-extractor. Only the configuration file, in particular Line 1, must be modified in order to use TypeChef instead of Undertaker. However, this can be seen as a refinement of the Undertaker-information as this also corresponds to code-blocks. This is actually how the information is represented: a source-code processor may provide variability-adorned code-blocks, which may contain more detailed information (e.g., AST). The data structures are defined in a way that further steps may ignore levels of detail that are not required in their processing increasing composability of the various plugins.

While the analysis of results itself is not part of KernelHaven, the infrastructure supports *R2* by supporting the export of the resulting data in analysis-friendly formats like text-files (e.g., csv) or Excel. The core analysis is then typically done either with Excel or using R-scripts.

This allows to execute the scenario described in Sect. 2. One can first test new analysis concepts based on the rather fast, but not so detailed Undertaker-extractor, which extracts variability elements as line ranges. After the analysis has been positively evaluated, one can perform a more detailed analysis using the macro-aware parser of TypeChef, which provides a code block as an AST-fragment where all elements have the same presence condition. So, what both extractors have in common is to provide source code elements tagged with presence conditions, which is sufficient for dead code analysis. An AST-based analysis like type-analysis requires code extractors, which extract an AST containing variability information. Currently KernelHaven supports this with TypeChef or srcML [30]. It is important to note that (a) these different types of analysis are all supported by KernelHaven, and (b), for switching among them, it is sufficient to change some configuration options; no implementation change for any extractor plugin or the analysis plugin is required as long as they all adhere to the interface conventions.

Here, KernelHaven realizes two different perspectives on experimentation workbenches. On the one hand, KernelHaven is a platform that provides support for various experiments in the domain of static product lines analyses. On the other, we derived different KernelHaven instances based on this platform. These instances consist of the common experimentation workbench, configuration parameters, and if necessary also experimentation-specific plugins that realize one specific analysis. In Sect. 6, we exemplary show some of the experiments, i.e., KernelHaven instances, which we realized based on the KernelHaven platform.

5 Challenges

While we believe the concept of experimentation workbenches is very fruitful for the research community and our own experiences with the KernelHaven implementation of it are so far very positive, there are still some challenges associated with the realization of an experimentation workbench.

Domain specifity. The first and most obvious challenge to experimentation workbenches is that they need to be constructed for a specific domain of experimentation. Thus, the requirements, we presented here, must be interpreted in the corresponding context and the capabilities of the workbench need to be scoped in terms of types of experiments (variations) to take into account. Thus, an experimentation workbench can be regarded as some form of product line [23] or open ecosystem [4]. Similar to product lines, of course, incremental development of it is possible.

Freedom of Implementation. It is fundamentally hard to guarantee full replicability, without significantly restricting the expressiveness used for realising specific parts of an experimental implementation. This is particularly the case for an experimentation workbench, like KernelHaven, that even allows pre-existing systems written in different languages and with arbitrary infrastructures as plugins. This issue is further compounded as in different domains different aspects may be important for replicability. For example, KernelHaven is purely functionality-related, i.e., as long as the same outputs are achieved for the same input, we can assume replicability. In other areas like performance engineering, the issue is different as similar timing behavior is required for replicability [8]. Hence, a corresponding experimentation workbench will have to address different issues. In this special case, special performance-rated environments have been proposed to promote replication [25].

Scope of Documentation. An important issue is the scope of an implementation that needs to be archived for replicability. In the example given in Sect. 4 only code artifacts related to the workbench implementation and the plugins are considered. The Java virtual machine and the operating system are not included. This yields rather lightweight packages where multiple archives can easily be stored locally. However, in other contexts the replication may require a copy of the virtual machine and the operating system. In such cases, an experimentation workbench may of course directly create a docker image or a virtual machine [3]. One can even imagine cases where a complex multi-machine setup needs to be archived like in large-scale adaptive systems.

Controlled Experiment Variation. A related issue are experiment variations. If some part of the analysis is replaced by something else, then this will result in changes to the experiment. Typically, this will also invoke undesirable changes. In the example given, a switch from the simple code extractor to the more detailed one does not only lead to a more precise analysis of variability information in header files, but can also impact the details of the analyzed blocks as they are analyzed in a different way. Whether these changes are acceptable or not, will depend very much on the specifics of the analysis performed. In case plugins are used that have been engineered from the beginning with an experimentation workbench in mind, we expect this also to be less of an issue than it is currently the case with the reengineered plugins that KernelHaven uses.

These challenges basically come down to the need of achieving a sufficient domain understanding. Either prior to the construction of such an environment or as part of the experimental process. In this regard the development of an experimentation workbench can be compared to the development of a software product line.

6   Experiences

So far, we described the general requirements for experimentation workbenches and how the research community can take advantage of them. In this section, we share our experiences when working with KernelHaven (cf. Sect. 4). We used this experimentation workbench for our own research in the ITEA3 project REVaMP2[4], which focuses on round-trip engineering of software product lines. Since KernelHaven supports the definition of various experiments (*R1*) in the domain of static SPL analysis, we were able to use KernelHaven for many different research activities, like for example reverse engineering of variability information for bootstrapping of SPL development, evolution support, and verification tasks. We provide an overview of the variety of analyses supported by Kernel-Haven and show how we could realize these very diverse analyses with limited development resources in a short time. Further, we present lessons learned when working with KernelHaven.

Together with the Robert Bosch GmbH, we worked on reverse engineering of a dependency management system for a large-scale industrial product line [10]. For this, we decided to adapt the feature effect analysis described by Nadi et al. [24] to the needs of Bosch. This kind of analysis requires usually much effort to combine various parsers that extract variability information from different information sources. By means of KernelHaven, we were able to develop a first prototype very quickly, since the combination of data from different sources is a major concern of KernelHaven and first suitable parsers were already present. As a result, we could focus on the integration of parsers specific to the development environment of Bosch [10], lifting the propositional analysis of feature effects to integer-based variability [19], and on providing visualization support for reverse engineered dependencies [17]. In addition, KernelHaven's reproduction support (*R4*) simplified the execution of configured algorithms at the two partners. Thus, we also achieved a significant benefit for industrial transfer of our research results.

---

[4] http://www.revamp2-project.eu/.

KernelHaven also supports the verification of various properties of SPLs through its data extraction and analysis capabilities. For instance, we can reproduce and freely combine a large number of published product line metrics [11] resulting in more than 23,000 variations of metrics for single systems and SPLs, many of which are not handled by any other tool [12]. Another very important aspect for SPLs, is the analysis of (un-)dead code with respect to its variability model [31]. This is a very time consuming task as it analyzes whether the variability model allows the (de-)selection of all configurable code parts, e.g., #ifdef-blocks. Thus, this kind of analysis is more suitable for daily builds than for a continuous analysis during the development. However, a commit analysis of the Linux kernel has shown that changes to variability information occur infrequently and only affect small parts [22]. Based on this insight, we implemented an incremental verification approach to reduce the overall time consumption by about 90% [14], which is suitable to be applied in a continuous development environment. The incremental verification is realized by combining previous results of an already available dead code analysis with a new analysis that detects changed variability information (*R5* and *R6*).

Through the broad range of conducted experiments in combination with tested variations of algorithms, KernelHaven evolved quickly to a highly configurable system. For this, we realized a documentation system that provides the user, based on installed plugins, a list of available configuration options, supported values, and default settings. However, this system does not scale well as it neither supports a documentation of suggested settings arising through the combination of multiple plugins nor does it provide a dependency management among the plugins, e.g., the metric analysis plugin requires code extractors that extract a variability-aware AST rather than a simple block structure as needed by most other analyses (cf. Sect. 4). Thus, for the future, we plan to address this issue by (1). limiting the amount of configuration possibilities for stable plugins and by (2). integrating dependency management systems suitable for software ecosystems [5], e.g., based on our EASyProducer implementation [28][5].

This does also strongly suggest that experimentation workbenches can be regarded as a special form of product line or open software ecosystem [27].

7   Conclusion

In this paper, we introduced the concept of an experimentation workbench as a way of thinking about scientific experimentation artifacts with a focus on the needs of the scientific process. We believe that thinking about experimental research software in terms of this concept provides significant advantages when developing research systems in software engineering. In the future, we believe that some powerful experimentation workbenches for specific software engineering domains may provide a major contribution and foster the development of better ecosystems that drive software engineering research.

---

[5] https://sse.uni-hildesheim.de/en/research/projects/easy-producer/.

Our main contributions besides the concept itself are the characterizing requirements, which define an "ideal" experimentation workbench along with an illustrative scenario. We further described KernelHaven as an example experimentation workbench situated in the domain of product line analysis. KernelHaven may provide a basis for a research ecosystem for product line analysis as it integrates already today a number of existing research tools and makes them significantly more accessible than is otherwise the case. Besides achieving already significant research benefits, as discussed, we also found that this approach significantly improves our potential of working with industrial partners.

We assume that the concept of an experimentation workbench always needs to be interpreted relative to the specific scientific area. However, we hope the general requirements we presented may guide the creation of such systems and thus support the scientific progress by fostering the creation of ecosystems around experimentation workbenches in a number of software engineering fields. For example, one may interpret our concept presented in this paper in the context of Natural Language Processing (NLP) in requirements engineering [13,15,16]. In particular, the NLP tool for requirements analysis [16] may provide an excellent foundation for extending it to an experimentation workbench for that domain in future.

Acknowledgements. This work is partially supported by the ITEA3 project REVaMP², funded by the BMBF (German Ministry of Research and Education) under grant 01IS16042H. Any opinions expressed herein are solely by the authors and not by the BMBF.

References

1. Association for Computing Machinery: Artifact review and badging (2018). http://www.acm.org/publications/policies/artifact-review-badging. Accessed 03 May 2019
2. Baker, M.: Over half of psychology studies fail reproducibility test. News article in Nature - International Weekly Journal of Science (2015). https://www.nature.com/news/over-half-of-psychology-studies-fail-reproducibility-test-1.18248. Accessed 03 May 2019
3. Boettiger, C.: An introduction to docker for reproducible research. ACM SIGOPS Operating Syst. Rev. **49**(1), 71–79 (2015)
4. Bosch, J.: From software product lines to software ecosystems. In: 13th International Software Product Line Conference (SPLC 2009), pp. 111–119 (2009)
5. Brummermann, H., Keunecke, M., Schmid, K.: Formalizing distributed evolution of variability in information system ecosystems. In: 6th International Workshop on Variability Modelling of Software-Intensive Systems (VaMoS 2012), pp. 11–19 (2012)
6. CADOS / VAMOS Team: Undertaker (2015). https://vamos.informatik.uni-erlangen.de/trac/undertaker. Accessed 03 May 2019
7. Dyer, R., Nguyen, H.A., Rajan, H., Nguyen, T.N.: Boa: A language and infrastructure for analyzing ultra-large-scale software repositories. In: 35th International Conference on Software Engineering (ICSE 2013), pp. 422–431 (2013)

8. Eichelberger, H., Sass, A., Schmid, K.: From reproducibility problems to improvements: a journey. In: Symposium on Software Performance (SSP 2016), Softwaretechnik-Trends, vol. 36, no. 4, pp. 43–45 (2016)
9. Eide, E., Stoller, L., Lepreau, J.: An experimentation workbench for replayable networking research. In: 4th USENIX Conference on Networked Systems Design & Implementation (NSDI 2007), pp. 16–16 (2007)
10. El-Sharkawy, S., Dhar, S.J., Krafczyk, A., Duszynski, S., Beichter, T., Schmid, K.: Reverse engineering variability in an industrial product line: observations and lessons learned. In: 22nd International Systems and Software Product Line Conference (SPLC 2018), vol. 1, pp. 215–225 (2018)
11. El-Sharkawy, S., Krafczyk, A., Schmid, K.: MetricHaven – more than 23,000 metrics for measuring quality attributes of software product lines. In: 23rd International Systems and Software Product Line Conference, SPLC 2019, vol. B. ACM (2019). Accepted
12. El-Sharkawy, S., Yamagishi-Eichler, N., Schmid, K.: Metrics for analyzing variability and its implementation in software product lines: A systematic literature review. Inf. Softw. Technol. **106**, 1–30 (2019)
13. Ferrari, A., Dell'Orletta, F., Esuli, A., Gervasi, V., Gnesi, S.: Natural language requirements processing: a 4D vision. IEEE Softw. **34**(6), 28–35 (2017)
14. Flöter, M.: Prototypical realization and validation of an incremental software product line analysis approach. Master thesis, University of Hildesheim (2018)
15. Gnesi, S., Ferrari, A.: Research on NLP for RE at CNR-ISTI: a report. In: 1st Workshop on Natural Language Processing for Requirements Engineering, vol. 4, pp. 1–5 (2018)
16. Gnesi, S., Trentanni, G.: QuARS: A NLP tool for requirements analysis. In: 2nd Workshop on Natural Language Processing for Requirements Engineering and NLP Tool Showcase, 1, pp. 1–5 (2019). Tool Demonstrations
17. Grüner, S., et al.: Demonstration of tool chain for feature extraction, analysis and visualization on an industrial case study. In: 17th IEEE International Conference on Industrial Informatics (INDIN 2019) (2019). Accepted
18. Kästner, C.: TypeChef (2013). https://ckaestne.github.io/TypeChef/. Accessed 03 May 2019
19. Krafczyk, A., El-Sharkawy, S., Schmid, K.: Reverse engineering code dependencies: converting integer-based variability to propositional logic. In: 22nd International Systems and Software Product Line Conference (SPLC 2018), vol. 2, pp. 34–41 (2018)
20. Kröher, C., El-Sharkawy, S., Schmid, K.: Kernelhaven – an experimentation workbench for analyzing software product lines. In: 40th International Conference on Software Engineering: Companion Proceedings (ICSE 2018), pp. 73–76 (2018)
21. Kröher, C., El-Sharkawy, S., Schmid, K.: Kernelhaven - an open infrastructure for product line analysis. In: 22nd International Systems and Software Product Line Conference (SPLC 2018), vol. 2, pp. 5–10 (2018)
22. Kröher, C., Gerling, L., Schmid, K.: Identifying the intensity of variability changes in software product line evolution. In: 22nd International Systems and Software Product Line Conference (SPLC 2018), vol. 1, pp. 54–64 (2018)
23. van der Linden, F., Schmid, K., Rommes, E.: Software Product Lines in Action: The Best Industrial Practice in Product Line Engineering, 1st edn, 333 pp. Springer, Heidelberg (2007). https://doi.org/10.1007/978-3-540-71437-8
24. Nadi, S., Berger, T., Kästner, C., Czarnecki, K.: Where do configuration constraints stem from? An extraction approach and an empirical study. IEEE Trans. Softw. Eng. **41**(8), 820–841 (2015)

25. Oliveira, A., Petkovich, J.C., Reidemeister, T., Fischmeister, S.: Datamill: rigorous performance evaluation made easy. In: 4th ACM/SPEC International Conference on Performance Engineering (ICPE 2013), pp. 137–149 (2013)
26. Project Jupyter: The Jupyter Notebook (2019). http://jupyter.org. Accessed 03 May 2019
27. Schmid, K.: Variability modeling for distributed development – a comparison with established practice. In: 14th International Conference on Software Product Line Engineering (SPLC 2010), pp. 155–165 (2010)
28. Schmid, K., Eichelberger, H.: Easy-producer: from product lines to variability-rich software ecosystems. In: 19th International Conference on Software Product Line (SPLC 2015), pp. 390–391 (2015)
29. Sim, S.E., Easterbrook, S.M., Holt, R.C.: Using benchmarking to advance research: a challenge to software engineering. In: 25th International Conference on Software Engineering (ICSE 2003), pp. 74–83 (2003)
30. srcML Team: srcML (2017). http://www.srcml.org/. Accessed 03 May 2019
31. Tartler, R., Lohmann, D., Sincero, J., Schröder-Preikschat, W.: Feature consistency in compile-time-configurable system software: facing the Linux 10,000 feature problem. In: 6th Conference on Computer Systems (EuroSys 2011), pp. 47–60 (2011)
32. The Eclipse Foundation: Eclipse IDE (2019). https://www.eclipse.org/. Accessed 03 May 2019
33. The R Foundation: R Project (2019). https://www.r-project.org/. Accessed 03 May 2019
34. Thüm, T., Apel, S., Kästner, C., Schaefer, I., Saake, G.: A classification and survey of analysis strategies for software product lines. ACM Computing Surveys 47(1), p. 45 (2014). Article 6

Formal Methods and Tools

Innovating Medical Image Analysis
via Spatial Logics

Gina Belmonte[1], Vincenzo Ciancia[2], Diego Latella[2], and Mieke Massink[2(✉)]

[1] Azienda Ospedaliera Universitaria Senese, Siena, Italy
[2] Consiglio Nazionale delle Ricerche - Istituto di Scienza e Tecnologie
dell'Informazione 'A. Faedo', CNR, Pisa, Italy
`Mieke.Massink@isti.cnr.it`

Abstract. Current computer-assisted medical imaging for the planning of radiotherapy requires high-level mathematical and computational skills. These are often paired with the case-by-case integration of highly specialised technologies. The lack of modularity at the right level of abstraction in this field hinders research, collaboration and transfer of expertise among medical physicists, engineers and technicians. The longer term aim of the introduction of spatial logics and spatial model checking in medical imaging is to provide an open platform introducing *declarative medical image analysis*. This will provide domain experts with a convenient and very concise way to specify contouring and segmentation operations, grounded on the solid mathematical foundations of Topological Spatial Logics. We show preliminary results, obtained using the spatial model checker `VoxLogicA`, for the automatic identification of specific brain tissues in a healthy brain and we discuss a selection of challenges for spatial model checking for medical imaging.

Keywords: Spatial logics · Closure Spaces ·
Spatial model checking · Medical imaging

1 Introduction

Spatial and Spatio-temporal logics and model checking are enjoying an increasing interest in Computer Science (see for instance [12,13,16,25,26,35]). The main idea of spatial and spatio-temporal model checking is to use specifications written in logical languages to describe spatial properties and to automatically identify patterns and structures of interest. Spatial and spatio-temporal model checking have recently been applied in a variety of domains, ranging from Collective Adaptive Systems [10,17,18] to signals [35] and images [4,13,26], just to mention a few. The origins of spatial logics can be traced back to the forties of the previous century when McKinsey and Tarski recognised the possibility of reasoning on space using topology as a mathematical framework for the interpretation of modal logic (see [9] for a thorough introduction). In their work, modal logic formulas are interpreted as sets of points of a topological space. In particular, in

© Springer Nature Switzerland AG 2019
M. H. ter Beek et al. (Eds.): Gnesi Festschrift, LNCS 11865, pp. 85–109, 2019.
https://doi.org/10.1007/978-3-030-30985-5_7

Fig. 1. Examples: open ball (left) and its topological closure (right)

that context, the modal operator $\Diamond$ is interpreted as the (logical representation of the) topological *closure* operator. Informally, this operator adds an (infinitely thin) border to an open set of points as illustrated in Fig. 1.

In recent work [12,13], Ciancia et al. pushed such theoretical developments further to encompass arbitrary graphs as models of space. In that work *Closure spaces*, a generalisation of topological spaces, are used as underlying model for *discrete spatial logic* inspired by recent work by Galton [21–23]. This resulted in the definition of the *Spatial Logic for Closure Spaces* (SLCS), and a related model checking algorithm. Furthermore, in [11], a spatio-temporal logic, combining *Computation Tree Logic* with the spatial operators of SLCS was introduced. An (extended) model checking algorithm has been implemented in the prototype *spatio-temporal model checker* topochecker[1].

A completely different and, so far, little explored domain of application for spatial model checking is that of medical imaging. Medical imaging is concerned with the creation of visual representations of parts of the human body for the purpose of clinical analysis and in preparation of medical intervention. In our recent work [4,6–8] we focused in particular on spatial model checking in the area of medical imaging for radiotherapy. One of the most important steps in the planning of radiotherapy is the accurate contouring of tissues and organs at risk in medical images, commonly produced by Computed Tomography (CT), Magnetic Resonance (MR), and Positron Emission Tomography (PET). Recent research efforts in the field of medical imaging are therefore focused on the introduction of automatic contouring procedures. These procedures are used to identify particular kinds of tissues. These can be for example parts of the brain (white matter[2], grey matter[3]) or tissues that could indicate diseases that need treatment. Such (semi-) automatic procedures would lead to an increase in accuracy and a considerable reduction in time and costs, compared to manual contouring – the current practice in most hospitals. The software for automatic contouring that is starting to appear on the market is, however, highly specialised for particular types of diseased tissue in particular parts of the body (e.g., "breast cancer", or "glioblastoma" – a kind of malign tumour in the brain), lacks transparency to its users, provides little flexibility, and its accuracy is still not always satisfactory. In the last few years also deep learning algorithms have become very popular for medical image analysis. They are reaching good results and are computationally efficient, but they are also posing their own limiting factors such as lack of

---

[1] Topochecker: *a topological model checker*, see http://topochecker.isti.cnr.it, https://github.com/vincenzoml/topochecker.
[2] Part of the central nervous system in the brain.
[3] Place where neurons are located in the outer part of the brain.

sufficiently large accurately labelled data sets, labelling uncertainty and problems to deal with rare cases (see for example a recent survey [29] and references therein) but also lack of explainability and transparency. Our recent work shows that, when comparing the accurate contouring of brain tumour tissue using a spatial model checking approach [8] with the best performing algorithms (among which many based on deep learning) on the public benchmark data set for brain tumours (BraTS 2017 [38]), our approach on 3D images is well in line with the state of the art, both in terms of accuracy and in terms of computational efficiency.

The work in the present paper is focusing on the identification of relevant tissues in the *healthy* brain such as white matter and grey matter rather than diseased tissue. As in our previous work, we do this using VoxLogicA, (*Voxel-based Logical Analyser*)[4] the free and open source spatial model checker described in [8] which efficiently implements the spatial logic SLCS enriched with a number of specific operators for the domain of medical imaging that were introduced in [4,8]. Furthermore, we provide a selection of challenges laying ahead for the use of spatial model checking in medical imaging as a valuable complementary method in this important area of research.

In Sect. 2, we briefly recall the spatial logic framework and some of the main aspects of spatial model checking based on Closure Spaces, and provide a number of illustrative examples that serve as a gentle introduction to the spatial logic. Section 3 illustrates further operators that are of particular interest in Medical Imaging. In Sect. 4 we show how these specific operators can be combined with the basic logic to identify tissues of interest in a healthy brain. In Sect. 5 we describe some of the main challenges for successful application of spatial model checking in the area of medical imaging for radiotherapy. Related work is described in Sect. 6. In Sect. 7 we provide some conclusions and an outlook for further research.

2   The Spatial Logic Framework

A 2D digital image can be modelled as an *adjacency space*, i.e. a set X of *cells* or *points*—each corresponding to a distinct *pixel*—together with an *adjacency relation* R among points. Usually, the so called *orthogonal* adjacency relation[5] is used, where only pixels which share an edge count as adjacent; on the other hand, in the *ortho-diagonal* adjacency relation (see Fig. 2) pixels are adjacent as long as they share at least either an edge or a corner. Each pixel of an image is associated with one or more (colour) *intensities*; we model this by equipping the points with *attributes*. We assume sets A and V of attribute *names* and *values*, and an *attribute valuation* function $\mathcal{A}$ such that $\mathcal{A}(x, a) \in V$ is the value of attribute a of point x. Attributes can be used in *assertions* α, i.e. boolean expressions, with standard syntax and semantics. Consequently, we abstract from related

---

[4] VoxLogicA: https://github.com/vincenzoml/VoxLogicA.

[5] Sometimes called von Neumann adjacency. The relation is reflexive and symmetric.

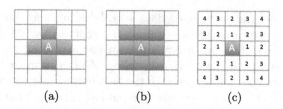

Fig. 2. Pixels that are orthogonally adjacent to pixel A (a) and orthodiagonally adjacent (b) are shown in blue. Distance transform (c) with distance to pixel A as attribute shown in each pixel for orthogonal adjacency and Manhattan distance function. (Color figure online)

details here and assume function $\mathcal{A}$ extended in the obvious way; for instance, $\mathcal{A}(x, a \leq c) = \mathcal{A}(x, a) \leq c$, for appropriate constant c.

A similar reasoning applies to 3D—or, in general, multi-dimensional—images, where *voxels* are used instead of pixels and the (chosen) adjacency relation needs to be extended in the obvious way (an extended introduction to these matters is given in [4]).

Given a set of (attributed) points X with a binary relation $R \subseteq X \times X$ we define function $\mathcal{C}_R : 2^X \to 2^X$ with $\mathcal{C}_R(Y) \triangleq Y \cup \{x | \exists y \in Y.y\,R\,x\}$. It turns out that $\mathcal{C}_R$ is a *closure* function and $(X, \mathcal{C}_R)$ is a *closure space*[6]. Thus, adjacency spaces are a subclass of closure spaces.

A (quasi-discrete) *path* π in $(X, \mathcal{C}_R)$ is a function $\pi : \mathbb{N} \to X$, such that for all $Y \subseteq \mathbb{N}$, $\pi(\mathcal{C}_{Succ}(Y)) \subseteq \mathcal{C}_R(\pi(Y))$, where π is implicitly lifted to sets in the usual way (i.e. $\pi(Y) = \{x \mid \exists y \in Y.\pi(y)\}$) and $(\mathbb{N}, \mathcal{C}_{Succ})$ is the closure space of natural numbers with the *successor* relation: $(n, m) \in Succ \Leftrightarrow m = n + 1$. Informally: the ordering in the path imposed by $\mathbb{N}$ is compatible with relation R, i.e. if $\pi(i) \neq \pi(i+1)$ then $\pi(i)\,R\,\pi(i+1)$[7].

A closure space $(X, \mathcal{C})$ can be enriched with a notion of *distance*, i.e. a function $d : X \times X \to \mathbb{R}_{\geq 0} \cup \{\infty\}$ such that $d(x, y) = 0$ iff $x = y$, leading to the *distance closure space* $((X, \mathcal{C}), d)$. The notion is easily lifted to sets $Y \neq \emptyset$: $d(x, Y) \triangleq \inf\{d(x, y) | y \in Y\}$, with $d(x, \emptyset) = \infty$.

In this paper, we use the version of the logic presented in [8], based on a reachability operator, as in [5], and recalled in the sequel. For given set P of *atomic predicates* p, and interval of $\mathbb{R}$ I, the *syntax* of the logic is given below:

$$\Phi ::= p \mid \neg\Phi \mid \Phi \vee \Phi \mid \mathcal{N}\Phi \mid \rho\,\Phi[\Phi] \mid \mathcal{D}^I\Phi \tag{1}$$

---

[6] The reader interested in the formal definition of closure spaces and on their properties is referred to the literature (see e.g. [12,13,21–23] and references therein). Here it suffices to say that $\mathcal{C}(Y)$ is essentially the set of points *close* to any point in Y; note that, since closure spaces generalize topological spaces, in the latter, the closure operator $\mathcal{C}$ coincides with topological closure, so that, for instance, in the monodimensional Euclidean space $\mathbb{R}$, $\mathcal{C}([0, 1)) = \mathcal{C}((0, 1)) = \mathcal{C}((0, 1]) = \mathcal{C}([0, 1]) = [1, 0]$.

[7] We refer to [13] for a discussion on paths on the more general class of closure spaces, including e.g. Euclidean spaces, including e.g. Euclidean spaces.

Satisfaction $\mathcal{M}, x \models \Phi$ of a formula Φ at point $x \in X$ in *distance closure model* $\mathcal{M} = (((X, \mathcal{C}), d), \mathcal{A}, \mathcal{V})$ is defined in Fig. 3 by induction on the structure of formulas. It is assumed that space is modelled by the set of points of a distance closure model; each atomic predicate $p \in P$ models a specific *feature* of *points* and is thus associated with the points that have this feature. A point x satisfies $\mathcal{N} \Phi$ if it belongs to the closure of the set of points satisfying Φ, i.e. if x is *near* (or *close*) to a point satisfying Φ; x satisfies $\rho \, \Phi_2[\Phi_1]$ if there is a path π rooted in x—i.e. with $x = \pi(0)$—and an index ℓ such that $\pi(\ell)$ satisfies Φ_2—i.e. $\mathcal{M}, \pi(\ell) \models \Phi_2$— and all intermediate points in π, if any, satisfy Φ_1—i.e. $\mathcal{M}, \pi(j) \models \Phi_1$, for all j with $0 < j < \ell$; x satisfies $\mathcal{D}^I \Phi$ if the distance of x from the set of points satisfying Φ falls in interval I; in the sequel we will use standard abbreviations for denoting intervals I of interest as parameter of $\mathcal{D}$, such as: '$< r$' for $[0, r)$ and '$\geq r$' for $[r, \infty)$. Finally, the logic includes logical negation ($\neg$) and disjunction ($\vee$); as usual, the true ($\top$) and false ($\bot$) constants as well as conjunction ($\wedge$) are defined as derived operators.

$$\mathcal{M}, x \models p \in P \quad \Leftrightarrow x \in \mathcal{V}(p)$$
$$\mathcal{M}, x \models \neg \Phi \quad \Leftrightarrow \mathcal{M}, x \models \Phi \text{ does not hold}$$
$$\mathcal{M}, x \models \Phi_1 \vee \Phi_2 \Leftrightarrow \mathcal{M}, x \models \Phi_1 \text{ or } \mathcal{M}, x \models \Phi_2$$
$$\mathcal{M}, x \models \mathcal{N} \Phi \quad \Leftrightarrow x \in \mathcal{C}(\{y | \mathcal{M}, y \models \Phi\})$$
$$\mathcal{M}, x \models \rho \, \Phi_2[\Phi_1] \Leftrightarrow \text{there exists a path } \pi \text{ and an index } \ell \text{ such that the following holds:}$$
$$\pi(0) = x \text{ and } \mathcal{M}, \pi(\ell) \models \Phi_2 \text{ and}$$
$$\mathcal{M}, \pi(j) \models \Phi_1, \text{ for all } j \text{ with } 0 < j < \ell$$
$$\mathcal{M}, x \models \mathcal{D}^I \Phi \quad \Leftrightarrow d(x, \{y | \mathcal{M}, y \models \Phi\}) \in I$$

where, whenever $p := \alpha$ is a definition for p, we assume $x \in \mathcal{V}(p)$ if and only if $\mathcal{A}(x, \alpha)$ yields the truth-value 'true'.

Fig. 3. Definition of the satisfaction relation

We provide a few simple examples to illustrate these basic spatial operators in Fig. 4. The examples are shown for a spatial model based on a 2D space of 100 points arranged as a 10×10 grid, with an orthogonal adjacency relation. We assume the set of atomic predicates P is the set $\{black, white, red\}$ and, in Fig. 4a, we show in black the points satisfying the atomic predicate *black* and similarly for *white* and *red*. In Fig. 4b the points satisfying formula *black* $\vee$ *red* are shown in green[8]; similarly, Fig. 4c shows the points satisfying $\neg(black \vee red)$, and Fig. 4d shows those satisfying $\mathcal{N} black$; all points of this model satisfy $\rho \, red[white]$, as shown in Fig. 4e while only the points satisfying *black* in the model satisfy also *black* $\wedge \rho \, red[white]$, as shown in Fig. 4f. Finally, Fig. 4g shows in green the points that satisfy $\mathcal{D}^{[2,3]} red$, i.e. those points that are at a distance of at least 2 and at most 3 from points satisfying *red* in Fig. 4a. In this case we assume that the underlying notion of distance is that of the Manhattan distance as shown in Fig. 2.

---

[8] Note that this colour does *not* correspond to any atomic predicate and so it is not part of the model; we use it only for illustration purposes.

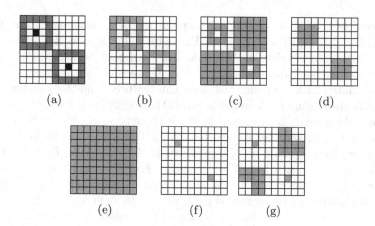

(a)   (b)   (c)   (d)

(e)   (f)   (g)

Fig. 4. An example model (a); the points shown in green are those satisfying *black* ∨ *red* (b), ¬(*black* ∨ *red*) (c), $\mathcal{N}$*black* (d), ρ *red*[*white*] (e), *black* ∧ ρ *red*[*white*] (f), and $\mathcal{D}^{[2,3]}$*red* (g). (Color figure online)

In the version of the logic presented in [12,13] a *surrounded* operator $\mathcal{S}$ was introduced for closure spaces, inspired by the *spatial until* operator discussed in [1] for topological spaces; x satisfies $\Phi_1 \mathcal{S} \Phi_2$ if it satisfies Φ_1 and in any path π with $x = \pi(0)$, if there is ℓ such that $\pi(\ell)$ does *not* satisfy Φ_1, then there is j, $0 < j \leq \ell$, such that $\pi(j)$ satisfies Φ_2; in other words, x belongs to an area satisfying Φ_1 and one cannot *escape* from such an area without hitting a point satisfying Φ_2, i.e. x is *surrounded* by Φ_2. In [8] it has been shown that the *surrounded* operator can be expressed using the *reaches* operator ρ as follows:

$$\Phi_1 \mathcal{S} \Phi_2 \equiv \Phi_1 \wedge \neg\rho \left(\neg(\Phi_1 \vee \Phi_2)\right)[\neg\Phi_2]$$

In this paper $\mathcal{S}$ will be considered as a derived operator. Again with reference to Fig. 4a we note that the two black points also satisfy *black* $\mathcal{S}(\mathcal{N}$*red*$)$.

3   Spatial Logic for Image Analysis

In this section we illustrate the use of the variant of SLCS briefly presented in Sect. 2 extended with a few additional operators introduced in [4,7,8], that are of particular interest for the domain of image analysis. In earlier work we focused on the contouring of diseased (brain) tissue [4,8]. In the next section we show how short but formal and unambiguous logic specifications can be used to identify typical parts of the human brain.

Before presenting the specifications, it is convenient to introduce a few additional derived operators, defined in Fig. 5.

Let us consider a point of a model which satisfies a formula of the form $\rho \, \Phi_2[\Phi_1]$; from the definition of the *reaches* operator, there is no guarantee that

$$touch(\Phi_1, \Phi_2) \triangleq \Phi_1 \wedge \rho \; \Phi_2[\Phi_1]$$
$$grow(\Phi_1, \Phi_2) \triangleq \Phi_1 \vee touch(\Phi_2, \Phi_1)$$
$$flt(r, \Phi_1) \quad\triangleq \mathcal{D}^{<r}(\mathcal{D}^{\geq r} \neg \Phi_1)$$

Fig. 5. Definition of the *touch*, *grow* and *flt* derived operators.

such a point would also satisfy Φ_1, i.e. the formula satisfied by the intermediate points of the path, if any. Such guarantee is ensured by the derived operator *touch*—i.e. a point satisfies $touch(\Phi_1, \Phi_2)$ if it satisfies Φ_1 and there is a path rooted in this point that reaches a point satisfying Φ_2 with all preceding points satisfying Φ_1; note that all such preceding points satisfy $touch(\Phi_1, \Phi_2)$ too. Figure 4c shows in green the points satisfying *touch(white, red)* in the model of Fig. 4a—that, by the way, in this specific model, happen to be the same as those satisfying $\neg(black \vee red)$.

The formula $grow(\Phi_1, \Phi_2)$ is satisfied by points that satisfy Φ_1 and by points that satisfy Φ_2 and that are on a path that reaches a point satisfying Φ_1. Figure 6a shows in green the points satisfying *grow(red, white)* in the model of Fig. 4a.

A point satisfies formula $flt(r, \Phi_1)$ if it is at a distance of less than r from the set of points that are at a distance at least r from the set of points that do *not* satisfy Φ_1. This operator works as a filter; only contiguous areas satisfying Φ_1 that have a minimal diameter of at least $2r$ are preserved; these are also smoothened if they have an irregular shape (e.g. protrusions of less than the indicated distance). An example of the effect of the *flt* operator is shown in Figs. 6b to e. Let us consider the model of Fig. 6b—defined on only two atomic predicates, namely *black* and *white*—and let us consider the formula $flt(2, black)$; Fig. 6c shows in green the points of the model of Fig. 6b satisfying $\neg black$, while those satisfying $\mathcal{D}^{\geq 2}(\neg black)$ are shown in Fig. 6d and finally Fig. 6e shows those satisfying $\mathcal{D}^{<2}(\mathcal{D}^{\geq 2}(\neg black))$—i.e. $flt(2, black)$.

Furthermore a statistical similarity operator is introduced (see [4,8]). It can search for tissue that has the same statistical texture characteristics as a provided texture sample by comparing the similarity of the histograms of the two textures. With reference to a point x, the statistical similarity operator $\triangle_{\bowtie c}\left[\begin{smallmatrix} m & M & k \\ r & a & b \end{smallmatrix}\right]\Phi$ compares the region of the image constituted by the sphere (hypercube) of radius r centred in x against the region characterised by Φ. The comparison is based on the cross correlation of the histograms of the chosen attributes of (the points of) the two regions, namely a and b and both histograms share the same range $([m, M])$ and the same bins $([1, k])$. In summary, the operator allows to check *to which extent* the *sphere (hypercube) around the point of interest* is *statistically similar* to a given region (specified by) Φ. This implements a form of *texture similarity*, which, in practice, works quite well for medical images, also since it is by definition invariant with respect to rotation. In Fig. 7 we report an example that was used in [4] as a benchmark. The benchmark uses a checkerboard-like pattern with areas having differently-sized squares (see Fig. 7a). Figure 7b shows the output of statistical cross-correlation—after thresholding—using as "target"

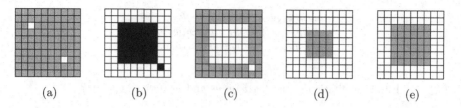

(a)	(b)	(c)	(d)	(e)

Fig. 6. With reference to the model in Fig. 4a, (a) shows in green the points satisfying *grow*(*red, white*). In (c) (d, e, respectively) the points of the model shown in (b) that satisfy ¬*black* ($\mathcal{D}^{\geq 2}$(¬*black*), $\mathcal{D}^{<2}$($\mathcal{D}^{\geq 2}$(¬*black*))—i.e. *flt*(2,*black*)—respectively) are shown in green. (Color figure online)

region the whole image. The associated histogram mostly consists of an equal number of black and white points (plus a smaller number of points having an intermediate value, due to grey lines separating the different areas of the image). Therefore the points that have high local cross-correlation with the whole image (depicted in green) are those that lay on the border of squares, whereas in the inner part of any square, the histogram only consists of either white or black points.

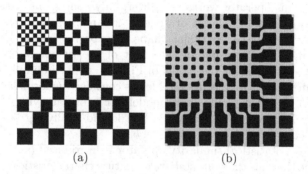

(a)	(b)

Fig. 7. A checkerboard-like pattern (a) and the result of the △ operator applied to it (b). (Color figure online)

The *maxvol* operator is another operator introduced for the domain of image analysis. A point satisfies *maxvol* Φ if it belongs to the *largest* connected component of (the subspace induced by the) points that satisfy Φ. If there are more than one of such largest components, then the points of all such largest components satisfy the property *maxvol* Φ.

Finally, a *percentiles* operator is introduced that assigns to each point of an image the percentile rank of its intensity among those that are part of the image. The interpretation of *percentiles*(*img, mask, c*) considers the set of points S identified by the Boolean-valued mask *mask* in the image *img*—an image with an intensity attribute value associated to each point—and returns an image in which the percentile attribute value of each voxel x is the fraction of points in S that have an intensity *below* that of x in *img*; c is a weight, between 0 and 1, used to take into account also the fraction of points that have intensity *equal* to that of x in the computation; more precisely, the percentile value v_x of each voxel x is defined by

$$v_x = \frac{l_x + (c \cdot e_x)}{N}$$

where l_x is the number of voxels in S having intensity *below* that of x, e_x is the number of voxels in S that have intensity *equal to* that of x, and N is the total number of voxels in S. This operator is used as a form of normalisation of the provided image so that the specification can be used on different cases without the need to recalibrate or explicitly normalise the intensities of the image which may differ in a similar way as normal photographs may show some over or under-exposition. To clarify this, let us just mention one example: the *hyperintense* areas of an image can be defined as those that have percentile rank higher than 0.95, no matter what is the range of the intensity of the source image, or even its numeric type and precision.

The spatial logic SLCS and the additional operators discussed in this section have been implemented in the free open source spatial model checker VoxLogicA. VoxLogicA is specifically designed for the analysis of (possibly multi-dimensional, e.g. 3D) digital images as a specialised image analysis tool, though it can also be used for 2D (general purpose) image analysis. It is tailored to usability and efficiency by employing state-of-the-art algorithms and open source libraries, borrowed from computational image processing, in combination with efficient spatial model checking algorithms. The source code and binaries of VoxLogicA as well as an exhaustive list of the available built-ins, a user manual and a mini-tutorial for the tool are available at the web site of the tool (see Footnote 4). Furthermore, a "standard library" is provided containing short-hands for commonly used functions, and for derived operators. For further details on the model checker and its implementation we refer to [8].

4 Illustration: Brain Segmentation

In previous work [4,7,8] we have focused on how the spatial model checker VoxLogicA can be used for contouring of brain tumours and associated oedema. In this section we present preliminary results on the identification of specific tissues in the healthy head and brain such as white and grey matter, the skull, the bone marrow and so on. For this purpose we use two simulated brain images[9] from a set of twenty [2,28]. Simulated brain images have the advantage that data is generated and therefore the 'ground truth' is know, i.e. it is know for sure which points belong to which kind of tissue. This is very useful for the quantitative testing of image analysis methods.

---

[9] See https://brainweb.bic.mni.mcgill.ca/brainweb/anatomic_normal_20.html (Publicly available).

The specifications that we present serve the purpose to illustrate the flexibility and the potential of the approach, although we expect that our method will be further improved to obtain more accurate results in future work.

The syntax we use for the specifications is that of VoxLogicA, namely: |,&,! are boolean *or, and, not*; distleq(c,phi) is the formula $\mathcal{D}^{\leq c}$phi (similarly, distgeq; distances are in millimeters); the *statistical similarity* operator (see Sect. 6) $\triangle_{\bowtie c} \left[\begin{smallmatrix} m & M & k \\ r & a & b \end{smallmatrix} \right] \Phi$ is written as crossCorrelation(r,a,b,phi,m,M,k) $\bowtie$ c; where the function crossCorrelation computes the relevant cross-correlation value. The >. and <. operators (greater than, and less than, respectively) perform thresholding of the attribute values of the points of an image; border is true on voxels that lay at the border of the image. Other operators should be self-explaining or will be explained in passing.

Specification 1: Derived operators in VoxLogicA

```
1 import "stdlib.imgql"

2 let grow(a,b) = (a | touch(b,a))
3 let flt(r,a) = distleq(r,distgeq(r,!a))
4 load imgT1 = "INPUTDIR/NAME_t1.nii.gz"
5 let t1 = intensity(imgT1)
6 let similarT1To(a) = crossCorrelation(3,t1,t1,a,min(t1),max(t1),30)
7 let similarT1Tor1(a) =
  crossCorrelation(1,t1,t1,a,min(t1),max(t1),30)
```

In the first part of the specification, shown in Specification 1, standard derived operators are imported from the file stdlib.imgql (they will be explained when they are used) and the derived operators that were presented in Sect. 3 are defined, i.e. the operators grow and flt.

In line 4 the 3D magnetic resonance image (MRI) is loaded (which in this case is of type T1, short for T1-weighted-Fluid-Attenuated Inversion Recovery). In this case, the file is encoded using the NIfTI file format (.nii file name extension)[10]. In line 5 the name t1 is bound to the attribute of each voxel of the image corresponding to the intensity of that voxel in the image. In line 6 and 7 two variants of the statistical similarity operator crossCorrelation are defined that share the same parameters, but use a different radius, 3 mm and 1 mm, respectively, around each point.

The second part of the specification is given in Specification 2, where the operations for the identification of the head and the background in the image are shown. Figure 8 shows a few intermediate results of Specification 2 that make it easier to follow the informal description below. Such figures across this section have been produced using the save command of the tool, which, when applied to a formula, generates and saves to disk a new binary image, where exactly those points satisfying the formula at hand are rendered using the boolean value *true*.

---

[10] The NIfTI file format is a special data format by the Neuro-imaging Informatics Technology Initiative, https://nifti.nimh.nih.gov/.

Specification 2: Segmentation of head and background

```
1 let bg = percentiles(t1,t1 >. 0,0.5)
2 let bg1 = touch(bg <. 0.6,border)
3 let head1 = maxvol(flt(2,!bg1))
4 let head2 = distleq(3,head1)
5 let bg2 = maxvol(!head2)
6 let background = distleq(3,bg2)
7 let head=!background
```

Such a binary image (also called *region of interest*) can be loaded in viewers to produce coloured overlays that are superimposed to the original image. In line 1 `bg` (short for 'background') is defined where each point in the image is associated with the value of its percentile ranking attribute w.r.t. the intensity of the points. In line 2 this is used to identify all points from which a border point can be reached passing only through relatively dark (low intensity) points that satisfy `bg < .0.6`, shown in red in Fig. 8b. Note that the formula is satisfied also by points inside the skull; this is due to the fact that the image under analysis is a 3D image, so there are (3D) paths which do not lay in the 2D projection shown in the figure. In line 3 this is used to obtain `head1`, a first approximation of the area of the head as the maximum volume that is not identified as background—after some smoothening using the filter operator (Fig. 8c). In line 4 also all points at a distance of less than 3 mm from points satisfying `head1` are included (Fig. 8d). This temporary enlargement of the head area is useful to separate points that are part of the background from those that are part of the head, so that in line 5 the operator `maxvol` can be used to identify all points of the background (in red in Fig. 8e). After this, the temporary enlargement is removed using the `distleq` operator in line 6 (in blue in Fig. 8f) and the points that satisfied it are again part of the background.

The separation of the background from the part of the image that is really of interest, namely the head, is important for the next steps. In particular, the percentiles can now be obtained considering only the area of the head. Since the anatomy of any adult human head is very similar, the number of points in each percentile, i.e. the normalised grey-level, have a very similar distribution for any head regardless of the possible fluctuations in the luminosity of the images due to differences in the registration. Therefore, in line 1 of Specification 3 the percentile rank for each point satisfying `head` is obtained in `pt1`. In line 2 the similarity coefficient (cross correlation) is computed (for each voxel) and in line 3 we define the interior part of the head, i.e. those points of the head that are at a distance of at least 30 mm from the background (Fig. 9a). The following steps use these definitions to identify the white matter of the brain. In line 4 we seek to obtain an area of the brain that is certainly composed of white matter and is defined as the largest area in the inner part of the brain each point of which is in a 3 mm ball that has a cross correlation coefficient with the complete head of between 0.4 and 0.6 (Fig. 9b). These values have been obtained experimentally

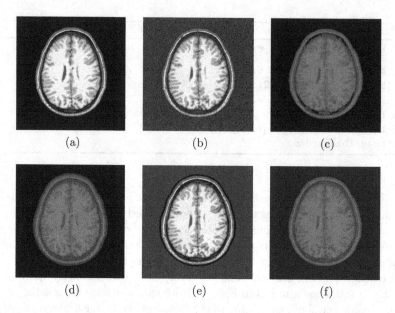

Fig. 8. Identification of head and background. Original axial view (a). In red points satisfying `bg1` (b); points satisfying `head1` (c); points satisfying `head2` (d); points satisfying `bg2` (e); points satisfying `head` (in red) and `background` (in blue) (f). (Color figure online)

in such a way that they correspond to points that are white matter and not other kind of tissue, such as the eyes, that also has a high intensity[11]. Then, in line 5, we look for all the points that are similar to `white1` using a rather small radius (1 mm) to obtain good accuracy (Fig. 9c). Subsequently, in line 6 the largest volume of points is selected that is sufficiently similar with a coefficient of at least 0.6 (Fig. 9d). This gives already a very good approximation. In line 7 this is somewhat refined by "closing tiny grey holes" in this area using a surrounded operator (Fig. 9e).

Specification 3: Segmentation of white matter

```
1 let pt1 = percentiles(t1,head,0.5)
2 let headSim = similarT1To(head)
3 let headInt = head & !(distleq(30,!head))

4 let white1 = maxvol((headSim <. 0.6) & (headSim >. 0.4) & headInt)
5 let whiteT1 = similarT1Tor1(white1)
6 let white2 = maxvol(whiteT1 >. 0.6)
7 let white = white2 | ((headSim >. 0.3) & surrounded((headSim >.
   0.3),white2))
```

---

[11] Again, note that we are processing a 3D image.

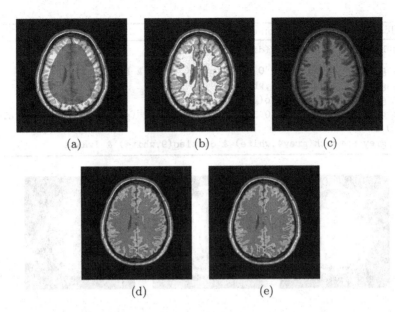

Fig. 9. Identification of white matter. In red points satisfying `headInt` (a); points satisfying `white1` (b); level of similarity `whiteT1` (c); points satisfying `white2` (d); points satisfying `white` (e). (Color figure online)

In Specification 4 we proceed by identifying the grey matter of the brain. In line 1 we take a larger internal portion of the head than that of `headInt` so that we are sure that the grey matter, which is mostly situated near the white matter towards the outside of the brain, is included. In line 2 an area is identified that is almost certainly part of the grey area, using expert knowledge on percentile ranking, similarity coefficient and position within the internal part of the head (Fig. 10a). In line 3 we use the knowledge that grey matter is attached to the white matter of the brain (Fig. 10b). We now have a good sample of grey matter, but there are some areas that are not covered (see the grey parts that are not red yet in the left and top part of the head in Fig. 10b). So we look for further texture that is similar to grey matter in line 4 and 5 (Fig. 10c and d). This indeed includes the previous grey areas that were missed out, but also includes other areas in the bottom outer part of the head. We use again the knowledge that grey and white matter are next to each other using `touch` and `distleq` and the knowledge that white and grey matter do not overlap, i.e. `!white` to exclude the areas on this outer part as they cannot be part of the grey matter for anatomical reasons. This gives us the final result for grey matter as shown in (Fig. 10e).

In a very similar fashion we can also identify the cerebrospinal fluid (CSF), the skull and the bone marrow for example. We omit the details here and only show the final results in Fig. 11. In the same figure we show some preliminary analysis of the quality of the described method by comparing our results with a 'ground truth' segmentation provided by the method in [2]. Figure 11 shows our

Specification 4: Segmentation of grey matter

```
1 let headInt2 = head & !(distleq(10,!head))
2 let grey1 = (headSim >. 0.6) & (pt1 <. 0.8) & headInt2
3 let grey2 = touch(grey1,white)
4 let greyT1 = similarT1To(grey2)
5 let grey4 = (greyT1 >. 0.3) & (pt1 <. 0.8) & (pt1 >. 0.4) & (whiteT1
    <. 0.8)
6 let grey = touch(grey4,white) & distleq(9,white) & !white
```

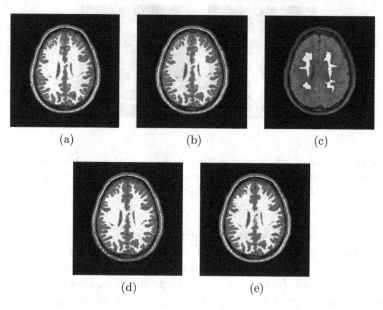

Fig. 10. Identification of grey matter. In red points satisfying `grey1` (a); points satisfying `grey2` (b); level of similarity `greyT1` (c); points satisfying `grey4` (d); points satisfying `grey` (e). (Color figure online)

results in red and the 'ground truth' segmentation of [2] for case study[12] Pat04 in blue. The points in pink are those where both analyses coincide.

Note that all the analyses are performed in 3D and can be viewed from all three directions. As an example, in Fig. 12 we show the three perspectives, axial, coronal and sagittal, for the grey matter for one particular cross-section.

We have applied the same specification also on case Pat05 of the same public database and have obtained very similar results. As a preliminary measure of similarity between the 'ground truth' segmentation and that obtained via spatial model checking we report here the Dice measure[13], and the sensitivity and

---

[12] See http://brainweb.bic.mni.mcgill.ca/brainweb/anatomic_normal_20.html.
[13] $Dice = 2 * TP/(2 * TP + FN + FP)$, where TP denotes True Positive and FN denotes False Negative.

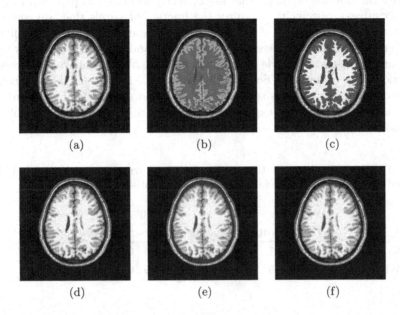

(a)   (b)   (c)

(d)   (e)   (f)

Fig. 11. Comparison with other results. Original axial view (a). In red the points satisfying our specification, in blue the 'ground truth' provided by the method in [2] for the case study of patient nr. 04 and in pink points that satisfy both analyses. White matter (b); grey matter (c); CSF (d); skull (e); bone marrow (f). (Color figure online)

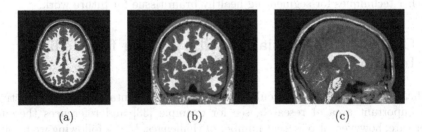

(a)   (b)   (c)

Fig. 12. Comparison in 3D perspective for grey matter. In red points satisfying our specification, in blue points identified by the 'ground truth' segmentation in [2] for the case study of patient nr. 04 and in pink points that satisfy both analyses. Axial (a), coronal (b) and sagittal (c) perspective. (Color figure online)

specificity measures for the grey and the white matter of the brain. Sensitivity measures the fraction of voxels that are correctly identified as part of a tumour (True Positives). Specificity measures the fraction of voxels that are correctly identified as *not* being part of a tumour (True Negatives). All these similarity coefficients give a result between 0 (no similarity) and 1 (perfect similarity) and are commonly used to provide a combined measure of the similarity of two segmentations. For example a Dice index of around 0.9 is considered as indicating very good similarity. This is so because there is no unique 'gold standard' for comparison as also manual expert markings have a certain level of variability (see also Sect. 5 and [32]).

Table 1. Similarity between the results of 'ground truth' segmentation and that obtained via spatial model checking for case studies Pat04 and Pat05

	Pat04			Pat05		
	Dice	Sensitivity	Specificity	Dice	Sensitivity	Specificity
Grey matter	0.90	0.91	0.98	0.89	0.88	0.99
White matter	0.89	0.85	1.0	0.90	0.85	1.0

Table 1 provides some first indication that the specification could be a good candidate to be applied to further cases for the segmentation of MRI images of healthy brains, much in the same way as we have done for tumour segmentation in [8]. Also from an execution time point of view our preliminary results obtained with VoxLogicA are encouraging as the complete segmentation (head, background, white matter, grey matter, CSF, skull and bone marrow) of the brain was obtained in less than 2 min on a MacBook Pro running MacOS Mojave, with 2.7 GHz Intel core i7 and 16 GB of memory. We leave the analysis of the other cases of the benchmark and a more complete comparison with the results of other techniques for segmenting healthy brain tissue for future work.

5   Challenges in Spatial Model Checking for Medical Imaging

Medical Imaging, and in particular brain tumour segmentation, is a very active and important area of research, see for example [33] and references therein. There are, however, also a great number of challenges. In the following we briefly describe some of them, and in particular those where we think that an approach based on spatial model checking may make a significant contribution to.

Modularity, Composition and Flexibility. An aspect that all logic-based model checking techniques have in common is their reliance on a relatively small set of basic logical operators. There are in general many choices for such minimal sets of operators. Ideally, this provides at the same time a good expressivity and also the basis for the definition of a useful set of *derived* operators that match the level of domain specific reasoning of the user. In case of medical imaging for radiotherapy, for example, that could be the neuro-radiologist. Derived operators exploit the *compositionality* of the basic operators so that more complicated operators can be constructed out of the basic building blocks. Furthermore, the basic set should allow for very *efficient verification algorithms* and be minimal, such that the *correctness* of the algorithms can be proven with reasonable and acceptable effort. Finally, we would also expect a certain *flexibility and generality* of the approach requiring that the operators are not too much specifically tied to a particular application or even a single case study or type of analysis.

Although these notions have been studied extensively in the wider field of model checking, the solutions in the sense of particular sets of basic operators, that have been proposed need to be reinterpreted in the case of spatial model checking and founded on other mathematical theories such as closure spaces. Restricting space to more regular structures than general graphs may also lead to very significant increases in the efficiency of spatial model checking algorithms at the cost of some generality. Such increase in efficiency may, however, make the difference between a tool that can effectively improve the daily work of, for example, neuro-radiologists and a tool that is very general but too slow or requiring too much memory to be of practical use. These increases in efficiency are also due to the fact that for example very efficient existing image processing algorithms and related software packages can be exploited. For example, in VoxLogicA [8] the state-of-the-art cross-platform and open source computational imaging library ITK[14] was used for the efficient implementation of the basic spatial operators. What exactly constitutes the best choice of basic spatial operators, given the trade-offs, is still not a fully answered question, however some promising candidate sets have been proposed for this area in some of our earlier work [12,13].

Interactive Feedback and Ease of Use. Whereas traditional model checkers and their extensions are in general used by experts in formal methods or by software engineers, in the case of spatial model checking for medical applications the expected users have a different background. Moreover, the specific analyses that clinicians or neuro-radiologists are envisioned to perform with these tools should be embedded into their daily activities and must be well-integrated with other environments that they use such as those for safe and secure archiving of images and their results. Furthermore, other aspects should be taken into account as well, such as cognitive fatigue and avoidance of information overload, allowing users to easily focus on their main critical(!) task at hand without being distracted by useless details. There are relatively few studies addressing these issues in some depth, even if the problem has been taken up by some research groups, see for example work by Gambino et al. [24] for a survey and some concrete proposals.

---

[14] The Insight Segmentation and Registration Toolkit, see https://itk.org and http://www.simpleitk.org.

Explainability, Independent Reproducibility and Transferability. In recent years, following the success of the use of artificial intelligence and neural networks for image recognition tasks, much of the research in medical imaging and segmentation tasks in particular, has focused on these (probabilistic) learning algorithms (see for example [33,38]). Such algorithms, however, usually depend on the availability of large and precisely annotated data sets for their learning phase. During such a learning phase the software is autonomously calibrating the value of thousands of parameters until the resulting program provides a satisfactory level of correct responses on the training data set. Deep learning is based on the use of artificial neural networks, consisting of several layers, that can extract a hierarchy of features from raw input data. Such learning algorithms may reach surprisingly good results, but they also pose some open challenges. First of all, developing large and precisely annotated data sets in delicate areas such as medical imaging and tumour segmentation is a time-consuming task that can only be performed, mostly manually, by specialists. This is difficult to achieve, not only because it is very laborious, but also because of the relatively high intra-expert and inter-expert variability; [32] quantifies the average of disagreement in identified contours by experts as $20 \pm 15\%$ and $28 \pm 12\%$, respectively, for manual segmentations of brain tumour images. Interactive approaches based on spatial model checking, in this context, may be of help to improve the generation of manual ground truth labels in a more efficient, transparent and reproducible way. Furthermore, the automatic algorithms that are obtained with a (deep) learning approach cannot provide human intelligible insight in why certain areas are identified as tumours. In other words, these procedures lack *explainability*. This is a more serious problem than it may seem, at first sight, since these algorithms (as any other in this context) do not *always* provide the correct results, and in the critical context of radiotherapy the preparations must comply to rigorous protocols where medical staff must be put in the condition to take responsibility for their decisions.

Extendability and Openness. Manual segmentation by experts is still the standard for in vivo images. This method is expensive and time-consuming, difficult to reproduce and possibly inaccurate due to human error. However, the expertise that has been gained by many practitioners in the field is very valuable and could in principle be exploited in improving segmentation procedures if such procedures could be easily expressed through and supported by computer assisted operations at the right level of abstraction. For example, if various segmentation procedures could be captured in an unambiguous way by the composition of a number of rather high-level operations in a formal specification, such specifications could be published, exchanged, discussed and improved directly by those experts working in the field. This challenge would call for an extendable framework, where new operations can be introduced, and that is sufficiently open to be used by a wider community.

Device Independence and Vendor Neutrality. Different research groups and institutions employ specific best-practices for image analysis, often locally built from home-made integration of different software technologies. This gives rise to a plethora of incompatible systems, very often of academic significance, but rarely used in clinical practice. Missing integration with existing hardware, hand-crafted procedures, lack of maintenance and accountability, difficult use, hard-coded dependence on the execution environment (e.g. specific operating system or hardware), are just some factors that hinder clinical application, medical procedure approval processes, and ethical scrutiny, creating a barrier between medical research and healthcare. Thus, successful technological transfer mostly happens by specialised, proprietary software solutions that are typically bundled with the hardware. The challenge here is to overcome the fragmentation of the medical imaging ecosystem, by providing a set of open standards and reference implementations, fostering a paradigm shift in the field in several ways such as by facilitating communication between research and healthcare providers and by providing technologies that are appropriate for intermediaries (such as manufacturers and vendors of Medical Imaging devices) to turn novel ideas into clinical practice. This may be pursued through the social computing capabilities of a spatial logic based language, that can attract experts of diverse fields to collaborate through a common communication infrastructure.

Privacy Issues. Regulation issues, especially related to privacy, may easily arise in an open platform. However, in the envisioned approach privacy is a key strength, rather than an issue. The definition of an open standard for image analysis, and its *free and open source software* implementation, will enable users to exchange analysis procedures, and establish common knowledge, without outsourcing the actual, privacy sensitive data, which can be handled on-site, obeying to the locally established practices.

The above is only a small selection of the many challenges in medical imaging for radiotherapy. We do by no means intend to present an exhaustive list. However, we think that the listed challenges are relevant and have shown where we expect that further research in a spatial logic-based method may lead to a useful contribution to advance this important field.

6   Related Work

Most of the present paper was dedicated to the potential of spatial model checking in the field of medical imaging, initiated in [7], and of image segmentation and contouring for the purpose of radiotherapy in particular (see [4,6,8]). However, spatial model checking has been explored in a number of other applications and it has been extended in several ways. In this section we provide a brief overview of recent related work.

A very valuable resource and reference on the topological origins of spatial logic is the *Handbook of Spatial Logics* [1]. This handbook describes several spatial logics, with applications far beyond topological spaces. Among them are not only logics that treat morphology, geometry, distance, or such as dynamic systems, but also a treatment of discrete models, that are particularly difficult to deal with from a topological perspective. See, for example [21], introducing the approach of Closure Spaces upon which the work in [12,13,16] is based.

Starting from a spatial formalism and from a temporal formalism, *spatio-temporal* logics may be defined, by introducing a mutually recursive nesting of spatial and temporal operators. Several combinations can be obtained, depending on the chosen spatial and temporal fragments, and the permitted forms of nesting of the two. A large number of possibilities are explored in [27], for spatial logics based on topological spaces. One such structure was investigated in the setting of closure spaces, namely the combination of the *Computation Tree Logic* (CTL) with SLCS, resulting in the *Spatio-Temporal Logic of Closure Spaces* (STLCS). In STLCS spatial and temporal fragments may be arbitrary and mutually nested.

STLCS is interpreted on a variant of Kripke models, where valuations are interpreted at points of a closure space. Fix a set P of proposition letters. STLCS em state and *path* formulas are defined by the grammars shown below, where p ranges over P.

$$\Phi ::= p \mid \neg\Phi \mid \Phi \vee \Phi \mid \mathcal{N}\Phi \mid \rho\,\Phi[\Phi] \mid A\varphi \mid E\varphi \tag{2}$$

$$\varphi ::= \mathcal{X}\Phi \mid \Phi\,\mathcal{U}\,\Phi \tag{3}$$

The logic features the CTL path quantifiers A ("for all paths"), and E ("there exists a path"). As in CTL, such quantifiers must necessarily be followed by one of the path-specific temporal operators, such as[15] $\mathcal{X}\Phi$ ("next"), $F\Phi$ ("eventually"), $G\Phi$ ("globally"), $\Phi_1\mathcal{U}\Phi_2$ ("until"), but, unlike CTL, in this case Φ, Φ_1 and Φ_2 are STLCS formulas that may make use of spatial operators, e.g. $\mathcal{N}$, ρ and operators derived thereof (see Sect. 2.) The mutual nesting of such operators permits one to express spatial properties in which the involved points are constrained to certain temporal behaviours.

As a proof of concept, a model checking algorithm has been defined, which is a variant of the classical CTL labelling algorithm [3,19], augmented with the algorithm in [10] for the spatial fragment. The algorithm, which operates on finite spaces, has been implemented as a prototype tool which is described in [11]. The same algorithm is also implemented in the tool `topochecker`.

The tool has been used to analyse a number of properties of vehicular movement in public transport systems in the context of *smart cities*. In [10], a bus transportation case study was developed, to detect problems in the automatic vehicle location (AVL) data that is provided as input to other systems that in

---

[15] Some operators may be derived from others; for this reason in the definition of the language we use a minimal set of connectives. As usual in logics, there are several different choices for such a set.

turn provide information to passengers and system operators such as bus arrival prediction systems. Such data may contain errors originating in a problem with the hardware of the measurement device or also indicate operational problems experienced by bus drivers that encountered unexpected road works or accidents and have to deviate from their planned route.

In [15], spatio-temporal model checking has been used to study a phenomenon known as *clumping*, which may occur in so-called "frequent" services – those where a timetable is not published. Clumping occurs where one bus catches up with – or at least comes too close to – the bus which is in front of it. In [17] spatio-temporal model checking has been used to detect the emergent formation of 'clusters' of full (and empty) stations in the simulation traces of a Markov Renewal Process (MRP) model of large bike sharing systems [31]. Subsequently, spatio-temporal model checking has been used in combination with statistical model checking in [18] to analyse further properties of bike sharing systems.

The logics discussed so far characterise properties of *single points* in space. In [13] an extended version of SLCS has been defined that is able to express properties that *sets* of points may satisfy *collectively*. The resulting logic, the *Collective* SLCS, CSLCS, can be used for example, for expressing that the points satisfying a certain formula Φ_1 are *collectively* surrounded by points satisfying formula Φ_2. The notion of *region* as set of points and related properties has been studied extensively in the literature, also in the context of discrete spaces (see [36,37] among others). For instance, RCC5D is a theory of region parthood for discrete spaces and RCC8D extends it with the topological notion of connection and the relations of disconnection, external connection, tangential and nontangential proper parthood and their inverse relations. In [14] an encoding of RCC8D into CSLCS is provided and it is shown how topochecker can be used for effectively checking the existence of a RCC8D relation between two given regions of a discrete space.

Two variants of the spatial modalities have also been added to the Signal Temporal Logic [20,30] leading to the Signal Spatio-Temporal Logic (SSTL). The first variant, the *bounded somewhere* operator $\diamondsuit_{[w_1,w_2]}$ is borrowed from [34], while the second one, the *bounded surround* operator $\mathcal{S}_{[w_1,w_2]}$, is inspired by SLCS. The logic comes with a boolean and quantitative semantics which can be found in [34,35]. The boolean semantics defines when a formula is satisfied, the quantitative semantics provides an indication of the robustness with which a formula is satisfied, i.e. how susceptible it is to changing its truth value for example as a result of a perturbation in the signals. In [5] an extension of SSTL is presented which uses a reachability operator as a basic operator of the logic.

In [25] a variant of spatial logic is proposed where spatial properties are expressed using quad trees. The authors show that very complex spatial structures can be identified with the support of model checking algorithms as well as machine learning procedures. However, the formulation of spatial properties becomes rather complex. The combination of this spatial logic with linear time signal temporal logic, defined with respect to continuous-valued signals, has recently led to the spatio-temporal logic SpaTeL [26].

7 Conclusions

Medical imaging is a very broad and active field of research with particular requirements. In this work we have illustrated the basic framework of spatial verification and how spatial logic and spatial model checking can be used to identify various kinds of tissues in the healthy brain. The field of medical imaging is posing very particular challenges, not only of technical nature, but in particular also in terms of responsibility, explainability, transparency and reproducibility. Formal verification and spatial model checking may provide interesting complementary methods in this important field.

The presented specifications are a first proof of concept to show that it is indeed possible to identify various (healthy) brain tissues with the available operators in the presented logic. The results are promising from different perspectives, however, we expect that the specifications can be further improved to obtain better accuracy. Improvements are also foreseen from the methodological point of view. More work is needed to refine the analyses and check applicability to a larger set of images in particular with respect to stability and accuracy of the results, and to make the approach available in a clinical setting. The latter requires the design of appropriate case studies and establishing experimental protocols for clinical validation. This is planned as part of future work.

Acknowledgments. This paper was written for the Festschrift in honour of Director of Research Dr. Stefania Gnesi. We would like to thank Stefania for the many years she has been coordinating our Formal Methods and Tools Laboratory at ISTI-CNR, and we hope she will continue to contribute to our Lab for many years to come. She guided the group safely through the many periods of instability of very different nature, and she did so with confidence and optimism. If now we have so many young (and less young) motivated formal methods researchers in our group, that explore and develop new and creative directions of formal methods research, both in theory and for applications, this is made possible, in a large part, thanks to her tireless efforts in all these years.

Part of this work has been developed in the context of the Italian MIUR-PRIN 2017 project "IT MaTTerS: Methods and Tools for Trustworthy Smart Systems".

References

1. Aiello, M., Pratt-Hartmann, I., van Benthem, J. (eds.): Handbook of Spatial Logics. Springer, Dordrecht (2007). https://doi.org/10.1007/978-1-4020-5587-4
2. Aubert-Broche, B., Griffin, M., Pike, G., Evans, A., Collins, D.: Twenty new digital brain phantoms for creation of validation image data bases. IEEE Trans. Med. Imaging **25**(11), 1410–1416 (2006). https://doi.org/10.1109/TMI.2006.883453
3. Baier, C., Katoen, J.: Principles of Model Checking. MIT Press, Cambridge (2008)
4. Banci Buonamici, F., Belmonte, G., Ciancia, V., Latella, D., Massink, M.: Spatial logics and model checking for medical imaging. Int. J. Softw. Tools Technol. Transf. (2019). https://doi.org/10.1007/s10009-019-00511-9. Online First

5. Bartocci, E., Bortolussi, L., Loreti, M., Nenzi, L.: Monitoring mobile and spatially distributed cyber-physical systems. In: Talpin, J., Derler, P., Schneider, K. (eds.) Proceedings of the 15th ACM-IEEE International Conference on Formal Methods and Models for System Design, MEMOCODE 2017, Vienna, Austria, 29 September–02 October 2017, pp. 146–155. ACM (2017). https://doi.org/10.1145/3127041.3127050

6. Belmonte, G., et al.: A topological method for automatic segmentation of glioblastoma in mr flair for radiotherapy - ESMRMB 2017, 34th annual scientific meeting. Magn. Reson. Mater. Phys. Biol. Med. **30**(S1), 437 (2017). https://doi.org/10.1007/s10334-017-0634-z

7. Belmonte, G., Ciancia, V., Latella, D., Massink, M.: From collective adaptive systems to human centric computation and back: spatial model checking for medical imaging. In: ter Beek, M.H., Loreti, M. (eds.) Proceedings of the Workshop on FORmal methods for the quantitative Evaluation of Collective Adaptive SysTems, FORECAST@STAF 2016, Vienna, Austria, 8 July 2016. EPTCS, vol. 217, pp. 81–92 (2016). https://doi.org/10.4204/EPTCS.217.10

8. Belmonte, G., Ciancia, V., Latella, D., Massink, M.: VoxLogicA: a spatial model checker for declarative image analysis. In: Vojnar, T., Zhang, L. (eds.) TACAS 2019, Part I. LNCS, vol. 11427, pp. 281–298. Springer, Cham (2019). https://doi.org/10.1007/978-3-030-17462-0_16. Preprint http://arxiv.org/abs/1811.05677

9. van Benthem, J., Bezhanishvili, G.: Modal logics of space. In: Handbook of Spatial Logics [1], pp. 217–298

10. Ciancia, V., Gilmore, S., Latella, D., Loreti, M., Massink, M.: Data verification for collective adaptive systems: spatial model-checking of vehicle location data. In: Eighth IEEE International Conference on Self-Adaptive and Self-Organizing Systems Workshops, SASOW, pp. 32–37. IEEE Computer Society (2014)

11. Ciancia, V., Grilletti, G., Latella, D., Loreti, M., Massink, M.: An experimental spatio-temporal model checker. In: Bianculli, D., Calinescu, R., Rumpe, B. (eds.) SEFM 2015. LNCS, vol. 9509, pp. 297–311. Springer, Heidelberg (2015). https://doi.org/10.1007/978-3-662-49224-6_24

12. Ciancia, V., Latella, D., Loreti, M., Massink, M.: Specifying and verifying properties of space. In: Diaz, J., Lanese, I., Sangiorgi, D. (eds.) TCS 2014. LNCS, vol. 8705, pp. 222–235. Springer, Heidelberg (2014). https://doi.org/10.1007/978-3-662-44602-7_18

13. Ciancia, V., Latella, D., Loreti, M., Massink, M.: Model checking spatial logics for closure spaces. Log. Methods Comput. Sci. **12**(4) (2016). http://lmcs.episciences.org/2067

14. Ciancia, V., Latella, D., Massink, M.: Embedding RCC8D in the collective spatial logic CSLCS. In: Boreale, M., Corradini, F., Loreti, M., Pugliese, R. (eds.) Models, Languages, and Tools for Concurrent and Distributed Programming. LNCS, vol. 11665, pp. 260–277. Springer, Cham (2019). https://doi.org/10.1007/978-3-030-21485-2_15

15. Ciancia, V., Gilmore, S., Grilletti, G., Latella, D., Loreti, M., Massink, M.: Spatio-temporal model checking of vehicular movement in public transport systems. STTT **20**(3), 289–311 (2018). https://doi.org/10.1007/s10009-018-0483-8

16. Ciancia, V., Latella, D., Loreti, M., Massink, M.: Spatial logic and spatial model checking for closure spaces. In: Bernardo, M., De Nicola, R., Hillston, J. (eds.) SFM 2016. LNCS, vol. 9700, pp. 156–201. Springer, Cham (2016). https://doi.org/10.1007/978-3-319-34096-8_6

17. Ciancia, V., Latella, D., Massink, M., Paškauskas, R.: Exploring spatio-temporal properties of bike-sharing systems. In: 2015 IEEE International Conference on Self-Adaptive and Self-Organizing Systems Workshops, SASO Workshops 2015, Cambridge, MA, USA, 21–25 September 2015, pp. 74–79. IEEE Computer Society (2015). https://doi.org/10.1109/SASOW.2015.17
18. Ciancia, V., Latella, D., Massink, M., Paškauskas, R., Vandin, A.: A tool-chain for statistical spatio-temporal model checking of bike sharing systems. In: Margaria, T., Steffen, B. (eds.) ISoLA 2016. LNCS, vol. 9952, pp. 657–673. Springer, Cham (2016). https://doi.org/10.1007/978-3-319-47166-2_46
19. Clarke, E.M., Grumberg, O., Peled, D.: Model Checking. MIT Press (2001). http://books.google.de/books?id=Nmc4wEaLXFEC
20. Donzé, A., Ferrère, T., Maler, O.: Efficient robust monitoring for STL. In: Sharygina, N., Veith, H. (eds.) CAV 2013. LNCS, vol. 8044, pp. 264–279. Springer, Heidelberg (2013). https://doi.org/10.1007/978-3-642-39799-8_19
21. Galton, A.: The mereotopology of discrete space. In: Freksa, C., Mark, D.M. (eds.) COSIT 1999. LNCS, vol. 1661, pp. 251–266. Springer, Heidelberg (1999). https://doi.org/10.1007/3-540-48384-5_17
22. Galton, A.: A generalized topological view of motion in discrete space. Theor. Comput. Sci. **305**(1–3), 111–134 (2003). https://doi.org/10.1016/S0304-3975(02)00701-6
23. Galton, A.: Discrete mereotopology. In: Calosi, C., Graziani, P. (eds.) Mereology and the Sciences. SL, vol. 371, pp. 293–321. Springer, Cham (2014). https://doi.org/10.1007/978-3-319-05356-1_11
24. Gambino, O., Rundo, L., Cannella, V., Vitabile, S., Pirrone, R.: A framework for data-driven adaptive GUI generation based on DICOM. J. Biomed. Inform. **88**, 37–52 (2018). https://doi.org/10.1016/j.jbi.2018.10.009
25. Grosu, R., Smolka, S., Corradini, F., Wasilewska, A., Entcheva, E., Bartocci, E.: Learning and detecting emergent behavior in networks of cardiac myocytes. Commun. ACM **52**(3), 97–105 (2009)
26. Haghighi, I., Jones, A., Kong, Z., Bartocci, E., Grosu, R., Belta, C.: SpaTel: a novel spatial-temporal logic and its applications to networked systems. In: Proceedings of the 18th International Conference on Hybrid Systems: Computation and Control, HSCC 2015, pp. 189–198. ACM, New York (2015)
27. Kontchakov, R., Kurucz, A., Wolter, F., Zakharyaschev, M.: Spatial logic + temporal logic = ? In: Handbook of Spatial Logics [1], pp. 497–564
28. Kwan, R.S., Evans, A., Pike, G.: MRI simulation-based evaluation of image-processing and classification methods. IEEE Trans. Med. Imaging **18**(11), 1085–1097 (1999)
29. Litjens, G.J.S., et al.: A survey on deep learning in medical image analysis. Med. Image Anal. **42**, 60–88 (2017). https://doi.org/10.1016/j.media.2017.07.005
30. Maler, O., Nickovic, D.: Monitoring temporal properties of continuous signals. In: Lakhnech, Y., Yovine, S. (eds.) FORMATS/FTRTFT 2004. LNCS, vol. 3253, pp. 152–166. Springer, Heidelberg (2004). https://doi.org/10.1007/978-3-540-30206-3_12
31. Massink, M., Paškauskas, R.: Model-based assessment of aspects of user-satisfaction in bicycle sharing systems. In: Sotelo Vazquez, M., Olaverri Monreal, C., Miller, J., Broggi, A. (eds.) 18th IEEE International Conference on Intelligent Transportation Systems, pp. 1363–1370. IEEE (2015). https://doi.org/10.1109/ITSC.2015.224
32. Mazzara, G., Velthuizen, R., Pearlman, J., Greenberg, H., Wagner, H.: Brain tumor target volume determination for radiation treatment planning through automated mri segmentation. Int. J. Radiat. Oncol. Biol. Phys. **59**(1), 300–312 (2004)

33. Menze, B., et al.: The multimodal brain tumor image segmentation benchmark (BRATS). IEEE Trans. Med. Imaging **34**(10), 1993–2024 (2015)
34. Nenzi, L., Bortolussi, L.: Specifying and monitoring properties of stochastic spatio-temporal systems in signal temporal logic. In: 8th International Conference on Performance Evaluation Methodologies and Tools, VALUETOOLS 2014, Bratislava, Slovakia, 9–11 December 2014. ICST (2014)
35. Nenzi, L., Bortolussi, L., Ciancia, V., Loreti, M., Massink, M.: Qualitative and quantitative monitoring of spatio-temporal properties. In: Bartocci, E., Majumdar, R. (eds.) RV 2015. LNCS, vol. 9333, pp. 21–37. Springer, Cham (2015). https://doi.org/10.1007/978-3-319-23820-3_2
36. Randell, D.A., Cui, Z., Cohn, A.G.: A spatial logic based on regions and connection. In: Nebel, B., Rich, C., Swartout, W.R. (eds.) Proceedings of the 3rd International Conference on Principles of Knowledge Representation and Reasoning (KR 1992), pp. 165–176. Morgan Kaufmann, Burlington (1992)
37. Randell, D.A., Landini, G., Galton, A.: Discrete mereotopology for spatial reasoning in automated histological image analysis. IEEE Trans. Pattern Anal. Mach. Intell. **35**(3), 568–581 (2013). https://doi.org/10.1109/TPAMI.2012.128
38. Spyridon (Spyros) Bakas, et al. (eds.): 2017 International MICCAI BraTS Challenge: Pre-conference Proceedings, September 2017. https://www.cbica.upenn.edu/sbia/Spyridon.Bakas/MICCAI_BraTS/MICCAI_BraTS_2017_proceedings_shortPapers.pdf

Formal Methods in Designing Critical Cyber-Physical Systems

Mehrnoosh Askarpour[1]($\boxtimes$), Carlo Ghezzi[1], Dino Mandrioli[1], Matteo Rossi[1],
and Christos Tsigkanos[2]

[1] Politecnico di Milano, DEIB, Milan, Italy
{mehrnoosh.askarpour,carlo.ghezzi,dino.mandrioli,matteo.rossi}@polimi.it
[2] Vienna University of Technology, Vienna, Austria
christos.tsigkanos@tuwien.ac.at

Abstract. Cyber-Physical Systems (CPS) are increasingly applied in critical contexts, where they have to support safe and secure operations, often subject to stringent timing requirements. Typical examples are scenarios involving automated living or working spaces in which humans operate, or human-robot collaborations (HRC) in modern manufacturing. Formal methods have been traditionally investigated to support modeling and verification of critical systems. In this paper, we review some of the main new challenges arising in the application of formal methods to modeling and verification of CPS. We do that by presenting two case studies (emergency response in a smart city and a smart manufacturing system), reflecting past work of the authors, from which some general lessons are distilled.

Keywords: Cyber-Physical Systems (CPS) · Formal model · Formal verification · Model-based design

1 Introduction

The revolutionary advancements of embedded computing have led to a generation of systems that integrate computing and physical processes, called cyber-physical systems (CPS) [2,22]. Such systems incorporate functions of sensing, actuation, and control while making decisions in a predictive or adaptive manner. This manifests in various novel fields such as the Internet of Things (IoT) [3]. The use of CPSs is growing every day with the developments of new application areas. For example, CPSs enable the creation of smart spaces [24,26], i.e., spatial environments including both cyber and physical elements and supporting new kinds of advanced functionalities. A particular case of smart spaces is smart factories [30], where computational and communication features are embedded in a manufacturing workspace to combine the flexibility of humans with the efficiency of machines and to allow for collaboration between them in a safe way [23]. To design such new kinds of complex systems, it is crucial to analyze, specify, and then verify their expected properties. Often properties

M. H. ter Beek et al. (Eds.): Gnesi Festschrift, LNCS 11865, pp. 110–130, 2019.
https://doi.org/10.1007/978-3-030-30985-5_8

are classified in functional vs non-functional ones, where the former capture the expected results of the system, whereas the latter correspond to its complementary properties—such as space, time, safety, security, fault tolerance, continuous adaptation, communication and process time, energy, or cost—and are no less relevant than the functional ones.

Model-based techniques could considerably simplify the design of such complex systems, and make the analysis of all of their required properties precise and rigorous. Although the separation of cyber and physical concerns in the modeling and design of CPSs could be beneficial for tractability, it complicates the assessment of the impacts and tradeoffs of the two domains [21]. The interplay between cyber and physical elements raises new challenges, and their effective orchestration requires semantic models that reflect properties of interest in both of them [18].

Formal languages should be defined to support specification both of a formal model of a CPS—e.g., a smart space—and of the properties it is expected to satisfy. These models could be input to automated formal verification tools to enable analysis and validation during design. Furthermore, the physical aspect of CPSs brings more uncertainty and dynamism into the picture w.r.t traditional embedded systems, due to the *runtime* physical intercommunication with the world (e.g., human-robot interaction, sensing or actuating on the elements of the environment). Thus, formal methods should also be brought to runtime, to support runtime verification and possible automatic adaptations to detected changes.

In this paper, we report the results of our analysis of the state of the art concerning the main issues regarding the modeling of CPSs and discuss the value of formal methods in resolving them. The paper reviews three issues that we found highly critical and then describes two case studies—a smart city and a smart factory—designed and verified by formal modeling and validation techniques.

The rest of this paper is structured as follows: Sect. 2 argues about the most important challenges in the modeling of CPSs and the use of formal methods to address them; Sect. 3 reports two case studies designed and verified in a formal manner; finally, Sect. 4 concludes.

2   Key Factors in the Design of CPSs

This section introduces a set of common, critical issues that have been raised in the literature concerning the design of CPSs.

2.1   Space and Time

From a software engineering perspective, cyber-physical systems live within a dynamic spatial environment populated with devices, human agents, changing context and/or localized resources. This can be abstracted into a cyber-physical space (CPSp), a structure indicating a spatial environment comprised of both computational and communication elements, which are interrelated and form some composite topological structure [26]. Such cyber-physical spaces are much more dynamic than traditional—physical—spatial environments used to be. Humans or devices moving around connecting and disconnecting from wireless networks are an example of entities dynamically performing actions while operating in a composite CPSp. Such dynamics have to be considered in the design of systems operating within spatial environments. Moreover, as for any other software-intensive system, maintaining a CPSp which operates in a dynamic environment is faced with the manifold challenges that evolution brings—in software, its composite environment and system—and demands for operational management to observe a constantly changing space and potentially react to environmental changes. Essentially, CPSp is a cyber-physical system operating in physical space and whose requirements and behaviors depend on space. This induces an extended notion of "space", which includes both the physical and the cyber dimension. Consider, for example, a bike-sharing system, which is typically made of internet-connected IoT devices; a bike has a distinct location in the physical space, but it is also located within a computer network, through its connection to a base station. In this particular case of a CPSp, we can define topological relations among entities that depend on the physical space (e.g., a currently available bike is located at an intersection that is "next" to the current location where a certain customer is standing) and also on the cyber space (a bike is logically connected to a customer's account when it is in use, to record its usage time). Topological relations may change over time, and we need to be able to specify requirements for the functionalities supported by the CPSp, which may predicate on topological relations that span both over the physical and the cyber space.

The physical environment in which CPSs operate or where CPSps are realized is perceived not only across space, but also over time. Hence, CPSs exhibit spatio-temporal features and their correct behavior is defined in both space and time. A formal representation of a CPS should predicate upon the flow of events along time, while reflecting spatial characteristics such as the distribution of systems in space [6], including positions or distances of different components. Such spatial characteristics also affect the timing of events within the system and the overall execution workflow, as only particular spatial distributions of objects would lead to the correct and safe execution of the business logic. Moreover, even though the resulting models should be a reflection of the physical reality, they should also suit formal verification. Hence, these models are usually an approximation of the reality resulting by appropriately abstracting the temporal [11] and spatial domains in which the system lives. In other words, the formal models of CPSs, like those of other types of systems, trade precision and exhaustiveness for simplicity and tractability and accept some level of abstraction.

Let us illustrate through an example the importance of capturing both space and time requirements in CPSs. Consider a manufacturing workspace in which humans and robots collaborate without any fences or physical segregation between them. A formal model of such a system needs to capture different temporal requirements of the collaboration (e.g., what the expected response time is, or what is the sequencing of jobs the robot should execute before the operator) and also spatial characteristics of the workspace (e.g., which mobility paths are more frequent for robots, where the exact place for execution of each job is, which areas are more prone to more frequent and dangerous contacts between humans and robots). It is important for robots and humans to perform the right action, at the right time and in the right place. For example, assume that a human and an industrial robotic arm with a screwdriver end-effector are expected to perform a collaborative pick-and-place task (e.g., picking workpieces with different shapes from a bin, then place and screwdrive them on a pallet). The correct way of performing this task is the following: "first the operator picks the workpieces one by one and places them on the pallet, then she removes her hand from the pallet; only then the robot end-effector moves above the pallet and starts to screwdrive the pieces". If the operator violates this instruction and, for example, tries to slightly move the workpiece while the robot is screwdriving it, then the execution may be interrupted—hence prolonged—or, worse, the operator could get hurt.

The interplay between space and time and its relevance to the satisfaction of requirements is exacerbated for novel types of pervasive systems, technologies and paradigms such as the Internet of Things (IoT), which often feature physically distributed entities roaming the physical space [27], exhibiting collective behaviors. Spatially-distributed IoT systems live within a dynamic spatial environment populated with devices, a changing context and/or localized resources. This spatial environment is often only partially known—or even unknown—at design time, which creates the need for suitable reasoning facilities and analyzable models used to observe, evaluate and react to a constantly changing space. Frequently, these activities must be performed during system operation, when analysis techniques working at runtime ensure that possible changes occurring due to the evolving spatial distribution and context—for example due to actions performed by active agents, or by the external environment—do not lead to violations of requirements [25]. This can be achieved through an autonomic, self-adaptive approach such as a MAPE loop [17]: (M)onitoring the spatial environment for changes, (A)nalyzing possible requirement violations, (P)lanning necessary countermeasures (e.g., moving a device from one point in space to another) and then (E)xecuting such actions and updating the shared model of space for the next loop.

2.2 Human-Robot Interaction

A distinguishing feature of many smart space applications is the presence of interactions between humans and robots. We can broadly classify the types of robots involved in these applications in the following categories:

- **Robots with interface devices** are such that the operator usually has no physical contact with the robot and the communication occurs via interface devices. They are used in a variety of domains such as healthcare, manufacturing, disaster management. Examples are medical and surgeon robots, large manufacturing robots and earthquake rescue robots.

- **Service provider or domestic robots** are usually employed as caregivers for elderly people or people with physical disabilities. Interaction with this type of robot occurs via interfaces, but it also features some level of physical contact with human operators (i.e., the care receivers). In the applications where these types of robots are used, the output of the robot is not continuously dependent on human inputs, and once a command is received from the interface device, the robot proceeds with its execution. In these scenarios humans are mostly passive receivers of services.
- **Collaborative robots** should attain a predefined goal by working in collaboration with humans. The specified objective—i.e., a job—is typically divided into atomic parts—i.e., actions— that must be carried out either by humans, or by robots, or by both of them concurrently. In these scenarios robots coordinate their actions with those of the humans—e.g., the operator must place a workpiece in position x before the robot can screwdrive it there.

These are general types of robots and could potentially be applied in very different areas, from disaster response to entertainment.

In general, the presence of humans (either as physical participants, or as command triggers)—who are, by their own nature, unpredictable agents—raises significant modeling issues when one wants to guarantee a certain level of safety and reliability for the application. To capture the unpredictable nature of human actions, stochastic models could be defined to describe the probability with which a certain behavior is taken, thus allowing designers to focus on the most probable ones. Building meaningful stochastic models, however, requires huge and reliable log data concerning human actions—and in particular human interactions with robots—to identify suitable probabilistic distributions (e.g., how probable it is for the operator to make an error and perform an action earlier or later than when it needs to be done). Unfortunately, such data logs are usually not available. To overcome this problem, nondeterministic modeling approaches can be used, which render unpredictability by describing alternative behaviors that are chosen in a nonobservable manner. Formal models could, for example, capture reasonably foreseeable human behaviors, for different types of human operators (experienced user vs novice user, attentive vs absent-minded, etc.). Nondeterministic and stochastic models could also be combined; for example, nondeterminism could be used to describe the choices that an operator can make based on her level of fatigue, but each fatigue level could have a different probability.

2.3   Managing Uncertainty at Runtime Through Self-adaptation

The difficulty of requirement validation for CPSs is exacerbated by the fact that they include both computational and physical aspects, they are susceptible to emergent behaviors, and their operational environment is often only partially known—or even unknown—at design time. Therefore, requirement analysis—preferably through formal verification—is a key activity in the design of CPSs. Requirement analysis consists in evaluating whether the system (as deployed in some environment) satisfies some intended behavior. However, the extent of the assurances obtained through the analysis depends on whether they address concerns that arise at design time or at runtime.

A consequence of relying only on design time verification is that the quality of provided guarantees depends strongly on the quality of the generated model. If the people who brainstormed to build the model have left out even only one possible situation, serious problems could occur during system operation (e.g., issues arising from people forgetting to take back their cards from an ATM). Consider, for example, a smart manufacturing facility where both humans and robots operate. In addition to the sources of uncertainty that are known at design time (e.g., human errors, malfunctioning sensors and actuators), unexpected events could occur during system operation, which had not been foreseen at design time. Examples of such events could be the unplanned entrance of another human operator in the workcell, or the unloading of workpieces to be grabbed by a robot that are geometrically unknown for the robot gripper. Even sources of uncertainty that are foreseeable at design time can be difficult to manage at runtime, as they could generate special sub-cases that have not been analyzed during design. For example, the fact that humans might make errors when interacting with a robot is quite expected, but it is very difficult to consider all such possible errors and their potential critical consequences.

The above example shows that satisfaction of certain requirements cannot always be guaranteed at design time. Instead, evaluation must be deferred at runtime, and subsequently their satisfaction must be ensured by adaptively generating counteractions that can prevent the system from violating requirements [28]. These counteractions, in turn, may threaten the satisfaction of system requirements. Uncertainty and its attributes have been investigated in the past [10,20], and classified [20] by (1) the place where it manifests, (2) its level—the spectrum between perfect knowledge and total lack of any knowledge—and (3) its nature—i.e., whether it originates from imperfect knowledge or from variability. Research on self-adaptive systems has long tackled managing uncertainty at runtime, considering both functional and non-functional requirements [4].

3   Case Studies

In this section we report on two exemplars of critical CPSs where formal methods prove to be highly useful. The first is a disaster scenario within a smart city, highlighting both design time reasoning of a space-intensive CPS as well as its runtime verification. The second is a smart factory, highlighting the validation of domain-specific requirements concerning the human operator's physical safety during the interaction with a robot system. Different formalisms and modeling approaches are adopted to enable reasoning on the two case studies, showing the potential that formal methods can bring to the design and analysis of complex CPSs.

Let us remark that the main concerns in the two case studies are different, hence different formalisms have been used to model them. The first example is more oriented towards the verification of general concepts (safety, reliability, integrity) with stronger focus on spatial aspects and their modeling; the second one verifies domain-specific requirements (physical safety of human while interacting with the robot system) with a stronger focus on temporal aspects. Hence, the modeling notation chosen for the first case was more oriented towards topological concerns (e.g., the capability of describing linking or containment relationships among entities), whilst for the second it was more oriented towards behavioral aspects (e.g., actions of system and human along time).

3.1 Case Study 1: Reasoning on Space-Intensive CPS

In this section, we introduce a case study concerning the emergency response in a smart city as an illustrative scenario of a space-intensive CPS, reasoning upon which is enabled by its consideration as a cyber-physical space (CPSp). We describe the scenario in a succinct manner; the interested reader can refer to [26] for a complete treatment. The scenario presented is a generalized case which can be instantiated for a variety of spatio-temporal reasoning cases. We begin with a brief description of the static structure of the cyber-physical space and then we consider its dynamics—i.e., how the space may change over time. Subsequently, we introduce two characteristic analysis scenarios exposing typical design challenges that are relevant for design and operation. We suggest that satisfaction of critical requirements arising from these scenarios can be either checked at design time, or at runtime.

Autonomous Unmanned Aerial Vehicles (UAVs) can be used as radio relay platforms in environments characterized by poor connectivity. These environments can be regions where no global connectivity exists, e.g., due to a disaster or even absence of line of sight between ground transmitters and receivers. We consider a setting of UAV-carried communication infrastructure [31] in a disaster scenario for smart city applications such as emergency response. The setting we present, including the model and its dynamics, is a generalized case [9] which can be concretized for a variety of urban warfare, search and rescue, homeland security or surveillance scenarios where autonomous UAVs operate in a space-dependent environment and global system properties need to be formally verified.

Emergency Response in a Smart City. Communication is disabled in a city due to a disaster; search and rescue must be performed. Parts of the city may be unsafe, and victims may be stranded in various locations. Autonomous UAVs are dispatched to locate and provide communication infrastructure to victims, leading them to safety. UAVs move in the city environment in specific ways, by flying over buildings. UAVs carry short-range antennas, and victims are able to connect when they are in the vicinity. If a UAV is close to a victim, it can lead her to a safe zone. A safe zone is some part of the city which can lead to a hospital. To utilize our approach, the designer specifies the model, the ways UAVs can move and desired properties of the system, specification steps illustrated in the following.

Modeling Space and Its Dynamics. In general, graphs are a natural way to model the topology of a CPSp, such as the urban scenario at hand. The basic intuition is that entities are represented by nodes, while relations between entities are represented by edges. We distinguish two fundamental kinds of relations between entities to which we refer to as *containment* and *linking*. Containment signifies that an entity is located within another, while linking expresses the fact that two entities are connected in some way. In Fig. 1, the topological structure of a city is presented, where buildings, roads and city blocks form a city. Various such entities may be connected, signifying that one can physically move from e.g., a building to an adjacent one. Such a model may enjoy formal semantics.

Bigraphs [19] are an emerging formalism for structures in ubiquitous computing, dealing with both containment and linking among entities and thus fit our intuition of modelling the topology of a cyber-physical environment. We use the basic notion of a *bigraph* which consists of two superimposed yet orthogonal graphs: a *place graph* is a forest, a set of trees defined over a set of nodes, and a *link graph* is a hypergraph over the same set of nodes, where edges between nodes can cross locality boundaries. Nodes are typed, and the node types are called *controls* in the bigraphical terminology.

We abstain from providing details of the formalism and instead rely on intuition; the interested reader can refer to the vast body of literature on the topic for complete definitions and proofs of the bigraphical theory [19]. Bigraphs can be described in algebraic terms according to Formulae (1a)–(1e). Basically, nodes are written in terms of their controls, i.e., names that define a node's type, such as P, Q, and U. The hierarchical structure of nodes through containment relationships is expressed according to Formula (1a), while the notation in Formula (1b) is used to indicate that two nodes are placed at the same hierarchical level. Bigraphs form rooted hierarchies; in Formula (1c), W and R indicate different roots. Bigraphs can contain *sites*, a special kind of node that denotes a placeholder, indicating the presence of unspecified nodes. A node may contain any number of sites, which are simply indexed in the context of their defining bigraph, as expressed in Formula (1d). Second, connections of an edge with its node are treated as separate elements of a bigraph, referred to as *ports*. Port names appear in the algebraic notation; in Formula (1e), the node of control K has port names in w. These port names are used to identify nodes, which may be omitted if a single instance node of a given type exists in the bigraph, and to express the linking structure: ports with the same name are connected forming a hyper-edge in the link graph. Port names prefixed by '@' are variables ranging over the names of a bigraph.

$$P.Q \qquad \textit{Nesting (P contains Q)} \qquad\qquad (1a)$$

$$P \mid Q \qquad \textit{Juxtaposition of nodes} \qquad\qquad (1b)$$

$$W \parallel R \qquad \textit{Juxtaposition of bigraphs} \qquad\qquad (1c)$$

$$-_i \qquad \textit{Site numbered i} \qquad\qquad (1d)$$

$$K_w \qquad \textit{Node with control K having ports w} \qquad\qquad (1e)$$

In practice, we can obtain a bigraphical model of space for our smart city case study from a domain model [29]; this occurs in two steps. To obtain the basic topological structure of a city, we automatically extract a bigraph from city models described in CityGML [13], a widely used XML-based standard for the exchange of city models, widely used within the architectural informatics discipline. Subsequently, further entities of interest such as UAVs (UAV_i) and disaster victims (Victim) are placed in that model represented by appropriate predicates. A conceptual representation of the topological structure extracted from a CityGML model with 20 buildings is illustrated in Fig. 1. A 2D projection of the roads and buildings is shown in light grey in the background, while the conceptual bigraphical structure is shown in the foreground. The bigraph exposes the following placing structure: A City node serves as root of the extracted bigraph. It contains nodes of type Road, which in turn contain nodes of type RoadSegment and Crossroad, a road segment representing the part of a road between two crossroads. Moreover, a City node contains nodes of type Block, a block representing the area surrounded by road segments. Blocks may contain an arbitrary number of Building nodes, each one representing a building. Auxiliary nodes (e.g., for City and Road) are not shown in Fig. 1 for the sake of readability. Other entities are present in the city as well, such as hospitals, airports, etc.

As for the linking structure of the extracted bigraph, it records an *accessibility* relation between city elements for the problem at hand—how UAVs may traverse the city. Each building is connected to the building next to it (represented by blue links in Fig. 1), and to a block's surrounding road segment if it is located in the respective block boundary (represented by green links). Moreover, road segments are linked to the crossroads being connected by that road segment (represented by red links). Links represent the fact that it is possible for a UAV to go from, e.g., a building to a road segment connected to it. An equivalent, partial algebraic representation of the city space is found in Formula (2); the formula shows how two buildings, Bld_2 and Bld_4 (found within the same block Blk_1), are connected through a link identified by port name 4.

Notice how the link signifies that two nodes of control C found in different parts of the model are connected, through the use of the same port name. A Hospital (not shown in Fig. 1) is also included in the city block. Other entities in various parts of the model are abstracted away in the formula representation using the formalism's sites facility. Hence, Formula (2) specifies the model of Fig. 1 only partially, as sites signify that unspecified entities are present in some parts of the containment hierarchy—for instance, Blk_1 (lower left) contains other buildings besides Blk_2 and Blk_4 (Fig. 1).

$$City.(Blk_1.(Bld_2.(UAV_3.(-_{11}) \mid Bg2Bg.(C_4 \mid -_1) \mid -_5)$$
$$\mid Hospital \mid Bld_4.(Bg2Bg.(C_4 \mid -_4) \mid -_3) \mid -_2) \mid -_9 \mid -_{10}). \qquad (2)$$

Space is rarely static, thus a formalism for modeling evolving space-intensive systems should also capture system *dynamics* to enable reasoning about the effects of changes in space. Bigraphical Reactive Systems (BRS) [19] extend bigraphs with well-defined semantics of dynamic behavior expressed as a set

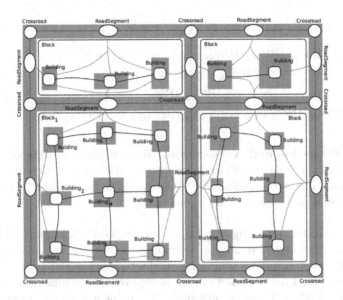

Fig. 1. Static bigraphical structure extracted from a CityGML model. The same structure is (partially) represented in algebraic form in Formula 2. (Color figure online)

of rules. BRS essentially allow describing possible ways in which the structure of the space can evolve through the application of transformation rules which selectively rewrite parts of a bigraph; they are called *reaction* rules. Reaction rules have the general form of R → R′, where R is called the *redex* and R′ is called the *reactum*; both the redex and reactum are bigraphs. If an occurrence of a redex can be found in a host bigraph, it may be replaced by the reactum, in a fashion similar to graph rewriting [8]. Redex and reactum can be considered as *patterns*, which are parametric; they describe some structure that can be transformed into another, which may not be concretely specified.

To this end, we can model the changes inherent in the disaster scenario using a BRS specification. For reasons of simplicity, we consider one such type of dynamics specification; how UAVs may move from a building to another. In Formula (3), a parametric reaction rule captures how a UAV moves from a building ($Bld_{@a}$) to another connected one (i.e., through a connection $C_{@b}$ which has the same port name). Essentially, the CPSp model is transformed, to record that the UAV is now found inside the $Bld_{@b}$. Note how the reaction is parametric; presence of other UAVs, buildings or other entities is not described, but merely that the UAV moves inside the specified structure. The parametric reaction can occur for instance, if a UAV is located in Bld_2, to move e.g., to Bld_4. Similarly to this reaction rule, we may additionally consider, e.g., that victims located by

UAVs move with them until a safe zone is reached.

$$\text{Blk}_{@w}.(\text{Bld}_{@a}.(\text{UAV}_{@UAVid}.(-_{11}) \mid \text{Bg2Bg}.(\text{C}_{@b} \mid -_1) \mid -_5)$$
$$\mid \text{Bld}_{@b}.(\text{Bg2Bg}.(\text{C}_{@a} \mid -_4) \mid -_3) \mid -_2) \mid -_9 \rightarrow$$
$$\text{Blk}_{@w}.(\text{Bld}_{@a}.(\text{Bg2Bg}.(\text{C}_{@b} \mid -_1) \mid -_5)$$
$$\mid \text{Bld}_{@b}.(\text{UAV}_{@UAVid}.(-_{11}) \mid \text{Bg2Bg}.(\text{C}_{@a} \mid -_4) \mid -_3) \mid -_2) \mid -_9. \qquad (3)$$

Analysis Scenarios and Verification. We consider two different analysis scenarios; the first aims at early requirements validation, as typically performed at design time. The second highlights validation at runtime, where the underlying system model is only known while in operation.

Scenario A: Verification of System Requirements. While bigraphs and bigraphical reaction rules are adequate for describing the topology of a CPSp and its inherent dynamics, a quality evaluation model to support systematic reasoning on the behaviour of the changing system is required. We assume that a CPSp is specified by a BRS as discussed previously. To enable automated reasoning, this specification can be transformed into an equivalent transition system generally known as a *(doubly) Labelled Transition System* (dLTS) [7]. States of this transition system describe bigraphical configurations of the CPSp, while transitions describe how the configuration of the system can change by moving from one state to its successors. Interpreting a BRS specification as a dLTS entails describing its possible evolution based on the application of reaction rules. Labelled transition systems are amenable to formal verification via explicit-state model checking. Model checking performs an exhaustive analysis of the state space to check the validity of a property. We abstain from describing the mechanisms behind this, and instead illustrate a characteristic case; the interested reader can refer to [26] for a complete treatment.

We consider the setting where victims and UAVs are positioned in various parts of the city; the initial state of the system is thus known. Victim and UAV are predicates describing entities, and their position within a bigraphical structure signifies their location in the city. Recall that there is a hospital in the city, and that victims are considered safe if they are in the hospital. UAVs roam inside the city, and if they locate a victim, they lead them to safety. Normally, UAVs follow some path planning strategy; from all possible movements of a UAV at any point, a strategy selects the optimal one, based on the strategy and local environmental conditions. Moreover, interesting problems arise with target search and surveillance scenarios, which can lead to complex controller algorithms; we are not concerned with the design of a controller here, but with verifying properties of the system which concern *any* decisions that the system of UAVs may take while operating within a city environment. Behaviors that may violate a global property of the system must be investigated, so every possible system behavior must be verified, possibly with an overall goal of using violating sequences to learn (or debug) a controller strategy. We consider a generic global requirement of the system, which states that if victims exist in the city, eventually all victims are found inside the hospital (i.e., no victims are located in other buildings). An LTL property (with the usual semantics) encoding the requirement is found in Formula (4), utilizing a parametric bigraphical pattern to express that no victim is eventually found in a building. Such a property can be used to validate the domain modeling, by verifying that the model and dynamics specified indeed lead to a valid system. Note how the formula utilizes a site in the same hierarchical level (within the building), thus allowing other entities to be inside the building, and a symbolic port name (?) denoting *any* building name.

$$\Box(\mathsf{Victim} \rightarrow \Diamond\neg\mathsf{Bld}_?.(\mathsf{Victim} \mid -_0)). \tag{4}$$

Scenario B: Spatial Verification at Runtime. In this scenario, we assume that UAVs are deployed in a spatial environment that is unknown at design time. The spatial model is instead built and updated at runtime, for example through a monitoring infrastructure in place [27]. Furthermore, we consider the following property, specifying that "all disaster victims are located in places in the city so that they can reach the hospital through road segments or crossroads". This is an example of a property of interest that would be not convenient to be expressed in LTL, since it does not predicate about the temporal evolution, but about certain relations in space—its topology. Hereafter, we illustrate the use of a spatial logic by which we can capture and verify the property at hand. We abstain from describing precisely the corresponding semantics and verification procedures, and instead illustrate an exemplar case; the interested reader can refer to [26] for a complete treatment.

The spatial reasoning approach we advocate uses the Spatial Logic for Closure Spaces (SLCS [6]), based on an extension of semantics of modal logics to closure spaces, a closure space being a generalization of a standard *topological* space [12]. A logical property will be evaluated accordingly on updated models of the CPSp obtained at runtime, assuming no knowledge about the structure of the model at design time, beyond the actual property specification. A spatial formula, in our case, consists of propositions representing bigraphical patterns along with SLCS operators. The logic features Boolean operators, a "one step" modality turning closure into a logical operator, and a "surrounds" operator. Informally, *closure* in space is similar to *next* in temporal logics, while *surrounds* is similar to *until*. The syntax of SLCS is defined by the following grammar:

$$\phi ::= \mathsf{p} \mid \top \mid \neg\phi \mid \phi \wedge \phi \mid \mathsf{C}\,\phi \mid \phi\,\mathsf{S}\,\phi \tag{5}$$

where p is drawn from a set of bigraph patterns, C is the *closure* operator, and S is the spatial *surrounds* operator. When used for the sake of spatial model checking, SLCS formulae are evaluated on bigraphical closure models [26]. While the elementary syntax presented above features the two fundamental spatial operators *closure* and *surrounds*, a set of more complex operators may be derived from them. In [5], for instance, complex operators reflecting the notions of nearness and reachability have been derived. In particular, the so-called "reach through" operator is defined as $\phi \; \Re(\psi) \; \zeta$. Informally, it is satisfied for a point x, if x satisfies ϕ and there is a sequence of points starting from x, all satisfying ψ, reaching a target point satisfying ζ.

Formula (6) below formally encodes a property which needs to be verified on a model monitored at runtime. Note that there is no information encoded on *how* a victim should reach the hospital, and the specification is able to capture every possible instance of a reachability realization through crossroads and road segments that may appear on a model.

$$\text{Victim} \; \Re(\text{RoadSegment}_? \vee \text{Crossroad}_?) \; \text{Hospital}.(-_1)). \tag{6}$$

To support runtime verification of the CPSp in our operational scenario, properties like the one presented in Formula (6) can be evaluated whenever the monitoring indicates a change in the CPSp, reflected in the bigraphical closure model. In the simplest case, an alarm may be generated if a critical property is violated. More advanced systems could be self-adaptive, counteracting property violations by triggering measures that ensure that requirements are satisfied. While the specification of such systems is beyond the scope of this paper, related research has proposed a number of such strategies (see e.g., [28] for security strategies). Although self-adaptation has been largely studied for temporal properties, we believe that the fundamentals may be adopted for the spatial domain as well.

3.2   Case Study 2: Reasoning on Temporal Modeling of CPS

In this scenario, we have analyzed a mobile robot unit which autonomously relocates in the layout shown in Fig. 2. This robot system is configured as a combination of a driverless truck (i.e., AGV) and a manipulator, which mainly moves between three assembly stations—①, ② and ③—and a sensor-based inspection station ④, as shown in Fig. 2(a). The robot unit can be manually relocated by operators around its predefined positions. The robot unit can travel and access the whole workspace (the blue area in Fig. 2(b)), including a load/unload area for raw materials and finished parts. Two human operators (OP_1 and OP_2) are employed in the application. OP_1 is mostly present in stations ① and ②, while OP_2 works mainly in ③ or executes auxiliary manual tasks on the workbench in ④. Both operators can freely hold and resume their tasks, swap posts, or join one another in some area. The main robot-assisted intended tasks are: pallet assembly at stations ① and ②, including bin-picking from a local storage carried by the mobile unit; pallet disassembly (reversal of assembly) at ① and ②, including bin-dumping; pallet inspection at station ③; lead-through programming of assembly, disassembly, and inspection tasks (trajectories, parameters, etc.) at stations ①, ② and ③; material handling on load/unload areas. Other manual tasks by OP_1 and OP_2 include manual loading of parts/boxes; (additional) visual inspection of pallet at stations ①, ② and ③; manual assembly/disassembly of pallet at stations ① and ②; manual measurements of parts at station ④;

cleaning pallets at stations ① and ②; kitting of tools and parts at stations ①, ② and ③; general supervision at stations ①, ② and ③. The generated formal model of the described system replicates *all* combinations of robot/manual task assignments (e.g., robot holds and OP_1 screw-drives jigs and vice versa, switching tasks on the fly, quitting a manual task and assigning the robot to proceed autonomously). Frequently, robot base and operators move side-to-side across the central aisle, or other operators transit along the aisle because the target area is part of a larger plant and access to it is not restricted (Fig. 2(b)).

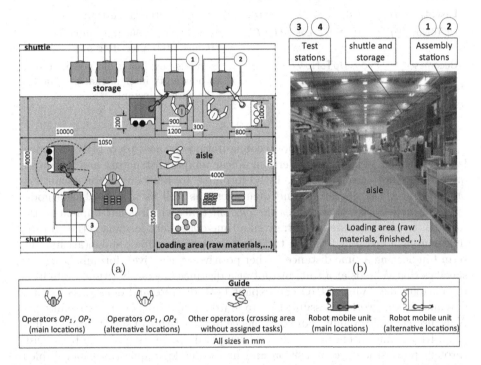

Fig. 2. Sketch of a cyber-physical space of a smart factory: (a) precise workcell depiction, (b) actual layout. (Color figure online)

Modeling Time and Its Dynamics. The model includes a descretized replica of human ({head, chest, leg, arm, fingers}) and robot $\{R_1, R_2, R_{ee}, R_{base}\}$. This example, unlike the previous one, focuses more strongly on time. This preference is driven by the overall goal of the project, which was centered on human physical safety analysis. As described in Sect. 2.2, different timings of human and robots actions could lead to different situations which could be harmful to humans. Harmful situations could also be of different intensities and need to be evaluated differently. For example if human and robot have a contact in ①, the harmfulness of the contact could differ if the robot is already there and then human enters ① and hits the robot or viceversa.

Table 1. List of derived TRIO operators; ϕ, ψ denote propositions, and v is a variable and d is a constant value.

TRIO Operator	Definition	Meaning
Past (ϕ, d)	$d > 0 \wedge \text{Dist}(\phi, -d)$	ϕ occurred d time units in the past
Alw (ϕ)	$\forall t(\text{Dist}(\phi, t))$	ϕ always holds
SomP (ϕ)	$\exists t(t > 0 \wedge \text{Dist}(\phi, t))$	ϕ occurs sometimes in the past
Lasted (ϕ, d)	$\forall t(0 < t < d \rightarrow \text{Dist}(\phi, -t))$	ϕ held for the last d time units
Lasts (ϕ, d)	$\forall t(0 < t < d \rightarrow \text{Dist}(\phi, t))$	ϕ held for the next d time units
Lasted$_{ie}$ (ϕ, d)	$\forall t(0 < t \leq d \rightarrow \text{Dist}(\phi, -t))$	ϕ held for the last d time units
UpToNow (ϕ)	$\exists t(t > 0 \wedge \text{Lasted}(\phi, t))$	ϕ holds in a nonempty interval immediately preceding now
Becomesϕ	$\phi \wedge \text{UpToNow}(\neg\phi)$	ϕ holds now but it did not hold for a nonempty interval that preceded the current instant

In order to model these temporal configurations we have used TRIO, a logical language which assumes an underlying linear temporal structure and features a quantitative notion of time [11]. TRIO formulae are built out of the usual first-order connectives, operators, and quantifiers, as well as a single basic modal operator, called Dist, that relates the *current time*, which is left implicit in the formula, to another time instant: given a time-dependent formula ϕ (i.e., a term representing a mapping from the time domain to truth values) and a (arithmetic) term t indicating a time distance (either positive or negative), formula $\text{Dist}(\phi, t)$ specifies that ϕ holds at a time instant at a distance of exactly t time units from the current one. While TRIO can exploit both discrete and dense sets as time domains, in this work we assume the standard model of the nonnegative integers N as discrete time domain. For convenience in the writing of specification formulae, TRIO defines a number of *derived* temporal operators from the basic Dist, through propositional composition and first-order logic quantification. Table 1 defines some of the most significant ones.

Yet, modeling the space is very important because of the placement of sensors and end effectors of the robot. The workspace is discretized in 23 regions with different characteristics and not all areas have static properties. An element (human or robot part) occupies one region at each time instant (e.g., if $p_{head} = L_k$ holds, it means that the human head is currently in L_k). The robot is constantly moving around and the areas mostly situated on the aisle could have different characteristics from time to time. In order to resemble the human reasoning about spatial properties and construct a 3D model of the workspace, each region is modeled in three layers: lower, middle and upper sections. The mobile base of the robot is always allowed in the lower layer, while the manipulator arm could move in the middle and upper layers.

To define different aspects of a system, we introduce several definitions in addition to basic TRIO operators. For example, predicate Sep_{ij} captures the distance between O_i and R_j with tree possible values: close (being in the same region), mid (being in adjacent regions), and far (any other case). Another example is predicate ArrivedBefore$_{ijk}$, which captures the contact in which the robot hits the operator, and which holds when human part $O_i \in$ {head, chest, leg, arm, fingers} hits robot part $R_j \in \{R_1, R_2, R_{ee}, R_{base}\}$ in layout section $L_k \in \{1, ..., 23\}$ because it arrived at k earlier than j. This formula is only an example of the interplay between time and space, as explained in Sect. 2.1. Examples of other formulae are presented in Table 2[1]. The relative values of force and velocity, that are very important when evaluating the danger of a contact, are captured by the model via two variables whose variations are discretized with four possible values none, low, mid, high. Temporal modeling allows for creating a meaningful and smooth fluctuation between these values. For example, the value of velocity cannot jump from none to high. These variations are modeled in Formulae 11 of Table 2. The same formulae hold also for the force.

Another important role that time plays in modeling is to reproduce the executing actions of human and robot that together create the full executing task (i.e., the job). As described in Sect. 2.3, a more thorough analysis would be provided by defining a rough sense of sequencing between different actions of a task, but not enforcing a static workflow. This is what we do by describing each action with a pair of pre- and post-conditions, which are combinations of temporal and spatial requirements, such as for example required positions of objects, or actions that should have been terminated beforehand. They enforce a realistic execution to the actions (e.g., the human operator cannot pick a workpiece if he or she is not in front of the bin, thus the pre-condition of the bin-picking action is the correct position for the operator), but generate and explore dynamically all the meaningful and possible workflows (e.g., what happens if that operator, instead of continuing the bin-picking, stops and switches to an inspection action). An action can be in one of several states: ns, when the action's preconditions are not yet satisfied; wt, when pre-conditions are satisfied and the human operator should start the execution; exe, when normative execution is ongoing; sfex, when execution is ongoing while some hazard is detected; hd, when, due to a risky hazard, the execution is on hold; exit, when the execution is aborted due to a high risk; dn, when the action is correctly performed and completed and its post-conditions are satisfied.

The model also contains definitions of physical hazards according to [15] and corresponding risk values [16] for detecting harmful contacts. For the sake of brevity, in this paper we do not provide details on the modeling of hazards and risks. It suffices to say that each hazard, based on the severity of the harm it could cause and its occurrence frequency, is assigned a risk value among $\{0, 1, 2\}$. If the value of risk is 0, everything is good, while a risk value equal to 1 is negligible. Otherwise, if there is a risk with value equal to 2, the human operator is in danger. Hence, the latter situation needs to be avoided.

---

[1] The full formal model is available on github/safer-hrc.

Table 2. Selected formulae of the second case study.

The parts of discretized operator, robot and layout are shown by O_i, R_j, L_k.

1. $\forall O_i \in \{$ head, chest, leg, arm, fingers $\}$
2. $\forall R_j \in \{R_1, R_2, R_{ee}, R_{base}\}$
3. $\forall O_i . \exists! L_k (p_i = L_k)$
4. $\forall R_j . \exists! L_k (p_j = L_k)$
5. $\text{Sep}_{ij} \in \{\text{close}, \text{mid}, \text{far}\}$
    a. $\text{Sep}_{ij} = \text{close} \leftrightarrow \exists L_k (p_i = p_j = L_k)$
    b. $\text{Sep}_{ij} = \text{mid} \leftrightarrow \text{Adj}(p_i, p_j)$
    c. $\text{Sep}_{ij} = \text{far} \leftrightarrow \text{Sep}_{ij} \neq (\text{mid}|\text{close})$
6. $\text{InSameL}_{ijk} \Leftrightarrow \text{Sep}_{ij} = \text{close}$
7. $\text{ArrivedBefore}_{ijk} \Leftrightarrow \text{InSameL}_{ijk} \wedge \text{Past}(p_i = L_k, 1) \wedge \text{Past}(p_j \neq L_k, 1)$
8. $\text{Reach}_{ijk} \Leftrightarrow \text{InSameL}_{ijk} \wedge \text{Past}(\text{Sep}_{ij} > close, 1)$
9. $\text{Leave}_{ijk} \Leftrightarrow \text{Past}(\text{InSameL}_{ijk}, 1) \wedge p_i \neq L_k \wedge p_j \neq L_k$
10. $\text{Contact}_{ijk} \Leftrightarrow \text{InSameL}_{ijk} \wedge \text{moving}_{R_j}$
11. $\forall R_j :$
    a. $v_i = \text{none} \Leftrightarrow \text{Lasted}_{ie}(p_j = L_k, 2)$
    b. $v_j = \text{low} \Leftrightarrow \text{Lasted}_{ie}(p_j = L_k, 1) \wedge past(p_j, 2) \neq L_k$
    c. $v_j = \text{mid} \Leftrightarrow past(p_j, 1) \neq p_j$
    d. $v_j = \text{high} \Leftrightarrow past(p_j, 2) \neq past(p_j, 1) \neq p_j$
    e. $past(p_j, 1) = p_j \vee \text{Adj}(past(p_j, 1), p_j)$
12. $\text{Sep}_{fingers, arm} \in \{\text{close}, \text{mid}\}$
Action 1. Robot moves to bin from an initial point (no other action has started, yet).
    Pre-condition 1 $\Leftrightarrow p_{base} = \text{initial\_point} \wedge \forall x_{\neq 1} : a_x^{sts} = \text{ns}$
    Post-condition 1 $\Leftrightarrow p_{base} = p_{bin}$
Action 2. Robot arm is stretching out towards bin right after action 1 is done.
    Pre-condition 2 $\Leftrightarrow a_1^{sts} = \text{dn} \wedge \neg\text{moving}_{base} \wedge \neg\text{moving}_{ee}$
    Post-condition 2 $\Leftrightarrow \neg\text{moving}_{base} \wedge p_{ee} = \text{bin}$

Analysis Scenarios and Verification

Scenario A: Detecting Hazards. The main requirement of this case study was to verify the physical safety of the human operator while working with the robot system. The physical safety itself needs to be interpreted in a general and standard way, and that is why the well-known industrial standards such as [14–16] are used in modeling the system. The formal verification procedure is supposed to detect and highlight any possible situation in which the movements of human and robot would violate the constraints imposed by the standards, which means detecting cases in which the risk value is 2. The formula below states the above property, and expresses that, for each hazardous situation involving human part i and robot part j in layout k, the risk should be below 2.

$$\forall O_i . \forall R_j . \forall L_k : \text{Alw}(\text{risk}_{ijk} \leq 1) \tag{7}$$

The verification was carried out through the Zot [32] formal verification tool, which reports the state of the system at each instant of time (e.g., positioning of the human and robot, state of task execution, level of criticality of human and robot interaction).

Scenario B: Detecting Human Errors at Runtime. The physical safety of humans is a critical issue that needs to be considered in the early stages of design. Anticipating hazardous situations and identifying proper remedies are tasks usually tackled at design time. However, not every situation is predictable in advance. For example, as discussed in Sect. 2.3, the presence of human operators introduces in the picture an unavoidable level of uncertainty, as their behavior during execution can never be fully predicted. To make the model more accurate, we have introduced a model of erroneous behavior that includes the formalization of the most frequent human errors that can influence the workflow, from the point of view of both time and space. The model is applicable also for runtime verification.

We categorize human errors in three main types: (i) space-related errors—the operator is in the wrong location, or places instruments in the wrong locations; (ii) goal-related errors—the operator does not follow instructions correctly and the action is performed poorly, which happens more frequently when the operator is not trained or skillful; and (iii) time-related errors—the operator does not follow the correct temporal ordering of actions. The latter group of errors could be represented by five error phenotypes: repetition, omission, early/late execution, and intrusion.

Let us here consider repetition errors. For example, assume that we want to model a task in which the operator and robot should pin a number of workpieces on a pallet by screwdriving them with some fixtures. Hence, the operator should prepare fixtures, then the robot should start moving towards the pallet. If the operator places the fixtures, but continues to play with them while the robot is moving, a collision between the operator's hand and the robot end-effector is very probable.

To formalize this kind of situations, for each action a_x we have defined two corresponding attributes, $\mathsf{opStarts}_x$ and $\mathsf{opStops}_x$, which correspond to human mental decisions about starting or stopping the execution of the action depending on what the operator may see, touch or feel.

$$\mathsf{Repetition}_x \Leftrightarrow (\mathsf{UpToNow}\,(posC_x) \wedge \mathsf{opStarts}_x) \vee (\mathsf{Becomes}\,(posC_x) \wedge \neg\mathsf{opStops}_x)$$

The formula above, which is a simplified version of the one appearing in [1], states that an action a_x is repeated when: it has already been done and its post-conditions are already satisfied, but the operator wants to start it over; or its post-conditions are just satisfied, but the operator does not realize this and continues to execute it. The formal definitions of other phenotypes and error types have been discussed in [1].

4 Conclusions

In this paper, we discussed why formal modeling and verification are needed in designing and operating CPSs, to offer assurances about their dependable use in many practical application areas in which they are increasingly deployed. We also discussed why and how modeling and verification methods need to accommodate the specific new requirements arising from interaction of computing elements with the physical environment, which is typical of CPSs. In particular, we focused on CPSs where the notion of *space* in which the system operates and *time* constraining operations are key. We also stressed how uncertainty, at different levels, heavily affects CPSs and asks for new approaches to formal methods that break the traditional boundary between design time and runtime. We also presented how in our past work we provided solutions to these problems, and case studies we developed in which we such solutions were applied.

The work we presented here, however, can only be viewed as a solution to some of the problems we need to face when formal methods are applied in the design and operation of CPSs. A community effort is needed to consolidate methods and provide both support tools and libraries including application-independent components and open to extensions to ad-hoc components specialized towards single application fields.

Dedication. It is an honor for us to dedicate this "gift" to Stefania. Stefania very much deserves recognition for her lasting, high-level research in computer science, covering and integrating theoretical and applicative fields. Mostly, her work in the organization of many events typical of the FM community has been intense, continuous and always worldwide appreciated. The oldest ones of us had the fortune to cooperate with her in many occasions since our common early steps in the academia. Among the many occasions of pleasant and productive cooperation we like to remember the superb organization of the 2003 FM symposium and the ever increasing success of the FORMALISE conference.

References

1. Askarpour, M., Mandrioli, D., Rossi, M., Vicentini, F.: Formal model of human erroneous behavior for safety analysis in collaborative robotics. Robot. Comput.-Integr. Manuf. **57**, 465–476 (2019)
2. Baheti, R., Gill, H.: Cyber-physical systems. Impact Control Technol. **12**(1), 161–166 (2011)
3. Bures, T., et al.: Software engineering for smart cyber-physical systems: challenges and promising solutions. ACM SIGSOFT Softw. Eng. Notes **42**(2), 19–24 (2017)
4. Cheng, B.H.C., et al.: Software engineering for self-adaptive systems: a research roadmap. In: Cheng, B.H.C., de Lemos, R., Giese, H., Inverardi, P., Magee, J. (eds.) Software Engineering for Self-Adaptive Systems. LNCS, vol. 5525, pp. 1–26. Springer, Heidelberg (2009). https://doi.org/10.1007/978-3-642-02161-9_1

5. Ciancia, V., Grilletti, G., Latella, D., Loreti, M., Massink, M.: An experimental spatio-temporal model checker. In: Bianculli, D., Calinescu, R., Rumpe, B. (eds.) SEFM 2015. LNCS, vol. 9509, pp. 297–311. Springer, Heidelberg (2015). https:// doi.org/10.1007/978-3-662-49224-6_24

6. Ciancia, V., Latella, D., Loreti, M., Massink, M.: Specifying and verifying properties of space. In: Diaz, J., Lanese, I., Sangiorgi, D. (eds.) TCS 2014. LNCS, vol. 8705, pp. 222–235. Springer, Heidelberg (2014). https://doi.org/10.1007/978-3-662-44602-7_18

7. Clarke, E.M., Grumberg, O., Peled, D.A.: Model Checking. MIT Press, Cambridge (1999)

8. Corradini, A., Montanari, U., Rossi, F., Ehrig, H., Heckel, R., Löwe, M.: Algebraic approaches to graph transformation-part I: basic concepts and double pushout approach. In: Rozenberg, G. (ed.) Handbook of Graph Grammars, pp. 163–246. University of Pisa, Pisa (1997)

9. Eaton, C.M., Chong, E.K., Maciejewski, A.A.: Multiple-scenario unmanned aerial system control: a systems engineering approach and review of existing control methods. Aerospace 3(1), 1 (2016)

10. Esfahani, N., Malek, S.: Uncertainty in self-adaptive software systems. In: de Lemos, R., Giese, H., Müller, H.A., Shaw, M. (eds.) Software Engineering for Self-Adaptive Systems II. LNCS, vol. 7475, pp. 214–238. Springer, Heidelberg (2013). https://doi.org/10.1007/978-3-642-35813-5_9

11. Furia, C.A., Mandrioli, D., Morzenti, A., Rossi, M.: Modeling Time in Computing. Monographs in Theoretical Computer Science. An EATCS Series, Springer (2012)

12. Galton, A.: A generalized topological view of motion in discrete space. Theoret. Comput. Sci. 305(1), 111–134 (2003)

13. Gröger, G., Kolbe, T.H., Czerwinski, A., Nagel, C., et al.: OpenGIS city geography markup language (CityGML) encoding standard, version 1.0. 0 (2008)

14. ISO 10218–1: Robots and robotic devices – Safety requirements for industrial robots - Part 1: Robots. International Organization for Standardization, Geneva, Switzerland (2011)

15. ISO 10218–2: Robots and robotic devices – Safety requirements for industrial robots - Part 2: Robot systems and integration. International Organization for Standardization, Geneva, Switzerland (2011)

16. ISO 12100: Safety of machinery – General principles for design – Risk assessment and risk reduction. International Organization for Standardization, Geneva, Switzerland (2010)

17. Kephart, J.O., Chess, D.M.: The vision of autonomic computing. Computer 36(1), 41–50 (2003)

18. Lee, E.A.: Cyber physical systems: design challenges. In: 2008 11th IEEE International Symposium on Object and Component-Oriented Real-Time Distributed Computing (ISORC), pp. 363–369, May 2008

19. Milner, R.: The Space and Motion of Communicating Agents. Cambridge University Press, New York (2009)

20. Perez-Palacin, D., Mirandola, R.: Uncertainties in the modeling of self-adaptive systems: a taxonomy and an example of availability evaluation. In: Proceedings of the 5th ACM/SPEC International Conference on Performance Engineering, ICPE 2014, pp. 3–14. ACM, New York, NY, USA (2014)

21. Rajhans, A., Cheng, S.W., Schmerl, B., Garlan, D., Krogh, B.H., Agbi, C., Bhave, A.: An architectural approach to the design and analysis of cyber-physical systems. Electronic Communications of the EASST 21, (2009)

22. Rajkumar, R.R., Lee, I., Sha, L., Stankovic, J.: Cyber-physical systems: the next computing revolution. In: Proceedings of the 47th Design Automation Conference, pp. 731–736. ACM (2010)
23. Tan, J.T.C., Duan, F., Zhang, Y., Watanabe, K., Kato, R., Arai, T.: Human-robot collaboration in cellular manufacturing: design and development. In: 2009 IEEE/RSJ International Conference on Intelligent Robots and Systems, pp. 29–34 (2009)
24. Tsigkanos, C., Kehrer, T., Ghezzi, C., Pasquale, L., Nuseibeh, B.: Adding static and dynamic semantics to building information models. In: Proceedings of the 2nd International Workshop on Software Engineering for Smart Cyber-Physical Systems, pp. 1–7. ACM (2016)
25. Tsigkanos, C., Kehrer, T., Ghezzi, C.: Architecting dynamic cyber-physical spaces. Computing **98**(10), 1011–1040 (2016)
26. Tsigkanos, C., Kehrer, T., Ghezzi, C.: Modeling and verification of evolving cyber-physical spaces. In: Proceedings of the 2017 11th Joint Meeting on Foundations of Software Engineering, ESEC/FSE 2017, pp. 38–48 (2017)
27. Tsigkanos, C., Nenzi, L., Loreti, M., Garriga, M., Dustdar, S., Ghezzi, C.: Inferring analyzable models from trajectories of spatially-distributed internet of things. In: Proceedings of the 14th International Symposium on Software Engineering for Adaptive and Self-Managing Systems, SEAMS@ICSE 2019, Montreal, QC, Canada, 25–31 May 2019, pp. 100–106 (2019)
28. Tsigkanos, C., Pasquale, L., Ghezzi, C., Nuseibeh, B.: On the interplay between cyber and physical spaces for adaptive security. IEEE Trans. Dependable Sec. Comput. **15**(3), 466–480 (2018)
29. Visconti, E., Tsigkanos, C., Hu, Z., Ghezzi, C.: Model-driven design of city spaces via bidirectional transformations (2019)
30. Wang, S., Wan, J., Li, D., Zhang, C.: Implementing smart factory of Industrie 4.0: an outlook. Int. J. Distrib. Sens. Netw. **12**(1), 3159805:1–3159805:10 (2016)
31. Xie, J., Al-Emrani, F., Gu, Y., Wan, Y., Fu, S.: UAV-carried long distance WI-FI communication infrastructure. In: AIAA Infotech@ Aerospace (2016)
32. ZOT: a bounded satisfiability checker (2012). github/fm-polimi/zot

Automata-Based Behavioural Contracts
with Action Correlation

Davide Basile[1]([✉]), Rosario Pugliese[1], Francesco Tiezzi[2], Pierpaolo Degano[3],
and Gian-Luigi Ferrari[3]

[1] Department of Statistics, Computer Science and Applications,
University of Florence, Florence, Italy
davide.basile@unifi.it
[2] School of Science and Technology, University of Camerino, Camerino, Italy
[3] Department of Computer Science, University of Pisa, Pisa, Italy

Abstract. The rigorous design of Service-Oriented Computing (SOC) applications has been identified as one of the primary research challenges for the next 10 years. Many foundational theories for SOC have been defined, but they often rely on mechanisms different from real-world SOC technologies, hindering actual service modelling and verification. In this paper, we propose a novel automata-based formalism of service contracts equipped with a mechanism, inspired by current web service technologies, exploiting correlation data to drive service interactions and with formal foundations enabling reasoning about service correctness.

1 Introduction

The increasing need of integrating functionalities of heterogeneous applications across multiple organisations has led to the emergence of an architectural approach for distributed systems supporting the Service-Oriented Computing paradigm (SOC) [12]. Systems are conceived as networks of loosely-coupled, interoperable and reusable components, called *services*, accessible by end-users and other system components. Services operate with little or no knowledge about their clients, and can be assembled in enterprise applications enacting complex business processes. They are created and published by possibly mutually distrusted organisations that may have conflicting goals. Services *cooperate* to achieve overall goals and at the same time they *compete* to perform specific tasks of their organisation. Ensuring reliability of a composite service is important, e.g. to avoid economic loss. Therefore, understanding and fulfilling a minimal number of behavioural obligations of services is crucial to determine whether the interactive behaviour is consistent with the requirements.

The most prominent instantiation of the SOC paradigm is given by so-called *Web services*, which provide operations that can be published, located and invoked in the Web via XML messages complying with standard formats. The interaction logic for composing Web services can be described by using the OASIS standard for orchestration of web services WS-BPEL [25].

In SOC, a service can engage in *conversations* with its partners in order to exchange the information necessary to fulfil all activities required by the service.

© Springer Nature Switzerland AG 2019
M. H. ter Beek et al. (Eds.): Gnesi Festschrift, LNCS 11865, pp. 131–151, 2019.
https://doi.org/10.1007/978-3-030-30985-5_9

For example, a hotel booking service typically interacts several times with a hotel service before finalising a room reservation. The loosely-coupled nature of SOC implies that, from a technological point of view, the connection between interacting partners cannot be assumed to persist for the whole duration of a conversation. Therefore, to enable the association, i.e., *correlation*, of a message with the right conversation, the message must include some value providing a form of context (e.g., a hotel identifier). The link among partners is hence determined by these correlation values, which are used to deliver each message to the appropriate interacting partner. Such message correlation mechanism is in fact at the basis of messaging in the WS-BPEL standard.

Whilst SOC is nowadays a well-established technology, the rigorous design of SOC applications is still identified as one of the primary research challenges for the next 10 years. The recent Service Computing Manifesto [12] points out that "Service systems have so far been built without an adequate rigorous foundation that would enable reasoning about them" and, moreover, that "The design of service systems should build upon a formal model of services". As a matter of fact, currently used software engineering technologies for SOC lack rigorous formal foundations.

In the last decade, behavioural contracts [4,11] have been proposed to formalise the externally observable behaviour of services in terms of *offers* of the service and *requests* by the service to be matched. *Agreement* of (a composition of) contracts relies on the fulfilment of all service requests through corresponding service offers. A precise semantics of service contracts permits to mechanically verify that a composition of contracts admits an agreement.

Process algebras, Petri Nets and Event Structures are some of the formalisms that have been adopted to specify behavioural contracts, their composition, and their agreement property (also known as compliance or conformance). *Modal Service Contract Automata* (MSCA) have been introduced in [7,10] to formalise service contracts and analyse contract agreement from a language-theoretic perspective. A contract automaton represents either a single service (in which case it is called a *principal*) or a multi-party composition of services. Service requests can be either necessary or permitted, where necessary requests must be matched whilst permitted requests can be optionally discarded without affecting the agreement. In a composition of contract automata, the goal of each principal is to reach a final state such that all its necessary requests and a subset of permitted requests are matched by complementary offers of other principals.

With the aim of narrowing the gap between the formalism and real-world SOC systems, in this paper we propose *Correlation-based Modal Contract Automata* (CMCA). CMCA extend MSCA with a mechanism for correlating interactions among each other. Whilst still oblivious of their partners, CMCA can indeed prescribe to whom their actions are directed depending on their previous interactions. A principal can establish conversations with other principals by exploiting variables within actions, firstly, to capture the 'identity' of the principal executing the complementary action matching the one starting a conversation and, then, to enforce that the same interacting principal do perform the complementary actions of the other actions belonging to the conversation. A principal can execute many such long-running conversations in parallel, as well as conversations formed of one interaction only that is not constrained to take place with a specific principal. Indeed, similarly to MSCA, a principal may also perform actions involving no variables at all so that they are not affected by previous interactions and do not affect future interactions.

Structure of the Paper. Further motivations on the advantages of introducing correlation in contract automata are illustrated through a motivating scenario presented in Sect. 2. Afterwards, CMCA and their composition are formally defined in Sect. 3. Results about CMCA validity are presented in Sect. 4, and an illustrative application of CMCA is described in Sect. 5. Finally, related work is discussed in Sect. 6, while concluding remarks and future work are sketched in Sect. 7.

2   Motivating Scenario

In this section we motivate the need for extending MSCA [7] to CMCA, which are equipped with a mechanism for correlating the interactions belonging to the same conversation. In MSCA all possible matches between offers and requests are dictated by the composition of contracts. In particular, a principal (i.e., a contract representing a single entity) *cannot* indicate on its own to which principal its offer or request is directed. Indeed, MSCA are oblivious of their communicating partners. Consider the following MSCA, each representing a different principal:

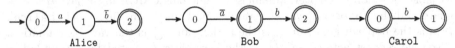

As usual, states and final states are depicted with a circle or two nested circles, respectively. The labels of MSCA are their actions, i.e. requests and offers. Thus, `Alice` prescribes to perform a request a and then an offer $\overline{b}$ (offers are overlined while requests are not). `Bob` offers $\overline{a}$ and then it can either terminate or require b. Finally, `Carol` either requires b or immediately terminates. Their composition, denoted by `Alice` $\otimes$ `Bob` $\otimes$ `Carol`, is the following MSCA:

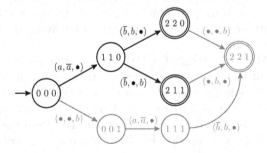

Since we are interested in contract agreement, we only focus on *match* actions, that is actions produced by a synchronisation between complementary offers and requests. Each state of the composed MSCA is characterised by a tuple indicating the current local state of each involved principal. In the initial state of the composition, the only enabled match action is $(a, \overline{a}, \bullet)$, which results from the matching between the request a of `Alice` and the offer $\overline{a}$ of `Bob`. In this action `Carol` is idle, denoted by $\bullet$. Afterwards, `Alice` may match her offer $\overline{b}$ either with the request b of `Bob`, denoted by the match action $(\overline{b}, b, \bullet)$, or with the request b of `Carol`, denoted by the match action $(\overline{b}, \bullet, b)$. Non-matching actions, corresponding to requests or offers of a single entity, are not relevant and, hence, are coloured grey in the composition; the same applies to states reached by non-matching actions, and consequently to all transitions and states originating from them. Thus, in the composition above, the request b of `Carol` from the initial state is grey, as well as all transitions and states reachable through this action.

Assume now, for the sake of the example, that `Alice` would like to constrain her offer $\overline{b}$ to be provided to the principal who has previously fulfilled her request a (`Bob` in this case). In the composition, `Alice` should have a way to somehow correlate the match $(a, \overline{a}, \bullet)$ with the match $(\overline{b}, b, \bullet)$, thus preventing $(\overline{b}, \bullet, b)$ from happening. This scenario, however, is not expressible through standard MSCA.

Instead CMCA can express and enforce the constraint above in the composition by exploiting a sort of correlation variables. Consider the following CMCA:

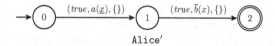

Alice'

The labels of CMCA are triples composed of a boolean guard, an action and a variable valuation. Moreover, all labels of principals CMCA must have *true* as a guard and the (empty) {} variable valuation. Thus, in the first label of `Alice'`, *true* is the boolean guard, $a(\underline{x})$ is the action, and {} is the variable valuation. Also, the request action $a(\underline{x})$ *binds* the variable x (denoted by the underline notation) in the continuation contract. The subsequent offer action $\overline{b}(x)$, instead, *uses* the variable x previously bound. As explained in more detail below, the resulting effect is that, in a composition involving `Alice'`, the variable x is first used to capture the 'identity' of the principal that executes the complementary action $\overline{a}$ and then to enforce that the complementary action b be executed by the same interacting principal. The variable x provides a sort of context that correlates the two actions $a(\underline{x})$ and $\overline{b}(x)$, which are now constrained to be both matched by the same principal. Thus, `Alice'` establishes a *conversation* with an interacting partner formed of two interactions involving the two actions and their complementary ones.

Similarly to MSCA, actions of a CMCA may also involve no variables at all. As a matter of fact, these actions belong to a conversation formed of one interaction only. This is the case of the actions of the CMCA `Bob'` and `Carol'` corresponding to the MSCA `Bob` and `Carol`, respectively. We do not explicitly report these two CMCA as they are trivially obtained from the original MSCA by simply extending the transition labels with the *true* guard and the empty valuation.

The composed CMCA Alice′ ⊗ Bob′ ⊗ Carol′ is:

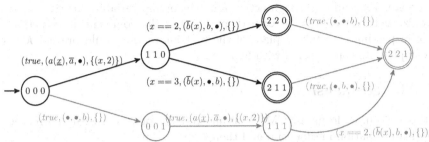

It is worth to notice that the composition assigns some indexes to the component principals according to the position they occupy. Thus, in the CMCA above, Alice′ gets index 1, Bob′ index 2 and Carol′ index 3. Now, the first label $(true, (a(\underline{x}), \overline{a}, \bullet), \{(x, 2)\})$ accounts for the matching between the request $a(\underline{x})$ of Alice′ and the offer $\overline{a}$ of Bob′. Since the request of Alice′ binds the variable x, the effect is to assign to x the index of Bob′. Thus, the valuation $\{(x, 2)\}$ is produced. After that, the composition has a choice between two labels. The label $(x == 2, (\overline{b}(x), b, \bullet), \{\})$ is generated by the matching between the offer $\overline{b}(x)$ of Alice′ and the request b of Bob′. This match can only take place if previously x has been bound to 2; this is checked by the guard $x == 2$. Similarly, the label $(x == 3, (\overline{b}(x), \bullet, b), \{\})$ is produced by the matching between the offer $\overline{b}(x)$ of Alice′ and the request b of Carol′; this time the guard is $x == 3$.

Hence, $(a(\underline{x}), \overline{a}, \bullet)(\overline{b}(x), b, \bullet)$ and $(a(\underline{x}), \overline{a}, \bullet)(\overline{b}(x), \bullet, b)$ are the only sequences of match actions that the CMCA Alice′ ⊗ Bob′ ⊗ Carol′ can potentially perform. However, the second sequence is not actually enabled because the guard of the second action requires that x is bound to 3 whilst the first, binding, action assigns 2 to x. This is instead not the case for the sequence $(a(\underline{x}), \overline{a}, \bullet)(\overline{b}(x), b, \bullet)$, which is then the only sequence that satisfies the constraint on the interactions specified by the contract Alice′.

Finally, consider the following CMCA David

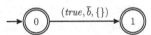

and the CMCA resulting from the composition of Alice′, Bob′, Carol′ and David shown below (where, for the sake of simplicity, we only show the match actions):

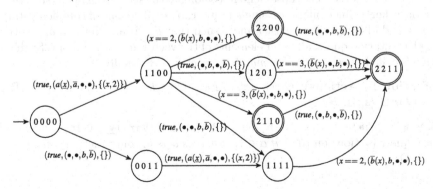

With respect to the CMCA $\texttt{Alice}' \otimes \texttt{Bob}' \otimes \texttt{Carol}'$, further interactions are now possible because, through action $\bar{b}$ not involving variables, $\texttt{David}$ can synchronize with either $\texttt{Bob}'$ or $\texttt{Carol}'$, performing the complementary action b. Note in passing that taking place of the first interaction could prevent $\texttt{Alice}'$ to complete its conversation with $\texttt{Bob}'$.

3   The Formalism

In this section, we formalise CMCA, as an extension of MSCA with a correlation-based coordination mechanism, and their composition.

3.1   Formal Definition and Semantics

Intuitively, a CMCA represents a multi-party composition of *principals*, which represent contracts that are not further decomposable. The number of principals of a CMCA is called its *rank*. The states of a CMCA are vectors of states of principals. In the following, notation $\vec{v}$ stands for a vector (whose indexes always start from 1), $\vec{v}_{(i)}$ is the ith element, $\bullet^m$ denotes a vector $(\bullet, \ldots, \bullet)$ of rank m, and the concatenation of two vectors $\vec{v}_1 = (a_1, a_2, \ldots, a_n)$ and $\vec{v}_2 = (b_1, b_2, \ldots, b_m)$ is denoted by $\vec{v}_1 \cdot \vec{v}_2 = (a_1, a_2, \ldots, a_n, b_1, b_2, \ldots, b_m)$. This definition is extended to the concatenation of n vectors $\vec{v}_\ell$, with $\ell \in 1 \ldots n$, denoted by $\oplus_{\ell=1}^{n} \vec{v}_\ell$.

We let R be a set of *requests* (depicted as non-overlined labels, e.g. a), O be a set of *offers* (depicted as overlined labels, e.g. $\bar{a}$) and $\bullet$ be a distinguished symbol representing the *idle* action. We assume that $\mathsf{R} \cap \mathsf{O} = \emptyset$ and $\bullet \notin \mathsf{R} \cup \mathsf{O}$. To establish if a pair of a request and an offer are *complementary*, we use the *involution* function $co : (\mathsf{R} \cup \mathsf{O}) \rightarrow (\mathsf{R} \cup \mathsf{O})$ defined as follows: $\forall a \in \mathsf{R} : co(a) \in \mathsf{O}$ and $\forall \bar{a} \in \mathsf{O} : co(\bar{a}) \in \mathsf{R}$ and $co \cdot co = id$. We also let Var be a finite set of variables (whose elements are $x, y, z, \ldots$). A *basic action* can be the idle action, or a request or an offer possibly with a variable argument. A variable occurring as an action argument can either be *used* by the action or *bound* by the action; in the second case it is underlined. Thus, for instance, $a(x)$ denotes request a using the variable x, $a(\underline{x})$ denotes request a binding variable x, and a denotes request a without a variable argument. For convenience, sometimes we will use the distinguished element $\circ \notin \texttt{Var}$ as action argument to explicitly denote absence of variable argument, so a and $a(\circ)$ are equivalent. Moreover, let $\underline{\mathsf{X}} = \{\underline{x} \mid x \in \mathsf{X} \subseteq \texttt{Var}\}$.

An *action* is a vector $\vec{a}$ whose elements belong to the set L given below such that there is either a single offer, or a single request, or a single pair of complementary request and offer, i.e. there exist i and j such that $\vec{a}_{(i)}$ is an offer and $\vec{a}_{(j)}$ is the complementary request; all other elements of the vector are the symbol $\bullet$. Such an action is called *request*, *offer*, or *match*, respectively. Formally:

Definition 1 (Actions). *Given a vector $\vec{a} \in \mathsf{L}^n$, where $\mathsf{L} = \{\bullet\} \cup \mathsf{R} \cup \mathsf{O} \cup ((\mathsf{R} \cup \mathsf{O}) \times (\texttt{Var} \cup \underline{\texttt{Var}}))$, if*

- *$\vec{a} = \bullet^{n_1} \alpha(u) \bullet^{n_2}$, $n_1, n_2 \geq 0$, $n_1 + n_2 + 1 = n$, $u \in (\texttt{Var} \cup \underline{\texttt{Var}} \cup \{\circ\})$, then $\vec{a}$ is a request (action) on $\alpha(u)$ if $\alpha \in \mathsf{R}$, whereas $\vec{a}$ is an offer (action) on $\alpha(u)$ if $\alpha \in \mathsf{O}$;*

- $\vec{a} = \bullet^{n_1}\alpha(u_1)\,\bullet^{n_2} co(\alpha)(u_2)\bullet^{n_3}$, $n_1, n_2, n_3 \geq 0$, $n_1 + n_2 + n_3 + 2 = n$, $u_1, u_2 \in$ $(\text{Var} \cup \underline{\text{Var}} \cup \{\circ\})$ then $\vec{a}$ is a match (action) on $\alpha(u_1)$ and $co(\alpha)(u_2)$, where $\alpha \in \mathsf{R} \cup \mathsf{O}$.

Actions $\vec{a}$ and $\vec{b}$ are complementary, *denoted by $\vec{a} \bowtie \vec{b}$, iff the following holds: (i) $\exists \alpha \in \mathsf{R} \cup \mathsf{O}$ s.t. $\vec{a}$ is either a request or an offer on $\alpha(u)$; (ii) $\vec{a}$ is an offer (request, resp.) on $\alpha(u)$ implies that $\vec{b}$ is a request (offer, resp.) on $co(\alpha)$. Given an offer or request action $\vec{a}$ on $\alpha(u)$, $uv(\vec{a})$ denotes $\{u\}$ if $u \in \text{Var}$ and $\circ$ otherwise, $bv(\vec{a})$ denotes $\{u\}$ if $u \in \underline{\text{Var}}$ and $\circ$ otherwise, and $pos(\vec{a}) = i$ iff $\vec{a}_{(i)} \neq \bullet$.*

Example 1. The action $\vec{a}_1 = (\bullet, \bullet, a(x))$ is a request on a of rank 3. The action $\vec{a}_2 = (\overline{a}, \bullet)$ is an offer on $\overline{a}$ of rank 2. It holds that $\vec{a}_1 \bowtie \vec{a}_2$ because $co(a) = \overline{a}$. The action $\vec{a}_3 = (\bullet, \bullet, a(x), \overline{a}, \bullet)$ is a match on actions $a(x)$ and $\overline{a}$. Moreover, $uv(\vec{a}_1) = \{x\}$, $bv(\vec{a}_1) = \circ$, $uv(\vec{a}_2) = bv(\vec{a}_2) = \circ$, $pos(\vec{a}_1) = 3$ and $pos(\vec{a}_2) = 1$.

Actions of CMCA can be classified using the *permitted* ($\Diamond$) and *necessary* ($\Box$) modalities. Intuitively, permitted actions represent optional behaviour and offers are always implicitly considered as permitted. With abuse of notation, modalities can be attached to basic actions or to their action vector (e.g. $(a\Box, \overline{a}) \equiv (a, \overline{a})\Box$), and if not specified otherwise, an action is assumed to be permitted.

In the following, we let $\bigcirc \in \{\Diamond, \Box\}$. We let $B(\text{Var})$ denote the set of constraints g generated by the grammar $g ::= true \mid (x{==}k) \mid g \wedge g$, where $k \in \mathbb{N}$. A *valuation* of the variables in Var is a partial function v from Var to $\mathbb{N}$ that is written $v \in \mathbb{N}^{\text{Var}}$.

Given $g \in B(\text{Var})$ and $v \in \mathbb{N}^{\text{Var}}$, the relation $v \models g$, meaning that v *satisfies* g, is defined by structural induction over the syntax of constraints through the following rules:

$$v \models true \qquad \text{is always true}$$
$$v \models (x{==}k) \qquad \text{if } v(x) = k$$
$$v \models g_1 \wedge g_2 \qquad \text{if } v \models g_1 \text{ and } v \models g_2$$

We let $v_0 = \{\}$ denote the valuation with empty domain, and $v[v']$ denote the valuation $\{(x, k) \mid v'(x) = k \vee (v(x) = k \wedge v'(x) \text{ undefined })\}$. The function $\texttt{shiftv}() : \mathbb{N}^{\text{Var}} \times \mathbb{N} \mapsto \mathbb{N}^{\text{Var}}$ is used to shift the values occurring within a valuation. Formally, $\texttt{shiftv}(v, n) = v'$ where $v' = \{(x, m + n) \mid x \in \text{Var}, m \in \mathbb{N}, (x, m) \in v\}$. Similarly, the function $\texttt{shiftg}() : B(\text{Var}) \times \mathbb{N} \mapsto B(\text{Var})$ is used to shift the values occurring within a constraint. Formally, $\texttt{shiftg}(g, n) = g'$ where $g = \bigwedge_{(x,m)\in I} (x{==}m)$ and $g' = \bigwedge_{(x,m)\in I} (x{==}m+n)$ for some set $I \subseteq \text{Var} \times \mathbb{N}$.

Example 2. The valuation $v = \{(x, 3), (y, 2)\}$ does not satisfy the guard $g = (x{==}1) \wedge (y{==}2)$ because x is mapped to 3 in v. Let $v' = \{(x, 1)\}$, the valuation $v[v'] = \{(x, 1), (y, 2)\}$ satisfies g, i.e. $v[v'] \models g$. Moreover, $\texttt{shiftv}(v[v'], 4) = \{(x, 5), (y, 6)\}$ and $\texttt{shiftg}(g, 4) = (x{==}5) \wedge (y{==}6)$.

We now formally define CMCA.

Definition 2 (Correlation-based Modal Contract Automata (CMCA)).
Assume as given a finite set of states $Q = \{q_1, q_2, \ldots\}$. *Then a* correlation-based
modal contract automaton $\mathcal{A}$ *of rank* $n \geq 1$ *is a tuple* $\langle Q, \vec{q_0}, A^r, A^o, \mathsf{X}, T, F \rangle$, *where*

- $Q \subseteq Q^n$;
- $\vec{q_0} \in Q$ *is the initial state;*
- $A^r = A^\diamond \cup A^\square \subseteq \mathsf{R}$ *is the finite set of requests partitioned into permitted and necessary requests, resp.;*
- $A^o \subseteq \mathsf{O}$ *is the finite set of offers;*
- $\mathsf{X} \subseteq \mathsf{Var}$ *is a finite set of variables;*
- $T = T^\diamond \cup T^\square \subseteq Q \times B(\mathsf{X}) \times A \times \mathbb{N}^\mathsf{X} \times Q$, *where* $A = (\{\bullet\} \cup [(A^r \cup A^o) \times (\mathsf{X} \cup \underline{\mathsf{X}} \cup \{\circ\})])^n$, *is the set of transitions partitioned into* permitted *transitions* $T^\diamond$ *and* necessary *transitions* $T^\square$ *and constrained as follows: given* $t = (\vec{q}, g, \vec{a}, v, \vec{q}') \in T$,
  * $\vec{a}$ *is either a request or an offer or a match,*
  * $\forall i \in 1 \ldots n,\ \vec{a}_{(i)} = \bullet$ *implies* $\vec{q}_{(i)} = \vec{q}'_{(i)}$,
  * $t \in T^\diamond$ *iff* $\vec{a}$ *is either a request or a match on* $a \in A^\diamond$ *or an offer on* $\overline{a} \in A^o$, *otherwise* $t \in T^\square$;
  * *if* $n = 1$ *then* $g = true$ *and* $v = \{\}$.
- $F \subseteq Q$ *is the set of final states.*

A *principal* is a CMCA of rank 1 with actions partitioned into offers or requests, formally $\forall a \in A^r, \exists \overline{b} \in A^o : co(a) = \overline{b}$, and $\forall \overline{b} \in A^o, \exists a \in A^r : co(\overline{b}) = a$.

From now on, we only consider automata where all states are connected (by sequence of transitions) to both the initial state and at least one final state.

Moreover, we assume as given the CMCA $\mathcal{A}$ of rank n defined as $\mathcal{A} = \langle Q_{\mathcal{A}}, \vec{q_0}_{\mathcal{A}}, A^r_{\mathcal{A}}, A^o_{\mathcal{A}}, \mathsf{X}, T_{\mathcal{A}}, F_{\mathcal{A}} \rangle$. Subscripts $\mathcal{A}$ may be omitted if no confusion can arise. We may write a transition t as a request, offer or match if its label is such. Similarly, the functions $\mathsf{pos}()$, $\mathsf{uv}()$ and $\mathsf{bv}()$, and the relation $\bowtie$ are extended from actions to labelled transitions in the obvious way.

Example 3. Let $t = (\vec{q_1}, [(y\texttt{==}3), (\overline{a}(y), a(\underline{x})), \{(x, 3)\}], \vec{q_2})$. We have $\mathsf{uv}(t) = \{y\}$ and $\mathsf{bv}(t) = \{x\}$.

We now define the traces of CMCA and its trace semantics, i.e. a language, over actions and their modalities.

Definition 3 (CMCA semantics). *Let* $(\mathbb{C}, c_0, \to)$ *be the labelled transition system associated to* $\mathcal{A}$, *where* $\mathbb{C} = Q \times \mathbb{N}^X$ *is the set of* configurations, $c_0 = (\vec{q_0}, v_0)$ *is the initial configuration, and the transition relation is such that there is a step* $(\vec{q_1}, v_1) \xrightarrow{\vec{a}\diamond} (\vec{q_2}, v_2)$ *iff* $(\vec{q_1}, g, \vec{a}, v_3, \vec{q_2}) \in T^\diamond$, *where* $v_1 \models g$ *and* $v_2 = v_1[v_3]$.
The semantics of $\mathcal{A}$ *is the language* $\mathscr{L}(\mathcal{A}) = \{\, w \mid (\vec{q_0}, v_0) \xrightarrow{w}{}^* (\vec{q}, v),\ \vec{q} \in F \,\}$, *where* $\xrightarrow{w}{}^*$ *is the reflexive and transitive closure of* $\xrightarrow{\vec{a}\diamond}$. *Any* $w \in \mathscr{L}(\mathcal{A})$ *is called a trace recognised by* $\mathcal{A}$, *where* $\mathscr{L}(\mathcal{A}) \subseteq A\mathsf{O}^*$.

3.2   Composition

A distinctive aspect of CMCA, w.r.t other automata-based models of services, is the composition operator $\otimes$ (formally defined in Definition 4), which generates statically an ensemble of service contracts by correlating their actions. Intuitively, the states of the composite automaton are elements of the cartesian product of the states of the component automata. The set of (used and bound) variables is the union of the set of variables of the component automata, that are assumed to be pairwise disjoint. The set of actions (requests and offers) is the union of the sets of actions of the component automata. The initial state is the concatenation of the initial states of the component automata, and similar for the final states.

Example 4. Let A be such that (transitions are discussed in the next example):

- $Q_A = \{(q_4, q_5, q_6), (q_4, q_7, q_6)\}$,
- $\vec{q}_{0_A} = (q_4, q_5, q_6)$,
- $A_A^r = \{d\square, b\square\}$,
- $A_A^o = \{\}$,
- $X_A = \{y\}$,
- $F_A = \{(q_4, q_7, q_6)\}$.

Moreover, let B be such that

- $Q_B = \{(q_0, q_1), (q_0, q_2), (q_9, q_3)\}$,
- $\vec{q}_{0_B} = (q_0, q_1)$,
- $A_B^r = \{a\Diamond\}$,
- $A_B^o = \{\bar{d}, \bar{a}, \bar{b}\}$,
- $X_B = \{x, z\}$,
- $F_B = \{(q_9, q_3)\}$.

The composition $A \otimes B$ will have the following components:

- $Q_{A\otimes B} = \{(q_4, q_5, q_6, q_0, q_1), (q_4, q_5, q_6, q_0, q_2), (q_4, q_5, q_6, q_9, q_3), (q_4, q_7, q_6, q_0, q_1), (q_4, q_7, q_6, q_0, q_2), (q_4, q_7, q_6, q_9, q_3)\}$;
- $\vec{q}_{0_{A\otimes B}} = (q_4, q_5, q_6, q_0, q_1)$;
- $A_{A\otimes B}^r = \{a\Diamond, b\square, d\square\}$;
- $A_{A\otimes B}^o = \{\bar{d}, \bar{a}, \bar{b}\}$;
- $X_{A\otimes B} = \{x, y, z\}$;
- $F_{A\otimes B} = \{(q_4, q_7, q_6, q_9, q_3)\}$.

We now discuss the set of transitions of the composite automaton. Intuitively, the composition interleaves the transitions of all component automata, unless two such automata are ready to execute two complementary transitions in which case only their match is allowed (and their interleavings are prevented). The match inherits the modality of the involved request. More in detail, a transition $t = (\vec{q}, g, \vec{a}, v, \vec{q}') \in T^\circ$ of the composed automaton can be obtained in one of the following two different ways.

The first way (case 1 of Definition 4) is when we consider two transitions of two component automata $t_i = (\vec{q}_i, g_i, \vec{a}_i, v_i, \vec{q}'_i) \in T_i^\bigcirc$ and $t_j = (\vec{q}_j, g_j, \vec{a}_j, v_j, \vec{q}'_j) \in T_j^\bigcirc \cup T_j^\diamond$ and the following three conditions hold: (i) the actions of t_i and t_j are complementary, i.e. $\vec{a}_i \bowtie \vec{a}_j$; (ii) the source states $\vec{q}_i$ and $\vec{q}_j$ of t_i and t_j are within the source state $\vec{q}$; (iii) the transition t_i has the same type $\bigcirc$ as the transition t, whilst t_j can possibly have the modality permitted. If t_i is necessary, so is also t (note that in this case t_j is an offer). Otherwise, if t_i is permitted then so is t (and t_j). The action $\vec{a}$ of t is a match between the two principals inside $\vec{a}_i$ and $\vec{a}_j$ with due care of their position in the vector $\vec{a}$. The guard g is *true* if $\vec{a}_i$ and $\vec{a}_j$ do not use variables previously bound. Otherwise, each used variable is constrained to be equal to the index of the other principal performing the complementary action. Similarly, the variable valuation v is empty if $\vec{a}_i$ and $\vec{a}_j$ do not bind variables. Otherwise, to each bound variable the index of the other principal performing the complementary action is assigned. Finally, the target state $\vec{q}'$ is obtained from $\vec{q}$ by only replacing the component states $\vec{q}_i$ and $\vec{q}_j$ with $\vec{q}'_i$ and $\vec{q}'_j$.

The second way (case 2 of Definition 4) is when only one transition of a component automaton is considered, namely $t_i = (\vec{q}_i, g_i, \vec{a}_i, v_i, \vec{q}'_i) \in T_i^\bigcirc$, and the following three conditions hold: (i) there exist no transitions of another component automaton that paired with t_i satisfy the three conditions of case 1 of Definition 4; (ii) the source states $\vec{q}_i$ is within the source state $\vec{q}$; (iii) the transition t_i has the same type $\bigcirc$ as the transition t. The action $\vec{a}$ is the concatenation of the action $\vec{a}_i$ with idle moves for all the other principals. The guard g and variable valuation v are defined by applying the functions $\texttt{shiftg}()$ and $\texttt{shiftv}()$ to, respectively, g_i and v_i, so to adjust their indexes. The target state $\vec{q}'$ is obtained from $\vec{q}$ by only replacing the component state $\vec{q}_i$ with $\vec{q}'_i$.

Example 5. Let A and B as in the Example 4. Suppose that the set T_A contains the following transitions (square brackets are used to enhance readability):

- $t_1 = (\ (q_4, q_5, q_6), \ [true, \ (\bullet, d\square, \bullet), \ \{\}], \ (q_4, q_7, q_6) \ )$,
- $t_2 = (\ (q_4, q_7, q_6), \ [true, \ (\bullet, \bullet, b(\underline{y})\square), \ \{\}], (q_4, q_7, q_6) \ )$,

and the set T_B contains the following transitions:

- $t_3 = (\ (q_0, q_1), \ [true, \ (\bullet, \overline{d}(\underline{x})), \ \{\}], \ (q_0, q_2) \ )$,
- $t_4 = (\ (q_0, q_2), \ [true, (a(\underline{z})\diamond, \overline{a}), \{(z, 2)\}] \ , (q_9, q_3) \ )$,
- $t_5 = (\ (q_9, q_3), \ [true, \ (\bullet, \overline{b}(x)), \ \{\}], \ (q_9, q_3) \ )$.

The transitions of the composition are computed as follows.

First consider the state $(q_4, q_5, q_6, q_0, q_1) \in Q_{A \otimes B}$. Call t^1 the transition of the composition we are building. Transitions t_1 and t_3 fall within the first case discussed above. In particular, the source states of t_1 and t_3 occur in $(q_4, q_5, q_6, q_0, q_1)$ and it holds that $(\bullet, d\square, \bullet) \bowtie (\bullet, \overline{d}(\underline{x}))$. Hence, the action of t^1 will be $\vec{a}_{t^1} = (\bullet, d\square, \bullet, \bullet, \overline{d}(\underline{x}))$. Since transition t_3 binds variable x, t^1 has assignment v_{t^1} containing $(x, 2)$, where $\vec{a}_{t^1(2)} = d\square$. There are no used variables, thus the guard is *true*. The target state will be $(q_4, q_7, q_6, q_0, q_2) \in Q_{\mathsf{A} \otimes \mathsf{B}}$, that is the concatenation of target states of t_1 and t_3. Overall, we have

$$t^1 = (\ (q_4, q_5, q_6, q_0, q_1),\ [true,\ (\bullet, d\square, \bullet, \bullet, \overline{d}(\underline{x})),\ \{(x, 2)\}],\ (q_4, q_7, q_6, q_0, q_2)\ )$$

Now consider the state $(q_4, q_7, q_6, q_0, q_2) \in Q_{\mathsf{A} \otimes \mathsf{B}}$ and build the transition named t^2 of the composition. Transition t_4 falls within the second case discussed above. Indeed, $(a(\underline{z})\Diamond, \overline{a})$ is neither a request nor an offer, hence no transitions of another component exist complementary to t_4. Moreover, the source state of t_4 occurs in $(q_4, q_7, q_6, q_0, q_2)$. The action of t^2 will thus be $\vec{a}_{t^2} = (\bullet, \bullet, \bullet, a(\underline{z})\Diamond, \overline{a})$. Note that all principals belonging to the operand A are idle in $\vec{a}_{t^2}$. The guard of t_4 is *true* and so will be the guard of t^2. The variable assignment is obtained by $\mathtt{shiftv}(\{(z, 2)\}, 3) = \{(z, 5)\}$ as 3 is the rank of A. Indeed, the principal at position 2 in B is shifted in position 5 in $\mathsf{A} \otimes \mathsf{B}$. Finally, the target state of t^2 is $(q_4, q_7, q_6, q_9, q_3)$, that is, only the principals involved in t_4 are moving to the target state of t_4 whilst the others remain in their source state. Overall we have

$$t^2 = (\ (q_4, q_7, q_6, q_0, q_2),\ [true,\ (\bullet, \bullet, \bullet, a(\underline{z})\Diamond, \overline{a}),\ \{(z, 5)\}],\ (q_4, q_7, q_6, q_9, q_3)\ )$$

Finally, we build the transition t^3 with source state $(q_4, q_7, q_6, q_9, q_3) \in Q_{\mathsf{A} \otimes \mathsf{B}}$. Transitions t_2 and t_5 fall within the first case discussed above. Indeed, their states occur in $(q_4, q_7, q_6, q_9, q_3)$ and their actions match. The action of t^3 is $\vec{a}_{t^3} = (\bullet, \bullet, b(\underline{y})\square, \bullet, \overline{b}(x))$. Since t_5 uses the variable x previously bound, t^3 will contain the guard $(x{=}{=}3)$ because the third principal in the composition is matching the basic action $\overline{b}(x)$. Since the transition t_2 binds variable y, the variable valuation of t^3 will be $\{(y, 5)\}$. The target state of t^3 is $(q_4, q_7, q_6, q_9, q_3)$. Overall we have

$$t^3 = (\ (q_4, q_7, q_6, q_9, q_3),\ [(x{=}{=}3), (\bullet, \bullet, b(\underline{y})\square, \bullet, \overline{b}(x)),\ \{(y, 5)\}],\ (q_4, q_7, q_6, q_9, q_3))$$

All remaining states in $Q_{\mathsf{A} \otimes \mathsf{B}}$, namely $(q_4, q_5, q_6, q_0, q_2)$, $(q_4, q_5, q_6, q_9, q_3)$, $(q_4, q_7, q_6, q_0, q_1)$, are not connected to either initial or final state and thus are ignored.

The formalisation of the composition operator follows.

Definition 4 (CMCA Composition). *Let $\mathcal{A}_i$ be CMCA of rank r_i, $i \in 1, \ldots, n$, with pairwise disjoint set of variables, and let $\bigcirc \in \{\Diamond, \square\}$. The composition $\bigotimes_{i \in 1 \ldots n} \mathcal{A}_i$ is the CMCA $\mathcal{A}$ of rank $m = \sum_{i \in 1 \ldots n} r_i$, where*

- $Q = Q_1 \times \cdots \times Q_n$,
- $\vec{q_0} = \oplus_{\ell \in 1}^n \vec{q}_{0\ell}$,
- $A^r = \bigcup_{i \in 1}^n A_i^r$,
- $A^o = \bigcup_{i \in 1}^n A_i^o$,
- $\mathsf{X} = \bigcup_{i \in 1 \ldots n} \mathsf{X}_i$,
- $T^\bigcirc \subseteq Q \times B(\mathsf{X}) \times A \times \mathbb{N}^\mathsf{X} \times Q$ *s.t.* $(\vec{q}, g, \vec{a}, v, \vec{q'}) \in T^\bigcirc$ *for a given* $\vec{q} = \oplus_{\ell \in 1}^n \vec{q}_\ell$ *iff*

1. *either* $\exists i, j \in 1 \dots n, i \neq j$ *s.t.* $(\vec{q}_i, g_i, \vec{a}_i, v_i, \vec{q}'_i) \in T^{\bigcirc}_i$, $(\vec{q}_j, g_j, \vec{a}_j, v_j, \vec{q}'_j) \in$ $T^{\bigcirc}_j \cup T^{\diamond}_j$, $\vec{a}_i \bowtie \vec{a}_j$ *and*

   - $\vec{a} = \, \bullet\!\sum_{\ell=1}^{i-1} r_\ell \ \vec{a}_i \ \bullet\!\sum_{\ell=i+1}^{j-1} r_\ell \ \vec{a}_j \ \bullet\!\sum_{\ell=j+1}^{n} r_\ell,$
   - $\vec{q}' = \, \oplus_{\ell \in 1}^{i-1} \vec{q}_\ell \, \cdot \, \vec{q}'_i \, \cdot \oplus_{\ell \in i+1}^{j-1} \vec{q}_\ell \, \cdot \vec{q}'_j \, \cdot \, \oplus_{\ell \in j+1}^{n} \vec{q}_\ell,$
   - $g = [\bigwedge\limits_{\substack{k_1, k_2 \in \{i,j\}, k_1 \neq k_2 \\ \exists x \in \mathsf{X}_{k_1} s.t. uv(\vec{a}_{k_1}) = \{x\}}} (x == ((\sum_{\ell=1}^{k_2-1} r_\ell) + pos(\vec{a}_{k_2})))] \wedge \mathit{true}$
   - $v = \{(x, (\sum_{\ell=1}^{k_2-1} r_\ell) + pos(\vec{a}_{k_2})) \mid k_1, k_2 \in \{i,j\}, k_1 \neq k_2, bv(\vec{a}_{k_1}) = \{x\} \ for \ x \in \mathsf{X}_{k_1}\},$

2. *or* $\exists 1 \leq i \leq n$ *such that* $(\vec{q}_i, g_i, \vec{a}_i, v_i, \vec{q}'_i) \in T^{\bigcirc}_i$, $\vec{a}_i \bowtie \vec{a}_j$ *does not hold* $\forall (\vec{q}_j, g_j, \vec{a}_j, v_j, \vec{q}'_j) \in T^{\bigcirc}_j \cup T^{\diamond}_j$ *with* $j \neq i$ *and* $1 \leq j \leq n$, *and*

   - $\vec{a} = \, \bullet\!\sum_{\ell=1}^{i-1} r_\ell \ \vec{a}_i \ \bullet\!\sum_{\ell=i+1}^{n} r_\ell,$
   - $\vec{q}' = \, \oplus_{\ell \in 1}^{i-1} \vec{q}_\ell \, \cdot \, \vec{q}'_i \, \cdot \oplus_{\ell \in i+1}^{n} \vec{q}_\ell,$
   - $g = \mathtt{shiftg}(g_i, \sum_{\ell=1}^{i-1} r_\ell),$,
   - $v = \mathtt{shiftv}(v_i, \sum_{\ell=1}^{i-1} r_\ell),$,

- $F = \{ \, \oplus_{\ell \in 1}^{n} \vec{q}_\ell \in Q \mid \vec{q}_\ell \in F_\ell, \ \ell \in 1 \dots n \}$

4   Validity

In this section we introduce the notion of validity of a CMCA. Intuitively, an automaton is not valid if it uses variables that have not been previously bound. We define two different notions, a semantic one and a syntactic one. We show that generally syntactic validity over-approximates semantic validity, and that they are equivalent under proper assumptions. In practice, checking syntactic validity can be done efficiently through static analyses, whilst this is not the case for semantics validity.

In the following, assume as given a CMCA $\mathcal{A} = \langle Q_{\mathcal{A}}, q^{\rightarrow}_{0_{\mathcal{A}}}, A^r_{\mathcal{A}}, A^o_{\mathcal{A}}, \mathsf{X}, T_{\mathcal{A}}, F_{\mathcal{A}} \rangle$. The following definition states that a trace $w \in \mathscr{L}(\mathcal{A})$ is *valid* if each action using a variable x is preceded by an action binding x, for any variable x. Formally:

Definition 5 (Semantic Validity). *Let* $w \in \mathscr{L}(\mathcal{A})$ *be a trace of length* n. *Then* w *is valid iff* $\forall i \in 1 \dots n$, *if* $w_{(i)} = \vec{a}$ *on action* $\alpha(x)$ *for some* $\alpha \in \mathsf{R} \cup \mathsf{O}$ *and* $x \in \mathsf{X}$ *then* $\exists j < i$ *such that* $w_{(j)} = \vec{b}$ *on action* $\beta(\underline{x})$ *for some* $\beta \in \mathsf{R} \cup \mathsf{O}$; w *is not valid otherwise.* $\mathcal{A}$ *is semantically valid if* $\forall w \in \mathscr{L}(\mathcal{A})$, w *is valid.*

Example 6. The trace $w_1 = (\bar{a}, a\diamond, \bullet)(\bullet, \bar{b}, b(\underline{x})\diamond)$ and the trace $w_2 = (\bar{a}, a\diamond, \bullet)(\bullet, \bullet, b(\underline{x})\diamond)$ are both valid traces, whilst $w_3 = (\bar{a}, a\diamond, \bullet)(\bullet, \bullet, b(x)\diamond)$ is not. Also the trace $w_4 = (\bullet, \bar{c}(\underline{x}), \bullet)(\bar{a}, a\diamond, \bullet)(\bullet, \bullet, b(\underline{x})\diamond)$ is valid. The automaton A whose language is $\mathscr{L}(\mathrm{A}) = \{w_1, w_2, w_4\}$ is valid, whilst the automaton B whose language is $\mathscr{L}(\mathrm{B}) = \{w_1, w_2, w_3, w_4\}$ is not valid.

Recall that the semantics of a CMCA is based on its configurations, which are tuples containing states and variable valuations. We are interested in analysing validity without computing all possible configurations. Indeed, even if it is possible to decide semantic validity (because the set of configurations of a CMCA is finite), the number of configurations is in general much bigger than the number of states. Therefore, we now introduce the notion of syntactic validity that only relies on the transitions of an automaton. Thus to establish it, we do not need to compute the automaton configurations. We first introduce the notion of a path.

Definition 6 (Path). *A path* π *within* $\mathcal{A}$ *from a state* $\vec{q_1}$ *to a state* $\vec{q_n}$ *is a finite sequence of transitions* $(\vec{q_1}, g_1, \vec{a_1}, v_1, \vec{q_2})$ $(\vec{q_2}, g_2, \vec{a_2}, v_2, \vec{q_3}) \cdots (\vec{q_{n-1}}, g_{n-1}, \vec{a_{n-1}}, v_{n-1}, \vec{q_n})$ *with* $(\vec{q_i}, g_i, \vec{a_i}, v_i, \vec{q_{i+1}}) \in T_{\mathcal{A}}$ *for all* $1 \leq i \leq n-1$; *it is* minimal *if no transition occurs more than once. Given a transition* $t \in T_{\mathcal{A}}$, *we let* $\mathtt{mpath}_{\mathcal{A}}(t)$ *be the finite set of* minimal *paths from the initial state of* $\mathcal{A}$ *to the source state of* t.

Notice that those paths where a cycle of transitions is unfolded more than once are not minimal. It is then easy to see that, while the set of all possible paths (from the initial state) leading to a given state could be infinite (because of cycles), the set of minimal paths is guaranteed to be finite. Differently from a trace, a minimal path can be computed by only considering the transitions of a CMCA.

Example 7. Consider the automaton A $\otimes$ B of Example 5 and its transitions t^1, t^2 and t^3. Let $\pi_1 = t^1$, $\pi_2 = t^1 t^2$, $\pi_3 = t^1 t^2 t^3$ and $\pi_4 = t^1 t^2 t^3 t^3$. We have $\mathtt{mpath}_{\mathsf{A} \otimes \mathsf{B}}(t^1) = \{\}$, $\mathtt{mpath}_{\mathsf{A} \otimes \mathsf{B}}(t^2) = \{\pi_1\}$, and $\mathtt{mpath}_{\mathsf{A} \otimes \mathsf{B}}(t^3) = \{\pi_2, \pi_3\}$. We also have $\pi_4 \notin \mathtt{mpath}_{\mathsf{A} \otimes \mathsf{B}}(t^3)$ since π_4 is not minimal.

The notions of a path and a trace of a CMCA differ. Indeed, no evaluation at all on guards or bindings on variables occur in determining a path, and only a check is done that states of transitions are correctly concatenated. Instead, variable bindings are updated while building a trace, and guards are to be true under those bindings. Therefore, any actual sequence of steps in the semantics (i.e. trace) corresponds to a path, whilst the contrary does not hold.

Example 8. Consider an automaton $\mathcal{A}$ with the following transitions $t_1 = (\vec{q_0}, [true, (\bar{a}, a(\underline{x})), \{(x, 1)\}], \vec{q_1})$, $t_2 = (\vec{q_1}, [(y{=}{=}2), (b(y), \bar{b}), \{\}], \vec{q_1})$, and assume that $\vec{q_0}$ is the initial state whilst $\vec{q_1}$ is a final state. There are two possible paths, i.e. $\pi_1 = t_1$ and $\pi_2 = t_1 t_2$. Instead, the only trace recognised by $\mathcal{A}$ is $w = (\bar{a}, a(\underline{x}))$. Indeed, the guard of t_2 is not satisfied in the configuration $(\vec{q_1}, \{\})$ reached from the initial configuration through the transition t_1 corresponding to the action $(\bar{a}, a(\underline{x}))$. Hence, the path π_1 corresponds to the trace w, whilst π_2 does not correspond to any trace.

Definition 7 (Syntactic Validity). $\mathcal{A}$ *is syntactically valid if and only if*

$$\forall t \in T_{\mathcal{A}}, \forall x \in uv(t), \forall \pi \in mpath_{\mathcal{A}}(t), \exists t' \in \pi \ s.t. \ x \in bv(t').$$

Example 9. Continuing Example 6. Let us focus on trace w_3 and let t_1 and t_2 be the transitions having respectively actions $(\bar{a}, a\diamond, \bullet)$ and $(\bullet, \bullet, b(x)\diamond)$. We have $\mathtt{mpath}_{\mathsf{B}}(t_2) = \{t_1\}$. Since $uv(t_2) = \{x\}$ but $x \notin bv(t_1)$ the automaton B is not valid.

We are now able to state the relation between syntactic and semantic validity. In particular, syntactic validity over-approximates semantic validity. Formally:

Theorem 1 (Syntactic Validity implies Semantic Validity). *If a CMCA is syntactically valid then it is semantically valid.*

Proof. Assume that $\mathcal{A}$ is syntactically valid and, by contradiction, that it is not semantically valid. This means that there exists a trace w of some length n and an index $i \in 1 \ldots n$ with $w_{(i)} = \vec{a}$ on action $\alpha(x)$ for some $\alpha \in R \cup O$ and $x \in X$, such that for all $j < i$ we have that $w_{(j)} = \vec{b}$ on action $\beta(u)$ for some $\beta \in R \cup O$ and $u \neq x$. Let t be the transition corresponding to the action $\vec{a}$ in w and, similarly, let π be the path formed of the transitions corresponding to the actions in w', where $w = w'\vec{a}w''$. By definition, it holds that $\forall t' \in \pi$, $x \notin \mathtt{bv}(t')$. If $\pi \notin \mathtt{mpath}_t(\mathcal{A})$, we take the minimal path $\pi' \in \mathtt{mpath}_t(\mathcal{A})$ obtained by removing from π all multiple occurrences of any transition. Of course, for such π' we have that $\forall t' \in \pi'$, $x \notin \mathtt{bv}(t')$. Hence $\mathcal{A}$ is not syntactically valid, which is a contradiction. □

The converse of Theorem 1 does not hold. For instance, the CMCA $\mathcal{A}$ of the Example 8 is semantically valid but not syntactically valid. In other words, by performing the proposed static analysis it is possible to reject (because not syntactically valid) a contract which turns out to only have valid traces.

However, in the case of principal automata, the next theorem proves that the two notions of validity do coincide. It is thus possible to avoid wrong rejections.

Theorem 2 (Validity Coincidence for Principals). *A principal CMCA is syntactically valid if and only if it is semantically valid.*

Proof. The 'if' part follows from Theorem 1. The 'only if' part follows from the fact that by Definition 2 all transitions of principals have guards equal to *true*, and therefore there is a one-to-one correspondence between traces and paths. □

The next lemma relates composition and syntactic validity.

Lemma 1 (Composition Preserves Syntactic Validity). *Let $\mathcal{A}$ be a CMCA obtained by composing the principals $\mathcal{A}_i$, $i \in 1 \ldots n$. Then, $\mathcal{A}$ is syntactically valid if and only if all $\mathcal{A}_i$, $i \in 1 \ldots n$ are syntactically valid.*

Proof. The statement directly follows from the fact that all principals have disjoint sets of variables and that the composition does not add any new variable. □

From the above results it is possible to prove a correspondence between syntactic validity and semantics validity of principals from whom a composite automaton is computed.

Corollary 1 (Validity Correspondence for Composed CMCA). *Let $\mathcal{A}$ be an automaton obtained by composing the principals $\mathcal{A}_i$ where $i \in 1 \ldots n$. Then, $\mathcal{A}$ is syntactically valid if and only if all $\mathcal{A}_i, i \in 1 \ldots n$ are semantically valid.*

Proof. The *'if'* part follows from Theorem 1 and Lemma 1. For the *'only if'* part, assume by contradiction that $\mathcal{A}$ is not syntactically valid. By Lemma 1 this means that some principal from whom $\mathcal{A}$ has been obtained by composition is not syntactically valid, and by Theorem 2 a contradiction is reached.   □

Example 10. Continuing Example 8, the automaton $\mathcal{A}$ is of rank 2 and it is composed of two principals, say A and B. $\mathcal{A}$ is not syntactically valid because principal A has transitions $t_3 = (q_0, (true, \overline{a}, \{\}), q_1)$ and $t_4 = (q_1, (true, b(y), \{\}), q_2)$ and it is not syntactically valid because in the path $t_3 t_4$ the variable y used in t_4 has not been previously bound in t_3. Moreover, A is also not semantically valid because of the trace $\overline{a} \, b(y)$.

5   CMCA at Work on a Hotel Booking Scenario

To show the effectiveness of our approach, in this section we use CMCA to model a hotel booking scenario, involving a number of clients, hotels and booking services. Each client makes use of a booking service to select and book a room for a given destination. When invoked, a booking service contacts a given number of hotels and proposes to the client only a limited number of the received offers (for the sake of presentation, in our example each booking service contacts five hotels and proposes three offers). A client can be of two different types, say A or B, according to his willingness of concluding the interaction with the booking service by sending or not the hotel review.

The CMCA of the four kinds of principals are in Fig. 1, where, for the sake of readability, we have omitted guards and variable valuations from labels, as they are *true* and $\{\}$, respectively, for all labels. Moreover, we use solid arrows for denoting transitions labelled by necessary actions, and dotted arrows for the permitted ones.

The overall scenario is rendered by the following composition:

$$\texttt{ClientA}_1 \otimes \ldots \otimes \texttt{ClientA}_n \otimes \texttt{ClientB}_1 \otimes \ldots \otimes \texttt{ClientB}_m$$
$$\otimes \texttt{HotelBooking}_1 \otimes \ldots \otimes \texttt{HotelBooking}_p \otimes \texttt{Hotel}_1 \otimes \ldots \otimes \texttt{Hotel}_r$$

Considered the large number of states of the full automaton, we omit its full graphical representation and just report in Fig. 2 an excerpt for the composition of one client of type A, one client of type B, two hotel booking services, and eight hotels.

Specifically, a client firstly contacts one booking service among those that are not currently serving another client (i.e., those HotelBooking CMCA that are in the state 0). Indeed, a booking service that is already engaged in a conversation cannot synchronise with the initial action of the client, at least until the conversation terminates and the service goes back to its initial state. The contacted booking service checks room availability of five hotels, each of which tries to send back its room offer. Once the booking service has received three out of five replies, it resets via the *timeout* action the other two hotels (bringing their CMCA back to the initial state) and sends the three room offers to the client, who selects one. Then, the booking service confirms the reservation to the

ClientA$_i$

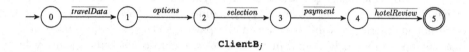

ClientB$_j$

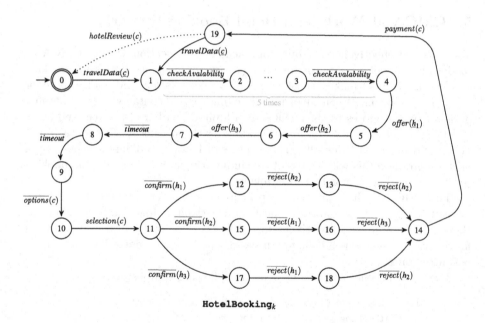

HotelBooking$_k$

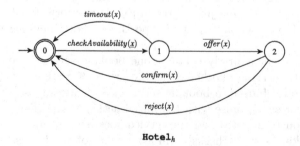

Hotel$_h$

Fig. 1. Hotel booking scenario: CMCA of Client, HotelBooking and Hotel

selected hotel and rejects the other two offers. Finally, the payment takes place and the client optionally sends a review about his stay to the service. In fact, since *hotelReview* is a permitted action, the booking service can interact with clients of both type A and B.

The scenario shows how correlation variables are used to prevent undesired matchings in the contract composition. Hotel uses x to ensure that, once contacted, it will always interact with the same booking service until it will come back to the initial state (where a new binding for x can be done). HotelBooking uses c to continue to interact with the same client, and $h1$, $h2$ and $h3$ to send the confirmation/rejection only to the three hotels that have made the offers, until it will come back to the initial state. Finally, ClientA and ClientB do not need to specify any correlation variable.

Consider the validity of the involved CMCA. The automata of both kinds of clients are trivially (syntactically and semantically) valid, as they do not use any correlation variable. The hotel automata are syntactically valid, because transitions labelled by actions $timeout(x)$, $\overline{offer}(x)$, $confirm(x)$ and $reject(x)$, which use variable x, are properly bound by the transition labelled by $checkAvailability(\underline{x})$ that occurs on the paths leading to the former transitions. By Theorem 1, the hotel automata are also semantically valid. In the same way, we can easily check that also the hotel booking service automata are syntactically, and hence semantically, valid. Finally, since all these CMCA are semantically valid principals, by Corollary 1 their composition is syntactically valid, and also, by Theorem 1, semantically valid.

6   Related Work

In the literature, there exist many formalisms for modelling and analysing (service) contracts, ranging from behavioural type systems, including behavioural contracts [1,15,22] and session types [13,14,17,20,24], to automata-based formalisms, including interface automata [2] and (timed) (I/O) automata [3,16,23]. Foundational models for service contracts and session types are surveyed in [4,11,21].

In [1,15,22], *behavioural contracts* of web services are described by CCS-like process algebrae, which model service features through input and output actions that synchronise. They have different, generally weaker notions of contract compliance than ours, e.g. only involving two parties. *Sessions* and *session types* [13,14,17,20,24] have been introduced to reason over the behaviour of services in terms of their interactions. Compared to CMCA, behavioural contracts and session types use process-algebraic frameworks, whilst CMCA are based on finite state machines. Indeed, CMCA are similar to other software engineering-based formalisms such as I/O automata [3,16,23], or semi-formal UML state machine diagrams, from which they benefit by being easily adaptable into the design phase of a software life-cycle. Different from CMCA, behavioural contracts are either bi-party or they do not use correlation variables to track their conversations, whilst session types have knowledge about other communicating partners.

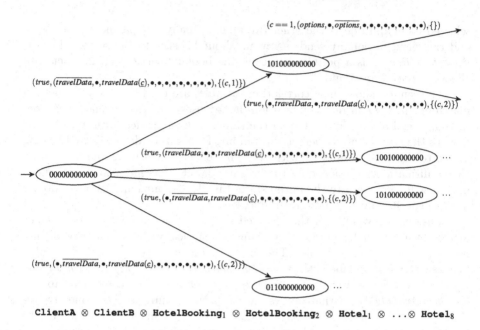

ClientA ⊗ ClientB ⊗ HotelBooking₁ ⊗ HotelBooking₂ ⊗ Hotel₁ ⊗ ...⊗ Hotel₈

Fig. 2. Hotel booking scenario: CMCA of a composition

CMCA builds upon contract automata [7] that have been used to study several issues arising in a composition of service contracts. Contract automata have been related to two intuitionistic logics introduced for modelling circular dependencies among contracts in [7], and have been related to session types in [8]. Moreover, contract automata have been extended to express real-time features in [6] and different necessary requests in [5,9]. Differently from CMCA, all these extensions do not include the possibility of specifying conversations between principals by using correlation variables.

Some form of correlation for directing a message to the correct interacting partner has already been used by a few formalisms aiming at providing a foundational understanding of the SOC paradigm among which COWS [26], SOCK [19], and SocL [18]. COWS is a process calculus whose design has been influenced by WS-BPEL. Correlation in COWS relies on a sophisticated pattern-matching mechanism that allows an input operation to selects the message to receive and, in case a message matches several input patterns, to direct the message to the input operation that requires fewer substitutions. Differently from COWS, the SOCK calculus was developed trying to be strongly related to the web services technology. This principle is also reflected in the used correlation mechanism. In SOCK, every process has a state consisting of valued variables. Some of them, called correlation variables, are explicitly indicated as those driving the correlation so that a message is directed to the process that contains in its correlation variables the same correlation values included in the message. SocL is a branching-time temporal logic that has been specifically designed to effectively express distinctive aspects of services, such as, e.g., acceptance of a request, provision of a response, and correlation among service requests and responses. The actions of the logic, that correspond to the actions performed by service providers and consumers, have correlation data among their attributes. Moreover, as in CMCA, the actions can use variables to capture correlation data. Differently from all the three formalisms mentioned above, where correlation data can be any sort of values that services can exchange in communication, the CMCA correlation mechanism only allows a principal to first introduce a variable for capturing the identity of an interacting partner and then use that variable for constraining further interactions to take place with the same partner. Indeed, the correlation data are implicitly generated as indexes of partners that are generated automatically.

7   Conclusion and Future Work

We have presented the foundational theory of Correlation-based Modal Contract Automata (CMCA). This formalism expresses behavioural contracts equipped with modalities (necessary and permitted actions) as well as a mechanism for correlating different actions. The correlation mechanism enables each interacting partner to use its past interactions to drive the future ones.

The original Contract Automata [7, 10] are equipped with an algorithm that permits the synthesis of the orchestration of multiple contracts. This orchestration represents the largest portion of behaviour of the composition that is in agreement. We plan to define the orchestration of CMCA. For this, it is first necessary to extend to CMCA the *refinement* relationship defined for Contract Automata. We also wish to extend the tool [9] supporting the design of Contract Automata and the automated calculation of their orchestration to include the correlation mechanism introduced in this paper.

The CMCA correlation mechanism, although expressive enough to enhance the original formalism and make it able to model interesting service scenarios and properties, is somehow more restrictive than that used by the foundational formalisms for SOC discussed in the previous section. Therefore, for modelling more complex interactions, we plan to integrate within CMCA a more general mechanism supporting explicit choice of correlation data, as well as their transmission to third party contracts.

Our long-term goal is to devise a methodology for verifying services against their contracts. Services could be expressed both as source code (e.g. WS-BPEL processes) or at a more abstract level (e.g. as COWS terms), while contracts would be expressed as CMCA. We want then to develop methods to automatically derive a contract out of a service and, vice versa, to derive a service (schema) out of a contract, while of course guaranteeing compliance of the service with its contract. This is at the base of a contract-based methodology to develop service applications that are *safe by design*.

Acknowledgements. We are pleased to point out that different subsets of authors of this paper have co-authored with Stefania Gnesi both the work on Service oriented computing Logic (SocL) [18] and on Modal Service Contract Automata (MSCA) [7,10]. Our paper is in fact an attempt to import the benefits of SocL (in particular, the correlation mechanism) into MSCA. Stefania has a long standing research history on both temporal logics and modal formalisms. Working with her on these subjects has been a great opportunity of growth. We also thank the anonymous reviewers for their useful comments.

References

1. Acciai, L., Boreale, M., Zavattaro, G.: Behavioural contracts with request-response operations. Sci. Comp. Program. **78**(2), 248–267 (2013)
2. de Alfaro, L., Henzinger, T.: Interface automata. In: ESEC/FSE, pp. 109–120. ACM (2001)
3. Alur, R., Dill, D.: A theory of timed automata. Theoret. Comp. Sci. **126**(2), 183–235 (1994)
4. Bartoletti, M., Cimoli, T., Zunino, R.: Compliance in behavioural contracts: a brief survey. In: Bodei, C., Ferrari, G.-L., Priami, C. (eds.) Programming Languages with Applications to Biology and Security. LNCS, vol. 9465, pp. 103–121. Springer, Cham (2015). https://doi.org/10.1007/978-3-319-25527-9_9
5. Basile, D., ter Beek, M.H., Di Giandomenico, F., Gnesi, S.: Orchestration of dynamic service product lines with featured modal contract automata. In: SPLC, pp. 117–122. ACM (2017)
6. Basile, D., ter Beek, M.H., Legay, A., Traonouez, L.-M.: Orchestration synthesis for real-time service contracts. In: Atig, M.F., Bensalem, S., Bliudze, S., Monsuez, B. (eds.) VECoS 2018. LNCS, vol. 11181, pp. 31–47. Springer, Cham (2018). https://doi.org/10.1007/978-3-030-00359-3_3
7. Basile, D., Degano, P., Ferrari, G.L.: Automata for specifying and orchestrating service contracts. Log. Meth. Comput. Sci. **12**(4) (2016)
8. Basile, D., Degano, P., Ferrari, G.L., Tuosto, E.: Relating two automata-based models of orchestration and choreography. J. Log. Algebr. Meth. Program. **85**(3), 425–446 (2016)
9. Basile, D., Di Giandomenico, F., Gnesi, S.: FMCAT: supporting dynamic service-based product lines. In: SPLC, pp. 3–8. ACM (2017)
10. Basile, D., Di Giandomenico, F., Gnesi, S., Degano, P., Ferrari, G.L.: Specifying variability in service contracts. In: Proceedings 11th International Workshop on Variability Modelling of Software-intensive Systems (VaMoS 2017), pp. 20–27. ACM (2017)
11. ter Beek, M.H., Bucchiarone, A., Gnesi, S.: Web service composition approaches: from industrial standards to formal methods. In: ICIW. IEEE (2007)
12. Bouguettaya, A., et al.: A service computing manifesto: the next 10 years. Commun. ACM **60**(4), 64–72 (2017)
13. Bruni, R., Lanese, I., Melgratti, H., Tuosto, E.: Multiparty sessions in SOC. In: Lea, D., Zavattaro, G. (eds.) COORDINATION 2008. LNCS, vol. 5052, pp. 67–82. Springer, Heidelberg (2008). https://doi.org/10.1007/978-3-540-68265-3_5
14. Castagna, G., Dezani-Ciancaglini, M., Padovani, L.: On global types and multiparty sessions. Log. Meth. Comp. Sci. **8**(1:24), 1–45 (2012)
15. Castagna, G., Gesbert, N., Padovani, L.: A theory of contracts for web services. ACM Trans. Program. Lang. Syst. **31**(5), 19:1–19:61 (2009)

16. David, A., Larsen, K.G., Legay, A., Nyman, U., Wasowski, A.: Timed I/O automata: a complete specification theory for real-time systems. In: HSCC, pp. 91–100. ACM (2010)
17. Dezani-Ciancaglini, M., de'Liguoro, U.: Sessions and session types: an overview. In: Laneve, C., Su, J. (eds.) WS-FM 2009. LNCS, vol. 6194, pp. 1–28. Springer, Heidelberg (2010). https://doi.org/10.1007/978-3-642-14458-5_1
18. Fantechi, A., Gnesi, S., Lapadula, A., Mazzanti, F., Pugliese, R., Tiezzi, F.: A logical verification methodology for service-oriented computing. ACM Trans. Softw. Eng. Methodol. 21(3), 16:1–16:46 (2012). https://doi.org/10.1145/2211616.2211619
19. Guidi, C., Lucchi, R., Gorrieri, R., Busi, N., Zavattaro, G.: SOCK: a calculus for service oriented computing. In: Dan, A., Lamersdorf, W. (eds.) ICSOC 2006. LNCS, vol. 4294, pp. 327–338. Springer, Heidelberg (2006). https://doi.org/10.1007/11948148_27
20. Honda, K., Yoshida, N., Carbone, M.: Multiparty asynchronous session types. In: POPL, pp. 273–284. ACM (2008)
21. Hüttel, H., et al.: Foundations of session types and behavioural contracts. ACM Comput. Surv. 49(1), 3:1–3:36 (2016)
22. Laneve, C., Padovani, L.: An algebraic theory for web service contracts. Form. Asp. Comp. 27(4), 613–640 (2015)
23. Lynch, N., Tuttle, M.: An introduction to input/output automata. CWI Q. 2, 219–246 (1989)
24. Michaux, J., Najm, E., Fantechi, A.: Session types for safe web service orchestration. J. Log. Algebr. Program. 82(8), 282–310 (2013)
25. OASIS WSBPEL TC: Web Services Business Process Execution Language Version 2.0. Technical report, OASIS, April 2007. http://docs.oasis-open.org/wsbpel/2.0/OS/wsbpel-v2.0-OS.html
26. Pugliese, R., Tiezzi, F.: A calculus for orchestration of web services. J. Applied Logic 10(1), 2–31 (2012). https://doi.org/10.1016/j.jal.2011.11.002

Logical Support for Bike-Sharing System Design

Ionuţ Ţuţu[1,2(✉)], Claudia Elena Chiriţă[2], Antónia Lopes[3],
and José Luiz Fiadeiro[2]

[1] Simion Stoilow Institute of Mathematics of the Romanian Academy,
Bucharest, Romania
ittutu@gmail.com
[2] Department of Computer Science,
Royal Holloway University of London, Egham, UK
claudia.elena.chirita@gmail.com, jose.fiadeiro@rhul.ac.uk
[3] LASIGE and Faculdade Ciências, Universidade de Lisboa, Lisbon, Portugal
malopes@ciencias.ulisboa.pt

Abstract. Automated bicycle-sharing systems (BSS) are a prominent
example of reconfigurable cyber-physical systems for which the locality
and connectivity of their elements are central to the way in which they
operate. These features motivate us to study BSS from the perspective
of Actor-Network Theory – a framework for modelling cyber-physical-
system protocols in which systems are networks of actors that are no
longer limited to programs but can also include humans and physical
artefacts. In order to support logical reasoning about information-flow
properties that occur in BSS, we use a logical framework that we have
recently developed for actor networks, which results from a two-stage
hybridization process. The first stage corresponds to a logic that captures
the locality and connectivity of actors in a given configuration of the
network; the second stage corresponds to a logic of possible interactions
between actors, which captures the dynamics of the system in terms of
network reconfigurations. To illustrate the properties that can be checked
using this framework, we provide an actor-network specification of a
particular BSS, and use a recently developed tool for hybridized logics to
highlight and correct an information-flow vulnerability of the system.

1 Introduction

Bike-sharing systems (BSS) facilitate urban transport by allowing users to borrow
bicycles from a location and return them at the destination of their journey. The
journeys are usually short, and the loan of a bicycle is conditioned by a fee.

The BSS model appeared in the 1960s and has since evolved through several
generations. The last decade in the history of BSS stands out for a rapid growth:
each year, they are more widespread and their number, sheer size and complexity,
keep increasing. This has led to reshaping cities, and has promoted bike-sharing
systems as one of the main means of urban transportation. If the first generations of BSS were vulnerable to vandalism and incorrect usage, the recent third

© Springer Nature Switzerland AG 2019
M. H. ter Beek et al. (Eds.): Gnesi Festschrift, LNCS 11865, pp. 152–171, 2019.
https://doi.org/10.1007/978-3-030-30985-5_10

generation has tackled issues concerning accessibility, automated payment, and bike and station distribution across cities.

We are now witnessing a major step forward through which dockless and electric bicycles feature as solutions to a more balanced distribution, more responsible parking and more equitable use of the public space. These features have contributed to the success of the fourth-generation BSS; from the few small schemes available in 2015, users can now benefit from city-scale systems with more than 17 million bikes across the globe [23]. In fact, one may even argue that BSS have become a victim of their own success: communities and owning organisations were not prepared for such a rapid spread. From the oversupply of bike-sharing systems in China that led to vast bicycle graveyards, to frequent attacks on the cyber-security of the systems and users' privacy breaches, fourth generation BSS are facing various new problems and threats.

In this paper, inspired by Stefania Gnesi's work on bike-sharing systems [2,3] (which is just one of her extensive contributions to formal methods in software engineering), we propose to model a BSS using tools and techniques that are specific to our field of work. We develop a formal specification of a BSS using an actor-network framework based on hybrid logic that we have recently presented in [14], and show how the logics advanced therein can be used in conjunction with off-the-shelf formal-specification tools and theorem provers in order to reason about the design of a BSS. To that end, we rely on H [7,10,11], a tool that extends the Heterogeneous Tool Set (HETS) [24] with support for hybridized logics based on theoretical developments presented in [12]. Through this, we hope to demonstrate how the development and analysis of such models can contribute towards the implementation of a viable BSS transport network. The analysis process could be part of the feasibility studies and project design processes that precede the implementation of a BSS, or part of the monitoring and evaluation that needs to be conducted throughout its operation

The BSS *Model Under Consideration.* The case study that we consider in this paper is simple. We focus on a fourth generation bike-sharing system operating in a city that is divided into several geographic regions (e.g., by geo-fencing). The regions of the city are connected through infrastructure elements such as roads, pathways, and bridges. To borrow a bicycle, users must connect to the system and make a request from the region where they are located. Once they collect a bicycle, users must input the destination of their journey before travelling. If, at any time during their travel, the destination region becomes full, with no free parking spaces, the system automatically offers rewards at that region. Rewards are an alternative to the usual (external) redistribution of bicycles across the city; they could be free rides or credit, and are meant to encourage nearby users to borrow bicycles from that region in order to make room for incoming bicycles. Once users reach their destination, they must secure their bicycles to physical docks or in designated parking spaces in order to end their journeys.

The Specification and Verification Process. In the following sections, we gradually formalize the BSS presented above using notions of actor-network theory and hybrid logic. Concepts and background information about the logics used are introduced on the fly as we progress towards the full specification of the system. In Sect. 2, we provide an informal overview of the main concepts involved in actor networks, which we illustrate with the BSS. This is continued with the presentation of the two hybrid-logic formalisms that we use in the paper, LNC (in Sect. 3) and LAN (in Sect. 4). Then, in Sect. 5, we discuss the hybrid-logic specification of the BSS. Lastly, in Sect. 6, we analyse the design and show that any implementation of the BSS has the following properties:

- If a region has a free dock, then no rewards are offered at that region.
- If a reward is offered at a region, then a user is expected to arrive there.

Whilst the first property is desired to hold, the second indicates a vulnerability because it discloses private information about the movement of users. We show how to address this through small changes in the design.

2   Actor Networks

Actor Networks (ANts) are a framework for modelling cyber-physical-system protocols originally proposed in [25] in the context of physical security. They are based on Latour's Actor-Network Theory [19] in recognition of the fact that such protocols involve a number of entities (called actors, which in concrete situations may correspond to people, devices, locations, etc.) that have shared agency, and for which interaction, rather than computation, is the major concern. Beyond that, ANts make location a primary concern, which is essential for physical security as well as other protocols. This brings ANts in line with spatial logics and frameworks that deal with the physical distribution of systems [1,6]; in contrast with those studies, which offer extensive support for topological properties, in ANts we only record the locality of actors in relation to other actors.

The Structure of Actor Networks. There are three major steps to follow when modelling a cyber-physical protocol using ANts. The first one requires the identification of the structural aspects of an actor network:

- The relevant *sorts* (or *kinds*) of actors.
  For the BSS case study that we consider in this paper, we distinguish the human *users* of the system, the *bicycles* that they can use to travel, the *docks* where the bicycles can be locked, as well as the various *regions* where docks are available for users to borrow or return bicycles.
- The means through which actors can store state attributes, knowledge or data, which for simplicity we capture through *propositional symbols*.
  For instance, in our running example, we use a propositional symbol (which may be regarded as a Boolean flag) specific to regions to indicate whether users are *offered rewards* (free rides) for borrowing bicycles at a given region.
- *Channel types*, which account for the ability of actors to connect to other actors. Every channel type has a source and a target, both of which are (actor) sorts, and can capture transfer of knowledge, intent, or specific actions.

For the BSS, we consider channels of type: *ask* through which users (the source of the channel) may request to borrow a bicycle at particular regions (the target of the channel); and *path* between regions (i.e. with the same source and target) to indicate the fact that users can travel directly between two given regions (if they choose to do so) – in other words, we use *path* to capture the physical topology of the BSS network.

Interactions in Actor Networks. In order to model cyber-physical-system protocols, we also need to consider the *network configurations* in which an ANt may find itself. Every such configuration gives a detailed account of:

- The exact channels that are available between every two actors – that is, the actor interconnectivity in a particular configuration.
- How each actor is *located* in relation to other actors. For instance, this can capture the fact that, at a given moment in the 'execution' of the BSS, a bicycle is locked *in* a specific dock *in* a region; or that a user is travelling *on* a specific bicycle, and that both the user and the bicycle are *in* a region.
- For every actor, the propositional symbols that are true for that actor.

Network configurations can change as a result of interactions taking place. Through an *interaction*, we identify specific conditions that should be met for a reconfiguration to occur, and we describe the effects of that reconfiguration. For the BSS, we consider four kinds of interactions, which correspond to:

- *borrowing/taking* a bicycle from a dock (in a region);
- *travelling* (on a bicycle) between two regions connected by a path;
- *returning* a bicycle (to a dock) once the destination is reached; and
- *offering rewards* (which is done automatically by the system) at full regions.

As an example of the conditions associated with interactions, we assume that a user can borrow a bicycle only if both the user and the bicycle are in the same region; moreover, the user must have requested to travel from that region, and the bicycle should be available in a dock in that region, where it is locked.

Specification for Actor Networks. Building on the above ingredients, the third major step in the development of an ANT-based design consists in describing the structure and the dynamics of the system by means of axioms written in a hybrid-logic language that is suitable for actor networks.

Through such axioms, we specify which configurations are well defined: for example, users can return bicycles at a region only if they are physically present at that region, on their bicycles, and if there are free docks available. Moreover, we also specify how networks evolve in time (as a result of reconfigurations) and the way their evolution is related to the interactions between actors.

We formalize and describe all these steps in detail, and give concrete examples of actors, channels, configurations, interactions, etc., in the following sections.

Logical Support for Actor Networks. The mathematical structures that support the development and analysis of ANts are provided by a kind of hybrid logic (which we have recently proposed in [14]) whose models are hierarchical Kripke structures with two layers:

1. a *base layer*, specific to the states/configurations of a network; in this case, the possible worlds correspond to the actors of the network, which are the same for all configurations, while the accessibility relations capture their locality and connectivity, which may vary from one configuration to another;
2. an *upper layer*, specific to the dynamics of a network; in this case, the possible worlds correspond to network configurations (i.e., base-layer structures), and the accessibility relations capture the transitions that are possible between configurations (i.e., discrete reconfigurations of the network).

There are several defining features of actor networks that distinguish them from ordinary two-layered Kripke structures:

- Firstly, as mentioned above, all configurations of a given network share the same underlying set of actors; this means that the cyber-physical systems modelled using actor networks are closed. However, structures can be of arbitrary size, even infinite.
- Secondly, the base-layer accessibility relation that corresponds to the locality of actors is necessarily functional and acyclic; this means that, for every configuration, the locality of actors in relation to one another is given by a forest (typically of finite depth) whose nodes are the actors of the network.
- Thirdly, every network reconfiguration is determined by a specific *interaction* between the actors at the source of that reconfiguration, where by *interaction* we mean a pre-defined set of locality and connectivity constraints.

The logic of actor networks, hereafter denoted LAN, can be obtained by way of a double constrained-hybridization process, along the lines of the original construction presented in [14]. In a nutshell, a *hybridization* of a logic, regarded as a base logic, consists in an exogenous enrichment of that logic (in the sense of [22]) with features that are characteristic of hybrid logic (see [4,5]); this is done both at the syntactic level – by introducing nominals, modalities, and hybrid-logic operators – and at the semantic level, through Kripke structures whose possible worlds are labelled with models of the base logic.

In many cases, this process is *constrained*, in the sense that the Kripke structures of the resulting hybridized logic are subject to additional semantic constraints. For instance, the base-logic models that label the possible worlds of a Kripke structure may share certain information (through what are usually referred to as *rigidity constraints*); or some of the accessibility relations may be required to be reflexive, preorders or, moreover, equivalences, as in the T, S4, and S5 variants, respectively, of hybrid propositional logic.

As this short introduction to hybridization suggests, the process is applicable to a broad spectrum of logics, and its result is not a single, definite logical system, but a class of logical systems, where variations arise from tuning hybridization parameters such as the precise hybrid features added to the base logic, or the semantic constraints imposed on Kripke structures. This idea is explored in [9, 21], where hybridization is formalized in the context of Goguen and Burstall's theory of institutions [17].[1] Actor-network logic(s) can be developed much in the same way: the main parameter is the base logical system, which by hybridization gives rise to a formalism for reasoning about the base layer of actor networks; and by hybridizing that logic further, we obtain an even richer logical system that provides support for both levels of actor networks.

Despite the logic-independent nature of the construction, for the purpose of this contribution, and to make the paper more accessible to readers who may not be familiar with hybridization or institution theory, we choose to focus on a concrete logical system. We build this logic in two steps: first, we define a logic of network configurations, called LNC, as a hybridization of propositional logic; then, we introduce the logic of actor networks (LAN) as a hybridization of LNC.

A short comparison with the developments reported in [14] is in order. Our previous work also deals with a two-stage constrained hybridization aimed at developing logics for actor networks, but there are subtle and important differences to consider. One is that the base logical system corresponds in that case to the three-valued Łukasiewicz logic. Another is that the presentation relies heavily on the graph-theoretic notion of an *actor-network schema*, which determines an upper bound for the size of the models considered – in [14], all models are finite. Last but not least, the use of quantifiers over state variables is no longer restricted to the base layer of the logic of actor networks; instead, we can combine such quantifiers freely with any of the other sentence-building operators.

3   Network Configurations

In what follows, we define the main building blocks of LNC: its *signatures* (structured collections of symbols), *models* (providing interpretations for the symbols declared in signatures), *sentences* (built from symbols declared in signatures), and *satisfaction relations* (establishing whether a property, formalized as a sentence, holds at a given model). All are interspersed with relevant fragments of the BSS specification that we are progressively building.

Definition 1. *An* LNC-*signature is a tuple* $\Sigma = \langle S, P, N, K \rangle$, *where:*

- *S is a set whose elements we call* sorts *or* kinds *of actors,*
- *$P = \{P_s\}_{s \in S}$ is an S-indexed family of sets of* propositional symbols,
- *$N = \{N_s\}_{s \in S}$ is an S-indexed family of sets of* actor names, *and*
- *$K = \{K_{s \to t}\}_{s,t \in S}$ is an $S \times S$-indexed family of sets of* channel types.

BSS Sorts. In line with the informal description of the actor-network model[2] of the BSS from Sect. 2, the LNC-signature that we consider here contains the following four sorts: User, Bike, Dock, and Region.

---

[1] The papers [15] and [13] can be regarded as precursors of [21]; both deal with enriching abstract logics – one with temporal features, and the other with modal features.

[2] Not to be confused with the formal concepts of *model* from Definitions 2 and 6.

BSS Propositional Symbols. We also declare four propositional symbols:

travelling: User[3] to indicate if a user is travelling or not towards some region;
freeDock: Dock to indicate that there is no bicycle locked in a particular dock;
fullRegion: Region to indicate that all docks in a region have bicycles in place;
rewardOffered: Region to capture the fact that users are offered free rides when
   borrowing bicycles from docks located in a particular region.

BSS Actor Names. At this stage, we use no actor names. However, actor names may be introduced on the fly when dealing with quantified sentences – and in that case they are sourced from variables. In LNC, a *state variable* (or *variable*, for short) for a signature $\Sigma = \langle S, P, N, K \rangle$ is a triple (x, s, N_s), usually denoted simply by $x: s$, where x is the name of the variable, and s is its sort.[4] Variables determine extensions of signatures as follows: for every S-sorted set X of Σ-variables, $\Sigma[X] = \langle S, P, N \cup X, K \rangle$ is an LNC-signature that includes Σ.

BSS Channel Types. We consider five channel types:

ask: User $\rightarrow$ Region to signal a user's intent to borrow a bicycle at a given region;
choose: User $\rightarrow$ Bike to capture the selection of a bicycle (to borrow) by a user;
choose: User $\rightarrow$ Dock for the selection of a dock (to return a bicycle) by a user;
travelTo: User $\rightarrow$ Region to specify the region towards which a user is travelling;
path: Region $\rightarrow$ Region to indicate that two regions are connected by a path.

The models of an LNC-signature Σ are Kripke structures that interpret the actor names in Σ as possible worlds, and the channel types as relations on worlds.

Definition 2. *Let $\Sigma = \langle S, P, N, K \rangle$ be an LNC-signature. A* model, *or* Kripke structure, *of Σ is a triple $\langle A, \lhd, M \rangle$, where $\langle A, \lhd \rangle$ is a* Kripke frame *defining, for every two sorts $s, t \in S$, actor name $n \in N_s$, and channel type $\kappa \in K_{s \rightarrow t}$:*

- *a set A_s of possible worlds, or* actors, *of sort s,*
- *an element $A_{s,n}$ of A_s, i.e., an actor of sort s corresponding to the name n,*
- *an* accessibility relation, *or* channel, *$A_{s \rightarrow t, \kappa}$ between the sets A_s and A_t,*
- *a functional and acyclic relation $\lhd$ on $\biguplus \{A_s \mid s \in S\}$ that captures the locality of actors, and for which $a \lhd a'$ reads as a is in/on/at a',*

and M is a family of sets $M_{s,a} \subseteq P_s$ (the propositions of sort s that hold at a) indexed by sorts $s \in S$ and actors $a \in A_s$. When there is no risk of confusion, we may drop the sorts from the notations of $A_{s,n}$, $A_{s \rightarrow t, \kappa}$, and $M_{s,a}$.

---

[3] We use this colon notation to separate a propositional symbol from its sort, and also to separate a channel type from the two sorts on which it is defined.

[4] We annotate the variables of sort s with the set of actor names of sort s in order to ensure that there are no accidental clashes between variables and actors names.

Note the properties of the second component of an LNC-model: $\lhd$ is a special kind of accessibility relation that is used here to capture the placement (location) hierarchy on actors. Equivalently, it could be presented as a (rooted) forest structure over the set of all actors. We denote its inverse by $\rhd$.

A typical example of a Kripke structure for the LNC-signature of the BSS can be seen in Fig. 1. We use graphical representations of LNC-models to make the correspondence between these semantic structures and the actual configurations of the BSS easier to perceive. The model is finite; it consists of six actors, depicted using circles, which are distributed and related as follows:

- $A_{\mathsf{User}} = \{\mathsf{U}\}$, $A_{\mathsf{Bike}} = \{\mathsf{B}\}$, $A_{\mathsf{Dock}} = \{\mathsf{D1}, \mathsf{D2}\}$, and $A_{\mathsf{Region}} = \{\mathsf{R1}, \mathsf{R2}\}$;
- the channels are represented using labelled arrows, and they are all singletons in this case; for instance, $A_{\mathsf{ask}} = \{(\mathsf{U}, \mathsf{R1})\}$ and $A_{\mathsf{path}} = \{(\mathsf{R1}, \mathsf{R2})\}$;
- the relation $\lhd$ is depicted through the nesting of nodes; we have, for example, $\mathsf{U} \lhd \mathsf{R1}$ to capture the fact that U is currently in the region $\mathsf{R1}$, $\mathsf{D1} \lhd \mathsf{R1}$ to capture the fact that $\mathsf{D1}$ is a dock in that region, and $\mathsf{B} \lhd \mathsf{D1}$ to capture the fact that the bicycle B is currently locked in $\mathsf{D1}$;
- the propositions that hold at given actors are indicated in a more coded way, by symbolic decorations placed on their corresponding circles; we use the symbols $>$ for travelling, $-$ for freeDock, $+$ for fullRegion, and $\star$ for rewardOffered; for instance, $M_{\mathsf{R1}} = \{\mathsf{rewardOffered}\}$, and $M_{\mathsf{D2}} = \{\mathsf{freeDock}\}$.

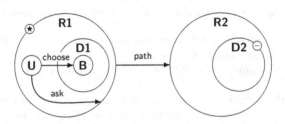

Fig. 1. An LNC-model for the BSS

The fact that the actors of a network are sorted has important consequences on the way we define the sentences of the logic of network configurations.

Definition 3. *Consider an* LNC-*signature* $\Sigma = \langle S, P, N, K \rangle$ *and let s be a sort in S. The sentences of sort s over Σ are defined by the following grammar:*

$$\varphi ::= p \mid n \mid \neg\varphi \mid \varphi \to \varphi \mid @_{n'}\,\varphi' \mid \langle\kappa\rangle\,\varphi^* \mid \langle\pi\rangle\,\varphi^\dagger \mid \exists X \cdot \varphi^\S$$

where $p \in P_s$ and $n \in N_s$ are propositional symbols and actor names of sort s, $n' \in N_{s'}$ is an actor name (of any sort s'), φ' is a Σ-sentence of sort s', $\kappa \in K_{s \to s^*}$ is a channel type with source sort s and target sort s^*, φ^* is a Σ-sentence of sort s^*, π is a distinguished and new parent modality, $\varphi^\dagger$ is a Σ-sentence (of any sort), X is a finite set of Σ-variables, and $\varphi^\S$ is a $\Sigma[X]$-sentence of sort s.

Other propositional connectives such as conjunction ($\wedge$), disjunction ($\vee$), and equivalence ($\leftrightarrow$) can be defined as usual. The dual modal operators $[\kappa]$, where κ is a channel type, and $[\pi]$ for the parent modality, as well as the universal quantifier over state variables can also be defined in the conventional way:

$$[\kappa]\,\varphi = \neg\,\langle\kappa\rangle\,\neg\,\varphi \qquad [\pi]\,\varphi = \neg\,\langle\pi\rangle\,\neg\,\varphi \qquad \forall x\cdot\varphi = \neg\,\exists x\cdot\neg\,\varphi$$

The satisfaction relation between LNC-models and sentences is defined, as for many logical systems, by induction on the structure of sentences, and is parameterized by actors (i.e., possible worlds of the Kripke structures considered).

Definition 4. *Let $\langle A, \lhd, M\rangle$ be a Σ-model and a an actor of sort s in A. Then:*

- $\langle A, \lhd, M\rangle \vDash^a p$ *if $p \in M_a$, when p is a propositional symbol of sort s;*
- $\langle A, \lhd, M\rangle \vDash^a n$ *if $a = A_n$, when n is an actor name of sort s;*
- $\langle A, \lhd, M\rangle \vDash^a \neg\,\varphi$ *if $\langle A, \lhd, M\rangle \nvDash^a \varphi$;*
- $\langle A, \lhd, M\rangle \vDash^a \varphi_h \rightarrow \varphi_c$ *if $\langle A, \lhd, M\rangle \vDash^a \varphi_h$ implies $\langle A, \lhd, M\rangle \vDash^a \varphi_c$;*
- $\langle A, \lhd, M\rangle \vDash^a @_{n'}\,\varphi'$ *if $\langle A, \lhd, M\rangle \vDash^{a'} \varphi'$, where $a' = A_{n'}$;*
- $\langle A, \lhd, M\rangle \vDash^a \langle\kappa\rangle\,\varphi^*$ *if there exists $(a, a^*) \in A_\kappa$ such that $\langle A, \lhd, M\rangle \vDash^{a^*} \varphi^*$;*
- $\langle A, \lhd, M\rangle \vDash^a \langle\pi\rangle\,\varphi^\dagger$ *if there exists $a^\dagger \rhd a$ such that $\langle A, \lhd, M\rangle \vDash^{a^\dagger} \varphi^\dagger$; this implicitly means that the actor $a^\dagger$ is of the same sort as $\varphi^\dagger$;*
- $\langle A, \lhd, M\rangle \vDash^a \exists X\cdot\varphi^\S$ *if there is a $\Sigma[X]$-expansion $\langle A^\S, \lhd, M\rangle$ of $\langle A, \lhd, M\rangle$ such that $\langle A^\S, \lhd, M\rangle \vDash^a \varphi^\S$, where by expansion of $\langle A, \lhd, M\rangle$ we mean a $\Sigma[X]$-model that interprets all symbols in Σ in the same way as $\langle A, \lhd, M\rangle$.*

Notice that the satisfaction relation is also sorted: we evaluate LNC-sentences φ of sort s only at actors whose sort is s. Given such a sentence φ of sort s, we write $\langle A, \lhd, M\rangle \vDash \varphi$ when $\langle A, \lhd, M\rangle \vDash^a \varphi$ for all actors $a \in A_s$.

As an example, consider the following sentence, which is satisfied by the BSS model in Fig. 1. Concerning the parsing of sentences, we rely on the usual precedence rules (e.g. unary sentence-building operators have a higher precedence than binary operators) and on parentheses to make sure no ambiguities arise.

$$\exists\{u\colon \mathsf{User}; b\colon \mathsf{Bike}; d\colon \mathsf{Dock}; r\colon \mathsf{Region}\}\cdot$$
$$@_u\,(\underbrace{\langle\pi\rangle\,(r \wedge \mathsf{rewardOffered})}_{(1)}) \wedge \underbrace{\langle\mathsf{ask}\rangle\,r}_{(2)} \wedge \underbrace{\langle\mathsf{choose}\rangle\,(b \wedge \langle\pi\rangle\,(d \wedge \langle\pi\rangle\,r))}_{(3)})$$

Intuitively, this sentence captures situations where a user (indicated by the operator $@_u$) is in a region r (in the sense that u and r are connected through the parent modality) where free rides are offered (as per part *1* of the sentence); the user u has requested to travel from that region (part *2* of the sentence), and has selected a bicycle available there (part *3* of the sentence).

4   Network Dynamics

The signatures, models, and sentences of the logic of actor networks (LAN) are obtained through a hybridization of LNC. In this case, we add nominals that identify initial configurations of networks, and *interactions* that act as modalities and are interpreted as transition relations between configurations.

By *interaction* for an LNC-signature Σ we mean a pair consisting of a *name* ι and an existentially quantified sentence $\exists X \cdot \varphi$ over Σ such that φ is quantifier-free. Intuitively, the sentence φ describes specific locality and connectivity relationships between the actors named in X (such as the fact that various regions of the BSS may be connected by paths). We usually denote interactions by $\iota \colon \exists X \cdot \varphi$.

Definition 5. *A LAN-signature is a tuple* $\Omega = \langle S, P, N, K, I, \Lambda \rangle$, *where:*

- $\langle S, P, N, K \rangle$ *is an* LNC-*signature,*
- *I is a set of* (names of) *initial configurations, and*
- *Λ is a set of* interactions *(with distinct names) for* $\langle S, P, N, K \rangle$.

In the context of the BSS, we extend the signature presented in Sect. 3 by adding a single name init for initial configurations, and four interactions. For each interaction, we also present a graphical representation (LNC-model) in Fig. 2.

Take: $\exists \{u \colon \mathsf{User}; b \colon \mathsf{Bike}; d \colon \mathsf{Dock}; r \colon \mathsf{Region}\} \cdot \varphi$
    where $\varphi = @_u (\langle \pi \rangle \, r \wedge \langle \mathsf{ask} \rangle \, r \wedge \langle \mathsf{choose} \rangle \, b) \wedge @_b \langle \pi \rangle \, (d \wedge \langle \pi \rangle \, r)$
    This means that users can begin their journeys at a region only if they have requested to travel from that region (through an ask channel) and there are bicycles available there that they could borrow (through a choose channel).

Travel: $\exists \{u \colon \mathsf{User}; b \colon \mathsf{Bike}; r_1, r_2 \colon \mathsf{Region}\} \cdot \varphi$
    where $\varphi = @_u (\mathsf{travelling} \wedge \langle \pi \rangle \, (b \wedge \langle \pi \rangle \, r_1)) \wedge @_{r_1} \langle \mathsf{path} \rangle \, r_2$
    That is, travellers can move only between regions that are connected by paths, and in order to do so, they must use bicycles.

Return: $\exists \{u \colon \mathsf{User}; b \colon \mathsf{Bike}; d \colon \mathsf{Dock}; r \colon \mathsf{Region}\} \cdot \varphi$
    where $\varphi = @_u (\langle \pi \rangle \, (b \wedge \langle \pi \rangle \, r) \wedge \langle \mathsf{travelTo} \rangle \, r \wedge \langle \mathsf{choose} \rangle \, (d \wedge \mathsf{freeDock} \wedge \langle \pi \rangle \, r))$
    This means that, in order to return a bicycle, a traveller should be in control of that bicycle and should have reached already the destination; moreover, there should be a free dock available at that region (to lock the bicycle).

Reward: $\exists \{u \colon \mathsf{User}; r \colon \mathsf{Region}\} \cdot @_u \langle \mathsf{travelTo} \rangle \, (r \wedge \mathsf{fullRegion})$
    That is, in order to pre-emptively free some of the docks in a region, that region should be full, and there should be a user travelling towards it.

Similarly to LNC, the models of a LAN-signature Ω are also Kripke structures, but the nominals are interpreted as configurations (i.e., LNC-models) and the interactions as transition relations between configurations.

Definition 6. *Consider a* LAN-*signature* $\Omega = \langle S, P, N, K, I, \Lambda \rangle$. *A* Kripke model $\langle D, C \rangle$ *of* Ω *consists of a* domain $|D|$, *i.e., a plain set of* worlds, *together with*

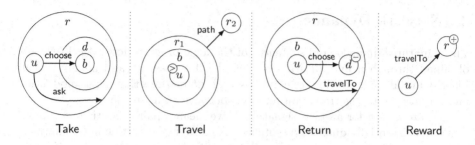

Fig. 2. Graphical representations of the four BSS interactions

– a possible world $D_i \in |D|$ for each configuration name $i \in I$,
– a transition relation $D_\iota \subseteq |D| \times |D|$ for each interaction name ι in Λ,

and a family of $\langle S, P, N, K \rangle$-models $C_w = \langle A_w, \lhd_w, M_w \rangle$, for $w \in |D|$, such that

– for all possible worlds $w, w' \in |D|$ and sorts $s \in S$ we have $(A_w)_s = (A_{w'})_s$;
– for every possible world $w \in |D|$ and interaction $\iota: \exists X \cdot \varphi$ in Λ, there exists
  a transition $(w, w') \in D_\iota$ if and only if $C_w \vDash \exists X \cdot \varphi$.

When there is no risk of confusion, we may also denote $(w, w') \in D_\iota$ by $w \xrightarrow{\iota} w'$.

Figure 3 depicts a model for the BSS that corresponds to the journey of a
user from one region (R1) to another (R2). This model has four possible worlds,
C0 − C3, of which C0 is the interpretation of init; and it has three transitions,
one for each of the following interactions: Take, Travel, and Return.

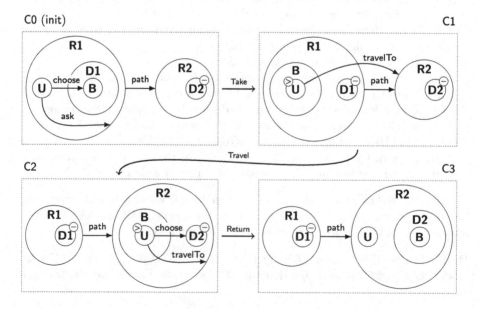

Fig. 3. A possible LAN-model for the BSS

In order to define the syntax of the logic of actor networks, we consider a different kind of extension of a signature: not only with state variables, but with network variables as well. In LAN, a *network variable* for a signature $\Omega = \langle S, P, N, K, I, \Lambda \rangle$ is a pair (y, I), where y is the name of the variable.[5] For any S-sorted set X of state variables for $\langle S, P, N, K \rangle$ and any set Y of network variables for Ω, we obtain the extended signature $\Omega[X; Y] = \langle S, P, N \cup X, K, I \cup Y, \Lambda \rangle$.

Definition 7. *The* LAN-*sentences over* $\Omega = \langle S, P, N, K, I, \Lambda \rangle$ *are given by:*

$$\psi ::= \varphi \mid i \mid \neg \psi \mid \psi \Rightarrow \psi \mid i : \psi \mid \langle\!\langle \iota \rangle\!\rangle \psi \mid \exists X; Y \cdot \psi'$$

where φ *is an* LNC-*sentence over* $\langle S, P, N, K \rangle$, $i \in I$ *is a configuration name,* ι *is an interaction name in* Λ, X *and* Y *are finite sets of state and network variables, respectively, and* ψ' *is a* LAN-*sentence over the extended signature* $\Omega[X; Y]$.

For quantified sentences, when the set Y *is empty, we also write* $\exists X \cdot \psi'$ *in place of* $\exists X; Y \cdot \psi'$. *Similarly, when* X *is empty, we write* $\exists Y \cdot \psi'$.

Notice that, similarly to LNC-sentences, LAN-sentences are built using hybrid-logic operators, but in this case we use a distinct double-symbol notation; moreover, the local-satisfaction operators (represented as @$_n$ in LNC) are denoted here by means of a colon. We extend the use of this notation to other Boolean connectives ($\mathbb{A}$, $\mathbb{V}$, $\Leftrightarrow$), to the dual modal operators ($[\![\_]\!]$), and to the universal quantifier ($\mathbb{V}$), which are defined as in Sect. 3.

Definition 8. *Let* $\langle D, C \rangle$ *be a* LAN-*model for a signature* $\Omega = \langle S, P, N, K, I, \Lambda \rangle$, *and* $w \in D$ *a possible worlds. The* local satisfaction *of* Ω-*sentences by* $\langle D, C \rangle$ *at* w *is defined by structural induction, as follows:*

- $\langle D, C \rangle \Vdash^w \varphi$ *if* $C_w \vDash \varphi$, *when* φ *is an* LNC-*sentence over* $\langle S, P, N, K \rangle$;
- $\langle D, C \rangle \Vdash^w i$ *if* $w = D_i$, *when* i *is a configuration name;*
- $\langle D, C \rangle \Vdash^w \neg \psi$ *if* $\langle D, C \rangle \nVdash^w \psi$;
- $\langle D, C \rangle \Vdash^w \psi_h \Rightarrow \psi_c$ *if* $\langle D, C \rangle \Vdash^w \psi_h$ *implies* $\langle D, C \rangle \Vdash^w \psi_c$;
- $\langle D, C \rangle \Vdash^w i : \psi$ *if* $\langle D, C \rangle \Vdash^{w'} \psi$, *where* $w' = D_i$;
- $\langle D, C \rangle \Vdash^w \langle\!\langle \iota \rangle\!\rangle \psi$ *if there exists a transition* $w \xrightarrow{\iota} w'$ *such that* $\langle D, C \rangle \Vdash^{w'} \psi$;
- $\langle D, C \rangle \Vdash^w \exists X; Y \cdot \psi'$ *if there exists a* $\Omega[X; Y]$-*expansion* $\langle D', C' \rangle$ *of* $\langle D, C \rangle$ *such that* $\langle D', C' \rangle \Vdash^w \psi'$, *where by expansion of* $\langle D, C \rangle$ *we mean a* $\Omega[X; Y]$-*model* $\langle D', C' \rangle$ *such that* (a) D' *has the same domain as* D *and gives the same interpretation as* D *for configuration names and interactions in* Ω, *and* (b) *for every world* $w \in |D'|$, C'_w *is an* $\langle S, P, N \cup X, K \rangle$-*expansion of* C_w.

We write $\langle D, C \rangle \Vdash \psi$ *when* $\langle D, C \rangle \Vdash^w \psi$ *for all possible worlds* $w \in |D|$.

The definition above justifies the use of different notations for the sentence-building operators of LAN. Formally, the relationship between the two kinds of operators is described in the list below, where $\langle D, C \rangle$ is an Ω-model with non-empty sets of actors for each sort, $w \in |D|$ is a possible world, φ, φ_h, φ_c, φ_1, φ_2 are $\langle S, P, N, K \rangle$-sentences, and φ' is an $\langle S, P, N \cup X, K \rangle$-sentence.

---

[5] Similarly to the logic LNC, we annotate LAN-variables with the set of configuration names in order to avoid accidental name clashes when building the extension.

- $\langle D, C \rangle \Vdash^w \neg \varphi$ only if $\langle D, C \rangle \Vdash^w \neg \varphi$
- $\langle D, C \rangle \Vdash^w \varphi_h \rightarrow \varphi_c$ only if $\langle D, C \rangle \Vdash^w \varphi_h \Rightarrow \varphi_c$
- $\langle D, C \rangle \Vdash^w \varphi_1 \wedge \varphi_2$ if and only if $\langle D, C \rangle \Vdash^w \varphi_1 \barwedge \varphi_2$
- $\langle D, C \rangle \Vdash^w \varphi_1 \vee \varphi_2$ if $\langle D, C \rangle \Vdash^w \varphi_1 \veebar \varphi_2$
- $\langle D, C \rangle \Vdash^w \varphi_1 \leftrightarrow \varphi_2$ only if $\langle D, C \rangle \Vdash^w \varphi_1 \Leftrightarrow \varphi_2$
- $\langle D, C \rangle \Vdash^w \exists X \cdot \varphi'$ if $\langle D, C \rangle \Vdash^w \overline{\exists} X \cdot \varphi'$
- $\langle D, C \rangle \Vdash^w \forall X \cdot \varphi'$ if and only if $\langle D, C \rangle \Vdash^w \overline{\forall} X \cdot \varphi'$

Most of the above properties are one-way implications ('if', or 'only if'), because the global satisfaction of LNC-sentences relies on an implicit universal quantification (over actors). Equivalences are guaranteed to hold only for those sentence-building operators that commute with universal quantifiers.

5   On the Design of a Bike-Sharing System

The two logical systems presented in this paper, LNC and LAN, enable us to give a detailed formal account of the way in which bike-sharing systems operate, hence opening the possibility for formal verification (using suitable proof techniques) at a later stage of development. To that end, in this section we discuss a formal specification of the BSS. By *formal specification* we mean a pair $\langle \Omega, \Gamma \rangle$, where Ω is a LAN-signature and Γ is a finite set of LAN-sentences over Ω. The actual bike-sharing networks defined by $\langle \Omega, \Gamma \rangle$ correspond to the Ω-models that satisfy all sentences in Γ. A specification of this kind is commonly known as a flat, or unstructured, specification. There are several ways to build structured specifications from these; for that purpose, various modularization techniques have been explored in the literature, especially around the notion of institution (see, e.g., the monograph [27]) – and they can be used in conjunction with LNC and LAN without special intervention. However, for the purpose of this work, and for simplicity, we describe the specification as a plain set of sentences over the LAN-signature for the BSS discussed in Sect. 4.

We consider three categories of sentences: *(a)* sentences that ensure that the base-layer Kripke structures (LNC-models) are actual, well-defined configurations of the BSS; *(b)* sentences that define the potential initial configurations of the BSS; *(c)* sentences that describe the effects that interactions have on the structure and properties of the configurations; and *(d)* sentences that deal with the frame problem[6] by specifying non-effects of the interactions in terms of attributes of the configurations that are preserved or reflected along transitions. For each category, we discuss below a few important examples. The full specification of the BSS is available in [29] through the repository engine Ontohub [8].

In order to make the following LNC and LAN-sentences easier to read, we make explicit all quantifiers over state variables; cf. Definition 8, where the satisfaction of a LNC-sentence at a world is implicitly quantified over actors of suitable sort.

---

[6] This problem is notorious for axiomatizing the way in which states change when an event occurs; various solutions have been proposed in connection to formalisms such as the situation calculus, event calculus, or default logic, among others; see, e.g. [28].

Well-Defined Configurations. The sentences in this category concern the locality and connectivity of the actors, as well as the way in which these structural aspects are related to propositional attributes such as travelling and rewardOffered.

Take, for instance, the following two LNC-sentences, which ensure that at most one traveller can use a bicycle at a given time (1), and that, in any configuration, at most one bicycle can be locked in one of the docks (2).

$$\forall\{u_1, u_2 \colon \mathsf{User}; b \colon \mathsf{Bike}\} \cdot @_{u_1} \langle \pi \rangle\, b \wedge @_{u_2} \langle \pi \rangle\, b \to @_{u_1}\, u_2 \tag{1}$$

$$\forall\{b_1, b_2 \colon \mathsf{Bike}; d \colon \mathsf{Dock}\} \cdot @_{b_1} \langle \pi \rangle\, d \wedge @_{b_2} \langle \pi \rangle\, d \to @_{b_1}\, b_2 \tag{2}$$

In regard to connectivity, there is a special relationship between the channels of type ask: User $\to$ Region and those of type choose: User $\to$ Bike. The aim is to ensure that whenever a user requests to travel from a region (through a channel of type ask), if there is a bicycle available in that region (i.e., a bicycle locked in a dock, and not claimed by another traveller), then the user can obtain a bicycle (perhaps even that bicycle) through a choose channel.

We specify this requirement in two steps: first, in (3) and (4) we provide preconditions for the existence of ask and choose channels; then, in (5) we describe choose as an injective partial mapping from users to bicycles (all in the same region), and in (6) we ensure that the interpretation of choose is maximal.

$$\forall\{u \colon \mathsf{User}; r \colon \mathsf{Region}\} \cdot @_u\, (\langle \mathsf{ask} \rangle\, r \to \langle \pi \rangle\, r) \tag{3}$$

$$\forall\{u \colon \mathsf{User}; b \colon \mathsf{Bike}\} \cdot @_u\, (\langle \mathsf{choose} \rangle\, b$$
$$\to \exists\{d \colon \mathsf{Dock}; r \colon \mathsf{Region}\} \cdot (\langle \mathsf{ask} \rangle\, r \wedge @_b \langle \pi \rangle\, (d \wedge \langle \pi \rangle\, r))) \tag{4}$$

$$\forall\{u_1, u_2 \colon \mathsf{User}; b_1, b_2 \colon \mathsf{Bike}\} \cdot$$
$$@_{u_1} \langle \mathsf{choose} \rangle\, b_1 \wedge @_{u_2} \langle \mathsf{choose} \rangle\, b_2 \to (@_{u_1}\, u_2 \leftrightarrow @_{b_1}\, b_2) \tag{5}$$

$$\forall\{u \colon \mathsf{User}; b \colon \mathsf{Bike}; d \colon \mathsf{Dock}; r \colon \mathsf{Region}\} \cdot$$
$$(@_u \langle \mathsf{ask} \rangle\, r \to \exists\{b_1 \colon \mathsf{Bike}\} \cdot @_u \langle \mathsf{choose} \rangle\, b_1)$$
$$\vee\, (@_b \langle \pi \rangle\, (d \wedge \langle \pi \rangle\, r) \to \exists\{u_1 \colon \mathsf{User}\} \cdot @_{u_1} \langle \mathsf{choose} \rangle\, b) \tag{6}$$

There is a similar relationship between the channels of type travelTo: User $\to$ Region and the channels of type choose: User $\to$ Dock. For space considerations, and because the entire specification is available in [29], we do not present it explicitly here.

For propositional attributes, we consider the following characterizations:

$$\forall\{u \colon \mathsf{User}\} \cdot @_u\, \mathsf{travelling} \leftrightarrow \exists r \colon \mathsf{Region} \cdot @_u \langle \mathsf{travelTo} \rangle\, r \tag{7}$$

$$\forall\{d \colon \mathsf{Dock}\} \cdot @_d\, \mathsf{freeDock} \leftrightarrow \neg\, \exists b \colon \mathsf{Bike} \cdot @_b \langle \pi \rangle\, d \tag{8}$$

$$\forall\{r \colon \mathsf{Region}\} \cdot @_r\, \mathsf{fullRegion} \leftrightarrow \forall d \colon \mathsf{Dock} \cdot @_d\, (\langle \pi \rangle\, r \to \neg\, \mathsf{freeDock}) \tag{9}$$

Initiality Constraints. The only restriction that we impose on the interpretation of init is that no user is travelling at that configuration, and no reward is offered.

$$\text{init} : (\neg \exists\{u\colon \mathsf{User}\} \cdot @_u \text{ travelling} \wedge \neg \exists\{r\colon \mathsf{Region}\} \cdot @_r \text{ rewardOffered}) \tag{10}$$

Interaction Effects. To axiomatize the effects of interactions, we make use of LAN-sentences of the form $\psi_h \Rightarrow \langle\!\langle \iota \rangle\!\rangle \, \psi_c$ or $\psi_h \Rightarrow [\![\iota]\!] \, \psi_c$, where ι is an interaction, ψ_h is a precondition for ι, and ψ_c is postcondition for ι – which holds either at one of the configurations reached through a ι-transition, or at all such configurations, depending on whether we use the *possibility* or the *necessity* operator.[7]

$$\forall\{u\colon \mathsf{User}; b\colon \mathsf{Bike}; d\colon \mathsf{Dock}; r\colon \mathsf{Region}\} \cdot$$
$$@_u (\langle\pi\rangle\, r \wedge \langle\mathsf{ask}\rangle\, r \wedge \langle\mathsf{choose}\rangle\, b) \wedge @_b \langle\pi\rangle\, (d \wedge \langle\pi\rangle\, r)$$
$$\Rightarrow [\![\mathsf{Take}]\!] \, @_u (\langle\pi\rangle\, (b \wedge \langle\pi\rangle\, r) \wedge \exists\{r_1\colon \mathsf{Region}\} \cdot \langle\mathsf{travelTo}\rangle\, r_1) \tag{11}$$
$$\forall\{u\colon \mathsf{User}; b\colon \mathsf{Bike}; r_1, r_2\colon \mathsf{Region}\} \cdot$$
$$@_u (\text{travelling} \wedge \langle\pi\rangle\, (b \wedge \langle\pi\rangle\, r_1)) \wedge @_{r_1} \langle\mathsf{path}\rangle\, r_2$$
$$\Rightarrow \langle\!\langle \mathsf{Travel} \rangle\!\rangle \, @_u \langle\pi\rangle\, (b \wedge \langle\pi\rangle\, r_2) \tag{12}$$
$$\forall\{u\colon \mathsf{User}; b\colon \mathsf{Bike}; d\colon \mathsf{Dock}; r\colon \mathsf{Region}\} \cdot$$
$$@_u (\langle\pi\rangle\, (b \wedge \langle\pi\rangle\, r) \wedge \langle\mathsf{travelTo}\rangle\, r \wedge \langle\mathsf{choose}\rangle\, (d \wedge \mathsf{freeDock} \wedge \langle\pi\rangle\, r))$$
$$\Rightarrow [\![\mathsf{Return}]\!] \, (@_b \langle\pi\rangle\, (d \wedge \langle\pi\rangle\, r) \wedge @_u (\langle\pi\rangle\, r \wedge \neg \text{ travelling})) \tag{13}$$
$$\forall\{r\colon \mathsf{Region}\} \cdot \exists\{u\colon \mathsf{User}\} \cdot @_u \langle\mathsf{travelTo}\rangle\, (r \wedge \mathsf{fullRegion})$$
$$\Rightarrow [\![\mathsf{Reward}]\!] \, @_r \text{ rewardOffered} \tag{14}$$

Consider, for instance, the sentence (12) describing the effects of the interaction Travel. By the definition of Travel (on page 10), we know that the interaction can lead to a change of any configuration where a traveller u, currently in a region r_1, can follow a path in order to reach another region, r_2. The axiomatization of Travel ensures that there exists indeed a reconfiguration of the system (as per the semantics in LAN of the *possibility* operator) such that u reaches the region r_2.

The Frame Problem. The sentences (11)–(14) above capture successfully the direct effects that the interactions may have, but convey no information about their non-effects. For example, Travel does not affect the relative locality of bicycles with respect to the docks. We specify this property in (15) and (16).

$$\forall\{b\colon \mathsf{Bike}; d\colon \mathsf{Dock}\} \cdot @_b \langle\pi\rangle\, d \Rightarrow [\![\mathsf{Travel}]\!] \, @_b \langle\pi\rangle\, d \tag{15}$$
$$\forall\{b\colon \mathsf{Bike}; d\colon \mathsf{Dock}\} \cdot \langle\!\langle \mathsf{Travel} \rangle\!\rangle \, @_b \langle\pi\rangle\, d \Rightarrow @_b \langle\pi\rangle\, d \tag{16}$$

---

[7] For (11), note that $\langle\mathsf{ask}\rangle\, r$ entails $\langle\pi\rangle\, r$; moreover, under the hypothesis $@_u \langle\mathsf{choose}\rangle\, b$, and by (3), (4) and the functionality of π, $@_u \langle\mathsf{ask}\rangle\, r$ and $\exists\{d\colon \mathsf{Dock}\} \cdot @_b \langle\pi\rangle\, (d \wedge \langle\pi\rangle\, r)$ are semantically equivalent. Still, to give a better picture of the configurations affected by Take (or by any of the other interactions), we write the precondition in full.

A considerable number of other trivial sentences of this kind need to be added to the BSS specification; see [29]. In addition, some of the sentences describing non-effects are necessarily conditional. For instance, the reward offered at a region is preserved by Take if no dock in that region can be freed by the interaction.

$$\mathbb{W}\{r\colon \mathsf{Region}\} \cdot @_r \, \mathsf{rewardOffered}$$
$$\land \neg \exists\{u\colon \mathsf{User}; b\colon \mathsf{Bike}; d\colon \mathsf{Dock}\} \cdot @_u \, \langle \mathsf{choose} \rangle \, (b \land \langle \pi \rangle \, (d \land \langle \pi \rangle \, r))$$
$$\Rightarrow \, [\![\mathsf{Take}]\!] \, @_r \, \mathsf{rewardOffered} \qquad (17)$$

A different situation arises when considering the 'reflection' of the rewardOffered properties. If, say, a reward is offered at a region r after a Reward-transition, then either the reward is also offered (at the same region r) at the source configuration of the transition (in which case, the property is preserved by the interaction), or it is generated by the transition as an effect of Reward.

$$\mathbb{W}\{r\colon \mathsf{Region}\} \cdot \langle\!| \mathsf{Reward} |\!\rangle \, @_r \, \mathsf{rewardOffered}$$
$$\Rightarrow \, @_r \, \mathsf{rewardOffered} \lor \exists\{u\colon \mathsf{User}\} \cdot @_u \, \langle \mathsf{travelTo} \rangle \, (r \land \mathsf{fullRegion}) \qquad (18)$$

It is important to highlight the fact that, under the current specification, Reward is the only interaction through which rewards can be offered at given regions. That is, for any interaction ι different from Reward, we have:

$$\mathbb{W}\{r\colon \mathsf{Region}\} \cdot \langle\!| \iota |\!\rangle \, @_r \, \mathsf{rewardOffered} \Rightarrow @_r \, \mathsf{rewardOffered} \qquad (19)$$

6 Information-Flow Properties

Generally, in the context of actor networks, by *information flow* we refer to the transfer of information from one configuration to another as a result of a reconfiguration process. A particular application of information-flow properties is to characterize invariants. For that purpose, suppose $\langle \Omega, \Gamma \rangle$ is the actor-network specification of the BSS described in Sect. 5. We say that a LAN-sentence ψ over some extension $\Omega[X; Y]$ of Ω is an *invariant* for $\langle \Omega, \Gamma \rangle$ when, for every interaction ι, $\forall X; Y \cdot \psi \Rightarrow [\iota] \, \psi$ is a semantic consequence of Γ – that is, when $\langle D, C \rangle \Vdash \forall X; Y \cdot \psi \Rightarrow [\iota] \, \psi$ for all models $\langle D, C \rangle$ that satisfy all sentences in Γ.[8]

We analyse the following two invariants of the BSS, denoted by FD and RO.

FD : If a region has a free dock, then no reward is offered at that region.

$$\forall\{d\colon \mathsf{Dock}\} \cdot @_d \, (\mathsf{freeDock} \to [\pi] \neg \, \mathsf{rewardOffered}) \qquad (20)$$

RO : If a reward is offered at a region, then a traveller is expected to arrive there.

$$\forall\{r\colon \mathsf{Region}\} \cdot @_r \, \mathsf{rewardOffered} \to \exists\{u\colon \mathsf{User}\} \cdot @_u \, \langle \mathsf{travelTo} \rangle \, r \qquad (21)$$

---

[8] When both X and Y are empty, we can further prove that ψ holds at all reachable configurations of the model of $\langle \Omega, \Gamma \rangle$ by verifying that Γ entails init : ψ.

To verify that the sentences FD $\Rightarrow$ $[\![\iota]\!]$ FD and RO $\Rightarrow$ $[\![\iota]\!]$ RO are indeed consequences of the actor-network specification $\langle \Omega, \Gamma \rangle$, where ι is any of the four interactions of the BSS, we use a recently developed extension of the Heterogeneous Tool Set (HETS) [24], called H [7,10,11], that provides support for formal specification and reasoning in hybridized logics.

In particular, for reasoning purposes, H implements a verification-by-translation method based on theoretical results presented in [12]. This involves three main steps: *(1)* translating the verification problem to first-order logic using a suitable encoding of the hybridized logic, *(2)* solving the problem there using automated-theorem-proving technologies that have already been developed for first-order logic (such as SPASS [30] or Vampire [26]), and *(3)* transferring the result of the verification process back to the hybridized logic.

Details of this process, including intermediate results that assist the theorem provers in establishing that FD and RO are invariants, can be found in [29].

Dealing with Vulnerabilities. As the two invariants discussed above show, the analysis of information-flow properties can be used to validate the design of the BSS by providing formal guarantees of desired properties such as FD; but the same process can also be used to prove the existence of vulnerabilities: by RO, it follows that any implementation of the current BSS design may inadvertently disclose information about the users' whereabouts.

What we briefly demonstrate next is that we can emend the design presented in Sect. 5 to prevent the vulnerability described by RO while maintaining the desired property FD. For that purpose, it suffices to examine the proof of RO (as provided through the H extension of HETS), which reveals that the invariant hinges on the fact that rewards are deterministically offered by Reward-transitions, and only by Reward-transitions. This suggests that one way to correct the design is by dropping the sentences described in (19), or by replacing them with sentences that express the fact that rewards can also be offered by Take, Travel, or Return when the region is full. Intuitively, the effect of the change is that rewards may now be non-deterministically offered by any of the four interactions. As a final verification, we have checked that the change does not affect FD.

To prove that RO is no longer deducible from the specification, all we need is to find a model of the specification that does not satisfy RO. We obtain such a model from the Kripke structure depicted in Fig. 3, by letting the Return-transition generate a reward at R2 in the configuration C3. This model satisfies all BSS axioms presented in Sect. 5 except (19), and does not satisfy RO.

7   Conclusions and Further Work

In this paper, we have presented an actor-network approach to the design and analysis of a bike-sharing system. We have shown how various aspects of the BSS can be formalized using a combination of two hybrid-logic formalisms: a logic of network configurations, which deals with static aspects of the BSS, and a logic of actor networks, which is defined on top of the logic of network configurations and deals with dynamic aspects of the system – i.e., the way reconfigurations occur as a result of interactions between actors.

The full specification of the BSS has been analysed using a recently developed extension of HETS that provides support for hybrid(ized) logics. This includes support for parsing, static analysis, as well as formal verification – which relies on a general encoding of hybridized logics into first-order logic. Using the toolset, we have confirmed two information-flow properties of the BSS: first, that the rewards at a region automatically cease to be offered when one of the docks in that region becomes free; and second, that all regions where rewards are offered have users travelling towards them. The latter shows that the system is vulnerable by design; we have used HETS again to identify (and then correct) the part of the specification that is responsible for the vulnerability.

Beyond the actual analysis of the BSS, one of the benefits of conducting a case study of this kind is that it confirms that the formal specification & verification tools that we have available today (thanks to a decades-long series of theoretical developments on the foundations of algebraic specification) are already well capable of dealing with complex, real-world reconfigurable systems. At the same time, it shows some of the limitations of the current technology – or, at least, of the one discussed in this paper. Currently, for the BSS, there is no way to ensure that all travellers can actually reach their destination (or that they eventually do). This is due to the limited expressive power of hybrid logics. A simple and elegant solution that we aim to pursue further is to consider dynamic-logic operators as in [16,18,20]. This raises a series of new and interesting challenges because some of the key results on hybrid logics, such as their encoding into first-order logic, cannot be generalized in a straighforward way to dynamic logics.

References

1. Bartocci, E., Bortolussi, L., Loreti, M., Nenzi, L.: Monitoring mobile and spatially distributed cyber-physical systems. In: Proceedings of the 15th ACM-IEEE International Conference on Formal Methods and Models for System Design, MEMOCODE 2017, Vienna, Austria, 29 September–2 October 2017, pp. 146–155. ACM (2017)
2. ter Beek, M.H., Fantechi, A., Gnesi, S.: Challenges in modelling and analyzing quantitative aspects of bike-sharing systems. In: Margaria, T., Steffen, B. (eds.) ISoLA 2014, Part I. LNCS, vol. 8802, pp. 351–367. Springer, Heidelberg (2014). https://doi.org/10.1007/978-3-662-45234-9_25
3. ter Beek, M.H., Gnesi, S., Latella, D., Massink, M.: Towards automatic decision support for bike-sharing system design. In: Bianculli, D., Calinescu, R., Rumpe, B. (eds.) SEFM 2015. LNCS, vol. 9509, pp. 266–280. Springer, Heidelberg (2015). https://doi.org/10.1007/978-3-662-49224-6_22
4. Blackburn, P.: Representation, reasoning, and relational structures: a hybrid logic manifesto. Logic J. IGPL 8(3), 339–365 (2000)
5. Braüner, T.: Hybrid Logic and its Proof-Theory. Applied Logic Series, vol. 37. Springer, Dordrecht (2011). https://doi.org/10.1007/978-94-007-0002-4
6. Ciancia, V., Latella, D., Loreti, M., Massink, M.: Model checking spatial logics for closure spaces. Log. Methods Comput. Sci. 12(4), 1–51 (2016)

7. Codescu, M.: Hybridisation of institutions in Hets. In: 8th Conference on Algebra and Coalgebra in Computer Science, CALCO 2019, London, 3–6 June 2019
8. Codescu, M., Kuksa, E., Kutz, O., Mossakowski, T., Neuhaus, F.: Ontohub: a semantic repository engine for heterogeneous ontologies. Appl. Ontol. **12**(3–4), 275–298 (2017)
9. Diaconescu, R.: Quasi-varieties and initial semantics for hybridized institutions. J. Log. Comput. **26**(3), 855–891 (2016)
10. Diaconescu, R.: Introducing H, an institution-based formal specication and verication language. CoRR abs/1908.09868 (2019)
11. Diaconescu, R., Codescu, M.: The H system. Developed in the project Formal Verication of Recongurable Systems (PN-III-P2-2.1-PED-2016-0494) at Simion Stoilow Institute of Mathematics of the Romanian Academy, Romania (2017–2018). http://imar.ro/~diacon/forver/forver.html
12. Diaconescu, R., Madeira, A.: Encoding hybridized institutions into first-order logic. Math. Struct. Comput. Sci. **26**(5), 745–788 (2016)
13. Diaconescu, R., Stefaneas, P.S.: Ultraproducts and possible worlds semantics in institutions. Theor. Comput. Sci. **379**(1–2), 210–230 (2007)
14. Fiadeiro, J.L., Ţuţu, I., Lopes, A., Pavlovic, D.: Logics for actor networks: a two-stage constrained-hybridisation approach. J. Log. Algebraic Methods Program. **106**, 141–166 (2019)
15. Finger, M., Gabbay, D.M.: Adding a temporal dimension to a logic system. J. Logic Lang. Inf. **1**(3), 203–233 (1992)
16. Găină, D., Ţuţu, I.: Birkhoff completeness for hybrid-dynamic first-order logic. In: Cerrito, S., Popescu, A. (eds.) TABLEAUX 2019. LNCS, vol. 11714, pp. 277–293. Springer, Cham (2019). https://doi.org/10.1007/978-3-030-29026-9_16
17. Goguen, J.A., Burstall, R.M.: Institutions: abstract model theory for specification and programming. J. ACM **39**(1), 95–146 (1992)
18. Hennicker, R., Madeira, A., Knapp, A.: A hybrid dynamic logic for event/data-based systems. In: Hähnle, R., van der Aalst, W. (eds.) FASE 2019. LNCS, vol. 11424, pp. 79–97. Springer, Cham (2019). https://doi.org/10.1007/978-3-030-16722-6_5
19. Latour, B.: Reassembling the Social: An Introduction to Actor-Network Theory. Oxford University Press, Oxford (2005)
20. Madeira, A., Barbosa, L.S., Hennicker, R., Martins, M.A.: A logic for the stepwise development of reactive systems. Theor. Comput. Sci. **744**, 78–96 (2018)
21. Martins, M.A., Madeira, A., Diaconescu, R., Barbosa, L.S.: Hybridization of institutions. In: Corradini, A., Klin, B., Cîrstea, C. (eds.) CALCO 2011. LNCS, vol. 6859, pp. 283–297. Springer, Heidelberg (2011). https://doi.org/10.1007/978-3-642-22944-2_20
22. Mateus, P., Sernadas, A., Sernadas, C.: Exogenous semantics approach to enriching logics. In: Essays on the Foundations of Mathematics and Logic. Advanced Studies in Mathematics and Logic, vol. 1, pp. 165–194. Polimetrica (2005)
23. Moon-Miklaucic, C., Bray-Sharpin, A., de la Lanza, I., Khan, A., Re, L.L., Maassen, A.: The evolution of bike sharing: 10 questions on the emergence of new technologies, opportunities, and risks. Technical report. World Resources Institute, Washington, DC (2019). http://www.wri.org/publication/evolution-bike-sharing
24. Mossakowski, T., Maeder, C., Lüttich, K.: The heterogeneous tool set (HETS). In: Proceedings of 4th International Verification Workshop in connection with CADE-21, vol. vol. 259. CEUR-WS.org (2007)

25. Pavlovic, D., Meadows, C.: Actor-network procedures (extended abstract). In: Ramanujam, R., Ramaswamy, S. (eds.) ICDCIT 2012. LNCS, vol. 7154, pp. 7–26. Springer, Heidelberg (2012). https://doi.org/10.1007/978-3-642-28073-3_2

26. Riazanov, A., Voronkov, A.: The design and implementation of VAMPIRE. AI Commun. **15**(2–3), 91–110 (2002)

27. Sannella, D., Tarlecki, A.: Foundations of Algebraic Specification and Formal Software Development. Monographs in Theoretical Computer Science. An EATCS Series. Springer, Heidelberg (2012). https://doi.org/10.1007/978-3-642-17336-3

28. Shanahan, M.: Solving the Frame Problem – A Mathematical Investigation of the Common Sense Law of Inertia. MIT Press, Cambridge (1997)

29. Țuțu, I., Chiriță, C., Lopes, A., Fiadeiro, J.: A hybrid-logic specification of a BSS. Ontohub (2019). https://ontohub.org/forver/BSS.dol

30. Weidenbach, C., Dimova, D., Fietzke, A., Kumar, R., Suda, M., Wischnewski, P.: SPASS version 3.5. In: Schmidt, R.A. (ed.) CADE 2009. LNCS (LNAI), vol. 5663, pp. 140–145. Springer, Heidelberg (2009). https://doi.org/10.1007/978-3-642-02959-2_10

A Generic Dynamic Logic
with Applications to Interaction-Based
Systems

Rolf Hennicker[(✉)] and Martin Wirsing[(✉)]

Ludwig-Maximilians-Universität München, Munich, Germany
{hennicker,wirsing}@ifi.lmu.de

Abstract. We propose a generic dynamic logic with the usual diamond and box modalities over structured actions. Instead of using regular expressions of actions our logic is parameterised by the form of the actions which can be given by an arbitrary language for complex, structured actions. In particular, our logic can be instantiated by languages that describe complex interactions between system components. We study two instantiations of our logic for specifying global behaviours of interaction-based systems: one on the basis of global session types and the other one using UML sequence diagrams. Moreover, we show that our proposed generic logic, and hence all its instantiations, satisfy bisimulation invariance and a Hennessy-Milner theorem.

Keywords: Propositional dynamic logic · Interaction-based systems · Global session types · UML sequence diagrams · Hennessy-Milner theorem

1 Introduction

Dynamic logic [8] is an established formalism to analyse, specify and verify properties of sequential programs represented by regular expressions over a set of atomic programs. It has been recognised in previous work [10,11] that a dynamic logic specification style can also be a useful tool to reason about systems of interacting, concurrent components if instead of atomic program statements atomic *interactions* are used to build complex, structured interactions. That way it is possible to specify abstract properties, like safety and liveness, of the global behaviour of ensemble-based systems, but it is also possible to specify desired and forbidden interaction scenarios. Our previous proposals were based on the assumption that complex interactions are built in accordance with the operators of regular expressions which are typical in dynamic logic. This assumption did impose some significant limitations. For instance, it was not possible to express parallel executions based on interleaving or other powerful structuring operators for interactions like weak sequencing and weak loops used in UML sequence diagrams. Thus we are interested to overcome these restrictions which leads to the

© Springer Nature Switzerland AG 2019
M. H. ter Beek et al. (Eds.): Gnesi Festschrift, LNCS 11865, pp. 172–187, 2019.
https://doi.org/10.1007/978-3-030-30985-5_11

proposal of a generic dynamic logic with interaction-based systems as a particular application domain.

Generic dynamic logic abstracts from the particular rules for the formation of actions and their interpretation which need not to be regular anymore. Thus the parameters of our logic are, additionally to a basic set A of atomic actions, an arbitrary set $Act(A)$ of structured actions over A and an interpretation function $\mathcal{L} : Act(A) \rightarrow \mathcal{P}(A^*)$ which assigns to any $\alpha \in Act(A)$ a language $\mathcal{L}(\alpha) \subseteq A^*$. Then formulae of the logic may involve diamond and box modalities, like $\langle \alpha \rangle \varphi$ and $[\alpha]\varphi$ resp., expressing possibility and necessity for an arbitrary structured action $\alpha \in Act(A)$. Since the construction of α is generic, the satisfaction of a formula in a state s of a labelled transition system M must be reformulated. The idea is that $M, s \models \langle \alpha \rangle \varphi$ holds if there is a state u of M reachable by a sequence w of atomic actions such that $w \in \mathcal{L}(\alpha)$ and φ is satisfied in u. We show that this generalisation indeed coincides with the standard satisfaction relation of propositional dynamic logic if we use for $Act(A)$ regular expressions of actions with the usual language interpretation. As a general result we show that generic dynamic logic, and hence all its instantiations, enjoy bisimulation invariance and satisfy a Hennessy-Milner theorem.

In the second part of this work we consider the application domain of interaction-based systems and two prominent specification formats for describing global behaviours: global types used for specifying global behaviours of session types [4], and UML sequence diagrams used in software engineering for specifying scenarios of distributed systems. Both languages offer operators to build structured interactions from smaller ones. As concrete formalisms we use [2] for global types and [13] for a formalisation of UML sequence diagrams. Our goal is to build on top of these formalisms a dynamic logic which allows us to use expressions of the respective specification styles inside the modalities of the logic. For instance, for a given global type $\mathcal{G}$, we can write $[\mathcal{G}]\varphi$ to express that after any execution of a sequence of interactions allowed by $\mathcal{G}$ property φ is valid; and similarly for sequence diagrams. That way we obtain powerful, logic-based specification languages on the basis of global types and sequence diagrams to specify properties of interaction-based systems which are not specifiable solely by expressions of the underlying formalisms. In the case of global types the resulting dynamic logic goes syntactically beyond regular expressions since it allows to specify unconstrained orders of interactions by interleaving. For the semantic interpretation a shuffling operator is used which is, however, still regular. Thus the logic is decidable. The situation is different when sequence diagrams are considered. Sequence diagrams can be structured by sequencing and by loops which both rely semantically on a weak sequencing operator which is not regular and not even context-free. Therefore our dynamic logic based on sequence diagrams is not decidable.

The paper is structured as follows: We start in Sect. 2 by recalling the basic definitions of (regular) propositional dynamic logic. In Sect. 3 generic dynamic logic is introduced and several instantiations, still parametric in the underlying sets of atomic actions, are discussed. Section 4, instantiates the generic logic by considering basic interactions as atomic actions. Two variants are considered: (structured) interactions expressed by global types (Sect. 4.1) and those specified by UML sequence diagrams (Sect. 4.2). We finish with some concluding remarks in Sect. 5.

Personal Note. Stefania and Martin know each other for many years and have closely collaborated in two EU projects AGILE [1] and SENSORIA [22] Martin was coordinating in 2002 - 2010. Rolf did not directly work with Stefania but has an ongoing cooperation with Maurice ter Beek who is a member of Stefania's team [19].

In AGILE Stefania and her team at ISTI started the design, implementation and experimentation of the verification system UMC for analysing and model checking UML state machines and used UMC for modelling the main "airport" case study [1]. The development of UMC [5] was continued in SENSORIA for supporting SRML modeling language and for modeling and verifying the main automotive and finance case studies. Stefania and her team developed also the model checker CMC [5] for verifying properties of service-oriented applications modeled in the Calculus for Orchestration of Web Services (COWS) [18]. These developments which had started in the end of the nineties and continue until now resulted in a family of model checkers, called KandISTI [20]. The name refers to the painter Wassily Kandinsky and was inspired by a visit of Stefania, Martin and other SENSORIA members to the museum Lenbachhaus[1] in Munich as part of a project meeting. In the SENSORIA project, Stefania performed also an excellent task in coordinating the work on the case studies and in this way assessing the applicability of the foundational results, giving feedback for refining the tools and methodologies developed in the project and bringing together the academic and industrial partners.

Cooperating and working with Stefania is always a pleasant experience. We are looking forward to many further inspiring exchanges with her.

2   Regular Propositional Dynamic Logic

In this section we recall the basic definitions of propositional dynamic logic (PDL) over regular expressions of actions as described in [8]. We use the test-free variant of dynamic logic and omit atomic propositions. Thus the logic described below is a Hennessy-Milner logic such that regular expressions of actions can be used in the diamond and box modalities.

In the following let A be a set of atomic actions. The set of *structured (regular) actions* $\mathrm{Act}^{\mathrm{rg}}(A)$ over A is defined by the grammar

$$\alpha ::= \mathbf{skip} \mid a \mid \alpha; \alpha \mid \alpha + \alpha \mid \alpha^{\star}$$

where $a \in A$. Thereby **skip** denotes the empty sequence of actions, ";" denotes sequential composition, "+" the union of actions and the Kleene star denotes

---

[1] Städtische Galerie im Lenbachhaus, München, https://www.lenbachhaus.de/?L=1.

iteration. If the set A of atomic actions is finite, i.e. $A = \{a_1, \ldots, a_n\}$, we write **all** for the structured action $a_1 + \ldots + a_n$. If, moreover, $B = \{b_1, \ldots, b_m\}$ is a finite subset of A, then $-(b_1 + \ldots + b_m)$ denotes the sum (union) of all actions in A which do not belong to B.

The set of sentences over A is defined by the grammar

$$\varphi :: = \textbf{true} \mid \neg\varphi \mid \varphi \vee \varphi \mid \langle \alpha \rangle \varphi$$

where $\alpha \in \text{Act}^{\text{rg}}(A)$. We use the usual abbreviations $\textbf{false} = \neg\textbf{true}, \varphi \wedge \psi = \neg(\neg\varphi \vee \neg\psi), [\alpha]\varphi = \neg\langle \alpha \rangle\neg\varphi$ etc.

Sentences $\langle \alpha \rangle \varphi$ with diamond operator denote *possibility* in the sense that in a current state an action described by α is possible and afterwards φ holds; sentences $[\alpha]\varphi$ with box operator denote *necessity* in the sense that whenever in the current state an action denoted by α is executed then afterwards φ holds. For the precise formalisation the semantics of PDL uses Kripke frames over A which we introduce in the following using the terminology of labelled transition systems.

Let A be a set of atomic actions. An *A-LTS* is a pair $M = (S, R)$ where S is a set of *states* and $R = (R_a \subseteq S \times S)_{a \in A}$ is a family of *transition relations*, one for each atomic action $a \in A$. The interpretation of structured, regular actions α in an A-LTS M extends the interpretation of atomic actions by the relations

- $R^{\text{rg}}_{\textbf{skip}} = \{(s, s) \mid s \in S\}$,
- $R^{\text{rg}}_a = R_a$ for each $a \in A$,
- $R^{\text{rg}}_{\alpha;\alpha'} = R^{\text{rg}}_\alpha \cdot R^{\text{rg}}_{\alpha'}$,
- $R^{\text{rg}}_{\alpha+\alpha'} = R^{\text{rg}}_\alpha \cup R^{\text{rg}}_{\alpha'}$,
- $R^{\text{rg}}_{\alpha*} = (R^{\text{rg}}_\alpha)^*$,

with the operations $\cdot$, $\cup$ and $*$ standing for relational composition, union and reflexive-transitive closure.

For any A-LTS $M = (S, R)$ and state $s \in S$ the *satisfaction* of sentences in state s of M is inductively defined by

- $M, s \models \textbf{true}$ holds;
- $M, s \models \neg\varphi$ if $M, s \models \varphi$ does not hold;
- $M, s \models \varphi \vee \varphi'$ if $M, s \models \varphi$ or $M, s \models \varphi'$;
- $M, s \models \langle \alpha \rangle\varphi$ if there is a state $u \in S$ with $(s, u) \in R^{\text{rg}}_\alpha$ and $M, u \models \varphi$.

An A-LTS $M = (S, R)$ satisfies a sentence φ, written $M \models \varphi$, if for any $s \in S$: $M, s \models \varphi$.

Note that regular PDL is decidable; see [8].

3   A Generic Dynamic Logic

In this section we abstract from the particular rules for the formation of actions and their interpretation. Thus we define a generic (propositional) dynamic logic which is parameterised by the following ingredients:

- a set A of atomic actions (as before),
- a set $\mathrm{Act}(A)$ of structured actions such that $A \subseteq \mathrm{Act}(A)$,
- an interpretation function $\mathcal{L} : \mathrm{Act}(A) \to \mathcal{P}(A^*)$ which assigns to any structured action $\alpha \in \mathrm{Act}(A)$ a language $\mathcal{L}(\alpha) \subseteq A^*$ such that $\mathcal{L}(a) = \{a\}$ for each $a \in A$.

The logic $\mathrm{PDL}(A, \mathrm{Act}(A), \mathcal{L})$ with parameters $A, \mathrm{Act}(A)$ and $\mathcal{L}$ has the sentences

$$\varphi ::= \mathbf{true} \mid \neg\varphi \mid \varphi \vee \varphi \mid \langle\alpha\rangle\varphi$$

as before but now $\alpha \in \mathrm{Act}(A)$. Of course, we use the same abbreviations as above for $\mathbf{false}, \varphi \wedge \psi, [\alpha]\varphi$ etc.

For the semantics of $\mathrm{PDL}(A, \mathrm{Act}(A), \mathcal{L})$ we use again labelled transition systems $M = (S, R)$ with transition relations $R = (R_a \subseteq S \times S)_{a \in A}$. The interpretation of structured actions $\alpha \in \mathrm{Act}(A)$ in the generic logic is given by the relations

$$\mathrm{R}_\alpha^{\mathrm{g}} = \{(s, u) \mid \exists w \in \mathcal{L}(\alpha) : s \xrightarrow{w}{}^* u\},$$

where $\xrightarrow{w}{}^* \subseteq S \times S$ is inductively defined for words $w \in A^*$ by

- $s \xrightarrow{\epsilon}{}^* s$ for all $s \in S$,
- if $s \xrightarrow{w}{}^* v$ and $(v, u) \in R_a$ for some $a \in A$, then $s \xrightarrow{wa}{}^* u$.

Hence $\mathrm{R}_\alpha^{\mathrm{g}}$ relates states s and u whenever u is reachable from s by some sequence $w = a_1 \ldots a_n$ of atomic actions such that w is a word in the language of α. Note that, for all $a \in A$ we have: $a \in \mathrm{Act}(A)$ and (*) $\mathrm{R}_a^{\mathrm{g}} = R_a$ which follows from the assumption that $\mathcal{L}(a) = \{a\}$ for each $a \in A$.

For any A-LTS $M = (S, R)$ and state $s \in S$ the satisfaction of sentences in state s of M is defined in the same way as in Sect. 2 with the difference that in the case of a diamond modality $\langle\alpha\rangle$ the relation $\mathrm{R}_\alpha^{\mathrm{g}}$ is used instead of $\mathrm{R}_\alpha^{\mathrm{rg}}$, i.e.

- $M, s \models \langle\alpha\rangle\varphi$ if there is a state $u \in S$ with $(s, u) \in \mathrm{R}_\alpha^{\mathrm{g}}$ and $M, u \models \varphi$.

As before, an A-LTS $M = (S, R)$ satisfies a sentence φ, written $M \models \varphi$, if for any $s \in S$: $M, s \models \varphi$.

As a semantic variant we may also consider A-LTSs *with initial state* s_0, i.e. triples $M = (S, s_0, R)$ with $s_0 \in S$. Then $M \models \varphi$ means that $M, s_0 \models \varphi$.

Remark 1. Chapter 9 of [8] considers different nonregular variants of PDL. For a given language L, [8] defines the logic PDL+L "exactly as PDL, but with the additional syntax rule stating that for any formula φ, the expression $\langle L \rangle\varphi$ is a new formula. ... Note that PDL+L does not allow L to be used as a formation rule for new programs or to be combined with other programs. It is added to the programming language as a single new stand-alone program only". It is shown in [8] (Theorem 9.3) that if L is any nonregular test-free language, then PDL+L is strictly more expressive than PDL. Moreover, for different variants of L decidability and undecidability results are provided.

We will now discuss some particular cases for the choice of structured actions $\mathrm{Act}(A)$ with interpretation function $\mathcal{L}$.

Example 1. First, let us take $\mathrm{Act}(A) = \mathrm{Act}^{\mathrm{rg}}(A)$ and let $\mathcal{L}^{\mathrm{rg}} : \mathrm{Act}^{\mathrm{rg}}(A) \to \mathcal{P}(A^*)$ be the standard interpretation of regular expressions. Note that the assumptions $A \subseteq \mathrm{Act}^{\mathrm{rg}}(A)$ and $\mathcal{L}(a) = \{a\}$ for all $a \in A$ are satisfied. Then the instantiation of generic PDL yields regular PDL.

For the proof we have to show that the satisfaction relation of $\mathrm{PDL}(A, \mathrm{Act}^{\mathrm{rg}}(A), \mathcal{L}^{\mathrm{rg}})$ coincides with the one of regular PDL as defined in Sect. 2. The critical case concerns the satisfaction of $\langle \alpha \rangle \varphi$. For this case we have to show that for any A-LTS $M = (S, R)$ and for all $\alpha \in \mathrm{Act}^{\mathrm{rg}}(A)$,

$$R_\alpha^{\mathrm{g}} = R_\alpha^{\mathrm{rg}}.$$

Proof. The proof of this equality is performed by structural induction on the form of $\alpha \in \mathrm{Act}^{\mathrm{rg}}(A)$:

If $\alpha = a \in A, R_a^{\mathrm{g}} =$ (see (*) above) $R_a =$ (by definition) R_a^{rg}.

If $\alpha = \mathbf{skip}$ we have that $(s, u) \in R_a^{\mathrm{g}}$ iff $s \xrightarrow{\epsilon}^* u$ iff $s = u$ iff $(s, u) \in R_{\mathbf{skip}}^{\mathrm{rg}}$.

If $\alpha = \beta; \gamma$ we have that $(s, u) \in R_{\beta;\gamma}^{\mathrm{g}}$ iff there exists $w \in \mathcal{L}^{\mathrm{rg}}(\beta; \gamma)$ with $s \xrightarrow{w}^* u$. Now we note that w must be of the form $w_1 w_2$ with $w_1 \in \mathcal{L}^{\mathrm{rg}}(\beta)$ and $w_2 \in \mathcal{L}^{\mathrm{rg}}(\gamma)$ and therefore there must exist $v \in S$ with $s \xrightarrow{w_1}^* v$ and $v \xrightarrow{w_2}^* u$. Hence $(s, v) \in R_\beta^{\mathrm{g}}$ and $(v, u) \in R_\gamma^{\mathrm{g}}$. Then, by induction hypothesis for β and γ we get $(s, v) \in R_\beta^{\mathrm{rg}}$ and $(v, u) \in R_\gamma^{\mathrm{rg}}$ which implies $(s, u) \in R_{\beta;\gamma}^{\mathrm{rg}}$. The proof can be easily conversed.

If $\alpha = \beta + \gamma$ we have that $(s, u) \in R_{\beta+\gamma}^{\mathrm{g}}$ iff there exists $w \in \mathcal{L}^{\mathrm{rg}}(\beta + \gamma)$ with $s \xrightarrow{w}^* u$. W.l.o.g. assume that $w \in \mathcal{L}^{\mathrm{rg}}(\beta)$ and thus $(s, u) \in R_\beta^{\mathrm{g}}$. By induction hypothesis, $R_\beta^{\mathrm{g}} = R_\beta^{\mathrm{rg}}$. Hence $(s, u) \in R_\beta^{\mathrm{rg}}$ and thus $(s, u) \in R_{\beta+\gamma}^{\mathrm{rg}}$. The proof can be easily conversed.

If $\alpha = \beta^\star$ we have that $(s, u) \in R_{\beta^\star}^{\mathrm{g}}$ iff there exists $w \in \mathcal{L}^{\mathrm{rg}}(\beta^\star)$ with $s \xrightarrow{w}^* u$. The result follows by induction on the number of iterations to construct $w \in \mathcal{L}^{\mathrm{rg}}(\beta^\star)$. Conversely, let $(s, u) \in R_{\beta^\star}^{\mathrm{rg}}$. Then the result follows again by induction, this time on the number of relational compositions to get $(s, u) \in R_{\beta^\star}^{\mathrm{rg}}$.   □

Example 2. Let us extend the syntax of structured regular actions by a *shuffle* operator $\sqcup\!\sqcup$ to express arbitrary interleavings of action sequences. The set of *structured (regular) actions* $\mathrm{Act}^{\mathrm{rg}+\sqcup\!\sqcup}(A)$ over A is defined by the grammar

$$\alpha ::= \mathbf{skip} \mid a \mid \alpha; \alpha \mid \alpha + \alpha \mid \alpha^\star \mid \alpha \sqcup\!\sqcup \beta$$

where $a \in A$. The interpretation $\mathcal{L}^{\mathrm{rg}+\sqcup\!\sqcup} : \mathrm{Act}^{\mathrm{rg}+\sqcup\!\sqcup}(A) \to \mathcal{P}(A^*)$ extends the interpretation function $\mathcal{L}^{\mathrm{rg}}$ for regular expressions by the case

$$\mathcal{L}^{\mathrm{rg}+\sqcup\!\sqcup}(\alpha \sqcup\!\sqcup \beta) = \mathcal{L}^{\mathrm{rg}+\sqcup\!\sqcup}(\alpha) \sqcup\!\sqcup \mathcal{L}^{\mathrm{rg}+\sqcup\!\sqcup}(\beta)$$

where for languages $L_1, L_2 \subseteq A^*$,

$$L_1 \sqcup L_2 = \bigcup_{w_1 \in L_1, w_2 \in L_2} w_1 \sqcup w_2,$$

and the shuffling $w_1 \sqcup w_2$ of two words $w_1, w_2 \in A^*$ is inductively defined by

- $\epsilon \sqcup w = w \sqcup \epsilon = \{w\}$,
- $a_1 w_1 \sqcup a_2 w_2 = \{a_1 w \mid w \in w_1 \sqcup a_2 w_2\} \cup \{a_2 w \mid w \in a_1 w_1 \sqcup w_2\}$.

Now we can instantiate generic dynamic logic by taking $\text{Act}(A) = \text{Act}^{\text{rg}+\sqcup}(A)$ and $\mathcal{L}(A) = \mathcal{L}^{\text{rg}+\sqcup}(A)$ for any arbitrary set A of atomic actions thus obtaining $\text{PDL}(A, \text{Act}^{\text{rg}+\sqcup}(A), \mathcal{L}^{\text{rg}+\sqcup})$. Note that regular languages are closed under shuffling and therefore our instantiation is still decidable. It just comes with a convenient and compact notation to denote interleaving which would be cumbersome to write down by using regular expressions only. As an example consider the structured action $(ab)^* \sqcup c^*$ whose language could be equivalently expressed by the complex and non-intuitive regular expression $(c^*; a; c^*; b; c^*)^*$. The practical usefulness of the shuffle operator to specify interactions of distributed computing entities will be shown in the next section.

Example 3. As a last general example we consider context-free PDL which is obtained by taking for $\text{Act}(A)$ the set of context-free grammars over A and for $\mathcal{L}(A)$ the usual interpretation in terms of context-free languages. In this case we can write, for instance, sentences of the form $\langle G \rangle \varphi$ with a context-free grammar G. It has been shown in [8] (Theorem 9.4) that validity of context-free PDL (and hence also the dual notion of satisfiability) is undecidable.

As an equivalence notion for labelled transition systems over A we use (strong) bisimulation. Let $M = (S, R)$ and $M' = (S', R')$ be two A-LTSs. A *bisimulation relation* between M and M' is a relation $B \subseteq S \times S'$ that satisfies for any $a \in A$ and $(s, s') \in B$:

(zig) if there exists $u \in S$ and a transition $(s, u) \in R_a$, then there is a $u' \in S'$ such that $(s', u') \in R'_a$ and $(u, u') \in B$;

(zag) if there exists $u' \in S'$ and a transition $(s', u') \in R'_a$, then there is a $u \in S$ such that $(s, u) \in R_a$ and $(u, u') \in B$.

Two states $s \in S$ and $s' \in S'$ are bisimilar if there exists a bisimulation relation $B \subseteq S \times S'$ between M and M' such that $(s, s') \in B$.

We can show that independently of the chosen set $\text{Act}(A)$ of structured actions and their language interpretation $\mathcal{L}$ the satisfaction of dynamic logic formulae is invariant under bisimulation. For this we need the following technical lemma.

Lemma 1. *Let $M = (S, R)$ and $M' = (S', R')$ be two A-LTSs and let $B \subseteq S \times S'$ be a bisimulation relation between M and M'. Then the following holds for all $\alpha \in \text{Act}(A)$ and for all $(s, s') \in B$:*

(zig_α) *if there exists $u \in S$ and $(s, u) \in R_\alpha^g$, then there is a $u' \in S'$ such that $(s', u') \in R'^g_\alpha$ and $(u, u') \in B$;*

(zag_α) *if there exists* $u' \in S'$ *and* $(s', u') \in \text{R}'^g_\alpha$, *then there is a* $u \in S$ *such that* $(s, u) \in \text{R}^g_\alpha$ *and* $(u, u') \in B$.

Proof. We prove case (zig_α). The other case is similar.

As an auxiliary step we show:

(aux) For all $w \in A^*$ and for all $(s, s') \in B$: If there exists $u \in S$ such that $s \xrightarrow{w}{}^* u$ then there exists $u' \in S'$ such that $s' \xrightarrow{w}{}^* u'$ and $(u, u') \in B$.

The proof of (aux) is by induction on the length of w:

If $w = \epsilon$ then $u = s$. Then we can take $u' = s'$ and obtain $s' \xrightarrow{\epsilon}{}^* u'$ and $(u, u') = (s, s') \in B$.

If $w = w_1 a$ with $a \in A$ then there must exist a state $v \in S$ such that $s \xrightarrow{w_1}{}^* v$ and $(v, u) \in R_a$. By induction hypothesis, there exists $v' \in S'$ such that $s' \xrightarrow{w_1}{}^* v'$ and $(v, v') \in B$. Since B satisfies (zig) there is a $u' \in S'$ such that $(v', u') \in R'_a$ and $(u, u') \in B$. Hence, $s' \xrightarrow{w}{}^* u'$ and $(u, u') \in B$. This completes the proof of (aux).

Now let $\alpha \in \text{Act}(A)$ and $(s, s') \in B$. Assume that $u \in S$ and $(s, u) \in \text{R}^g_\alpha$. Then there exists $w \in \mathcal{L}(\alpha)$ such that $s \xrightarrow{w}{}^* u$. By (aux) there exists $u' \in S'$ such that $s' \xrightarrow{w}{}^* u'$ and $(u, u') \in B$. Hence, since $w \in \mathcal{L}(\alpha)$, $(s', u') \in \text{R}'^g_\alpha$ and $(u, u') \in B$. $\square$

Theorem 1. *Let* $M = (S, R)$ *and* $M' = (S', R')$ *be two A-LTSs and let* $s \in S$ *and* $s' \in S'$.

1. *If* s *and* s' *are bisimilar, then for any sentence* φ: $M, s \models \varphi$ *iff* $M', s' \models \varphi$.
2. *If* M *and* M' *are image-finite[2] then the converse of (1) holds: If for any sentence* φ, $M, s \models \varphi$ *iff* $M', s' \models \varphi$, *then* s *and* s' *are bisimilar.*

Proof. The proof of (1) is, as usual, by induction on the form of the sentences. For the case $\langle \alpha \rangle \varphi$ Lemma 1 is used. The proof of (2) is just the usual one since generic dynamic logic subsumes Hennessy-Milner logic [9]. $\square$

4   Specification of Interaction-Based Systems

In [11] and [10] we have shown that (propositional) dynamic logic on the basis of regular expressions of actions can be a useful tool for the specification of scenarios and other properties of interaction-based systems. In this section we go further and apply our generic dynamic logic to two well-known formalisms: global types and UML sequence diagrams.

For illustration purposes we use the UML sequence diagram in Fig. 1 which is based on an example in [2]. It models a bargaining interaction between a seller and a buyer making use of several interaction operators like par for parallel execution, loop for iteration, and alt for alternatives. Moreover there is implicitly a sequential composition operator combining the single fragments. The idea of

---

[2] This means that for any atomic action a and any state s there are at most finitely many outgoing transitions labelled with a.

the bargaining interaction is that first the seller sends, in an arbitrary order, a description and a price of the product to sell. Then the buyer can negotiate sending arbitrarily often an offer to which the seller reacts by sending a (new) price. When the negotiation is finished two alternative continuations are possible: Either the buyer pays the price and then the seller sends the product or the buyer quits the bargaining.

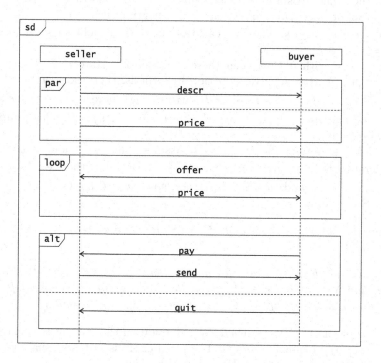

Fig. 1. Sequence diagram for a bargaining interaction

4.1   A Dynamic Logic for Global Types

Global types are a family of formalisms, see, e.g., [2,4,15,21], for the formal description of the global behaviour of interacting, distributed computing entities, often called *participants* or *roles*. They play a major role for the specification of multi-party session types [12]. In this section we follow the global type specification framework of [2]. We propose a dynamic logic built on top of global types which is particularly useful for formal requirements specifications to express abstract properties like safety and liveness. For this purpose we instantiate generic dynamic logic with the sets of atomic actions A^{gt}, structured actions $Act^{gt}(A^{gt})$ and interpretation $\mathcal{L}^{gt}$ explained in the following.

[2] assumes given a set Π of participants (roles) and a set of message types, let's call it $\mathcal{M}$. An atomic action is an *interaction*, i.e. a triple $\pi \xrightarrow{\ m\ } p$ expressing

that all participants in a finite (nonempty) subset $\pi \subseteq \Pi$ send a message $m \in \mathcal{M}$ to participant $p \in \Pi$. Self messages are not allowed, i.e. it is assumed that $p \notin \pi$. If $\pi = \{s\}$ is a singleton set then $s \xrightarrow{m} p$ stands for $\pi \xrightarrow{m} p$. The set A^{gt} is the set of all interactions.

The set $\mathrm{Act}^{\mathrm{gt}}(\mathrm{A}^{\mathrm{gt}})$ of structured actions over A^{gt} is the set of *gobal types* defined by the grammar

$$\mathcal{G} ::= \mathbf{skip} \mid \pi \xrightarrow{m} p \mid \mathcal{G};\mathcal{G} \mid \mathcal{G}\,\mathbf{or}\,\mathcal{G} \mid \mathcal{G}\,\mathbf{and}\,\mathcal{G} \mid \mathcal{G}^*$$

where $(\pi \xrightarrow{m} p) \in \mathrm{Act}^{\mathrm{gt}}(\mathrm{A}^{\mathrm{gt}})$.

In the global type expressions ";" denotes sequential composition, **or** alternativeness, and **and** denotes unconstrained order, and * iteration. The original syntax in [2] uses $\vee$ for **or** and $\wedge$ for **and**. We have changed the notation here to avoid confusion with the disjunction and conjunction symbols used in dynamic logic. According to [2] "global types denote languages of legal interactions that can occur in a multi-party session". Hence, the semantics of a global type $\mathcal{G}$ is given in terms of the set of (finite) traces of interactions associated to $\mathcal{G}$. The interpretation function $\mathcal{L}^{\mathrm{gt}} : \mathrm{Act}^{\mathrm{gt}}(\mathrm{A}^{\mathrm{gt}}) \to \mathcal{P}((\mathrm{A}^{\mathrm{gt}})^*)$ is inductively defined as follows

- $\mathcal{L}^{\mathrm{gt}}(\mathbf{skip}) = \{\epsilon\}$,
- $\mathcal{L}^{\mathrm{gt}}(\pi \xrightarrow{m} p) = \{\pi \xrightarrow{m} p\}$,
- $\mathcal{L}^{\mathrm{gt}}(\mathcal{G}_1;\mathcal{G}_2) = \mathcal{L}^{\mathrm{gt}}(\mathcal{G}_1) \cdot \mathcal{L}^{\mathrm{gt}}(\mathcal{G}_2)$,
- $\mathcal{L}^{\mathrm{gt}}(\mathcal{G}_1\,\mathbf{or}\,\mathcal{G}_2) = \mathcal{L}^{\mathrm{gt}}(\mathcal{G}_1) \cup \mathcal{L}^{\mathrm{gt}}(\mathcal{G}_2)$,
- $\mathcal{L}^{\mathrm{gt}}(\mathcal{G}_1\,\mathbf{and}\,\mathcal{G}_2) = \mathcal{L}^{\mathrm{gt}}(\mathcal{G}_1) \sqcup\!\sqcup \mathcal{L}^{\mathrm{gt}}(\mathcal{G}_2)$,
- $\mathcal{L}^{\mathrm{gt}}(\mathcal{G}^*) = \mathcal{L}^{\mathrm{gt}}(\mathcal{G})^*$.

with the operations $\cdot$, $\cup$ and $*$ standing for sequential composition, union and reflexive-transitive closure of languages and $\sqcup\!\sqcup$ stands for the shuffling of languages as defined in Example 2. In particular, a global type $s \xrightarrow{m} p$ and $s' \xrightarrow{m'} p'$ allows any order for exchanging messages m *and* m'.

Obviously, the assumptions for building a generic dynamic logic over global session types are satisfied since $\mathrm{A}^{\mathrm{gt}} \subseteq \mathrm{Act}^{\mathrm{gt}}(A)$ and $\mathcal{L}^{\mathrm{gt}}(a) = \{a\}$ for all $a \in \mathrm{A}^{\mathrm{gt}}$. Thus, we obtain the dynamic logic $\mathrm{PDL}(\mathrm{A}^{\mathrm{gt}}, \mathrm{Act}^{\mathrm{gt}}(\mathrm{A}^{\mathrm{gt}}), \mathcal{L}^{\mathrm{gt}})$ where diamond and box modalities are equipped with global types. This is the same logic as $\mathrm{PDL}(\mathrm{A}^{\mathrm{gt}}, \mathrm{Act}^{\mathrm{rg}+\sqcup\!\sqcup}(\mathrm{A}^{\mathrm{gt}}), \mathcal{L}^{\mathrm{rg}+\sqcup\!\sqcup})$ in Example 2 if we take interactions as atomic actions, **or** for + and **and** for $\sqcup\!\sqcup$. Hence dynamic logic for global types is decidable. For the semantics we use the semantic variant mentioned in Sect. 3 where models $M = (S, s_0, R)$ are labelled transition systems with initial state s_0. Hence $M \models \varphi$ means that $M, s_0 \models \varphi$.

Example 4. Let us assume that we want to specify some abstract requirements for a bargaining interaction with participants $\Pi = \{\mathsf{seller}, \mathsf{buyer}\}$ and with message types $\mathcal{M} = \{\mathsf{descr}, \mathsf{price}, \mathsf{offer}, \mathsf{pay}, \mathsf{send}, \mathsf{quit}\}$. Then the set A^{gt} is finite and therefore we can use the shorthand notation **all** to express the disjunction (i.e. semantically the union) of all interactions in A^{gt}. Thus, with a sentence of the form $[\mathbf{all}^*]\varphi$ we can require that a sentence φ is satisfied in all reachable states of an LTS M, i.e. in all states of M reachable from the initial state by a finite set of interactions in A^{gt}. For interactions $a_1, \ldots, a_k \in \mathrm{A}^{\mathrm{gt}}$ we will also use the shorthand notation $-\{a_1, \ldots, a_k\}$ to denote the (finite) union of all interactions in A^{gt} which are different from any a_i $(i = 1, \ldots, k)$. For a bargaining session we require the following properties. Thereby we use the following abbreviations:

m stands for seller $\xrightarrow{\ m\ }$ buyer if m $\in$ {descr, price, send},

m stands for buyer $\xrightarrow{\ m\ }$ seller if m $\in$ {offer, pay, quit}.

- "Whenever the seller has sent a description and a price, it is eventually possible that the buyer pays for the product and it is also eventually possible that the buyer quits the interaction."

$$[\mathbf{all}^*; \text{descr and price}](\langle \mathbf{all}^*; \text{pay}\rangle \mathbf{true} \wedge \langle \mathbf{all}^*; \text{quit}\rangle \mathbf{true}) \tag{1}$$

- "Whenever the buyer has paid, it is possible that the seller sends immediately the product and no other interaction is allowed." (Hence the seller must send the product when the price has been paid.)

$$[\mathbf{all}^*; \text{pay}](\langle \text{send}\rangle \mathbf{true} \wedge [(-\text{send})^*]\mathbf{false}) \tag{2}$$

- "Whenever the seller has sent the product or the buyer has quit the interaction, the bargaining process is finished."

$$[\mathbf{all}^*; \text{send or quit}; \mathbf{all}]\mathbf{false} \tag{3}$$

- "The interaction cannot stop before either the product is sent or the buyer has quit."

$$[(-\{\text{send}, \text{quit}\})^*]\langle \mathbf{all}\rangle \mathbf{true} \tag{4}$$

- "A product cannot be sent before the price has been paid."

$$[(-\text{pay})^*; \text{send}]\mathbf{false} \tag{5}$$

- "When the interaction starts the seller can send a description and a price to the buyer."

$$\langle \text{descr and price}\rangle \mathbf{true} \tag{6}$$

□

Dynamic logic is a powerful tool to express abstract requirements which cannot be expressed by global types. (Well-formed) global types, however, can be considered as more concrete specifications from which by projection to local session types, a correct implementation can be derived. Methodologically this means that dynamic logic specifications may be used for requirements while global types may be used for designs and the definition of a refinement relation between the two may be worth to be investigated in future research.

4.2   A Dynamic Logic Based on UML Sequence Diagrams

UML sequence diagrams are a popular tool in software engineering to model requirements for communications between several components (and also users) of a system. In particular they are used to model scenarios that an intended system should realise. The semantics of sequence diagrams is informally described in the UML specification [7]. A survey on different choices for a formal semantics of UML sequence diagrams is given in [16]. In this section we follow the formalisation of [13] as a basis for instantiating our generic dynamic logic with the sets of atomic actions A^{sd}, structured actions $Act^{sd}(A^{sd})$ and interpretation $\mathcal{L}^{sd}$ defined in the following.

In UML *lifelines* represent the partners of interaction. Therefore [13] assumes given a set L of lifelines and a set $\mathcal{M}$ of messages. The following atomic actions are used: $\mathsf{snd}(s, r, m)$ expresses that lifeline s sends message m to lifeline r and action $\mathsf{rcv}(s, r, m)$ denotes that lifeline r receives m from lifeline s. Hence, in contrast to global types, sending and receiving are separate events. UML sequence diagrams can also model open systems where messages are sent to the environment or received from the environment represented by atomic actions $\mathsf{snd}(s, m)$ and $\mathsf{rcv}(r, m)$ respectively. Thus the grammar defining the set A^{sd} of atomic actions is

$$a:: = \mathsf{snd}(s, r, m) \mid \mathsf{rcv}(s, r, m) \mid \mathsf{snd}(s, m) \mid \mathsf{rcv}(r, m)$$

where $s, r \in L$ and $m \in \mathcal{M}$.

Complex interactions are constructed by combining *interaction fragments*. The UML specification contains a series of operators to form complex interactions. We restrict here to those considered in [13] and add the formation of loops; for a more comprehensive treatment (including loops) see [3]. Interaction fragments (and hence complex interactions) are formed in accordance with the following grammar which defines the set $Act^{sd}(A^{sd})$

$$F:: = \mathbf{skip} \mid a \mid \mathsf{strict}(F_1, F_2) \mid \mathsf{seq}(F_1, F_2) \mid \mathsf{alt}(F_1, F_2) \mid \mathsf{par}(F_1, F_2) \mid \mathsf{loop}(F)$$

where $a \in A^{sd}$. The following explanations of the structuring operators are due to [13]: "$\mathsf{strict}(F_1, F_2)$ is strict sequencing of interactions, i.e., all events in F_1 must occur before those in F_2. $\mathsf{seq}(F_1, F_2)$ is weak sequencing, only imposing the restriction that events keep their lifeline-wise order. $\mathsf{par}(F_1, F_2)$ allows for any parallel interleaving of F_1 and F_2. $\mathsf{alt}(F_1, F_2)$ chooses either F_1 or F_2." Moreover, $\mathsf{loop}(F)$ expresses arbitrarily many iterations of F with a weak sequencing interpretation in each iteration; see below. Therefore we may call these loops "weak" loops.

[13] provides a trace-based semantics for interactions. The interpretation function $\mathcal{L}^{sd} : Act^{sd}(A^{sd}) \to \mathcal{P}((A^{sd})^*)$ is inductively defined as follows

- $\mathcal{L}^{sd}(\mathbf{skip}) = \{\epsilon\}$,
- $\mathcal{L}^{sd}(a) = \{a\}$,
- $\mathcal{L}^{sd}(\mathsf{strict}(F_1, F_2)) = \mathcal{L}^{sd}(F_1) \cdot \mathcal{L}^{sd}(F_2)$,
- $\mathcal{L}^{sd}(\mathsf{seq}(F_1, F_2)) = \mathcal{L}^{sd}(F_1) \cdot_{\mathbb{X}} \mathcal{L}^{sd}(F_2)$,

- $\mathcal{L}^{sd}(\mathsf{alt}(F_1, F_2)) = \mathcal{L}^{sd}(F_1) \cup \mathcal{L}^{sd}(F_2),$
- $\mathcal{L}^{sd}(\mathsf{par}(F_1, F_2)) = \mathcal{L}^{sd}(F_1) \sqcup\!\sqcup \mathcal{L}^{sd}(F_2),$
- $\mathcal{L}^{sd}(\mathsf{loop}(F)) = \mathcal{L}^{sd}(F)^{*\!\bar{\varkappa}}.$

There are two operators for languages not considered yet. The first one is the operator $\cdot_{\bar{\varkappa}}$ for weak sequencing. It allows, like $\sqcup\!\sqcup$, interleaving of atomic actions but only for those actions which are not in conflict. For actions a_1, a_2 which are in conflict, denoted by $a_1 \bar{\varkappa} a_2$, strict sequencing is applied. Two atomic actions are in conflict if they have the same active lifeline. The active lifeline of a send event is the sender and the active lifeline of a receive event is the receiver. Weak sequencing is formally defined, for any two languages $L_1, L_2 \subseteq (\mathrm{A}^{sd})^*$, by

$$L_1 \cdot_{\bar{\varkappa}} L_2 = \bigcup_{w_1 \in L_1, w_2 \in L_2} w_1 \cdot_{\bar{\varkappa}} w_2,$$

where weak sequencing $w_1 \cdot_{\bar{\varkappa}} w_2$ of two words $w_1, w_2 \in (\mathrm{A}^{sd})^*$ is inductively defined by

- $\epsilon \cdot_{\bar{\varkappa}} w = w \cdot_{\bar{\varkappa}} \epsilon = \{w\},$
- $a_1 w_1 \cdot_{\bar{\varkappa}} a_2 w_2 = \{a_1 w \mid w \in w_1 \cdot_{\bar{\varkappa}} a_2 w_2\} \cup \{a_2 w \mid w \in a_1 w_1 \cdot_{\bar{\varkappa}} w_2, \neg(a_1 \bar{\varkappa} a_2)\}.$

The second new operator $^{*\!\bar{\varkappa}}$, defined in [3], computes iterations using weak sequencing instead of standard concatenation in each iteration. It is defined, for any language $L \subseteq (\mathrm{A}^{sd})^*$, by

$$T^{*\!\bar{\varkappa}} = \bigcup_{0 \leq i} T^{(i)\bar{\varkappa}} \text{ where } T^{(0)\bar{\varkappa}} = \{\varepsilon\}, T^{(i+1)\bar{\varkappa}} = T \cdot_{\bar{\varkappa}} T^{(i)\bar{\varkappa}}.$$

Note that the languages for sequence diagrams go beyond regular languages. For instance, the interaction fragment

$$\mathsf{loop}(\mathsf{strict}(\mathsf{snd}(s, r, m), \mathsf{rcv}(s, r, m)))$$

expresses words of send and receive actions such that in any prefix no more receptions can occur than sends. This example models a typical buffered asynchronous communication. The languages obtained by loops with weak sequencing are even not context-free (if more than two communication partners are involved) but they are context-sensitive; see [17].

Obviously, the assumptions for building a generic dynamic logic over sequence diagrams are satisfied since $\mathrm{A}^{sd} \subseteq \mathrm{Act}^{sd}(A)$ and $\mathcal{L}^{sd}(a) = \{a\}$ for all $a \in \mathrm{A}^{sd}$. Thus, we obtain the dynamic logic $\mathrm{PDL}(\mathrm{A}^{sd}, \mathrm{Act}^{sd}(\mathrm{A}^{sd}), \mathcal{L}^{sd})$ where diamond and box modalities can be equipped with interaction fragments. As a consequence of Example 3 this logic is not decidable. As semantic models we use again labelled transition systems with initial states such that $M \models \varphi$ means $M, s_0 \models \varphi$.

Example 5. Let us come back to the bargaining interaction, now with lifelines $L = \{\mathsf{seller}, \mathsf{buyer}\}$ and with messages $\mathcal{M} = \{\mathsf{descr}, \mathsf{price}, \mathsf{offer}, \mathsf{pay}, \mathsf{send}, \mathsf{quit}\}$ as before. Since the set A^{sd} is finite we can again use shorthand notations like **all** to denote finite alternatives, similarly to what has been done in Example 4. For a bargaining interaction we require similar properties as in Example 4 but now we must distinguish between send and receive events. Therefore the specifications become more complex.

– "Whenever the seller has sent a description and a price to the buyer, it is eventually possible that the seller receives a payment for the product from the buyer and it is also possible that the seller receives a notification that the buyer has quit the interaction."

$$[\text{strict}(\text{loop}(\textbf{all}), \text{par}(\text{snd}(\text{seller}, \text{buyer}, \text{descr}), \text{snd}(\text{seller}, \text{buyer}, \text{price})))]$$
$$(\langle\text{strict}(\text{loop}(\textbf{all}), \text{rcv}(\text{buyer}, \text{seller}, \text{pay}))\rangle\textbf{true} \wedge$$
$$\langle\text{strict}(\text{loop}(\textbf{all}), \text{rcv}(\text{buyer}, \text{seller}, \text{quit}))\rangle\textbf{true})$$

We omit specifications of the other properties in Example 4 which can be formulated in a similar way.   □

Dynamic logic sentences allow us to express abstract requirements which cannot be expressed by sequence diagrams. Let us now discuss whether requirements stated by sequence diagrams can be expressed by sentences of our logic. For this it is necessary to clarify when a system is considered as a correct realisation of a sequence diagram, or, formally, of an interaction fragment F. In accordance with [13] a realisation can be given by a system of communicating state machines. By asynchronous composition such a system is formalised as a labelled transition system with a set of initial states thus corresponding to the models of dynamic logic (when we restrict, for simplicity, to one initial state only). [13] compute the traces of such an LTS. If the intersection of these traces with the language associated to F is not empty then the realisation is considered to be correct w.r.t. F. In other words, there must exist a trace w of the LTS (representing the realisation) such that $w \in \mathcal{L}^{\text{sd}}(F)$. This can, however, be easily expressed by the sentence $\langle F\rangle\textbf{true}$ of our logic. Thus correct models of an interaction fragment F are exactly those LTS which satisfy the sentence $\langle F\rangle\textbf{true}$.

Let us remark that in this way a correct realisation can have traces which do not comply to F. To eliminate undesirable traces the general syntax of UML sequence diagrams offers a neg construct such that $\text{neg}(F)$ declares all words in $\mathcal{L}^{\text{sd}}(F)$ as invalid and therefore not allowed by a realisation. This requirement can be again easily formalised with our logic by the sentence $\neg\langle F\rangle\textbf{true}$ or, equivalently, $[F]\textbf{false}$.

5   Conclusion

We have proposed a generic dynamic logic which allows to go beyond regular expressions of actions. In contrast to temporal logics our approach uses explicit (structured) actions which is particularly useful for specifying collaborations in interaction-based systems. As a proof of concept we have considered two instantiations of our logic, one based on global types and the other one based on (a formalisation of) UML sequence diagrams. In both cases there are operators to build complex interaction expressions from smaller ones, which can be used inside diamond and box modalities but go beyond regular expressions. In the global type case, however, the semantic interpretation is still regular since the shuffling operator which interprets unconstrained order of interactions preserves regularity of languages. Thus dynamic logic on the basis of global types is decidable. This is not the case if sequence diagrams are used inside the modalities since the interpretation of loops uses weak sequencing in each iteration.

In future work we are interested to apply our logics in a systematic development process for interaction-based systems. In particular this concerns notions of refinement, proof methods and the development of tools. A formal proof system for generic dynamic logic would use those axioms and rules of the (sound and complete) calculus for propositional dynamic logic presented in [8], Chap. 5.5, which are independent of the form of the actions. If they are regular, the proof system in [8] could be reused as it is. Otherwise it must be appropriately adjusted, for instance to deal with weak sequencing of UML interactions. Appropriate tools for model checking would also depend on the form of structured actions at hand. In the case of regular actions the toolset of mCRL2 [6] would be appropriate. In particular, it could also be applied for the global type instance of our logic if occurrences of unconstrained order are first resolved by a preprocessor to their equivalent regular forms. Concerning the dynamic logic based on UML sequence diagrams the model checking approach described in [14] would be an appropriate candidate. It allows to check "whether an interaction can be satisfied by a given set of message exchanging UML state machines". Hence, it allows us to verify formulas of the form $\langle F \rangle$**true** with an arbitrary interaction fragment F. An interesting task would be to extend [14] in order to verify more complex formulas of our logic.

Acknowledgement. We would like to thank Alexander Knapp for very helpful comments and remarks concerning the interpretation of UML sequence diagrams and corresponding tools.

References

1. Andrade, L., et al.: AGILE: software architecture for mobility. In: Wirsing, M., Pattinson, D., Hennicker, R. (eds.) WADT 2002. LNCS, vol. 2755, pp. 1–33. Springer, Heidelberg (2003). https://doi.org/10.1007/978-3-540-40020-2_1
2. Castagna, G., Dezani-Ciancaglini, M., Padovani, L.: On global types and multiparty sessions. Log. Methods Comput. Sci. **8**(1), 1–45 (2012)
3. Cengarle, M.V., Knapp, A., Mühlberger, H.: Interactions. In: Lano, K. (ed.) UML 2-Semantics and Applications, pp. 205–248. Wiley, Hoboken (2009)
4. Deniélou, P.-M., Yoshida, N.: Multiparty session types meet communicating automata. In: Seidl, H. (ed.) ESOP 2012. LNCS, vol. 7211, pp. 194–213. Springer, Heidelberg (2012). https://doi.org/10.1007/978-3-642-28869-2_10
5. Gnesi, S., Mazzanti, F.: An abstract, on the fly framework for the verification of service-oriented systems. In: Wirsing and Hölzl [22], pp. 390–407
6. Groote, J.F., Mousavi, M.R.: Modeling and Analysis of Communicating Systems. MIT Press, Cambridge (2014)
7. Object Management Group. Unified Modeling Language 2.5. http://www.omg.org/spec/UML/2.5. Accessed 21 May 2019
8. Harel, D., Kozen, D., Tiuryn, J.: Dynamic Logic. MIT Press, Cambridge (2000)

9. Hennessy, M., Milner, R.: Algebraic laws for nondeterminism and concurrency. J. Assoc. Comput. Mach. **32**, 137–162 (1985)
10. Hennicker, R.: Role-based development of dynamically evolving esembles. In: Fiadeiro, J.L., Ţuţu, I. (eds.) WADT 2018. LNCS, vol. 11563, pp. 3–24. Springer, Cham (2019). https://doi.org/10.1007/978-3-030-23220-7_1
11. Hennicker, R., Wirsing, M.: Dynamic logic for ensembles. In: Margaria, T., Steffen, B. (eds.) ISoLA 2018. LNCS, vol. 11246, pp. 32–47. Springer, Cham (2018). https://doi.org/10.1007/978-3-030-03424-5_3
12. Honda, K., Yoshida, N., Carbone, M.: Multiparty asynchronous session types. In: Proceedings of the 35th Annual ACM SIGPLAN-SIGACT Symposium on Principles of Programming Languages (POPL 2008), pp. 273–284. ACM (2008)
13. Knapp, A., Mossakowski, T.: UML interactions meet state machines-an institutional approach. In: Bonchi, F., König, B. (eds.) 7th Conference on Algebra and Coalgebra in Computer Science, CALCO 2017, 12–16 June 2017, Ljubljana, Slovenia, LIPIcs, vol. 72, pp. 15:1–15:15. Schloss Dagstuhl - Leibniz-Zentrum fuer Informatik (2017)
14. Knapp, A., Wuttke, J.: Model checking of UML 2.0 interactions. In: Kühne, T. (ed.) MODELS 2006. LNCS, vol. 4364, pp. 42–51. Springer, Heidelberg (2007). https://doi.org/10.1007/978-3-540-69489-2_6
15. Lange, J., Tuosto, E., Yoshida, N.: From communicating machines to graphical choreographies. In: POPL 2015, pp. 221–232 (2015)
16. Micskei, Z., Waeselynck, H.: The many meanings of UML 2 sequence diagrams: a survey. Softw. Syst. Model. **10**(4), 489–514 (2011)
17. Morin, R.: Recognizable sets of message sequence charts. In: Alt, H., Ferreira, A. (eds.) STACS 2002. LNCS, vol. 2285, pp. 523–534. Springer, Heidelberg (2002). https://doi.org/10.1007/3-540-45841-7_43
18. Pugliese, R., Tiezzi, F.: A calculus for orchestration of web services. J. Appl. Log. **10**(1), 2–31 (2012)
19. ter Beek, M.H., Carmona, J., Hennicker, R., Kleijn, J.: Communication requirements for team automata. In: Jacquet, J.-M., Massink, M. (eds.) COORDINATION 2017. LNCS, vol. 10319, pp. 256–277. Springer, Cham (2017). https://doi.org/10.1007/978-3-319-59746-1_14
20. ter Beek, M.H., Gnesi, S., Mazzanti, F.: From EU projects to a family of model checkers. In: De Nicola, R., Hennicker, R. (eds.) Software, Services, and Systems. LNCS, vol. 8950, pp. 312–328. Springer, Cham (2015). https://doi.org/10.1007/978-3-319-15545-6_20
21. Tuosto, E., Guanciale, R.: Semantics of global view of choreographies. J. Log. Algebr. Meth. Program. **95**, 17–40 (2018)
22. Wirsing, M., Hölzl, M. (eds.): Rigorous Software Engineering for Service-Oriented Systems. LNCS, vol. 6582. Springer, Heidelberg (2011). https://doi.org/10.1007/978-3-642-20401-2

Requirements Engineering

Ambiguity in Requirements Engineering: Towards a Unifying Framework

Vincenzo Gervasi[1,3]([✉]), Alessio Ferrari[2], Didar Zowghi[3], and Paola Spoletini[4]

[1] Dipartimento di Informatica, University of Pisa, Pisa, Italy
gervasi@di.unipi.it
[2] Istituto di Scienza e Tecnologie dell'Informazione "Alessandro Faedo", CNR,
Pisa, Italy
[3] Faculty of Engineering and IT, University of Technology, Sydney, Australia
[4] SWEGD, Kennesaw State University, Kennesaw, USA

Abstract. A long stream of research in RE has been devoted to analyzing the occurrences and consequences of *ambiguity* in requirements documents. Ambiguity often occurs in documents, most often in natural language (NL) ones, but occasionally also in formal specifications, be it because of abstraction, or of imprecise designation of which real-world entities are denoted by certain expressions. In many of those studies, ambiguity has been considered a defect to be avoided. In this paper, we investigate the nature of ambiguity, and advocate that the simplistic view of ambiguity as merely a defect in the document does not do justice to the complexity of this phenomenon. We offer a more extensive analysis, based on the multiple linguistic sources of ambiguity, and present a list of real-world cases, both in written matter and in oral interviews, that we analyze based on our framework. We hope that a better understanding of the phenomenon can help in the analysis of practical experiences and in the design of more effective methods to detect, mark and handle ambiguity.

1   Introduction

The study of properties of software requirements specifications (SRS) has been an important and recurring theme throughout the evolution of requirements engineering (RE) research. Fundamental issues concerning the *contents* of requirements, such has how to avoid or detect inconsistencies in SRS (and whether to remove or tolerate them), or how to ensure completeness of the requirements, have been a mainstay in RE. The reasons are clear: no implementation can satisfy an inconsistent SRS, and an incomplete SRS, once implemented, will not satisfy all the needs of the users of the corresponding software system. In fact, consistency and completeness have been regarded in our earlier work [1,2] as the two main factors for requirements correctness, i.e. as two quality features that an SRS must, eventually, possess.

Another related stream of research has been concerned with properties of the *form* of requirements, rather than of their content. Properties such as understandability, conciseness, etc. have been studied and discussed, and techniques to ensure an SRS exhibits such properties (or to identify and fix their negative dual properties) have been proposed.

In this paper, we focus mainly on *ambiguity*, i.e. the phenomenon by which multiple distinct meanings can be assigned to the same requirement (or, more generally, sets

© Springer Nature Switzerland AG 2019
M. H. ter Beek et al. (Eds.): Gnesi Festschrift, LNCS 11865, pp. 191–210, 2019.
https://doi.org/10.1007/978-3-030-30985-5_12

of requirements), and discuss the relationships between ambiguity and certain related phenomena which are often observed in requirements. The process of transforming an intended meaning into a set of signs (the documented form of a requirement), and then back from signs to meanings, is complex enough – even in the case of formal or diagrammatic languages – that an accurate understanding of its different facets is needed for an effective management of the requirements. Given the complexity of the ambiguity phenomenon and of its relationship with requirements, this work does not have the ambition of being a comprehensive analysis of neither of the two. Certain areas, such as for example how interactions between certain requirements can generate ambiguity that were not present in the requirements in isolation, are not dealt with in the paper.

We do not provide in this work advice on how to avoid introducing ambiguity in an SRS, nor on how to remedy it when it is detected. Rather, we focus on understanding what ambiguity *is* (with particular reference to its role in requirements engineering), on how, when and by whom it is introduced in SRS, and on what the effects of its various forms are. We posit that ambiguity is not necessarily a defect, and in fact can play an important positive role both in the requirements as a document, and in the requirements elicitation process. In short, this paper is not about a solution to a problem, but rather about exploring and characterizing the nature of a phenomenon, with supporting evidence from real-world practice.

At the same time, the paper constitutes a call to fellow researchers to draw more freely on the vast amount of knowledge that scholarly work in semiotics and linguistics has produced in the past. While requirements specifications are a very peculiar type of document, with very specific uses, and often the language employed in them is highly stylized when not entirely formalized, yet the fundamental situation is still that of two parties communicating through some form of language, and most results from established discourse theories in linguistics apply equally well to requirements engineering.

The rest of this paper is organized as follows: Sect. 2 discusses our basic model of ambiguity in the interpretation of RE documents (e.g., SRS); this is followed by an analysis and classification of the different levels at which ambiguity can be introduced. Section 3 presents a discussion on linguistic sources of ambiguity. Section 4 then discusses the relationships between ambiguity, abstraction and absence, and presents both a theoretical framework and a classification of different forms of ambiguity. Sections 5 and 6 present a number of real-world cases of ambiguity, in written text and in oral interviews respectively, which are characterized according to our framework. This is followed by a short survey of related works (where we restrict ourselves to the RE literature) and by some conclusion.

The present paper is a substantially extended and revised version of our previous work in [3].

2   Ambiguity and Interpretation in Requirements Engineering

As has been recognized in the literature (see Sect. 7), ambiguity is a complex, multi-level phenomenon. While the general concept of "having multiple meanings" is relatively easy to describe, locating the original source – or root cause – of the ambiguity may be challenging. Moreover, ambiguity may or may not be detected by the several parties involved in requirements elicitation or analysis, and be intentional or accidental; its extent can be confined to a minor detail or encompass some major aspect of the system.

It is clear that the simple intuitive definition of "having multiple meanings" is insufficient for a deep understanding of ambiguity. We will instead use as reference frame that of the classical denotational approach, where semantics is given by a function mapping from a source domain (the text of the requirements) to a target domain (the denotation of their semantics). Which particular semantics we want to observe (e.g., input/output semantics, performances, labeled transition system, development cost estimates, etc.) is immaterial for our discussion, and we can imagine that the semantics domain will in fact be different for different purposes[1]. Of course we will not insist on all the properties that characterize domains according to the Scott-Strachey definition [4] (e.g., that domains are partial orders, or that the mapping is Scott-continuous), nor on the compositionality of the mapping function. In requirements engineering, all these three elements — source domain, target domain, mapping function—are fuzzy at best. The source domain can include, in addition to written text, spoken information, observed behavior, references to pre-existing systems or work practices, etc. The target domain (i.e. the semantics of the requirements) should in theory be such that it is possible to determine if a given specification or implementation satisfies the requirements, but in practice it is often in itself vague. And finally, the mapping is ill-defined, and often – even when a strict formal definition exists – may well be misunderstood by at least some of the stakeholders (e.g., an end-user will probably be incapable of understanding the meaning of a fragment of Z [5] from a complex requirements specification). This last point is worth stressing. For the purpose of assessing the effects of ambiguity, it is not the *intrinsic* meaning of a requirement or set thereof that is of interest (even when we have such a thing, e.g. in formal languages), but the *interpretation* placed on it by a cognitive agent or interpreter.

We will thus accept the fuzziness of all our elements, while still keeping the general framework of denotational semantics, and asking only that any semantics, in order to be considered acceptable, must allow for testing an implementation for satisfaction of the requirements. This is in keeping with Dana Scott's position [6] that

> It is not necessary for the semantics to determine an implementation, but it should provide criteria for showing that an implementation is correct.

Figure 1 shows an overview of how we define the various steps and transformations which can lead to multiple meanings. The details will be elucidated in the next section; for now it suffices to say that the meaning of a stated requirement is determined on a purely symbolic base, based on which symbols constitute the requirement, and on the

---

[1] In fact, a statement can be ambiguous or not depending on which particular semantics we observe. For example, a requirement asking for a given feature in ambiguous terms could be interpreted in several different ways for the purpose of implementing the feature, and thus be ambiguous; however, if the possible interpretations all have the same implementation costs, the meaning would be unique for cost-estimate purposes, and thus no ambiguity would arise in that particular denotation.

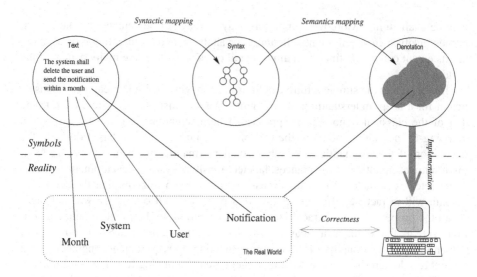

Fig. 1. The theoretical framework for the occurrence of ambiguity.

grammar and interpretation rules of the language used (in Fig. 1 we are using natural language as an example, but the same holds for any other notation used to express the requirements). The denotation of the semantics of the requirements is then what drives the implementation, whose purpose is to build a computer-based system (in the real world) which will interact with its environment and modify it in such a way that the original intention expressed through the requirements is satisfied.

In the following, we outline a more structured analysis of ambiguity, with particular reference to its potential sources, and the roles that ambiguity can play in requirements specifications.

3   Linguistic Sources of Ambiguity

Different forms of ambiguity are introduced in a requirements document at different levels. As ambiguity is essentially a linguistic phenomenon, in that it pertains to how meaning is associated to a certain statement or set of statements in some language, it is appropriate to analyze sources of ambiguity according to the usual linguistics paradigm of lexicon, syntax, semantics. In this paper, we will not explicitly consider the fourth possible source of ambiguity, namely pragmatics, which could generate ambiguity due to contextual information (e.g. about the nature or intent of a document), or to the identities or roles of the actors in the exchange, or based on the stated or presumed intentions of the author or speaker, etc. However, these are informally addressed in the examples presented in Sect. 6.

The distinction is not new; in relation to requirements quality it has been introduced in [7] and maintained in subsequent studies, such as [8–10]. We will briefly outline the main issues that occur at different levels here, not delving into all the details since our main interest is only on one particular form, as will be discussed in the following.

3.1 Levels of Ambiguity

Lexical Level. Ambiguity in lexicon occurs typically when the same term is used to denote different things. This can be an inherent feature of the language being used (for example: homonyms in natural language, as in *bank* account vs. *bank* of a river), or happen even in more formal languages due to lack of or imprecise *designations* [11]. In fact, even in formal languages such designations are invariably rooted in the informal real world, and all stakeholders must *a-priori* agree on their meaning (thus establishing a common base of reference). Of course, this rarely happens in practice; even when using a particular domain's jargon, it is often the case that certain terms are found to be ambiguous.

It is worth remarking that even approaches based on lexical semantics (e.g., Wordnet [12]) or ontologies (e.g., LEL [13]) cannot rule out the risk of lexical ambiguity: in these approaches, relations between terms are spelled out, but the meaning of a term is only given by other terms. And after all, words are conventional and do not derive from things as Cratylus used to believe [14]. The only thing keeping Humpty Dumpty from really going by his statement "When I use a word, it means just what I choose it to mean – nothing more nor less." is the need of making himself clear to Alice [15]— unfortunately, not something to rely upon when analyzing software requirements.

In Fig. 1, terms appearing in the requirement (in the Text circle), such as "user" or "month" are just lexical tokens. They can correspond to different designations, e.g. "month" could mean a 30-days period, or a 31-days period, or till the same-numbered day in the next month, or go with the moon phases, or even some fancier period[2]. Without a more precise designation, the term "month" is seriously ambiguous: for example, which date is "a month after January 30"?

Syntactic Level. Ambiguity on the syntactic level is in a sense easier to define. It stems from there existing multiple parse trees for a single sentence (or, more generally, a given segment of the linear stream of language); to each possible parse tree, a different meaning is attached, hence the ambiguity. Berry, Kamsties and Krieger in [8] have provided a large number of delightful examples of ambiguities in several natural languages (and guidelines on how to avoid the most common pitfalls).

In Fig. 1, multiple possible parse trees exist for our sample requirement. In fact, the sentence could be parsed as "The system shall delete the user and (send the notification within a month)" (Fig. 2, left) or as "The system shall (delete the user and send the notification) within a month" (Fig. 2, right), where the parentheses have been used to indicate the two critically different parsings.

Interestingly, syntactic ambiguity can be avoided by design in certain languages, and in fact most formal languages are so designed that their grammar does not allow ambiguous parsing (this allows the construction of simple and efficient parsers). This is the case in fact of almost all programming and formal specification languages, but is also claimed of some engineered spoken language, e.g. Loglan [16].

---

[2] The Bahá'í calendar, for example, has 19 months of 19 days each, plus 4 intercalary days (5 in leap years) which are not part of any month. How would our requirement be interpreted in a Bahá'í community?

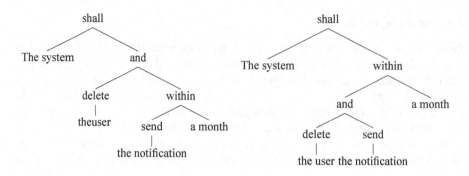

Fig. 2. Two different parse trees for our sample requirement: a case of syntactic ambiguity. This situation is termed *coordination ambiguity*.

Semantic level. Semantic ambiguity is our main concern in this paper. This happens when the source text is uniquely determined in both lexicon and syntax, i.e. the exact meaning of all terms is established, and there is only one correct parsing of the text. Nevertheless, multiple meanings can be assigned to the sentence. In this case, the ambiguity lies not in the source, but in the function assigning meaning to the source, labeled in Fig. 1 as the *semantics mapping* function.

In holding this view we differ from [8, 10, 17], where semantic ambiguity is ascribed to coordination ambiguity (properly deciding the operands of *and*, *or* or other sentence constructors), referential ambiguity (resolving pronominal references and anaphora), and scope ambiguity (delimiting the scope of quantifiers). We rather consider that these phenomena stem from the syntax of the language: in fact, if natural language had some form of parentheses (for scoping) and indexing (for references), these problems would disappear (as shown, accidentally, by our previous example in Fig. 2 about syntactic ambiguity). In practice, typography and layout can at times serve to mark parenthetical structure when the language does not offer it: for example, we could have written our requirement as:

> The system shall:
> – delete the user, and
> – send the notification within a month.

or rather

> The system shall:
> – delete the user, and
> – send the notification
> within a month.

to make our intention clear. In fact, some systems for the automated analysis of NL requirements such as [18] have used layout to help infer parenthetical structure in such cases.

Another proof that types of ambiguity cited above are syntactic phenomena lies in the fact that semantic ambiguity can also happen in formal languages, where the lexicon and syntax are perfectly defined. In this case, the *understanding* of the semantics of the language on the part of a reader can cause a certain statement to be interpreted ambiguously. Whether a standard semantics for the language exist or not is somewhat irrelevant to the phenomenon itself (e.g., it is often the case that even skilled programmers ignore some subtle point of the formal semantics of a programming language[3] or that the description of the semantics in itself is ambiguous). In practice, the standardized semantics of some language can be, and often is, so large and complex that it can be considered for all practical purposes to be cognitively inaccessible to the reader: hence, the semantics mapping function really used by a reader can be different from the official one, of which it will be just one of many possible approximations. And of course, different approximations by different readers, or at different times, will produce different meanings.

In Fig. 1, even if we have precise designations for "month", "system", "user" etc., and even if we are told in some way which of the two syntactic interpretation to take, we could still have doubts on the intended semantics. For example, "shall send a notification" means the system will attempt to do it, but how? Is it sufficient to print out a form and hope that some operator will put it in an envelope and give to the Post Office for delivery? What if the notification is sent, but not delivered? Is there some sort of acknowledgment to be expected? Maybe the notification could be sent via a text message to the user's mobile phone? Or maybe, the notification is not intended for the user, but for his manager? And so on (endlessly).

We will devote the rest of the paper to semantic ambiguity: that is, the form of ambiguity which arises irrespective of lexicon and syntax. We will have much to say about its role in requirements elicitation and analysis.

3.2 Ambiguity vs. Vagueness

It is important not to unduly conflate *ambiguity* with *vagueness*, a different (yet related) linguistic phenomenon. Ambiguity denotes the existence of multiple distinct meanings, with an implicit assumptions that they are individually well-defined – so that solving the ambiguity means making a choice between a discrete set of possible interpretations, eventually leading to a certain implementation. In contrast, vagueness refer instead to cases where the meaning itself is fuzzily defined (Fig. 3); the possible implementations form a continuous space, no longer a discrete set. Consequently, requirements cannot be said to be satisfied or not; rather, the notion of *degree of satisfaction* comes into play. This is often the case with non-functional requirements, and the topic has been extensively researched in requirements literature: in fact, both techniques to explicitly model the vagueness (e.g. by using fuzzy logic or the concept of satisficing in goal models) and recommendations to avoid vagueness (e.g., by substituting every non-functional requirement of this kind with some measurable proxy, as in service level agreements) have been advocated [19].

In natural languages, ambiguity and vagueness are often intertwined, due to one of the parties assuming a vague meaning, and the other assuming two (or more) different

---

[3] For a concrete example, even an experienced C language programmer might look puzzled at a statement like `long c=3["test"];` which is perfectly legal and unambiguous in the language. But then, `int x=*(char *)&c;`, which is again legal, produces results which are not specified by the semantics, and is thus ambiguous (probably, x would be either 0 or 116).

Fig. 3. A visual rendition of the difference between ambiguity (left) and vagueness (right).

points inside the continuous space to be two (or more) distinct meanings. In practice, it is not uncommon for a stakeholder to use a vague term to signify a genuine lack of preference, whereas an analyst might insist in setting on a single non-vague choice.

4   Ambiguity, Abstraction, Absence

We have seen in the previous section how even a simple sentence like our example

The system shall delete the user and send the notification within a month.

which could appear among the old-fashioned requirements, say, for a library loan system when membership expires, is actually riddled by lexical, syntactic, and semantic ambiguity, so that its correct implementation, missing further information, is probably beyond hope.

One could then believe that ambiguity is thus a pernicious defect, to be eradicated with ruthless determination from any self-respecting requirements specification. Unfortunately, this noble determination often leads to the practical impossibility of writing down, analyzing, and implementing, the requirements for even the simplest of software systems, while huge amounts of effort are devoted to writing beautifully complex and extensive specifications.[4]

We believe instead that ambiguity can also play a positive role in requirements specifications, beyond its well-known political role in negotiations. To this end, we need first to distinguish among three related concepts:

- **Ambiguity** is the existence of multiple denotations for the same source text in the semantics space. Whether this is caused by syntactic ambiguity (as in Fig. 4, bottom) or by semantics ambiguity (as in Fig. 4, top), or by lexical issues (e.g., uncertain designations) is irrelevant: the essence of the phenomenon is in having multiple (distinct) semantics for the same source. Ambiguity has often been considered a defect in requirements, in account of the lack of a single, well-defined, shared semantics that can be used to drive implementation (and, later, verification).
- **Abstraction** is the omission of some details (or more properly, of some information content). Ambiguity can be used as a form of abstraction, in that the detail missing is the information needed to discriminate between multiple semantics in order to

---

[4] In fact, we rather believe that it is essentially impossible to write unambiguous specifications, with space for doubt for some purely symbolic processing system (such as lexical domains in [11]), that start with Peano axioms [20] and work up from those.

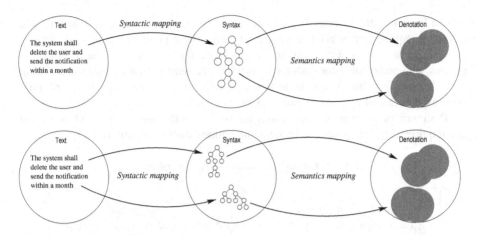

Fig. 4. Cases of ambiguity: semantics ambiguity (top), syntactic ambiguity (bottom).

identify the right ones (in the eye of the requirement author). Abstraction is generally considered a desirable quality in requirements, up to a point, in that it avoids over-specification, a flaw that may cause waste of time or generation of new errors [21], and thus simplifies the requirements, keeping them manageable and allowing stake-holders to focus on the important parts.

– **Absence** is the total lack of details on some specific aspect; as such, it is the extreme case of abstraction, where certain information content is abstracted to nothingness (hence, it is at times called *silence*). Being a special case of abstraction, absence as well can be related to ambiguity as discussed above. Absence is the major motivation for requirements elicitation: knowledge holes are usually considered dangerous in specifications, and need to be filled-in by investigating the problem and its domain in more depth.

In witness of the pervasiveness of ambiguity in requirements, our sample require-ment also contains instances of both abstraction and absence. Using the term "month" can be seen as a not very precise way to refer to some specific duration of time, essen-tially conveying the idea of "I don't care about the *exact* duration, but it should be close to 30 days", hence this is a case of abstraction. At the same time, nothing is said about the actual contents of the "notification", e.g. which text should be sent. Of course, the implemented system will have to send some specific text (we cannot keep the actual message abstract in the implementation), so the missing information is needed, and hence this is really a case of absence.

Since ambiguity can play both negative and positive roles, the question arises natu-rally: when is bad ambiguity turned into good abstraction, and when is the latter turned again into bad absence? We believe this question, in this crude form, is too simplistic, and more about the *intentions* of the stakeholders working on and with the requirements must be considered.

As a fist step, let us identify two roles in interacting with requirements, those of *author* and of *reader*. The author is the stakeholder that commits a requirement to a written form: it is not necessarily the customer or the problem owner, and in fact it could also be a requirement analyst, a consultant, or the long-gone author of a procedures manual that has since left the company. The reader is the participant to the development process who needs the information conveyed by the requirements in order to perform his or her own job. Implementors, testers, customer (in validation), developers of other systems, etc. can all play the role of readers.

Both writers and readers may or may not recognize the ambiguity which is present in a requirement. This gives rise to the combinations shown in Table 1.

Table 1. Recognized and unrecognized ambiguity.

		Reader	
		recognized	unrecognized
Writer	recognized	**(a)** ambiguity used by writer as abstraction device, recognized as such: good use of ambiguity, any implementation correct.	**(b)** writer used ambiguity as abstraction device, reader only recognized one possible meaning: loss of design space.
	unrecognized	**(c)** writer wrote ambiguous requirement without realizing, reader assumed all meanings are acceptable: potential incorrect implementation.	**(d)** ambiguity gone unnoticed: if both reader and writer agree on meaning, correct implementation possible by chance, otherwise incorrect implementation.

We assume for now that recognizing an ambiguity means being cognizant of all the possible meanings, whereas not recognizing it means considering only one meaning (which may or may not be the intended one), and not realizing that there is a potential ambiguity. Naturally, in practice we can be faced with fuzzy cases, in which we can suspect that there is an ambiguity but cannot determine for certain (e.g., for lexical or semantic ambiguity), or the different meanings conveyed by an ambiguous statement can themselves be vague and blend into each other without clear distinction. For the sake of exposition, we will oversimplify the issue in the following analysis.

When the ambiguity is recognized by the writer (cases (a) and (b) in Table 1), we can assume that it is *intentional*: the writer is using ambiguity as a means of abstracting away unnecessary details, signifying that all possible meanings are all equally acceptable to her as correct implementations of the requirements. For example, in our previous example from Fig. 1, the clause "within a month" could be intentionally ambiguous, meaning that the writer (e.g., the customer) is not interested in the exact limit, as long as there is a fixed term, and the term is *approximately* a month. In case (a), the reader (e.g., the implementor) also recognizes the ambiguity, and is free to choose, among all possible implementations that satisfy the requirement in any of its possible ambiguous meanings, the one that best suits him: for example, a simple `limit=today()+30;` in code will suffice. In case (b), the reader may not realize that the writer has given him freedom to implement a vague notion of *month*, and might implement a full calendar, taking into account leap years and different month lengths, possibly synchronizing with time servers on the Internet to give precise-to-the-millisecond months, etc. The resulting implementation will be correct, but unnecessarily complex. The design space for the solution has been restricted without reason, and maybe opportunities for improving the quality of the implementation in other areas (e.g., robustness or maintainability) have been lost.

If the ambiguity is not recognized by the writer (cases (c) and (d) in Table 1), we can assume it is *not intentional*: in a sense, it has crept in against the writer's intention. Hence, only one of the possible meanings is correct, whereas others are incorrect. Of course, once the ambiguity has entered the meaning chain, it is impossible to establish which of the various possible meanings was the intended one. The implementation can still be correct, but only by chance (because, among the possible interpretations, the correct one was chosen). Moreover, when multiple readers are involved, as is the case in every real-life project, the chances of *every* reader taking up the correct interpretation by chance becomes smaller as the number of readers increases: so, this type of ambiguity will probably lead to a wrong implementation, or to a correct implementation which is tested against the wrong set of test cases, or to a correct implementation which is tested correctly but then erroneously documented in users' manuals according to a wrong interpretation, etc.

5   Ambiguity Cases in Requirements Documents

In this section we review some typical cases of ambiguity in requirements documents, based on publications available from the literature [22], and we show how such real-world ambiguities can be explained by means of the presented framework.

Pronouns: Anaphora occurs in a text whenever a pronoun (e.g., *he, it, that, this, which,* etc.) refers to a previous part of the text. The referred part of the text is normally called *antecedent*. An anaphoric ambiguity occurs if the text offers more than one antecedent options [23], either in the same sentence (e.g., *The system shall send a message to the receiver, and it provides an acknowledge message—it = system* or *receiver?*) or in previous sentences. The potential antecedents for the pronouns are noun phrases (NP), which can be detected by means of a shallow parser.

Whenever the ambiguity can be resolved by identifying a proper textual antecedent, we can assume this to be a type of syntactic ambiguity. However, at times a proper antecedent will be missing entirely: in such cases, *context* might provide a resolution. For example, "them" might be a signifier for "our competitors" if the document serves the role of a strategic market analysis, even if no antecedent appear in the text.

Coordinating Conjunctions: coordination ambiguity occurs when the use of coordinating conjunctions (e.g., *and* or *or*) leads to multiple potential interpretations of a sentence [24]. Two types of coordination ambiguity are considered here. The first type includes sentences in which more than one coordinating conjunction is used in the same sentence (e.g., *There is a 90° phase shift between sensor 1 **and** sensor 2 **and** sensor 3 shall have a 45° phase shift*). The second type includes sentences in which a coordinating conjunction is used with a modifier (e.g., *Structured approaches and platforms—Structured* can refer to *approaches* only, or also to *platforms*).

Coordinating conjunctions are invariably a case of syntactic ambiguity, as the difficulty lies with producing the correct parse tree, not with the interpretation of the meaning once the correct parse tree is provided.

Vague Terms: Vagueness is associated with the usage of terms that admit a continuous set of possible interpretations (Sect. 3.2), such as *minimal, as much as possible, later, taking into account, based on, appropriate*, etc. Typical example requirements are as follows: *In case the boolean logic evaluates the permissive state, the system shall activate <u>a certain</u> redundant output* – which output shall be activated?

Modal Adverbs: Modal adverbs (e.g., *positively, permanently, clearly*) are modifiers that express a quality associated to a predicate. Example of ambiguous requirements using modal adverbs are: *The system shall respond positively when the no fault is identified*—the requirement does not specify what type of message should be sent. The term "positively" is thus an abstraction device (Sect. 4): we state only the single property of the message we are interested in (i.e., that it will be interpreted by the receiver as the positive outcome), and not all other properties the message might have, thus leaving the implementor free in that respect.

Passive Voice: The use of passive voice is a defect of clarity in requirements, and can lead to ambiguous interpretations in those cases in which the passive verb is not followed by the subject that performs the action expressed by the verb (e.g., *The system shall be shut down*—by which actor?). Omitting the actor is a case of absence of information, and as such an opportunity for further elicitation. Also, different meanings could be intended by the writer, e.g. "The system shall be shut down *on condition*", or "The system shall be shut down *by operator*" or "It shall be possible to shut down the system *for whom*", etc.

It is interesting to observe that the rules of standard English grammar allow omitting the actor, hence this is no syntactic ambiguity. However, other languages which have an *ergative case*[5] in their grammar that cannot be omitted, would rather consider this a syntax error; or if the ergative case is unmarked, this could give rise to a proper syntactic ambiguity. The fact that different languages exhibit different cases of syntactic ambiguity should come as no surprise—and in fact, that is exactly one of the reasons in support of using controlled languages in RE.

6   Ambiguity Cases in Requirements Elicitation Interviews

In this section we present typical cases of ambiguity in requirements elicitation interviews, based on publications on the topic available from the literature [25, 26], and we show how these real-world ambiguities can be explained by means of the presented framework. The cases are presented based on typical categories of ambiguity cues in interviews, namely under-specified terms, vague terms, quantifiers and pronouns.

---

[5] Ergative is the grammatical case for nouns that identify the intentional agent of a verb (especially a transitive verb), often marked by a special suffix or prefix.

Under-Specified Terms. This category includes terms with a high degree of generality, i.e., terms that identify a class of concepts or actions, but do not specify some required detail. Examples are names such as *people, knowledge, movement, area, rule, data, category, interface, thing, detail, etc.* and – less frequently – verbs such as *use, make, search, etc.* As such, under-specified terms are a form of abstraction, applied at the lexical level.

These terms might characterize a *specific* concept in the mind of the customer, which might not be accessible to the analyst, and that can be clarified with a more detailed specification. In other cases, they can characterize a concept that is not well defined in the mind of the customer, and that hence deserves to be made more concrete. In general, using the term "under-specified" implies a desire for a greater specificity, hence this particular designation has a negative connotation, and is often used to stigmatize cases of nocuous ambiguity. Below we present real-world examples of under-specified terms, adapted from [26].

> *Example 1. A bio-medical engineer wants to develop a system that patients can use to measure their blood pressure. The system shall include a mobile application, which sends the data about the blood pressure to the general practice doctor. When asked how blood pressure is currently measured, the customer said:* There is this <u>device</u>. *The analyst correctly understood that a specific device is used. The analyst thought that a precise name, or brand, for the device was needed, to develop an interface between the mobile phone and the device. After asking, it was clarified that the bio-medical engineer did not know the name of the device (i.e., blood pressure monitor).*

> *Example 2. A customer wants to develop a mobile application that monitors the use that she makes of her mobile phone. She said:* Maybe the system could give me also some <u>recommendations</u>. *The analyst thought that the term* recommendations *could have two acceptable meanings: (a) negative recommendations on applications and mobile features that she should not use; (b) positive recommendations on applications that could be downloaded, and mobile features that could be used. After clarification, the first meaning resulted correct.*

We have presented examples in which only one under-specified term is used. However, we saw also situations in which several under-specified terms are used together, possibly with vague expressions (discussed in the next sub-section), giving a too abstract level to the conversation, and causing interpretation difficulties. An interesting example is presented below.

> *Example 3. One of our customers is a public administration officer. He started the interview saying:* [I want to develop] a <u>data-base</u> in which there are *several* <u>profiles</u> of <u>users</u> that can <u>access</u> to different <u>levels</u> of <u>information</u>, but, most of all, can do *different* <u>operations</u> *depending on* their <u>profile</u>. *We have underlined under-specified terms, and emphasised vague ones. The analyst could not assign a clear meaning to this fragment and asked:* What is the application field? *Basically, the analyst did not have a contextual ground over which the under-specified*

terms could make sense. Afterwards, it was clarified that the application field was the monitoring and assessing of EU-funded projects. The different users were the receivers of the funds, who are required to provide evidence of their expenses, and the officer, who is required to assess the projects.

Vague Terms. Vague terms are terms that admit a continuous set of possible interpretations (Sect. 3.2) such as *minimal, as much as possible, later, taking into account, based on, appropriate, etc.* We already discussed these in the previous section; however, in interviews their use is generally more widespread and less damaging. In fact, vague terms are often use as an effort-saving device, so that the speaker needs not focus on retrieving the more precise term, an effort that would render the conversation less natural and impede its flow. In addition, in interviews the context is often more immediately clear to both the interviewer and the interviewee (at least, at that point in time), and moreover there is usually an underlying assumption that the material will eventually end up in written form, and at that point more precise designations may be substituted for vague terms used in the oral form.

Example 4. One of our customers wants to develop a system to automatically sketch the map of apartments. The goal is to use the system before buying an apartment, to have an idea of how the place could be rearranged. The analyst suggested a robot that follows the walls when the user visits the apartment, and provides a sketch of the map that can be visualized through a tablet. The customer asked: Can I do adjustments later? *The term* later *triggered a multiple understanding phenomenon. Indeed, the analyst could intend* later *as (a) when the user was not anymore in the apartment, e.g., to actually rearrange the map, or (b) right after the map was sketched, e.g., to account for errors made by the system. When asked, the customer specified that the first interpretation was correct.*

Notice again how, by itself, *later* is non-ambiguous: it has a single meaning (i.e., at some time subsequent the initial mapping), but the degree of vagueness was incompatible with the needs of the analyst, who (arbitrarily) chose two possible interpretations that were compatible with the vague semantics, yet more precise. We could have imagined even more compatible interpretations, e.g. (c) after the apartment is sold, maybe for tax-avoidance purposes!

Quantifiers. Quantifiers are the Natural language expressions that serve to select certain elements from a typically larger set of similar elements, and are thus akin to the universal quantifier $\forall$ and the existential quantifier $\exists$ in logic. These terms include *all, for each, any, some, both, etc.*

Example 5. A customer wants to develop a virtual phone-chain, i.e., a system that alerts her when she is more than five meters from her mobile phone. The system is composed of an application to be installed in the mobile, and by a device that the user shall wear. The customer said: From the device I can switch off all of them. *The term* all *could be interpreted in multiple ways: the device allows to switch* *itself and the application simultaneously (*for all*); the device can switch itself and the application off in a given sequence (*for each*); the device allows to switch itself and the application separately (*any*) based on user's choice. The first interpretation resulted to be valid.*

Pronouns. Personal pronouns such as *he, she, it*, possessive pronouns as *her, his, its*, relative pronouns such as *that, which*, demonstrative pronouns such as *this, those, etc.*, are all potential sources of ambiguity (i.e., when the target of the reference is not uniquely determined by grammatical rules), which we have considered at the semantic level.

Example 6. A customer wants to develop an electronic business card, to be passed from the mobile of the sender to the one of the receiver by means of a Bluetooth connection. Along the discussion, the electronic business card was decided to be associated with an image, like paper business cards. He said: If we are in the same area, <u>it</u> gets transferred. *The analyst thought that it could be referred to the information only, or also to the image, and asked:* You want to transfer just the information, or you want also the image of the card? *The customer – quite surprisingly – replied:* Just the information.

Example 7. A real-estate appraisal expert says that, when she has to estimate the value of a property, she searches for the price of similar properties in the same area. Then, she compares the characteristics of those properties with the property under evaluation, to estimate the price. She said that her problem is that: <u>This</u> *work takes a lot of time.*[6] *The analyst assumed that the time consuming work was the comparison. But, when the analyst summarised what he understood, the customer said:* No, the search [of similar properties is time consuming].

In both these examples, the pronouns are used in an anaphoric function, i.e. they refer to a noun or noun phrase that had already been mentioned in the context. Syntactic concordance rules (e.g., the pronoun must be compatible in number and gender with the referred noun) help in resolving the reference, yet may not be sufficient to identify a single possible interpretation. More candidates can be discarded by having recourse to semantics (e.g., in our example 6 *it* can only refer to something that can be transferred via a Bluetooth connection), and if multiple possible candidates still exists, to pragmatics (e.g., also in example 6, the analyst is assuming from social context that people might be more interested in the textual details of the business card, so the options for clarification offered to the customer are just two: (a) only textual information, (b) textual information+image—but the third possible interpretation, (c) only image, is discarded on pragmatic grounds).

It is worth to notice that pronouns can also serve other functions, e.g. as deictic[7] instead of anaphora. This is particularly common in interviews. Our customer from

---

[6] The reader will notice that the ambiguity is not raised by the vague expression *a lot*, which appeared acceptable at that stage of the conversation.

[7] A deictic expression refers to something that only exist in the context, e.g. "here" referring to the current location of the speaker, never appearing in text.

example 6 could have said *I want this transferred.* while holding in his hand a traditional, paper-based business card, and looking down at the printed face of the card while saying it. Deictics may also introduce ambiguity, which would clearly be at the contextual level.

7   Related Work

Although not one of the most popular subjects, ambiguity in requirements has received some degree of attention from researchers, especially in recent years. Not always the phenomenon has been correctly described, and at times it has been mixed up with related phenomena; also, the connection with classical studies of ambiguity in the humanities is a relatively recent acquisition.

Early studies generally have considered ambiguity in relation to completeness, i.e. only in its capacity as abstraction or absence (although often the terms used are more pertaining to vagueness), and not as an independent and significant phenomenon. Among those, Boehm [27] mentions indeterminacy as a form of incompleteness, and attributes it to missing information. There is no distinction between information that the writer might want to convey and is missing due to forgetfulness (absence), information that the writer positively wanted to omit (abstraction), and information that the writer wanted to convey, but was unable to articulate (tacit knowledge). Hence, several distinct phenomena are confused into one "indeterminacy", and the latter is itself flattened into incompleteness. In [21], Meyer lists ambiguity as one of the seven deficiencies requirements specification can suffer of. In his view, ambiguity together with inadequacies with respect to the real needs, incompletenesses, and contradictions are errors that may have disastrous effects on the subsequent development steps and on the quality of the resulting software product.

Gause and Weinberg [28] correctly identified these variations, but still defined ambiguity as related to missing information and communication errors. As causes, they cite the fact that humans make errors in observation and recall (absence), tend to leave out evident information, and generalize incorrectly (wrong abstraction); communications error that occur between writers and readers are ascribed to expression inadequacies in the writing. The fact that ambiguity can be introduced by lexicon, syntax, semantics (and that these different causes call for different remedies, given that they only consider the case of unwanted ambiguity) is not explored in [28].

A similar position is taken in the later work of Schneider et al. [29], where ambiguity is defined as

> An important term, phrase, or sentence essential to an understanding of system behavior has either been left undefined or defined in a way that can cause confusion and misunderstanding. Note, these are not merely language ambiguities such us uncertain pronoun reference, but ambiguities about the actual system and its behavior.

so ambiguity is considered either as absence (examples at the lexical and syntactic levels are provided) or as confusion. Unfortunately, the definition offered defines "ambiguity" in terms of "misunderstandings" and of "ambiguities about the system", which makes it shallow and circular, preventing a more in-depth analysis. Once again, only absence and vagueness are identified, and equated to ambiguity.

In his 2002 paper [30], Kovitz sees ambiguity as a defect, and recommends to add redundancy relating to the context (i.e., everything outside the description and its subject matter that relates to it in any way) in order to remove ambiguity. It is unclear if his view is closer to consider ambiguity as absence, and thus adding relevant material would help in that it provides more information, or if it is closer to what we have called the pragmatic source of ambiguity, in which case the added material only serves to introduce the reader to the same context. In any case, most probably the added material is not really redundant nor irrelevant, since it serves a precise purpose.

A first step in separating the different levels of ambiguity (still seen as a defect *tout court*) was taken in [7], where syntactic, structural (referring to documents' structure), semantic and pragmatic levels were identified. That stream of works then continued, eventually producing tools to identify the presence of known forms of lexical and syntactic ambiguity in NL requirements [31,32].

Bubka et al. [33] highlighted the exaggerated attention given to ambiguity (as a defect), since ambiguous statements may be "comprehended in such a way that the intended meaning is chosen" and, hence, "it would seem that under the appropriate circumstances, there is no ambiguity."; in our framework the "appropriate circumstances" would entail a form of pragmatic ambiguity resolution.

The most complete analysis of linguistic causes of ambiguity (in RE) is probably the one in [8,9,17,34], which we have already discussed. The one that more closely matches our own is that by Chantree et al. [24]: Their work, though, focuses mostly on a technique to automatically identify problematic cases of coordination ambiguity in requirements, while discounting the easy cases in which lexical statistics techniques let them judge misinterpretation unlikely. However, their distinction between *nocuous* and *innocuous* ambiguity is based only on whether misunderstandings are more or less likely, in that different interpretations are preferred by different readers, and they do not consider the intent of the writer. Similarly, their distinction between *acknowledged* and *unacknowledged* ambiguity coincides with our *recognized* and *unrecognized* ambiguity, but only on the reader's side. They do not investigate the relationship between ambiguity, abstraction, and absence, nor how ambiguity can be used purposefully for a variety of reasons (including negotiation).

A thorough analysis of tools to identify and manage ambiguity is provided in [10]; they also report on experiments that indicate that reasonable performance can be obtained in certain recognition tasks.

Other works focusing on the development of tools for ambiguity detection are those of Gleich et al. [35] and Tjong and Berry [36]. Recent advances in natural language processing technologies [37], and the rising awareness about requirements quality in industry have led to the application of this previous research in extensive industrial case studies [22,38]. Furthermore, different companies have developed commercial tools to support automated ambiguity detection, as well as other defects or smells. Among these companies, Qualicen GmbH[8], developed Requirements Scout, a tool to analyze requirements specifications aiming to uncover requirements smells; QRA Corp[9], developed QVscribe, a tool for requirements analysis for quality and consistency;

---

[8] https://www.qualicen.de/en/.
[9] https://qracorp.com.

OSSENO Software GmbH[10], developed ReqSuite, a tool to support requirements writing and requirements analysis.

8 Conclusions

This paper presented a comprehensive exploration of the nature of the ambiguity phenomena in requirements specifications. We have conducted a thorough examination of the relationship between ambiguity and two other phenomena, that of abstraction and absence of information. Furthermore, we have explored a subtle variation of ambiguity, referred to as vagueness.

This in depth analysis of different forms of ambiguity has resulted in offering as characterization of the different levels at which ambiguity can be manifested in requirements specification documents. This systematic exploration of the ambiguity phenomena and its relationship to other relevant concepts has thus enabled us to offer a theoretical framework to study different forms of ambiguity.

We thus argue that each instance of ambiguity cannot be merely considered as useful or damaging, nocuous or innocuous, good or bad just by itself, but that these characteristics can only be defined with reference to a particular set of stakeholders—and, in particular, with reference to the original author of the requirement. We believe that our exploration and classification of ambiguity presented in this paper has achieved significant steps towards an increased understanding of the important and crucial issues in identifying and handling ambiguity is requirements specifications.

We assert that an improved understanding of the nature and effect of ambiguity can help clear the way for a more positive view of ambiguity in requirements, and suggest ways to improve the current state of practice. In particular, tools and techniques aimed at identifying instances of ambiguity in requirements could incorporate the classification presented in this paper, assisting their users focus on identifying and properly handling the different types of ambiguity, particularly critical and risky cases.

Far from being just little more than the result of unapt use of the language, ambiguity has proven in our research to be an excellent instrument to expose more subtle features, which play an important role in requirements analysis [39]. Future work will focus on better exploring and exploiting the beneficial relation between ambiguity and the elicitation of tacit knowledge [25]. Furthermore, we aim to study the relationships between intentional ambiguity and *markedness* [40,41], a typical linguistic phenomenon that received little attention so far in RE.

Acknowledgment. The authors would like to thank Stefania Gnesi for her pioneering work on ambiguity in requirements documents, and for the many scientific collaborations with her, on several subjects, that they have enormously enjoyed along the years. The first author wishes to acknowledge the financial support of the Centre for Human-Centred Technology Design Research at UTS which partially sponsored the present work. This work was partially supported by the National Science Foundation under grant CCF-1718377.

---

[10] https://www.osseno.com/en/.

References

1. Zowghi, D., Gervasi, V.: The 3Cs of requirements: consistency, completeness, and correctness. In: Salinesi, C., Regnell, B., Pohl, K. (eds.) Proceedings of REFSQ 2002, Essener Informatik Beitrage, pp. 155–164, September 2002
2. Zowghi, D., Gervasi, V.: On the interplay between consistency, completeness, and correctness in requirements evolution. Inf. Softw. Technol. **46**(11), 763–779 (2004)
3. Gervasi, V., Zowghi, D.: On the role of ambiguity in RE. In: Wieringa, R., Persson, A. (eds.) REFSQ 2010. LNCS, vol. 6182, pp. 248–254. Springer, Heidelberg (2010). https://doi.org/10.1007/978-3-642-14192-8_22
4. Scott, D., Strachey, C.: Toward a mathematical semantics for computer languages. Technical report PRG-6, Oxford Programming Research Group (1971)
5. ISO: Information Technology - Z Formal Specification Notation - Syntax, Type System and Semantics. ISO (2002)
6. Scott, D.S.: Lambda calculus: some models, some philosophy. In: Barwise, J., Keisler, H.J., Kunen, K. (eds.) The Kleene Symposium, pp. 223–265. North-Holland Publishing Company, Amsterdam (1980)
7. Fabbrini, F., Fusani, M., Gervasi, V., Gnesi, S., Ruggieri, S.: On linguistic quality of natural language requirements. In: Dubois, E., Opdahl, A.L., Pohl, K. (eds.) Proceedings of REFSQ 1998, 57–62. Presses Universitaires de Namur, Pisa (1998)
8. Berry, D., Kamsties, E., Krieger, M.: From contract drafting to system specification: linguistic sources of ambiguity (2003)
9. Berry, D., Bucchiarone, A., Gnesi, S., Lami, G., Trentanni, G.: A new quality model for natural language requirements specifications. In: Proceedings of REFSQ 2006, Luxembourg (2006)
10. Kiyavitskaya, N., Zeni, N., Mich, L., Berry, D.M.: Requirements for tools for ambiguity identification and measurement in natural language requirements specifications. Requir. Eng. **13**(3), 207–239 (2008)
11. Jackson, M.: Problem Frames. Addison Wesley, Harlow (2001)
12. Fellbaum, C. (ed.): WordNet: An Electronic Lexical Database. MIT Press, Cambridge (1998)
13. Breitman, K.K., Sampaio do Prado Leite, J.C.: Lexicon based ontology construction. In: Lucena, C., Garcia, A., Romanovsky, A., Castro, J., Alencar, P.S.C. (eds.) SELMAS 2003. LNCS, vol. 2940, pp. 19–34. Springer, Heidelberg (2004). https://doi.org/10.1007/978-3-540-24625-1_2
14. Plato: Cratylus. In: Cooper, J.M., Hutchinson, D.S. (eds.) Plato Complete Works. Hackett Publishing (1997)
15. Carroll, L.: Through the Looking-Glass, and What Alice Found There. Macmillan, London (1871). (pseudonym of C. L. Dodgson)
16. Rice, S.L.: Loglan 3: Understanding Loglan. Master's thesis, University of Alaska at Fairbanks, May 1994. (Reprinted in serialized form by the Loglan Institute, Inc. in La Logli issues 1997/1, 1997/2 and 1997/3)
17. Berry, D.M., Kamsties, E.: Ambiguity in requirements specifications. In: do Prado Leite, J.C.S., Doorn, J.H. (eds.) Perspectives on Software Requirements, vol. 753, pp. 7–44. The Kluwer International Series in Engineering and Computer Science. Springer (2004)
18. Gervasi, V.: Environment Support for Requirements Writing and Analysis. Ph.D. thesis, University of Pisa, March 2000
19. Chung, L., Nixon, B., Yu, E., Mylopoulos, J.: Non-functional Requirements in Software Engineering. Kluwer Academic Publishers, Massachusetts (2000)
20. Peano, G.: Arithmetices principia, nova methodo exposita. Fratres Bocca, Turin (1889). (in Latin)

21. Meyer, B.: On formalism in specifications. IEEE Softw. **2**(1), 6–26 (1985)
22. Ferrari, A., et al.: Detecting requirements defects with NLP patterns: an industrial experience in the railway domain. Empirical Softw. Eng. **23**(6), 3684–3733 (2018)
23. Yang, H., Deroeck, A., Gervasi, V., Willis, A., Nuseibeh, B.: Extending nocuous ambiguity analysis for anaphora in natural language requirements. In: Proceedings of the 18th IEEE International Requirements Engineering Conference, Sydney (2010)
24. Chantree, F., Nuseibeh, B., de Roeck, A., Willis, A.: Identifying nocuous ambiguities in requirements specifications. In: Proceedings of 14th IEEE International Requirements Engineering Conference (RE 2006), Minneapolis/St. Paul, Minnesota, September 2006
25. Ferrari, A., Spoletini, P., Gnesi, S.: Ambiguity and tacit knowledge in requirements elicitation interviews. Requirements Eng. **21**(3), 333–355 (2016)
26. Ferrari, A., Spoletini, P., Gnesi, S.: Ambiguity cues in requirements elicitation interviews. In: IEEE 24th International Requirements Engineering Conference (RE), pp. 56–65. IEEE (2016)
27. Boehm, B.: Some experiences with automated aids to the design of largescale reliable software. IEEE Trans. Software Eng. **1**(1), 125–133 (1975)
28. Gause, D.C., Weinberg, G.M.: Exploring Requirements: Quality Before Design. Dorset House, New York (1989)
29. Schneider, G.M., Martin, J., Tsai, W.T.: An experimental study of fault detection in user requirements documents. ACM Trans. Softw. Eng. Methodol. **1**(2), 188–204 (1992)
30. Kovitz, B.: Ambiguity and what to do about it. In: Proceedings of the 10th International Conference on Requirements Engineering. IEEE Computer Science Press, Los Alamitos (2002)
31. Fabbrini, F., Fusani, M., Gnesi, S., Lami, G.: An automatic quality evaluation for natural language requirements. In: Proceedings of REFSQ 2001, Interlaken (2001)
32. Gnesi, S., Lami, G., Trentanni, G., Fabbrini, F., Fusani, M., et al.: An automatic tool for the analysis of natural language requirements. Int. J. Comput. Syst. Sci. Eng. **20**(1), 53–62 (2005)
33. Bubka, A., Gorfein, D.S.: Resolving semantic ambiguity: an introduction. In: Gorfein, D.S. (ed.) Resolving Semantic Ambiguity, pp. 3–12. Springer, New York (1989). https://doi.org/10.1007/978-1-4612-3596-5_1
34. Kamsties, E., Berry, D., Paech, B.: Detecting ambiguities in requirements documents using inspections. In: Workshop on Inspections in Software Engineering (WISE 2001), Paris, pp. 68–80 (2001)
35. Gleich, B., Creighton, O., Kof, L.: Ambiguity detection: towards a tool explaining ambiguity sources. In: Wieringa, R., Persson, A. (eds.) REFSQ 2010. LNCS, vol. 6182, pp. 218–232. Springer, Heidelberg (2010). https://doi.org/10.1007/978-3-642-14192-8_20
36. Tjong, S.F., Berry, D.M.: The design of SREE — a prototype potential ambiguity finder for requirements specifications and lessons learned. In: Doerr, J., Opdahl, A.L. (eds.) REFSQ 2013. LNCS, vol. 7830, pp. 80–95. Springer, Heidelberg (2013). https://doi.org/10.1007/978-3-642-37422-7_6
37. Ferrari, A., Dell'Orletta, F., Esuli, A., Gervasi, V., Gnesi, S.: Natural language requirements processing: a 4D vision. IEEE Softw. **34**(6), 28–35 (2017)
38. Femmer, H., Fernández, D.M., Wagner, S., Eder, S.: Rapid quality assurance with requirements smells. J. Syst. Softw. **123**, 190–213 (2017)
39. Ferrari, A., Spoletini, P., Gnesi, S.: Ambiguity as a resource to disclose tacit knowledge. In: Zowghi, D., Gervasi, V., Amyot, D. (eds.) 23rd IEEE International Requirements Engineering Conference, RE 2015, Ottawa, 24–28 August 2015, pp. 26–35. IEEE Computer Society (2015)
40. Merlini Barbaresi, L.: Markedness in English Discourse: A semiotic approach. Edizioni Zara, Parma (1988)
41. Chandler, D.: Semiotics: The Basics, 2nd edn. Routledge, London (2007)

QuARS: A Pioneer Tool for NL Requirement Analysis

Giuseppe Lami[✉], Mario Fusani, and Gianluca Trentanni

Consiglio Nazionale delle Ricerche,
Istituto di Scienza e Tecnologie dell'Informazione "A. Faedo", Pisa, Italy
{giuseppe.lami,mario.fusani,gianluca.trentanni}@isti.cnr.it

Abstract. This paper summarizes the achievements of Stefania Gnesi's research activity in the area of the natural language requirements analysis and quality evaluation. The development of the QuARS tool has been the pivotal step of this research stream led by Stefania Gnesi at ISTI–CNR. A functional description of the QuARS tool is provided as well as a short report of its evolutions over a decade. The wide use of QuARS in several research and industrial contexts demonstrates the validity and the originality of Stefania's contribution in such an area of software engineering.

Keywords: NLP (Natural Language Processing) ·
Software Engineering · Requirement Analysis

1 Introduction

The achievement of software requirement quality is the first step towards software quality. The process leading to requirement quality starts with the analysis of the requirements expressed in natural language (NL).

NL requirements are massively used in software industry, even when formal or semi-formal methods are applied to requirement representation. Although NL has the advantage of being universal and flexible, it is inherently ambiguous. The Oxford English dictionary states that the 500 most used words in English have on average 23 meanings. NL requirements are then inherently prone to errors and this is mainly due to interpretation problems of NL itself. Addressing the evaluation of NL requirements to address part of the interpretation problems due to linguistic problems has been considered an interesting research issue since late '90s by Stefania Gnesi and her research group at the CNR.

There are several techniques to reduce the ambiguity of NL requirements. Some of them adopt a restrictive approach based on the definition of writing rules that introduce limitations of freedom in writing requirements aimed at avoiding defects, some adopt analytic approaches aimed at identify and remove linguistic defects in requirements. The research referred in this paper follows the analytic approach.

The research has been conducted on two interdependent tracks: (1) the definition of an effective quality model for NL requirements in order to define and

© Springer Nature Switzerland AG 2019
M. H. ter Beek et al. (Eds.): Gnesi Festschrift, LNCS 11865, pp. 211–219, 2019.
https://doi.org/10.1007/978-3-030-30985-5_13

classify linguistic defects in requirements; (2) the development of technical solutions to perform the quality evaluation against the quality model in an automatic way.

The aim of this paper is to retrospectively provide an overall description of the main phases of such a research and to highlight the principal effects they produced in the last two decades. To do this we first provide a synthetic description of the tool called QuARS (Quality Analyzer for Requirements Specification) and of its evolution, as well as the underlying quality model in Sect. 2. Then a survey of the principal research results based on the use of QuARS is presented in Sect. 3. Finally some conclusions are provided in Sect. 4.

2 QuARS: Genesis, Evolution and Functional Characteristics

Evaluating something means first comparing some properties of an entity with a reference model and then determining the extent of the distance between the entity's property and the model itself. The same for quality analysis of NL requirements. In order to evaluate the quality of NL requirements, it is necessary that a quality model exists.

The quality model defined by Stefania's team was originally [1–4] composed of 4 high level quality properties:

o TESTABILITY: the capability of each requirement to be assessed in a pass/fail or quantitative manner.
o COMPLETENESS: the capability of the requirements to refer precisely identified entities.
o UNDERSTANDABILITY: both the capability of each requirement to be fully understood when used for developing software and the capability of the requirement specification document to be fully understood when read by the user.
o CONSISTENCY: the capability of the requirements to avoid potential or actual discrepancies.

For each quality property a set of quality indicators for NL requirements were being defined as shown in the table in Fig. 1.

The quality model was successively refined [5] to avoid those ambiguities, which were not already included in the initial quality model, described by Berry, Kamsties, and Krieger [6].

The quality model was the basis for implementing a prototype tool called QuARS with the purpose to provide an automatic linguistic analysis of NL requirements based on the developed quality model [7].

QuARS allows the requirements engineers to perform an initial parsing of the requirements for automatically detecting potential linguistic defects that can determine interpretation problems at the subsequent development stages of software development.

Property	Indicator	Description	Notes
Testability	Optionality	An Optionality Indicator reveels a requirement sentence containing an optional part (i.e. a part that can or cannot considered)	Optionality-revealing words: possibly, eventually, if case, if possible, if appropriate, if needed, ...
	Subjectivity	A Subjectivity Indicator is pointed out if sentence refers to personal opinions or feeling	Subjectivitt-revealing wordings: similar, better, similarly, worse, having in mind, take into account, take into consideration, as [adjective] as possible
	Vagueness	A Vagueness Indicator is pointed out if the sentence includes words holding inherent vagueness, i.e. words having a non uniquely quantifiable meaning	Vagueness-revealing words: clear, easy, strong, good, bad, efficient, useful, significant, adequate, fast, recent, far, close.
	Weakness	Weakness Indicator is pointed out in a sentence when it contains a weak main verb	Weak verbs: can, could, may.
Completeness	Under-specification	An Under-specification Indicator is pointed out in a sentence when the subject of the sentence contains a word identifying a class of objects without a modifier specifying an instance of this class	This indicator deals with the syntactic and semantics of the sentence under evaluation
Consistency	Under-reference	An Under-reference Indicator is pointed out in a NLSRS document when a sentence contains explicit references to: · not numbered sentences of the NLSRS document itself · documents not referenced into the NLSRS document itself · entities not defined nor described into the NLSRS document itself	
Understandability	Implicity	An Implicity Indicator is pointed out in a sentence when the subject is generic rather than specific.	Subject expressed by: Demonstrative adjective (this, these, that, those) or Pronouns (it, they, ..). Subject specified by: Adjective (previous, next, following, last,..) or Preposition (above, below, ..).
	Multiplicity	A Multiplicity Indicator is pointed out in a sentence if the sentence has more than one main verb or more than one direct or indirect complement that specifies its subject	Multiplicity-revealing words: and, or, and/or, ...
	Comment Frequency	It is the value of the CFI (Comment Frequency Index). [CFI= NC / NR where NC is the total number of requirements having one or more comments, NR is the number of requirements of the NLSRS document]	
	Readability Index	It is the value of ARI (Automated Readability Index) [ARI=WS + 9*SW where WS is the average words per sentence, SW is the average letters per word]	
	Directives Frequency Unexplanation	It is the rate between the number of NLSRS and the pointers to figures, tables, notes, ... An Unexplaination Indicator is pointed out in a NLSRS document when a sentence contains acronyms not explicitly and completely explained within the NLSRS document itself	

Fig. 1. Quality indicators

The QuARS tool has been developed in an incremental way, starting from an initial prototypal version. Then, more complete and reliable versions have been released, and several specialized versions have been developed for specific uses.

In the following the evolution steps of the QuaRS are shortly presented as well as their use in industrial and research environment.

The first complete version of QuARS [3] was structured as described in Fig. 2.

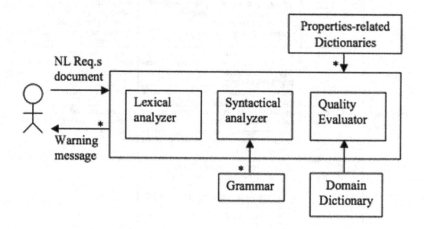

Fig. 2. The QuARS tool functional scheme.

The input was a plain text file containing NL requirements to analyze. The phases of the SRS Quality Evaluation made by the QuARS tool are described in the following.

o The files containing the SRS (Software Requirements Specification) document are analyzed by the Lexical Analyzer in order to verify if a correct English Dictionary has been used.

o The output of the Lexical Analyzer (i.e. the lexical category associated to each word of the sentences) is the input of the Syntactical Analyzer that, using a special purpose grammar, builds the derivation trees of each sentence. During the analysis process, each syntactic node is associated with a feature structure, which specifies morpho-syntactic data of the node and application-specific data, such as errors with respect to our quality criteria.

o The set of derived trees is the input of the Quality Evaluator module of the QuARS tool. The Quality Evaluator module receives also the Properties-related Dictionaries as input. These Dictionaries contain the words and the syntactical elements that allow the detection of inaccuracies in the requirements. Another Dictionary is used by the Quality Evaluator module: the Domain Dictionary that will contain specific terms of the particular application domain. The Domain Dictionary is used to avoid the detection as defective of terms that belong to the Properties-Related Dictionaries and in the same time they are typical of the application domain. The Quality Evaluator module, according to the rules of the Quality Model and by reading the dictionaries, performs the evaluation of the sentences.

○ QuARS provides the user with Warning Messages that are able to point out those sentences of the SRS Document having potential defects. Furthermore, some metrics (Readability Index, Comment Frequency and Directives Frequency) are provided too.

The GUI of the first release of QuARS is shown in Fig. 3.

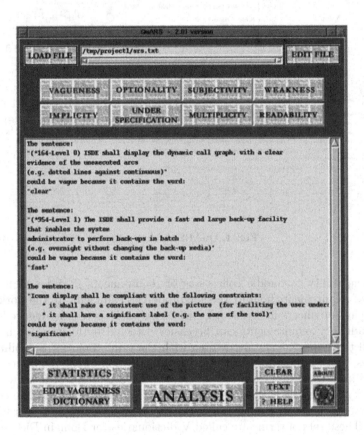

Fig. 3. First version of the QuARS GUI.

The functionalities and the GUI of QuARS were later improved in order to enlarge the scope of the analysis and to make the tool more usable. QuARS ver. 4.1 was released with a brand new graphical user interface as shown in Fig. 4.

From a functional point of view the novelty of the ver. 4.1 was the capability of provide a clustering of requirements according to specific domain dictionaries or topics. Such a clustering function was aimed at supporting the consistency and completeness analysis of [8].

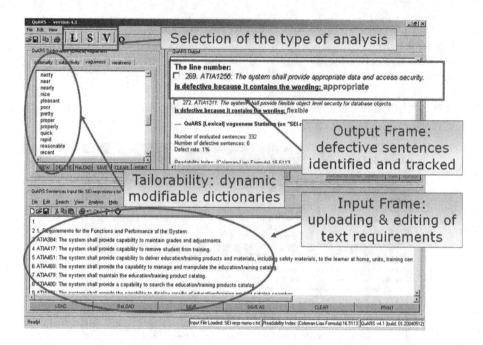

Fig. 4. QuARS version 4.1.

The capability to handle collections of requirements in order to highlight clusters of requirements holding specific properties can facilitate the work of the requirements engineers in terms of Consistency analysis (conflicting, redundant or contradictory requirements can be easier detected by focusing on a cluster where all the requirements are dealing with the same topic), Traceability with test cases, and Verification of the correct organization of the requirement document [8]. These clusters are called Views. The derivation of a View from a document relies on the availability of special sets of terms each of them containing the appropriate corpus that can be put in relation with a particular factor of interest. These sets of terms are called V-dictionaries (or Domain Dictionaries), Fig. 5.

The quite simple clustering approach of QuARS was later improved by the application of a clustering algorithm to exploit lexical and syntactic relationships occurring between natural language requirements for grouping together similar requirements contained in a requirements document [9].

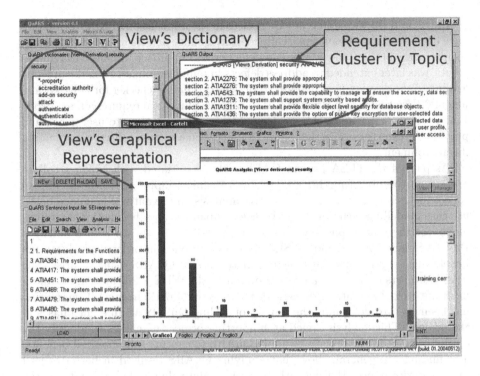

Fig. 5. Clustering in QuARS v4.1.

3 QuARS: A Launch Pad for Requirements Engineering Automation

The QuARS tool has been a trigger for many initiatives aimed at evaluating and refining the effectiveness of the automatic evaluation of NL requirements. QuARS has been also used in several research and industrial initiatives.

Empirical experiments to assess the impact in terms of effectiveness and efficacy of the automation in the requirements review process of a software company are need to evaluate to usability and applicability of NLP based tools for the quality analysis of textual requirements [10]. Three different experiments may be cited in this direction. One concerns the use of QuARS, in collaboration with Siemens CNX R&D Labs, on telecommunication requirement documents [11]. In [12] a customization of QuARS, QuARS Express was used to evaluate the quality of a large set of requirements developed in a EU project. In [13] we report the experience done within a collaboration between a world-leading railway signalling company, the University of Florence, and ISTI-CNR to investigate the feasibility of using NLP for defect identification in the requirements documents of the company.

In [12] and [13] two different experiences in the application of NLP techniques have been developed to automatically identify quality defects in natural language requirements in the Railway Domain. The QuARS approach, oriented to requirements, was later extended to address defects in public administration documents, leading to the development of online tool QuOD (Quality checker for Official Documents). Use cases are powerful tools to capture functional requirements for software systems. They allow structuring requirements according to user goals, and provide a means to specify the interaction between a certain software system and its environment.

As part of the ITEA project CAFE [15], we initiated with Nokia a collaboration on the use of methods based on a linguistic approach with the aim to collect metrics and perform a qualitative analysis on the natural-language-based use case modelling technique used by the company to specify functional requirements for the mobile phone software user interface [15,16]. In [14], a Software Process Simulation Method (P-SIM) has been applied in order to evaluate the benefits (including financial benefits) of the use of QuARS using a large-scale NASA projects that utilize a process similar to the IEEE 12207 systems development life cycle. In addition to assessing the value of QuARS in general, simulation has been used to determine the impact of adding QuARS at different phases in the project. This analysis aimed at supporting project managers to identify the optimum point in the process to apply QuARS to capture full potential benefits. The findings, in general, show that applying QuARS resulted in better overall project performance. However, the degree of the value added depends on the insertion point and step order in which QuARS is applied.

4   Conclusions

This paper presents the research activity led by Stefania Gnesi in the last two decades in the field of NL requirements evaluation. Such a research experience is a demonstration that an idea arisen in a research environment, if properly developed and led, can produce a really positive impact both in the research community and in industrial contexts.

The contribution of Stefania's team in automatic NL requirements evaluation, represented by the QuARS tool and the other derivative tools, has been outstanding and represents even today a milestone.

Acknowledgment. The research activity described in this paper has been conducted with the active contribution of our friend and colleague Fabrizio Fabbrini departed in 2017.

References

1. Fabbrini, F., Fusani, M., Gervasi, V., Gnesi, S., Ruggieri, S.: On Linguistic quality of natural language requirements. In: 4th REFSQ, Presses Universitaires de Namur, pp. 57–62 (1998)
2. Fabbrini, F., Fusani, M., Gnesi, S., Lami, G.: Software requirements verification by natural language analysis: a CNR initiative for italian SME's. ERCIM News **40**, 52–53 (2000)
3. Fabbrini, F., Fusani, M., Gnesi, S., Lami, G.: The linguistic approach to the natural language requirements quality: benefit of the use of an automatic tool. In: 26th Annual NASA Software Engineering Workshop, pp. 97–105, IEEE (2001)
4. Fabbrini, F., Fusani, M., Gnesi, S., Lami, G.: An automatic quality evaluation for natural language requirements. In: 7th REFSQ (2001)
5. Berry, D.M., Bucchiarone, A., Gnesi, S., Lami, G., Trentanni, G.: A new quality model for natural language requirements specifications. In: 12th REFSQ (2006)
6. Berry, D.M., Kamsties, E., Krieger, M.M.: From Contract Drafting to Software Specification: Linguistic Sources of Ambiguity. University of Waterloo, Waterloo (2017)
7. Gnesi, S., Lami, G., Trentanni, G.: An automatic tool for the analysis of natural language requirements. Computer Systems: Science & Engineering, vol. 20, no. 1. CRL Publishing (2005)
8. Fabbrini, F., Fusani, M., Gnesi, S., Lami, G.: Automatic clustering of non-functional requirements. In: IASTED Conference on Software Engineering and Applications 2004, IASTED/ACTA Press, pp. 672–677 (2004). http://fmt.isti.cnr.it/nlreqdataset/
9. Ferrari, A., Gnesi, S.: Using collective intelligence to detect pragmatic ambiguities. In: 20th RE, pp. 191–200. IEEE (2012)
10. Lami, G., Ferguson, R.W.: An empirical study on the impact of automation on the requirements analysis process. J. Comput. Sci. Technol. **22**(3), 338–347 (2007)
11. Bucchiarone, A., Gnesi, S., Pierini, P.: Quality analysis of NL requirements: an industrial case study. In: 13th RE, pp. 390–394. IEEE (2005)
12. Bucchiarone, A., Gnesi, S., Trentanni, G., Fantechi, A.: Evaluation of natural language requirements in the MODCONTROL project. ERCIM News **75**, 52–53 (2008)
13. Rosadini, B., et al.: Using NLP to detect requirements defects: an industrial experience in the railway domain. In: Grünbacher, P., Perini, A. (eds.) REFSQ 2017. LNCS, vol. 10153, pp. 344–360. Springer, Cham (2017). https://doi.org/10.1007/978-3-319-54045-0_24
14. Raffo, D.M., Ferguson, R., Setamanit, S., Sethanandha, B.D.: Evaluating the impact of the QuARS requirements analysis tool using simulation. In: Wang, Q., Pfahl, D., Raffo, D.M. (eds.) ICSP 2007. LNCS, vol. 4470, pp. 307–319. Springer, Heidelberg (2007). https://doi.org/10.1007/978-3-540-72426-1_26
15. Fantechi, A., Gnesi, S., Lami, G., Maccari, A.: Application of linguistic techniques for use case analysis. In: 10th RE, pp. 157–164. IEEE (2002)
16. Fantechi, A., Gnesi, S., Lami, G., Maccari, A.: Applications of linguistic techniques for use case analysis. Requir. Eng. **8**(3), 161–170 (2003)

Detecting Feature Interactions
in FORML Models

Sandy Beidu(⊠) and Joanne M. Atlee

University of Waterloo, Waterloo, ON N2L 3G1, Canada
{sbeidu,jmatlee}@uwaterloo.ca

Abstract. Requirement engineers must know how features (units of functionality) interact, in order to resolve undesired interactions. Model checking has been proposed as an effective method for detecting feature interactions. We propose a method for (1) modelling features as distinct modules (explicating intended interactions with other features), (2) composing feature modules into a system model that preserves intended interactions, (3) translating this rich model into the input language of a model checker, and (4) automatically generating correctness properties whose violations reveal unintended feature interactions.

Keywords: Feature modelling · Feature interactions · Model checking

1 Introduction

A software system is often thought of in terms of its constituent features, where each **feature** is "an optional or incremental unit of functionality" [24]. Users view features as capabilities (e.g., cut, copy, and paste; Caller ID; Cruise Control). Software developers use features as a criterion for incremental development, to ease system development and evolution, because features can be developed in isolation, in parallel, or by third-party vendors. Feature orientation is particularly relevant in software product lines, in which a family of software products shares a common set of mandatory features and products are differentiated by their variable (optional or alternative) features [23].

The downside of feature orientation is that engineers must consider how features interact when deriving a product from a selection of features. A **feature interaction** occurs when "one feature affects the operation of [the other] feature" [10]. Some features interact by design: for example, Advanced Cruise Control features are *designed* to extend and override basic Cruise Control. Other features interact by accident as a consequence of operating in a shared context [16,19]. To be safe, the engineer needs to be able to specify, understand, control, and reason about the behaviours of features in combination.

Stefania Gnesi is one of the earliest researchers to employ and extend Modal Transition Systems (MTSs) to model and reason about variability in software behaviour. Her group's contributions have included new variants of MTSs that express different types of variability in behavioural models [14,15]; logics such as MHML for expressing variability constraints and behaviour properties over

M. H. ter Beek et al. (Eds.): Gnesi Festschrift, LNCS 11865, pp. 220–235, 2019.
https://doi.org/10.1007/978-3-030-30985-5_14

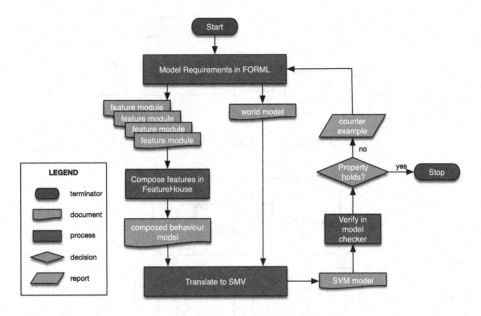

Fig. 1. FORML analysis process

MTSs [3,4]; and reasoners [5,8] for deriving valid products from product-line models and for analyzing properties of products and product families.

We aim to emulate Stefania's work in modelling and analyzing behaviour models of feature-rich software, but we start from the premise of wanting to model features modularly. The Feature-Oriented Requirements Modelling Language (FORML) [21,22] enables modular specifications of features. Models of features are composed into models of products or a family of products, which can subsequently be model checked. Our work is most similar to work by Stefania and colleagues on detecting conflicts among policies [7]. In their approach, policies and policy actions are expressed as simple UML State Machines, operations on policy rules specify how to compose policy actions (and state machines), and the resulting composite machines can be model checked using the UMC model checker [6].

In this paper, we describe our process of using model checking to detect interactions in FORML models. Figure 1 shows our process: FORML models of distinct features are composed together and translated into the input language of the NuSMV model checker [11]. Importantly, as part of the translation phase, CTL properties [1] for detecting conflicts among features' actions are also generated, automatically. Generating CTL properties to detect feature interactions is possible because the individual features serve as specifications of how the features ought to behave. That is, CTL properties derived from feature specifications relate to how a feature behaves in isolation; and the violation of a generated property indicates that some behaviour of the feature no longer holds when the feature is composed with other features.

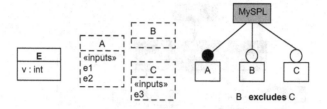

Fig. 2. World model of *MySPL*

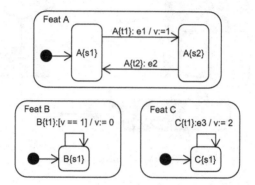

Fig. 3. Behaviour model of *MySPL*

2 Overview of FORML

This section provides a brief overview of FORML. Details can be found in [21].

A FORML model is decomposed into a static model (*world model*) and a dynamic model (*behaviour model*). A FORML **world model** is an ontology of a software product's environment, expressed as a UML-based concept model. Each **concept** represents a type of environmental variable. A concept instance is an **object** that is characterized by **attributes**, **inputs** and **outputs**, and **relationships** with other objects (e.g., a car has a speed and direction, a road has lanes, and a car travels on a road). The values of world objects comprise the **world state**. Actions in the behaviour model change the values of world objects. A **feature concept** is a FORML-specific concept, distinguished by a dashed border, that specifies feature-specific data (attributes, inputs, outputs) that are visible to the environment (e.g., *cruisingSpeed* is introduced by the Cruise Control feature). A FORML world model includes a **feature model** [18] that constrains the valid feature configurations of an SPL. Figure 2 shows the world model of a toy SPL called *MySPL*, consisting of a concept *E*, having an attribute *v* of type integer, and three feature concepts, with input events that the features receive from the environment; and a feature model.

A FORML **behaviour model** comprises a set of feature modules, one for each feature object. Figure 3 shows the feature modules of *MySPL*'s three features. Each **feature module** is a set of *feature machines* and *feature-machine* *fragments.* A **feature machine** is an extended state-machine model, based on the UML state-machine notation [20]. A state may be a basic state or a super-state containing one or more orthogonal *regions*; each region models a sub state-machine that executes concurrently with the sub machines in sibling regions. A transition between states has a label of the form:

$$id : te \ [gc] \ / \ id_1 : [c_1]a_1, \ldots, id_n : [c_n]a_n$$

where id is the name of the transition; te is an optional triggering event; gc is a boolean guard condition; and $a_1...a_n$ are concurrent actions, each with its own name id_i and guard condition c_i.

A **feature fragment** extends a specified feature machine with new or modified behaviours. Specifically, a fragment can *add* new behaviours at specific points in an existing feature machine:

– A *new region* added to an existing state
– A *new transition* (and possibly new states) added to an existing machine.
– A *new action* added to an existing transition
– A *weakening clause* that extends the guard condition of an existing transition or action with a disjunct, thereby weakening the guard condition.

A fragment can *restrict* the behaviour of a feature machine by adding a conjunct, called a *strengthening clause*, to the guard condition of a transition or action. Strengthening a guard condition results in the condition being satisfied less often, and therefore leads to *"removed"* behaviours. Lastly, a new feature machine or fragment can *replace* existing behaviour by specifying a new transition that is enabled under similar conditions as an existing transition, but has higher priority. There is distinct syntax to specify that a new transition has **priority** over an existing transition; or **overrides** an existing transition[1]. Fragments, transition priorities, and overrides all specify **intended feature interactions**, in that they express explicit changes to the behaviour of existing features.

3   Composing Behaviour Models

Feature composition in FORML composes feature machines in parallel, and applies fragments (new regions, new transitions, new actions; new clauses in guard conditions; prioritized and overriding transitions) to the feature machines that they extend. The behaviour of a composed model is the concurrent execution of the extended feature machines; each execution step comprises the simultaneous execution of all enabled transitions and their actions [21]. The composition preserves intended interactions specified as weakening/strengthening clauses, and prioritized and overriding transitions. Our analysis does not report intended feature interactions.

Feature composition is commutative and associative [21], which has considerable advantages. For one, engineers do not need to identify an order of composition in order to derive a product from a collection of features. More importantly,

---

[1] An *overriding transition* implicitly has the same enabling conditions as the transition it override, whereas a *prioritized transition* has unique enabling conditions.

it means that the order of composition does not affect analysis results. A third advantage is that new features can be composed with an existing composed model, thereby enabling incremental composition and analysis.

We implemented FORML feature composition [9] using the FeatureHouse framework [2]. FeatureHouse provides a generic framework for the structural composition of feature modules using superimposition. The input to the composer are the feature modules of the selected features; the output is a FORML model representing the composed behaviour model of the software product. The result of composing $MySPL$'s three features from Fig. 3 is a single state machine (not shown) with three concurrent regions, one for each feature.

4   Translation of FORML to SMV

We analyze FORML models using the NuSMV model checker [11]. NuSMV is a symbolic model checker, which is the best choice when analyzing concurrent models with non-interleaving semantics. Symbolic model verifier (SMV) is the input language to NuSMV.

An SMV model consists of a set of variable declarations (VAR) and a set of variable assignments (ASSIGN). Variables can be of type Boolean, integer subranges (e.g., 0..10), enumerated types (e.g. {on, off}) or an array of any of these types. SMV expression operators include ! (not), | (or), & (and), → (implies) and ↔ (iff). Assignment expressions specify variables' initial values (INIT) at the start of a model's execution, and their next values (NEXT) in every SMV execution step. A variable can be assigned a specific value or expression over current variable values; a set of values $\{val_1, ..., val_n\}$, meaning that the next value is non-deterministically selected from this set; or there can be no assignment, meaning that the next value is non-deterministically selected from the range of values in the variable's defined type. In this manner, the variable declarations define the model's state space and the assignments define the model's transition relation. Macros can be defined (DEFINE) to represent any valid expression. In our translation from FORML to SMV, we use macro definitions instead of variable declarations wherever possible (because macros are not typed and do not contribute to the model's state space).

SMV modules (MODULE) are used to encapsulate sub-models of variables and assignments. An SMV model can contain several modules, but must have one high-level module called main. An SMV module can be instantiated as a variable in other modules. Given a module instance a, the expression a.x identifies a variable or macro named x inside the instance a. SMV invariants (INVAR) are constraints on SMV variable values. We use invariants to constrain when a transition can execute. SMV comments are preceded by the symbol −−.

We implemented a translator from FORML to SMV using BSML2SMV [13], which is useful for translating *big-step modelling languages (BMSL)* [12] into SMV. BSMLs are a family of behaviour modelling languages that have multi-step execution semantics; the family of BSMLs includes UML State-Machines, various statechart variants, and process algebras. We extended BSML2SMV to the

```
                                MODULE snapshot
                                  DEFINE
                                    -- macros for non-basic states
                                  VAR
                                    ws : WS;
                                    ws_pre : WS;
                                    A_t1_exec : boolean;
                                    A_t2_exec : boolean;
                                    B_t1_exec : boolean;
                                    C_t1_exec : boolean;
MODULE WS                         ASSIGN
  DEFINE                            next(ws_pre.E_v) := ws.E_v;
    -- scope variables             next(ws_pre.A_e1) := ws.A_e1;
    E_v_max : 2;                   next(ws_pre.A_e2) := ws.A_e2;
  VAR                               ...
    E_v : 0..E_v_max;              next(ws.A_s1) := case
    A_e1 : boolean;                  A_t1_exec : 0;
    A_e2 : boolean;                  A_t2_exec : 1;
    C_e3 : boolean;                  1 : ws.A_s1;
    -- basic states of MySPL       esac;
    A_s1 : boolean;                 ...
    A_s2 : boolean;                next(ws.E_v) := case
    B_s1 : boolean;                  A_t1_exec & B_t1_exec & C_t1_exec : {1,0,2};
    C_s1 : boolean;                  A_t1_exec & B_t1_exec : {1,0};
  ASSIGN                             B_t1_exec & C_t1_exec : {0,2};
    -- initial values of            A_t1_exec & C_t1_exec : {1,2};
    -- variables and states         A_t1_exec : 1;
    init(E_v) : 0;                   B_t1_exec : 0;
    init(A_s1) : TRUE;               C_t1_exec : 2;
    init(A_s2) : 0;                  1 : ws.E_v;
    init(B_s1) : TRUE;             esac;
    init(C_s1) : TRUE;              ...
```

Fig. 4. SMV module for WS   **Fig. 5.** SMV model of an execution state

execution semantics of concurrently executing transitions that have conflicting actions, and to translate the rich world model of a FORML model.

4.1   World State (WS) Module

The FORML-to-SMV translator generates an SMV module called WS, which specifies valid world states of a FORML world model. The WS module models the world concepts, their attributes, and associations between these concepts. This module also contains a boolean *state variable* for each basic state in the FORML composed behaviour model. A state variable has value true whenever it is one of the current execution states of the model. Two instances ws_pre and ws of this module are declared in the snapshot module to represent the current and previous world states. (The previous world state is needed to specify properties for detecting feature interactions.) Fig. 4 shows the WS module for MySPL. WS variables are assigned next values in the snapshot module, described below.

Specifying Bounds for Analysis: Many model checkers, including SMV, verify only *finite-state* systems. Thus, the engineer must specify bounds on the number of objects of each type in the world model and on the value ranges of variables[2]. For example, the SMV model in Fig. 4 binds the value of attribute E_v to the range 0..2. Specifying a small bound is often sufficient, based on the

---

[2] Although bounds may need to be specified, this is for the purpose of analysis alone; the bounds do not reflect the specified size of the model.

small-scope hypothesis [17], which claims that a high percentage of bugs can be found by checking a model on all possible inputs within some small bound. One verification strategy is to analyze a model with respect to increasingly larger bounds, until the engineer is satisfied that no bugs are likely to be found deep in the model.

4.2 Snapshot Module

The snapshot module specifies the current execution state of a FORML model. It includes two instances of the WS module: (1) ws, which represents the current world state, and (2) ws_pre, which represents the previous world state. The snapshot module also declares for each transition in the composed FORML model a boolean *execution variable*, which indicates whether the transition will execute in the next execution step. The values of the execution variables are defined in the *state* modules, described in the next subsection.

The snapshot module updates all of the WS variables. Consider the snapshot module for our MySPL model, shown in Fig. 5, which includes four types of assignments: (1) The next values of ws_pre variables are always the current values of ws variables. (2) The next value of each state variable is false if it is the source state of an executing transition; true if it is the destination state of an executing transition; and otherwise does not change. (3) The next value of a WS variable reflects the assignments made by the executing transitions. If more than one transition assigns values to the same variable, these actions are merged into the same SMV assignment expression. For example, in *MySPL* (Fig. 3), there are three transitions $A\{t1\}$, $B\{t1\}$, $C\{t1\}$ that assign $E.v$ to the values 1, 0, and 2, respectively. In the corresponding SMV model (Fig. 5), the next value of E_v depends on the combination of transitions that executes; if more than one transition executes, the value is non-deterministically one of the executing transitions' assignments[3]. (4) There are no assignments to the input events A_e1, A_e2 and C_e3 because these are environmental inputs whose values are not controlled by the model; their values are non-deterministically set in each execution step.

4.3 State Module

An SMV module is generated for each non-basic state and region of the composed behaviour model - including the model's root state. Each of these modules is passed as a parameter the snapshot instance, ss, declared in the main SMV module. The snapshot parameter gives the state module access to all information defined in the snapshot module. Each state module declares a flag for each

---

[3] The order of the branch conditions in an SMV case statement matters. The branch conditions are considered in sequential order. Thus, branches should be ordered such than no branch condition is a subcase of a subsequent branch condition. In the next(ws.E_v) assignment in Fig. 5, where the branch conditions are the possible subsets of executing transitions, the branches are listed in decreasing size of the set of executing transitions.

```
MODULE MySPL_root (ss)
  VAR
    a_reg : A_Reg(ss);
    b_reg : B_Reg(ss);
    c_reg : C_Reg(ss);
  DEFINE
    enabled := a_reg.enabled |
               b_reg.enabled |
               c_reg.enabled ;
    execute := a_reg.exec |
               b_reg.exec |
               c_reg.exec ;
  INVAR
    (enabled -> execute) &
    (execute -> (
       (a_reg.enabled -> a_reg.exec)&
       (b_reg.enabled -> b_reg.exec)&
       (c_reg.enabled -> c_reg.exec)))
```

```
MODULE A_Reg (ss)
  DEFINE
    A_t1_enabled := ss.ws.A_s1 & ss.ws.A_e1;
    A_t2_enabled := ss.ws.A_s2 & ss.ws.A_e2;
    enabled := A_t1_enabled | A_t2_enabled;
    exec := ss.A_t1_exec | ss.A_t2_exec;
  INVAR
    (ss.A_t1_exec -> A_t1_enabled) &
    (ss.A_t2_exec -> A_t2_enabled) &
    (exec -> (
       (A_t1_enabled -> ss.A_t1_exec) &
       (A_t2_enabled -> ss.A_t2_exec)))
```

Fig. 6. SMV model of the root state   **Fig. 7.** SMV model of a non-basic state

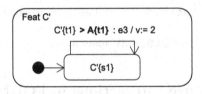

Fig. 8. Modified feature C, whose transition has priority over $t1$ in feature A

transition within its scope (i.e., the state is the lowest-common parent of the transition's source and destination states); the flag is a boolean macro that indicates whether the transition is enabled with respect to its source state and enabling conditions (events and variables). Each state module also declares two flags (macros) that indicate its own enabledness and execution: the *enabled* flag indicates whether there is any enabled transition within the scope of that state or any of its descendants, and the *exec* flag indicates whether any of these enabled transitions will execute in the next execution step.

Figure 6 shows the root state module for *MySPL*. It declares variables for three regions, one for each of the feature machines in the composed behaviour model. Figure 7 shows the SMV module generated for feature A's region.

Intended Interaction (Priority): Intended interactions, such as prioritized transitions or overrides, are encoded as invariants expressed over the transitions' *enabled* and *exec* flags. Specifically, if one transition has priority over another, the translator adds an invariant that states that when the higher-priority transition is enabled the lower transition cannot be executed even if the lower-priority transition is enabled.

For example, Fig. 8 presents a modified feature C whose transition $C'\{t1\}$ has priority over $A\{t1\}$. This is an intended interaction, and is translated to the following SMV invariant:

```
INVAR ( C'_t1_enabled -> !ss.A_t1_exec )
```

4.4   Main Module

The SMV `main` module pulls all of the pieces together. The SMV `main` module of our running example (in Fig. 9) contains (1) an instance of the *snapshot* module, (2) an instance of the root-state module, with a snapshot parameter, and (3) the temporal logic properties to be checked. Our translation process automatically generates the properties: one for each transition action. We describe our process for generating interaction-detection properties in the next section.

```
MODULE main
  VAR
    ss : snapshot;
    model_root : MySPL_root(ss);
  SPEC
    -- interaction-detection properties
```

Fig. 9. SMV main module

5   Detecting Feature Interactions in FORML

In this paper, we focus on feature interactions that are caused by conflicting actions on shared variables. Note that detecting conflicting assignments is not simply a matter of detecting transitions whose actions effect the same variables – because those transitions might not be reachable, or might never be simultaneously enabled. We need a dynamic analysis, like model checking, to detect realizable conflicts among features' actions.

A barrier to effective model checking is the need to identify correctness properties to be checked of the model, and to express those properties in temporal logic. In our work, we are able to generate properties for detecting feature interactions automatically from the feature modules. We can do this precisely because of the nature of feature interactions: feature interactions are effectively deviations from how features would behave in isolation. Thus we use features' FORML behavioural models as specifications of expected behaviours of individual features; and check whether the features' specified behaviours vary when the features are composed into a product.

5.1   Running Example

This section employs a running example to demonstrate how correctness properties are generated and used to detect interactions. For pedagogical reasons, we consider an SPL called `AutoSoft`, which has four features that correspond to various basic functions of a car. These features are:

- `Ignition Control` (`IC`), responds to commands to turn the vehicle's ignition on and off (shown in Fig. 11).

- Acceleration control (AC), responds to commands to increase the vehicle's acceleration (shown in Fig. 12).
- Braking control (BC), responds to commands to decrease the vehicle's acceleration (shown in Fig. 13).
- Steering control (SC), responds to commands to change the vehicles's direction (shown in Fig. 14).

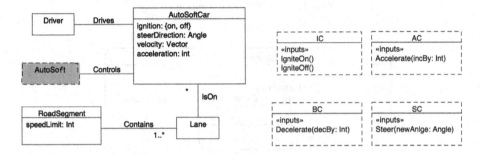

Fig. 10. The AutoSoft World Model

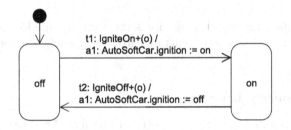

Fig. 11. The IC feature module

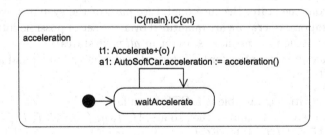

Fig. 12. The AC feature module.

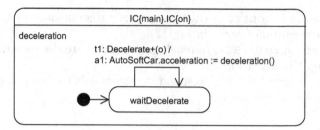

Fig. 13. The BC feature module.

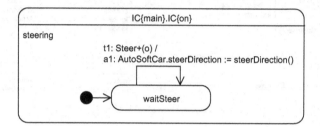

Fig. 14. The SC feature module.

Figure 10 shows the world model for AutoSoft. Figure 15 shows the composed behaviour model that is generated from composing the four features of AutoSoft.

5.2   CTL Property Language

The feature-interaction detection properties to be model checked are expressed as formulae in the **Computational Tree Logic (CTL)** branching-time temporal logic [1]. Branching-time temporal formulae are evaluated with respect to a particular execution state, based on the set of possible execution paths emanating from the state. Because *the* future path of the system's execution is unknown, temporal operators are quantified over the set of possible futures (e.g., a property p is true in *some* next state or in *all* next states).

The syntax and semantics for CTL formulas are defined in [1] and are simply summarized below:

1. Every propositional variable is a CTL formula.
2. If f and g are CTL formulas, then so are: $!f$, $f\&g$, $f\,|\,g$, AXf, EXf, $A[fUg]$, $E[fUg]$, AFf, EFf, AGf, EGf.

The symbols ! (*not*), & (*and*), and | (*or*) are logical connectives and have their usual meanings. X is the *nextstate* operator, and formula $EX\phi$ ($AX\phi$) is true in state s_i iff formula ϕ is true in some (in every) successor state of s_i. U is the

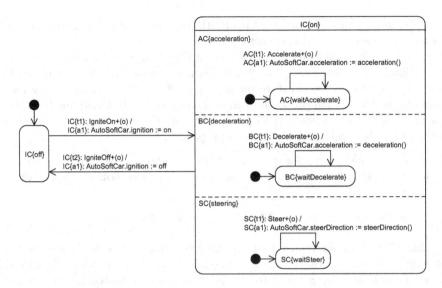

Fig. 15. Composed behaviour model of `AutoSoft`

until operator, and formula $E[\phi \; U \; \psi]$ $(A[\phi \; U \; \psi])$ is true in state s_i iff along some (every) path emanating from s_i there exists a future state s_j at which ψ holds and ϕ is continuously true until state s_j is reached. F is the *future* operator, and $EF\phi$ $(AF\phi)$ is true in state s_i iff along some (every) path from s_i there exists a future state in which ϕ holds. Finally, G is the *global* operator, and $EG\phi$ $(AG\phi)$ is true in state s_i if ϕ holds in every state along some (every) path emanating from s_i.

5.3   Generating Feature-Interaction Detection Properties

According to the execution semantics of FORML, if a transition **t** executes in a given world state, the effects of its actions should be realized in the next world state. If the effects are not realized, it means that some action(s) from other transition(s) have assigned value(s) to some of the same world-model variables, thereby interfering with **t**'s actions. Such interference can occur among actions performed by a single feature or actions performed by multiple features.

Recall from Sect. 4.2 that, when translating FORML transition actions into SMV assignments, if two or more transitions write to the same world-state variable, the actions need to be merged into the same SMV assignment expression. The outcome is a single (case-based) assignment expression that reflects exactly one transition's actions if only one transition executes; and that reflects a race condition among actions if several of the transitions execute simultaneously. If these transitions can ever execute together, then a race condition is possible – revealing a feature interaction: an executing transition that loses a race condition has a post-condition that is unsatisfied. Our goal is to specify properties that can detect unsatisfied post-conditions.

We do this by generating automatically a CTL property for each transition action. Each property states that if a transition executes in the current world state, then in the next world state the expected effect of the transition's actions should be realized. Such properties can be generated solely based on the state-machine model and do not require any user input. We define below the general template for these interaction-detection properties.

RULE 1. *For each action of a transition* t *that assigns a value* x *to an attribute* C_a *in the world model, add the following CTL specification to the main module:*

SPEC AG (t_exec -> **AX** (ws.C_a = ws_pre.x))

This CTL formula states that in **A**ll execution paths, it is always (or **G**lobally) true that if the value of t_exec is true, then (in **A**ll ne**X**t states) the next value of C_a is equal to the value of x as evaluated in the current world state; if x is an expression, then the next value of C_a is the value of the expression as applied over the current world-state variable values[4].

Listing 1.1 shows the three example CTL properties that are generated for the three actions: a1 from transition AC_t1, a1 from BC_t1, and a1 from SC_t1. The expressions acceleration_fn and deceleration_fn correspond to the unspecified functions *acceleration()* and *deceleration()*, respectively, in Fig. 15. If any of the correctness properties fails, it indicates an interaction among feature actions.

AG(AC_t1_execute->**AX**(ws.AutoSoftCar_acceleration =   (P1)
                          ws_pre.acceleration_fn))

AG(BC_t1_execute->**AX**(ws.AutoSoftCar_acceleration =   (P2)
                          ws_pre.deceleration_fn))

AG(SC_t1_execute->**AX**(ws.AutoSoftCar_steerDirection =   (P3)
                          ws_pre.steerDirection_fn))

Listing 1.1. CTL properties of AutoSoft2 to detect action conflicts

We now show how our approach detects interactions in our AutoSoft example. In Fig. 15, the transitions $AC\{t1\}$ and $BC\{t1\}$ both have actions that assign values to the same variable *AutoSoftCar.acceleration*. Our translator combines these actions into a single conditional assignment expression that makes a

---

[4] Note that current and next values in the current world state are previous and current values in the next world state AX().

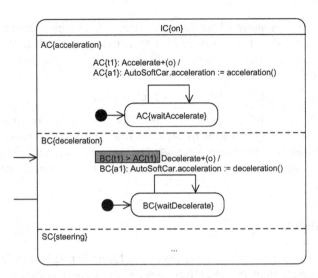

Fig. 16. Composed behaviour model of `AutoSoft`, modified to include an intended interaction.

non-deterministic choice if both transitions execute; assigns a unique value if exactly one transition executes; and makes no assignment if neither transition executes:

```
next(ws.AutoSoftCar_acceleration) := case
   AC_t1_exec & BC_t1_exec : {ws.acceleration_fn,
                                    ws.deceleration_fn};
   AC_t1_exec : ws.acceleration_fn;
   BC_t1_exec : ws.deceleration_fn;
   1 : ws.AutoSoftCar_acceleration;
esac;
```

If both transitions execute simultaneously (which is possible because they reside in concurrent regions and do not have conflicting enabling conditions), then `AutoSoftCar_acceleration` will nondeterministically be assigned to either `acceleration_fn` or `deceleration_fn`. In this scenario, only one of the properties P1 or P2 of Listing 1.1 is satisfied. If `AutoSoftCar_acceleration` is assigned the value of `acceleration_fn`, property P1 will hold but not P2, and vice versa.

In the real world, this feature interaction represents the case where a driver requests to accelerate and decelerate a vehicle simultaneously, for example by pressing both the gas and brake pedals at the same time. We can resolve this interaction by modifying the model to give one transition priority over the other (in this case, it makes sense to prioritize the transition that decelerates the vehicle) The result is an intended interaction, in which transition `BC_t1` can supersede transition `AC_t1`.

Figure 16 shows a modified version of Feature BC in which transition `BC_t1` is explicitly specified to have priority over transition `AC_t1`. If both transitions are enabled, only `BC_t1` can execute. This transition priority is represented in the SMV model as an invariant:

```
INVAR (BC_t1_enabled -> !AC_t2_exec)
```

When this invariant is part of the SMV model, it is impossible for `AC_t1_exec` and `BC_t1_exec` to both be true at the same time. Therefore, the first case branch in the `next(AutoSoftCar_acceleration)` assignment never executes; and there is no longer any reported violation of properties `P1` and `P2`.

6   Conclusion

In this paper, we present an approach and tools for detecting feature interactions due to conflicting actions in FORML models. The approach consists of first composing FORML models of features into a composed FORML behaviour model, and then translating the composed model and the FORML world model into the SMV language. As part of the translation process, CTL properties for detecting feature interactions are automatically generated from the translated model. Each CTL property states for some transition action that the post-condition of that action should hold if the transition executes. Lastly, the CTL properties are model checked; any violation of a property indicates a conflict among feature actions. We are currently evaluating the effectiveness of our approach on a case study of 11 automotive drive-assist features from an industrial partner.

Acknowledgement. We are grateful to Stefania Gnesi in whose honour this Festschrift is held, not only for her pioneering work on modelling and analysis of behaviour models of software product lines (which inspired our work in this area), but also for her service and leadership in the formal methods and SPL communities, for many thought-provoking technical discussions, and for her friendship.

References

1. Alur, R., Courcoubetis, C., Dill, D.: Model checking for real-time systems. In: Proceedings of the 5th Annual Symposium on Logic in Computer Science, pp. 414–425 (1990)
2. Apel, S., Kästner, C., Lengauer, C.: FeatureHouse: language-independent, automated software composition. In: International Conference on Software Engineering, pp. 221–231 (2009)
3. Asirelli, P., ter Beek, M.H., Gnesi, S., Fantechi, A.: Formal description of variability in product families. In: International Software Product Line Conference, pp. 130–139 (2011)
4. Asirelli, P., ter Beek, M.H., Fantechi, A., Gnesi, S.: A logical framework to deal with variability. In: Méry, D., Merz, S. (eds.) IFM 2010. LNCS, vol. 6396, pp. 43–58. Springer, Heidelberg (2010). https://doi.org/10.1007/978-3-642-16265-7_5

5. Basile, D., Di Giandomenico, F., Gnesi, S.: FMCAT: supporting dynamic service-based product lines. In: International Systems and Software Product Line Conference, SPLC 2017, vol. B, pp. 3–8 (2017)
6. ter Beek, M.H., Fantechi, A., Gnesi, S., Mazzanti, F.: A state/event-based model-checking approach for the analysis of abstract system properties. Sci. Comput. Program. **76**(2), 119–135 (2011)
7. ter Beek, M.H., Gnesi, S., Montangero, C., Semini, L.: Detecting policy conflicts by model checking UML state machines. In: International Conference on Feature Interactions (2009)
8. ter Beek, M.H., Mazzanti, F., Sulova, A.: VMC: a tool for product variability analysis. In: Giannakopoulou, D., Méry, D. (eds.) FM 2012. LNCS, vol. 7436, pp. 450–454. Springer, Heidelberg (2012). https://doi.org/10.1007/978-3-642-32759-9_36
9. Beidu, S., Atlee, J.M., Shaker, P.: Incremental and commutative composition of state-machine models of features. In: International Workshop on Modeling in Software Engineering (MiSE 2015), (ICSE Workshop), pp. 13–18, May 2015
10. Bowen, T.F., Dworack, F.S., Chow, C.H., Griffeth, N., Herman, G.E., Lin, Y.-J.: The feature interaction problem in telecommunication systems. In: International Conference on Software Engineering for Telecommunication Switching Systems, pp. 59–62 (1989)
11. Cimatti, A., Clarke, E., Giunchiglia, F., Roveri, M.: NUSMV: a new symbolic model checker. Int. J. Softw. Tools Technol. Transf. **2**(4), 410–425 (2000)
12. Esmaeilsabzali, S., Day, N.A., Atlee, J.M., Niu, J.: Deconstructing the semantics of big-step modelling languages. Requirements Eng. J. **15**(2), 235–265 (2010)
13. Faghih, F.: Model translations among big-step modeling languages. In: International Conference on Software Engineering, Doc. Sym., pp. 1555–1558 (2012)
14. Fantechi, A., Gnesi, S.: Formal modeling for product families engineering. In: International Software Product Line Conference, pp. 193–202 (2008)
15. Fantechi, A., Gnesi, S.: A behavioural model for product families. In: European Software Engineering Conference/Foundations of Software Engineering: Companion Papers, pp. 521–524 (2007)
16. Hay, J.D., Atlee, J.M.: Composing features and resolving interactions. In: Foundations of Software Engineering, pp. 110–119 (2000)
17. Jackson, D., Damon, C.A.: Elements of style: analyzing a software design feature with a counterexample detector. IEEE Trans. Softw. Eng. **22**(7), 484–495 (1996)
18. Kang, K.C., Cohen, S.G., Hess, J.A., Novak, W.E., Peterson, A.S.: Feature-Oriented Domain Analysis (FODA) Feasibility Study. Technical report CMU/SEI-90-TR-21, Carnegie-Mellon University Software Engineering Institute (1990)
19. Nhlabatsi, A., Laney, R., Nuseibeh, B.: Feature interaction as a context sharing problem. In: International Conference on Feature Interaction, pp. 133–148 (2009)
20. Rumbaugh, J., Jacobson, I., Booch, G.: Unified Modeling Language Reference Manual, The, 2nd edn. Pearson Higher Education, Boston (2004)
21. Shaker, P.: A feature-oriented modelling language and a feature-interaction taxonomy for product-line requirements. Ph.D. thesis, University of Waterloo (2013)
22. Shaker, P., Atlee, J.M., Wang, S.: A feature-oriented requirements modelling language. In: International Requirements Engineering Conference, pp. 151–160 (2012)
23. Weiss, D., Lai, R.: Software Product Line Engineering: A Family Based Development Process. Addison Wesley, Boston (1999)
24. Zave, P.: Requirements for evolving systems: a telecommunications perspective. In: International Symposium on Requirements Engineering, pp. 2–9 (2001)

Natural Language Processing

Comparing Results of Natural Language Disambiguation Tools with Reports of Manual Reviews of Safety-Related Standards

Isabella Biscoglio[1], Attilio Ciancabilla[2], Mario Fusani[1], Giuseppe Lami[1],
and Gianluca Trentanni[1(✉)]

[1] Istituto di Scienza e Tecnologie dell'Informazione "A. Faedo" (ISTI–CNR),
Pisa, Italy
{isabella.biscoglio,mario.fusani,giuseppe.lami,
gianluca.trentanni}@isti.cnr.it
[2] Rete Ferroviaria Italiana (RFI, Infrastructure Manager for the Italian State
Railways), Rome, Italy
a.ciancabilla@rfi.it

Abstract. Methods and tools for detecting and measuring ambiguity in texts have been proposed for years, yet their efficacy is still under study for improvement, encouraged by results in various application fields (requirements, legal documents, interviews, ...). The paper presents a fresh-started process aimed at validating such methods and tools by applying some of them to a semi-structured data corpus. This corpus represents results of manual reviews, done by international experts, along with their source texts. The purpose is to check how much results of automated analysis are consistent with the reviewers reports. The application domain is that of safety-related system/software Standards in Railway. Thus, if we increase confidence in tools, then we also increase confidence in Standard correctness, which in turn impacts in conforming products. Care is taken in using, for scientific purpose only, sensitive, unpublished source data (the comments, protected by NDAs), that are kept reviewer-anonymous before statistical results are produced, while the Standards are publicly available texts. The results will also be used to improve the tools themselves, even if much elaboration is still to be carried out: the research is still at its beginning, so metrics for tool evaluation is a goal, whose characteristics are just sketched and discussed in the paper.

Keywords: Natural Language Processing · Disambiguation ·
Tool validation · Safety-related Standards

1 Introduction

Requirements expressed in Natural Language (NL) are often uneasy to be checked against, particularly when it comes to process requirements. For product requirements, checking if they are satisfied can be usually done by measurement, which can give more objective evidence, and even rigorous one when

© Springer Nature Switzerland AG 2019
M. H. ter Beek et al. (Eds.): Gnesi Festschrift, LNCS 11865, pp. 239–249, 2019.
https://doi.org/10.1007/978-3-030-30985-5_15

Formal Methods are used to express product properties. Process conformance, instead, implies searching for evidence, by document inspection and interviews, that certain actions are done: this is where the typical limitations of NL (clarity problems, ambiguity) mostly create uncertainty.

There has been a rich, continuously evolving literature about methods and tools able to cope with the problems of NL-expressed requirements in general, where ISTI–CNR has been playing an important role since pioneering work done by Stefania Gnesi's group [1,2], and up to the most recent activity reports [3,4, 17]. The need to propose and check solutions to problems with NL understanding led to implement a NLP (Natural Language Processing) tool, called QuARS (see Sect. 4), useful to assist in text preparation and analysis [2,5].

In this paper we introduce a just-started research project, made possible by the availability of a particularly interesting literary corpus on process requirements. This 2.3-gigabyte corpus represents more than a decade-long effort by an international group of experts in creating some of the recent international Standards for the European Committee for Electrotechnical Standardization (CEN-ELEC), namely EN 50126 and EN 50128 [6,7]. These Standards consist of a set of norms that regulate the life-cycle processes of safety-related systems and software in railway applications. Some of the authors of this paper have also been participating in official Working Groups for the creation and review of these Standards. This allows, once privacy restrictions (NDA-covered) are granted, to work on the material to issue anonymous, statistically-processed results. One outstanding feature of this corpus is that it contains the full story of document versions, including Standards drafts, along with comments and suggestions that made each version evolve into the next one. We believe that this opportunity allows to investigate a rare documentation of a review process, made particularly precious as it engaged a relevant number of experts, bound to follow defined review procedures [8,9]. Our aim is being able to reproduce, by using NLP techniques and tools, processes similar to those that were followed by the actors of the standardization work.

Another feature, useful in NLP, is that all the Standards drafts as well as their final, publicly available versions, are structured into hierarchically organized, uniquely-labelled requirements (the clauses and sub-clauses of the Standards).

At the beginning of our investigation, in order to plan this likely long activity, we can envision the following research questions:

RQ1: What are the conditions that make reviewers to propose a change, particularly to increase clarity and remove non-ambiguity?

RQ2: How to automate, by using NLP, the detection of such conditions?

RQ3: To what extent could the deployment of the proposed changes be considered as a reference model to validate different NLP tools?

RQ4: Could the application of NLP help finding new possible situations of lack of clarity and understandability in Standards, different from the ones recurring in procedure-guided reviews, so that NLP methods and tools can enter in the Standards creation process?

The purpose of this paper is by no means that of responding to such questions. For now, we can present the framework in which this research project, driven by the same questions, can evolve. Such evolution will start with QuARS as a NLP tool applied to single documents and then progressing towards other, more recent approaches and tools. In an advanced research stage the whole CENELEC corpus, hopefully enriched with material from other standardisation bodies, such as ISO and IEC, would be viewed as a sandbox for the application of a selection of existing data analytics methods and also new versions of QuARS itself.

The paper is organized as follows:

In Sect. 2, reasons are given about why safety-related Standards describing lifecycle processes are best fitted for NLP and particularly for this research project.

In Sect. 3, a short description of the corpus under examination is presented, and the CENELEC review regulation, a norm itself, is also shown.

In Sect. 4, NLP-related work is referred, and it is shown how QuARS, of which a brief description is given, has been used to help disambiguating requirements in different application domains.

In Sect. 5, an example of using QuARS on two successive clause versions, taken from the CENELEC corpus, is shown.

In Sect. 6, a perspective of a possible, long-term research activity is sketched.

2   Why Safety-Related Standards?

We have some reasons to refer to safety-related Standards as a target for our NLP project.

1. The safety-related Standards we are interested in are very popular process-oriented Standards and so, as mentioned in Sect. 1, they are prone to suffer the typical NL problems.
2. The set of documents leading to publicly available international Standards are submitted to a thorough, procedure-driven analysis by experts of all interested Countries. Then, a full report of their step-by-step evolution can be considered as a best model for understanding why and how a given text is evolved into an improved text.
3. Being involved in standardization Working Groups of some safety-related Standards, the authors happen to have access, although with restrictions regarding disclosure of sensitive CENELEC material, to their related documentation, from the first draft to the final, public issue. This is an unique occasion indeed. Without this opportunity, any analysis would have been done only with the publicly available versions (nominally, one every five years), thus missing essential data of the review process.
4. Since safety-related Standards, including the CENELEC Standards, prescribe adoption of state-of-the-art techniques in system and software lifecycle processes, their qualities do impact in the resulting products, and then in the life of human beings using such products (trains, in our case), and in the

environment as well. This impact is stronger than in other disciplines that have seen similar research approaches (such as product requirements, legal acts, handbooks).
5. Granted all the value attributable to the standardization work and its actors, safety-related Standards have not been free from criticism. Since the 1990's, papers expressing concern on their quality and efficacy have appeared now and then, typically about means and actions for safety assurance when the target of comparison for conformity (the Standard text) may mix process and product requirements, as well as different abstraction levels, and carry some ambiguity in clause texts [10, 14–16]. We believe that results of our research project will help clarifying such criticism so to be able to improve the Standard review process itself: in fact this could be aided by tools assisting reviewers to mitigate the risks of ambiguity, unclarity, and other recurrent defects of NL.

3 Documenting a CENELEC Standard Definition Process

3.1 CENELEC Standard Regulations and Activity

Quoting from [8]:

"CENELEC is the European Standardization Body in the field of electrotechnology and related technologies, facilitating and organizing contacts with all interested parties: producers, users, governments, public bodies, consumers, trade unions, etc."

Most of the standardization work is done in the area of Technical Committees (TC). TC are established by a Technical Board with precise titles and scopes, mainly to prepare CEN/CENELEC publications (EN, etc.). A TC is normally organized in Sub-Committees (SC) and in operating Working Groups (WGs).

An European Standard (EN) is a Standard adopted by CEN/CENELEC and carrying with it an obligation of implementation as an identical national standard and withdrawal of conflicting national standards. EU directives and regulations can prescribe conformance to an EN in some application domains such as railway domain.

There are written rules on how to prepare an EN, that include analysing draft-documents produced by a WG through formal internationally organized Enquiries and international Formal Votes aimed to approve an EN [9].

Regarding activities of WG's, they use and produce a fair amount of documentation, namely:

1. Source documents (formerly approved EN, Standards from other organizations, related technical literature)
2. Draft EN documents
3. Comments on specific drafts, including the rationale for comments
4. Reports on discussions and decision of comments disposition
5. Formal and informal meeting minutes
6. Organization and managing documents (schedule, plans, participants lists).

3.2   Our Reference CELELEC Corpus

CENELEC TC's cover several technical areas. The material of our literary corpus has been produced within TC9X, whose mission is: "Electrical and electronic applications for railways, dealing with standardization of electrical and electronic systems, equipment and associated software for use in all railway applications, whether on vehicles or fixed installations, including urban transport".

More in detail, our literary corpus consists of a set of documents, including type 2, 3, 4, 5 documents listed in Sect. 3.1. It is a collection of different standard projects, created by different WG's. WG 14 of TC 9X has been working on EN 50126 from 2008 to 2014. In SC 9XA (a Sub Committee of TC 9X), WG11 worked from 2006 to 2010 producing EN 50128:2011 and WG18 has been active since 2017, working on the amendment of EN 50128.

An interesting type of documents, on which QuARS can work with moderate pre- and post-processing, includes spreadsheets in which old and new clauses are listed almost synoptically, along with some explanations and discussion notes. One of these documents has been used for the example shown in Sect. 5.

4   Related Work: A Short Overview of NLP Applied to Requirements

This paper belongs to a research line started in the 1990's at the ISTI–CNR FMT Lab, led by Stefania Gnesi. The FMT Lab was working by then in Use Case Analysis [11] and investigating the relationship between NL requirements and requirements formalisation using NL2ACTL [1]. In particular, NL2ACTL proposed a way to transform NL requirements into more rigorous formal and semi-formal models and languages. Since then, interest has been focused, at ISTI–CNR and in other research environments, on providing quality models for textual expressions (organized as structured sets of linguistic attributes), against which sets of requirements can be checked. A survey of the role of ISTI–CNR in this activity is shown in [12]. Early along this research line, the tool QuARS (Quality Analyzer for Requirements Specifications) was developed at ISTI–CNR. QuARS (referred in literature many times since [5] up to recent [13]), performs sentence-bound analyses with the objective of finding evidence of indicators of lexical and syntactical characteristics and sub-characteristics, structured as the Quality Model shown in Fig. 1. In spite of the nice deal of effort devoted to using NLP in requirement engineering at various institutions worldwide, no application to Standards are known to be reported outside ISTI–CNR, where some related work was initiated by the Stefania Gnesi's group in 2010 [15].

5   Example

In Fig. 2 an example of applying QuARS to two consecutive versions (Old and New) of some EN 50128 clauses, from a document belonging to the CENELEC corpus, is shown.

Quality Characteristics and Sub-characteristics	
Lexical	
	Un-ambiguity: the capability of each requirement to have a unique interpretation
	Vagueness: items having a non-uniquely quantifiable meaning appear in a requirement
	Subjectivity: personal opinions or feelings are expressed in a requirement
	Optionality: optional parts (i.e. a parts that may or may not be considered) are contained in a requirement
	Weakness: weak verbs (e.g. may, might, to manage, to process, ..) are used in a requirement
Syntactical	
	Implicity: subjects or objects are not expressed by means of their specific name but by pronouns or other indirect references in a requirement
	Specification Completion: the capability of each requirement to uniquely identify its object or subject
	Under-specification: Generic terms are used instead of specific ones in a requirement
	Understandability: the capability of each requirement to be fully understood when used for developing software
	Multiplicity: more than one main verb or subject occur in a requirement

Fig. 1. Quality model adopted by QuARS

CLAUSE	status	no. of Words	Findings	Total h Clause	Warning Density	Warnings minus False Positive Density	Optionality	Subjectivity	Vagueness	Weakness	Implicity	Multiplicity	Under-specification
5.2.1	Old	72	warnings	3	0.042				1			2	
	Old	72	False Pos	3	0.042	0.000			1			2	
	New	62	warnings	4	0.065							2	2
	New	62	False Pos	2	0.032	0.032						2	
5.2.2	Old	33	warnings	0	0.000								
	Old	33	False Pos	0	0.000	0.000							
	New	36	warnings	0	0.000								
	New	36	False Pos	0	0.000	0.000							
5.2.3	Old	53	warnings	3	0.057					1		2	
	Old	53	False Pos	3	0.057	0.000				1		2	
	New	45	warnings	5	0.111			1		1	1	2	
	New	45	False Pos	5	0.111	0.000		1		1	1	2	
5.2.5	Old	59	warnings	5	0.085				1	1	1	2	
	Old	59	False Pos	5	0.085	0.000			1	1	1	2	
	New	39	warnings	0	0.000								
	New	39	False Pos	0	0.000	0.000							
6.2.1	Old	30	warnings	2	0.067				1			1	
	Old	30	False Pos	1	0.033	0.033						1	
	New	31	warnings	2	0.065				1			1	
	New	31	False Pos	0	0.000	0.065							
6.2.2	Old	38	warnings	3	0.079				1			2	
	Old	38	False Pos	2	0.079	0.026						2	
	New	26	warnings	3	0.115					3			
	New	26	False Pos	0	0.000	0.115							

Fig. 2. Results from clause analysis (Old vs. New clauses)

In Fig. 3 a summary is shown regarding 20 clauses.

In this example, false positive Warnings are decided (and removed) by manually inspecting all the Warnings reported by QuARS, on the basis of experience in safety-related Standard applications to railway projects. We do not have sufficient resulting data here to express quantitative considerations with any confidence: Fig. 2 is just to show one of the different possible ways of comparing clauses before (Old) and after (New) the changes suggested by the appointed Standard reviewers. Among the hypotheses to be tested statistically, which we

no. of clauses		Words Total		Total		Average Warning density
20	Old	788	warnings	60		0.017
			False P	51		
	New	911	warnings	70		0.014
			False P	55		

Fig. 3. Results from 20 clause analysis

will do as one of the first analyses, there will be one about the percentage of the potential defects detected by QuARS shared by the expert reviewers (see Research Question 3 and 4). Here, out of 24 non-false-positive warnings (9 in Old clauses and 15 in New ones) only a few seem to be agreed upon by the reviewers, whose purpose was more oriented to technical issues than to comprehension aspects. This should not be considered as a conclusion, for the just stated reasons.

6   Working with Our Research Questions

Looking ahead from the beginning of our work, that will likely last a couple of years, we can foresee that the activity with the CENELEC corpus (and possibly other similar corpora) will mostly be focused in the analysis of Standard reviewers' change proposals, also comparing them with tools results.

One difficulty that we can perceive right now is that the two approaches have different quality objectives, or models. Whilst a defined quality model (call it NLP-QM) is used by QuARS (Fig. 1) and by other similar tools, the process of the manual review, instructed by formal CENELEC enquiries [9], produces a more general spectrum of type of issues, or comments, which could still be related to a quality model, let us call it R-QM. R-QM can be thought of being made of a basic set of issues, denoted as Technical, General and Editorial issues, to be possibly associated, after manual inspection, with a given Standard clause.

A somehow loose relationship can be established between NLP-QM and R-QM (see Fig. 4): common features could be found for Editorial issues, even if in some occasions there is no sharp bound between Editorial and Technical. Of course we expect that most Technical problems found by the reviewers that generate changes in clauses would not be found also by tools such as QuARS, that is oriented to intrinsic, generally non-technical characteristics within a single clause.

Just one Editorial/Under-spec match was found by QuARS after the 20-clause run that produced the results shown in Fig. 3).

NLP-QM R-QM	Vagueness	Subjectivity	Optionality	Weakness	Implicity	Under-spec	Multiplicity
Technical	X	X				X	X
Editorial	X	X	X	X		X	X
General							

Fig. 4. Possible partial matches (X) between R-QM and NLP-QM

6.1 Planning the Work

Granted the problem just mentioned and others that will occur, our envisioned research framework will start with a thorough data preparation (cleaning, pre-processing, normalizing the parts of the CENELEC corpus) and partition (training data sets, testing data sets), according to a data model, still to be defined, partly constrained by the actual structure of the corpus. QuARS and other tools would then be run on defined parts of data sets. Among the results in which both the issues raised by the reviewers (Reviewer Warnings) and the warnings detected by NLP tools (Tool Warnings) will be reported (after pruning false positives), the following groups can be considered of particular interest:

(1) Reviewer Warnings not matched by any Tool Warnings;
(2) Reviewer Warnings matched by Tool Warnings;
(3) Tool Warnings NOT matched by Reviewer Warnings.

Group 1 would solicit research for better QM, methods and tools. Group 2 would be used for tool validation and for comparison among tools. Group 3 would give rise to recommendations for the WG's working in Standards definition, which is also valid, for the advantages due to automation, for the case of Group 2.

We want to stress again here that the idea to start a new research arises from the (unexpected) availability of a corpus containing information about reviews in standards, the most interesting parts being: text to be changed, comments and new proposed text. As pointed out in the Introduction, this availability is happening in the same research group that has been involved for years (yet non continuously) in textual requirements analysis, not only with the aim of disambiguation but also for other purposes (consistency, usability, concept representation). However exciting this opportunity may be, it is too early to define a detailed research work. What we can do now is to plan for an exploratory survey of the available material, with the research questions (see Sect. 1) in mind, starting with RQ1 ("What are the conditions that make reviewers to propose a change, particularly to increase clarity and remove non-ambiguity?"), which is at the basis of the other ones.

We plan to extract, from the CENELEC corpus, only the Group 1 and Group 2 warnings (Reviewer Warnings), to obtain a set C of proposed changes of Standard clauses.

If N changes are proposed, then

C = set of $c(i)$ $(i = 1, ..., N)$, where

$c(i)$ = [Set(i) of Old-Clauses, Related-Comments, Set(i) of New-Proposed-Clauses].

In general, we could have even more sets of new proposed clauses for the same old clause, however the simplest and most frequent case is when just one clause is requested to be changed into a single new clause (possibly with no comments), so our element of investigation becomes the triplet:

$c(i)$ = [Old-Clause(i), Related Comments, New-Proposed-Clause(i)].

A comparison will then be done between Old-Clause(i) and New-Proposed-Clause(i) $(i = 1, ..., N)$, according to criteria to which some metrics can be associated. An example of such metrics could be represented by the following measurable attributes of a proposed change:

- Word count change;
- Percentage of new words or lemmas in New-Proposed-Clause(i);
- Percentage of deleted words or lemmas in New-Proposed-Clause(i);
- Change in density of Tools Warnings (e.g., by QuARS tool), for each kind of warnings according a defined QM.

Results of some of this metrics was shown in Fig. 2.

Also changes of various parameters in sentence complexity and readability indexes could be considered.

From an analysis of the results of measuring an entire set C of changes, we hope to find a way to appreciate the reviewer effort to make a clause more understandable to its users (e. g.: implementers, testers, assessors).

Technical motivations for changes will be a real challenge: however we think we will be able to discover some of them, or to confirm some related hypotheses, by considering frequency of words belonging to the domain jargon, the comment part of each triplet $c(i)$, and the glossaries included in the Standard.

6.2   Concluding Remarks

Considering the research questions mentioned in Sect. 1, our activity will be aimed at:

Investigating the technical aspects at the basis of the clause changes, by considering also inter-clause relationships, both in a document and across documents, also referring to glossaries, definitions and different use of the same expressions (RQ1 and RQ2).

Categorising the Reviewer Warnings into some detailed QM and studying the way to automate their detection (RQ1).

Using, besides typical NLP tools, currently available data analytics tools on the corpus as a whole, with a strategy still to be established, to discover new relationships between clause contents and reviewers' comments (RQ1 and RQ3).

One practical and final achievement would be to provide a handbook and a tool set to assist WG's in their Standard definition work (RQ4).

The authors feel very indebted to Stefania Gnesi, who had, more than two decades ago, the idea of applying automated textual analysis to NL requirements (see Sect. 4).

References

1. Fantechi, A., Gnesi, S., Ristori, G., Carenini, M., Vanocchi, M., Moreschini, P.: Assisting requirement formalization by means of natural language translation. Formal Methods Syst. Des. **4**(3), 243–263 (1994)
2. Fabbrini, F., Fusani, M., Gnesi, S., Lami, G.: An automatic quality evaluation for natural language requirements. In: Proceedings of 7th REFSQ (2001)
3. Fantechi, A., Ferrari, A., Gnesi, S., Semini, L.: Hacking an ambiguity detection tool to extract variation points: an experience report. In: Proceedings of the 12th International Workshop on Variability Modelling of Software-Intensive Systems, pp. 1–13 (2018)
4. Ferrari, A., Trentanni, G., Gnesi, S.: An automatic quality evaluation for natural language requirements. In: Proceedings of 1st Workshop on Natural Language Processing for Requirements Engineering and NLP Tool Showcase, RESFQ 2018, March 19th - Utrecht, The Netherlands (2019)
5. Gnesi, S., Lami, G., Trentanni, G.: An automatic tool for the analysis of natural language requirements. IJCSSE **20**(1) (2005)
6. CENELEC: EN 50128 - Railway applications - Communication, signalling and processing systems - Software for railway control and protection systems (2011)
7. CENELEC: EN 50126–1 - Railway Applications - The Specification and Demonstration of Reliability, Availability, Maintainability and Safety (RAMS) - Part 1: Generic RAMS Process (2017)
8. CENELEC: Internal Regulations Part 2: Common Rules For Standardization Works (2017)
9. CENELEC: Internal Regulations Part 3: Principles and rules for the structure and drafting of CEN and CENELEC documents (2017)
10. Fenton, N., Neil, M.: A strategy for improving safety related software engineering standards. IEEE Trans. Software Eng. **24**(11), 1002–1013 (1998)
11. Fantechi, A., Gnesi, S., Lami, G., Maccari, A.: Application of linguistic techniques for use case analysis. In: Proceedings of IEEE 10th RE, pp. 157–164 (2002)
12. Ferrari, A., Trentanni, G., Gnesi, S.: Research on NLP for RE at CNR-ISTI: a Report. In: Proceedings of 1st Workshop on Natural Language Processing for Requirements Engineering and NLP Tool Showcase, RESFQ 2018, 19th March 2018, Utrecht, The Netherlands (2018)
13. Gnesi, S: Trentanni, G.: QuARS: a NLP tool for requirements analysis. In: Proceedings of 2nd Workshop on Natural Language Processing for Requirements Engineering and NLP Tool Showcase, RESFQ 2019, 18th March 2019, Essen, Germany (2019)
14. Graydon, P., Holloway, C.: Planning the unplanned experiment: assessing the efficacy of standards for safety critical software. NASA/TM-2015-218804, September 2015
15. Biscoglio, I., Coco, A., Fusani, M., Gnesi, S., Trentanni, G.: An approach to ambiguity analysis in safety-related standards. In: Proceedings of International Conference on the Quality of Information and Communications Technology (QUATIC 2010), pp. 146–176 (2010)

16. Ferrari, A., Fusani, M., Gnesi, S.: Are standards an ambiguity-free reference for product validation? In: Fantechi, A., Lecomte, T., Romanovsky, A. (eds.) RSSRail. Lecture Notes in Computer Science, vol. 10598. Springer, Cham (2017). https:// doi.org/10.1007/978-3-319-68499-4_17
17. Ferrari, A., et al.: Detecting requirements defects with NLP patterns: an industrial experience in the railway domain. IEEE Empir. Softw. Eng. **23**(6), 3684–3733 (2018)

Looking Inside the Black Box: Core Semantics Towards Accountability of Artificial Intelligence

Roberto Garigliano[1] and Luisa Mich[2(✉)]

[1] Journal of Natural Language Engineering (Founding Editor), Cambridge, UK
[2] University of Trento, Trento, Italy
luisa.mich@unitn.it

Abstract. Recent advances in artificial intelligence raise a number of concerns. Among the challenges to be addressed by researchers, accountability of artificial intelligence solutions is one of the most critical. This paper focuses on artificial intelligence applications using natural language to investigate if the core semantics defined for a large-scale natural language processing system could assist in addressing accountability issues. Core semantics aims to obtain a full interpretation of the content of natural language texts, representing both implicit and explicit knowledge, using only 'subj-action-(obj)' structures and causal, temporal, spatial and personal-world links. The first part of the paper offers a summary of the difficulties to be addressed and of the reasons why representing the meaning of a natural language text is relevant for artificial intelligence accountability. In the second part, a-proof-of-concept for the application of such a knowledge representation to support accountability, and a detailed example of the analysis obtained with a prototype system named CoreSystem is illustrated. While only preliminary, these results give some new insights and indicate that the provided knowledge representation can be used to support accountability, looking inside the box.

Keywords: Artificial intelligence · Natural language processing · Knowledge representation · Semantics · Rules · Accountability

1 Introduction

Thanks to more powerful hardware and to a new generation of learning algorithms [1], artificial intelligence (AI) supports the automation of a widespread number of tasks and activities, changing not only the job landscape, but also everyday life [2, 3]. Embedded in almost any device and software system, AI solutions support decisions and control systems giving advice and recommendations that may imply serious risks [4–7]. The first step to address such risks is to be able to explain why a given solution or behavior has been chosen, providing information on the data and knowledge used, and on their processing, thus including stakeholders. This feature of an AI system is named accountability [8]. The problem is that many AI systems run programs based on algorithms whose particular output cannot usually be traced back to specific parts of the input. The new generation algorithms, based on deep learning, are even more inscrutable

© Springer Nature Switzerland AG 2019
M. H. ter Beek et al. (Eds.): Gnesi Festschrift, LNCS 11865, pp. 250–266, 2019.
https://doi.org/10.1007/978-3-030-30985-5_16

due to the complexity of the processing steps and the huge size of data required and produced [9]. Focusing on AI systems using natural language, whose role is relevant in a variety of areas, we assume that a 'core' semantic representation of the content of natural language text could assist to address accountability issues, looking inside the box. A core semantic approach aims at obtaining a full interpretation of a natural language text representing both implicit and explicit knowledge: in this way it could support explanation of the output of AI systems embedding any form of natural language processing (NLP), e.g., translators, chatbot, information extraction systems. Furthermore, a core semantic representation could be applicable also to systems which do not have natural language as their normal input or output (e.g., a medical system which takes patient data and produces a structured output), but which would benefit from being able to store their knowledge in core semantics and explain it in a comprehensible manner using natural language.

In this paper we will investigate if and how the core semantic representation defined for a large-scale domain independent NLP system could be used to support accountability of AI. The system, a prototype that in this paper is referred as CoreSystem, represents the content of natural language texts using only 'subj-action-(obj)' structures and causal, temporal, spatial and personal-world links, the basic elements of the 'core semantics'. To be able to explain is the first, crucial step in 'accounting', which can be seen as detecting causes and then allocating responsibilities. Beyond that, the two key elements in allocating responsibilities are causal relationship and 'personal-world' relationships (those produced by relations which move into a person's inner world, such as 'think', 'want', 'need', etc.). These are exactly the two elements which CoreSystem uses as basic links in its model.

As a-proof-of-concept, a detailed example is illustrated, showing the representation of a complex sentence's content produced by CoreSystem, and how it could be used to answer some simple questions in order to explain its interpretation. The results of the analysis, albeit preliminary, indicate that the core semantics approach produces a knowledge representation that can be understood and checked towards accountability goals.

The rest of the paper is structured as follow. Section 2 illustrates the concept of accountability and the difficulties involved in making an AI system accountable. Section 3 summarizes the problems of NLP in the light of accountability and the benefit of a core semantic representation of a text. In Sect. 4, the core semantics defined for CoreSystem is illustrated focusing on the output of the system. Section 5 gives an example of how the analysis produced by an NLP system able to implement a core semantics could be used to support accountability goals. Conclusions are drawn in Sect. 6.

2 Accountability for Artificial Intelligence

In AI, accountability is the ability to explain how a given result has been obtained from a given input, to justify why a certain decision or behaviour has been suggested and to identify roles and responsibilities. The accountability concept is connected to that of explainability, interpretability and transparency [5, 10, 11]. Accountability problems were raised since the very first AI systems, as automatic systems and processes are based on algorithms and the problem of accountability for their output is not a new one. Many authors have underlined the risks connected with applications of algorithms in different fields. AI has elevated the complexity of algorithms and the related risks to unprecedented levels. Besides, many people are unaware of the use of the results of a software system and accept suggestions without critical reflection. For a given AI system, accountability is challenged since the first activities of definition and choice of the input data. Data and knowledge used in deep-learning AI algorithms are:

- unstructured: textual documents, audio, video, images;
- extracted from large data sets and knowledge bases;
- analysed applying data analytics or other techniques of big data analysis.

The higher risk is that of data-bias, that is of data reflecting values of the people who design and realize the data sets [12]. A number of cases have been reported in literature and in newspapers [11, 13, 14].

As regards algorithms, the need to have explanations for decisions by being able to inspect the system or the code – looking inside the box – can be defined as external accountability. Unfortunately, learning algorithms, especially unsupervised and deep learning algorithms, are based on models that do not allow tracking and understanding of the internal steps [15, 16]. Complex multilayer neural networks and large inputs cannot be described in details at the level of their inner processing and, in turn, it is difficult to understand the relationship between inputs and outputs. For expert systems, one of the first type of AI applications and usually based on if-then rules, accountability is guaranteed through 'why?' and 'how?' explanation capabilities, allowing, e.g., a doctor to know why a given diagnose was suggested for the specified symptoms, but this is not the case for the new generation of AI algorithms. Even for supervised algorithms, in which it would be possible to use (a subset of) the training sets to show the input for a given output to explain why a solution was obtained, usability problems could arise [17].

Finally, the output of an AI system comes in a variety of forms; each of them can be more or less difficult to be traced-back to the input and to justify the results.

3 Natural Language Processing and Accountability

3.1 Representing Meaning in a Text

Natural language processing is one of the main areas of AI. Natural language texts are traditionally analysed in a sequential process, starting with lexical and structural elements, parsing text to identify the most suitable parsing tree and then applying more or less complex techniques to interpret the semantic content, that is, to understand the meaning.

Parsing trees and semantic representations are typically dependent on the particular form of the sentence; in this sense, they give a surface representation. For example, the parsing and shallow semantic analysis of the following sentence:

(a) A 59-year-old man from York has been arrested on suspicion of murdering missing chef Claudia Lawrence.

would allow identifying two instances of 'named entity', 'York' and 'Claudia Lawrence'; the first part of the sentence as the syntactical subject of an 'arrest'; 'missing' as an adjective and (possibly) 'chef' as a 'role' of the named entity 'Claudia Lawrence'; the last part of the sentence as the object of the 'suspicion'. The difference between a shallow and a core semantics can be illustrated comparing sentence (a) with the following:

(b) Police have arrested a York man, aged 59, because they suspect him to be the murderer of Claudia Lawrence, the chef who has disappeared.

Phrase (b) has the same meaning for any competent native speaker as phrase (a), but it produces completely different parse tree and surface semantics. It should be noticed that there is a large amount of ways (surface structures) in which this same meaning could be expressed.

To fully understand that meaning, an NLP system needs a core semantics, that is, an approach based on an internal representation of the content of sentences in which both explicit and implicit knowledge is showed.

There are many reasons why an internal representation for natural language is necessary and the most important for an NLP system are the following:

– To deal with *problems in the natural language inputs*: an NLP system has to be able to address possible problems of incorrect data, incomplete data or skewed data, all problems quite frequent in real natural language texts.
– To show *how the NLP system reached its result*: to this end, the system has to be able to look from outside at an internal representation or 'record', a characteristic that is relevant to developers of the system but also to support accountability.
– To *reason on its internal representation independently from the surface form* of its NLP input.
– To implement *self-awareness* (more philosophical): in order for any system to reason and evaluate its own beliefs and actions autonomously, it needs an internal accessible representation of at least part of it [7, 18].

Focusing on the application of NLP systems to accountability goals, an example for the need of an internal representation is the recent case of the Amazon assistant Alexa, which was faced with the request from a teenager about what to do with annoying parents, and which replied "murder them", because it had found a perfect match to the input in a 'for-laughs' site (https://tinyurl.com/ybedgm6f). The system deals with speech (i.e. natural language) input all the time in millions of home, yet has no model of what is doing or what the request-answers mean.

As regards AI systems processing different media, images or videos, when human analyze the accountability implications, they do it using natural language. For example in the government-sponsored panel in Germany to define guidelines for automated and connected driving (https://tinyurl.com/y3rf6mgx), experts had to deal with questions like: "In case of possible accident, should the car prioritize the driver, the passengers or passer-by?" (with various sub-categories considered). The natural language answers then becomes suitable for analysis by a system like CoreSystem, as are the simplified output of the experts. The results can then be fed-back to the car designers, in a more formal and interactive way, helping to bridge the gap between moral experts on the panel and engineers.

3.2   Core Semantic Representation

A core semantic representation in NLP is an internal representation of the text that attempts to describe its meaning in a form that can be (very) different from the original one. Internal semantic representation can be categorised in various ways according to the supported functionalities:

- Disambiguation: does it disambiguate the text; normally disambiguation is understood to cover lexical (nouns and verbs) and some structural (e.g., attachment) elements; a core semantic approach covers also other structures such as prepositions, implicit elements (especially causal and temporal ones, events underlying nouns), redundant structures, etc.
- Normalization: does it normalize the representation, i.e., does it produce the same output for inputs that human would recognize as equivalent, even if the surface forms are very different.
- Relationships: does it make explicit all the implicit relationships: causal, temporal, spatial, and personal.
- Point of views: can the system extrapolate from the narrative point of view in the description; e.g., giving and receiving: "Tom gives a book to Mary" and "Mary receives a book from Tom" have the same deep meaning, but told from different viewpoints.
- Reasoning: does it help reasoning and query answering, by avoiding unnecessary searches, combinatorial explosions, match-failure due to surface elements, etc.

There are some difficulties in implementing such explicit representation using a deep learning approach on its own. The main problems are related to the following issues:

- Lack of data: while there are huge repositories of text translations (e.g., the EU translation repositories) [19, 20] and question answering (large repos exist in call centre databases, etc.), there are fewer such databases of text-internal representation pairs, usually of much smaller dimensions. Note that deep learning usually requires huge amount of data, from millions to billions; e.g., DeepL [21].
- While it can be used on smaller data sets, its general correct coverage on new input decreases noticeably. Parsing is a different issue, in that the parse tree is fundamentally a grammatical structure. Deep learning has been successfully used on TreeBank [22], but this has two key features: (1) all the text used is correct; (2) the representation pairs stored includes semantic decisions (e.g., on attachment) that usually cannot correctly be solved at that scale; (3) the representation is surface-based anyway.

– Existing deep semantic approaches still do not achieve the above requirements. Example of such deep semantics models are: the Mental models [18], based on instantiation, separation of possibilities in different models (cognitive bias), elimination of non-compatible models, self-centred models, etc.; the Conceptual dependency theory model [23], based on primitives chosen away from language, negation of parsing role, no explicit rules for extractions, pre-constructed scripts, difficult handling of negation, etc. Many semantic representation systems carry surface-based elements such as the absence of personal worlds (e.g., AMR, https:// amr.isi.edu); a case-structure (e.g., FrameNet, https://framenet.icsi.berkeley.edu) or the inability to extract implicit causal links.

"Deep semantics" is also used to indicate a number of approaches in which 'deep' denotes specific characteristics of the task or of the output. For example, in [24] it is used to indicate a latent semantic model exploiting neural networks to semantic role labelling; the authors propose an approach that does not run any parsing, does not actually recover the full meaning of the sentences and is dependent on various surface elements.

4   CoreSystem

CoreSystem[1] is a prototype NLP system. Its final goal is to obtain an internal representation of the meaning of sentences independent of the surface description and able to explicit the key implicit elements. The current version of the system is based on a sequence of compositional rules. These rules tend to be linked to general semantic properties of the terms or language structures: once specific information is acquired, it can then be used to supplement the analysis with specific domain dependent information. The design is based on the principle of doing what can be done straight away, according to an economy principle, since keeping options open costs efforts (in human is also limited by working memory), while at the same time leaving open the decisions for which there is not enough information at that stage (e.g., for attachment at parsing stage). This can be done without overload by a technique that allows localizing structural ambiguities. Vice versa, where semantic information can be used efficiently early on (e.g., semantic restrictions on verbs), it is incorporated in the parsing stage. Once a surface semantic representation is achieved – i.e., one which transforms the parsing tree into a graph, in which same entities or events are unified, the process to transform it into core semantics begins.

CoreSystem deals only with English, however, given the present proficiency of automatic translation systems, for other languages it is possible to do the following: automatically translate an input in English, convert it in the internal semantics, elaborate it as required, get CoreSystem to generate an English text from such elaboration

---

[1] The following brief description of the prototype system is provided in order to outline what has been used to produce the analysis below. The system is at present not available for external testing; furthermore, as it is under development, no claims are made here to its coverage or efficiency with respect to other NLP systems.

as required, re-translate in the desired language. Initial experiments in this sense with Italian and Spanish have given positive results.

The analysis process is a step-by-step one, in which a set of rules has been elaborated looking at many written texts from different sources (e.g., Economist, Wikipedia, BBC, Telegraph, Mirror, Bloomberg, Reuters); these rules turn out to be by-and-large domain independent. A version for different types of input (e.g., speech transcription, dialogue, chat, etc.) is under development. CoreSystem satisfies, albeit at different levels, all the requirements described in Sect. 3.2. Its core semantic approach tackles the combinatorial explosion of meaning representations following a strongly minimalist approach that leads to a representation of the content independent of the surface description, including hidden casual, spatial and temporal connections.

The core of the present version is written in Haskell (www.haskell.org). Haskell, a purely functional, strongly typed, lazy, referentially transparent, higher order programming language, is particularly suited for representing very complex set of rules; also, because of its referential transparency, it is not dependent on side effects, which greatly help the managing of a large number of rules working together. Haskell can be run in parallel, either internally or using orchestrating systems such as Erlang. The user interface is implemented in JavaScript, with the logic controlling the display managed from Haskell.

The last version of CoreSystem has been used and preliminary validated, in a national project (Sintesys, http://www.cerict.it/it/progetti-nazionali-conclusi/281-sintesys-ricerca.html) and in a European project (LASIE, http://www.lasie-project.eu). In these projects, CoreSystem was tasked with analysing texts from similar domains (terrorism for the national project and crime for the European project), while the type of text was different (short, information rich Reuters flash news in Sintesys; long newspaper articles and blogs in LASIE). In both cases, the goal was to produce an analysis that helped investigators in the following ways:

- provide a clear representation of the information and the underlying structures;
- find common references to people, places, organizations, events, etc.;
- connect events along temporal causal and spatial chains;
- extract modal information, such as desires, beliefs, plans, likes, duties, etc.

In order to reach these objectives, the core semantic representation has proved the key feature, since it has allowed to unify apparently different entities and events and to connect them using implicit deep temporal, causal and spatial chains. It has also been essential in extracting motivations, likely actions, elements of planning and other mental structures.

As regards self-awareness, a deep neural network may embody such knowledge, beliefs, etc., but it is distributed, so there is not a part that represents it. For some scholars, such representation has to be symbolic in nature, and separated from the underlying one, in order to avoid infinite regressions [7].

5   Core Semantics and Accountability

To investigate how a core semantic representation could be used to support accountability of AI, in this section the output produced by CoreSystem for sentence (a) is analysed.

A 59-year-old man from York has been arrested on suspicion of murdering missing chef Claudia Lawrence.

In this sentence, a lot of knowledge is implicit, but a reader would be able to interpret it, understanding it as follows: Claudia Lawrence worked as a chef, she disappeared, she may have been murdered, then police suspected that a man murdered her and so they arrested him. The man had been in York before police arrested him, and he was 59 years of age when the police arrested him.

Its surface representation (parsing or semantic) is very distant from its core semantics (Figs. 1a and 1b give the output created by the NLP system split for the sake of readability).

Core semantics means that all the implicit information, as for example the events hidden inside nouns such as 'suspicion', adjective such as 'missing', or roles such as 'chef', has to be extracted and organized in small atomic unit, which then are put together in the correct temporal and causal sequence.

In CoreSystem, information is represented in a graph as objects and events. For the above sentence, the system creates 3 new objects ('man', 'York' – used in the event which describes the man's position before the arrest – and 'police'), an object created for a previous analysis ('Claudia Lawrence') and 14 events. Figure 2 presents an extract of the analysis obtained by the CoreSystem applying a core semantics for the sentence: the *event* 'arrest', the *object* 'police' and the event created to explicit the fact that the man is 59 years old when he is arrested by the police. Both events are interpreted according the 'subj-action-(obj)' structure, supplemented by other meta-level information, as the time of the action, the source of the information and the links with other objects and events used by CoreSystem to represent the content of the sentence.

The final analysis is rather distant from the original text, although it is close to how a native speaker would mentally visualize the story [18]. The full analysis is given in the appendix, and the number of the nodes used for the internal representation is reported in what follows. 'Arrest' (109608) is an example of a general event marked as 'proto-typical', which allows to explicit police (172748) as the subject of the arrest. A proto-type is a 'best initial guess' structure, based on causal models. It is not probabilistic and it can be overruled by more specific information. Other prototypes used to represent the meaning of the sentence are that of 'murder' (172705) and 'suspicion' (172745). 'Police' is also used as the subject of the *event* "Police suspects a man murdering Claudia Lawrence" (172745), the event representing the reason of the arrest, i.e. the causal link between suspicion and arrest. The content of the last part of the sentence is

(a)

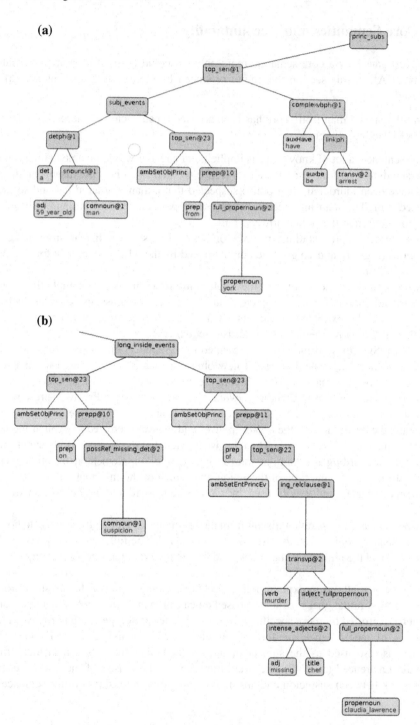

Fig. 1. Parse tree for sentence (a) first subtree (b) second subtree

represented by the following *events:* "Claudia Lawrence works as Chef" (171759), "Claudia Lawrence disappears" (172744), and "Claudia Lawrence works as Chef, before she disappears" (172780). The murder, the suspicion and the arrest are then connected by the *event* "Police suspects a man murdering Claudia Lawrence so they arrest him" (170891). The other events are needed to represent the causal, spatial and temporal relations among the events in the original sentence.

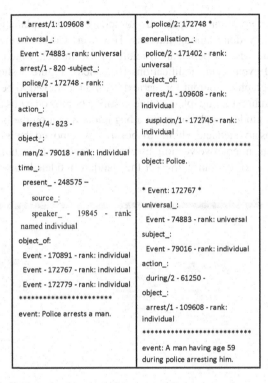

Fig. 2. Examples of events and objects used for representing core semantics

Notice that the fact that the arrested man murdered Claudia Lawrence is marked as hypothetical, since it exists at present only in police's suspicion. This, as well as other phenomena such as negation, desires, different beliefs etc., is modelled using a many-worlds semantics, some of which may be incompatible with each other.

For what concerns accountability, such representation could be used to explain some facts and actions, answering questions as "Who was arrested?"; "Where is he from"; "Why was he arrested?"; "What was she doing for a living" but also "Who arrested him", even if this information is not explicited in the sentence. While, what is the name of the arrested man could be answered saying "I do not know", being that a statement about the knowledge in the AI system and not about not being able to extract such knowledge from the text. Also important is the source information given for an event (Fig. 2).

Question answering is an obvious way to achieve both explanation and accountability, as is normally done among humans. However, CoreSystem also produces a graphical view of the causal-personal structure of the model, which allows for easy understanding (and even hand-modifications if needed). Figure 3 shows a simplified screen shot for the graphical output for the text "A man, believed to be a member of an unknown Muslim militant group, planted five gasoline bombs on a bus carrying German tourists in Cairo. A guide saw the man put a bag under a seat on the bus and called the police. The man was arrested and a bomb disposal crew removed the bombs. No injuries were reported." In the interactive version, by clicking on the various links the viewer can see the different types of causality, inspect the standard models behind etc.

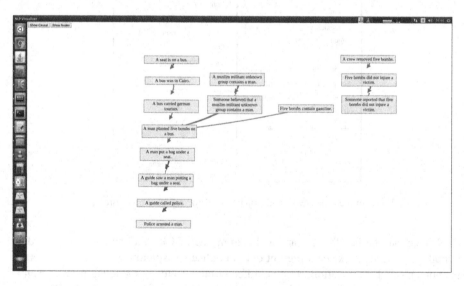

Fig. 3. Screenshot of the graphical representation produced by CoreSystem

6 Conclusions

The importance of accountability and the need for a core semantics which can fully understand the meaning of natural language processing texts have recently been underlined in two interventions by leading AI scientists [25, 26]. Focusing on AI systems embedding any form of NLP, in this paper we investigated how a core semantic approach could be used to address those concerns. In general, core semantics embedded in various AI applications would greatly help in assessing systems' performance, as well as allowing the systems themselves to have an image of their own high-level processing. The final goal of an NLP system is to extract from natural language documents core semantic version that clearly shows the crucial causal and temporal links, and this is a pre-requisite to use the NLP system to support accountability. As a proof-of-concept, the practicability of the core semantics has been tested using a prototype large-scale NLP system. For accountability goals, the example illustrated in Sect. 5 indicates that a core semantics produces textual representations that can be easily understood and checked by human. The next step is to provide also a graphical representation and the NLP query answering. To design and implement accountability functionalities as NLP system module, the large amount of knowledge used for the analysis of a single statement highlights that it is critical to be able to deal with the combinatorial explosion of the graph. Besides, according to software engineering best practices, interfaces supporting final users, and not only developers, have to satisfy usability and performance requirements.

Acknowledgments. As researchers in natural language processing and requirements engineering, authors shared a number of papers with Stefania Gnesi and her research group since the early 1990s. She is a passionate scientist, and these exchanges resulted in a fruitful and enriching relationship.

Appendix A

Representation of the Meaning of the Sentence: "A 59-year-old man from York has been arrested on suspicion of murdering missing chef Claudia Lawrence".

* Event: 79016 *
universal_:
Event - 74883 - rank: universal
subject_:
man/2 - 79018 - rank: individual
action_:
have_age/1 - 258771 -
object_:
59 - 258887 - rank: universal
time_:
present_ - 248575 -
source_:
speaker_ - 19845 - rank: named individual
subject_of:
Event - 172767 - rank: individual
****
event:
A man has age 59.
****

* man/2: 79018 *
universal_:
man/2 - 79015 - rank: universal
murderer/1 - 150961 - rank: universal
suspect/3 - 189089 - rank: universal
subject_of:
Event - 79016 - rank: individual
Event - 79021 - rank: individual
murder/2 - 172705 - rank: individual - hypothe-
sis_
object_of:
arrest/1 - 109608 - rank: individual
****
object:
A man.
****

* Event: 79021 *
universal_:
Event - 74883 - rank: universal
subject_:
man/2 - 79018 - rank: individual
action_:
be/12 - 15902 -
location_:
position_ - 79022 - rank: individual

time_:
past_ - 248407 -
source_:
speaker_ - 19845 - rank: named individual
subject_of:
Event - 172779 - rank: individual
****
event:
A man was in York.
****

* position_: 79022 *
universal_:
position_ - 11456 -
subject_of:
Event - 79023 - rank: individual
location_of:
Event - 79021 - rank: individual
****
object:
In York.
****

* Event: 79023 *
universal_:
Event - 74883 - rank: universal
subject_:
position_ - 79022 - rank: individual
action_:
in/1 - 119448 -
object_:
york/5 - 247198 - rank: named individual
****
event:
Is in York.
****

* arrest/1: 109608 *
universal_:
Event - 74883 - rank: universal
arrest/1 - 820 -
subject_:
police/2 - 172748 - rank: universal
action_:
arrest/4 - 823 -
object_:
man/2 - 79018 - rank: individual

time_:
present_ - 248575 -
source_:
speaker_ - 19845 - rank: named individual
object_of:
Event - 170891 - rank: individual
Event - 172767 - rank: individual
Event - 172779 - rank: individual
****
event:
Police arrests a man.
****

* Event: 170891 *
universal_:
Event - 74883 - rank: universal
subject_:
suspicion/1 - 172745 - rank: individual
action_:
cause/3 - 33341 -
object_:
arrest/1 - 109608 - rank: individual
source_:
speaker_ - 19845 - rank: named individual
****
event:
Police suspects a man murdering Claudia Lawrence so they arrest him.
****

* Event: 171759 *
universal_:
Event - 74883 - rank: universal
subject_:
claudia_lawrence/1 - 258841 - rank: named
individual
action_:
work_as/1 - 172933 -
object_:
chef/1 - 44708 - rank: universal
source_:
speaker_ - 19845 - rank: named individual
subject_of:
Event - 172780 - rank: individual
****
event:
Claudia Lawrence works as Chef.
****

* murder/2: 172705 *
universal_:

murder/2 - 157791 - rank: universal
subject_:
man/2 - 79018 - rank: individual
action_:
murder/1 - 154816 -
object_:
claudia_lawrence/1 - 258841 - rank: named
individual
source_:
speaker_ - 19845 - rank: named individual
status_:
hypothesis_ - 248409 -
subject_of:
Event - 172750 - rank: individual
object_of:
Event - 172766 - rank: individual
suspicion/1 - 172745 - rank: individual
****
event:
A man may murder Claudia Lawrence.
****

* Event: 172744 *
universal_:
Event - 74883 - rank: universal
subject_:
claudia_lawrence/1 - 258841 - rank: named
individual
action_:
disappear/1 - 70373 -
source_:
speaker_ - 19845 - rank: named individual
subject_of:
Event - 172766 - rank: individual
object_of:
Event - 172780 - rank: individual
****
event:
Claudia Lawrence disappears.
****

* suspicion/1: 172745 *
universal_:
suspicion/1 - 189007 - rank: universal
subject_:
police/2 - 172748 - rank: universal
action_:
suspect/4 - 189090 -
object_:

murder/2 - 172705 - rank: individual - hypothe-
sis_
time_:
present_ - 248575 -
subject_of:
Event - 170891 - rank: individual
object_of:
Event - 172750 - rank: individual
****
event:
Police suspects a man murdering Claudia Lawrence.
****

* police/2: 172748 *
generalisation_:
police/2 - 171402 - rank: universal
subject_of:
arrest/1 - 109608 - rank: individual
suspicion/1 - 172745 - rank: individual
****
object:
Police.
****

* Event: 172750 *
universal_:
Event - 74883 - rank: universal
subject_:
murder/2 - 172705 - rank: individual - hypothe-
sis_
action_:
before/2 - 15971 -
object_:
suspicion/1 - 172745 - rank: individual
****
event:
A man may murder Claudia Lawrence, before
police suspects this.
****

* Event: 172766 *
universal_:
Event - 74883 - rank: universal
subject_:
Event - 172744 - rank: individual
action_:
before/2 - 15971 -
object_:

murder/2 - 172705 - rank: individual - hypothe-
sis_
****
event:
Claudia Lawrence disappears, before a man
may murder her.
****

* Event: 172767 *
universal_:
Event - 74883 - rank: universal
subject_:
Event - 79016 - rank: individual
action_:
during/2 - 61250 -
object_:
arrest/1 - 109608 - rank: individual
****
event:
A man having age 59 during police arresting
him.
****

* Event: 172779 *
universal_:
Event - 74883 - rank: universal
subject_:
Event - 79021 - rank: individual
action_:
before/2 - 15971 -
object_:
arrest/1 - 109608 - rank: individual
****
event:
A man was in York, before police arrests him.
****

* Event: 172780 *
universal_:
Event - 74883 - rank: universal
subject_:
Event - 171759 - rank: individual
action_:
before/2 - 15971 -
object_:
Event - 172744 - rank: individual
****
event:
Claudia Lawrence works as Chef, before she
disappears.

References

1. LeCun, Y., Yoshua, B., Geoffry, H.: Deep learning. Nature **521**(7553), 436 (2015)
2. Davis, A.: How artificial intelligence has crept into our everyday lives. IEEE Special Report (2016). http://theinstitute.ieee.org/static/special-report-artificial-intelligence
3. LinkedIn: Global recruiting trends 2018 (2018). https://business.linkedin.com/talent-solutions/recruiting-tips/2018-global-recruiting-trends?trk=bl-ba_global-recruiting-trends-launch_maria-ignatova_011018
4. Kaplan, J.: Artificial intelligence: think again. Commun. ACM **60**(1), 36–38 (2016). https://doi.org/10.1145/2950039
5. Internet Society: Artificial Intelligence and Machine Learning: Policy paper (2017). https://www.internetsociety.org/resources/doc/2017/artificial-intelligence-and-machine-learning-policy-paper
6. Parnas, D.L.: The real risks of artificial intelligence. Commun. ACM **60**(10), 27–31 (2017). https://doi.org/10.1145/3132724
7. Shanahan, M.: The Technological Singularity. MIT Press, New York (2015)
8. Anthes, G.: Artificial intelligence poised to ride a new wave. Commun. ACM **60**(7), 19–21 (2017). https://doi.org/10.1145/3088342
9. Guidotti, R., Monreale, A., Pedreschi, D.: The AI black box explanation problem. ERCIM News **116**, 12–13 (2019)
10. ACM U.S. Public Policy Council, ACM Europe Policy Committee: Statement on algorithmic transparency and accountability (2017). https://www.acm.org/binaries/content/assets/public-policy/2017_joint_statement_algorithms.pdf
11. Doshi-Velez, F., et al.: Accountability of AI under the law: the role of explanation. CoRR abs/1711.01134 (2017)
12. O'Neil, C.: Weapons of math destruction: how big data increases inequality and threatens democracy. New York Time (2016)
13. Pell, D.: The 10 algorithms that rule the world and other fascinating news on the web. Time (2014). http://time.com/111313/the-10-algorithms-that-rule-the-world-and-other-fascinating-news-on-the-web
14. Barry-Jester, A.M., Casselman, B., Goldestein, D.: The Marshall Project. The new science of sentencing (2015). https://www.themarshallproject.org/2015/08/04/the-new-science-of-sentencing#.bwuhXcwqn
15. Buregess, M.: Holding AI to account: will algorithms ever be free from bias if they're created by humans? Wired, UK (2016). http://www.wired.co.uk/article/creating-transparent-ai-algorithms-machine-learning
16. Kirkpatrick, K.: Battling algorithmic bias: how do we ensure algorithms treat us fairly? Commun. ACM **59**(10), 16–17 (2016). https://doi.org/10.1145/2983270
17. Gaines, B.: Designing expert systems for usability. In: Shackel, B., Richardson, S.J. (eds.) Human Factors for Informatics Usability, pp. 207–246. Cambridge University Press, New York (1991)
18. Johnson-Laird, P.: How We Reason. Oxford University Press, New York (2006)
19. Wong, S.: Google Translate AI invents its own language to translate with. Daily News (2016). https://www.newscientist.com/article/2114748-google-translate-ai-invents-its-own-language-to-translate-with
20. Reynolds, M.: Google uses neural networks to translate without transcribing. Daily News (2017). https://www.newscientist.com/article/2126738-google-uses-neural-networks-to-translate-without-transcribing

21. Coldewey, D., Lardinois, F.: DeepL schools other online translators with clever machine learning. Techcrunch (2017). https://techcrunch.com/2017/08/29/deepl-schools-other-online-translators-with-clever-machine-learning
22. Mitchell, M.P., Santorini, B., Marcinkiewicz, M.A., Taylor, A.: Treebank-3 LDC99T42 Web Download. Linguistic Data Consortium, Philadelphia (1999)
23. Schank, S., Abelson, R.: Scripts, Plans, Goals and Understanding. An Inquiry into Human Knowledge Structures. Lawrence Erlbaum, Hillsdale (1997)
24. He, L., Lee, K., Lewis, M., Zettlemoyer, L.: Deep semantic role labeling: what works and what's next. In: Proceedings of the 55th Annual Meeting Association for Computational Linguistics, vol. 1, pp. 473–483 (2017)
25. Jordan, M.: Artificial Intelligence. The revolution hasn't happened yet. Medium (2018). https://medium.com/@mijordan3/artificial-intelligence-the-revolution-hasnt-happened-yet-5e1d5812e1e7
26. Hutson, M.: AI researchers allege that machine learning is alchemy. Science 360(6388), 861 (2018). http://www.sciencemag.org/news/2018/05/ai-researchers-allege-machine-learning-alchemy

QuOD: An NLP Tool to Improve the Quality of Business Process Descriptions

Alessio Ferrari[1]([⊠]) [iD], Giorgio O. Spagnolo[1], Antonella Fiscella[2],
and Guido Parente[2]

[1] ISTI–CNR, Pisa, Italy
{alessio.ferrari,spagnolo}@isti.cnr.it
[2] Narwhal Software, Florence, Italy
info@narwhal.it

Abstract. [**Context and Motivation**] In real-world organisations, business processes (BPs) are often described by means of natural language (NL) documents. Indeed, although semi-formal graphical notations exist to model BPs, most of the legacy process knowledge—when not *tacit*—is still conveyed through textual procedures or operational manuals, in which the BPs are specified. This is particularly true for public administrations (PAs), in which a large variety of BPs exist (e.g., definition of tenders, front-desk support) that have to be understood and put into practice by civil servants. [**Question/problem**] Incorrect understanding of the BP descriptions in PAs may cause delays in the delivery of services to citizens, or, in some cases, incorrect execution of the BPs. [**Principal idea/results**] In this paper, we present the development of an NLP-based tool named QuOD (QUALITY ANALYSER FOR OFFICIAL DOCUMENTS), oriented to detect linguistic defects in BP descriptions and to provide recommendations for improvements. [**Contribution**] QuOD is the first tool that addresses the problem of identifying NL defects in BP descriptions of PAs. The tool is available online at http://narwhal. it/quod/index.html.

Keywords: NLP · Business process · Requirements engineering

1 Introduction

Public Administrations (PAs) are socio-technical systems whose goal is to provide services to citizens in accordance with the law. Services are performed by civil servants following business processes (BPs), which are sequences of activities to be carried out to deliver a service [5]. In PA, as in other organisations, BP specifications are available in the form of written procedures, or operational manuals [15,16,22]. As typical also for system/software requirements specifications, these documents are expressed in informal natural language, which is inherently open to different interpretations [2,20,23]. Hence, the content of these documents might be incorrectly interpreted by those who have to put the process

© Springer Nature Switzerland AG 2019
M. H. ter Beek et al. (Eds.): Gnesi Festschrift, LNCS 11865, pp. 267–281, 2019.
https://doi.org/10.1007/978-3-030-30985-5_17

into practice. It is therefore important to identify linguistic defects in written BP specifications, to ensure that BPs are properly carried out [12,19,23].

In the context of the EU Project Learn PAd (http://www.learnpad.eu) [8–10], we developed a tool, named QuOD (QUALITY ANALYSER FOR OFFICIAL DOCUMENTS), which is specifically oriented to identify language defects in written BP specifications and official documents of PAs. The tool is based on the evaluation of a set of quality attributes, with associated indicators of potential defects. Specifically, QuOD deals with four main quality attributes, namely *simplicity, non-ambiguity, content clarity* and *correctness*, and identifies defects such as the usage of difficult jargon, syntactic ambiguities, unclear actors or acronyms as well as grammatical errors. To this end, QuOD leverages a set of patterns expressed by means of the JAPE grammar, supported by the GATE (General Architecture for Text Engineering)[1] tool.

In this paper, we present the quality model developed within the context of Learn PAd, which was used as a reference to define the defect detection patterns of QuOD. Furthermore, we describe each pattern in details and we present the web interface of the tool. Further information about the development of the tool, and the role of its patterns in the context of Learn PAd can be found in our public deliverable [15].

The remainder of the paper is structured as follows. In Sect. 2 we briefly present background on the Learn PAd project and the quality model. In Sects. 4 to 6 we present the patterns associated to each quality attribute of the quality model. Section 7 presents the interface of QuOD, and Sect. 8 concludes the paper.

2   The Learn PAd Quality Model

The Learn PAd EU project [8–10] aims to improve the sharing of knowledge among civil servants, and as a consequence the perceived quality of services delivered by the public administration (PA). The overall idea of Learn PAd is to use the business process modeling notation (BPMN) [4] to teach civil servants how the procedures shall be implemented in practice and to complement the models expressed according to the BPMN with BP descriptions that give details in natural language about the procedures.

In the context of the project, a quality model was defined comprising a set of defects to be automatically identified in the BP descriptions. The quality model is based on a throughout domain analysis published in a recent work [16], and focuses on those defects that can be automatically checked by means of a rule-based system, i.e., a system that is based on pattern matching algorithms.

A quality model is a reference model against which a certain artifact—a PA procedure expressed in natural language, i.e., a BP description, in our case—can be evaluated [17]. A quality model is defined by means of a set of quality attributes, which are high-level quality properties that the PA procedure shall exhibit. The general quality model for PA procedures comprises seven general quality attributes, namely:

---

[1] https://gate.ac.uk.

- **Clarity:** this attribute indicates that the PA procedure is understandable, both in terms of *content*, in terms of presentation, and in terms of practical applicability.
- **Non-ambiguity:** this attribute indicates that the content of the PA procedure has only one interpretation, independently of the reader. The attribute considers the non-ambiguity of terms, and the non-ambiguity of the syntax used in the sentences of the PA procedure.
- **Simplicity:** this attribute indicates that the content of a PA procedure is easy to read. The attribute considers both the difficulty of the terms and the difficulty of the syntax.
- **Completeness:** this attribute indicates that all the required fields of a given template for PA procedures are filled with content. The attribute requires a reference template to be defined.
- **Conciseness:** this attribute indicates that the PA procedure is sufficiently synthetic, and does not have any irrelevant detail or repetition.
- **Correctness:** this attribute indicates that the content of the PA procedure is correct in terms of grammar, and does not include copy-paste errors.
- **Coherence:** this attribute indicates that the content of the PA procedure is not contradictory or illogical. The attribute takes into account the internal coherence, the external coherence (i.e., the coherence with other documents), and the coherence with respect to the real world (referred as applicability incoherence).

Among the different quality attributes, in this paper we focus on those that have been addressed with the definition of a set of patterns implemented in QuOD. Specifically, we focus on (content) clarity, non-ambiguity, simplicity, and correctness. The other quality attributes can be enforced by means of the guidelines for writing BP descriptions collected by Ferrari et al. [16] and the BP description template presented therein. For each quality attribute, we have identified a set of *indicators*, which can be automatically detected and provide information about a particular attribute [17]. Indicators can be regarded as *defects* to be matched by means of defect detection patterns. Patterns are regular expressions that might involve characters or more complex linguistic constructs, such as words, and phrases. To express simple patterns we generally use an intuitive semi-formal notation that use natural language and symbols. To express more complex patterns we use a notation inspired to the JAPE grammar [27], which is the one employed by the tool GATE and that is used to implement the patterns in QuOD. Each pattern has been designed to identify the majority of potential defects. The idea, borrowed from the requirements engineering domain [1], is that the system raises the possibility of a defect in the text, and that the user considers whether such defect is an actual defect, or can be ignored. The rationale here is that a user can easily discard those potential defects that are not actual flaws from their point of view, while more severe consequences can be expected (e.g., procedure not correctly performed or not performed at all [22]) in case a defect is not detected. Each of the following sections is dedicated to a quality attribute, and to the associated indicators.

3   Quality Attribute: Non-ambiguity

The *non-ambiguity* quality attribute defines the degree of non-ambiguity of a BP description. Such quality attribute considers both the ambiguity of the terms and the ambiguity of the syntax. The following sections describe the indicators that we consider for this attribute.

3.1   Indicator: Lexical Ambiguity

In general, a lexical ambiguity occurs whenever a term can have different meaning (e.g., the word "bank" can be the bank of a river, or the bank as "establishment for custody, loan, exchange, or issue of money") [2]. However, in this context, we will not refer to this definition of lexical ambiguity – cases as the one exemplified will be treated as *pragmatic* ambiguity, since the interpretation of "bank" depends on the context. Instead, we will refer to the model defined by Gnesi *et al.* [17], for checking the quality of natural language requirements specification. According to such model, lexical ambiguity occurs whenever a sentence includes an adverb, adjective or conjunction, possibly combined with prepositions, that might lead to different interpretations of the sentence. In practice, the considered model does not take into account *names* or *verbs* with potentially different interpretations, but solely typical expressions that are commonly source of potential misunderstandings. Four categories of lexical ambiguity are defined in [17], namely vagueness, subjectivity, optionality and weakness. The first category includes the usage of vague expressions, with a non uniquely quantifiable meaning, such as "accurate", "suitable", "appropriate", "clearly", etc. The second category includes expressions that refers to personal opinions or feelings, such as "better", "accordingly", "depending on", etc. The third category includes expressions that reveal the presence of an optional part in the sentence, such as "if necessary", "if needed", "and/or". The fourth category include cases when a weak main verb, such as "can", "may", etc., is used. Examples for the first three categories are provided below:

- **Vagueness:** *The field office will forward the application to the **appropriate** official for a final decision.* Here, the term "appropriate" is vague, and the editor shall specify which is the specific official that is in charge of taking the final decision.
- **Subjectivity:** *Support staff may be called in from other teams **depending on** the extent of the scene.* Here, the expression "depending on" leaves the reader with the freedom to personally evaluate the extent of the scene.
- **Optionality:** *The director of the group must transfer 10% of the funded loans to the institute **and/or** to the department.* Here the expression "and/or" leaves the freedom of sending the funded loans to just one organisation.

In the context of Learn PAd, we do not consider cases of "weakness", since this indicator was specifically designed for natural language requirements specifications, and appeared less suitable for PA documents. Indeed, in the context of PA procedure descriptions, we have found that it is rather frequent to find verbs such as "can" or "may" (e.g., 63 cases of "can", and 124 cases of "may" are found in our dataset [15]), and these are normally acceptable (as, e.g., in the following example *"Ensure you can meet the deadlines"*).

To check the presence of vagueness, subjectivity or optionality in a sentence, we define three patterns. Let V, U and O be sets of vague, subjective, or optional terms. Let S be a sentence, and let $T(S)$ be any sequence of words in the sentence. The patterns are the following:

- **VAG:** $\forall v \in V, \forall t \in T(S)$, if $t = v$, mark t as vague.
- **SUB:** $\forall u \in U, \forall t \in T(S)$, if $t = u$, mark t as subjective.
- **OPT:** $\forall o \in O, \forall t \in T(S)$, if $t = o$, mark t as optional.

If a sentence has at least one term that is detected to be vague, subjective of optional according to the at least one of the previous patterns, such sentence is marked as defective. In QuOD, we employ the dictionaries used by QuARS [17], to check the three categories of lexical ambiguity exemplified above. Therefore, the sets V (446 terms), S (19 terms) and O (11 terms) are composed of all the terms used by QuARS.

3.2 Indicator: Syntactic Ambiguity

Syntactic ambiguity manifest itself whenever the sentence can have more than one grammatical structure, each one with a different meaning. Four types of syntactic ambiguity are defined in the literature [2], namely *analytical* (i.e., a complex noun group with modifiers [18]), *attachment* (i.e., a prepositional phrase can be attached to two parts of the sentence), *coordination* (i.e., when more than one conjunction "or", or "and" is used in a sentence), *elliptical* (i.e., when words are omitted because they are expected to be deduced from the context), and *anaphoric/referential* (i.e., when pronouns or other words refer to other elements, but there is more than one possibility). This latter type of ambiguity may involve different sentences, and the literature often categorise it as pragmatic ambiguity. However, given its strong relation with the syntax, and its similarity with, e.g., attachment ambiguity, we consider more reasonable to include it among the syntactic ambiguities.

Examples of each category are provided below:

- **Analytical:** *The Italian office director.* Here, "Italian" can be referred to the office or to the director.
- **Attachment:** *The officer edits a resumee with a template for the final assessment.* Here "for" can be referred to the "template", or to the "resumee" or can specify a deadline (i.e., before the final assessment).
- **Coordination:** *The employee met the council and the head of office and the secretary assessed his presence.* Here, the sentence can have several parses. For example, it is unclear whether both the head of office and the secretary assessed the presence of the employee, or just the secretary.

- **Elliptical:** *The successful candidate receives the letter on Sept. 12, and the unsuccessful doesn't.* Here, the ambiguity is whether the unsuccessful candidate receives a notification in another date, or does not receive any notification.
- **Anaphoric:** *The delegate assesses the presence of the candidate, and* **he** *provides his signature.* Here "he" can be referred to both the delegate or the candidate.

We decided to focus on a sub-set of the syntactic ambiguity categories and to provide pattern-based approaches for them. The chosen categories are coordination and anaphoric ambiguities. The choice has fallen on these categories since they are more clearly defined in the literature, and can be in principle associated to the presence of specific keywords (e.g., "and", "or" for coordination ambiguities, and pronouns for anaphoric ambiguities). The other types of syntactic ambiguities are more likely to be identifiable with machine learning approaches.

Coordination Ambiguities. Potential coordination ambiguities may occur when we have more than one coordinating conjunction in the form "or" or "and" in the same sentence, as in the example provided above. Moreover, they may occur when a conjunction is used with a modifier, as e.g., in the sentence *"Novel employees and directors are required to provide summaries of their work at the end of the year"* (is "novel" referred to employees only, or to both employees and directors?). To detect these types of ambiguity, two patterns, one for each type, can be provided.

- **CAMB-1:** (Token)* (and | or) (Token.kind != "punct")* (and | or) (Token)*
- **CAMB-2:** (JJ) (NN | NNS) (and | or) (NN | NNS).

The first pattern searches for at least two occurrences of "and" or "or", not separated by punctuation (e.g., commas, semicolons, separator such as "-", etc.). As reported in [2], commas, and other types of punctuation may clarify the syntactic structure. Coordination ambiguity may occur also in presence of punctuation. However, we have evaluated these cases are sufficiently rare to be negligible. The second pattern matches cases where an adjective (JJ) precedes a couple of singular (NN) or plural nouns (NNS), joined by "and" or "or".

Anaphoric Ambiguities. Anaphora occurs in a text whenever a linguistic expression (e.g., personal pronouns such as "he/she/it", possessive pronouns as "her/his", relative pronouns such as "that", "which", demonstrative pronouns such as "this", "who", etc.) refer to a previous part of the text. The referred part of the text is normally called *antecedent*. An anaphoric ambiguity occurs if the text offers one or more antecedent options, either in the same sentence or in previous sentences [28]. Here, we focus on anaphoric ambiguities that involve third personal subject/object pronouns and possessive pronouns, of the three genders, namely male ("he", "his", "him", "himself"), female ("she", "her", "hers", "herself"), and neuter ("it", "its", "itself", "they", "their", "theirs", "them", "themselves"). We do not focus on first and second person pronouns, since these are less frequent in PA documents.

The potential antecedents for these pronouns are noun phrases (NP) [28]. Therefore, we define the following two patterns to identify potential cases of anaphoric ambiguities.

- **AAMB-1:** (NounChunk) (NounChunk)+ (Pronoun)
- **AAMB-2:** (NounChunk) (NounChunk)+ (Split) (Pronoun)

The first pattern matches any single sentence with a pronoun and two or more potential antecedents. The second pattern searches for potential antecedents in the previous sentence (the notation "Split" indicates the sentence separator).

4   Quality Attribute: Simplicity

The *simplicity* quality attribute defines how easy is to read a BP description. It is a quality attribute that, in a sense, shall give an overall degree of readability of each sentence, and compute an aggregate value of readability. Such quality attribute takes into account the difficulty of the terms. The difficulty associated to the syntax – a topic that is still a matter of research, see. e.g., [11] – instead is considered by simply evaluating the length of the sentences. We use the term "simplicity" and not "readability", since readability in the literature is a more domain-generic concept, which involves also typographical aspects and degree of interest that a text raises [16]. Here, we wish to highlight that the defects that we address are those that makes *difficult* the understanding of PA procedure descriptions, such as, e.g., juridical jargon and difficult jargon. Therefore, we have considered the term simplicity to be more appropriate. The following sections describe the indicators that we consider for this attribute.

4.1   Indicator: Excessive Length

This indicator indicates that a sentence is too long. The length of a sentence is a rather intuitive indicator of its complexity. Normally a long sentence includes multiple concepts that have to be processes by the reader, and is more likely to include complex syntactic constructions that require higher reading effort. An example of long sentence is provided below:

- **Long Sentence:** *Further distribution of vote sheets within the staff is permissible upon issuance of the vote, but distribution outside the agency is permissible only after the final collegial decision is recorded by the Secretary in an SRM to the action office and the votes have been released to the public.* This sentence is 49 words, and 293 characters, and it requires multiple readings to be understood.

This indicator can be easily checked with this basic pattern:

- **LEN:** N = number of words in a sentence, $N < \tau$.

The *The Plain English Guide* by Cutts [6] states that sentences should be 15–20 words in average, and should not exceed 40 words. Moreover, the style guidelines of the English government [26] recommends sentences to not exceed 25 words. Therefore, in the context of Learn PAd, we take the threshold τ of 26 words as basic rule to check whether a sentence is too long.

4.2 Indicator: Juridical Jargon

Juridical jargon is the usage of terms and constructions that belong to the juridical domain. This domain has defined a specific jargon that is understood by domain experts, and in a sense, is oriented to establish clear concepts and to avoid ambiguity. Nevertheless, studies as [25] have shown that even technical experts prefer text that use plain English instead of legal jargon, and that the more specialist the knowledge of the reader, the higher the preference for plain English. These studies have been used also by the UK government to define their guidelines for editing the content of their Web pages [26], where they recommend to minimize the usage of juridical jargon, and latin terms, which are typical in legal writing. Moreover, our interviews and questionnaires show that the presence of juridical jargon is one of the main linguistic problems found in their current procedure descriptions.

To address this problem, we define the current indicator – i.e., juridical jargon – which aims to identify juridical words and expressions in the Learn PAd content. It is worth mentioning that the term "jargon" includes not only words and expressions, but also the syntax. Here, we focus solely on the terms (i.e., words and expressions), since other indicators are defined in Learn PAd that address problem with ambiguous syntax (see Sect. 3.2), a typical problem of juridical jargon.

Let J be a set of juridical terms, let S be a sentence and let $T(S)$ be the set of any ordered sequence of words in a sentence (i.e., any potential single or multi-word term). The following pattern checks the presence of juridical terms.

– **JUR:** $\forall j \in J, \forall t \in T(S)$, if $t = j$, mark t as juridical jargon.

The set J of juridical terms used in Learn PAd is composed of 877 terms in total. To compose this set, we have merged comprehensive glossaries selected from the Web. In particular, we have merged juridical terms from (a) the glossary provided by NY-COURTS.GOV, the New York State Unified Court System[2], (b) the glossary provided by the Judicial Branch of the State of Connecticut [3], and (c) the list of legal Latin terms in Wikipedia[4].

4.3 Indicator: Difficult Jargon

This indicator quantifies the amount of sentences using terms (single and multi-words) that are considered difficult, either because they are rare, or because

---

[2] http://www.nycourts.gov/lawlibraries/glossary.shtml.
[3] http://www.jud.ct.gov/legalterms.htm.
[4] https://en.wikipedia.org/wiki/List_of_legal_Latin_terms.

they are overly complex expressions that can be substituted with simpler ones. The Dale-Chall formula [3] measures the readability of a text by taking into account the percentage of words in the text not included in a list of 3,000 words considered easy-to-read. Such formula has two primary defects in our context: (1) It gives only an index and does not indicate the editor which term is defective, i.e., hard to read; (2) the set of 3,000 words is too restricted and risks to raise too many warnings. Indeed, a 5–6 years old child normally already uses 2,500–5,000 common words [26], and by age 9, people normally build the set of words that they use every day. This set is normally composed of two sub-sets, a primary set (around 5,000 terms), and a secondary set (around 10,000 terms). Though also the secondary set includes terms that are used in every day life, such set includes also terms that are less common, and, hence, more difficult. Therefore, to identify the usage of difficult jargon, we define a pattern that, for each sentence, checks that each term is contained in the primary set. More formally, let S be a sentence, and let $W(S)$ be any word in the sentence. Moreover, let E be the set of 5,000 terms that belong to the primary set of easy-terms. The following pattern checks the presence of difficult jargon:

- **DIF-1:** $\forall w \in W(S)$, if $w \notin E$, mark w as difficult jargon.

If a sentence has at least one word that is detected to be difficult, according to the previous pattern, such sentence will be marked as defective. As set E, we have used the set of top-5000 most common terms available at [7].

The previous pattern checks that terms used in a sentence are easy-to-read for a general public, and it is domain independent. Indeed, the list of common words is based on the selection of the most frequent words in genre-balanced corpus [7]. To detect difficult expressions that are *specific* of PA documents, we resort to use the list of pompous terms that litter official writing [21]. Such list of terms has been edited by the Plain English Campaign[5], with the objective of making official writing easier to read. While the list of easy words include only single-word terms, this list includes also multi-word terms (e.g., "acquaint yourself with", "despite the fact that", *etc.*). Therefore, we define a pattern to check the presence of difficult jargon according to such list. Let D be the set of difficult terms. Let S be a sentence, and let $T(S)$ be any sequence of words in the sentence. The pattern is as follows:

- **DIF-2:** $\forall d \in D, \forall t \in T(S)$, if $t = d$, mark t as difficult jargon.

If a sentence has at least one term that is detected to be difficult according to one of the previous patterns, such sentence is marked as defective. As set D, we have used the mentioned set of 407 difficult terms listed in [21].

5 Quality Attribute: Clarity

The *content clarity* quality attribute defines the degree of clarity of a BP description. Clarity of content is associated to specific aspects of sentences that make

---

[5] http://www.plainenglish.co.uk.

them more *understandable* from the procedural point of view. In other terms, this attribute focuses on aspects associated to the applicability of a procedure, such as the presence of well-defined actors in a sentence, and the presence of clear time constraints. The following sections describe the indicators that we consider for this attribute.

5.1 Indicator: Actor Unclear

This indicator indicates that the actor of an action is unclear. This might occur in different cases, as e.g., in the following examples:

- *The **officer** shall send the review form within 5 days from the reception of the review request.*
- *The procedure shall be carried out before the end of March 2015.*

In the first case, it is unclear which officer is in charge of sending the review form. This situation might be resolved though the other sentences of the documents—where the concept of officer might be defined—, and can be apportioned to the cases of potential *pragmatic ambiguities* [13], not considered here. The second case, instead, is using the passive voice, and this is a typical case where the subject of the action, i.e., the actor, is not specified in the sentence, and he/she is therefore unclear. However, a simple "by" could help specifying the actor, as in the following rephrasing:

- *The procedure shall be carried out by the certification authority before the end of March 2015.*

In this section, we will define patterns to identify cases similar to the one shown in the second example. The pattern below has been defined such cases:

- **ACT:** (Auxiliary) (RegularPP | IrregularPP)+ ($\neg$ "by")

The pattern matches any case where we have a term that indicates the presence of at least an auxiliary verb (i.e., "am", "are", "were", "being", "is", "been", "was", "be") followed by one or more past participle in regular form (i.e., any term terminating with "-ed") or irregular form (e.g., "written", "spent", "proven", etc. – a list of 175 irregular verbs have been used). Moreover, the pattern checks the presence of the preposition "by" following the verbs, as indicator of the potential specification of an actor.

5.2 Indicator: Unclear Acronym

An acronym is word made from the initial letters or parts of other words, generally used to identify organisations (e.g., NATO, NASA, etc.) or domain specific concepts (e.g., BPMN, SQL, etc.). An acronym is normally composed of capital letters, which can be separated by full stops (e.g., F.A.O.), or not (e.g., FAO). This indicator checks for acronyms that are never expressed in their extended form (e.g., North Atlantic Treaty Organization for NATO). We have seen that undefined acronyms are a relevant problem in the real-world BP descriptions collected within the Learn PAd project [15]. Indeed, such BP descriptions include a large amount of sentences with acronyms, and in most of the cases the meaning of such acronyms is not defined in any part of the text. Though some acronyms are commonly used, many acronyms found are domain specific, or even procedure specific and need to be defined to clarify their meaning.

We define an algorithm that makes use of regular expressions to check the presence of unclear acronyms in a document. The algorithm first searches for potential acronyms (**Step 1**). Then scans the document to search for sentences where the potential acronym occurs together with its definition; if no sentence is found, the acronym is marked as unclear (**Step 2**).

Step 1. The following regular expression is used to find potential acronyms:

- **Find Acronyms:** $[A - Z|\.]\{2, \}$

The expression matches any string of text with capital letters or full stops, if it is composed of at least two characters. This expression includes cases of sequences of full stops, and terms written in capital letters (e.g., "PROTOCOL" in a capitalized title). After the execution of the regular expression, these cases are discarded from the list of potential acronyms. In practice, all potential acronyms made of full stops are discarded, as well as sequence of capital letters longer than 5 character.

Step 2. In each sentence where the acronym appears, the algorithm checks if a sequence of words exist that express the acronym in its extended version. The following regular expression is used to find the presence of a potential extended version of an acronym of length "len" in a sentence. The value of "len" is computed without counting the full stops (CNR and C.N.R. have both len = 3).

- **Find Acronym Definition:** $([A - Z] + \w + ([\ ]|))\{len\}$

The regular expression searches for sequences of length "len". The sequences are required to be composed of one or more capital letters, followed by any word character ($\w$), followed by a space ([ ]), or not (to detect final words). Finally, the algorithm checks that each capital letter in the matched string matches the capital letters found in the candidate acronym.

If the extended version of an acronym is found in at least one sentence in the document, the acronym is marked as ``clear'', and no defect will be raised if the acronym appears in the rest of the document without its extended version. If no sentence exist where the acronym appears together with its extended version, such acronym is marked as ``unclear'' in each sentence where the acronym appears. In turn, each sentence including an ``unclear'' acronym will be marked as defective.

6 Quality Attribute: Correctness

The *correctness* quality attribute defines the degree of grammatical correctness of a BP description. Hence, in this case, the quality attribute is equivalent to the indicator. Grammatical correctness is a fluid concept that evolves according to the evolution of a language and its grammar. Therefore, in our context, we have decided to give a more operational definition of correctness (i.e., a text is correct, if a grammar checker does not find any defect). To this end, we use a set of prescriptive rules, which are embedded in a tool, namely Language Tool[6], which has the advantage of embedding grammar checks that can be extended with the contributions of the user community. Therefore, as the grammar of a language evolves, we expect to easily plug additional patterns – or remove old ones –, so that the computed degree of correctness of a sentence is up-to-date with the rules of language.

7 The QuOD Tool

The different patterns have been implemented in the form of JAPE rules, deployed within a web service, and embedded in the content analysis component of the Learn PAd platform [10,15]. Furthermore, the QUOD web application has been implemented that, through RESTful APIs, interacts with the web service and allows users to check the quality of their BP descriptions and official documents in general. The web application was developed by Narwhal Software[7] and it is publicly available at http://narwhal.it/quod/.

Figure 1 reports a screenshot of QUOD when applied to a sample BP description named EPBR (European Project Budget Reporting), see Thönssen et al. [24] for more details. On the top-left panel, the user can select the quality attributes to check (named Criteria), the Language, and the Document type. After performing the analysis, the system outputs a summary of the numerical scores associated to each quality attribute, indicating the percentage of defective sentences over the whole document for each attribute (bottom-left). On the right panel, the user can see the actual occurrences of the defects, highlighted with the color of the associated attribute. By hovering the mouse on the highlighted defect, the user can see the recommendation. For example, in the figure, we have an unclear actor in the sentence *[...] the authorization of the involved school has to be asked [...]*, and we see a pop-up window with a recommendation concerning Content Clarity: *The sentence does not specify the subject: asked by whom? Please specify.*

By selecting the lens icon on the top-right corner, the user can also inspect the single defects. In the figure, we see the list of defects associated to the non-ambiguity attribute. This is particularly useful when overlapping defects are present in the original document, which may not be clearly visible in the central panel. For example, in the figure, we have two potential, and overlapping,

---

[6] https://www.languagetool.org.
[7] http://narwhal.it.

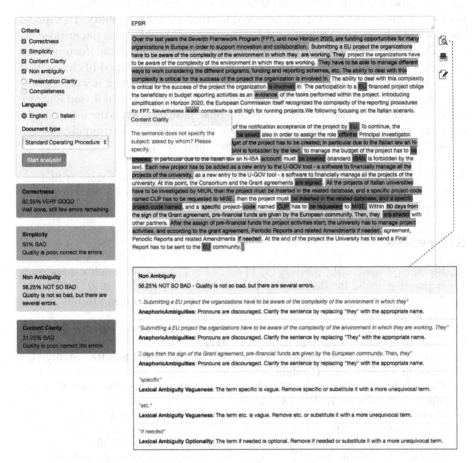

Fig. 1. The interface of QuOD when applied to a BP description.

anaphoric ambiguities: one is referred to the usage of "they" in the sentence *"Submitting a EU project the organizations have to be aware of the complexity of the environment in which they are working."*, identified with **AAMB-1** of Sect. 3.2. The other is referred to the usage of "They" in the following sentence, which refers to the previous one, and which was identified based on **AAMB-2** of Sect. 3.2.

8   Conclusion

Public administrations (PAs) typically use natural language to describe their business processes (BPs). As natural language is inherently ambiguous, descriptions of BPs need to be carefully reviewed for their linguistic quality. To support the work of editors and reviewers of BP descriptions in PAs, this paper presents QuOD, a tool oriented to detect linguistic quality defects in official documents in general, and in PA documents in particular. The tool is developed in the context of the EU project Learn PAd, and is publicly available through a web application. In the future, we plan to gather data from the users of the tool, and improve the defect detection capabilities to reduce *false positives*, as pattern-based systems are known to suffer from this problem [14]. A validation campaign is also foreseen with PA users, to assess and further improve the tool.

Acknowledgments. This work was possible thanks to the seminal work of Stefania Gnesi and co-authors on the usage of rule-based NLP techniques for detecting ambiguity and other quality issues in requirements specifications [17].

References

1. Berry, D., Gacitua, R., Sawyer, P., Tjong, S.F.: The case for dumb requirements engineering tools. In: Regnell, B., Damian, D. (eds.) REFSQ 2012. LNCS, vol. 7195, pp. 211–217. Springer, Heidelberg (2012). https://doi.org/10.1007/978-3-642-28714-5_18
2. Berry, D.M., Kamsties, E., Krieger, M.M.: From contract drafting to software specification: linguistic sources of ambiguity (2003)
3. Chall, J.S., Dale, E.: Readability Revisited: The New Dale-Chall Readability Formula. Brookline Books, Cambridge (1995)
4. Chinosi, M., Trombetta, A.: BPMN: an introduction to the standard. Comput. Stand. Interfaces **34**(1), 124–134 (2012)
5. Corradini, F., et al.: A guidelines framework for understandable BPMN models. Data Knowl. Eng. **113**, 129–154 (2018)
6. Cutts, M.: The Plain English Guide. Oxford University Press, Oxford (1996)
7. Davies, M.: Word frequency data. http://www.wordfrequency.info/free.asp. Accessed 1 Aug 2015
8. De Angelis, G., Ferrari, A., Gnesi, S., Polini, A.: Collaborative requirements elicitation in a European research project. In: Proceedings of the 31st Annual ACM Symposium on Applied Computing, pp. 1282–1289. ACM (2016)
9. De Angelis, G., Ferrari, A., Gnesi, S., Polini, A.: Requirements elicitation and refinement in collaborative research projects. J. Softw. Evol. Process **30**(12), e1990 (2018)
10. De Angelis, G., Pierantonio, A., Polini, A., Re, B., Thönssen, B., Woitsch, R.: Modeling for learning in public administrations—the learn PAd approach. Domain-Specific Conceptual Modeling, pp. 575–594. Springer, Cham (2016). https://doi.org/10.1007/978-3-319-39417-6_26
11. Dell'Orletta, F., Montemagni, S., Venturi, G.: Read-it: assessing readability of Italian texts with a view to text simplification. In: Proceedings of the Second Workshop on Speech and Language Processing for Assistive Technologies, pp. 73–83. Association for Computational Linguistics (2011)

12. Ferrari, A., Dell'Orletta, F., Esuli, A., Gervasi, V., Gnesi, S.: Natural language requirements processing: a 4D vision. IEEE Softw. **34**(6), 28–35 (2017)
13. Ferrari, A., Gnesi, S.: Using collective intelligence to detect pragmatic ambiguities. In: 20th IEEE International Requirements Engineering Conference (RE), pp. 191–200. IEEE (2012)
14. Ferrari, A., et al.: Detecting requirements defects with NLP patterns: an industrial experience in the railway domain. Empir. Softw. Eng. **23**(6), 3684–3733 (2018)
15. Ferrari, A., Spagnolo, G.O., Witschel, H.F.: Learn PAd - deliverable D4.2 quality assessment strategies for contents (2019). https://doi.org/10.5281/zenodo.2643293
16. Ferrari, A., Witschel, H.F., Spagnolo, G.O., Gnesi, S.: Improving the quality of business process descriptions of public administrations: resources and research challenges. Bus. Process Manag. J. **24**(1), 49–66 (2018)
17. Gnesi, S., Lami, G., Trentanni, G.: An automatic tool for the analysis of natural language requirements. IJCSSE **20**(1), 53–62 (2005)
18. Hirst, G.: Semantic Interpretation and the Resolution of Ambiguity. Cambridge University Press, Cambridge (1992)
19. Leopold, H., Smirnov, S., Mendling, J.: On the refactoring of activity labels in business process models. Inf. Syst. **37**(5), 443–459 (2012)
20. Massey, A.K., Rutledge, R.L., Anton, A., Swire, P.P., et al.: Identifying and classifying ambiguity for regulatory requirements. In: IEEE 22nd International Requirements Engineering Conference (RE), pp. 83–92. IEEE (2014)
21. Plain English Campaign: The A to Z of alternative words. http://www.plainenglish.co.uk/files/alternative.pdf
22. Sanne, U., Ferrari, A., Gnesi, S., Witschel, H.F.: Ensuring action: identifying unclear actor specifications in textual business process descriptions. In: Proceedings of the 8th International Conference on Knowledge Management and Information Sharing (KMIS). Springer (2016)
23. Silva, T.S., Thom, L.H., Weber, A., de Oliveira, J.P.M., Fantinato, M.: Empirical Analysis of Sentence Templates and Ambiguity Issues for Business Process Descriptions. In: Panetto, H., Debruyne, C., Proper, H., Ardagna, C., Roman, D., Meersman, R. (eds.) OTM 2018. LNCS, vol. 11229. Springer, Cham (2018). https://doi.org/10.1007/978-3-030-02610-3_16
24. Thönssen, B., Witschel, H.F., Rusinov, O.: Determining information relevance based on personalization techniques to meet specific user needs. In: Dornberger, R. (ed.) Business Information Systems and Technology 4.0. SSDC, vol. 141, pp. 31–45. Springer, Cham (2018). https://doi.org/10.1007/978-3-319-74322-6_3
25. Trudeau, C.R.: The public speaks: an empirical study of legal communication. Scribes J. Leg. Writ. **14**(2011–2012), 32 (2012)
26. UK Government: Content design: planning, writing and managing content. https://www.gov.uk/guidance/content-design/writing-for-gov-uk. Accessed 1 Aug 2015
27. University of Sheffield: JAPE: regular expressions over annotations. https://gate.ac.uk/sale/tao/splitch8.html. Accessed 1 Aug 2015
28. Yang, H., Roeck, A.N.D., Gervasi, V., Willis, A., Nuseibeh, B.: Analysing anaphoric ambiguity in natural language requirements. Requir. Eng. **16**(3), 163–189 (2011)

Software Product Lines

A Decade of Featured Transition Systems

Maxime Cordy[1] , Xavier Devroey[2] , Axel Legay[3], Gilles Perrouin[4(✉)] ,
Andreas Classen[5], Patrick Heymans[4], Pierre-Yves Schobbens[4] ,
and Jean-François Raskin[6]

[1] SnT, University of Luxembourg, Luxembourg, Luxembourg
maxime.cordy@uni.lu
[2] Delft University of Technology, Delft, The Netherlands
x.d.m.devroey@tudelft.nl
[3] UCLouvain, Louvain-la-Neuve, Belgium
axel.legay@uclouvain.be
[4] PReCISE/NaDI, Faculty of Computer Science, University of Namur,
Namur, Belgium
{gilles.perrouin,patrick.heymans,pierre-yves.schobbens}@unamur.be
[5] INTEC Software Engineering, St. Vith, Belgium
andreas.classen@intecsoft.com
[6] ULB, Brussels, Belgium
jraskin@ulb.ac.be

Abstract. Variability-intensive systems (VIS) form a large and heterogeneous class of systems whose behaviour can be modified by enabling or
disabling predefined features. Variability mechanisms allows the adaptation of software to the needs of their users and the environment. However,
VIS verification and validation (V&V) is challenging: the combinatorial
explosion of the number of possible behaviours and undesired feature
interactions are amongst such challenges. To tackle them, Featured Transitions Systems (FTS) were proposed a decade ago to model and verify
the behaviours of VIS. In an FTS, each transition is annotated with a
combination of features determining which variants can execute it. An
FTS can model all possible behaviours of a given VIS. This compact
model enabled us to create efficient V&V algorithms taking advantage
of the behaviours shared amongst features resulting in a reduction of the
V&V effort by several orders of magnitude. In this paper, we will cover
the formalism, its applications and sketch promising research directions.

Keywords: Variability-intensive systems · Modeling ·
Model-checking · Testing

1 Introduction

Variability-intensive systems (VISs) form a vast and heterogeneous class of software systems that encompasses: *Software Product Lines* [2,84], operating system

---

Gilles Perrouin is a research associate at the FNRS. This research was partially funded
by the EU Project STAMP ICT-16-10 No. 731529, the NIRICT 3TU.BSR (Big Software
on the Run) project, the EOS project VeriLearn under FNRS Grant O05518F-RG03.

M. H. ter Beek et al. (Eds.): Gnesi Festschrift, LNCS 11865, pp. 285–312, 2019.
https://doi.org/10.1007/978-3-030-30985-5_18

kernels, web development frameworks/stacks, e-commerce configurators, code generators, *Systems of Systems (SoS)*, *software ecosystems* (*e.g.*, Android's "Play Store"), autonomous systems, *etc.* While being very different in their goals and implementations, VIS see their behaviour affected by the activation or deactivation of one or more *feature(s)*, *i.e.*, units of variability, or configuration *options*. Configurable systems may involve thousands of features with complex dependencies. The set of valid combinations of features of a VIS can be represented in a tree-like structure, called *feature model* (FM) [60]. Each valid combination is a configuration of the VIS, which can be derived as a *variant* or a *product*, terms we will use interchangeably in this paper both at the model and code level. Each feature may be decomposed into sub-features and additional constraints may be specified amongst the different features. Within feature models, features can be mandatory (present in every configuration) or selected depending on the groups they belong to (OR, XOR, etc.) and cross-tree constraints (dependence on or exclusion of other feature selections). To support automated reasoning, feature models have been equipped with formal semantics and in particular based on first-order logic [88]. Thanks to their formal semantics, operations on feature models such as inconsistency reasoning can be automated thanks to SAT solvers [75].

Considering that some VIS such as the Linux kernel can easily have more than 10,000 features and that the number of possible variants grows exponentially with the number of features, considering each variant independently for verification and validation (V&V) activities is intractable. As an example, Halin *et al.* [54] report their effort to perform a complete product-based testing of JHipster, an open-source generator for Web applications with 48 features. It took 8 person/month to set up the testing infrastructure, 5.2 TB of disk space, and 4,376 h (around 182 days) computation time to test all 26,256 products. It is therefore desirable to analyse VIS behaviours without requiring to build and run tests for each variant by reasoning on a behavioural model rather than on the system itself (which may not be implemented yet). However, while providing a transition system for each variant and performing model-checking [6] or model-based testing (MBT) activities allows to find bugs early in the process, this does not solve *per se* the combinatorial explosion problem due to variability, as providing a transition system for each variant is also intractable. A family-based approach is required to model all the variants in a compact manner without having to enumerate them. Almost a decade ago, Classen *et al.* [27] defined *Featured Transition Systems* (FTSs) as transition systems (TSs) annotated with combination of features on their transitions: each combination describes the set of products that can execute the behaviour defined by the transition. It is thus possible to model all the variants of a VIS with a unique FTS and its associated feature model. This compact formalism allows to take advantage of sharing between variants leading to drastic reductions of the analysis time, both for formal verification or test generation.

This paper reviews the foundations and applications of featured transition systems, connecting them to other formalisms, such as modal transition systems, and considering extensions such as quantities and probabilities which are required to address V&V challenges induced by, for instance, cyber-physical or learning systems. The rest of this paper is structured as follows. Section 3 introduces the formalism and describes how the modified VIS model-checking problem can be solved efficiently. Section 3.4 reviews other model-checking techniques for VIS, placing FTS-based verification in a broader context. Section 4 explores how the FTS formalism was used to provide a framework for model-based testing for VIS, notably extending existing coverage criteria for transition systems. Section 5 provides an outlook into the future of VIS V&V. Finally, Sect. 6 concludes the paper.

2 Grazie Mille

The content of this paper, although being a synthesis of a 10-year collective research effort, is only a very small sample of the many ways in which the work and personality of Stefania Gnesi have inspired us. The scope of this chapter lies at the intersection of formal methods and software product lines, two areas to which Stefania offered both seminal contributions and devoted a continuous effort over several decades. If that was all Stefania had done, she could already be proud of herself and happily retire without regrets. But this is actually only part of the story we are celebrating, a story that produced significant scientific contributions in a variety of other areas too, including requirements engineering, software engineering, critical systems and natural language processing; a story of relentlessly passing knowledge to her students and peers; a story of coordinating international research efforts; a story of organizing memorable scientific events and of serving research communities; and, in spite of all that, a story of remaining a humble, attentive and kind colleague with whom it is a constant pleasure to work and discuss. Stefania does not deserve a simple applause, she deserves a standing ovation. Thank you from all of us!

3 Verifying Variability-Intensive Systems with FTS

We model the space of variants in terms for feature models following the semantics as provided by Schobbens et al. [88]. A FM fm is a tuple (F, r, DE) where F is a set of features, $r \in F$ is the root, and $DE \subseteq F \times F$ is the set of decomposition edges between features. A product (or variant) is defined as a set of features $P = \{f_1, \ldots, f_n\}$, such that $f_i \in P$ if and only if f_i is part of the product. The semantics of a FM fm, noted $[\![fm]\!]$, is the set of valid products (whose features satisfy the FM constraints), i.e. a set of sets of features: $[\![fm]\!] \in 2^{2^F}$. We also assume the presence of a behavioural model M_v for all variants – which we will formalise below – in order to introduce the VIS model-checking problem. This problem is more complex than for single systems because it requires to verify all the variants that can be built against a given property. More precisely, it is desired to identify exactly which VIS variants violate the property [25].

Definition 1 (VIS model checking). *Let fm be a feature model, M_v be a behavioural model of all variants in $[\![fm]\!]$, and ϕ a property. Model checking M_v against ϕ is the problem of:*

1. *Determining for each product $p \in [\![fm]\!]$ whether p satisfies ϕ in M_v, that is, whether the behaviour of p expressed in M_v satisfies ϕ.*
2. *Providing for each product p that does not satisfy ϕ a counterexample of behaviour of p that violates ϕ.*

A simple method to address this problem consists of modelling every valid product of a VIS in a separate transition system (TS), and then applying single-system model checking on each of these TS individually. This method, named *enumerative* [26] or product-based [85], violates the principles of VIS engineering: the variants should not be modelled separately. Instead, one should build a core model, which is subsequently specialized into desired variants. In addition to the modelling task, performance is also a major concern. State explosion, a problem inherent to model checking, is amplified when considering VISs, especially when these consist of a huge number of variants. Being part of a VIS, these variants likely share commonalities in both their structure and their behaviour. This observation illustrates the fact that single-system verification techniques are suboptimal to address the VIS model-checking problem. Clearly, VIS model checking would benefit from models that can concisely represent the behaviour of a set of variants, and algorithms that can exploit the information about the commonalities between these variants to speed-up verification.

3.1   A Formalism to Model VIS Behaviour

In [25, 27], we proposed Featured Transition Systems (FTSs) as a compact representation of the behaviours of a set of variants. FTSs are an extension of TSs equipped with an FM and whose every transition is annotated with the exact set of variants able to execute it. For the sake of conciseness, these sets are encoded as feature expressions.

Definition 2 (Feature expression). *Let $F = \{f_1, \ldots, f_{|F|}\}$ be a set of features. Then a feature expression over F is a Boolean formula $b \in 2^{2^F}$ in which each variable corresponds to a unique element of F, and whose semantics is a function $2^F \rightarrow \{\bot, \top\}$ encoding a set of products. A product $p \in 2^F$ is included in the set represented by b, noted $[\![b]\!]$, if and only if $b(p) = \top$, or equivalently: $\bigwedge_{f \in p} f \bigwedge_{g \in F \backslash p} \neg g \models b$. In this case, p is said to satisfy b, noted $p \models b$. We also denote by $\mathbb{B}(px)$ the feature expression encoding the set of products px, that is, $\mathbb{B}(px) = \bigvee_{p \in px} \left(\bigwedge_{f \in p} f \bigwedge_{g \in F \backslash p} \neg g \right)$.*

Definition 3 (Featured transition systems). *An FTS is a tuple $(S, Act, Trans, I, AP, L, fm, \gamma)$, where*

- *S is a set of states named the state space;*
- *Act is a set of actions;*

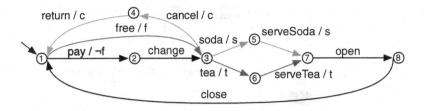

Fig. 1. The FTS modelling the vending machine VIS.

- $Trans \subseteq S \times Act \times S$ is the transition relation, where $(s, \alpha, s') \in Trans$ (also noted $s \xrightarrow{\alpha} s'$) means that there is a transition from state s to state s' labelled with action α;
- $I \subseteq S$ is a set of initial states;
- AP is a set of atomic propositions;
- $L : S \rightarrow 2^{AP}$ is a function that associates every state with the set of atomic propositions satisfied by this state.
- fm is an FM over a set of features F;
- $\gamma : Trans \rightarrow 2^{2^F}$ is a total function that associates a transition with a feature expression over F.

An FTS can be seen as the merging of the TSs of all the variants that compose the VIS. The TS model of a specific product is obtained from the FTS by applying a *projection* function. In simple terms, this function suppresses in the FTS all the transitions whose feature expression is not satisfied by the considered product [27], and then removes all feature expressions.

Definition 4 (Projection of FTS). *Let* $fts = (S, Act, Trans, I, AP, L, fm, \gamma)$ *be an FTS and* $p \in [\![fm]\!]$ *be a variant. The projection of* fts *onto* p, *noted* $fts_{|p}$, *is the TS* $(S, Act, Trans', I, AP, L)$ *where* $Trans' = \{t \in Trans \mid p \models \gamma(t)\}$.

Example 1. Figure 1 depicts an FTS modelling an VIS of vending machines, while Fig. 2 shows its associated FM. This VIS consists of 12 variants, each of which has its behaviour modelled by the FTS. For instance, the transition from state 3 to state 6 is labelled with the feature expression t, meaning that it can be executed only by variants including the corresponding feature *Tea*. Transition from state 1 to state 2 is labelled with $\neg f$, and thus can be executed only by variants that do not have the feature *Free*.

Since an FTS represents the behaviour of a *set* of variants, its semantics is defined as a function that associates a variant with the traces of the corresponding projection.

Definition 5 (FTS Semantics). *Let* fts *be an FTS over an FM* fm. *The semantics of the* fts *is a total function* $[\![fts]\!] : [\![fm]\!] \rightarrow 2^{(2^{AP})^\omega}$ *such that* $\forall p \in [\![fm]\!] \bullet [\![fts]\!](p) = [\![fts_{|p}]\!]$.

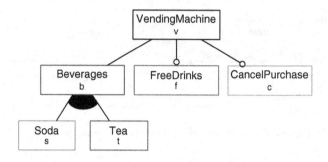

Fig. 2. The FM of the vending machine VIS.

3.2 FTS Model Checking

Contrary to single systems, a binary result is not sufficient to appropriately address the model-checking problem for VIS. In case of property violation, a model checker is expected to identify all variants responsible for the violation. There is thus a need for generalizing the definition of model checking. We already gave an intuitive definition at the beginning of this paper. Here, we rephrase this definition formally, by considering a FTS as a model for VIS behaviour.

Beforehand, let us remark that a property may only be relevant for certain variants. For instance, a property may refer to characteristics that only occur in a subset of the VIS. To address this requirement, we proposed to extend temporal logic with a *product quantifier*, i.e. a feature expression that defines for which variants the property must be checked [25]. The resulting variant of LTL is defined as follows.

Definition 6 (fLTL). *Let F be a set of features. An fLTL formula ψ is an expression $\psi = [\chi]\phi$ where χ is a feature expression over F and ϕ an LTL formula. Let fts be an FTS over an FM fm over F and let $p \in [\![fm]\!]$. Then p satisfies ψ in fts if and only if $\chi(p) \Rightarrow fts_{|p} \models \phi$.*

We are now ready to generalise the concept of satisfiability.

Definition 7 (F-satisfiability). *Let fts be a FTS over an FM fm, and $\psi = [\chi]\phi$ be an fLTL formula. Then, the variants that F-satisfy ψ in fts are encoded as the feature expression*

$$(fts \models \psi) = \neg\chi \vee \mathbb{B}(\{p \in [\![fm]\!] \mid fts_{|p} \models \phi\}).$$

Conversely, the variants that F-unsatisfy ψ in fts are encoded as the feature expression

$$(fts \not\models \psi) = \chi \wedge \mathbb{B}(\{p \in [\![fm]\!] \mid fts_{|p} \not\models \phi\}).$$

Given an FTS and an fLTL formula, a VIS model-checker should thus compute F-satisfiability expressions, and associate each F-unsatisfying product with one of its traces that violates the formula.

3.3   Algorithms

Given its explicit notion of features, FTSs constitute a suitable formalism to concisely model behaviour subject to variability. Yet there remains a second challenge to solve, i.e. an efficient verification of the behaviour of a set of variants. To achieve that, we designed algorithms to check FTS against LTL [25] and CTL [26] formulae that exploit common transitions among variants to reduce the verification effort. As opposed to the product-based approach, a given behaviour is not always checked as many times as the number of variants in which it occurs.

Regardless of the logic used to express properties, the verification process can be reduced to the computation of reachability relations. A major difference is that the reachability of a state now depends on variability: the variants that can reach a target state a from an initial state i are those that can execute any sequence of transitions starting from i and ending in a. Fundamentally, the difference with single-system model-checking is the definition of successor state. In TS, state s' is a successor of a given state s if and only if there exists a transition from s to s'. In FTSs, variability can influence the set of successors as a transition may exist for only a subset of the variants. The definition of successor has thus to be revisited according to variants as well. It is given as follows.

Definition 8 (Successors in FTS). *Let* $fts = (S, Act, Trans, I, AP, L, fm, \gamma)$ *be an FTS. The successor function in* fts *is defined as* $Post : S \to (S \to 2^{(2^F)})$ *such that:*

$$Post(s_i)(s_{i+1}) = \mathbb{B}(\{p \in \cup_\alpha [\![\gamma(s_i, \alpha, s_{i+1})]\!]\})$$
$$= \bigvee_\alpha \gamma(s_i, \alpha, s_{i+1})$$

with $(s_i, \alpha, s_{i+1}) \in Trans$.

Intuitively, for a given pair of states (s, s'), the function $Post(s)(s')$ is the feature expression encoding the variants that can execute a transition from s to s'.

From the definition of successor, one can define reachability relation in FTS. Similarly to successor, reachability takes the form of a function. It associates two states, say s_0 and s_n, to a feature expression encoding the variants able to reach s_n from s_0. These variants are those able to follow at least one path from s_0 to s_n. Let $s_0, \ldots, s_n$ be a path in a given FTS. A variant can follow this path if and only if it satisfies the feature expression $\bigwedge_{0 \le i < n} Post(s_i)(s_{i+1})$. To obtain the variants that can reach s_n from s_0, we can existentially quantify the above expression over the paths from s_0 to s_n.

Definition 9 (Reachability in FTS). *Let* $fts = (S, Act, Trans, I, AP, L, fm, \gamma)$ *be an FTS. Reachability in fts is a function* $R : S \rightarrow (S \rightarrow 2^{(2^F)})$ *such that:*

$$R(s_0)(s_n) = \mathbb{B}(\{p \in 2^F \mid \exists s_1, \ldots, s_{n-1} \bullet p \in [\![\bigwedge_{i=0}^{n-1} Post(s_i)(s_{i+1})]\!]\})$$

$$= \mathbb{B}(\{p \in [\![\bigvee_{s_1, \ldots, s_{n-1} \in S^{n-1}} \bigwedge_{i=0}^{n-1} Post(s_i)(s_{i+1})]\!]\})$$

$$= \bigvee_{s_1, \ldots, s_{n-1}} \bigwedge_{i=0}^{n} Post(s_i)(s_{i+1})$$

where $\forall j \bullet 0 \leq j < n \bullet \exists \alpha \in Act \bullet (s_j, \alpha, s_{j+1}) \in Trans.$

To efficiently compute the reachability function in an FTS, we designed a depth-first search algorithm that accumulates the conjunction of the feature expressions of all transitions executed on a given path in order to keep track of the variants able to reach any state met along this path. The algorithm separates the verification of different sets of variants only if they discover a behavioural discrepancy between them. This optimisation is called *late splitting* [3].

Algorithm 1 formalises the computation of the reachability function of a given state s_0. The algorithm consists of a loop that iterates over a stack of pairs (s, γ) where s is a state and γ is a feature expression. Initially, the stack contains only the element (s_0, fm) in order to start the search from s_0 while considering all the variants. At each iteration, the algorithm takes the top element (s, γ) of the stack, computes the successors of s and associates each successor with the variants that satisfy γ and can reach the successor from s (Lines 4–5). This results in a set of couples $(s', \gamma') \in S \times 2^{2^F}$. For each such pair, the algorithm first determines whether $[\![\gamma']\!]$ contains at least one valid product; otherwise it is not needed to pursue the search from s'. This verification is achieved by checking the satisfiability of γ' (Line 6). If that is the case, we enter an inner loop (Lines 7–17).

During the search, the algorithm may visit a given state more than once (Lines 7–13). In single-system model checking, it should not pursue the search since it already knows that the revisited state is reachable. In our case, however, it may happen that the algorithm discovers a new path to an already visited state s' which is executable by variants that were not known to be able to reach s'. Formally, let $R(s')$ be the feature expression encoding the set of variants that were known to reach s'. Then $\neg R(s') \wedge \gamma'$ encodes the set of variants that are newly known to reach s (noted γ_{new} at Line 8). If there is at least one valid product satisfying this feature expression, the search continues from s' considering only the variants in γ_{new} (Lines 9–12). Indeed, any state reachable from s for variants $[\![R(s')]\!]$ may have already been visited for these variants. Therefore, the paths starting from s are worth re-exploring only for the variants in γ_{new}. Before pursuing the exploration, the feature expression $R(s')$ is updated accordingly.

Input: $fts = (S, Act, Trans, I, AP, L, fm, \gamma), s_0 \in S.$
Output: $R(s_0).$

```
1  R ← ⊥;
2  Stack ← push((s_0, fm), []);
3  while Stack ≠ [] do
4      (s, γ) ← pop(Stack);
5      succ ← {(s', γ') | s' ∈ dom(Post(s)) ∧ γ' = Post(s)(s') ∧ γ};
6      foreach (s', γ') ∈ succ • γ' ⊭⊥ do
7          if s' ∈ dom(R) then
8              γ_new ← ¬R(s') ∧ γ';
9              if γ_new ⊭⊥ then
10                 R(s') ← R(s') ∨ γ';
11                 push((s', γ_new), Stack);
12             end
13         end
14         else
15             R(s') ← γ';
16             push((s', γ'), Stack);
17         end
18     end
19 end
20 return R
```

Algorithm 1: Reachables(fts, s_0)

The theoretical complexity of the above algorithm is given as follows.

Theorem 1. *[25] Let fts be an FTS over a set of features F. The worst-case time complexity of computing Algorithm 1 is bounded by $\mathcal{O}(|fts|.2^{2 \cdot |F|})$.*

Intuitively, in the worst-case each valid product has a different behaviour starting from the initial state. In this case, Algorithm 1 behaves as the product-based approach. Moreover, the number of valid variants is in the worst-case the size of the power set of F, i.e. $2^{|F|}$. Furthermore, there is an overhead in the FTS algorithm that does not exist in the product-by-product method: At each iteration, a satisfiability check on feature expression is performed, which also has a time complexity of $\mathcal{O}(2^{|F|})$. Although the FTS algorithm has a worse theoretical complexity, experiments tend to show that in practice it outperforms the product-based approach [23,25,26]. The FTS theory is thus a solid candidate solution for the VIS model-checking problem.

3.4 Related FTS-Based Verfication Work

Modal Automata, i.e., automata with optional and compulsory transitions, precede FTS as a formal model for software product lines. As an example, in [49], Gnesi and Fantechi proposed a behavioural model, namely the Extended Modal Labeled Transition Systems (EMLTS), as a basis for the formalisation of the different notions of variability usually present in the definitions of product families. In particular, an EMLTS is able to define a family of products by telling at any state of the system whether transitions are optional or compulsory for the products of the family. The work was then pursued by Leucker and co-authors [52] and compared with FTS in [4]. One of the main drawbacks of EMLTS is that there is no causality on transition choice from state to state. This causality is captured by FTS constraints and also by a constraint-based extension of EMLTS proposed in [7,8], but without the family-based analysis. It should be also noted that, contrary to FTS, EMLTS have not been extended to the quantitative setting.

Our FTS formalism has been extended in various directions. The first of them was to consider other types of logic in order to specify product line requirements. As an example in [24], we have showed how to extend symbolic model-checking of computational tree logic to FTS. We showed how to encode features as extra variables in BDDs representing symbolic behaviors of multiple products without blowing up the representation. Later, in [10], Ter Beek *et al.*, have showed how to consider the entire mu-calculus. Their main contribution was to introduce μL_f, a logic that combines mu-calculus modalities with feature expressions. They showed how to define and model-check this logic on FTS. Their work has been implemented in a tool called mCRL2 [96].

In parallel, we have also extended our approach to conformance model-checking (also known as refinement-based model-checking), that is the problem of comparing the behaviors of several products. Simulation relation allows us to decide whether all behaviors of a system are covered by those of another system. In product lines, the problem reduces to check if all products from one line are covered by products from another line. One way to do so is to perform a pairwise comparison between the products of the two lines, which is expensive. In order to avoid this enumerative comparison, we have showed how to generalize the notion of simulation from systems to family. The work, which is presented in [31], shows clear benefit in using this approach. Branching bisimulation for FTS was also studied by Belder *et al.* [11]. Later, in collaboration with University of Waterloo Canada, we have showed that these new relations can be used to quantify the impact of change when introducing or removing features from a given system. This was one of the first extensions of FTS has been used to handle problems that are not related to product lines. Indeed, here features are used to label behaviors of a system, not to distinguish products in a specific line. Results related to this topic are available in [5].

Abstraction is a technique that permits to reduce the size of a system by merging states or transitions. The resulting system is generally smaller and easier to verify. Abstraction is behaviorally conservative, but may introduce extra fake behaviors. In [32], we have showed how to abstract states and transitions of FTS. The situation is more complex than for single systems. Indeed, we need not only to merge states, but also to simplify formulas representing set of features over FTS's transitions. In order to remove fake behaviors (when needed), we have entirely redeveloped a CEGAR-based model-checking for FTS. Another

CEGAR procedure was developed by Wasowski for LTL and latter CTL [43–45]. Contrary to us, they only focus on abstracting features, but not states. Their approach uses games and modal automata as FTS abstractions, hence showing that FTS is practically more convenient than modal automata to represent complex behavioral relations between products.

Another trend has been the one of extending FTS with quantitative information. The first attempt was when we showed how to combine FTS and timed automata in order to handle timed product lines. In [34], we have showed how to combine timed constraints of real-time clocks with feature constraints. We have then showed that the model-checking procedure from [25] applies directly to our case by using the well-known region construction from timed automata. Our timed extension has been reused and extended in various directions. As an example, Beohar and Mousavi introduced IOFTS that is an input/output extension of timed FTS for model-based testing of software product lines [14]. Their main contributions were to define a notion of test suite and test cases generated from an IOFTS. They also defined two notions of refinement, one at the level of IOFTS and another one at the level of test suites.

Later, probabilistic extensions of FTS were also considered. In [86], we have combined FTS with stochastic information coming from a Markov Decision Process representation of the environment. In this context, one has to compute which product satisfies a given requirement with a specified probability. We have defined family-based algorithms to analyze the resulting quantitative FTS. One of them directly extends the classical algorithm for bounded quantitative logic. The other one uses parameter synthesis in stochastic systems to extract products that do satisfy a quantitative behavior. In [39], we have showed how learning algorithms and Markov Decision processes can be used to abstract environment behaviors. We then showed how the result can be used to restrict FTS behaviors in a model-testing based approach. Our work also paved the way for compositional reasoning and analysis of probabilistic queries for software product lines. In [47], Baier et al. give a clear adaptation of compositional reasoning to this context. This is implemented in the ProFeat tool [21] that uses similar techniques to those in [86]. It is worth mentioning that other research groups are also working of verifying stochastic and even quantitative behaviors of product lines. As an example, in [9,89], Ter Beek et al. have proposed an algebra to defined quantitative relations between features. This algebra is static in the sense that it relates features with quantitative information (cost, constraints on costs, etc.) and dynamic in the sense that it allows us to specify when features can appear and disappear in system's execution at runtime (hence opening the door to the analysis of dynamic software product lines). The verification process used in these works relies on a dynamic extension of statistical model-checking [66].

In a series of recent works e.g., [79], we have also extended FTS to handle quantitative problems such as long run average. Quantitative problems were already handled at feature diagram level, but not yet at behavioral level. Unfortunately, the family-based approach advantages decrease in this context. Indeed, those weighted automata-based problems require to compute specific quantities that differ from products to product. A solution to this problem could be to use abstraction-based approaches over quantities.

4   Testing Variability-Intensive Systems with FTSs

In this section, we focus on *Model-Based Testing* (MBT) [93] at the SPL level. Test cases are defined during domain engineering [84] for the SPL by associating each test to the set of products able to execute it. Intuitively, if one wants to test a particular product, she will consider only the tests associated to that particular product. In the other way around, if one wants to test an SPL, she will start by building the product with the highest number of associated tests and execute those tests on that product.

MBT requires to define a model of the expected behaviour of the System Under Test (SUT), *i.e.*, a specification, that serves as input to an automated test suite selection tool. The model should be small enough to be cheaper than the analysis of the actual system, but accurate enough to describe the characteristics to test. The tool uses this model to generate a sequence of input (*i.e.*, a *test case*) and an oracle for each one of those sequences. For most systems, selecting all the possible test cases from the model is intractable. The test engineer relies on selection algorithms that maximize a given *coverage criterion*, measuring the adequacy of a test suite [73].

4.1   Test Concepts for FTSs

Since FTSs are derived from TSs, a natural starting point to adapt model-based testing in the context of software product lines is to consider existing coverage criteria for transition systems [93] and extend them to make them meaningful with respect to FTSs.

Abstract Test Case over an FTS. In an MBT approach, test cases are automatically selected from a model of the system under test. This derivation is done in several steps: first, *abstract test case* are selected from the model, an FTS in our case, using a given criterion; those abstract test cases are then refined, using additional information in order to be executable by the SUT. The remainder of this section cover the first step: abstract test case selection.

First, let us define the notion of abstract test case for FTS. We define an abstract test case over an FTS as a sequence of *actions* from this FTS, such that there exists a sequence of *transitions* in this FTS with the given actions.

Definition 10 (Abstract test case). *Let fts = $(S, Act, Trans, I, AP, L, fm, \gamma)$ be an FTS. An abstract test case t is a finite sequence $(\alpha_1, \ldots, \alpha_n)$, where $\alpha_1, \ldots, \alpha_n \in Act$ and there exists a sequence of transitions in trans such that*

$$\exists i \in I : i \xrightarrow{\alpha_1} s_k \xrightarrow{\alpha_2} \ldots \xrightarrow{\alpha_n} s_l$$

Positive and Negative Abstract Test Cases. We distinguish two kinds of test cases: *positive test cases* trigger a desired/expected behaviour of the system under test; and *negative test cases* trigger an undesired behaviour of the system under test [93]. At the SPL level, a positive abstract test case is defined as a sequence of actions executable by the *fts* (*i.e.,* executable by at least one product), while a negative abstract test case is a sequence of actions not executable by the *fts* (*i.e.,* not executable by any product). Once concretized (*i.e.,* transformed into executable code) [95], negative abstract test cases typically represent sequences of actions that every product of the product line should forbid. Note that a positive test case for a SPL may become a negative test case for one particular product of the SPL if this product is not allowed to exercise the behavior described in the test case. In the remainder of this section, we focus on test case selection at the SPL level.

In a LTS (*lts*), an abstract test case $t = (\alpha_1, \ldots, \alpha_n)$ is executable, denoted $lts \stackrel{t}{\Longrightarrow}$, if there exists a sequence of transitions starting from an initial state and labelled with $\alpha_1, \ldots, \alpha_n$ [91,92]. For an FTS (*fts*), to be executable, the sequence of transitions must moreover have feature expressions compatible with the associated FM (or its projection on a subset of the product line if one wants to test only a given set of products). In other words, when selecting test cases for a product line, a sequence of actions is executable by *fts* if there exists at least one product (p) which, when *fts* is projected onto p (denoted $fts_{|p}$), is able to execute it:

$$\left(fts \stackrel{\alpha_1, \ldots, \alpha_n}{\Longrightarrow} \right) \Leftrightarrow \left(\exists p \in [\![fm]\!] : fts_{|p} \stackrel{\alpha_1, \ldots, \alpha_n}{\Longrightarrow} \right)$$

In testing, unlike model-checking [6], we only consider finite sequences of actions. Since FTS (as LTS) do not have an observable final/accepting state *per se*, in order to decide if a sequence of actions represents a desired behaviour of the system, we chose to consider the initial states of an FTS as accepting states, observable for the tester (contrarily to Tretmans *et al.* [91,92], we do not partition the set of actions into inputs and observable outputs, this will be part of our future work). Positive abstract test cases have to end their execution in an initial state (*e.g.,* state 1 in the soda vending machine FTS) in order to observe that the test case was executed successfully.

Definition 11 (Positive abstract test case). *Let fts = (S, Act, Trans, I, AP, L, fm, γ) be an FTS. A positive abstract test case $t = (\alpha_1, \ldots, \alpha_n)$, where $\alpha_1, \ldots, \alpha_n \in Act$, is a finite sequence of actions such as there is at least one product from fm able to execute t, and this execution ends in an initial state:*

$$\exists p \in [\![fm]\!], \exists i \in I : fts_{|p} \stackrel{t}{\Rightarrow} i$$

Definition 12 (Negative abstract test case). *Let fts = (S, Act, Trans, I, AP, L, fm, γ) be an FTS. A negative abstract test case $t = (\alpha_1, \ldots, \alpha_n)$, where $\alpha_1, \ldots, \alpha_n \in Act$, is a finite sequence of actions such as for every product from fm, the product is not able to execute t or this execution does not end in an initial state:*

$$\forall p \in [\![fm]\!], \nexists i \in I : fts_{|p} \stackrel{t}{\nRightarrow} i$$

When derived from the soda vending machine FTS, a positive abstract test case has to start from 1 and end in 1 and only fire transitions with compatible feature expressions. For instance, abstract test case *(free, soda, serveSoda, open, close)* is a positive abstract test case, while *(free, soda, serveSoda)* is a negative abstract test cases as it does not end in an initial state when it is executed on the FTS (and hence one cannot observe if the test is successfull or not). Other negative abstract test cases include sequences of actions that mix the behaviour of two incompatible products.

In the remainder, we mainly focus on positive abstract test cases and simply write *test case*. A *test suite*, defined for a SUT, is a set of test cases.

Test Suite Product Selection. When abstract test cases are concretized, the result (*i.e.,* concrete test cases, represented as a sequence of operations on the system) has to be executed on one or more products of the SPL. The set of products able to execute a test case may be calculated from the FTS (and the FM). It corresponds to all the products (*i.e.,* set of features) of the FM that satisfy all the feature expressions associated to the transitions fired by the abstract test case when it is executed on the FTS:

Definition 13 (Test case product selection). *Given an FTS fts = (S, Act, Trans, I, AP, L, fm, γ) and a positive abstract test case $t = (\alpha_1, \ldots, \alpha_n)$ with $(\alpha_1, \ldots, \alpha_n) \in Act$, the set of products able to execute t is defined as:*

$$prod(fts, t) = \{p \in [\![fm]\!] \mid \exists i \in I : fts_{|p} \xRightarrow{t} i\}$$

From a practical point of view, the set of products contains all the products satisfying the conjunction of the feature expressions $\gamma(s_k \xrightarrow{\alpha_i} s_{k+1})$ on the path(s) of t and the FM fm. When fm is Boolean, it may be transformed to a Boolean formula [38]. The existence of a product for a test case is equivalent to the satisfiability of the following formula, that can be checked by a SAT solver:

$$\bigvee_{pt \in paths} \left(\bigwedge_{i=1}^{n_{pt}} \left(\gamma(s_k \xrightarrow{\alpha_i} s_l) \right) \right) \wedge fm$$

For instance, the set of products for the test case *(free, soda, serveSoda, open, close)*, derived from the vending machine FTS, contains all the products of the SPL that offer free soda. Similarly, for a test suite, we have:

Definition 14 (Test suite product selection). *Given an FTS fts = (S, Act, Trans, I, AP, L, fm, γ) and a test suite $s = \{t_1, \ldots, t_n\}$, where $t_1, \ldots, t_n$ are positive abstract test cases, the set of products able to execute the test suite:*

$$prod(fts, s) = \bigcup_{t_i \in s} prod(fts, t_i)$$

If we have a test suite (s) with two test cases *(free, soda, serveSoda, open, close)* and *(free, tea, serveTea, open, close)*, the set of products contains all the products of the SPL that offers free soda or free tea.

We will consider that for a given test suite (s), a set of products (M) is adequate, if M contains enough products to execute the test cases in s:

Definition 15 (s-adequate set of products). *Let fts be an FTS and $s = \{t_1, \ldots, t_n\}$ be an abstract test suite where $t_1, \ldots, t_n$ are positive abstract test cases. The set of products M is s-adequate, denoted $M \stackrel{s}{\Longrightarrow}$, if each test case in s may be executed by at least one product in M:*

$$\forall t \in s : \exists p \in M, \exists i \in I, fts_{|p} \stackrel{t}{\Longrightarrow} i$$

Since one of the main concerns in SPL testing is to reduce the number of products needed to execute the tests, we also define the selection of the minimal s-adequate set of products required to execute a test suite:

Definition 16 (P-Minimal test suite product selection). *Let fts be an FTS and $s = \{t_1, \ldots, t_n\}$ be an abstract test suite where $t_1, \ldots, t_n$ are positive abstract test cases. A minimal s-adequate set of products needed to execute the test suite, denoted $mprod(fts, s) = M$, is a subset of $prod(fts, s)$ such that M is s-adequate and there is no subset of M that is s-adequate:*

$$\left(M \stackrel{s}{\Longrightarrow} \right) \wedge \left(\forall M' \subset M, M' \stackrel{s}{\not\Longrightarrow} \right)$$

For instance, there are two products able to execute all the test cases in the test suite s: one that allows to cancel purchase and one that doesn't. The p-Minimal set of products for s is a set with only one of those two products. The decision of the products to include (or not) should be taken by the test engineer, depending for instance on the cost linked to the derivation of each product.

4.2 Selection Criteria

In order to efficiently select test cases, the test engineer has to provide *selection criteria* [73,93], defined hereafter as a function, returning for a given FTS and a test suite, a value between 0 and 1 specifying the coverage degree of the executable abstract test suite over the FTS: 0 meaning no coverage and 1 the maximal coverage.

Definition 17 (coverage criterion). *A coverage criterion is a function cov that associates an FTS and a test suite over this FTS to a real value in $[0, 1]$.*

Structural Coverage. Classical structural coverage criteria are expressed using the structural elements of the model [73,93] (in this case, FTSs) covered by the execution of a test case.

Definition 18 (State/All-states coverage). *The state coverage criterion is related to the ratio between the states visited by the test cases pertaining to the test suite and all the states of the FTS. When the value of the function equals to 1, the test suite satisfies the all-states coverage.*

Definition 19 (Action/All-actions coverage). *The action coverage criterion is related to the ratio between the actions triggered by the test cases pertaining to the test suite and all the actions of the FTS defined. When the value of the function equals 1, the test suite satisfies* all-actions coverage.

Definition 20 (Transition/All-transitions coverage). *Transition coverage is related to the ratio between transitions covered when running test cases on the FTS and the total number of transitions of the FTS. When this ratio equals to 1, then the test suite satisfies* all-transitions *coverage.*

Definition 21 (Transition-pair/All-pairs coverage). *The transition-pairs coverage considers adjacent transitions successively entering and leaving a given state. When the coverage function reaches the value of 1, then the test suite covers* all-transition-pairs.

Definition 22 (Path/All-paths coverage). *Path coverage takes into account simple executable paths (i.e., paths that does not fire the same transition twice), that is sequences of transitions starting from and ending in an initial state. If the coverage function value computing the ratio between the number of simple executable paths covered by the test cases and total number of simple executable paths in the FTS is 1,* all-paths *coverage has been reached.*

The all-path coverage is the strongest coverage criterion. It specifies that each simple executable path in the FTS should be followed at least once when executing the test suite. Depending on the FTS, this coverage criterion might not be scalable.

Dissimilarity-Based Coverage. Dissimilarity testing is a technique used to select a test suite among all possible test cases, which aims to maximise the fault detection rate by increasing diversity among test cases [20,55]. This diversity is characterized by a *dissimilarity distance* defined over the different test cases. For instance, Henard *et al.* [57] applied dissimilarity testing to SPL in order to sample and prioritize products to test. The idea was to mimic the combinatorial interaction testing (CIT) sampling for SPLs [69,83], in which valid combinations of features are covered at least once.

Applied to FTS, dissimilarity-based coverage extends Henard *et al.*'s work [57] by formulating the abstract test case selection as a bi-objective problem [40] where one wants to maximize dissimilarity between the products, but also the exercised behaviors. Formally, we define the dissimilarity between two test cases as follows:

Definition 23 (Test cases dissimilarity). *Given an FTS fts and two test cases $t_1 = (\alpha_1, \ldots, \alpha_n)$ and $t_2 = (\beta_1, \ldots, \beta_n)$ derived from fts, the dissimilarity between t_1 and t_2 is defined as:*

$$diss(fts, t_1, t_2) = diss_p(prod(fts, t_1), prod(fts, t_2))$$
$$\otimes \ diss_a((\alpha_1, \ldots, \alpha_n), (\beta_1, \ldots, \beta_n))$$

Where $diss_p : \llbracket d \rrbracket \times \llbracket d \rrbracket \to [0,1]$ *computes a dissimilarity distance between the* products, $diss_a : Act^+ \times Act^+ \to [0,1]$ *computes a dissimilarity distance between* the actions of the test cases, and $\otimes : [0,1] \times [0,1] \to [0,1]$ *is an operator combin-* ing the products and actions distances to return a global dissimilarity distance between the two test cases.

The dissimilarity between products $(diss_p)$ may for instance be the Jaccard index (*i.e.*, the the ratio between the number of products common to $prod(fts, t_1)$ and $prod(fts, t_2)$, and the total number of products in both) [57,58]. In our previous work [40], we defined several dissimilarity distances $diss_a$ for the actions executed by two test cases (including the Jaccard index which gave best results in our evaluation) and used Definition 23 to drive the selection of abstract test cases using a (1+1) evolutionary algorithm [46].

4.3   Test Case and Test Suite Minimality

Usually, when performing test case selection, one wants to have a test suite as small as possible while ensuring the best coverage. Contrary to single systems where only the size of the test suite is taken into account, when performing SPL testing, we also have to consider the number of products needed to execute the test suite. We define the *size* of a test suite as the number of transitions triggered by its test cases.

Definition 24 (Test suite size). *The size of a test suite s corresponds to the* number of transitions triggered in a FTS fts when executing the test cases of s on fts, denoted

$$fts \overset{s}{\Longrightarrow}$$

This allows to differentiate a test suite s_1 with test cases only triggering a min-imal set of transitions to satisfy a coverage criterion from a test suite s_2 also satisfying this coverage criterion, but with longer test cases triggering transitions that do not contribute to the coverage. For a given FTS *fts*, we denote $s_1 < s_2$ if

$$\left(fts \overset{s_1}{\Longrightarrow}\right) < \left(fts \overset{s_2}{\Longrightarrow}\right)$$

As opposed to current practice, the size of the test suite does not take the number of test cases into account. Two test suites with the same size may have different number of test case. This metric is more representative of the behaviour of the SPL covered by a test suite. As for test suites, we define the size of a test case as the number of transitions triggered by this test case.

Definition 25 (Test case size). *The size of a test case t corresponds to the* number of transitions triggered in a FTS fts when executing t on fts, denoted

$$fts \overset{t}{\Longrightarrow}$$

Depending on the product line under test, the test engineer decides if the test suite has to contain lots of small test cases, to ease the debugging process when a test case fails for instance, or few longer test cases, if the setup required to execute each test is expensive for instance.

For such a distribution of test cases sizes in a test suite, the selection process compromises between the size of the test suite and the number of products needed to execute this test suite. We define the former as the *minimal* test suite property, and the latter as the *P-minimal* test suite property.

Property 1 (Minimal test suite). A test suite s over a given FTS $fts = (S, Act, trans, i, d, \gamma)$ is minimal *w.r.t.* a selection criteria cov iff $\nexists s'$ such that $s' < s$ and $cov(fts, s') \geq cov(fts, s)$.

Property 2 (P-minimal test suite). A test suite s over a given FTS $fts = (S, Act, trans, i, d, \gamma)$ is product-minimal (p-minimal) regarding a selection criteria cov iff $\nexists s'$ such that $(cov(fts, s') \geq cov(fts, s)) \wedge (\# mprod(fts, s') < \# mprod(fts, s))$.

In other words, a test suite is minimal if there exists no smaller test suite with a better coverage, and a p-minimal test suite represents the minimal set of test cases (with the best coverage) such that the number of products needed to execute all of them is minimal.

4.4 Related Work

The first approaches of SPL testing considered the impact of the intertwined domain engineering and application engineering processes on test planning, design and execution activities [74,84]. Early contributions focused notably on the relationship between SPL use cases [17] and tests [18]. In the latter, Bertolino and Gnesi adapt the SPL use cases into test plans with tags. These tags allows to specify which scenarios and which properties must be tested depending on the activated features (mandatory, alternative, optional, etc.). Another approach is to combine high-level "test patterns" during product derivation and synthesize such scenarios as LTS in order to take advantage of model-based test generation techniques [76]. Incremental testing approaches have also been more recently adapted in the SPL context [63,70,81,94]. For example, Lochau *et al.* [68,70] proposed a model-based approach that shifts from one product to another by applying *deltas* to state machine models. These deltas enable automatic reuse and adaptation of the test model and derivation of retest obligations. Oster *et al.* [81] extend combinatorial interaction testing with the possibility to specify a predefined subset of products in the set of products to test. These approaches assume that *we know already* which products to test.

Sampling techniques, such as t-wise approaches [28,29,59,83], strive to answer to this question by exploring configurations allowed by the feature model. These techniques are based on the systematic coverage of the interaction of two more features, a criteria that has been shown empirically to cover 80% of bugs [64]. T-wise sampling being NP-complete in the presence of constraints, various heuristics have been proposed [71], from greedy algorithms [28,59] to meta-heuristics [48,50]. Meta-heuristics are also at the heart of dissimilarity sampling techniques that maximize distances between configurations [1,57]. There are also approaches that combines several objectives (coverage, cost of configurations, *etc.*) [53,56,87].

Efforts to combine sampling techniques with modelling ones (*e.g.,* [69]) exist. These approaches are product-based, meaning that they may miss opportunities to reuse tests among sampled products [85]. There are also approaches focused on the SPL code by building variability-aware interpreters for various languages [61]. Based on symbolic execution techniques such interpreters are able to run a very large set of products with respect to one given test case [77]. Cichos *et al.* [22] use the notion of 150% test model (*i.e.,* a test model of the behaviour of a product line) and test goal to derive test cases for a product line but do not redefine coverage criteria at the SPL level. At the code level, Li *et al.* [67] focuses on test specification and values reuse from one product to another by using a genetic algorithm that integrates software fault localization techniques and structural coverage of the program. Finally, Beohar *et al.* [13,15,16] propose to adapt the *ioco* framework proposed by Tretmans [91] to FTSs.

As we have seen, the FTS formalism offers an ideal language to study model-based testing of SPLs. Though we initially focused on family-based approaches to exploit the sharing opportunities amongst test cases, the impact of sampling techniques can be assessed and we can envision both in a multi-objective setting [40]. We believe that the FTS formalism, natively equipped with features as a first-class concept, is pivotal to inter-model verification support and supports combination of quality assurance techniques both at the domain and application engineering levels.

5 Perspectives

Ten years after the inception of featured transition systems, we (and others) demonstrated its relevance to lay the foundations for model-based and formal quality assurance of variability-intensive systems. This in turn enabled us to derive efficient algorithms and to integrate them in the ProVeLines and ViBES frameworks [36,42]. In this section, we would like to discuss some perspectives that would possibly lead us to work on and extend FTS for next decade.

5.1 Optimisation of Quality Requirements

The initial endeavour surrounding FTS and the work presented in this paper mainly targets the verification and validation of functional requirements in VIS. FTS-based approaches for checking non-functional (aka quality) requirements have also been targeted in the recent years, most of them focusing on one particular non-functional aspect (e.g. execution time [30,72], reliability [86], income [80], quality of service [78]). Our recent work [65] proposes an end-to-end framework to efficiently assess multiple quality attributes across all variants and find the variant optimizing the trade-off between those attributes.

This quest for optimum paves the way for future research that exploit sampling techniques to efficiently search for such optimal variants. Our preliminary work [33] shows that this problem is non trivial and call for new endeavour lying at the intersection of VIS verification, configuration sampling and statistical model checking.

5.2   Grand Verification Challenges: Cyber-Physical and Learning Systems

The last decade has seen a tremendous increase in the integration of hardware and software in number of connected devices and sensors, leading to the advent of the internet-of-things (IoT). IoT has pervaded every domain of our lives from the most useless gadget to more safety-critical Cyber-Physical Systems (CPS) embedded in cars and planes. According to Briand *et al.*, even a simple car controller can be *untestable* [19]. Indeed, the large input space and the necessity to evaluate the outputs continuously over a time period is not adapted to discrete testing and verification approaches. The fact that CPS are also VIS, in the sense that they can dynamically adapt to their environment and the difficulty to predict this environment precisely forms an additional challenge.

Connected devices and sensors produce an enormous amount of data that are processed by intelligent systems increasingly relying on artificial intelligence (AI) algorithms. AI-enabled systems have shown their power in a variety of domains from the game of Go to autonoumous driving. "With great power comes great responsibility" is a cliché that perfectly applies to artificial intelligence (AI). As technology is progressing faster than ever before towards software with more and more abilities, adaptation and autonomy, the risks are becoming increasingly apparent. Adversarial machine learning [51] has shown how to have a given AI algorithm to misclassify a panda as a gibbon thanks to a few transformations to the image, sometimes invisible. Slight changes in luminosity may lead to the wrong turn on the road [90]. With recent work showing that learnability may be undecidable, the hope of fully verifiable AI vanishes [12].

5.3   Extended FTS for Cyber-Physical and AI-Ready Systems

The aforementioned challenges suggest two research directions in order to extend the FTS formalism and its verification and validation algorithms for these highly complex, dynamic and configurable systems.

Anytime FTS. FTS were initially thought in the usual product line setting where all the features and their relationships could be specified in advance ans were not allowed to change. Adaptation to the environment and learning imply that this assumption does not hold anymore: features will disappear and new ones may appear as normal operation of the system. We previously envisioned the scenario where cars receive new features such as autopilot that can be downloaded and activated on demand via a software marketplace [82]. Since these cars dynamically adapt - the behaviour of the car is itself variability-aware and context-dependent - verifying if the introduction of a new feature is safe, the car should itself embeds its FTS and model-checker. To be efficient, on-the-fly reduction techniques of the verification space must be employed: for example, Kim *et al.* prune statically configurations that cannot violate a given property, reducing the number of configurations to monitor at runtime [62]. Cordy *et al.* have proposed incremental verification of software product lines to deal with partial configurations [35], though this technique has not been extended to runtime scenarios yet. These challenges lead us to conjecture that the upcoming techniques should be able to mix design time and runtime V&V techniques in a seamless manner.

Stochastic FTS. The uncertain nature of the targeted systems lead us to pursue the work on stochastic FTS and their relation with other formalisms such as markov chains, markov decision processes or modal transition systems (see Sect. 3.4). As we have seen, there is no predetermined winning strategy between family-based and product-based scenarios. It has to be noted that stochasticity does not only concern behaviour but also decisions as it is the nature of machine learning algorithms to take decisions on probabilities rather than on logic. In other words, V&V algorithms will have to deal with feature models that are themselves probabilistic [37].

6 Conclusion

In this paper, we covered almost a decade of VIS modelling, verification and testing for and with Featured Transition Systems. Initially dedicated to model-checking it also demonstrated it suitability for model-based testing and supported applications even beyond VIS such as offering solutions to speed up the analysis of mutants [41]. We believe that the universality and simplicity of FTS contributed to this diversity of FTS-related contributions. From a more personal perspective, it enabled the dialogue between the authors issued from the formal verification and testing communities, yielding fruitful collaborations. Given the challenges ahead, we are convinced that the combination of techniques and the removal of the frontiers between these communities is a prerequisite to future advances in VIS V&V and we look forward to it.

References

1. Al-Hajjaji, M., Thüm, T., Meinicke, J., Lochau, M., Saake, G.: Similarity-based prioritization in software product-line testing. In: 18th International Software Product Line Conference, SPLC 2014, Florence, Italy, 15–19 September 2014, pp. 197–206 (2014). https://doi.org/10.1145/2648511.2648532
2. Apel, S., Batory, D., Kästner, C., Saake, G.: Feature-Oriented Software Product Lines: Concepts and Implementation. Springer, Heidelberg (2013). https://doi.org/10.1007/978-3-642-37521-7

3. Apel, S., von Rhein, A., Wendler, P., Größlinger, A., Beyer, D.: Strategies for product-line verification: case studies and experiments. In: ICSE 2013, pp. 482–491 (2013)
4. Asirelli, P., ter Beek, M.H., Gnesi, S., Fantechi, A.: Formal description of variability in product families. In: 15th International Conference on Software Product Lines, SPLC 2011, Munich, Germany, 22–26 August 2011, pp. 130–139 (2011)
5. Atlee, J.M., Beidu, S., Fahrenberg, U., Legay, A.: Merging features in featured transition systems. In: Proceedings of the 12th Workshop on Model-Driven Engineering, Verification and Validation Co-located with ACM/IEEE 18th International Conference on Model Driven Engineering Languages and Systems, MoDeVVa@MoDELS 2015, Ottawa, Canada, 29 September 2015, pp. 38–43. CEUR-WS.org (2015)
6. Baier, C., Katoen, J.P.: Principles of Model Checking. MIT Press, Cambridge (2008)
7. ter Beek, M.H., Damiani, F., Gnesi, S., Mazzanti, F., Paolini, L.: From featured transition systems to modal transition systems with variability constraints. In: Calinescu, R., Rumpe, B. (eds.) SEFM 2015. LNCS, vol. 9276, pp. 344–359. Springer, Cham (2015). https://doi.org/10.1007/978-3-319-22969-0_24
8. ter Beek, M.H., Fantechi, A., Gnesi, S., Mazzanti, F.: Modelling and analysing variability in product families: model checking of modal transition systems with variability constraints. J. Log. Algebr. Meth. Program. **85**(2), 287–315 (2016). https://doi.org/10.1016/j.jlamp.2015.11.006
9. ter Beek, M.H., Legay, A., Lluch-Lafuente, A., Vandin, A.: Statistical analysis of probabilistic models of software product lines with quantitative constraints. In: Proceedings of the 19th International Conference on Software Product Line, SPLC 2015, Nashville, TN, USA, 20–24 July 2015, pp. 11–15. ACM (2015)
10. Ter Beek, M.H., de Vink, E.P., Willemse, T.A.C.: Family-based model checking with mCRL2. In: Huisman, M., Rubin, J. (eds.) FASE 2017. LNCS, vol. 10202, pp. 387–405. Springer, Heidelberg (2017). https://doi.org/10.1007/978-3-662-54494-5_23
11. Belder, T., ter Beek, M.H., de Vink, E.P.: Coherent branching feature bisimulation. In: Atlee, J.M., Gnesi, S. (eds.) Proceedings 6th Workshop on Formal Methods and Analysis in SPL Engineering, FMSPLE@ETAPS 2015, London, UK, 11 April 2015. EPTCS, vol. 182, pp. 14–30 (2015). https://doi.org/10.4204/EPTCS.182.2
12. Ben-David, S., Hrubeš, P., Moran, S., Shpilka, A., Yehudayoff, A.: Learnability can be undecidable. Nat. Mach. Intell. **1**(1), 44–48 (2019). https://doi.org/10.1038/s42256-018-0002-3
13. Beohar, H., Mousavi, M.R.: Input-output conformance testing based on featured transition systems. In: Proceedings of the 29th Annual ACM Symposium on Applied Computing, SAC 2014, pp. 1272–1278. ACM Press (2014). https://doi.org/10.1145/2554850.2554949
14. Beohar, H., Mousavi, M.R.: Input-output conformance testing for software product lines. J. Log. Algebr. Meth. Program. **85**(6), 1131–1153 (2016). https://doi.org/10.1016/j.jlamp.2016.09.007
15. Beohar, H., Mousavi, M.: Spinal test suites for software product lines. ArXiv e-prints (2014)
16. Beohar, H., Varshosaz, M., Mousavi, M.R.: Basic behavioral models for software product lines: expressiveness and testing pre-orders. Sci. Comput. Program., July 2015. http://www.sciencedirect.com/science/article/pii/S0167642315001288

17. Bertolino, A., Fantechi, A., Gnesi, S., Lami, G.: Product line use cases: scenario-based specification and testing of requirements. In: Käköla, T., Duenas, J.C. (eds.) Software Product Lines, pp. 425–445. Springer, Heidelberg (2006). https://doi.org/10.1007/978-3-540-33253-4_11

18. Bertolino, A., Gnesi, S.: PLUTO: a test methodology for product families. In: van der Linden, F.J. (ed.) PFE 2003. LNCS, vol. 3014, pp. 181–197. Springer, Heidelberg (2004). https://doi.org/10.1007/978-3-540-24667-1_14

19. Briand, L., Nejati, S., Sabetzadeh, M., Bianculli, D.: Testing the untestable: model testing of complex software-intensive systems. In: Proceedings of the 38th International Conference on Software Engineering Companion, ICSE 2016, pp. 789–792. ACM, New York, NY, USA (2016). https://doi.org/10.1145/2889160.2889212

20. Cartaxo, E.G., Machado, P.D.L., Neto, F.G.O.: On the use of a similarity function for test case selection in the context of model-based testing. Softw. Test. Verification Reliab. **21**(2), 75–100 (2011). https://doi.org/10.1002/stvr.413

21. Chrszon, P., Dubslaff, C., Klüppelholz, S., Baier, C.: ProFeat: feature-oriented engineering for family-based probabilistic model checking. Formal Asp. Comput. **30**(1), 45–75 (2018). https://doi.org/10.1007/s00165-017-0432-4

22. Cichos, H., Oster, S., Lochau, M., Schürr, A.: Model-based coverage-driven test suite generation for software product lines. In: Whittle, J., Clark, T., Kühne, T. (eds.) MODELS 2011. LNCS, vol. 6981, pp. 425–439. Springer, Heidelberg (2011). https://doi.org/10.1007/978-3-642-24485-8_31

23. Classen, A., Cordy, M., Heymans, P., Legay, A., Schobbens, P.Y.: Model checking software product lines with SNIP. STTT **14**(5), 589–612 (2012)

24. Classen, A., Cordy, M., Heymans, P., Legay, A., Schobbens, P.: Formal semantics, modular specification, and symbolic verification of product-line behaviour. Sci. Comput. Program. **80**, 416–439 (2014). https://doi.org/10.1016/j.scico.2013.09.019

25. Classen, A., Cordy, M., Schobbens, P., Heymans, P., Legay, A., Raskin, J.: Featured transition systems: foundations for verifying variability-intensive systems and their application to LTL model checking. IEEE Trans. Software Eng. **39**(8), 1069–1089 (2013). https://doi.org/10.1109/TSE.2012.86

26. Classen, A., Heymans, P., Schobbens, P.Y., Legay, A.: Symbolic model checking of software product lines. In: ICSE 2011, pp. 321–330. ACM (2011)

27. Classen, A., Heymans, P., Schobbens, P.Y., Legay, A., Raskin, J.F.: Model checking lots of systems: efficient verification of temporal properties in software product lines. In: ICSE 2010, pp. 335–344. ACM (2010)

28. Cohen, M., Dwyer, M., Shi, J.: Constructing interaction test suites for highly-configurable systems in the presence of constraints: a greedy approach. IEEE Trans. Software Eng. **34**(5), 633–650 (2008)

29. Cohen, M.B., Dwyer, M.B., Shi, J.: Coverage and adequacy in software product line testing. In: Proceedings of the ISSTA 2006 Workshop on Role of Software Architecture for Testing and Analysis - ROSATEA 2006, pp. 53–63 (2006). http://portal.acm.org/citation.cfm?doid=1147249.1147257

30. Cordy, M., Classen, A., Perrouin, G., Heymans, P., Schobbens, P.Y., Legay, A.: Simulation-based abstractions for software product-line model checking. In: ICSE 2012, pp. 672–682. IEEE (2012)

31. Cordy, M., Classen, A., Perrouin, G., Schobbens, P., Heymans, P., Legay, A.: Simulation-based abstractions for software product-line model checking. In: 34th International Conference on Software Engineering, ICSE 2012, 2–9 June 2012, Zurich, Switzerland, pp. 672–682. IEEE Computer Society (2012)

32. Cordy, M., Heymans, P., Legay, A., Schobbens, P., Dawagne, B., Leucker, M.: Counterexample guided abstraction refinement of product-line behavioural models. In: Proceedings of the 22nd ACM SIGSOFT International Symposium on Foundations of Software Engineering, (FSE-22), Hong Kong, China, 16–22 November 2014, pp. 190–201. ACM (2014)

33. Cordy, M., Legay, A., Lazreg, S., Collet, P.: Towards sampling and simulation-based analysis of featured weighted automata. In: FORMALISE@ICSE 2019, pp. 61–64 (2019)

34. Cordy, M., Schobbens, P., Heymans, P., Legay, A.: Behavioural modelling and verification of real-time software product lines. In: 16th International Software Product Line Conference, SPLC 2012, Salvador, Brazil, 2–7 September 2012, vol. 1, pp. 66–75. ACM (2012)

35. Cordy, M., Schobbens, P.Y., Heymans, P., Legay, A.: Towards an incremental automata-based approach for software product-line model checking. In: Proceedings of the 16th International Software Product Line Conference, vol. 2, pp. 74–81. ACM (2012)

36. Cordy, M., Schobbens, P.Y., Heymans, P., Legay, A.: ProVeLines: a product-line of verifiers for software product lines. In: SPLC 2013, pp. 141–146. ACM (2013)

37. Czarnecki, K., She, S., Wasowski, A.: Sample spaces and feature models: There and back again. In: Proceedings of the 2008 12th International Software Product Line Conference, SPLC 2008, pp. 22–31. IEEE Computer Society, Washington, DC, USA (2008). https://doi.org/10.1109/SPLC.2008.49

38. Czarnecki, K., Wasowski, A.: Feature diagrams and logics: there and back again. In: SPLC 2007, pp. 23–34. IEEE Computer Society (2007)

39. Devroey, X., et al.: Statistical prioritization for software product line testing: an experience report. Softw. Syst. Model. **16**(1), 153–171 (2017). http://link.springer.com/10.1007/s10270-015-0479-8

40. Devroey, X., Perrouin, G., Legay, A., Schobbens, P.Y., Heymans, P.: Search-based similarity-driven behavioural SPL Testing. In: Proceedings of the Tenth International Workshop on Variability Modelling of Software-intensive Systems - VaMoS 2016, pp. 89–96. ACM Press, Salvador, Brazil, January 2016

41. Devroey, X., Perrouin, G., Papadakis, M., Legay, A., Schobbens, P., Heymans, P.: Featured model-based mutation analysis. In: Dillon, L.K., Visser, W., Williams, L. (eds.) Proceedings of the 38th International Conference on Software Engineering, ICSE 2016, Austin, TX, USA, 14–22 May 2016, pp. 655–666. ACM (2016). https://doi.org/10.1145/2884781.2884821

42. Devroey, X., Perrouin, G., Schobbens, P.Y., Heymans, P.: Poster: VIBeS, transition system mutation made easy. In: 2015 IEEE/ACM 37th IEEE International Conference on Software Engineering, ICSE 2015, vol. 2, pp. 817–818. IEEE, Florence, Italy, May 2015. https://doi.org/10.1109/ICSE.2015.263, http://ieeexplore.ieee.org/document/7203084/

43. Dimovski, A.S., Legay, A., Wasowski, A.: Variability abstraction and refinement for game-based lifted model checking of full CTL. In: Hähnle, R., van der Aalst, W. (eds.) FASE 2019. LNCS, vol. 11424, pp. 192–209. Springer, Cham (2019). https://doi.org/10.1007/978-3-030-16722-6_11

44. Dimovski, A.S., Wąsowski, A.: From transition systems to variability models and from lifted model checking back to UPPAAL. In: Aceto, L., Bacci, G., Bacci, G., Ingólfsdóttir, A., Legay, A., Mardare, R. (eds.) Models, Algorithms, Logics and Tools. LNCS, vol. 10460, pp. 249–268. Springer, Cham (2017). https://doi.org/10.1007/978-3-319-63121-9_13

45. Dimovski, A.S., Wąsowski, A.: Variability-specific abstraction refinement for family-based model checking. In: Huisman, M., Rubin, J. (eds.) FASE 2017. LNCS, vol. 10202, pp. 406–423. Springer, Heidelberg (2017). https://doi.org/10.1007/978-3-662-54494-5_24

46. Droste, S., Jansen, T., Wegener, I.: On the analysis of the (1+1) evolutionary algorithm. Theoret. Comput. Sci. **276**(1), 51–81 (2002). http://www.sciencedirect.com/science/article/pii/S0304397501001827

47. Dubslaff, C., Klüppelholz, S., Baier, C.: Probabilistic model checking for energy analysis in software product lines. In: 13th International Conference on Modularity, MODULARITY 2014, Lugano, Switzerland, 22–26 April 2014, pp. 169–180. ACM (2014)

48. Ensan, F., Bagheri, E., Gašević, D.: Evolutionary search-based test generation for software product line feature models. In: Ralyté, J., Franch, X., Brinkkemper, S., Wrycza, S. (eds.) CAiSE 2012. LNCS, vol. 7328, pp. 613–628. Springer, Heidelberg (2012). https://doi.org/10.1007/978-3-642-31095-9_40

49. Fantechi, A., Gnesi, S.: A behavioural model for product families. In: Proceedings of the 6th Joint Meeting of the European Software Engineering Conference and the ACM SIGSOFT International Symposium on Foundations of Software Engineering, 2007, Dubrovnik, Croatia, 3–7 September 2007, pp. 521–524 (2007)

50. Garvin, B.J., Cohen, M.B., Dwyer, M.B.: Evaluating improvements to a meta-heuristic search for constrained interaction testing. Empir. Softw. Eng. **16**(1), 61–102 (2011)

51. Goodfellow, I., Shlens, J., Szegedy, C.: Explaining and harnessing adversarial examples. In: International Conference on Learning Representations (2015). http://arxiv.org/abs/1412.6572

52. Gruler, A., Leucker, M., Scheidemann, K.: Modeling and model checking software product lines. In: Barthe, G., de Boer, F.S. (eds.) FMOODS 2008. LNCS, vol. 5051, pp. 113–131. Springer, Heidelberg (2008). https://doi.org/10.1007/978-3-540-68863-1_8

53. Guo, J., et al.: SMTIBEA: a hybrid multi-objective optimization algorithm for configuring large constrained software product lines. Softw. Syst. Model., July 2017. https://doi.org/10.1007/s10270-017-0610-0

54. Halin, A., Nuttinck, A., Acher, M., Devroey, X., Perrouin, G., Baudry, B.: Test them all, is it worth it? assessing configuration sampling on the JHipster web development stack. Empir. Softw. Eng. **24**(2), 674–717 (2019). https://doi.org/10.1007/s10664-018-9635-4

55. Hemmati, H., Arcuri, A., Briand, L.: Achieving scalable model-based testing through test case diversity. ACM Trans. Softw. Eng. Methodol. **22**(1), 1–42 (2013). http://dl.acm.org/citation.cfm?id=2430536.2430540

56. Henard, C., Papadakis, M., Harman, M., Le Traon, Y.: Combining multi-objective search and constraint solving for configuring large software product lines. In: Proceedings of the 37th International Conference on Software Engineering, vol. 1, ICSE 2015, pp. 517–528. IEEE Press, Piscataway, NJ, USA (2015). http://dl.acm.org/citation.cfm?id=2818754.2818819

57. Henard, C., Papadakis, M., Perrouin, G., Klein, J., Heymans, P., Le Traon, Y.: Bypassing the combinatorial explosion: using similarity to generate and prioritize T-wise test configurations for software product lines. IEEE Trans. Softw. Eng. **40**(7), 650–670 (2014)

58. Jaccard, P.: Étude comparative de la distribution florale dans une portion des Alpes et des Jura. Bulletin del la Société Vaudoise des Sciences Naturelles **37**, 547–579 (1901)

59. Johansen, M.F., Haugen, Ø., Fleurey, F.: An algorithm for generating t-wise covering arrays from large feature models. In: Proceedings of the 16th International Software Product Line Conference on - SPLC 2012, vol. 1, p. 46. ACM Press (2012)

60. Kang, K., Cohen, S., Hess, J., Novak, W., Peterson, S.: Feature-oriented domain analysis (FODA) feasibility study. Technical report CMU/SEI-90-TR-21, Carnegie Mellon University (1990)

61. Kästner, C., et al.: Toward variability-aware testing. In: Proceedings of the 4th International Workshop on Feature-Oriented Software Development, FOSD 2012, pp. 1–8. ACM Press (2012). http://doi.acm.org/10.1145/2377816.2377817

62. Kim, C.H.P., Bodden, E., Batory, D., Khurshid, S.: Reducing configurations to monitor in a software product line. In: Barringer, H., et al. (eds.) RV 2010. LNCS, vol. 6418, pp. 285–299. Springer, Heidelberg (2010). https://doi.org/10.1007/978-3-642-16612-9_22

63. Knapp, A., Roggenbach, M., Schlingloff, B.H.: On the use of test cases in model-based software product line development. In: Proceedings of the 18th International Software Product Line Conference, vol. 1, SPLC 2014, pp. 247–251. ACM Press (2014). http://doi.acm.org/10.1145/2648511.2648539

64. Kuhn, D., Wallace, D., Gallo, A.: Software fault interactions and implications for software testing. IEEE Trans. Softw. Eng. 30(6), 418–421 (2004)

65. Lazreg, S., Cordy, M., Collet, P., Heymans, P., Mosser, S.: Multifaceted automated analyses for variability-intensive embedded systems. In: ICSE 2019, pp. 854–865 (2019)

66. Legay, A., Delahaye, B., Bensalem, S.: Statistical model checking: an overview. In: Barringer, H., et al. (eds.) RV 2010. LNCS, vol. 6418, pp. 122–135. Springer, Heidelberg (2010). https://doi.org/10.1007/978-3-642-16612-9_11

67. Li, X., Wong, W.E., Gao, R., Hu, L., Hosono, S.: Genetic algorithm-based test generation for software product line with the integration of fault localization techniques. Empir. Softw. Eng., pp. 1–51 (2017). https://doi.org/10.1007/s10664-016-9494-9

68. Lochau, M., Lity, S., Lachmann, R., Schaefer, I., Goltz, U.: Delta-oriented model-based integration testing of large-scale systems. J. Syst. Softw. 91, 63–84 (2014). https://doi.org/10.1016/j.jss.2013.11.1096. http://linkinghub.elsevier.com/retrieve/pii/S0164121213002781

69. Lochau, M., Oster, S., Goltz, U., Schürr, A.: Model-based pairwise testing for feature interaction coverage in software product line engineering. Software Qual. J. 20(3–4), 567–604 (2012). http://www.springerlink.com/index/10.1007/s11219-011-9165-4

70. Lochau, M., Schaefer, I., Kamischke, J., Lity, S.: Incremental model-based testing of delta-oriented software product lines. In: Brucker, A.D., Julliand, J. (eds.) TAP 2012. LNCS, vol. 7305, pp. 67–82. Springer, Heidelberg (2012). https://doi.org/10.1007/978-3-642-30473-6_7

71. Lopez-Herrejon, R.E., Fischer, S., Ramler, R., Egyed, A.: A first systematic mapping study on combinatorial interaction testing for software product lines. In: 2015 IEEE Eighth International Conference on Software Testing, Verification and Validation Workshops (ICSTW), pp. 1–10. IEEE (2015)

72. Luthmann, L., Stephan, A., Bürdek, J., Lochau, M.: Modeling and testing product lines with unbounded parametric real-time constraints. In: Proceedings of the 21st International Systems and Software Product Line Conference - Volume A, SPLC 2017, pp. 104–113. ACM, New York, NY, USA (2017). http://doi.acm.org/10.1145/3106195.3106204

73. Mathur, A.P.: Foundations of Software Testing. Pearson Education, India (2008)
74. McGregor, J.D.: Testing a software product line. In: Borba, P., Cavalcanti, A., Sampaio, A., Woodcook, J. (eds.) PSSE 2007. LNCS, vol. 6153, pp. 104–140. Springer, Heidelberg (2010). https://doi.org/10.1007/978-3-642-14335-9_4
75. Mendonca, M., Branco, M., Cowan, D.: S.P.L.O.T.: Software product lines online tools. In: Proceedings of OOPSLA 2009, pp. 761–762. ACM, New York, NY, USA (2009). http://doi.acm.org/10.1145/1639950.1640002
76. Nebut, C., Pickin, S., Le Traon, Y., Jézéquel, J.M.: Automated requirements-based generation of test cases for product families. In: 2003 Proceedings of 18th IEEE International Conference on Automated Software Engineering, pp. 263–266. IEEE (2003)
77. Nguyen, H.V., Kästner, C., Nguyen, T.N.: Exploring variability-aware execution for testing plugin-based web applications. In: Proceedings of the 36th International Conference on Software Engineering - ICSE 2014, pp. 907–918. ACM Press (2014). http://dl.acm.org/citation.cfm?doid=2568225.2568300
78. Olaechea, R., Atlee, J., Legay, A., Fahrenberg, U.: Trace checking for dynamic software product lines. In: Proceedings of the 13th International Conference on Software Engineering for Adaptive and Self-Managing Systems, SEAMS 2018, pp. 69–75. ACM (2018)
79. Olaechea, R., Fahrenberg, U., Atlee, J.M., Legay, A.: Long-term average cost in featured transition systems. In: Proceedings of the 20th International Systems and Software Product Line Conference, SPLC 2016, Beijing, China, 16–23 September 2016, pp. 109–118. ACM (2016)
80. Olaechea, R., Fahrenberg, U., Atlee, J.M., Legay, A.: Long-term average cost in featured transition systems. In: Proceedings of the 20th International Systems and Software Product Line Conference, SPLC 2016, pp. 109–118. ACM, New York, NY, USA (2016). http://doi.acm.org/10.1145/2934466.2934473
81. Oster, S., Markert, F., Ritter, P.: Automated incremental pairwise testing of software product lines. In: Bosch, J., Lee, J. (eds.) SPLC 2010. LNCS, vol. 6287, pp. 196–210. Springer, Heidelberg (2010). https://doi.org/10.1007/978-3-642-15579-6_14
82. Perrouin, G., Acher, M., Davril, J., Legay, A., Heymans, P.: A complexity tale: web configurators. In: Proceedings of the 1st International Workshop on Variability and Complexity in Software Design, VACE@ICSE 2016, Austin, Texas, USA, 14–22 May 2016, pp. 28–31. ACM (2016). https://doi.org/10.1145/2897045.2897051
83. Perrouin, G., Oster, S., Sen, S., Klein, J., Baudry, B., le Traon, Y.: Pairwise testing for software product lines: comparison of two approaches. Softw. Qual. J. 20(3–4), 605–643 (2011). http://dx.doi.org/10.1007/s11219-011-9160-9
84. Pohl, K., Böckle, G., van der Linden, F.: Software Product Line Engineering - Foundations, Principles, and Techniques. Springer, Heidelberg (2005). https://doi.org/10.1007/3-540-28901-1
85. von Rhein, A., Apel, S., Kästner, C., Thüm, T., Schaefer, I.: The PLA model: on the combination of product-line analyses. In: VaMoS, p. 14 (2013)
86. Rodrigues, G.N., et al.: Modeling and verification for probabilistic properties in software product lines. In: 16th IEEE International Symposium on High Assurance Systems Engineering, HASE 2015, Daytona Beach, FL, USA, 8–10 January 2015, pp. 173–180 (2015)
87. Sayyad, A.S., Menzies, T., Ammar, H.: On the value of user preferences in search-based software engineering: a case study in software product lines. In: ICSE 2013, pp. 492–501 (2013)

88. Schobbens, P.Y., Heymans, P., Trigaux, J.C., Bontemps, Y.: Feature diagrams: a survey and a formal semantics. In: RE 2006, pp. 139–148 (2006)
89. Ter Beek, M., Legay, A., Lluch Lafuente, A., Vandin, A.: A framework for quantitative modeling and analysis of highly (re)configurable systems. IEEE Trans. Softw. Eng., p. 1 (2018). https://doi.org/10.1109/TSE.2018.2853726
90. Tian, Y., Pei, K., Jana, S., Ray, B.: DeepTest: automated testing of deep-neural-network-driven autonomous cars. In: ICSE 2018, pp. 303–314. ACM, New York, NY, USA (2018)
91. Tretmans, J.: Model based testing with labelled transition systems. In: Hierons, R.M., Bowen, J.P., Harman, M. (eds.) Formal Methods and Testing. LNCS, vol. 4949, pp. 1–38. Springer, Heidelberg (2008). https://doi.org/10.1007/978-3-540-78917-8_1. http://www.springerlink.com/index/y390356226x154j0.pdf
92. Tretmans, J.: Model-based testing and some steps towards test-based modelling. In: Bernardo, M., Issarny, V. (eds.) SFM 2011. LNCS, vol. 6659, pp. 297–326. Springer, Heidelberg (2011). https://doi.org/10.1007/978-3-642-21455-4_9
93. Utting, M., Legeard, B.: Practical Model-Based Testing: A Tools Approach. Morgan Kaufmann, San Francisco (2007)
94. Uzuncaova, E., Khurshid, S., Batory, D.: Incremental test generation for software product lines. IEEE Trans. Softw. Eng. **36**(3), 309–322 (2010)
95. Vanhecke, J., Devroey, X., Perrouin, G.: AbsCon : a test concretizer for model-based testing. In: 2019 IEEE Twelfth International Conference on Software Testing, Verification and Validation Workshops (ICSTW), A-MOST 2019. IEEE, Xi'an, China (2019)
96. Vojnar, T., Zhang, L. (eds.): TACAS 2019. LNCS, vol. 11428. Springer, Cham (2019). https://doi.org/10.1007/978-3-030-17465-1

Product Line Verification via Modal Meta Model Checking

Tim Tegeler, Alnis Murtovi, Markus Frohme, and Bernhard Steffen$^{(\boxtimes)}$

Chair for Programming Systems, TU Dortmund University, Dortmund, Germany
{tim.tegeler,alnis.murtovi,markus.frohme,steffen}@cs.tu-dortmund.de

Abstract. Modal Meta Model Checking (*M3C*) is a method and tool supporting meta-level product lining and evolution that comprises both context-free system structure and modal refinement. The underlying Context-Free Modal Transition Systems (CFMTSs) can be regarded as loose specifications of meta models, and modal refinement as a way to increase the specificity of allowed domain specific languages (DSLs) by constraining the range of allowed syntax specifications. Model checking with *M3C* allows one to verify properties specified in a branching-time logic for all DSLs of a given level of specificity in one go. The paper illustrates the impact of *M3C* in an industrial setting where well-formed documents serve as contracts between a provider and its customers in two steps: it establishes CFMTS as a formalism to specify product lines of document description types (DTDs – or related formalisms like JSON schema), and it shows how *M3C*-based product line verification can be used to guarantee that violations of essential well-formedness constraints of a corresponding user document are detected by standard DTD-checkers. The resulting hierarchical product line verification allows Creios GmbH, a service provider for E-commerce systems to provide a wide range of tailored shop applications whose essential business rules are checked by a standard DTD-checker.

Keywords: Modal Transition Systems ·
Context-free/Procedural transition systems · Modal refinement ·
Second-order model checking · Meta model ·
Domain-specific languages · Predicate/property transformers ·
Compositionality · Product lines · Variation · Document description

1 Introduction

Generalizing system validation and control from individual systems to product lines [31] is a topic of my (Bernhard's) heart since the GAIN project on telephony services in 1995/96 with Siemens Nixdorf [35]. Unfortunately, due to certain non-disclosure agreements this work has never been decently published. Stefania Gnesi was one of the first who went in the same direction, first from a testing perspective [6,7] and later [1–4,18] to also use modal transition systems (MTS) [26] in order to capture classes of implementation in one specification. However, her work did not (explicitly) exploit the property-preservation of modal refinement [26] for showing that the successful verification of a property of an MTS

© Springer Nature Switzerland AG 2019
M. H. ter Beek et al. (Eds.): Gnesi Festschrift, LNCS 11865, pp. 313–337, 2019.
https://doi.org/10.1007/978-3-030-30985-5_19

captures all products that can be constructed via refinement – an "inheritance property" which can be regarded as the conceptual backbone of this paper.

An alternative way to impose/control properties beyond single instances is the way of tailored domain specific languages (DSLs): all systems developed in such a language are typically guaranteed to satisfy the properties/constraints imposed by the DSLs' meta model (cf. [38]). Corresponding checks are typically done by parsers, but using context-free model checking [9–11], it is also possible to model check interesting properties of DSLs, whose impact on the individual systems typically increases with the specificity of the considered DSL. [36] proposes an approach that elaborates on the idea to control/guide software evolution and product lining by lifting the software evolution process (in part) to the meta level.

In fact, work on featured transition systems (FTSs) [13–15] can be regarded as an approach in this direction: FTSs are an expressive and concise graphical specification language, and they allow for techniques that help avoiding (some) redundancy when verifying all the corresponding admissible product variants with significant performance gains.[1] However, similarly to Stefania's work, there is no discussion of property preservation along product specialization like the MTS-based inheritance of temporal properties along modal refinement. The work on FTSs rather focuses on expressivity, which contrasts our approach that focuses on simplicity [28]. Our extension towards the meta level maintains all the nice properties known for MTSs, while it introduces property-preserving language refinement: Properties of MTS specifications are inherited for all systems specified as (refined) MTS specifications with additional constraints like, e.g., that declarations have to precede uses. Similarly, all properties of those languages are preserved when adding constraints of the final products, e.g., that every terminating run has to execute a certain action. In our accompanying example this could define a payment feature that guarantees that every complete order process has to pass a payment action.

$M3C$ is a method and tool supporting meta-level product lining and evolution that comprises both context-free system structure and modal refinement [37]. The underlying Context-Free Modal Transition Systems (CFMTSs) can be regarded as loose specifications of meta models, and modal refinement as a way to increase the specificity of allowed DSLs constraining the range of allowed syntax specifications. Model checking with $M3C$ allows one to verify properties specified in a branching-time logic for all DSLs of a given level of specificity in one go. For example see Fig. 1 where the initial CFMTS contains two may transitions (a and c). In the following CFTS these transitions are either turned into must transitions or eliminated.

In this paper we illustrate the impact of $M3C$ in an industrial setting where well-formed documents serve as contracts between a provider and its customers. In our setup CFMTSs serve as a formalism to specify product lines of document description types (DTDs – or related formalisms like JSON schema) and $M3C$

---

[1] Our meta tooling suite CINCO [29] would, indeed, be ideally suited to generate an FTS-based development environment.

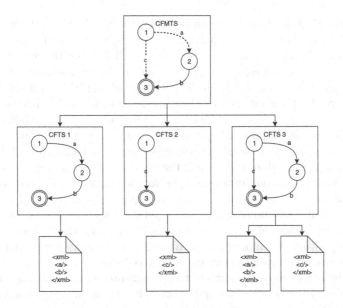

Fig. 1. Example of CFMTS with CFTS refinements and XML documents

as a method to verify that the specified product lines satisfy essential well-formedness constraints. Each user document (see XML documents in Fig. 1) that conforms to one of the corresponding document description types (i.e. to a product of the product line) has certain guaranteed properties.

The functioning and impact of this hierarchical approach to product line verification may become clearer when looking at a concrete example:

- The product line specification may describe certain online-shop applications for selling customized print goods.[2]
- Typical properties concern configuration constraints, e.g., business cards will always be guaranteed to have 120 g grammage (paper density), and business constraints, like that goods are only shipped when the payment is confirmed in the document.

In this setting, the shipping requirement may be regarded as a general policy binding for all products, whereas the property concerning business cards may only be true for certain shops.[3]

Please note, that the properties verified for DTDs (and therefore for their corresponding online shops) via $M3C$ at the meta-level automatically guarantee that corresponding violations within a print good document are automatically detected

---

[2] We avoid the standard notion print product here in order to avoid confusion: the products of the product line are shop applications which allow customers to configure their print goods.

[3] It is accidental that it holds for the four products discussed in Sect. 4.1.

by standard DTD-checkers. This can be exploited, e.g., by Creios GmbH[4] to provide a wide range of tailored shop applications whose essential business rules are automatically checked without requiring to install any additional checking software for the customer. Responsible for this fact is the approach to turn essential properties into what we call *rigid archimedean points* in [38], i.e. into primary language features that are enforced by the underlying meta model. The (meta) DSL for specifying the print good DSLs and its corresponding graphical IDE described in this paper was developed with our meta tooling suite CINCO [29].

Technically, $M3C$ is based on second-order model checking [9–11] which determines how procedure calls *affect* the validity of the properties of interest. The corresponding second-order analysis for determining the predicate transformers (the effects) for the individual procedures is characterized by its hierarchical fixpoint iteration: a higher-level iteration for exchanging approximate predicate transformers of the involved procedures, and a (local) lower level iteration for updating the individual predicates transformers on the basis of the current approximate transformers for the procedures.

The inherent compositionality of the second-order approach leads to a runtime complexity linear in the size of the procedural system representation, whose corresponding transition systems typically have infinitely many states. In fact, second-order model checking can be regarded as a means to tame state explosion via "procedural abstraction", a technique which may well be beneficial also for regular (recursion-free) systems: during higher-level iterations, entire subsystems are just considered as predicate transformers, i.e., as second-order versions of the predicate abstractions introduced in [22].

Abstraction, the art of focusing on the essential details, is also a guiding principle for modal refinement. In a sense, the may transitions of MTSs can be regarded as a form of don't-care-transition, providing future implementations with a freedom of choice, which may profitably be used for optimization or future system evolution. The fact that modal refinement supports a notion of property-preserving abstraction in the sense of [27] allows one to cover even infinite classes of implementations with one check or to minimize given implementations in a don't-care fashion along the lines of [21, 23, 24].

Outline. We continue with introducing formal notions and definitions in Sect. 2 and present the model-checking concepts of $M3C$ in Sect. 3. Section 4 presents the use-case of Creios GmbH and how our $M3C$ approach can be used to verify product line properties in an industrial environment. Section 5 concludes the paper.

2   Preliminaries

In this section we recall *Context-Free Modal Transition Systems* (CFMTSs) which extend *Modal Transition Systems* (MTSs) to mutually recursive systems of

---

[4] https://www.creios.net.

MTSs [37][5] and the considered property language, the (alternation-free) modal μ-calculus.

2.1   Context-Free Modal Transition Systems

MTSs and their extension with mutual recursion presented in this section come with a notion of refinement that establishes a powerful specification-implementation relation. They allow one to model check properties at the specification-level that are then guaranteed to hold for each implementation.

Definition 1 (Modal Transition Systems [25]). *Let S be a set of states and Act an alphabet of action symbols. $M = (S, s_0, Act, \dashrightarrow, \longrightarrow)$ is called a (rooted) Modal Transition System (MTS) with root s_0 if the following condition holds:*

$$\longrightarrow \,\subseteq\, \dashrightarrow \,\subseteq\, (S \times Act \times S)$$

Elements of $\dashrightarrow$ are called may transitions, those of $\longrightarrow$ must transitions. As usual, we will write $s \xrightarrow{a} s'$ iff $(s, a, s') \in \longrightarrow$ and $s \xrightarrow{a}$ to abbreviate $\exists s'.\, s \xrightarrow{a} s'$, $s \overset{a}{\dashrightarrow} s'$ and $s \overset{a}{\dashrightarrow}$ are defined analogously.

MTSs denote sets of *Labeled Transition Systems* (LTSs), which can simply be defined as MTS where all transitions are *must* transitions. Modal refinement, the corresponding specification-implementation relation, defines these sets as the minimal elements of the refinement ordering:

Definition 2 (MTS refinement [25]). *Let $M_1 = (S_1, s_0^1, Act_1, \dashrightarrow_1, \longrightarrow_1)$, $M_2 = (S_2, s_0^2, Act_2, \dashrightarrow_2, \longrightarrow_2)$ be two MTSs. A relation $\leq_r \,\subseteq\, (S_1 \times S_2)$ is called a refinement if the following holds for all $(p, q) \in \leq_r$:*

1. $\forall (p, a, p') \in \dashrightarrow_1, \exists (q, a, q') \in \dashrightarrow_2 : (p', q') \in \leq_r$
2. $\forall (q, a, q') \in \longrightarrow_2, \exists (p, a, p') \in \longrightarrow_1 : (p', q') \in \leq_r$

An MTS M_1 refines an MTS M_2, written $M_1 \leq_r M_2$, if there exists a refinement $\leq_r$ with $(s_0^1, s_0^2) \in \leq_r$. Intuitively, refinement is closed under node-splitting/duplication of states and allows may transitions to be either turned into must transitions or to be eliminated, while it requires all must transitions to be maintained. Like *bisimulation*, it preserves all temporal properties of finite state systems [26]. In fact, the restriction to finite state is not essential for the induction proof along the structure of the temporal formulas, which makes modal refinement an ideal tool for product line verification also for the here considered infinite state case.

The following notion of procedural modal transition systems (PMTSs) extends MTSs to comprise *call transitions* that allows one to define mutually recursive sets of MTSs, later formalized as Context-Free Modal Transition Systems (CFMTSs).

---

[5] Alternatively, one can regard CFMTSs also as an extension of Context-Free Process Systems [9] to also allow *may transitions*.

Definition 3 (Procedural Modal Transition Systems). *A procedural modal transition system is defined as* $P = (\Sigma_P, Trans := Act \cup N, \dashrightarrow_P, \longrightarrow_P, \sigma_P^s, \sigma_P^e)$, *where:*

- *Σ_P is a set of state classes,*
- *$Trans := Act \cup N$ is a set of transformations (Act is a set of actions, N is a set of procedure names),*
- *$\longrightarrow_P := \longrightarrow_P^{Act} \cup \longrightarrow_P^N$ is the must transition relation*
- *$\dashrightarrow_P := \dashrightarrow_P^{Act} \cup \dashrightarrow_P^N$ is the may transition relation,*
  where $\longrightarrow_P^{Act} \subseteq \dashrightarrow_P^{Act} \subseteq \Sigma_P \times Act \times \Sigma_P$ and $\longrightarrow_P^N \subseteq \dashrightarrow_P^N \subseteq \Sigma_P \times N \times \Sigma_P$
- *$\sigma_P^s \in \Sigma_P$ is a class of start states and $\sigma_P^e \in \Sigma_P$ is a class of end states.*

A procedural MTS can be seen as an MTS that is extended by the possibility of having transitions whose effect is described by another MTS. For technical reasons, we require a PMTS P to satisfy the following two constraints:

1. The class of *end states* σ_P^e must be terminating in P, i.e. $\sigma_P^e \overset{\alpha}{\dashrightarrow}$ does not hold.
2. P must be guarded, i.e. all initial transitions of P must be labeled with atomic actions.

Definition 4 (Context-Free Modal Transition Systems (CFMTSs)). *A context-free modal transition system is a quadruple $P = (N, Act, C, P_0)$, where:*

- *$N := \{N_0, \ldots, N_{n-1}\}$ is a set of names,*
- *Act is a set of actions,*
- *$C := \{N_i = PMTS_i \mid 0 \le i < n\}$ is a finite set of PMTS definitions where $PMTS_i$ is a finite PMTS with name $N_i \in N$ and*
- *P_0 is the main PMTS. Moreover we denote $\Sigma = \bigcup_{i=0}^{n-1} \Sigma_{P_i}$, $\longrightarrow = \bigcup_{i=0}^{n-1} \longrightarrow_{P_i}$ and $\dashrightarrow = \bigcup_{i=0}^{n-1} \dashrightarrow_{P_i}$.*

As detailed in [9,19,20],[6] CFMTSs serve as finite representations of the complete, typically infinite-state expansion of the corresponding main PMTS P_0.

2.2   The Alternation-Free Modal μ-Calculus

The *modal μ-calculus* is a branching-time logic that is used to specify properties of transition systems. Characteristic are its greatest fixed point operator ν and a least fixed point operator μ that provide an enormous expressive power, however at the price of increased intricacy [8].

Let Var be a (countable) set of variables, AP a set of atomic propositions and Act a set of Actions. Furthermore let $X \in Var$, $A \in AP$ and $a \in Act$. The syntax is then given by the following Backus-Naur form:

$$\phi ::= A \mid X \mid \phi \vee \phi \mid \phi \wedge \phi \mid \langle a \rangle \phi \mid [a]\phi \mid \nu X.\phi \mid \mu X.\phi.$$

---

[6] In [19,20] a conceptually similar structure to CFMTSs is called *Systems of Procedural Automata* (SPAs) to better match the terminology used in the field of automata learning.

The semantics are given with respect to an MTS $(S, Act, \dashrightarrow, \longrightarrow)$, a valuation V which maps atomic propositions to subset of states of S and an environment e, mapping variables to subsets of S. The semantic function $[\![\cdot]\!]_e$ maps a formula to the set of states which satisfy the formula [9].

$$[\![A]\!]_e = V(A)$$
$$[\![X]\!]_e = e(X)$$
$$[\![\phi_1 \vee \phi_2]\!]_e = [\![\phi_1]\!]_e \cup [\![\phi_2]\!]_e$$
$$[\![\phi_1 \wedge \phi_2]\!]_e = [\![\phi_1]\!]_e \cap [\![\phi_2]\!]_e$$
$$[\![\langle a \rangle \phi]\!]_e = \{s \mid \exists s'.s \xrightarrow{a} s' \wedge s' \in [\![\phi]\!]_e\}$$
$$[\![[a]\phi]\!]_e = \{s \mid \forall s'.s \overset{a}{\dashrightarrow} s' \wedge s' \in [\![\phi]\!]_e\}$$
$$[\![\nu X.\phi]\!]_e = \bigcup\{T \subseteq S \mid T \subseteq [\![\phi]\!]_{e[X:=T]}\}$$
$$[\![\mu X.\phi]\!]_e = \bigcap\{T \subseteq S \mid [\![\phi]\!]_{e[X:=T]} \subseteq T\}$$

Thus an atomic proposition A is true in a state s if $s \in V(A)$, s satisfies X if $s \in e(X)$, and conjunction and disjunction are defined as usual. Special are the *diamond*-operator $\langle a \rangle$ and *box*-operator $[a]$. The diamond-operator is true if there exists a $s' \in S$ with $s \xrightarrow{a} s'$ that satisfies ϕ, while the box-operator is true if all successors of s that are connected by an edge labeled by the action a satisfy ϕ.

The modal μ-calculus is not very "user friendly". On the other hand, it is a very good basis for a tool as many more convenient temporal logics, like CTL, can easily be expressed in the μ-calculus [12,17]. This property is, e.g., also exploited by KandISTI[7] [5], the model checker suite of Stefania's research group.

3   Model Checking Context-Free Modal Transition System

In this section we sketch the approach of [37] for extending the second-order model checking algorithm described in [9] to capture CFMTSs. Like there, our algorithmic description also requires the representation of the modal μ-calculus formulas that serve as input in terms of hierarchical equational systems.

3.1   Hierarchical Equational Systems

Hierarchical equational systems are composed of equational blocks which, due to the underlying hierarchy, can be evaluated in a hierarchical fashion.

Definition 5 (Equational Block [9]). *An equational block has one of two forms, $min\{E\}$ or $max\{E\}$, where E is a list of (mutually recursive) equations*

$$X_1 = \phi_1, \ldots, X_n = \phi_n$$

---

[7] http://fmt.isti.cnr.it/kandisti/.

where $\phi_1, \ldots, \phi_n$ are basic formulas, i.e., can be written using the following grammar:

$$\phi^{basic} ::= A \mid X \vee X \mid X \wedge X \mid \langle a \rangle X \mid [a]X$$

The set of all variables X_i appearing in a block B are denoted by V_B, or simply by V in case B is clear from the context.

Min-blocks are used for capturing the least fixed point operator and Max-blocks for capturing the greatest fixed point operator, respectively. An *equational system* is a list of equational blocks $B = (B_1, \ldots, B_m)$ where the variables appearing on the left-hand side of some block are all distinct.

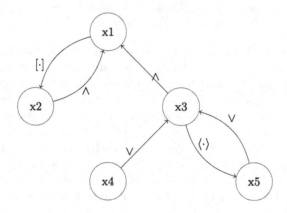

Fig. 2. Dependency graph of the equational system of ϕ

Example 1. Let $\phi = \nu X.[\cdot]X \wedge (\mu Y.A \vee \langle \cdot \rangle Y)$. The formula ϕ specifies that "it is always possible that A will hold". The dot '$\cdot$' specifies that the box-/diamond-operator holds regardless of the transition label. In CTL we could express this as AG EF A [8]. The equational system consists of two blocks. We need one block for greatest fixed point νX and one for the least fixed point μY. The equational system corresponding to ϕ then looks as follows:

$$max\{ \; X_1 = X_2 \wedge X_3 \qquad\qquad min\{ \; X_3 = X_4 \vee X_5$$
$$X_2 = [\cdot]X_1\} \qquad\qquad\qquad\qquad X_4 = A$$
$$X_5 = \langle \cdot \rangle X_3\}$$

"Hierarchical" in the term hierarchical equational systems means that there are no cyclic dependencies between blocks in the sense defined below:

Definition 6 (Hierarchical Equational System [9]). *An Equational System $B = (B_1, \ldots, B_n)$ is hierarchical if the existence of a left-hand side variable of a block B_j, $1 \leq j \leq n$, appearing in a right-hand side formula of a block B_i implies $i \leq j$.*

The constraint to exclude cyclic dependencies between blocks limits the expressive power of hierarchical equational systems to the alternation-free fragment of the modal μ-calculus [16].

The model checking algorithm presented in the next subsection propagates information between the variables of equational blocks in an ordering reverse to the dependency relation: Fig. 2 shows the dependency graph of the formula $\phi = \nu X.[\cdot]X \wedge (\mu Y.A \vee \langle \cdot \rangle Y)$ presented in the previous example. Please note, that in this graph every loop has an edge labeled with some box or diamond modality, a property of equational systems which we can enforce without loosing expressive power, and which is sufficient to guarantee a hierarchical evaluation/updating strategy for each state. In the following we will therefore assume that the dependency graphs of all equational blocks have this property.

The specification language used to specify the properties in Sect. 4 is CTL (Computation Tree Logic) with slightly extended operators. The label for a diamond or box operator can either be defined over a single transition label $a \in Act$ or over the disjunction of a set of labels. The box operator for e.g. $[a \vee b]\phi$ holds in a state iff all successor states reached by an transition labeled by an 'a' or a 'b' satisfy ϕ.

$$
\begin{aligned}
\phi ::= \; & Act \mid tt \mid ff \mid \phi \wedge \phi \mid \phi \vee \phi \\
& \mid [Act_\vee]\phi \mid \langle Act_\vee \rangle \phi \\
& \mid AG\phi \mid EG\phi \mid AF\phi \mid EF\phi \\
& \mid A(\phi\, U\, \phi) \mid E(\phi\, U\, \phi) \mid A(\phi\, WU\, \phi) \mid E(\phi\, WU\, \phi)
\end{aligned}
$$

It is common knowledge that formulas of this kind can easily be translated into the modal μ-calculus and therefore also in hierarchical equational systems.

3.2 The Second-Order Model Checking Algorithm

(Classical) first-order model checking for a block B computes a mapping that associates each state s of the considered MTS with the subset of V that contains all formulas that are valid at s. This means that model checking computes a fixpoint in the power set lattice 2^V. Second-order model checking lifts the fixpoint computation to the lattice of corresponding (monotonic) predicate transformers $D = 2^V \longrightarrow 2^V$. This allows one to formulate model checking as a fixpoint computation that computes a predicate transformer $PT_\sigma \in D$ for each state class σ of a PMTS P in the considered CFMTS that aggregates the effect of the fragment of P that starts in σ and terminates with P's end state σ_P^e in the following sense: For any $V' \in 2^V$, $PT_\sigma(V')$ is the set of all variables of V that hold at σ in case that all formulas of V' hold at the end state of P. After this fixpoint computation the original model checking problem can be answered for the considered CFMTS simply by checking whether the input formula X_1 lies in $PT_{\sigma_P^e}(V_{deadlock})$, where $V_{deadlock}$ denotes the set of variables that hold for the deadlocked state. For example, for the block whose dependency graph is shown in Fig. 2 this would only be X_4 in case A happens to hold at the considered deadlocked state, otherwise $V_{deadlock}$ would just be the empty set.

In the following we sketch how $PT_{\sigma_P^s}$ can be computed for all CFMTSs P and equational systems E while focusing on the peculiarities of the second-order approach and, in particular, of the implications of allowing also may transitions.

The global structure for hierarchically dealing with hierarchical equational systems in a depth-first fashion is identical to the first-order case. Thus we only need to consider the treatment of blocks in more detail, and we can focus on min blocks only, as the treatment of max blocks is completely dual.

Algorithm 1 shows the classical workset pattern for the corresponding fixpoint computation, which consists of an initialization phase, an iterative update of the property transformers, and the update of the workset.

Initialize the property transformers PT_σ of all state classes σ.
workset $= \Sigma$
while *workset* $\neq \emptyset$ **do**
> LET $\sigma \in$ workset;
> workset $=$ workset$\setminus\{\sigma\}$;
> $PT_\sigma.old = PT_\sigma$;
> $\alpha_1, \ldots \alpha_n =$ outgoing edge labels of σ;
> $PT_\sigma = \diamond^\sigma_{j=1,\ldots,n} PT_{[a_j]} \circ PT_{\sigma_j}$;
> **if** $PT_\sigma \neq PT_\sigma.old$ **then**
> > **if** $\sigma = \sigma^s_{P_i}$ *for some* $i \in N$ **then**
> > > workset $=$ workset $\cup \{\sigma' \mid \sigma' \xrightarrow{P_i} \}$;
> > **end**
> > workset $=$ workset $\cup \{\sigma' \mid \sigma' \xrightarrow{\alpha} \sigma\}$;
> **end**
end

Algorithm 1: Algorithm: Model checking of CFMTSs [9]

The property transformers associated with end states are generally initialized with the identity function, and this setting is maintained during the fixpoint computation. As we are considering min blocks, all other property transformers are initialized to the constant function *false*. Also the update of the workset is simple. As in the classical case of a backward analysis, all predecessors of a state whose property transformer has changed are added to the workset. Special is only the situation for start states. Changes there affect all states that *call* the corresponding PMTS. Thus they must also be added to the workset.

The most intricate part is the iterative update of the property transformers for a state class σ which proceeds in two steps: the determination of the property transformers for the individual choices of σ's outgoing transitions, and the aggregation of the common effect of all these individual property transformers on σ's property transformer.

The property transformer for an outgoing transition $\sigma \xrightarrow{\alpha} \sigma'$ is defined as

$$PT_{[\alpha]} \circ PT_{[\sigma']}$$

where $PT_{[\alpha]}$, the effect of taking step α, is defined as follows:

In case $\alpha = P_i$, we have $PT_{[\alpha]} = PT_{[P_i]} = PT_{\sigma^s_{P_i}}$, i.e., $PT_{[\alpha]}$ is the current approximation of the effect of P_i. Otherwise, i.e., in case $\alpha = a \in Act$, $PT_{[\alpha]}$ is characterized by

$$X_i \in PT_{[\alpha]}(M) \text{ iff } \left\{ \begin{array}{l} \phi_i = \langle a \rangle X_j \text{ and } X_j \in M \text{ and } \xrightarrow{\alpha} \in \longrightarrow \\ \phi_i = [a] X_j \text{ and } X_j \in M \\ \phi_i = [b] X_j \text{ and } b \neq a \end{array} \right\}$$

for $M \subseteq V$ and an equation $X_i = \phi_i$ of block B.

Please note, that may transitions do not contribute when considering diamond-subformulas, as they cannot be guaranteed to exist in an actual implementation. In contrast, box subformulas are insensitive to the nature of may and must transitions.

Finally, the aggregation of the common effect of all the individual property transformers for outgoing transitions on σ's property transformer is defined by the function $(\diamond^\sigma_{i=1,\ldots,k} PT_i(M)) = M'$ which is characterized by

$$X_j \in M' \text{ iff } \left\{ \begin{array}{ll} \phi_j = A & \text{and } \sigma \in V(A) \\ \phi_j = X_{j_1} \wedge X_{j_2} & \text{and } (X_{j_1} \in M' \text{ and } X_{j_2} \in M') \\ \phi_j = X_{j_1} \vee X_{j_2} & \text{and } (X_{j_1} \in M' \text{ or } X_{j_2} \in M') \\ \phi_j = \langle a \rangle \psi & \text{and } \exists.1 \leq i \leq k \text{ with } X_j \in \boldsymbol{PT_i}(M) \\ \phi_j = [a] \psi & \text{and } \forall.1 \leq i \leq k \text{ with } X_j \in PT_i(M) \end{array} \right\}$$

for $M \subseteq V$, equations $X_j = \phi_j$ of B, and the convention that property transformers belonging to outgoing must transitions are emphasized in bold face (see line four). Like before, also here only the diamond subformulas are sensitive to the distinction between may and must transitions.

4 Verifying Software Product Lines Using $M3C$

In this section, we show how our $M3C$ approach can be used in practice to verify software properties over product lines. For this example, we especially focus on software for data processing, i.e. software that either collects some kind of data or transforms existing data. Characteristic of this kind of software is that it produces some form of document that is consumed by subsequent software processes within a larger workflow. For a successful execution it is required that the created documents adhere to certain constraints. This often not only includes syntactical properties (e.g. the documents' content must be encoded in XML or JSON) but also semantic properties (i.e. no data should be missing, data should be verified or documented, etc.).

In the following, we first present the concept of *document-driven process verification*, which describes our approach to handle the importance of data integrity/document integrity. We motivate our example by the real-world use case of Creios GmbH, which is a german service provider for E-commerce systems. After presenting the specifics of their data aggregation process, we present how the required properties can be modeled via CFMTSs and how the $M3C$ approach can be used to guarantee required properties over software products.

4.1 Document-Driven Process Verification

The main task of the software systems discussed in this example is the aggregation of data for either further processing or storage. Key requirement for a successful completion of this task is, that the aggregated document adheres to certain syntactical constraints (e.g. file-format) as well as semantic constraints (e.g. order contains an unique identifier). To leverage this emphasis on data integrity, we introduce the concept of *document-driven process verification*:

Instead of describing the actual process of aggregating the data, we use CFMTSs to describe the syntactical meta-structure of the documents that the software should produce and use *M3C* to verify semantic properties on these documents. We see multiple benefits in this approach:

Abstraction from syntactical details. Instead of directly specifying the explicit document structure (e.g. XML or JSON), we introduce a layer of abstraction in which the actions of the CFMTSs represent *abstract* structural elements. Consequently, we use CFMTSs to describe the meta-structure of documents. To yield an explicit specification for a software product, we exploit the fact, that many of the prominent file formats provide syntactical validation frameworks. For example, the context-free meta specification described in a CFMTSs may be easily translated into a document type definition (DTD) for XML documents. In a similar fashion, translating the meta specification into a JSON schema definition would automatically yield a parser for JSON documents.

While we are still able to describe arbitrary context-free document structures, any syntactical details (such as the well-matchedness of XML tags) do not matter on the meta-level as this property is guaranteed by the respective, format-specific document validator. Instead, due to our abstraction, we can ignore these syntactical details and focus on the semantic structure of the resulting documents, which will be subject to our *M3C* verification.

Loose coupling of software and documents. Nowadays, it is expected that software adapts to changing requirements. The trend of agile software development endorses this approach. Modern software architectures (e.g. microservices and self-contained systems) and especially the practice of continuous software engineering aim at rapid develop and deployment cycles [30,32]. This results in quickly evolving software and enlarging systems. Our approach enables to react to those chances by having a loose coupling of software and documents. While the implementation of processes can change, the resulting documents and especially their properties have to stay consistent.

Guaranteeing correctness for further processing. Especially for E-Commerce systems, having correct documents (i.e. orders) is crucial. Not only further processing like manufacturing and delivery processes build upon correct data, but also national institutions like finance authorities. For example the german law demands consecutively numbered invoice numbers. Our approach can easily verify and guarantee such requirements.

4.2   Example

Our example is motivated by the real-world company Creios GmbH. This company is primarily specializing in custom tailored E-commerce systems for professional printing of business equipment (e.g. envelopes, letter paper and business cards). The E-commerce system targets business-to-business relationships, where Creios GmbH is responsible to develop and operate the system for customers. Every instance is based upon the same code base but custom tailored for the requirements of the customer. This results in a product line with various features and properties. With growing numbers of customers also the E-commerce systems become more complex over time. A system like that is hard to maintain while documents (e.g. orders) produced by processes have to stay correct. The $M3C$ approach is ideal to support the further development.

Ontology. In our example we present the order process, one of the central components of the E-commerce system. Guaranteeing correctness of an order is crucial. This section introduces the ontology of the order process to define properties and relations between the entities. It contains a lot of different entities, but we will focus just on the most important ones for simplicity. The major entities are ORDER, CART, ITEM, PRODUCT, DATA, CHECK, DELIVERY and PRIVACY.

- ORDER: Top level entity and condenses all other entities.
  - validated: Proof that the order was successfully validated.
- CART: Summarizes one or more ITEMs.
- ITEM: Stores the amount and the price of a PRODUCT.
  - amount: How many objects of the product are ordered.
  - price: Price of all requested products of the given type.
- PRODUCT: Can be personalized and purchased.
  - business_card: Product that can be purchased.
  - colored: Product should be color printed.
  - embossing: Product has a special embossing (e.g. for the logo)
  - envelope: Product that can be purchased.
  - letter_paper: Product that can be purchased.
  - sealed: Envelope can be sealed.
  - 120g: Higher grammage of the paper for premium products.
- DATA: Used to personalize a PRODUCT.
  - position: Job position a person owned in a company.
  - title: Academic title of a person.
  - first_name: First name of a person.
  - last_name: Last name of a person.
  - email: Email address of a person.
  - chk: Verification of user-provided data.
- CHECK: Documents that an ORDER is valid.
  - escalation: Order has to be validated by a supervisor.
  - nok: The order is not validated.
  - ok: The order is validated.

- DELIVERY: Summarizes the shipping of an order.
  - appointment: The appointment to pick up the order in house.
  - express: Shipping has high priority.
  - in_house: Shipping is picked up in house.
  - deadline: Latest shipping date for an express shipment.
  - default: Shipping has normal priority.
- PRIVACY: Documents the decision of an user if personal data can be stored or should be deleted.
  - address: The personal data to process the shipment.
  - keep_data: Decision that the personal data can be stored.
  - consent: The consent of the user to store the data.
  - delete_data: Personal data has to be deleted.

Product Line Refinement. We begin demonstrating our hierarchical product line (Fig. 4) with the weakest modal specification in Fig. 3. In this weakest modal specification every procedure has the same basic structure. For reasons of clarity we refrain from displaying every procedure on its own. ORDER serves as an example for the omitted procedures (CART, ITEM, PRODUCT, DATA, CHECK, DELIVERY and PRIVACY). The ORDER model only contains a single *final* state whose outgoing transitions are all self-loops. Note, that for this presentation we use a more compact MTS visualization, whereas our $M3C$ model checker used the corresponding adapted models, with e.g. only a single *final* state without any outgoing transitions, etc.

While the weakest specification does not allow to verify any of the semantic properties, the nature of translating our CFMTS to a syntactic validator, guarantees syntactic validity. Even in the weakest semantic case, our approach allows full syntactical verification (e.g. well-matched XML tags in case of a DTD validator). Consequently, the following refinements allow to solely focus on semantic aspects of the document. The abstract specification in Fig. 5 already satisfies properties of interest and therefore guarantees the validity of these properties in all of its refinements. The functionality of each procedure has already been described in Sect. 4.2. It serves as a basis for the refinements which will be described in the following.

Fig. 3. The ORDER procedure within the weakest specification (WS)

The following four refinements, PREMIUM, PICKUP, DEFAULT and DELIVERY, each draw attention to a different aspect of a webshop.

The PREMIUM refinement is characterized as the abstract specification PRODUCT procedure is defined as seen in Fig. 6. The procedure is refined such that each option for each product, i.e. business_card, envelope and letter_paper, can be chosen. A letter paper can for example be colored, embossed and use paper with 120 grams per square meter.

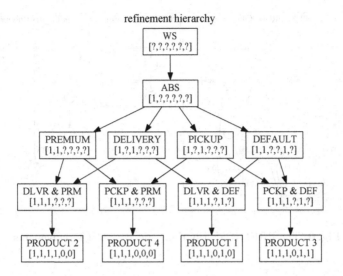

Fig. 4. Refinement ordering of the variations

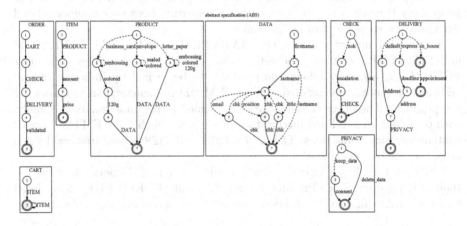

Fig. 5. The abstract specification

The PICKUP, DEFAULT and DELIVERY refinements are defined analogously. The PICKUP refinement characterizes webshops which only offer the products to be picked up by the customer and there is no option to ship the products to the customer.

The DEFAULT refinement can be regarded as the complement of the PREMIUM refinement as it offers no additional options for the products, i.e. the may transitions `embossing`, `colored`, `sealed` and `120g` are omitted in this refinement.

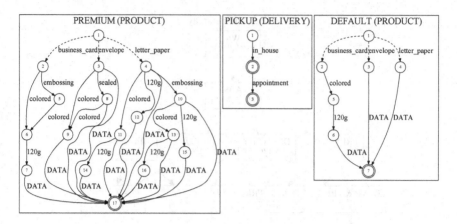

Fig. 6. The PREMIUM, PICKUP and DEFAULT refinements

The DELIVERY refinement in Fig. 7 adapted the PRIVACY and DELIVERY procedures. In contrast to the PICKUP refinement, products can only be shipped either as default or express and they cannot be picked up by the customer. The keep_data transition is here set to a must transition because customer related data must be stored within the document.

Four additional refinements, i.e. DLVR&PRM, PCKP&PRM, DLVR&DEF and PCKP&DEF combine the refinements described above. The refinement PCKP&PRM e.g. only allows the products to be picked up in-house and all additional features, as described in the PREMIUM refinement, can be chosen for the products. The other combinations are defined in the same manner. Finally, each combination is refined further to a product in which the CFMTS does not contain any may transitions. The ORDER, CART and ITEM procedures are defined as in the abstract specification.

Product 1 in Fig. 8 offers business cards, with no additional features, as their only product. Since Product 1 is a refinement of DELIVERY, the ordered business cards can only be shipped and not be picked up in-store. As the may

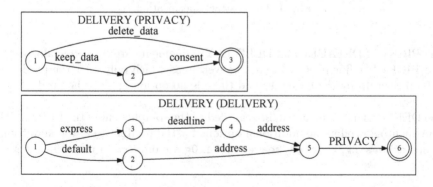

Fig. 7. The DELIVERY refinement

transition **nok** within the **CHECK** procedure is set to a must transition, it is possible that certain orders must first be approved and this approval must be documented. The **DATA** procedure states that the data input for the product must at least contain the first and last name and in addition either two titles, an email address or the position within the company can be input.

The second product is derived from the DLVR&PRM refinement. It offers business cards and envelopes as their product and the **CHECK**, **DELIVERY** and **PRIVACY** are defined in the same manner as in the first product. Compared to Product 1 the **DATA** procedure allows for more information to be input.

Figure 10 shows the LTSs of Product 3 and Product 4. They are both derived from the PICKUP refinement and therefore only offer the ordered products to be picked up in-house. Product 3 is the most basic shop. It does not require the order to be approved and the only data which must and can be input is the first and last name. Product 4 differs from Product 1 only in the aspect that the business cards cannot be shipped and can only be picked up.

In the following the impact of the refinements will be illustrated by means of properties specified by CTL formulas. While some properties can already be verified for the abstract specification and therefore for all of its refinements, some properties only hold for the products.

Properties to Verify. When maintaining software for different customers through a product line, challenges arise. It is crucial that every software product satisfies the features requested by the customer while the main (integral) properties stay intact. We will illustrate the corresponding impact of $M3C$ using six exemplary properties.

(A) Since further processing relies on correct orders we ensure that every order is validated.
(B) Business cards are premium products that are intended for repeated use. Therefore they are printed typically on paper with higher grammage.
(C) Picking "default" or "express" as the delivery option requires the customer to input information about his address. Because address information are personal the company must have the user's consent to save this information for later reuse.
(D) The E-commerce system offers the complete range of products requested by a customer, like business equipment for correspondence.
(E) Embossing and sealed are options only available in premium instances. Both options require more complex manufacturing processes.
(F) Products of customers (e.g. letter papers) can have certain design guidelines (i.e. corporate identity) that regulates which information is allowed to be printed.

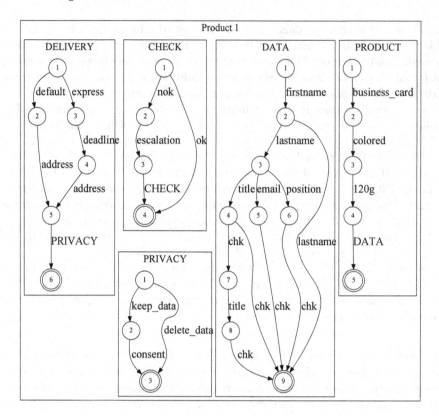

Fig. 8. Product 1

We are going to use these six discussed properties as input for the specification of the various refinements, seen in Fig. 4. The same figure also summarizes the corresponding model checking results. A question mark indicates that it is unknown whether the formula holds in this system as refinements exist in which the property holds but there are also refinements which do not satisfy the property. As can be seen the products do not have any question marks in their row as they do not contain any may transitions and can therefore not be refined further.

(A) $\mathbf{A}(\neg validated\,\mathbf{WU}\,ok)$

Since further processing relies on correct orders we ensure that every order is validated. While the first property (A) does not hold within the weakest specification, it does hold in the abstract specification and thus in all of its refinements. The property specifies that it is not possible to perform a **validated** transition until an **ok** is seen. The **validated** transition can be regarded as the end of the document which should not be reachable until the order has been approved by an **ok**.

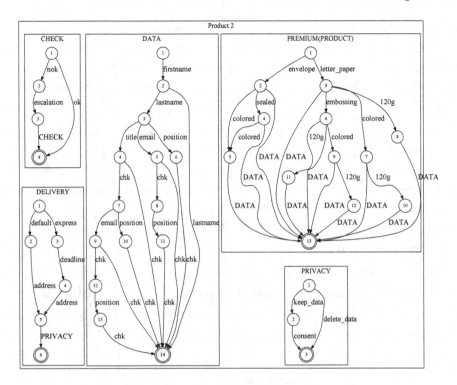

Fig. 9. Product 2

(B) **AG**[*business_card*](**AF** 120*g*)

Business cards are premium products that are intended for repeated use and therefore printed typically on paper with higher grammage. The second property specifies that whenever a transition labeled by business_card is seen, the option 120g will always be picked for the business_card. The reason that this property does not hold in some of the refinements is that it is possible to infinitely often choose embossing and never reach the 120g transition.

(C) (**AG**[*default* ∨ *express*](**EF**⟨*keep_data*⟩*consent*))

The DELIVERY and PICKUP refinements are separated from the PRE-MIUM and DEFAULT refinements by the third property which states that whenever a transition labeled by default or express is seen, it is possible that a transition labeled by keep_data is seen which is then followed by a consent transition. Since picking default or express as the delivery option requires the customer to input information about his address, the company must have the user's consent to save this information.

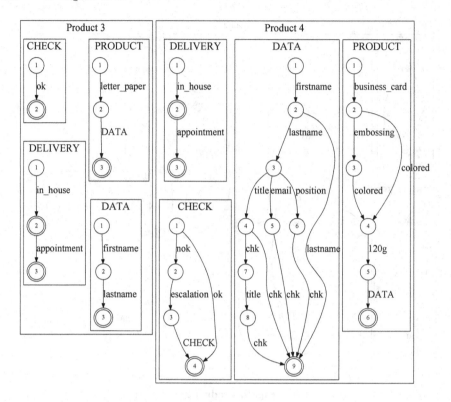

Fig. 10. Product 3 & 4

(D) (**EF** *letter_paper*) ∧ (**EF** *envelope*)

Property (D) specifies that the E-commerce system is guaranteed to offer both, `letter_paper` and `envelope`, as their products. This property can only hold in refinements in which the `letter_paper` and `envelope` transitions within the PRODUCT procedure are must transitions. As seen in Fig. 4 this only holds for Product 2 because Product 1 does not offer envelopes and Product 3 offers neither of them. In all other refinements the transitions labeled by `letter_paper` and `envelope` are may transitions and thus not guaranteed to exist in actual products.

(E) **AG**(¬*embossing* ∧ ¬*sealed*)

Embossing and sealed are options only available in premium web shops, because they require more complex manufacturing processes. The fifth property is satisfied by a refinement if `embossing` and `sealed` are not possible options within the refinement. This is the case for the DEFAULT system and all of its refinements as DEFAULT does not offer these options.

(F) **AG**($\neg email \wedge \neg title \wedge \neg position$)

Products of customers (e.g. letter papers) can have certain design guidelines (i.e. corporate identity) that regulates which information is allowed to be printed. Property (F) states that email, title and position are no information that will be stored within the document. This property is satisfied only by Product 3 which offers letter papers as the only product and the data needed for this consists of the first and last name.

Technical Note. As we have mentioned in Sect. 3, there are well-known problems in expressing certain properties for LTSs in branching-time logic [33, 34]: Our intention to say that ok must have definitely happened before validated happens (property (A)) cannot be expressed in our branching-time logic, as there is no state, e.g. in product 1, for which we can say that ok will definitely happen, as there is always the possibility to (indefinitely) expand the recursion branch. That is, the corresponding formula **A**($\neg validated$ **WU** ok) (where we use ok as a "derived" atomic proposition for states where ok will definitely happen in the next step) is invalid, even though from the linear-time perspective, it is clear that we cannot reach validated without going through ok. As we are only interested in the linear-time perspective and use branching-time logic only for technical reasons, i.e. for having efficient context-free model checking, we solve this problem by transforming the CFMTS into a *precondition* CFMTS [33, 34], which introduces additional helper states that allow us to prove the intended property. Figure 11 illustrates this simple model transformation for the check procedure of product 1, which now has a state where the atomic proposition ok is true. Please note, that the proof of equivalence for this transformation is out of scope for this paper.

We decided to not force the modelers to provide precondition models and to apply the corresponding transformations automatically on demand for simplicity

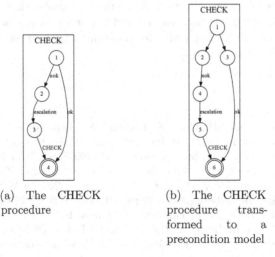

(a) The CHECK procedure

(b) The CHECK procedure transformed to a precondition model

Fig. 11. Transformation to a precondition model

reasons [28]. We consider it a good compromise to not clutter the models from the modeler's perspective and to be nevertheless able to use the efficient model checking procedure.

5   Conclusion

In this paper we have illustrated the impact of Modal Meta Model Checking ($M3C$) in an industrial setting where well-formed documents serve as contracts between the provider and its customers. The point of the presented $M3C$-based approach is that it exploits the well-formedness constraints of the required documents as requirement specification at two levels:

- During the design of the products of Creios GmbH in order to guarantee essential properties of the shop applications, and
- at print good definition time, i.e when the customers of Creios GmbH configure their print goods.

The point of this approach is that print good configurations passing the check of a standard DTD-checker are guaranteed to obey the intended business constraints. In addition, using CFMTS as specification language allows one to apply this approach not only to individual products, but to entire product lines as has been illustrated in Sect. 4. Technically, the paper is special in that it exploits the leeway in the linear-time/branching time spectrum: It uses model transformations (hidden from the user) that preserve a linear-time semantics to subsequently apply an efficient branching-time algorithm in order to allow simple user-level specifications that can be efficiently verified (only) after the transformation. This approach is correct as we only need to preserve the linear-time semantics. It is our experience that the document-based specifications are a good basis for narrowing the so-called semantic gap, in particular when using adequate DSLs for their specification. As mentioned above, these DSLs may look quite different for different stakeholders, and in particular for the model checker. In fact, for the user level often a simple constraint language should be sufficient, and models may not be required at all.

References

1. Asirelli, P., ter Beek, M.H., Gnesi, S., Fantechi, A.: Formal description of variability in product families. In: 2011 15th International Software Product Line Conference, pp. 130–139, August 2011. https://doi.org/10.1109/SPLC.2011.34
2. Asirelli, P., ter Beek, M.H., Fantechi, A., Gnesi, S.: A logical framework to deal with variability. In: Méry, D., Merz, S. (eds.) IFM 2010. LNCS, vol. 6396, pp. 43–58. Springer, Heidelberg (2010). https://doi.org/10.1007/978-3-642-16265-7_5
3. Asirelli, P., ter Beek, M.H., Fantechi, A., Gnesi, S.: A model-checking tool for families of services. In: Bruni, R., Dingel, J. (eds.) FMOODS/FORTE -2011. LNCS, vol. 6722, pp. 44–58. Springer, Heidelberg (2011). https://doi.org/10.1007/978-3-642-21461-5_3

4. ter Beek, M.H., Fantechi, A., Gnesi, S., Mazzanti, F.: Modelling and analysing variability in product families: model checking of modal transition systems with variability constraints. J. Log. Algebraic Methods Program. **85**(2), 287–315 (2016). https://doi.org/10.1016/j.jlamp.2015.11.006
5. ter Beek, M.H., Fantechi, A., Gnesi, S., Mazzanti, F.: States and events in KandISTI. In: Margaria, T., Graf, S., Larsen, K.G. (eds.) Models, Mindsets, Meta: The What, the How, and the Why Not? LNCS, vol. 11200, pp. 110–128. Springer, Cham (2019). https://doi.org/10.1007/978-3-030-22348-9_8
6. Bertolino, A., Fantechi, A., Gnesi, S., Lami, G., Maccari, A.: Use case description of requirements for product lines. In: Proceedings of the International Workshop on Requirements Engineering for Product Lines 2002 - REPL 2002. Technical report: ALR2002-033, AVAYA, pp. 12–18 (2002)
7. Bertolino, A., Gnesi, S.: PLUTO: a test methodology for product families. In: van der Linden, F.J. (ed.) PFE 2003. LNCS, vol. 3014, pp. 181–197. Springer, Heidelberg (2004). https://doi.org/10.1007/978-3-540-24667-1_14
8. Blackburn, P., van Benthem, J.F.A.K., Wolter, F.: Handbook of Modal Logic. Studies in Logic and Practical Reasoning, vol. 3. Elsevier Science Inc., New York (2006)
9. Burkart, O., Steffen, B.: Model checking for context-free processes. In: Cleaveland, W.R. (ed.) CONCUR 1992. LNCS, vol. 630, pp. 123–137. Springer, Heidelberg (1992). https://doi.org/10.1007/BFb0084787
10. Burkart, O., Steffen, B.: Pushdown processes: parallel composition and model checking. In: Jonsson, B., Parrow, J. (eds.) CONCUR 1994. LNCS, vol. 836, pp. 98–113. Springer, Heidelberg (1994). https://doi.org/10.1007/978-3-540-48654-1_9
11. Burkart, O., Steffen, B.: Model checking the full modal mu-calculus for infinite sequential processes. Theor. Comput. Sci. **221**(1–2), 251–270 (1999). https://doi.org/10.1016/S0304-3975(99)00034-1
12. Clarke Jr., E.M., Grumberg, O., Peled, D.A.: Model Checking. MIT Press, Cambridge (1999)
13. Classen, A., Cordy, M., Heymans, P., Legay, A., Schobbens, P.Y.: Model checking software product lines with SNIP. Int. J. Softw. Tools Technol. Transfer **14**(5), 589–612 (2012). https://doi.org/10.1007/s10009-012-0234-1
14. Classen, A., Cordy, M., Schobbens, P.Y., Heymans, P., Legay, A., Raskin, J.F.: Featured transition systems: foundations for verifying variability-intensive systems and their application to LTL model checking. IEEE Trans. Software Eng. **39**(8), 1069–1089 (2013). https://doi.org/10.1109/TSE.2012.86
15. Classen, A., Heymans, P., Schobbens, P.Y., Legay, A., Raskin, J.F.: Model checking lots of systems: efficient verification of temporal properties in software product lines. In: Proceedings of the 32nd ACM/IEEE International Conference on Software Engineering, ICSE 2010, vol. 1, pp. 335–344. ACM, New York (2010). https://doi.org/10.1145/1806799.1806850
16. Cleaveland, R., Steffen, B.: A linear-time model-checking algorithm for the alternation-free modal mu-calculus. Form. Methods Syst. Des. **2**(2), 121–147 (1993). https://doi.org/10.1007/BF01383878
17. Emerson, E.A.: Model checking and the mu-calculus. In: DIMACS Series in Discrete Mathematics, pp. 185–214. American Mathematical Society (1997)
18. Fantechi, A., Gnesi, S.: Formal modeling for product families engineering. In: 2008 12th International Software Product Line Conference, pp. 193–202, September 2008. https://doi.org/10.1109/SPLC.2008.45

19. Frohme, M., Steffen, B.: Active mining of document type definitions. In: Howar, F., Barnat, J. (eds.) FMICS 2018. LNCS, vol. 11119, pp. 147–161. Springer, Cham (2018). https://doi.org/10.1007/978-3-030-00244-2_10

20. Frohme, M., Steffen, B.: Compositional Learning of Mutually Recursive Procedural Systems (2018, under submission)

21. Garavel, H., Lang, F., Mounier, L.: Compositional verification in action. In: Howar, F., Barnat, J. (eds.) FMICS 2018. LNCS, vol. 11119, pp. 189–210. Springer, Cham (2018). https://doi.org/10.1007/978-3-030-00244-2_13

22. Graf, S., Saidi, H.: Construction of abstract state graphs with PVS. In: Grumberg, O. (ed.) CAV 1997. LNCS, vol. 1254, pp. 72–83. Springer, Heidelberg (1997). https://doi.org/10.1007/3-540-63166-6_10

23. Graf, S., Steffen, B.: Compositional minimization of finite state systems. In: Clarke, E.M., Kurshan, R.P. (eds.) CAV 1990. LNCS, vol. 531, pp. 186–196. Springer, Heidelberg (1991). https://doi.org/10.1007/BFb0023732

24. Graf, S., Steffen, B., Lüttgen, G.: Compositional minimisation of finite state systems using interface specifications. Formal Aspects Comput. **8**(5), 607–616 (1996). https://doi.org/10.1007/BF01211911

25. Larsen, K.G., Thomsen, B.: A modal process logic. In: Proceedings of the Third Annual Symposium on Logic in Computer Science, pp. 203–210. IEEE (1988). https://doi.org/10.1109/LICS.1988.5119

26. Larsen, K.G.: Modal specifications. In: Sifakis, J. (ed.) CAV 1989. LNCS, vol. 407, pp. 232–246. Springer, Heidelberg (1990). https://doi.org/10.1007/3-540-52148-8_19

27. Loiseaux, C., Graf, S., Sifakis, J., Bouajjani, A., Bensalem, S.: Property preserving abstractions for the verification of concurrent systems. Formal Methods Syst. Des. **6**(1), 11–44 (1995). https://doi.org/10.1007/BF01384313

28. Margaria, T., Steffen, B.: Simplicity as a driver for agile innovation. IEEE Comput. **43**(6), 90–92 (2010). https://doi.org/10.1109/MC.2010.177

29. Naujokat, S., Lybecait, M., Kopetzki, D., Steffen, B.: CINCO: a simplicity-driven approach to full generation of domain-specific graphical modeling tools. STTT **20**(3), 327–354 (2018). https://doi.org/10.1007/s10009-017-0453-6

30. O'Connor, R., Elger, P., Clarke, P.: Continuous software engineering—a microservices architecture perspective. J. Softw. Evol. Process **29** (2017). https://doi.org/10.1002/smr.1866

31. Pohl, K., Böckle, G., van der Linden, F.J.: Software Product Line Engineering. Foundations Principles and Techniques. Springer, Heidelberg (2005). https://doi.org/10.1007/3-540-28901-1

32. Shahin, M., Babar, M.A., Zhu, L.: Continuous integration, delivery and deployment: a systematic review on approaches, tools, challenges and practices. CoRR abs/1703.07019 (2017). http://arxiv.org/abs/1703.07019

33. Steffen, B.: Data flow analysis as model checking. In: Ito, T., Meyer, A.R. (eds.) TACS 1991. LNCS, vol. 526, pp. 346–364. Springer, Heidelberg (1991). https://doi.org/10.1007/3-540-54415-1_54

34. Steffen, B.: Generating data flow analysis algorithms from modal specifications. Sci. Comput. Program. **21**(2), 115–139 (1993). https://doi.org/10.1016/0167-6423(93)90003-8

35. Steffen, B.: Method for Incremental Synthesis of a Discrete Technical System (1998). https://patents.google.com/patent/WO1998024022A1/en

36. Steffen, B., Gossen, F., Naujokat, S., Margaria, T.: Language-driven engineering: from general-purpose to purpose-specific languages. In: Steffen, B., Woeginger, G. (eds.) Computing and Software Science: State of the Art and Perspectives, LNCS, vol. 10000. Springer (2018). https://www.springer.com/gp/book/9783319919072

37. Steffen, B., Murtovi, A.: $M3C$: modal meta model checking. In: Howar, F., Barnat, J. (eds.) FMICS 2018. LNCS, vol. 11119, pp. 223–241. Springer, Cham (2018). https://doi.org/10.1007/978-3-030-00244-2_15

38. Steffen, B., Naujokat, S.: Archimedean points: the essence for mastering change. Trans. Found. Mastering Chang. **1**, 22–46 (2016). https://doi.org/10.1007/978-3-319-46508-1_3

Towards Model Checking Product Lines in the Digital Humanities: An Application to Historical Data

Ciara Breathnach[1], Najhan M. Ibrahim[1], Stuart Clancy[1],
and Tiziana Margaria[2(✉)]

[1] Department of History, Health Research Institute and Lero, Dublin, Ireland
{Ciara.Breathnach,najhan.ibrahim,stuart.clancy}@ul.ie
[2] Department of Computer Science and Information Systems, Lero and HRI,
University of Limerick, Limerick V94 T9PX, Ireland
tiziana.margaria@ul.ie

Abstract. Rapid development in computing techniques and databases' systems have aided in the digitization of, and access to, various historical (big) data, with significant challenges of analysis and interoperability. The Death and Burial Data, Ireland project aims to build a Big Data interoperability framework loosely based on the Knowledge Discovery Data (KDD) process to integrate Civil Registration of Death data with other data types collated in Ireland from 1864 to 1922.

For our project, we resort to a Document Type Description (DTD) product line to represent and manage various representations and enrichments of the data. Well-formed documents serve as contracts between a provider (of the data set) and its customers (the researchers that consult them). We adopt the Context-Free Modal Transition Systems as a formalism to specify product lines of DTDs. The goal is to then proceed to product line verification using context-free model checking techniques, specifically the M3C checker of [14] to ensure that they are fit for purpose. The goal is to later implement and manage the corresponding family of data models and processes in the DIME framework, leveraging its flexible data management layer to define and efficiently manage the interoperable historical data framework for future use.

The resulting hierarchical product line verification will allow our technical platform to act as a high-quality service provider for digital humanities researchers, providing them with a wide range of tailored applications implementing the KDD process, whose essential business rules are easily checked by a standard DTD checker.

Keywords: Digital humanities · Big Data Interoperability · Data integration · Historical data · Product lines · CFMTS · DIME · Workflow processes · Model checking

M. H. ter Beek et al. (Eds.): Gnesi Festschrift, LNCS 11865, pp. 338–364, 2019.
https://doi.org/10.1007/978-3-030-30985-5_20

1 Introduction

Death and Burial Data, Ireland 1864–1922 (DBDIrl), a project funded by the Irish Research Council, is original in its approach as it will be the first national project to create linkages between historical registered deaths and other data types in an open access environment using both an open access framework and open source analytical tools. Vast quantities of *historical Big Data* (hBD) are in the public domain but they exist as silos. Much of it is unstructured or structured in accordance with its original historical ontologies and consequently the data sets cannot naturally interact or are not *interoperable* with one another. Advances in computational power and linked data techniques, which are "a set of best practices for publishing and connecting structured data on the Web" [1], provide extraordinary opportunities to create relationships between disparate data collected for specific purposes. DBDIrl proposes to create and analyze the relationships between individual level historical death and burial data to understand how the concept of Nikolas Rose's (2007) "biological citizenship" [2] advanced in Ireland, and how power dynamics operated regionally and from gendered and religious perspectives. It is to state and judicial instruments of Civil Registration (CR), specifically birth, death and marriage registration, census returns and court records that this project turns as primary sources of Big Data.

Big Data (BD) is simply defined by Graham, Milligan and Weingart (2017) as "more data that you could conceivably read yourself in a reasonable amount of time … information that requires computational intervention to make new sense of it" [3]. We contend that our core data, Civil Registration (CR) of deaths, meets the requirements identified by Graham et al. Over the past few decades these CR data have been digitized in the form of a Microsoft Excel index and corresponding TIFF files containing high resolution scans of the original handwritten documents. Although Rob Kitchin considers the measurement of the "bigness" of BD in terms of its ability to fit in a Microsoft Excel spreadsheet as "a trite proclamation", it is nonetheless a characteristic of the CR data used here [4]. Indeed, we received our raw CR data as a Microsoft Excel index of 4.3 million registered deaths each entry containing 11 fields (see Table 1). Due to the limited functionality of Microsoft Excel to process files in excess of 1 million entries it was necessary to break it into smaller files. BD can be also defined as database/ datasets, which conventional spreadsheet software like Microsoft Excel is unable to handle, process and manipulate. Further to size, BD definitions also encompass the use of data analytics methods to analyze the data and extract information and knowledge from data patterns in given sets of data. We will soon receive a data drop of census records from the National Archives of Ireland, which will be similar in volume to our CR data. Thus we will face a data integration and interoperability challenge: in order to manipulate our hBD, a set of techniques and technologies will be required to integrate and discover potential patterns from these diverse datasets that are in multiple record forms. In this paper we also argue that data interoperability should form a core part of academic discourse on BD frameworks to ensure that large scale digitization projects can take place with reasonable effort. We consider this as a potential longer-term goal, to be tackled in collaboration with computer science experts who work on innovative IT system integration using model-based frameworks.

In this paper, we provide some background about the DBDIrl project (Sect. 2), then briefly describe why it is a case of Big Data analysis (Sect. 3) and the proposed big data interoperability framework for DBDIrl (Sect. 4). We then discuss issues related to the current data representations in the hDB (Sect. 5) introducing and discussing corresponding initial models. Sections 6 and 7 introduce a series of refinements: flat, hierarchical and recursive, together with simple initial product lines. The models here span Transition Systems, Modal Transition Systems and Context-free Modal Transitions Systems. Section 8 is devoted to the formulation of some initial constraints and their model checking. Finally, Sect. 9 draws some reflections and conclusions, in the context of Stefania Gnesi's work.

2   Background

In 1864 CR of births, deaths and marriages (for Roman Catholics) was introduced to Ireland. This involved the collation of large amounts of hand-written personal metadata about individuals and their next of kin. Because of mass Irish emigration in the period under review our initial focus is on death data as it enables us to close off a life course in Ireland, which in turn permits a data verification exercise with other data types like birth registrations, marriages and census returns gathered during the life course. By taking death and burial as key themes this study adopts a *life events* approach to the study of social class, gender and power in Ireland from macro and microhistory perspectives (Ginzburg, 1993) [5]. Table 1 shows an example of the type of information collated at a death registration: number, date and place of death, name and surname, sex, condition (marital status), age last birthday, rank, profession or occupation, certified cause of death and duration of illness, signature, qualification and residence of informant, when registered and signature of informant. It is currently partially indexed online and available to search for free on irishgenealogy.ie by name, civil registration district/office, year range and life event level. For end-users each indexed death is linked to an image (TIFF file) of the original entry and each page can contain up to 10 entries. Users have to solve a Captcha which is followed by an application to search the records on an individual level under section 61 of the Civil Registration Act, 2004. Our aim is to find ways of integrating these categories into domain-specific modeling frameworks as discussed from Sect. 5 onwards.

Table 1. Structure of the Irish Civil Registration data as required by statute (GROdata) [41].

Deaths registered in the District of [ ] in the Union of [ ] in the County of [ ]									
No	Date and place of death	Name and Surname	Sex	Condition	Age last birthday	Rank, Profession or Occupation	Certified Cause of Death and Duration of Illness	Signature, Qualification and Residence of Informant	When registered	Signature of Registrar
1	24 January 1864, 10 High Street, Kingstown	James Green	Male	Married, Bachelor or Widower (as the case may be)	43 Years	Carpenter	Pneumonia, Two months, Certified	Sarah Green, Widow, High Street, present at death	25 January 1864	John Cox, Registrar

In the longer term, we are particularly interested in automating the process of data entry to flesh out the partial index to provide a fuller impression of cause of death data, especially contagious diseases. We intend, with the aid of BD analytics and other tools, to visualize and map our data to street and household level to identify micro epidemics, disease under-reporting and to discuss reasons why these patterns emerge.

Historical data presents many opportunities for breakthroughs in BD science and analytics as it constitutes the necessary components of volume, variety and variability as defined by (NIST Big Data operability Framework, p. 7) [6] although the veracity of the indexed data will need to be quality assured and cleaned to ensure uniformity. The project will initially use a sample from the CR data to create a set of linkages with other data types. One of our first tasks will be the creation of unique URIs for every death entry to ensure the veracity of our work. Among our challenges will be the quality assurance of our data linkages and issues associated with common surnames and the reuse of ancestral first names.

3 Big Data Analysis

In 1996 Fayad et al. argued the urgency of finding new ways and theoretical under-pinnings to deal with the "rapidly growing volumes of digital data". Building on Platesky-Shapiro's 1989 theories they identified Knowledge Discovery Databases (KDD) as a sensible way forward. KDDs quickly became and continue to form the cornerstone of data analytics [7].

BD analysis encompasses the gathering, management and examination of huge datasets from various data sources to discover hidden patterns, unknown correlations, trends preference and other useful information. The hBD that we analyze are not just large in volume, but also complex in their content. BD also has the ability to identify the unique properties of the content (multi-dimension, heterogeneous, unstructured, incomplete, and erroneous) which may require a specific method or approach for typical data types. The advance of technologies makes it possible to collect more data to find more useful information, however the generation of more data means potentially also more ambiguous or abnormal data. Therefore, it is important to find an analytical method to identify relevant particulars of our data for the specific purpose of the research study.

The practice of finding useful information/knowledge in data has been defined broadly as including data mining, knowledge extraction, information discovery, data pattern processing, etc. The KDD approach comes with a multi-phased process [8] encompassing several workflow processes such as data selection, data preprocessing, data transformation, data mining, data interpretations and evaluation as presented in Fig. 1. According to surveys, KDD is one of the most successful approaches to big data management [9]. Applied to our research, an adequate implementation of the KDD approach will enable the development of a complete data analysis cycle that is capable of identifying useful information and knowledge patterns, and make them available to a wider range of researchers through adequate user interfaces.

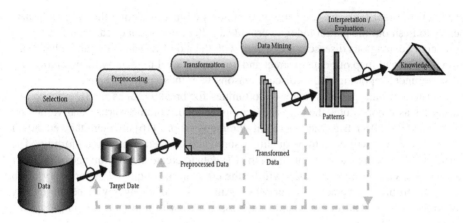

Fig. 1. Knowledge discovery databases (KDD) process [8]

4 The Proposed Big Data Interoperability Framework for DBDIrl

In the hDB context and in particular in our DBDIrl project, we face the central issues of data interoperability across various sources, amenability of data to be analyzed and manipulated automatically, and the need to support in the best way fellow researchers and also the general public to pose more or less specialized queries. In all three aspects, we need to address data modelling issues concerning among others integrity, suitability, compatibility, equivalence, and other more specialized properties. We approach it through a product line approach and by adopting and adapting the meta-model checking techniques introduced in detail in [14].

4.1 Heterogeneous Datasets

Figure 2 shows the heterogeneous dataset for our project. The four main data sources consist of CR Data and Census Data, which are hBD, and Coroners' records and miscellaneous databases, which are smaller data. These data can be further classified as describing life course, life grid, life event and verification data. For example, a death registration combined with a birth provides the parameters of a life course while a comparative analysis of the 1901 and 1911 census can produce a life grid of 10 years. On the other hand, coroners' records and miscellaneous data can enrich the picture of an individual's microhistory by adding other life events or independent verification data. We concentrate in this paper on the discussion of how to deal with the various sources and formats available for the CR data (cf. introduction in Sect. 1). We have yet to determine the census data file type and expect them to be available in a database. Coroners' records are not yet fully digitized, and we have experimented with Text Encoding Initiative to mark up the text in a meaningful way for our research. Several miscellaneous databases available online are likely to be accessible via structured query language (SQL). Therefore, the proposed framework needs to be able to integrate these different types of available data.

The integration process between multiple types of data sources will bring the four main local data models into **one local model aggregation** and then to **one final data model.** CR data will be used to generate the life course data model and Census data will provide a life grid data model. At the same time, coroners' record will lead to a life event data model and miscellaneous sources may provide a verification data model. Ideally, already these 4 distinct models should be crafted in the same technology, to provide the basis for the data integration model of each individual typical data source. The local data aggregation model is the main interoperability engine of the proposed framework. It serves to integrate the local data model types into one schema that refers to each individual local model of the available data sources. Then a further step will generate the final model to be used for the research questions, e.g. to identify potential applications for modern-day global health problems associated with under-reporting of life events and the implications that this has for public health planning.

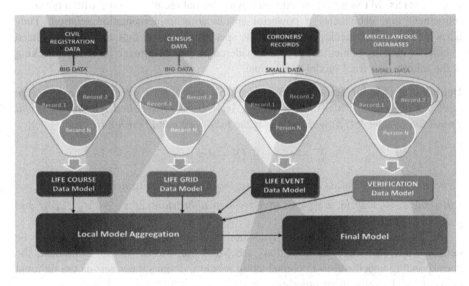

Fig. 2. Big Data Interoperability conceptual reference model.

Technically, as the KDD-related processes will be modelled and implemented in DIME [10, 11], the developers responsible for the data integration need to define a small domain-specific language (DSL) based on the API of the technology underlying the dataset, e.g. actions to access Excel data, import or export tables. The developers will make these actions available to DIME users as language elements for the process models and data models. We expect such a model DSL to be needed for each type of data source to be integrated (i.e. Excel, Microsoft's Access database, etc.). Once this DSL is available, the creation, management, and interpretation of those data components are automatically generated by DIME. The impact of such DSL model libraries becomes significant when looking at the standardization of the process model to develop a complex application system: once a specific database is integrated as a technology with its DSL, any data set stored in that technology becomes easily accessible. Therefore, it is strongly argued that using DIME with its underlying DyWA [29] data integration library concept can assist in the development of complex applications and realize reusable DSLs for hBD.

We have at this moment a top-level DIME model for the phased KDD approach of Fig. 1, but it is not yet operational because any automated dataset manipulation hinges on the existence of automatable, checked, interoperable data models fit for purpose, that can populate the collection of DyWA schemata for the DBDIrl project shown in Fig. 2.

4.2   The Models: From LTS to MTS and CFMTS

We recall Context-Free Modal Transition Systems (CFMTSs) along the definitions in [14] as an extension of Modal Transition Systems (MTSs) to mutually recursive systems of MTSs. MTSs and their extension with mutual recursion come with a notion of refinement that establishes a powerful specification-implementation relation. They allow one to model check properties at the specification-level that are then guaranteed to hold for each implementation. The considered property language for model checking is the (alternation-free) modal μ-calculus.

Definition 1 (Modal Transition Systems [25]). *Let S be a set of states and Act an alphabet of action symbols. $M = (S, s_0, Act, \dashrightarrow, \longrightarrow)$ is called a (rooted) Modal Transition System (MTS) with root s_0 if the following condition holds:*

$$\longrightarrow \subseteq \dashrightarrow \subseteq (S \times Act \times S)$$

Elements of $\dashrightarrow$ are called may transitions, those of $\longrightarrow$ must transitions. As usual, we will write $s \xrightarrow{a} s'$ iff $(s, a, s') \in \longrightarrow$ and $s \xrightarrow{a}$ to abbreviate $\exists s'.s \xrightarrow{a} s'$, $s \overset{a}{\dashrightarrow} s'$ and $s \overset{a}{\dashrightarrow}$ are defined analogously.

MTSs denote sets of Labeled Transition Systems (LTSs), which can simply be defined as MTS where all transitions are Must transitions. Modal refinement, the corresponding specification-implementation relation, defines these sets as the minimal elements of the refinement ordering.

Definition 2 (MTS refinement [25]). *Let, $M_1 = (S_1, s_0^1, Act_1, \dashrightarrow_1, \longrightarrow_1)$, $M_2 = (S_2, s_0^2, Act_2, \dashrightarrow_2, \longrightarrow_2)$ be two MTSs. A relation $\leq_r \subseteq (S_1 \times S_2)$ is called a refinement if the following holds for all $(p, q) \in \leq_r$:*

1. $\forall (p, a, p') \in \dashrightarrow_1, \exists (q, a, q') \in \dashrightarrow_2: (p', q') \in \leq_r$
2. $\forall (q, a, q') \in \longrightarrow_2, \exists (p, a, p') \in \longrightarrow_1: (p', q') \in \leq_r$

Intuitively, refinement allows May transitions to be either turned into Must transitions or to be eliminated, while it requires all Must transitions to be maintained. Like bisimulation, it preserves all temporal properties of finite state systems. In fact, modal refinement is an ideal tool for product line verification also for the here considered infinite state case, where procedural MTS are involved.

A procedural MTS can be seen as an MTS that is extended by the possibility of having transitions whose effect is described by another MTS.

Definition 3 (Procedural Modal Transition Systems). *A procedural modal transition system is defined as* $P = (\Sigma_P, Trans := Act \cup N, \dashrightarrow_P, \longrightarrow_P, \sigma_P^s, \sigma_P^e)$, *where:*

- Σ_P *is a set of state classes,*
- *Trans* $:= Act \cup N$ *is a set of transformations (Act is a set of actions, N is a set of procedure names),*
- $\longrightarrow_P := \longrightarrow_P^{Act} \cup \longrightarrow_P^N$ *is the must transition relation,*
- $\dashrightarrow_P := \dashrightarrow_P^{Act} \cup \dashrightarrow_P^N$ *is the may transition relation,*
  where $\longrightarrow_P^{Act} \subseteq \dashrightarrow_P^{Act} \subseteq \Sigma_P \times Act \times \Sigma_P$ *and* $\longrightarrow_P^N \subseteq \dashrightarrow_P^N \subseteq \Sigma_P \times N \times \Sigma_P$,
- $\sigma_P^s \in \Sigma_P$ *is a class of start states and* $\sigma_P^e \in \Sigma_P$ *is a class of end states.*

We consider only PMTSs P where end states σ_P are terminating in P and all initial transitions of P are labeled with atomic actions, i.e. they are guarded.

Call transitions allow one to define mutually recursive sets of MTSs, formalized as Context-Free Modal Transition Systems (CFMTSs):

Definition 4 (Context-Free Modal Transition Systems (CFMTSs)). *A context-free modal transition system is a quadruple* $P = (N, Act, C, Po)$, *where:*

- $N := \{N_0, \ldots, N_{n-1}\}$ *is a set of names,*
- *Act is a set of actions,*
- $C := \{N_i = PMTS_i \mid 0 \leq i < n\}$ *is a finite set of PMTS definitions where PMTS$_i$ is a finite PMTS with name $N_i \in N$ and*
- P_0 *is the main PMTS. Moreover we denote* $\Sigma = \bigcup_{i=0}^{n-1} \Sigma_{P_i}, \longrightarrow \bigcup_{i=0}^{n-1} \longrightarrow P_i$ *and* $\dashrightarrow = \bigcup_{i=0}^{n-1} \dashrightarrow_{P_i}$

CFMTSs serve as finite representations of the complete, typically infinite-state expansion of the corresponding main PMTS P_0.

5 Current Data Representations in the hDB

In this and the following sections, we present the currently ongoing interdisciplinary work by historians and computer scientists on the data comprehension, organization, ontology creation, and modelling. We show some of the most obvious benefits of adopting the M3C approach as a conceptual guidance and practical tool.

Referring to the KDD approach (Fig. 2), we address its first three steps:

- **Selection:** we concentrate right now on the data sets relative to deaths recorded in Dublin in the year 1901. This subset spans ca. 9500 deaths.
- **Preprocessing:** we work at this stage with the Irish CR data. They are available in a number of different formats and levels of aggregation of the information, that need to be examined from the point of view of their suitability to address the research questions we need to answer.
- As a consequence of their shortcomings, we need to undertake some **Transformations** of data format and granularity of information.

Once this preparation work is done, trained individuals will be able to enter the data that is not yet available in a digitally analyzable form, and specialists will then check the data entry quality and its conformity with the original data sources. It is foreseen to offer the data entry activity (which includes also interpretation of the original sources) as a research-based project to the ca 20–25 students of module HI4187 - Health, State And Irish Medical Care, 1837–1948. In this Problem Based Learning project, they will develop and apply *skills of historical analysis and interpretation, demonstrate knowledge of basic research methods, including the conventions of documentation, in the context of a specific research project.* The DIME application using the data models designed and refined in this paper and the corresponding DTD checkers will be used by the students and researchers.

5.1   The Original CR Data Set and the GRO Data

At the outset of our investigations, our immediate aim is to transform the historical Document Type Definition (DTD) shown in Table 1 into a finer grained and better searchable format. This historical DTD was devised as part of a digitization project between the data owners and Accenture resulting in the 9-field Excel index of the GROdata that was provided as a large CSV with several million entries. As shown in Table 2, the GROdata 9-field Excel index provides

(1)   a unique ID for each entry (column A),
(2)   the essential data about the death, and
(3)   a link to a page of the original handwritten register. This link is provided via a pathway to a scan in TIFF format of that page.

Table 2.   Sample of CSV file from the GROdata.

Group Registration ID	Deceased Forename	Deceased Surname	Deceased Age at Death	SR District/ Reg Area	Deceased Date of Death	Deceased Year of Death	Deceased Civil Status	TIFF File Path
4519165	CAROLINE	DOBBIN	55	Dublin North	NULL	1901	NULL	Deaths_Returns\ deaths_1901\ 05712\ 4611332. tif
4529269	JOHN	ONEILL	43	Dublin North	NULL	1901	NULL	Deaths_Returns\ deaths_1901\ 05712\ 4611353A.tif
4527402	JULIA	MOORE	1	Dublin North	NULL	1901	NULL	Deaths_Returns\ deaths_1901\ 05712\ 4611348. tif

The Excel export to a CSV enclosed text file stores the flat data, as numbers and/or text, in rows (lines) each corresponding to one record and columns, each corresponding to a data field, in plain text format. Table 2 shows the 9 data fields (columns A to M) and five sample records (rows 1 to 5). While CSV can be considered as a simple, conventional and popular data exchange format supported by most organizations and institutions, it is not at a professional *data exchange* standard. Using commas as field separators is simple, but amenable to ambiguity when data fields can themselves contain commas and other characters like dashes, underscores or any unsupported values (for example, an ampersand & or a currency symbol like £ or $) that could be used as alternatives to the comma. Dealing with big data, it is essential to establish automated ways to search, manipulate, transform and analyze the data at any granularity, and this is impossible if there are inherent ambiguities in the representation and storage formats. The CSV representation makes it very difficult to maintain and control the accuracy of data in an automated way. For instance, numeric values may be mistakenly stored in the alphabetic data fields during the import and export process. Because Excel does not support value control mechanisms in each row and column data, there is also a risk that redundancy can occur during the exchange process.

For our project, we resort to a DTD product line to represent and manage various representations and enrichments of the data. For our purposes well-formed documents form the basis of the contracts between the provider (the data set) and its customers (the researchers that consult them. In a first step, we intend to establish the Context-Free Modal Transition Systems (CFMTS) of [14] as a formalism to specify product lines of Document Type Descriptions (DTDs) – or related formalisms like JSON schema. The goal is to then proceed to product line verification using the M3C model checking techniques of [14, 19] to ensure that they are fit for purpose. We need in fact to guarantee that violations of essential well-formedness constraints of a corresponding user document are detected by standard DTD-checkers.

The goal is to later implement and manage the corresponding family of data models and processes in DIME [10], leveraging its flexible DyWA [29] data management layer to define and efficiently manage the interoperable hDB framework for future use. The resulting hierarchical product line verification will allow our hDB platform to act as a **high-quality service provider** for digital humanities researchers, providing them with a wide range of tailored applications implementing the KDD process, whose essential business rules are easily checked by a standard DTD-checker.

5.2   Initial Ontology and Initial Models

In the notation of [14], we have the following two initial ontologies for the CR data:

(A)   CR data (GROdata): it contains the following 11 fields (see Table 1)

no	rank_profession_or_occupation
date_and_place_of_death	certified_cause_of_death_and_duration_of_illness
name_and_surname	signature_qualification_and_residence_of_informant
sex	when_registered
condition	signature_of_registrar
age_last_birthday	

(B) CSV data (GROdata): it contains the following 9 fields (see Table 2)

group_registration_id,	deceased_date_of_death
deceased_forename,	deceased_year_of_death
deceased_surname,	deceased_civil_status
deceased_ age_ at_death	tiff_file_path
sr_district_reg_area,	

As we see, there are only syntactically basic types, one per column. While some are also semantically basic (like deceased_forename), many contain a complex aggregation of semantically rich information items, like certified_cause_of_death_and_du-ration_of_illness. For our research they need to be individually analyzable, thus we need to introduce a granularity transformation step already on this individual dataset, just in order to make the data collection fit for the research purpose.

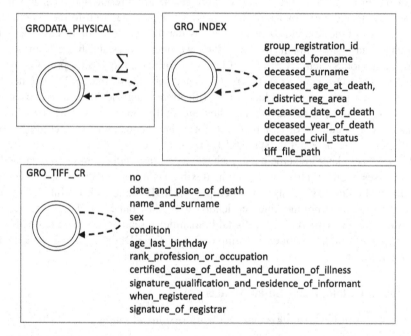

Fig. 3. Initial models (MTS) for the physical archive GRODATA_PHYSICAL (top left), the CSV schema GRO_INDEX (top right) and the original GRO_TIFF_CR data schema (bottom).

Their respective specifications in terms of MTS [14] are amenable to provide for example a syntactic validator, guaranteeing the syntactic validity for each satisfying data entry with that structure. As we see in Fig. 3, these checkers are not very useful. In particular GRODATA_PHYSICAL, corresponding to the original physical archive, does not rule out any entry because it accepts all symbols as indicated by the label Σ (i.e. "any category") in Fig. 3 (top left). The other two MTS compactly represent one May transition for each set of label A) and B): they at least restrict acceptance to the "correct" set of categories present in the respective representations.

5.3   The Product Models for the CSV and CR Representations

The MTSs of the concrete products for Tablea 1 and 2 are in Fig. 4 and 5, respectively. There are no May transitions, therefore taken in isolation these are strictly speaking LTS. In the context of the set of very abstract MTS reported in Fig. 3, we note that CR_GRODATA (Fig. 4) is a refinement of GRO_TIFF_CR, and CSV_GRODATA (Fig. 5) is a refinement of GRO_INDEX.

We see that these concrete products have differences: for example, they use **different terminology** and **different granularity** for the same information, like <name_and_surname> in the CR schema vs. <deceased_forename, deceased_surname> in the CSV schema. In this sense, we face an **ontology mapping** problem in order to reconcile different representations arising at different times for the same (physical) data collection.

Even more crucially, as it is clear from the product model in Fig. 5, the CSV representation we received does not contain many fields necessary for our research in an automatically searchable and analyzable form. It provides details on the personal data of the deceased person, but not for example the location nor the cause of death.

The full CR information can be manually retrieved from the CSV in the linked TIFF, which contains the entire CR information as in Fig. 4. Also here we see that there is no "proper" date of birth: deceased_age_last_birthday is a simple number, not the full date/month/year. People had no concept of age in the modern sense back then.

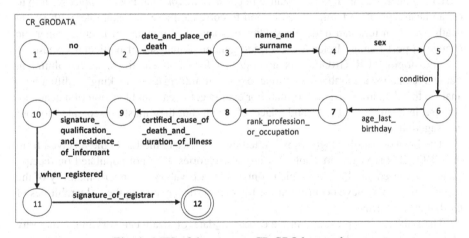

Fig. 4. MTS of the concrete CR GROdata product.

As it is not possible to automatically search the TIFFs, in order to carry out our research we need to undergo a tedious and manual process of extracting the additional information needed from the TIFFs and enhance the available CSV information with these new fields. This manual process is expensive (it uses in fact a large part of the project resources) and error prone, so each record needs to be checked by trained experts once its additional data is entered in the extended records. In fact, this incompleteness of the data de facto available for automated analysis is the reason why we have limited ourselves for the moment to a single year (1901) and a single location (Dublin).

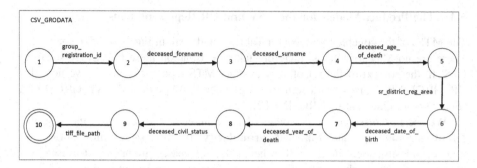

Fig. 5. MTS of the CSV GROdata product.

For a precise and comfortable study of the questions central to this project, we need therefore to create a new, **fine grained** and well-organized representation, easily amenable to a number of future adaptations, extensions, filters, and uses.

6   Subject Domain Refinement: The Fine Grained Data Representation

DBDIrl is interested in the first instance in *cause of death* data. For example, we aim to create heatmaps of particular diseases and to correlate these, for example, with age at death, which in turn can underpin studies of social determinants of health, epigenetic change in post-Famine Ireland, cohort and gendered analyses of particular diseases.

The original CR GROdata is not optimal for these enquiries: each column in Table 1 contains a number of unique pieces of information, making it difficult to analyse this data in its original format. For example, the date and location of a death are coupled in a single field date_and_place_of_death, but they must be separated for our envisaged analysis.

The breakdown of categories is limited even further in the Excel file received from the GRO. This is visible in Table 2. Certain categories were not populated on receipt, such as deceased_civil_status, which contains NULL values in the vast majority of the entries, which may have occurred in the file export, thus exposing the vulnerabilities of the Excel file format.

The same issue is prevalent in the deceased_date_of_death category in the majority of the records provided to us. Our project aims cannot be met unless we conduct further data entry and subdivide the categories to a finer grained level that corresponds to the atomic granularity of enquiry and thus of query. This in turn led to the creation of fifteen additional fields, which are populated with the relevant data derived from the TIFF files.

Table 3. The GROdata-fine representation with 24 individually meaningful categories.

Group Registration ID	District	Date of Death	Place of Death	Where Resident	Sex (M/F)	Deceased Forename	Deceased Surname	Deceased Age at Death	Civil Status of Deceased (M/W/S/B)	SR District/Reg Area	Rank, Profession or Occupation
4519165	No. 1 East	17/10/1 901	166 North strand Road		F	CAROLINE	DOBBIN	55	W	Dublin North	Housekeeper
4529269	No. 1 North City	19/11/1 901	M.M. Hospital	66 Rosemount Kilmainham	M	THOMAS	O'NEILL	43	M	Dublin North	Clerks Widow
4527402	No.1 North City	28/10/1 901	St. Joseph's Hospital		F	JULIA	MOORE	1	S	Dublin North	Poulters Child
Cause of Death 1	Duration of Illness 1	Cause of Death 2	Duration of Illness 2	Certified (C/U)	Name of Informant	Qualification of Informant	At Time of Death (P/N)	Residence of Informant	Date of Registration	Name of Registrar	Tiff File Path
Cardiac Failure				C	Charlotte		P	15 Turlough Terrace	31-10-1901	J. Donnelly	Deaths_Returns\ deaths_1901\ 05712\ 4611332.tif
Heart Failure		Appendicitis		C	P. Allen	Inmate			19-11-1901	J.H Mcauley Asst.	Deaths_Returns\ deaths_1901\ 05712\ 4611353A.tif
General Tuberculosis	1 Day	Tubercular MeningitisTubercular Meningitis	2 h	C	M.J. Byrne	Inmate			30-10-1901	J. H Mcauley Asst.	Deaths_Returns\ deaths_1901\ 05712\ 4611348.tif

Note: The top and bottom sections are concatenated. NULL fields are left empty.

Table 3 (top) and (bottom) shows how we transformed the individual entries by conducting data entry and splitting, for example, alphabetic from numerical data. This is a **refinement step in the subject domain**[1]. These additional categories provide a more meaningful granularity that is fit for purpose for our research agenda. To illustrate this, Tables 2 and 3 have been populated with sample data from the 1901 GRO records for Dublin and include a woman (top row), a man (middle row), and a child (bottom row).

The corresponding product LTS is provided in Fig. 6. The CSV_DATA_R1 refines the LTS of the CSV GROdata product model of Fig. 5 by incorporating some of the TIFF file categories and reformulating some other categories. For example, there is no deceased_year_of_death anymore because it is contained in the date_of_death provening from the CR model. It also keeps the finer grained category pair for the deceased forename and surname. As a principle, we choose systematically the most precise (full date of death vs. only the year) and disaggregated (separate forename and surname) alternative.

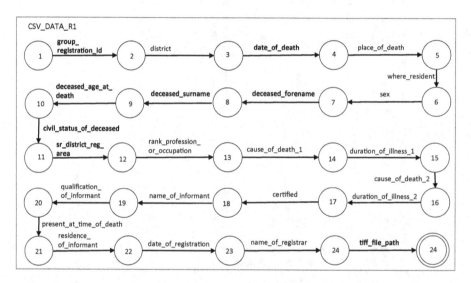

Fig. 6. CSV_DATA_R1: LTS of the GROdata fine-grained representation of Table 3.

Fitness for Purpose: Key to the geographical analysis of disease presence is the *District* and *Place Of Death* data. The *Where Resident* category accounts for deaths in institutions such prisons, hospitals, infirmaries and asylums. The separation of the *Date Of Death* category not only allows us to divide our sample studies into select time periods but allow us to also examine the data in a linear format. This has the potential to show a timeline of disease outbreaks and provides us with the ability to factor

---

[1] This refinement should not be confused with the MTS refinement of Definition 2, that concerns the May/Must modalities and will play a role in Sect. 7.

seasonality. These categories can be combined with existing categories in the original Excel document such as *Deceased Age Of Death.*

Multiple Occurrence of Categories: Another problematic category in the TIFF files is *Certified Cause Of Death And Duration Of Illness* as it contains too many unique attributes. Our original breakdown included *Cause Of Death, Duration Of Illness* and *Certified (Y/N)* as the only categories clarifying these attributes. On further analysis it became clear that the tripartite breakdown would have to be extended to allow for the large number of entries that list more than one cause of death and illness duration. So *Cause Of Death 2* and *Duration Of Illness 2* were added. Examples of this need can be seen in Table 3 in the entries for Julia Moore and Thomas O'Neill.

7   May/Must Refinements, Minimum Specifications and Roles

To prepare our data for automated analysis purposes our source fields should be further categorised into a series of attributes that Must or May be there. Here we adopt taxonomy as opposed to an ontological approach and at this preliminary stage we are also remaining faithful to the original hierarchies defined in Table 1. For a death to be properly registered we Must have a register number, a name and gender ("unknown" is entered in cases of unidentified bodies found), a date of death and registration, Table 4 lists how Fig. 1 can be crudely represented in these terms. The Must categories are typographically evidenced in boldface in Fig. 4.

Table 4. May and Must categories for Table 1.

Must	May
Number of Registration	Condition
Date and place of death	Age last birthday
Name and surname	Duration of Illness
Sex	
Certified Cause of Death Duration of Illness	
Signature, Occupation and Residence of Informant	
When registered	
Signature of Registrar	

7.1   Minimum Specification and Roles

A more refined way of expressing the minimum specifications principles for analysis purposes revolves around the three people involved in the record creation: the **Dead person**, the **Informant** and the **Registrar**. Under these hierarchical taxonomies are the associated attributes that we can assign to each person. The only granular data that Must be or is consistently present for a death to be lawfully registered are the properties associated with the Registrar. The deceased person May/or may not have a name, address or gender. For example, a badly decomposed body found in a waterway would be returned as an unknown infant or adult, without a name, address and sometimes gender as even this might not have been ascertainable. While such instances would have occasioned a coronial court inquiry, post mortem examinations were not always comprehensively undertaken [42].

In Table 5 the Registrar's Taxonomy includes a new field *Data Associated with Admin*: this corresponds to the pro forma typed header to each register page (see Table 1). Here we include the number of the registration as it was generated by that office and Must be present, although arguably it could be an attribute associated with the deceased.

Table 5. Minimum Specifications for each role

Dead Person	Informant	Registrar
Name and Surname	Signature, Occupation and Residence of Informant	Data associated with admin Deaths registered in the District of [ ] in the Union of [ ] in the County of [ ]
Sex	Certified Cause of Death, Duration of Illness	Number of registration
	Date and place of death	When registered
		Signature of Registrar

7.2 Hierarchy: Introducing Procedures

The model for this minimum specification becomes hierarchical, and as such introduces procedures and CFMTS. As shown in Fig. 7, a main MTS DBD_IRL_MIN organizes the essential information relative to the three roles, DEAD_PERSON, INFORMANT and REGISTRAR. This happens by DBD_IRL_MIN referring to the three role-specific own MTS, each implementing the pertaining categories listed in the role-describing columns of Table 5.

In this hierarchical description we start to see potential for local refinement that takes into consideration the May part of the descriptions. In this case, the refinement is role based.

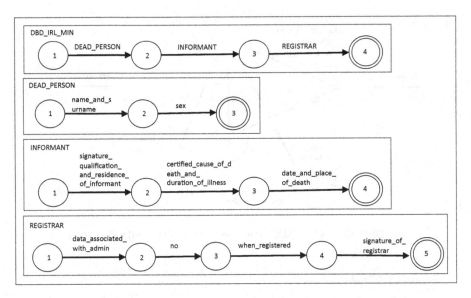

Fig. 7. CFMTS for the hierarchical role-based minimum specification DBD_IRL_MIN.

7.3 Refinements Including May Categories

We can now enrich the description including also the May categories of Table 4 (right column) as required categories. This can happen in either of two ways:

- At the DBD_IRL_MIN level. This choice results in the refined model DBD_IRL_WITH_MAY in Fig. 8, which foresees the new states 5, 6, 7, and 8. There, path 2 → 5 covers the presence of one May category, paths 2 → 6 → 5 and 2 → 7 → 5 the presence of 2 categories and path 2 → 7 → 8 → 5 the presence of all three categories.
- Observing that all the May fields semantically are pertaining to the DEAD_-PERSON role, they can be associated with the deceased and enrich their profile as in the DEAD_PERSON_WITH_MAY model (Fig. 9).
  DEAD_PERSON_WITH_MAY includes the original DEAD_PERSON model, and leads to an alternative refinement DBD_IRL_WITH_MAY_R2 of the entire description, shown in Fig. 10.

From the point of view of achieving a product line of descriptions, we see that the refinement so far is still happening through successive creation of new **individual products** that incorporate the missing or desirable traits as required: there are no May transitions yet in these MTS. In the non-technical terms of common-sense understanding, the natural reaction to deficiencies is to try to formulate a concrete "super-product" that covers all the needs. The fact that it may require too much in many occurring cases is shadowed by the more compelling desire to achieve completeness.

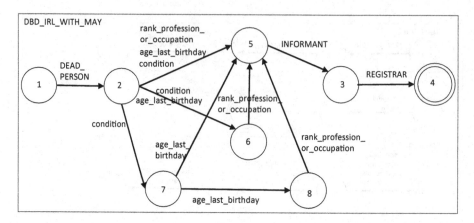

Fig. 8. DBD_IRL_WITH_MAY refinement of DBD_IRL_MIN (Fig. 7 top).

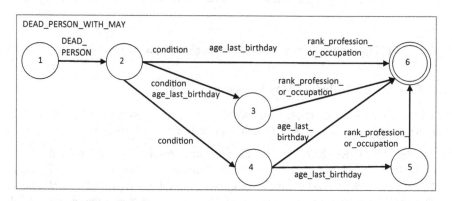

Fig. 9. DEAD_PERSON_WITH_MAY refinement of DEAD_PERSON (Fig. 7)

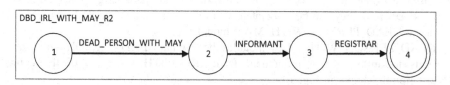

Fig. 10. DBD_IRL_WITH_MAY_R2   Refinement   of   DBD_IRL_MIN,   including DEAD_PERSON_WITH_MAY.

7.4   Including Administrative Data in the Registrar Role

At this point, we can easily observe that also the Registrar role is amenable to further refinement on the basis of the additional administrative data included in Table 5. These data come from the registration page header information of the original GRO data, as shown in Table 1. The REGISTRAR_R1 refinement shown in Fig. 11 includes the

DATA_ASSOCIATED_WITH_ADMIN model and goes therefore beyond even the categories of CSV_DATA_R1, which was the extended CFMTS for the GROdata-fine representation of Table 3.

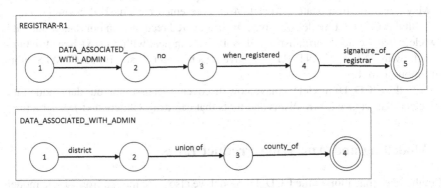

Fig. 11. REGISTRAR_R1 refinement of REGISTRAR including administrative data.

7.5 Multiple Occurrence of Categories: Recursion in the Informant Role

As described in Sect. 6 and shown in Table 3 for Thomas O'Neill and Julia Moore, there can be more than one *Certified Cause Of Death* and relative *Duration Of Illness*. The temporary solution adopted in Table 3, just adding a second pair of columns called *Certified Cause Of Death 2* and relative *Duration Of Illness 2* is an expedient and not a clean systematic modelling solution. We decide that there can be **one or more** such category pairs, therefore it is opportune to define a sub-model CCD_DI to deal with the multiplicity aspect.

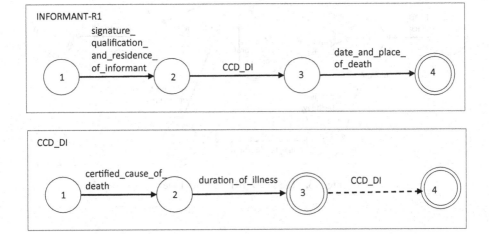

Fig. 12. CFMTS INFORMANT_R1 refinement of INFORMANT with the recursive CCD_DI.

As shown in Fig. 12 (bottom), in the CCD_DI model the accepting state 3 covers the case of single occurrence of the <certified_cause_of_death, duration_of_illness> information, while accepting state 4 is reached when more than one pair occurs. The additional pairs are **optional**, therefore, following the notational conventions for MTS, the May-transition from state 3 to state 4 is represented by a dashed arrow.

With this CCD_DI model we have now discovered recursion in our data model: it is now clear that we need formalisms and tools that can deal with context-free structures. In fact, with INFORMANT_R1 we have reached our first proper CFMTS along Definitions 1 to 4.

With this CCD_DI model we have now discovered recursion in our data model: it is now clear that we need formalisms and tools that can deal with context-free structures.

8   Modelling and Analyzing Product Lines

With the May-transition in the CCD_DI model we also have moved from single models (products) to a **product line**: this model summarizes the shape of any element of the family of <certified_cause_of_death, duration_of_illness> we wish to consider. It is a very simple product line, but it is sufficient for us to be able to express properties that can be checked on the CFMTS by the higher order model checker of [14].

Taken together, the CFMTS for DBD_IRL_WITH_MAY in Fig. 8 and DBD_IRL_MIN (Fig. 7 top) define a simple product line too: its CFMTS, shown in Fig. 13, foresees as alternatives either zero or any combination of the May categories from Table 4.

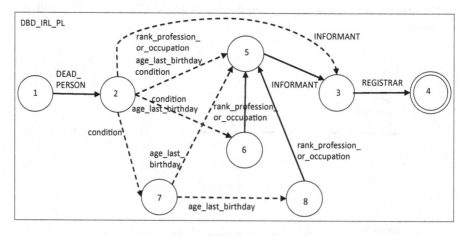

Fig. 13. The DBD_IRL Product Line.

8.1   Model Checking Product Lines

Our work is just starting. We are still discovering the many ways this style of modelling can be useful to simplify the work for both the historians, who are burdened with many manual data entries and checks, and the system designers, who try to be supportive of the researcher's needs and automate its most tedious and error prone bits.

Automation in our case works through formulation of properties for these products and product lines and the construction of mechanisms that enforce or check such properties.

Looking at the DBD_IRL Product Line of Fig. 13, it seems reasonable to ask that
P1: *"A Must-specification is sufficient"*.

In Hennessy-Milner logic, which is included in the modal mu-calculus [40] internally adopted by the context-free model checker in [19], this property is formulated as

$$< DEAD\_PERSON > \; < INFORMANT > \; < REGISTRAR > \; true$$

P1 is satisfied by the DBD_IRL_MIN product, but not by the DBD_IRL_-WITH_MAY refinement, as there the INFORMANT does not directly follow DEAD_PERSON.

On the DBD_IRL_PL, P1 is satisfied by the upper path only, corresponding to DBD_IRL_MIN.

P2: *"The information about the* INFORMANT *follows immediately the* DEAD_-PERSON *information"*.

$$< DEAD\_PERSON > \; < INFORMANT > \; true$$

This property is a looser version of P1, but still sufficient in the current product line as the only location where there are differences among the products is between the call to DEAD_PERSON and the call to INFORMANT.

As already P1, also this property is satisfied in the DBD_IRL_PL by the DBD_IRL_MIN product but not by the DBD_IRL_WITH_MAY refinement.

P3: *"The May information categories precede the* INFORMANT *information"*.
Using the derived **Before** operator of CTL, this property is formulated as
(condition ∨ age_last_birthday ∨ rank_profession_or_occupation) **Before** INFORMANT
and using the definition of Before in terms of the weak until operator it ultimately becomes
A   [(¬ INFORMANT) **WU** (condition ∨ age_last_birthday ∨ rank_profession_or_occupation)]
which is satisfied in the DBD_IRL_PL by DBD_IRL_WITH_MAY but not by DBD_IRL_MIN.

P4: The converse property is (by negation, using the Strong Until operator)
E   [¬ (condition ∨ age_last_birthday ∨ rank_profession_or_occupation) **SU** INFORMANT]
and it is satisfied on the DBD_IRL_PL by the upper path only, corresponding to DBD_IRL_MIN.

9 Conclusion

As we proceed in the project, we are quickly progressing the project from the current stage of unstructured and mostly manual approach to variability and its management that used to be common among bio-scientists over a decade ago [16] to a level of structure and meta-structure that leverages the experts' understanding as well as standards and ties into leading edge tools and techniques from the MDD world. The still manual orientation of the history discipline is exemplified by the Captcha-barrier posed to the access to the data scans, preventing an automatic access to the data - even if in image form and thus very difficult to analyse automatically for information extraction. The automation of search, analysis and management of the data collection is in fact going to be one of the most precious contributions of the DBDIrl project to the advancement of the field – additionally to the insights expected of course in the subject matter. Big Data interoperability has become in fact a significant area of research in the digital humanities due to the variety of data types and data sources available.

The lack of interoperability awareness in big database and small datasets integration motivates this research to focus on the development of a reusable Big Data interoperability framework. The main objective of this project is to provide a conceptual big data interoperability framework that supports flexible Big Data integration between different sources of historical data. This is to ensure the seamlessness for the process of collecting, integrating, and analyzing the data. We intend to apply the eXtreme Model Driven Development environment DIME to design an advanced data integration workflow for history Big Data amenable to be extended to the special purpose integration of various data sources. The distant aim is to assess its potential application for modern-day public health using history Big Data to illustrate its flexibility and robustness.

So far, we have seen the problems that arise from having different ontologies for the representation of ultimately the same data collection, different granularities of the information, and different research purposes to fulfill. These differences have been traditionally solved with manual data capture, data entry, transcription, and checks, with immensely tedious work at exorbitant costs.

With this work, we intend to leverage the XMDD approach [30, 31] and the previous work on evolution-oriented software engineering, be it under the aspect of simplicity [21], continuous systems engineering [22] and the fundamental attention to usability by non-IT specialists [13]. We build upon over a decade of previous experiences gathered in various application domains, facing problems and settings that are amenable to transfer to the DBDIrl project and possibly to the domain of digital humanities. Specifically, our own work in scientific workflows summarized in [12] included experiences gathered to build platforms for the access to complex genetic data manipulations in the bioinformatics domain (the Bio-jETI platform of [23, 27] and the agile Gene-Fisher-P [32]). Similarly, the GIS-related work in the analysis of data concerning sea-level-rise in [24] and the work on flexibilizing the popular ci:grasp platform of PIK [33] will be useful here: the advanced project aims concern creating with GIS technologies heatmaps of particular diseases and to correlate them, for example, with age at death, which in turn can underpin studies of social determinants of health, epigenetic change in post-Famine Ireland, cohort and gendered analyses of particular diseases.

The tools we intend to use span from the CINCO-products [11] DIME and DyWA to the most recent context free model checking approach to product lines of [14] and its underlying M3C model checker [18] for Modal Meta Model Checking. Their deep roots are in works like the original seminal paper on context-free model checking [39] and the Fixpoint Analysis Machine [26] that addressed even the model checking of the full mu-calculus implicitly as a two-dimensional product line for the efficient computation of homogeneous, hierarchical, and alternating fixpoints over regular, context-free/push-down and macromodels.

By resorting to DSLs for the data integration and the KDD process implementation and by adopting the meta-level data modelling approach using product lines we also hope to leverage the language-driven engineering approach of [18], which proposes language and tools specialization down to the single-use level, as well as the Archimedean-point related insights of [20] about what to consider stable or variable, for which purposes and in what contexts.

The DTD checkers resulting from the MTS and CFMTS model checking of a much larger set of properties on a widely expanded and refined product line of (data) models will allow the inheritance of properties established at the meta-level across individual data sources and across a growing selection of complementary data sources that need to be linked and overlaid. For example, the choice of 1901 as sample year is due to the fact that Irish Census Data are available meanwhile for 1901 and 1911. How to relate locations, individuals and other information for Irish historical data as well as for other countries in approximately the same period could well lead to a standardized and highly declarative knowledge base of product lines expressed as CFMTS together with various sets of properties expressing equivalence, identity, complementarity, and other research domain and research question specific characteristics, including data precision, and trust level, e.g. based on the reputation of who input and checked the data.

The connection with the lifetime work and many outstanding achievements of Stefania lies in our joint quest of over a quarter century towards a systematic methodology for coping with complexity, variability and change. Our joint initiative within the FMICS Working Group of ERCIM brought us to co-edit an ambitious book on Formal Methods for Industrial Critical Systems [28] that appeared in 2012 and was later translated in Chinese, that surveyed both the techniques and tools (on the research side) as well as the applications and case studies (on the translational research side). Her significant cluster of works on product lines spans requirements [35], modelling [36, 37], analysis and verification [37, 38] and testing [34] in over a decade of activity, and it arose in various national and international collaborations.

Our own work in the DBDIrl project connects most closely to Stefania's long line of work concerning feature based descriptions [44] up to the most recent Featured Modal Contract Automata [43] and relative FMCAT tool. We too used features for a long time to model variability [17], introduced various categories of constraints to define structural and behavioural aspects of variability [15], provided constraint-driven safe service customization adapting features to various contexts [], ultimately aiming to rich descriptions of product lines in a fashion as much as possible declarative. We hope to reap the benefits of this investment in the ontological and technical infrastructure in the later phases of the project, when the Data mining and Interpretation/Evaluation phases of the KDD process of Fig. 8 will translate in an entire community of researchers answering rich, custom and meaningful questions on the basis of our integrated system.

Acknowledgments. This research is funded by the Irish Research Council Laureate Award 2017/2018 and by Science Foundation Ireland grant 13/RC/2094 to Lero - the Irish Software Research Centre (www.lero.ie). We are grateful for the full cooperation of the Registrar General of Ireland for permission to use these data for research purposes.

References

1. Bizer, C., Heath, T., Berners-Lee, T.: Linked Data — the story so far. In: Hepp, M., Bizer, C.: (eds.) Special Issue on Linked Data, International Journal on Semantic Web and Information Systems, pp. 1–26 (2009). http://tomheath.com/papers/bizer-heath-berners-lee-ijswis-linked-data.pdf
2. Rose, N.: The politics of life itself: biomedicine, power, and subjectivity in the twenty-first century. Princeton University Press, Princeton (2007)
3. Graham, S., Milligan, I., Weingart, S.: Big Digital History: Exploring Big Data through a Historian's Macroscope. Imperial College Press, London (2015)
4. Kitchin, R.: Big data, new epistemologies and paradigm shifts', Big Data & Society, pp. 1–12, April–June 2014. https://doi.org/10.1177/2053951714528481
5. Ginzburg, C., Tedeschi, J., Tedeschi, A.C.: Microhistory: two or three things that i know about it. Crit. Inq. **20**, 10–35 (1993)
6. National Institute of Standards and Technology (NIST): U.S. Department of Commerce, Big Data Interoperability Framework, vol. 1, Definitions (2015)
7. Fayyad, U., Piatetsky-Shapiro, G., Smyth, P.: From data mining to knowledge discovery in databases. AI Mag. **17**(3), 37–54 (1996)
8. Singh, R.K.: Taxonomy of big data analytics: methodology, algorithms and tools. Int. J. Future Revolution Comput. Sci. Commun. Eng. **4**(12), 101–104 (2018)
9. Gyamfi, N.K., Appiah, P., Sarpong, K.A., Gah, S.K., Katsriku, F., Abdulai, J.: Big data analytics: survey paper. In: Conference Proceeding: Dialogue on Sustainability and Environmental Management, Accra, pp. 101–112, 15–16 February 2017
10. Boßelmann, S., et al.: DIME: a programming-less modeling environment for web applications. In: Margaria, T., Steffen, B. (eds.) ISoLA 2016. LNCS, vol. 9953, pp. 809–832. Springer, Cham (2016). https://doi.org/10.1007/978-3-319-47169-3_60
11. Naujokat, S., Lybecait, M., Kopetzki, D., Steffen, B.: CINCO: a simplicity-driven approach to full generation of domain-specific graphical modeling tools. Int. J. Softw. Tools Technol. Transfer **20**, 327–354 (2018)
12. Lamprecht, A.-L., Steffen, B., Margaria, T.: Scientific workflows with the jABC framework - a review after a decade in the field. STTT **18**(6), 629–651 (2016)
13. Margaria, T.: Knowledge management for inclusive system evolution. Trans. Found. Mastering Chang. **1**, 7–21 (2016)
14. Tegeler, T., Murtovi, A., Frohme, M., Steffen, B.: Product line verification via modal meta model checking. In: ter Beek, M.H., et al. (eds.) Gnesi Festschrift. LNCS, vol. 11865, pp. 313–337. Springer, Cham (2019)

15. Jörges, S., Lamprecht, A.L., Margaria, T., Schaefer, I., Steffen, B.: A constraint-based variability modeling framework. Int. J. Softw. Tools Technol. Transfer **14**(5), 511–530 (2012)
16. Lamprecht, A.-L., Margaria, T., Steffen, B.: Seven variations of an alignment workflow - an illustration of agile process design and management in bio-jETI. In: Măndoiu, I., Sunderraman, R., Zelikovsky, A. (eds.) ISBRA 2008. LNCS, vol. 4983, pp. 445–456. Springer, Heidelberg (2008). https://doi.org/10.1007/978-3-540-79450-9_42
17. Karusseit, M., Margaria, T.: Feature-based modelling of a complex, online-reconfigurable decision support service. Electron. Notes Theor. Comput. Sci. **157**(2), 101–118 (2006)
18. Steffen, B., Gossen, F., Naujokat, S., Margaria, T.: Language-driven engineering: from general-purpose to purpose-specific languages. In: Steffen, B., Woeginger, G. (eds.) Computing and Software Science: State of the Art and Perspectives. LNCS, vol. 10000. Springer (2018, in print)
19. Steffen, B., Murtovi, A.: *M3C*: modal meta model checking. In: Howar, F., Barnat, J. (eds.) FMICS 2018. LNCS, vol. 11119, pp. 223–241. Springer, Cham (2018). https://doi.org/10.1007/978-3-030-00244-2_15
20. Steffen, B., Naujokat, S.: Archimedean points: the essence for mastering change. Trans. Found. Mastering Chang. **1**, 22–46 (2016). https://doi.org/10.1007/978-3-319-46508-1_3
21. Margaria, T., Steffen, B.: Simplicity as a driver for agile innovation. IEEE Comput. **43**(6), 90–92 (2010). https://doi.org/10.1109/MC.2010.177
22. Margaria, T., Lamprecht, A.L., Steffen, B.: Continuous Model-Driven Engineering. Software Technology: 10 Years of Innovation in IEEE Computer, pp. 141–154. Wiley (2018)
23. Lamprecht, A.L., Margaria, T., Steffen, B.: Bio-jETI: a framework for semantics-based service composition. BMC Bioinformatics **10**(10), S8 (2009). https://doi.org/10.1186/1471-2105-10-S10-S8
24. Al-Areqi, S., Lamprecht, A.-L., Margaria, T.: Constraints-driven automatic geospatial service composition: workflows for the analysis of sea-level rise impacts. In: Gervasi, O., et al. (eds.) ICCSA 2016. LNCS, vol. 9788, pp. 134–150. Springer, Cham (2016). https://doi.org/10.1007/978-3-319-42111-7_12
25. Larsen, K.G., Thomsen, B.: A modal process logic. In: Proceedings. Third Annual Symposium on Logic in Computer Science, pp. 203–210. IEEE (1988). https://doi.org/10.1109/LICS.1988.5119
26. Steffen, B., Claßen, A., Klein, M., Knoop, J., Margaria, T.: The fixpoint-analysis machine. In: Lee, I., Smolka, S.A. (eds.) CONCUR 1995. LNCS, vol. 962, pp. 72–87. Springer, Heidelberg (1995). https://doi.org/10.1007/3-540-60218-6_6
27. Margaria, T., Kubczak, C., Steffen, B.: Bio-jETI: a service integration, design, and provisioning platform for orchestrated bioinformatics processes. BMC Bioinformatics **9**(4), S12 (2008). https://doi.org/10.1186/1471-2105-9-S4-S12
28. S. Gnesi, T. Margaria. Formal methods for industrial critical systems: A survey of applications. John Wiley & Sons, 2012. Book
29. Neubauer, J., Frohme, M., Steffen, B., Margaria, T.: Prototype-driven development of web applications with DyWA. In: Margaria, T., Steffen, B. (eds.) ISoLA 2014. LNCS, vol. 8802, pp. 56–72. Springer, Heidelberg (2014). https://doi.org/10.1007/978-3-662-45234-9_5
30. Margaria, T., Steffen, B.: Agile IT: thinking in user-centric models. In: Margaria, T., Steffen, B. (eds.) ISoLA 2008. CCIS, vol. 17, pp. 490–502. Springer, Heidelberg (2008). https://doi.org/10.1007/978-3-540-88479-8_35
31. Margaria, T., Steffen, B.: Service-Orientation: Conquering Complexity with XMDD. In: Hinchey, M., Coyle, L. (eds.) Conquering Complexity. Springer, London (2012). https://doi.org/10.1007/978-1-4471-2297-5_10

32. Lamprecht, A.L., Margaria, T., Steffen, B., Sczyrba, A., Hartmeier, S., Giegerich, R.: GeneFisher-P: variations of GeneFisher as processes in Bio-jETI. BMC bioinformatics **9**(4), 1–17 (2008). S13

33. Al-areqi, S., Lamprecht, A.L., Margaria, T., Kriewald, S., Reusser, D., Wrobel, M.: Agile workflows for climate impact risk assessment based on the ci: grasp platform and the jABC modeling framework. In: 7th International Congress on Environmental Modelling and Software, International Environmental Modelling and Software Society (iEMSs), pp. 470–477 (2014)

34. Bertolino, A., Gnesi, S.: PLUTO: a test methodology for product families. In: van der Linden, F.J. (ed.) PFE 2003. LNCS, vol. 3014, pp. 181–197. Springer, Heidelberg (2004). https://doi.org/10.1007/978-3-540-24667-1_14

35. Bertolino, A., Fantechi, A., Gnesi, S., Lami, G., Maccari, A.: Use case description of requirements for product lines. In: Proceedings of the International Workshop on Requirements Engineering for Product Lines - REPL 2002. Technical report: ALR2002-033, AVAYA, pp. 12–18 (2002)

36. Asirelli, P., ter Beek, M.H., Fantechi, A., Gnesi, S.: A model-checking tool for families of services. In: Bruni, R., Dingel, J. (eds.) FMOODS/FORTE -2011. LNCS, vol. 6722, pp. 44–58. Springer, Heidelberg (2011). https://doi.org/10.1007/978-3-642-21461-5_3

37. ter Beek, M.H., Fantechi, A., Gnesi, S., Mazzanti, F.: Modelling and analysing variability in product families: model checking of modal transition systems with variability constraints. J. Log. Algebraic Methods Program. **85**(2), 287–315 (2016)

38. Asirelli, P., ter Beek, M.H., Gnesi, S., Fantechi, A.: Formal description of variability in product families. In: 15th International Software Product Line Conference, pp. 130–139, August 2011. https://doi.org/10.1109/SPLC.2011.34

39. Burkart, O., Steffen, B.: Model checking for context-free processes. In: Cleaveland, W.R. (ed.) CONCUR 1992. LNCS, vol. 630, pp. 123–137. Springer, Heidelberg (1992). https://doi.org/10.1007/BFb0084787

40. Blackburn, P., van Benthem, J.F.A.K., Wolter, F.: Handbook of Modal Logic. Studies in Logic and Practical Reasoning, vol. 3. Elsevier Science Inc., New York (2006)

41. An Act for the Registration of Births and Deaths in Ireland. 26 & 27 - Vict. c.11

42. Breathnach, C., O'Halpin, E.: Registered "unknown" infant fatalities in Ireland, 1916-1932. Ir. Hist. Stud. **38**(149), 70–88 (2012). https://doi.org/10.1017/S0021121400000638

43. Basile, D., ter Beek, M.H., Gnesi, S.: Modelling and analysis with featured modal contract automata. SPLC **2**, 11–16 (2018)

44. ter Beek, M.H., Gnesi, S., Njima, M.N.: Product lines for service oriented applications - PL for SOA. In: Kovács, L., Pugliese, R., Tiezzi, F. (eds.) Proceedings 7th International Workshop on Automated Specification and Verification of Web Systems (WWV 2011) (EPTCS), vol. 61, pp. 34–48. Open Publishing Association (2011). https://doi.org/10.4204/eptcs.61.3

45. Braun, V., Margaria, T., Steffen, B., Yoo, H., Rychly, T.: safe service customization. In: Proceedings of the IEEE Intelligent Network Workshop: 'Meeting the Challenges of Converging Networks and Global Demand'. IEEE, May 1997. https://doi.org/10.1109/inw.1997.601576

Variability Modelling and Analysis During 30 Years

David Benavides[(✉)] [iD]

Department of Computer Languages and Systems, University of Seville, Seville, Spain
benavides@us.es

Abstract. Variability modelling and analysis are among the most important activities in software engineering in general and in software product line engineering in particular. In 1990, the FODA report supposed a revolution in the importance of modelling and analysing of variability. In 2020, 30 years of variability modelling and analysis will be celebrated. In this paper, a short overview of the history and the importance of variability modelling and analysis is given, in concordance to that anniversary and on the occasion of Stefania Gnesi's retirement. She was part of this amazing history.

Keywords: Software product lines · Feature models · Variability modelling

1 Variability Modelling as a Key Activity

Software systems are one of the engineering creations where variability is most important, to such an extent that variability is an intrinsic element of any software system. Variability can be defined as the ability of a software system to be adapted to different situations such as different users, operational environments or quality requirements. For example, a piece of code that calculates the shortest path for graphs can be prepared to calculate it for different types of graphs such as directed or undirected. We can even envision a graph library that can include this and other graph operations that could be assembled to support different kinds of graphs [12].

Variability management becomes very important to any kind of software system and more important when managing what is called a *software product line* [15]. A software product line can be defined as a set of software systems that share more commonalities than variabilities and that are able to operate in a given domain. Examples of software product lines can be found in many different domains such as operating systems (e.g. Android operating systems in different platforms such an mobile phones, TV sets or smart watches); car control systems (e.g. adaptations of a system for different car models); or web commerce solutions (e.g. different adapted solutions for different specific online stores). Variability management is defined as the set of activities that have to

© Springer Nature Switzerland AG 2019
M. H. ter Beek et al. (Eds.): Gnesi Festschrift, LNCS 11865, pp. 365–373, 2019.
https://doi.org/10.1007/978-3-030-30985-5_21

be performed to correctly deal with variability in this kind of scenarios to better profit from the commonalities of the systems while reducing cost and increasing quality in software production.

One of the crucial activities when managing variability is its modelling. Variability modelling can be done at different levels of abstraction. From top level activities such as requirements engineering to more concrete activities such as coding, delivery or deployment. For example, a requirements engineer may want to express the different elements that can be of interest to a given user (such as the supported graph types in the example above) and how these elements could depend on each other (for instance, that an algorithm of cycle detection is only available if a directed graph is selected). Likewise, during deployment, developers may want to express the different configurations available for deployment with different storage capabilities, different memory consumption or different number of processors.

Variability modelling has been present in the general software engineering literature since its infancy. As an example, in 1968 McIlroy's text in the NATO conference [13] one can already divine that variability modelling had to be one of the key activities when mass producing software products. Nevertheless, it is in 1990 that Kang *et al.* presented the FODA report and explicitly gave a way of modelling variability in the form of feature models.

2   The FODA Report in 1990

The FODA report can be considered as the kickoff for variability modelling and analysis [10]. It had and still has an immense impact in the software engineering literature in general and in the software product line engineering research and practice in particular. However, as shown in Fig. 1 it is remarkable that the recognition of the importance of the FODA report started only around 2005, that is, 15 years after its publication. There was still another peak in 2010 that was basically due to the consolidation of a new line of research, as we will explain further in Sect. 3.

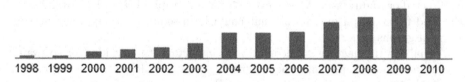

Fig. 1. Citations evolution of the FODA report (taken from Google scholar)

In 2020, 30 years of the FODA report will be celebrated, making this a good moment to remember some of the novelties that were presented at that time. It is not easy to find scientific contributions in software engineering that pass the test of time, but the FODA report is one such contribution. It is remarkable that a scientific text with more than 4.500 citations in Google scholar was produced as a technical report instead of being a journal paper or a conference proceedings contribution. The report was produced in the Software Engineering Institute (SEI) where leading projects on software product line engineering were run. Not in vain, in 2000 one of the most well-known books on software product line engineering was produced [5].

One of the main outputs of the FODA report was what they called "feature models" as part of the domain modelling activity. A feature model is a compact representation of all possible products of a software product line and it is represented in a feature diagram as a tree-like structure composed of features and relationships among them [3]. A feature is defined as an increment in product functionality [1] and is a widely used concept in software product line engineering. Since the appearance of the FODA report there have been a lot of different notations for feature modelling, most of them well surveyed by Schobbens *et al.* [17]. There are different concepts and elements in the different notations, but most of them have the basic elements of what we often call "basic feature models".

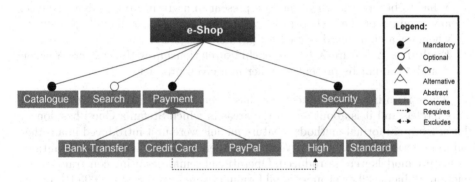

Fig. 2. Feature model of an e-shop software product line (from [16])

In basic feature models, features are depicted as boxes and relationships among features are depicted as arrows. Figure 2 shows a feature model of an e-shop software product line where the root is an abstract feature (i.e. it's used to model the concept, but it has no concrete implementation) and the other features are so-called concrete features (i.e. features that have concrete implementations). Relationships among features are divided in hierarchical relationships and cross-tree constraints. The hierarchical relationships are:

- **Mandatory**: A parent feature X has a mandatory relationship with a child feature Y when Y has to be present whenever X is present in a given product. For instance, any product of the e-shop product line of Fig. 2 has to have a catalogue of products.
- **Optional**: A parent feature X has an optional relationship with a child feature Y when Y can be present or not whenever X is present in a given product.

For instance, a product of the e-shop product line can optionally have a search feature.

- **Or**: A parent feature X has an or relationship with a set of child features $Y_1, \ldots, Y_n$ when any of the children can be present or not whenever X is present in a given product. For instance, a product of the e-shop product line can optionally have different payment methods such as bank transfer, credit card, paypal or any combination of the three.
- **Alternative**: A parent feature X has an alternative relationship with a set of child features $Y_1, \ldots, Y_n$ when one and only one of the children can be present whenever X is present in a given product. For instance, a product of the e-shop product line can only have high or standard security, but not both.

Furthermore, cross-tree constraints can be used to model restrictions among features. These constraints can be complex constraints on the form of propositional formulas [1]. However, very often we see two kinds of cross-tree constraints:

- **Requires**: A feature X has a requires relationship with a feature Y when Y has to be present whenever X is present in a given product. For instance, any product of the e-shop product line of Fig. 2 has to have high security whenever a credit card is used for payment purposes.
- **Excludes**: A feature X has an excludes relationship with a feature Y when X and Y cannot be present together in a given product.

There is an important aspect that has to be underlined in the history of feature models and it is about one of the areas in which Stefania Gnesi has done a lot of research: formal methods. Feature models were first introduced in a rather informal form. Only around 10 years after their introduction, formal definitions of feature models were introduced. Operational semantics using constraint satisfaction problems [2] or propositional formulas were introduced in 2005 [1]. Later, formal syntax and semantics of feature models were conscientiously developed [6,17]. Feature models were then extended to work with more complex models, analysis and domains. It is remarkable that Stefania Gnesi's team worked in depth to use feature models together with modal transition systems with clean and formal semantics to perform complex analysis in highly (re)configurable systems [7,18,19].

With the formalisation achievement, a new line of research –that was already marginally mentioned in the original FODA report– took the scene: the automated analysis of variability models.

3   Automated Analysis of Variability Models

The automated analysis of variability models is about the computer-aided extraction of information from variability models [3]. Figure 3 shows a simplification of the analysis process. First, a variability model is taken as input. Second, the variability model is translated to a given logical representation following several rules. Third, an off-the-shelf solver is used to perform different analysis operations over the logical representation. And finally, an analysis result is constructed as a final output of the process.

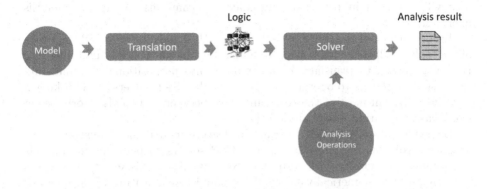

Fig. 3. Process of the automated analysis of variability models

An example of an analysis operation can be to count the number of products represented by the feature models. In the model of Fig. 2, the total number of potential products is 20. This operation could be done manually for small feature model examples as the one in Fig. 2 but when dealing with large-scale feature models, this operation become complex and even infeasible in some cases due to the computational complexity required. For instance, it is known that the feature model representing the Linux kernel can have more configurations than there are atoms in the universe!

Another often used operation is "valid configuration" that takes a set of features representing a configuration after which the analysis process determines whether the configuration is valid or not. For instance, the configuration A below is a valid configuration for the feature model of Fig. 2, but the configuration B is not valid because it has a credit card payment but a standard security system.

$$A = \{eShop, Catalogue, Payment, BankTransfer, Security, High\}$$
$$B = \{eShop, Catalogue, Search, Payment, CreditCard, Security, Standard\}$$

Imagine that we include a new cross—tree constraint that states that a catalogue feature excludes any payment method. In such a case, the feature model becomes "void" in the sense that the feature model would represent no product.

Also, imagine that we add a new cross-tree constraint that states that the Security feature excludes Bank Transfer. In such a case, we can still derive products from the feature model. For instance, the product B in the example above. However, the feature Bank Transfer becomes what is known as a "dead feature". A dead feature is a feature that is present in the feature model, but can never be present in any product derived from the feature model.

In 2005, there were two papers [1,2] that emphasised the importance of the automated analysis of feature models and gave a new impetus to the study of modelling and analysis of variability. Independently but complementary, the teams of Batory (University of Texas at Austin) and Benavides (University of Sevilla) worked in proposing automated mechanisms to support analysis operations[1].

Batory proposed the usage of SAT solvers [1], Benavides proposed the usage of CSP solvers [2]. The idea was quite similar, but the solution was a bit different. Batory proposed to translate feature models into propositional formulas and then use SAT solvers to operate over the formulas. SAT solvers are well known to perform fast in most of the cases and have been proved to also work fast in many cases of feature model analysis [14].

Benavides *et al.* proposed to translate feature models into Constraint Satisfaction Problems (CSP) and then use CSP solvers to perform the analysis operations. The novelty with respect to SAT-based analysis was that in CSPs you can also have numerical values and not only Boolean features. Feature models could then be extended with attributes. For example, imagine that we add an integer attribute to the payment feature stating the maximum amount for a given transaction.

When adding attributes to feature models the kind of analysis that can be performed becomes even more complex [11]. For instance, you can try to optimise some attributes so that a line of research was born dealing with optimisation in feature model analysis.

In 2010, an extensive review of the analysis proposed up-to-date was presented [3]. A total of 30 different analysis operations were reported. As well as SAT and CSP solvers, also description logic solvers, BDD solvers and ad-hoc algorithms were reported. In 2010, the conceptual underpinnings of the discipline were settled and the automated analysis of feature models was added to software product line tools in commercial and open-source formats. For instance, Pure::Variants and FeatureIDE are examples of commercial and open-source tools that incorporate feature model analysis among their capabilities.

After that, the decade of the applications was started and is at the point of finishing with this anniversary. More and more applications were found specially in the following areas, as reported in [9]:

- product configuration and derivation: the automated analysis of feature models is used to configure and derive products, for instance, using consistency checking capabilities to avoid compiling or linking incompatible configurations.
- testing and evolution: there is a still active part of the research in software product lines that deals with the problem of testing these kind of systems, which is another area where Stefania Gnesi contributed early on [4,8]. Testing software product lines adds an extra level of difficulty and complexity from

---

[1] These two works were recently recognised with the Test-of-Time Award and the Most Influential Paper Award by the software product line community.

the traditional testing of a single product. The automated analysis of feature models has been used, for instance, to select representative combinations of features when the testing of all the configurations becomes infeasible.

- reverse engineering: another still active area of research is how to build variability models from existing artefacts. It is quite common that software product lines are built from existing products and artefacts rather than building them from the beginning. One of the ideas is to extract variability models from these assets. The automated analysis of feature models can be used in these scenarios to check the consistency among the assets and the produced models.
- multi-model variability-analysis: it is common that variability is not expressed in a single model or by a single stakeholder and in the same variability modelling language. In this cases, we have to deal with heterogeneous scenarios where the automated analysis has to be adapted
- variability modelling: variability modelling is still being studied because for different scenarios, different variability constructs might be used. In different domains, different adaptations of the variability language constructs have to be defined. The automated analysis has to be adapted as well to these different scenarios.
- variability-intensive systems: the automated analysis of variability models is going beyond software product lines to a wider scope that can be named as "variability-intensive systems". These are systems that are not built following a software product line philosophy specially from a process engineering perspective, but that have to deal with variability. The Linux kernel, the Android ecosystem, and the Eclipse IDE framework are examples of these systems. The automated analysis of variability models is also being used and extended in this kind of new environments.

4   Conclusions

Variability modelling and analysis has progressed in the last three decades. One of the points were the discipline progressed faster and better was when formal approaches were considered by the researchers. One of those researchers was Stefania Gnesi and she was an important part of the health of the community. As well as technically, she contributed with community service chairing the Systems and Software Product Line Conference (SPLC) in 2014 in Florence and being active part of the Steering Committee of SPLC in the recent past. The community will lose a very important active researcher with her retirement, but we will be lucky to have both her already established contributions and their fellows that are still active in the field. This book is only a small piece of the immense gratitude that the community owes Stefania. Thank you very much for sharing your time and talent with us and all the best for the future.

Acknowledgements. This work has been partially funded by the EU FEDER program, the MINECO project OPHELIA (RTI2018-101204-B-C22); the TASOVA network (MCIU-AEI TIN2017-90644-REDT); and the Junta de Andalucia META-MORFOSIS project. I would like to give special thanks to Maurice ter Beek for taking care of the book, the ceremony and the gratitude to Stefania. This acknowledgement is extended to all her team.

References

1. Batory, D.: Feature models, grammars, and propositional formulas. In: Obbink, H., Pohl, K. (eds.) SPLC 2005. LNCS, vol. 3714, pp. 7–20. Springer, Heidelberg (2005). https://doi.org/10.1007/11554844_3

2. Benavides, D., Trinidad, P., Ruiz-Cortés, A.: Automated reasoning on feature models. In: Pastor, O., Falcão e Cunha, J. (eds.) CAiSE 2005. LNCS, vol. 3520, pp. 491–503. Springer, Heidelberg (2005). https://doi.org/10.1007/11431855_34

3. Benavidges, D., Segura, S., Ruiz-Cortés, A.: Automated analysis of feature models 20 years later: a literature review. Inf. Syst. **35**(6), 615–636 (2010)

4. Bertolino, A., Gnesi, S.: PLUTO: a test methodology for product families. In: van der Linden, F.J. (ed.) PFE 2003. LNCS, vol. 3014, pp. 181–197. Springer, Heidelberg (2004). https://doi.org/10.1007/978-3-540-24667-1_14

5. Clements, P., Northrop, L.: Software Product Lines: Practices and Patterns. The SEI Series in Software Engineering. Addison-Wesley, Boston and London (2001)

6. Durán, A., Benavides, D., Segura, S., Trinidad, P., Ruiz-Cortés, A.: FLAME: a formal framework for the automated analysis of software product lines validated by automated specification testing. Softw. Syst. Model. **16**(4), 1049–1082 (2017)

7. Fantechi, A., Gnesi, S.: Formal modeling for product families engineering. In: Proceedings of the 12th International Software Product Line Conference (SPLC 2008), pp. 193–202. IEEE (2008)

8. Fantechi, A., Gnesi, S., Lami, G., Nesti, E.: A methodology for the derivation and verification of use cases for product lines. In: Nord, R.L. (ed.) SPLC 2004. LNCS, vol. 3154, pp. 255–265. Springer, Heidelberg (2004). https://doi.org/10.1007/978-3-540-28630-1_16

9. Galindo, J.A., Benavides, D., Trinidad, P., Gutiérrez-Fernández, A.-M., Ruiz-Cortés, A.: Automated analysis of feature models: quo vadis? Computing (2018)

10. Kang, K.C., Cohen, S.G., Hess, J.A., Novak, W.E., Spencer Peterson, A.: Feature-oriented domain analysis (FODA) feasibility study. Technical report, DTIC Document (1990)

11. Lettner, M., Rodas, J., Galindo, J.A., Benavides, D.: Automated analysis of two-layered feature models with feature attributes. J. Comput. Lang. **51**, 154–172 (2019)

12. Lopez-Herrejon, R.E., Batory, D.: A standard problem for evaluating product-line methodologies. In: Bosch, J. (ed.) GCSE 2001. LNCS, vol. 2186, pp. 10–24. Springer, Heidelberg (2001). https://doi.org/10.1007/3-540-44800-4_2

13. Douglas McIlroy, M., Buxton, J., Naur, P., Randell, B.: Mass-produced software components. In: Proceedings of the 1st International Conference on Software Engineering, Garmisch Partenkirchen, Germany, pp. 88–98 (1968)

14. Mendonca, M., Wąsowski, A., Czarnecki, K.: SAT-based analysis of feature models is easy. In: Proceedings of the 13th International Software Product Line Conference, pp. 231–240. Carnegie Mellon University (2009)

15. Pohl, K., Böckle, G., van der Linden, F.J.: Software Product Line Engineering: Foundations, Principles and Techniques. Springer, Heidelberg (2005). https://doi.org/10.1007/3-540-28901-1
16. Rodas-Silva, J., Galindo, J.A., García-Gutiérrez, J., Benavides, D.: Selection of software product line implementation components using recommender systems: an application to wordpress. IEEE Access 7, 69226–69245 (2019)
17. Schobbens, P.-Y., Heymans, P., Trigaux, J.-C., Bontemps, Y.: Generic semantics of feature diagrams. Comput. Netw. **51**(2), 456–479 (2007)
18. ter Beek, M.H., Damiani, F., Gnesi, S., Mazzanti, F., Paolini, L.: On the expressiveness of modal transition systems with variability constraints. Sci. Comput. Program. **169**, 1–17 (2019)
19. ter Beek, M.H., Fantechi, A., Gnesi, S., Mazzanti, F.: Modelling and analysing variability in product families: model checking of modal transition systems with variability constraints. J. Log. Algebraic Methods Program. **85**(2), 287–315 (2016)

Formal Verification

A Systematic Approach to Programming and Verifying Attribute-Based Communication Systems

Rocco De Nicola[1]([⊠]), Tan Duong[2]([⊠]), Omar Inverso[2]([⊠]),
and Franco Mazzanti[3]([⊠])

[1] IMT School for Advanced Studies Lucca, Lucca, Italy
rocco.denicola@imtlucca.it
[2] Gran Sasso Science Institute, L'Aquila, Italy
{tan.duong,omar.inverso}@gssi.it
[3] ISTI–CNR, Pisa, Italy
franco.mazzanti@isti.cnr.it

Abstract. A methodology is presented for the systematic development of systems of many components, that interact by relying on predicates over attributes that they themselves mutually expose. The starting point is a novel process calculus AbC (for Attribute-based Communication) introduced for modelling collective-adaptive systems. It is shown how to refine the model by introducing a translator from AbC into UML-like state machines that can be analyzed by UMC. In order to execute the specification, another translator is introduced that maps AbC terms into $ABEL$, a domain-specific framework that offers faithful AbC-style programming constructs built on top of $Erlang$. It is also shown how the proposed methodology can be used to assess relevant properties of systems and to automatically obtain an executable program for a non-trivial case study.

1 Introduction

Collaboration between Stefania Gnesi (to whom this work is dedicated) and the first author of this paper dates back to the late eighties, when they were both working at CNR and interested in devising formal methods to provide models and techniques to guarantee correctness of concurrent systems. Together with other colleagues, they developed a model checker [1] for proving logical properties of concurrent systems using ACTL [2], an action-based version of the branching time logic CTL. Stefania has since continued to work on developing variants of ACTL and tailored model checkers for new classes of systems she has been confronted with. Stefania and the last author of this paper, together with other colleagues, developed the FMC model checker [3] adopting as models and logic, respectively, transition systems and a version of ACTL extended with fixed-point operators; they then developed the UMC [4] model checker, where the model was instead directly inspired by UML statecharts and the logic, UCTL, could express properties of both actions and states.

In this paper we build on Stefania's work and show how UMC can be used to prove properties of so-called collective-adaptive systems (CAS). These are

© Springer Nature Switzerland AG 2019
M. H. ter Beek et al. (Eds.): Gnesi Festschrift, LNCS 11865, pp. 377–396, 2019.
https://doi.org/10.1007/978-3-030-30985-5_22

systems formed by anonymous components that can dynamically join and leave, and adapt their behaviour to the environment in pursuit of an individual or collective goal.

To describe CAS, we rely on a specifically conceived process calculus, *AbC* [5,6] whose distinguishing features are the interaction primitives, based on the concept of *attribute-based communication*, which permits groups of partners to communicate according to predicates over attributes that they expose. Communication takes place anonymously in an implicit multicast fashion without a prior agreement among the involved peers. Groups are dynamically formed by considering, among the potential receivers, those that satisfy the predicates of the sender; run-time changes of attribute values allow opportunistic interactions between components. By parameterising the interaction predicates with local attributes, groups can be implicitly changed and adaptation is naturally captured. Sending operations are non-blocking while receiving operations are; this breaks synchronisation dependencies between interacting partners, and permits modelling systems where agents can enter or leave at any time without perturbing the overall behaviour.

When devising new languages for a new class of systems, following [7], we think that it is important to consider three main ingredients:

1. a specification language equipped with a formal semantics, which associates mathematical models to each term of the language to precisely capture the expected behaviour of systems;
2. a set of techniques and tools, built on top of the models, to express and verify the properties of interest;
3. a programming framework together with an associated run-time environment, to actually execute the specified systems.

In this paper, we rely on *AbC* as our specification language, on UMC as the tool for property verification and on *Erlang* [8] to set up the programming framework that we call *ABEL* [9]. The execution and verification flows of our approach are summarised by the following diagram.

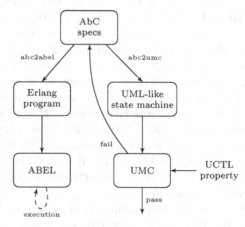

Starting from AbC specifications we obtain a UMC model whose properties we can express with UCTL and then model check with the tool. We see this as an iterative process that calls for a progressive revision of the specification in case any property of interest is not satisfied. Once satisfactory specifications are obtained, they are translated into $ABEL$ and can finally be executed.

The main contributions of this paper, are thus the two translators (i) from AbC to the language of UMC and (ii) from AbC to the language of $ABEL$. The former is a refinement of a translation already presented in [10] while the latter is presented here for the first time to take advantage of the $ABEL$ implementation presented in [9].

The feasibility of the approach is vindicated by considering a case study dealing with distributed graph colouring. We first show how errors in an initial specification can be detected by exploiting the counterexample facility of UMC, then we show how properties of interest of a new version can be formally verified, finally we provide an executable $Erlang$ program obtained from the correct specification.

2   Background

In this section we briefly review the main ingredients of our approach, i.e., the AbC process calculus, the UMC verification framework, and the $ABEL$ framework. We also illustrate AbC programming via a non-trivial example.

2.1 AbC Process Calculus

AbC (Attribute-based Communication calculus) is a process calculus specifically conceived for collective adaptive systems. In AbC [6], a system is a collection of interacting components; each component C is either a process P associated with an attribute environment Γ and an interface I, or the parallel composition of two components. The environment Γ is a partial mapping from attribute names to values, representing the component state. The interface I is a set of exposed attribute names which other components may use when specifying their predicates.

(Components)	$C ::= \Gamma :_I P \mid C_1 \parallel C_2$
(Processes)	$P ::= 0 \mid (\tilde{E})@\Pi.U \mid \Pi(\tilde{x}).U \mid \langle \Pi \rangle P \mid P_1 + P_2 \mid P_1 \vert P_2 \mid K$
(Update)	$U ::= [a := E]U \mid P$
(Expressions)	$E ::= v \mid x \mid a \mid this.a \mid f(\tilde{E})$
(Predicates)	$\Pi ::= \text{tt} \mid p(\tilde{E}) \mid \Pi_1 \wedge \Pi_2 \mid \neg \Pi$

Process P can be either an inactive process 0, a prefixing process $\alpha.P$, an update process U, an awareness process $\langle \Pi \rangle P$, a choice process $P_1 + P_2$, a parallel process $P_1 \vert P_2$, or a process call K (with a unique definition $K \triangleq P$). The derived syntax allows no sequential composition between AbC processes, similar to TAPAs [11].

AbC prefixing actions exploit run-time attributes and predicates over them to determine the internal behaviour of components and the communication partners. Specifically:

$(\tilde{E})@\Pi$ is an output action that evaluates expressions $\tilde{E}$ under the local environment and sends the result to those components whose attributes satisfy predicate Π;

$\Pi(\tilde{x})$ is an input action that binds to the variables $\tilde{x}$ the message received from any component whose attributes and the communicated values satisfy the receiving predicate Π;

$[a := E]$ is an attribute update that assigns the evaluation of expression E under the local environment to attribute a;

$\langle \Pi \rangle$ blocks the following process until Π is satisfied under the local environment.

Attribute updates and awareness predicates are local to components and their execution includes the associated communication action, atomically.

An expression E may be a constant value v, a variable x, an attribute name a, or a reference $this.a$ to attribute a in the local environment. Predicate Π can be either tt, or can be built using comparison operators $\bowtie$ between two expressions and logical connectives $\wedge$, $\neg$, ... Both expressions and predicates can take more complex forms, of which we deliberately omit the precise syntax; we just refer to them as n-ary operators on subexpressions, i.e., $f(\tilde{E})$ and $p(\tilde{E})$.

In AbC, the output action is non-blocking while the input action waits for synchronization on available messages. Parallel processes inside a single component do not communicate; they simply interleave their actions and have access to the shared environment. According to the system semantics, message passing is performed in a broadcast fashion. An outbound message is attached with the portion of environment limited by the senders' interface and the sending predicate. Every component which can execute an input action, upon receiving a message checks both the sending and receiving predicates to decide whether to use the message or discard it.

We now illustrate AbC constructs by considering a distributed variant of graph colouring (borrowed from [12]). The problem amounts to labelling the vertices of a graph with a colour (in our case, positive integers) such that adjacent vertices have a different colour. We model the vertices as separate components of the form $\Gamma_i :_{\{id,nbr\}} V$, with public attributes a unique identifier, id, and a set, nbr, of neighbours. Additionally, the environment Γ_i maintains the following private attributes for local computations:

- colour, assigned: the proposed colour and the colouring status
- round: the current round of computation
- counter: the number of un-assigned neighbours operating in the same round
- constraints: the set of colours proposed by greater neighbours in the same round
- done: the number of neighbours who have finished colour selection
- used: the set of colours already used by neighbours
- send: a flag controlling when to send colour proposals

The vertices operate in rounds and use predicates of the form $this.\text{id} \in \text{nbr}$ to communicate with neighbours. Each vertex has the same behaviour, and consists of four parallel processes $V \triangleq (F \mid T \mid D \mid A)$. Initially, assigned = false, round

= counter = done = colour $= 0$, constraints = used $= \emptyset$ and send = true. Any unassigned vertex repeatedly performs two consecutive actions:

$$F \triangleq \langle \text{send} \wedge \neg \text{assigned} \rangle()@(\text{ff}).[\text{colour} := \min\{i \notin \text{used}\}]$$
$$(\text{`try'}, this.\text{colour}, this.\text{round})@(this.\text{id} \in \text{nbr}).[\text{send} := \text{ff}]F$$

to update the current colour (after an empty output action), and to send a 'try' message of the form $(\text{`try'}, c, r)$ to inform neighbours that it wants to take colour c at round r. Note that $\min\{i \notin \text{used}\}$ denotes the smallest element not in used.

Each vertex counts the number of 'try' messages from its neighbours as described by the following expression:

$$T \triangleq (x = \text{`try'} \wedge this.\text{id} > \text{id} \wedge this.\text{round} = z)(x, y, z).$$
$$[\text{counter} := \text{counter} + 1]T$$
$$+ \; (x = \text{`try'} \wedge this.\text{id} < \text{id} \wedge this.\text{round} = z)(x, y, z).$$
$$[\text{counter} := \text{counter} + 1, \text{constraints} := \text{constraints} \cup \{y\}]T$$
$$+ \; (x = \text{`try'} \wedge this.\text{id} > \text{id} \wedge this.\text{round} < z)(x, y, z).$$
$$[\text{send} := \text{tt}, \text{round} := z, \text{counter} := 1, \text{constraints} := \emptyset]T$$
$$+ \; (x = \text{`try'} \wedge this.\text{id} < \text{id} \wedge this.\text{round} < z)(x, y, z).$$
$$[\text{send} := \text{tt}, \text{round} := z, \text{counter} := 1, \text{constraints} := \{y\}]T$$

where the first two branches deal with messages from neighbours in the same round (i.e., $this.\text{round} = z$); to avoid conflicts, the proposed colours from neighbours with greater ids are stored in constraints: only the vertex with the greatest id among un-assigned neighbours can take a conflict colour. Messages associated with a greater round are instead handled by the two branches. Any message of this kind will denote the beginning of a new round at the receiving end, by updating round, counter, constraints, and enabling send in order to activate process F.

Upon succeeding in deciding a colour, a vertex sends a message of the form $(\text{`done'}, c, r + 1)$ to notify the others that the colour c has been taken at round r, setting assigned to true and terminating:

$$A \triangleq \langle\langle (\text{counter} + \text{done} = |\text{nbr}|) \wedge \text{colour} > 0 \wedge \text{colour} \notin \text{constraints} \cup \text{used}) \rangle\rangle$$
$$(\text{`done'}, this.\text{colour}, this.\text{round} + 1)@(this.\text{id} \in \text{nbr}).[\text{assigned} := \text{tt}]0$$

this process is activated if the vertex has collected all neighbours information (i.e., counter + done $= |\text{nbr}|$) and there are no conflicts (i.e., colour $\notin$ constraints $\cup$ used). At the other endpoint, a vertex receiving notification messages from neighbours updates done and the set of used colours, and, in case the message is associated with a greater round, triggers the execution of a new round:

$$D \triangleq (x = \text{`done'} \wedge this.\text{round} \geq z)(x, y, z).$$
$$[\text{done} := \text{done} + 1, \text{used} := \text{used} \cup \{y\}]D$$
$$+ \; (x = \text{`done'} \wedge this.\text{round} < z)(x, y, z).$$
$$[\text{done} := \text{done} + 1, \text{used} := \text{used} \cup \{y\},$$
$$\text{send} := \text{tt}, \text{round} := z, \text{counter} := 0, \text{constraints} := \emptyset]D$$

2.2   UMC Model Checker

UMC [4] is one of the model checkers belonging to the KandISTI [13] formal verification framework used for analyzing functional properties of concurrent systems. In UMC, a system is represented as a set of UML-like communicating state machines, each associated with an active object in the system. UMC adopts doubly-labelled transition systems (L2TS) [14] as semantic model of systems behaviours. A L2TS is essentially a directed graph in which nodes and edges are labelled with sets of predicates and of events, respectively. The model checker allows to interactively explore graphs and to verify behavioural properties specified in the state-event logic UCTL [15]. UCTL allows to express state predicates and event predicates and to combine them with temporal and boolean operators in the style of CTL [16] and ACTL [2].

The main building block of a concurrent system in UMC is a class definition, that defines the structure a UML-like state machine. The active components of a system are represented by class instances, i.e. objects. A class definition has the following structure:

```
class Name is
  Signals
  -- asynchronous events accepted by the class
  Operations
  -- synchronous events accepted by the class
  Vars
  -- local variables of this object
  --
  -- state properties
  Behavior
  -- transitions that determine the behaviour of the class
end Name
```

The `Signals` and `Operations` sections contain the set of events to which an active object may react by triggering some transition of the state machine. The `Vars` section contains the private (non statically-typed) local variables of the class and optionally their initial value. Values can denote object names, boolean values, integer values or, recursively, (dynamically sized) sequences of values. The `Vars` section can be followed by a list of `state` definitions that allow to specify special properties of some of the states, like the list of events deferred inside those states. The `Behaviour` section contains a set of transition rules that describe the behaviour of the class and have the following general form:

```
source -> target {trigger [guard] / actions}
```

Source and target denote internal states of the state machine and may be defined by composite names in presence of composite (sequential or parallel) states. A single evolution step of a state machine has the semantics of a run-to-completion step as defined in [17]. At each step one event is extracted from the events queue of the object and dispatched to the set of active states for which it may trigger a transition. A transition is enabled not only if the requested trigger is being currently dispatched, but also when its `guard` expression (if any) is satisfied by the current object state and trigger arguments. If different conflicting transitions are concurrently enabled, one of them is nondeterministically selected for firing, taking into account possible priorities. Concurrent non conflicting transitions are instead executed in the same run-to-completion step. Transitions not requiring a triggering event (completion transitions) have a higher priority than normally triggered transitions. When a transition is fired the execution of its actions may change the state of the object and send further events to the same or other objects. UMC supports a fairly rich language to specify actions and guards. Actions, in particular, can be composite actions like finite loops or conditionals, and can use local temporary transition variables. The reader is referred to the UMC website [18] and to the documentation therein for additional details.

While the operational semantics in terms of state machine of a UMC specification is directly defined by the system behaviour, the evaluation of logical formulas on the system is carried out by reasoning on an abstract L2TS derived from systems behaviour by a set of Abstraction rules. These rules allow to decorate the states and the edges of the L2TS with relevant state predicates and abstract relevant events. They are defined inside the Abstractions section:

```
Abstractions {
  Action: <internal event> -> <edge label>
  ...
  State:  <internal system state> -> <node label>
  ...
}
```

The labels exposed can be visualized, to provide a compact summary of the computation trees, and can be referred when specifying UCTL formulae.

2.3 *ABEL*

ABEL [9] is a faithful implementation of *AbC* in *Erlang* with the support of APIs closely corresponding to *AbC* primitives. *ABEL* relies on provable-correct coordination strategy [19] for preserving *AbC* execution semantics. This is an advantage over previous proposals; using *ABEL* in our framework makes automatic translation immediate.

An *ABEL* program is essentially an *Erlang* program which uses *ABEL* APIs. It consists of the process definitions of the components, and of top-level statements for initialization. The syntax of components and processes is given in Fig. 1, where [*elem*] is used to denote a list of *elems*. A component is created by invoking *new_component* which takes as parameters an attribute environment *Env* (a map) and an interaction interface *I* (a list). The command returns a component address *C* which can be used by *start_component* to start the execution of *C* from an initial behaviour referenced by *BRef*. The main building block of a process definition is function definition *BDef*. A definition takes two parameters: a component address *C* and the current list *V* of *bound variables* of the process. *V* is initially empty and may be gradually updated with the messages received by input actions. The body of a definition contains a single command *Com* determining the process behaviour.

A reference *BRef* to a definition is a function of one parameter that may alter the list of bound variables of the wrapped function. A reference can be passed as parameter to commands so that they can continue with the referred behaviour. This way of programming is reminiscent of continuation passing style.

$$
\begin{aligned}
C ::= \ & \textbf{new\_component}(Env, I) & \text{Create} \\
& \textbf{start\_component}(C, BRef) & \text{Start} \\
BDef ::= \ & beh\_name(C, V) \to Com. & \text{Definition} \\
BRef ::= \ & \textbf{fun}(\_V) \to beh\_name(C, \_V) \ \textbf{end} & \text{Reference} \\
& \mid \textbf{nil} & \\
Com ::= \ & \textbf{prefix}(C, V, \{Act, BRef\}) & \text{Prefix} \\
& \mid \textbf{choice}(C, V, [\{Act, BRef\}]) & \text{Choice} \\
& \mid \textbf{parallel}(C, V, [BRef]) & \text{Parallel} \\
& \mid \textbf{call}(C, V, BRef) & \text{Call} \\
Act ::= \ & \{`!\text', g, \tilde{m}, s, [u]\} & \text{Output} \\
& \mid \{`?\text', g, r, \tilde{x}, [u]\} & \text{Input}
\end{aligned}
$$

Fig. 1. ABEL API for process definitions.

A command Com has parameters C, V bounded by those of an outer function, and a third parameter specifying basic actions possibly paired with references, depending on the command type. It is worth mentioning that C and V are names that simply act as place holders in commands and processes definitions. *ABEL* supports the following commands.

prefix - takes as parameter an action Act and a continuation $BRef$. Act can be either input ('?') or output ('!') action and its description is a tuple where g, s, and r denote awareness, sending and receiving predicates, respectively, while $\tilde{m}$ denotes the message, $\tilde{x}$ denotes input-binding variables and u denotes an attribute update. If g or u are omitted, *ABEL* treats them as *true* and empty list [], respectively. This command executes Act and then the behaviour encapsulated in $BRef$. The execution of an input action (if successful) returns a message; *ABEL* then continues by calling $BRef$ on an updated list of bound variables, calculated by appending the message to the current list V. If Act is an output action, the continuation is determined by applying $BRef$ to V.

choice - takes as parameter a list of pairs, each providing a description of the prefixing action Act and a continuation $BRef$. This command executes one of the actions and continues with the associated behaviour. Currently, *ABEL* does not support mixed choices between input and output actions.

parallel - takes as parameter a list of $BRef$ functions and creates new processes, executing a behaviour resulting from the application of $BRef$ functions to V.

call - executes the behaviour referenced by $BRef$ by applying $BRef$ to V.

The representation of AbC basic terms is based on *Erlang*. Function g is parameterized with the local environment, $(fun(L) \to \ldots end)$. The tuple $\tilde{m}$ is composed of functions parameterized with the local environment, $(fun(L) \to \ldots end)$. $\tilde{x}$ is a tuple of atoms. Function s is parameterized with the local environment and the environment of other components $(fun(L, R) \rightarrow \dots end)$, while r is parameterized also with the incoming message $(fun(L, M, R) \rightarrow \dots end)$. Finally, u is a pair whose first element is an attribute name and the second is a function parameterized with the local environment, and a message, in case the update is associated with an input operation $(fun(L, \langle M \rangle) \rightarrow \dots end)$.

In order to properly model the semantics of these elements, several helper functions are available: $att(a, E)$ refers to the value of attribute a in an environment E; $msg(i, M)$ refers to the ith element of a message M, and $var(x, V)$ refers to the value of x in a list V of bound variables.

3   From *AbC* to UMC

We now show how to model an *AbC* system as a unique UML state machine whose state is the union of the states of the components in the system. The behaviour of each component is modelled by a concurrent region of a global parallel system state. This yields several advantages. First, the receivers of a sending predicate can be easily determined, because components can read the attribute environments of the others. Second, message broadcasting can be effectively modelled via signals to the state machine itself, to allow all targeted components to receive in parallel.

Our translation takes as input a collection of *AbC* components of the form $\Gamma_k : \langle D_k, P_{init_k} \rangle$, where Γ_k, D_k, and P_{init_k} denote the environment, the process definitions, and the initial behaviour, respectively. The output of our translation is a UMC class whose structure is depicted in Fig. 2.

```
0   [[(Γ0 : ⟨D0, Pinit0⟩, Γ1 : ⟨D1, Pinit1⟩ ..., Γs : ⟨Ds, Pinits⟩)]] =
1       Class System with RANDOMQUEUE is
2       Signals: allowsend(i:int),
3               bcast(tgt,msg,j:int);
4       Vars:
5           receiving:bool := false;
6           pc:int[];
7           bound:obj[];
8           /* Attribute vectors - attr1:int[]; attr2:int[]; ...*/
9       State Top Defers allowsend(i)
10      Transitions:
11          /* Initial movement of the system */
12          init → SYS {-/
13          for i in 0..pc.length-1 {
14              self.allowsend(i);
15          }}
16          /* Transitions of all components */
17          [[⟨D0, Pinit0⟩]]
18          [[⟨D1, Pinit1⟩]]
19          ...
20      end System
```

Fig. 2. Structure of the UMC encoding for *AbC*

The System class includes fixed code snippets such as the necessary signals and data structures to model AbC input and output actions. Attributes (line 8) are represented as vectors whose values are accessible via component indexes. Transitions model the components' behaviour (lines 17 - 20). The Transitions section contains the sets of transitions, for each component. Specifically, for component k, our translation visits all actions (of all processes) starting from P_{initk} and uses D_k for looking up new definitions when needed.

In the following we first explain the structural part of the translation, where we combine AbC actions according to the process structure, and then the behavioural part, where AbC input and output actions are modelled.

To model process interleaving we introduce program counters: pc[k][p] is the program counter for process p of component k. Furthermore, for each action in p we calculate two values: an *entry point* C_{in} and an *exit point* C_{out} based on the process structure. These values can be worked out by recursively visiting the process structure, following the approach of [10]. Figure 3 gives an idea of how different transitions can be combined by using program counters and entry and exit points: (a) is the graphical representation of a single transition; (b) an action-prefixing process $\alpha.P$ has the entry point of α as C_{in}, and the entry point of P as the exit point of α (C_{out}); (c) a choice process $P_1 + P_2$ has the same entry point on both sub-processes P_1 and P_2; (d) the entry points of sub-processes P_1 and P_2 in a parallel process $P_1|P_2$ contain their entry points, possibly combined with the exit point of a previous action. An action is then encoded as a transition of the following form:

```
SYS.Ck.s0 -> Ck.s0 {Trigger[... & pc[k][p]=Cin]/
    -- transition body
    pc[k][p]:=Cout;
}
```

A guard $pc[k][p] = C_{in}$ makes sure that the program counter points to the correct transition to be executed next. Right after a transition, pc[k][p] is assigned a new value to correctly enable the next set of feasible transitions.

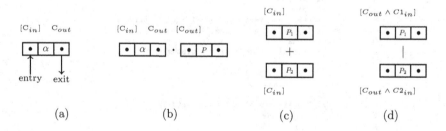

| | | | |
| (a) | (b) | (c) | (d) |

Fig. 3. Structural composition of UMC transitions with program counters

In order to model communication, we introduce two unique events to model attribute-based input and output actions. The event bcast(tgt, msg, j) carries out the set tgt of component indexes allowed to receive the message msg, and the index j of the sending component and triggers all the input actions in all components. The event `allowsend(i)`, where i is a component index, schedules the components through interleaving when sending messages. The event queue of the state machine stores a set of `allowsend(i)` signals for each AbC component. These signals are declared in the top state of the system as `Defers`, to prevent them from being removed from the event queue when they do not trigger any transition. The queue is defined as `RANDOM` so that the relative ordering of signals is not considered relevant. In this way, whenever an AbC output action is allowed, a single `allowsend(i)` signal is nondeterministically selected from the queue to enable a single component, with index i, to proceed.

Output and Input Actions. We encode an output action as two separate transitions that do occur strictly sequentially: a sending operation to self (i.e., the state machine) of the `bcast` event (that will be dispatched to all the parallel components), and a discarding of this very message.

```
[⟨Πₐ⟩(Ẽ)@Πₛ.[ã := Ẽ]]^{k,p,cᵢₙ,cₒᵤₜ} =
SYS.Ck.s0 -> Ck.s0 {
    allowsend(i)[i=k & receiving=false & [[Πₐ]] & pc[k][p] = cᵢₙ]/
    tgt: int[];
    for j in 0..pc.length-1 {
        if ([[Πₛ]]) then {tgt[j]:=1;} else {tgt[j]:=0;}
    };
    receiving:=true;
    self.bcast(tgt,[[Ẽ]],k);
    [[ã := Ẽ]];
    pc[k][p] = cᵢₙ + 1;
}
SYS.Ck.s0 -> Ck.s0 {
    bcast(tgt,msg,j)[pc[k][p] = cᵢₙ + 1]/
    receiving:=false;
    self.allowsend(k);
    pc[k][p] = cₒᵤₜ;
}
```

Note that an action may be preceded by an awareness predicate Π_a and followed by an attribute update $[\tilde{a} := \tilde{E}]$. The global variable `receiving` of the state machine works as a lock, to guarantee the correct ordering of the two transitions. Here the (main) transition is enabled if the component k is selected by UMC (i.e., `i=k`) and no other component is performing an output action, (i.e., `receiving=false`), and the awareness predicate Π_a, if any, holds. The transition body includes the computation of the set of potential receivers `tgt`, a sending operation `self.bcast(tgt, msg, k)` where `msg` is the result of translating expressions $\tilde{E}$ and of any attribute updates. This transition also sets the global variable `receving` to prevent other components from performing further transitions of this kind, and to allow only transitions triggered by `bcast(tgt, msg, k)`. The second transition resets `receiving`, updates the program counter of the current process to the correct exit point c_{out}, and pushes the `allowsend(k)` signal on the event queue of the state machine.

An input action is instead translated into a single UMC transition, as below.

$[\![\langle \Pi_a \rangle \Pi_r(\tilde{x}).[\tilde{a} := \tilde{E}]]\!]^{k,p,c_{in},c_{out}} =$
```
SYS.Ck.s0 -> Ck.s0 {
    bcast(tgt,msg,j)[tgt[k]=1 & [[Πa]] & [[Πr]] & pc[k][p]= cin ]/
    bound[k][p] = msg;
    [[ã := Ẽ]];
    pc[k][p] = cout;
}
```

The transition is enabled, for a component k (if k is in the target set **tgt** of receivers), when the receiving predicate Π_r and (possibly) the preceding aware-ness predicate Π_a are satisfied. Variable binding is achieved by assigning the received message **msg** to a global vector **bound** indexed by k and p. This allows other transitions of the same process to use the message. Like for output actions, the transition body may contain attribute updates.

For brevity, we have omitted the detailed treatment for other syntactic ele-ments such as expressions and predicates. Their translations are quite straight-forward since in each transition, we have full information of component and process indexes for accessing components attributes and bound variables.

4   From *AbC* to *ABEL*

We now describe the translation from *AbC* into *ABEL*. We make the follow-ing assumptions on the input: (i) any process involved in a choice is preceded (guarded) by an action, although the choice branches can still initially appear in the form of process calls; (ii) the guarded actions in a choice are not mixed, i.e., all of them are either input actions or output actions; (iii) the names of input-binding variables in the code of a sequential process definition are unique.

Our translation is structured in two phases. A *normalization phase* that con-sists in refactoring process definitions (of all components) in the input *AbC* spec-ification to match the structure of the forms provided by *ABEL*'s programming interface, and a *generation phase* that produces the actual *Erlang* code.

Normalization. Let D be the set of process definitions; X be either a process name K or process code P. We define a function $\mathcal{N}$ that rewrites the defini-tions, and while doing so may produce auxiliary definitions. A fresh definition is introduced if any of the following conditions holds: (i) the continuation of a prefixing process is not a process name; (ii) any branch of a choice process is not a prefixing process; and (iii) any branch of a parallel process is not a process name.

Figure 4 presents the rewriting rules for normalization. We note that the rules are applied exhaustively until all definitions in D, including the newly created ones, are processed.

In a prefixing definition, the generic action denoted by α may be associated with awareness and attributes updates. The procedure generates another def-inition with the same structure, except that the continuation X needs to be processed by a helper function $\mathcal{R}$: if X is a name, $\mathcal{R}$ returns that name, other-wise, if X is a process code P, $\mathcal{R}$ creates a fresh name K, adds a new definition $\{K \triangleq P\}$ and returns K.

$$\text{(prefix)} \quad \mathcal{N}[\![K \triangleq \alpha X]\!] \qquad = \quad K \triangleq \alpha \cdot \mathcal{R}[\![X]\!]$$

$$\text{(choice)} \quad \mathcal{N}[\![K \triangleq X_1 + X_2]\!] = K \triangleq \mathcal{N}[\![X_1]\!] + \mathcal{N}[\![X_2]\!]$$
$$\mathcal{N}[\![K]\!] \qquad\qquad = \mathcal{N}[\![P]\!] \quad \text{where } P = D(K)$$
$$\mathcal{N}[\![\alpha X]\!] \qquad\qquad = \alpha \cdot \mathcal{R}[\![X]\!]$$
$$\mathcal{N}[\![X_1 + X_2]\!] \qquad = \mathcal{N}[\![X_1]\!] + \mathcal{N}[\![X_2]\!]$$

$$\text{(parallel)} \quad \mathcal{N}[\![K \triangleq X_1 \mid X_2]\!] = K \triangleq \mathcal{R}[\![X_1]\!] \mid \mathcal{R}[\![X_2]\!]$$
$$\mathcal{N}[\![X_1 \mid X_2]\!] \qquad = \mathcal{R}[\![X_1]\!] \mid \mathcal{R}[\![X_2]\!]$$

$$\text{(call)} \quad \mathcal{N}[\![K \triangleq K']\!] \qquad = \quad K \triangleq K'$$

$$\text{(new def.)} \quad \mathcal{R}[\![K]\!] \qquad\qquad = \quad K$$
$$\mathcal{R}[\![P]\!] \qquad\qquad = \quad K \text{ for K fresh and } D = D \cup \{K \triangleq P\}$$

Fig. 4. Normalizing process definitions

In a choice definition, the procedure recursively processes all the branches of the choice. For process names, $\mathcal{N}$ looks up the definition of that name and continues the normalization for the corresponding code. For prefixing process, $\mathcal{N}$ behaves similarly to the prefixing case. If one of the branches is again a choice process, $\mathcal{N}$ normalizes its sub-processes.

In a parallel definition, the procedure recursively normalizes all the branches. Finally, any call definition remains unchanged. The above procedure is guaranteed to terminate because the input specification contains a finite number of definitions and $\mathcal{N}$ processes them only once.

Code Generation. This phase produces *Erlang* code from a set of normalized definitions. The generated code consists of a module for each component type wherein each normalized definition is translated into one function. The rules for code generation ($\mathcal{G}$) are reported in Fig. 5. The first four rules capture all possible forms of a definition and generate the corresponding $BDef$ definitions in $ABEL$ style (see Fig. 1). The next two rules do generate references $BRef$. The other next two rules deal with AbC actions. The remaining nine rules are responsible for the actual translation of the basic elements of such actions: Namely, they consider awareness, sending and receiving predicates Π_a, Π_s, Π_r, attribute updates $[\tilde{a} := \tilde{E}]$ and the message $\tilde{E}$ to be sent. The translation is parameterized with input-binding variables $\tilde{x}$ because the expressions contained in receiving predicates or in attribute updates may need them.

Please, notice that the details of the translation of the last five rules are omitted. The definition of $[\![\cdot]\!]$ is quite standard and is based on the actual syntax of AbC predicates and expressions. However, we would like to add some consideration about some special cases. In an awareness predicate Π_a, the two terms a and $this.a$ have the same meaning, therefore $[\![a]\!] = [\![this.a]\!] = \text{att}(a,L)$. The translation for interaction predicates (Π_s, Π_r) instead differs between a

$$\mathcal{G}[\![K \triangleq \alpha \cdot K']\!] \qquad\qquad = \mathrm{k(C,V)} \to \mathtt{prefix(C,V,\{\mathcal{G}[\![\alpha]\!],\mathcal{G}[\![K']\!]\}).}$$
$$\mathcal{G}[\![K \triangleq \alpha_1 \cdot K_1 + \ldots + \alpha_n \cdot K_n]\!] = \mathrm{k(C,V)} \to \mathtt{choice(C,V,[\{\mathcal{G}[\![\alpha_1]\!],\mathcal{G}[\![K_1]\!]\},\ldots,\{\mathcal{G}[\![\alpha_n]\!],\mathcal{G}[\![K_n]\!]\}]).}$$
$$\mathcal{G}[\![K \triangleq K_1|\ldots|K_m]\!] \qquad = \mathrm{k(C,V)} \to \mathtt{parallel(C,V,[\mathcal{G}[\![K_1]\!],\ldots,\mathcal{G}[\![K_m]\!]]).}$$
$$\mathcal{G}[\![K \triangleq K']\!] \qquad\qquad = \mathrm{k(C,V)} \to \mathtt{call(C,V,\mathcal{G}[\![K']\!]).}$$
$$\mathcal{G}[\![K]\!] \qquad\qquad\qquad = \mathtt{fun(\_V)} \to \mathtt{k(C,\_V)}\ \mathtt{end}$$
$$\mathcal{G}[\![nil]\!] \qquad\qquad\qquad = \mathtt{nil}$$
$$\mathcal{G}[\![\langle \Pi_a \rangle(\tilde{E})@(\Pi_s).[\tilde{a} := \tilde{E}]]\!] = \{\mathtt{'!'}, \mathcal{G}[\![\Pi_a]\!], \mathcal{G}[\![\tilde{E}]\!], \mathcal{G}[\![\Pi_s]\!], \mathcal{G}[\![[\tilde{a} := \tilde{E}]]\!]\}$$
$$\mathcal{G}[\![\langle \Pi_a \rangle(\Pi_r)(\tilde{x}).[\tilde{a} := \tilde{E}]]\!] = \{\mathtt{'?'}, \mathcal{G}[\![\Pi_a]\!], \mathcal{G}[\![\Pi_r]\!]^{\tilde{x}}, \mathcal{G}[\![\tilde{x}]\!], \mathcal{G}[\![[\tilde{a} := \tilde{E}]]\!]^{\tilde{x}}\}$$
$$\mathcal{G}[\![\tilde{E}]\!] \qquad\qquad\qquad = \{\mathcal{G}[\![E_1]\!],\ldots,\mathcal{G}[\![E_k]\!]\}$$
$$\mathcal{G}[\![\tilde{x}]\!] \qquad\qquad\qquad = \{\mathtt{x_1},\ldots,\mathtt{x_l}\}$$
$$\mathcal{G}[\![[\tilde{a} := \tilde{E}]]\!] \qquad\quad = [\{\mathtt{a_1},\mathcal{G}[\![E_1]\!]\},\ldots,\{\mathtt{a_i},\mathcal{G}[\![E_i]\!]\}]$$
$$\mathcal{G}[\![[\tilde{a} := \tilde{E}]]\!]^{\tilde{x}} \qquad = [\{\mathtt{a_1},\mathcal{G}[\![E_1]\!]^{\tilde{x}}\},\ldots,\{\mathtt{a_j},\mathcal{G}[\![E_j]\!]^{\tilde{x}}\}]$$
$$\mathcal{G}[\![\Pi_a]\!] \qquad\qquad\qquad = \mathtt{fun(L)} \to [\![\Pi_a]\!]\ \mathtt{end}$$
$$\mathcal{G}[\![\Pi_s]\!] \qquad\qquad\qquad = \mathtt{fun(L,R)} \to [\![\Pi_s]\!]\ \mathtt{end}$$
$$\mathcal{G}[\![\Pi_r]\!]^{\tilde{x}} \qquad\qquad = \mathtt{fun(L,M,R)} \to [\![\Pi_r]\!]^{\tilde{x}}\ \mathtt{end}$$
$$\mathcal{G}[\![E]\!] \qquad\qquad\qquad = \mathtt{fun(L)} \to [\![E]\!]\ \mathtt{end}$$
$$\mathcal{G}[\![E]\!]^{\tilde{x}} \qquad\qquad\quad = \mathtt{fun(L,M)} \to [\![E]\!]^{\tilde{x}}\ \mathtt{end}$$

Fig. 5. Code generation

and *this.a* being a interpreted as a remote attribute: $[\![a]\!] = \mathtt{att(a,R)}$ while $[\![this.a]\!] = \mathtt{att(a,L)}$. Next, consider a variable x. The special case is when x appears in input-binding variables $\tilde{x}$, to which the parameterized translation output is $\mathtt{msg}(i,\mathtt{M})$ where i denotes the index of x in $\tilde{x}$, otherwise $\mathtt{var(x,V)}$. Finally, for complex expressions $f(\tilde{E})$ (or predicates) which do not have a closed form in *AbC* syntax, the translation generates a function call as a place holder, i.e., $\mathtt{f}(\mathcal{G}[\![\tilde{E}]\!])$, and users need to provide the *Erlang* definition for f afterward.

5   Experiments

In this section we report some experiments that we have conducted adopting as a case study the graph colouring algorithm of Sect. 2.1 by taking advantage of the two tools[1] that permit translating *AbC* systems into UMC models and into *ABEL*.

Experimenting with UMC. In order to model check the UMC model for graph colouring, we instrumented it as follows.

```
Abstractions {
    -- Auto generated
    Action sending($1,$2) -> send($1,$2)
    Action received($1,$2) -> received($1,$2)
    State SYS.colour[0]=$2 -> has_colour(C1,$2)
    State SYS.assigned[0]=$2 -> has_assigned(C1,$2)
    ...
    -- Manual instruments
    -- Soundness
    State SYS.matrix[0][1]>0 and SYS.colour[0]=SYS.colour[1] -> not_sound
    State SYS.matrix[0][2]>0 and SYS.colour[0]=SYS.colour[2] -> not_sound
```

---

[1]   https://doi.org/10.5281/zenodo.3234713.

```
...
-- \delta + 1 algorithm
State SYS.maxt<SYS.colour[0] -> bad_alg
State SYS.maxt<SYS.colour[1] -> bad_alg
...
}
```

First, we introduce abstraction rules for the `colour` and `assigned` attributes of each vertex. Second, whenever the `colour` of any two adjacent vertices is the same, we label the state as `not_sound`. For this we rely on a global variable storing the adjacency `matrix` of the graph under consideration. Finally, a label `bad_alg` is exposed if the maximum degree + 1 (stored in `maxt`) is smaller than the colour value of any vertex. We can now specify a number of properties concerning the termination and soundness of the graph colouring procedure:

G_1 *(termination)* The system converges to final states:
   `AF FINAL`

G_2 *(completeness of colouring)* Every vertex has a valid colour:
   `AF (FINAL and not has_colour(*,0))) and not has_assigned(*,false))`

G_3 *(soundness of colouring)* Adjacent vertices do not share the same colour:
   `AF (FINAL and not not_sound)`

G_4 *(not bad algorithm)* The algorithm is $(\Delta + 1)$ - colouring:
   `AF (FINAL and not bad_alg)`

We have verified the system under consideration for *all* possible graphs with 2 from 5 vertices. Property G_1 holds, showing that our colouring algorithm terminates, while property G_2 does not hold, because some vertex eventually is not `assigned`.

Figure 6 reports the UMC counterexample for a connected graph of 2 vertices. After being assigned a colour, vertex C2 still sends a 'try' message (the grey line), which affects the counting of the neighbours for vertex C1 (the line after the grey one). This prevents the halting condition for colour selection, i.e., $|\text{nbr}| = \text{done} + \text{counter}$ to ever happen to the vertex C1. This happens because in the specifications (Sect. 2.1), process F performs colour selection and sends a 'try' message as two separate actions, therefore there is the possibility that these two actions are interleaved with process A.

We can fix the specifications by modifying process F as follows:

$$F' \triangleq \langle \text{send} \wedge \neg \text{assigned} \rangle (\text{'}try\text{'}, \min\{i \notin \text{used}\}, this.\text{round})@(this.\text{id} \in \text{nbr}).$$
$$[\text{colour} := \min\{i \notin \text{used}\}, \text{send} := \text{ff}]F'$$

where basically the two actions of F are combined into a single action wherein the sending action sends the value of the expression $\min\{i \notin \text{used}\}$, and `colour` is atomically set via an attribute update. After these changes, we can perform the verification again. The results are summarised in Table 1. UMC successfully verified that, for all possible graphs of the considered degrees, all the above properties do hold for the fixed version of the specifications. The number of states generated when verifying the property AF FINAL is also included, giving an idea of the state space for each set of inputs.

```
AF (FINAL and not has_assigned(*,false)) is FOUND_FALSE in State C1
This happens because:
...
C13 --> C68   {} /* nbr:=[[2],[1]]; matrix:=[[-1,1],[1,-1]]; */
C68 --> C69   {} /* colour[0]:=1; */
C69 --> C70   {send(C1,[try,1,0])} /* send[0]:=false; */
C70 --> C71   {receive(C2,[try,1,0])} /* counter[1]:=1; */
C71 --> C228  {} /* colour[1]:=1; */
C228 --> C238 {send(C2,[donec,1,1])} /* assigned[1]:=true; */
C238 --> C239 {receive(C1,[donec,1,1])} /* round[0]:=1; done[0]:=1;
                   send[0]:=true; counter[0]:=0; used[0]:=[1];
                   constraints[0]:=[]; */
C239 --> C240 {} /* colour[0]:=2; */
C240 --> C241 {send(C1,[try,2,1])} /* send[0]:=false; */
C241 --> C242 {receive(C2,[try,2,1])} /* send[1]:=true; counter[1]:=1;
                   constraints[1]:=[]; */
C242 --> C245 send(C2,[try,1,1]) /* send[1]:=false; */

C245 --> C246 receive(C1,[try,1,1]) /* counter[0]:=1; constraints[0]:=[1]; */
(C246 is final)
```

Fig. 6. Counterexample for property G_2

Table 1. Verification results for the initial and the refined specifications

Property	G_1	G_2	G_3	G_4
original spec	✓	×	n/a	n/a
fixed spec	✓	✓	✓	✓
n. of vertices	2	3	4	5
state space	85	1,469	52,068	2,859,341

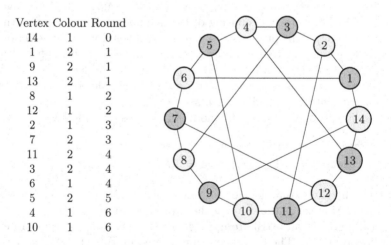

Vertex	Colour	Round
14	1	0
1	2	1
9	2	1
13	2	1
8	1	2
12	1	2
2	1	3
7	2	3
11	2	4
3	2	4
6	1	4
5	2	5
4	1	6
10	1	6

Fig. 7. Execution trace of the automatically generated *ABEL* program

Experimenting with ABEL. Using the second translator, we generated an *Erlang* program for the considered case study from the correct version of the specifications. We ran this program on some random graphs from [20], and observed the outcome of the colouring procedure. Below we report the outcome of the *ABEL* program that received as input the `Heawood` graph shown on the right in Fig. 7; the corresponding run of the *ABEL* program is reported in the left part of the figure.

It is worth observing that *ABEL* can deal with systems with a very large number of components. For instance, we have also experimented with graphs up to 1000 vertices (components), measuring critical parameters such as the number of message exchanges, the total size of messages for each scenario. For detailed performance evaluations, we refer the reader to [9].

6 Concluding Remarks and Future Work

We have presented an integrated framework for programming and verifying systems that are formally described by a theoretically well-founded process calculus, namely *AbC*. Starting from *AbC* specifications, our framework can be used for verifying and executing *AbC* systems by relying on external tools. Indeed, while this work selects only two environments for executing *AbC* programs and verifying their properties, we think that the outlined methodology is sufficiently general to be extended to analyze and execute *AbC* with other verification and programming environments.

For automatic verification, we would like to experiment with adapting our translation to other frameworks and model checkers such as SPIN, for which the work in [21] can be the starting point. Recent surveys [22,23] have described a possible approach to translating simple state machines into a formalism supported by different frameworks, but further analysis is needed to fully assess the complexity of the effort. Moreover, it has still to be understood whether the modeling language is sufficiently expressive to define the properties required for an *AbC* specification.

For programming environments, other approaches have been considered to provide implementations of *AbC*, see e.g., [24–26]. However, these works do not fully capture the original *AbC* semantics or exhibit a significant gap between their programming constructs and the *AbC* primitives, making the translation not obvious. Among the above mentioned implementations, the most promising alternative to *ABEL* appears to be GoAt [25], although some revisions are required also in this case.

Closely related to our work is the one presented in [27] which generates the Java code from the verified spi-calculus specification. They assume correctness of an underlying Java implementation, and focus on proving correctness of code translation and generation. We have not yet considered the correctness of our translators but plan to do it in the close future.

Static verification may be out of reach for large systems. Some lines of work such as the P programming language [28] promote systematic testing within a limit on formal models as an alternative to verification; runtime-monitoring techniques [29] offload the verification to post deployment. The latter typically employs a special entity called monitor to record the interesting events (i.e., send and receive) of a running system and validate the runs against a desired correctness property. It would be interesting to investigate whether these alternatives would fit our model-driven approach to the development of AbC systems.

References

1. De Nicola, R., Fantechi, A., Gnesi, S., Ristori, G.: An action-based framework for verifying logical and behavioural properties of concurrent systems. Comput. Networks ISDN Syst. **25**(7), 761–778 (1993)
2. De Nicola, R., Vaandrager, F.: Action versus state based logics for transition systems. In: Guessarian, I. (ed.) LITP 1990. LNCS, vol. 469, pp. 407–419. Springer, Heidelberg (1990). https://doi.org/10.1007/3-540-53479-2_17
3. Gnesi, S., Mazzanti, F.: On the fly verification of network of automata. In: Arabnia, H.R. (Ed) Proceedings of the International Conference on Parallel and Distributed Processing Techniques and Applications, PDPTA, CSREA Press, Georgia, pp. 1040–1046 (1999)
4. ter Beek, M.H., Fantechi, A., Gnesi, S., Mazzanti, F.: A state/event-based model-checking approach for the analysis of abstract system properties. Sci. Comput. Program. **76**(2), 119–135 (2011)
5. Abd Alrahman, Y., De Nicola, R., Loreti, M.: On the power of attribute-based communication. In: Albert, E., Lanese, I. (eds.) FORTE 2016. LNCS, vol. 9688, pp. 1–18. Springer, Cham (2016). https://doi.org/10.1007/978-3-319-39570-8_1
6. Abd Alrahman, Y., De Nicola, R., Loreti, M.: A behavioural theory for interactions in collective-adaptive systems. CoRR, vol. abs/1711.09762 (2017). http://arxiv.org/abs/1711.09762
7. De Nicola, R., Ferrari, G.L., Pugliese, R., Tiezzi, F.: A formal approach to the engineering of domain-specific distributed systems. In: Di Marzo Serugendo, G., Loreti, M. (eds.) COORDINATION 2018. LNCS, vol. 10852, pp. 110–141. Springer, Cham (2018). https://doi.org/10.1007/978-3-319-92408-3_5
8. Armstrong, J.: Making reliable distributed systems in the presence of software errors. Ph.D. dissertation, The Royal Institute of Technology, Stockholm (2003)
9. De Nicola, R., Duong, T., Loreti, M.: ABEL - a domain specific framework for programming with attribute-based communication. In: Riis Nielson, H., Tuosto, E. (eds.) COORDINATION 2019. LNCS, vol. 11533, pp. 111–128. Springer, Cham (2019). https://doi.org/10.1007/978-3-030-22397-7_7
10. De Nicola, R., Duong, T., Inverso, O., Mazzanti, F.: Verifying properties of systems relying on attribute-based communication. In: Katoen, J.-P., Langerak, R., Rensink, A. (eds.) ModelEd, TestEd, TrustEd. LNCS, vol. 10500, pp. 169–190. Springer, Cham (2017). https://doi.org/10.1007/978-3-319-68270-9_9
11. Calzolai, F., De Nicola, R., Loreti, M., Tiezzi, F.: TAPAs: a tool for the analysis of process algebras. In: Jensen, K., van der Aalst, W.M.P., Billington, J. (eds.) Transactions on Petri Nets and Other Models of Concurrency I. LNCS, vol. 5100, pp. 54–70. Springer, Heidelberg (2008). https://doi.org/10.1007/978-3-540-89287-8_4

12. Abd Alrahman, Y., De Nicola, Loreti, R.: Programming the interactions of collective-adaptive systems by relying on attribute-based communication. CoRR, vol. abs/1711.06092 (2017). http://arxiv.org/abs/1711.06092
13. ter Beek, M.H., Gnesi, S., Mazzanti, F.: From EU projects to a family of model checkers. In: De Nicola, R., Hennicker, R. (eds.) Software, Services, and Systems. LNCS, vol. 8950, pp. 312–328. Springer, Cham (2015). https://doi.org/10.1007/978-3-319-15545-6_20
14. De Nicola, R., Vaandrager, F.W.: Three logics for branching bisimulation. J. ACM, 42(2), 458–487 (1995). http://doi.acm.org/10.1145/201019.201032
15. Fantechi, A., Gnesi, S., Lapadula, A., Mazzanti, F., Pugliese, R., Tiezzi, F.: A logical verification methodology for service-oriented computing. ACM Trans. Software Eng. Methodol. (TOSEM) 21(3), 16 (2012)
16. Clarke, E.M., Emerson, E.A., Sistla, A.P.: Automatic verification of finite-state concurrent systems using temporal logic specifications. ACM Trans. Program. Lang. Syst. (TOPLAS) 8(2), 244–263 (1986)
17. OMG, "Unified modeling language version 2.5 - behavioral statemachines," Object Management Group, Technical Report (2015). https://www.omg.org/spec/UML/2.5/PDF
18. The UMC verification framework. http://fmt.isti.cnr.it/umc
19. Alrahman, Y.A., De Nicola, R., Garbi, G., Loreti, M.: A distributed coordination infrastructure for attribute-based interaction. In: Baier, C., Caires, L. (eds.) FORTE 2018. LNCS, vol. 10854, pp. 1–20. Springer, Cham (2018). https://doi.org/10.1007/978-3-319-92612-4_1
20. Brinkmann, G., Coolsaet, K., Goedgebeur, J., Mélot, H.: House of graphs: a database of interesting graphs. Discrete Appl. Math. 161(1–2), 311–314 (2013)
21. De Nicola, R., et al.: Programming and verifying component ensembles. In: Bensalem, S., Lakhneck, Y., Legay, A. (eds.) ETAPS 2014. LNCS, vol. 8415, pp. 69–83. Springer, Heidelberg (2014). https://doi.org/10.1007/978-3-642-54848-2_5
22. Mazzanti, F., Ferrari, A., Spagnolo, G.O.: Towards formal methods diversity in railways: an experience report with seven frameworks. STTT 20(3), 263–288 (2018). https://doi.org/10.1007/s10009-018-0488-3
23. Mazzanti, F., Ferrari, A.: Ten diverse formal models for a CBTC automatic train supervision system. In: Proceedings Third Workshop on Models for Formal Analysis of Real Systems MARS/VPT@ETAPS 2018, Thessaloniki, Greece, pp. 104–149, 20 April 2018. https://doi.org/10.4204/EPTCS.268.4
24. De Nicola, R., Duong, T., Inverso, O., Trubiani, C.: AErlang: empowering erlang with attribute-based communication. In: Jacquet, J.-M., Massink, M. (eds.) COORDINATION 2017. LNCS, vol. 10319, pp. 21–39. Springer, Cham (2017). https://doi.org/10.1007/978-3-319-59746-1_2
25. Abd Alrahman, Y., De Nicola, R., Garbi, G.: GoAt: Attribute-based interaction in google go. In: Margaria, T., Steffen, B. (eds.) ISoLA 2018. LNCS, vol. 11246, pp. 288–303. Springer, Cham (2018). https://doi.org/10.1007/978-3-030-03424-5_19
26. Abd Alrahman, Y., De Nicola, R., Loreti, M.: Programming of CAS systems by relying on attribute-based communication. In: Margaria, T., Steffen, B. (eds.) ISoLA 2016. LNCS, vol. 9952, pp. 539–553. Springer, Cham (2016). https://doi.org/10.1007/978-3-319-47166-2_38
27. Pironti, A., Sisto, R.: Provably correct java implementations of spi calculus security protocols specifications. Comput. Secur. 29(3), 302–314 (2010)

28. Desai, A., Gupta, V., Jackson, E., Qadeer, S., Rajamani, S., Zufferey, D.: P: safe asynchronous event-driven programming. ACM SIGPLAN Not. **48**(6), 321–332 (2013)
29. Cassar, I., Francalanza, A., Aceto, L., Ingólfsdóttir, A.: A survey of runtime monitoring instrumentation techniques. In: Francalanza, A., Pace, G.J. (Eds.) Proceedings Second International Workshop on Pre- and Post-Deployment Verification Techniques, PrePost@iFM 2017, series EPTCS, vol. 254, pp. 15–28 (2017)

On the Prediction of Smart Contracts' Behaviours

Cosimo Laneve$^{(\boxtimes)}$ [iD], Claudio Sacerdoti Coen [iD], and Adele Veschetti [iD]

Department of Computer Science and Engineering,
University of Bologna – INRIA Focus, Bologna, Italy
{cosimo.laneve,claudio.sacerdoticoen,adele.veschetti2}@unibo.it

Abstract. Smart contracts are pieces of software stored on the blockchain that control the transfer of assets between parties under certain conditions. In this paper we analyze the bahaviour of smart contracts and the interaction with external actors in order to maximize objective functions. We define a core language of programs with a minimal set of smart contract primitives and we describe the whole system as a parallel composition of smart contracts and users. We therefore express the system behaviour as a first logic formula in Presburger arithmetics and study the maximum profit for each actor by solving arithmetic constraints.

1   Introduction

Smart contracts are programs that run on distributed networks with nodes storing a common state in the form of a blockchain. These programs are gaining more and more interest because they implement the so-called *decentralized applications*, which are applications that can handle and transfer assets of considerable value (usually, in the form of cryptocurrency like Bitcoin). Several decentralized applications have already been applied to asset management scenarios ranging from food supply chain management to energy market management and to identity notarization. The smart contracts of such applications are written in programming languages that are targeted to different blockchains. Two such languages are Solidity for Ethereum (which is imperative) [7] and Liquidity for Tezos (which is functional) [14].

Decentralized applications consist of smart contracts and users, such as humans performing either computer actions or physical ones. Since they run on systems that have no coercing central authority, the uncertainty of the overall emerging behaviour is very high and this is a critical issue when asset movements are at the core of applications. Therefore it becomes important to understand the protocols between interacting parties and, when possible, use smart contracts to regulate behaviours of users that systematically try to maximize their revenues or to minimize losses. For example, a client behaves in different ways in order to minimize the cost κ of a good (e.g. he may choose one company or another).

Research partly supported by the H2020-MSCA-RISE project ID 778233 "Behavioural Application Program Interfaces (BEHAPI)".

M. H. ter Beek et al. (Eds.): Gnesi Festschrift, LNCS 11865, pp. 397–415, 2019.
https://doi.org/10.1007/978-3-030-30985-5_23

On the other hand, the interacting company tries to maximize its revenue; therefore it strives for the greatest value κ such that the client has still a convenience in acquiring its own good. Determining the least value κ is complex because it may not only depend on the price, but also on the trademark, the delivery type, etc.

In this paper, to suitably address the foregoing issues, (i) we adhere to a formal modelling approach, (ii) define an analysis technique and (iii) prototype the verification process. A precise account of the work follows.

As regards the formal modelling, since (human) users and smart contracts act concurrently and independently, we adopt methods and techniques from the domain of process algebras. As such, we depart from most of the literature on application of formal methods to smart contracts that study their properties as sequential programs. In Sect. 2 we introduce a unified calculus of actors – both contracts and users, the scl calculus – that is expressive enough (it is Turing complete) and features method invocations, field updates, conditional behaviour, recursion and failures. According to the semantics of scl, systems, which are parallel compositions of smart contracts and users, perform *transactions*, e.g. sequences of smart contract operations that are triggered by users. Transactions may return a value or may fail; in the first case the states of smart contracts that have taken part in the transaction are committed; in the second case the states backtrack to the last committed one. In parallel to transactions, users may evolve internally in a nondeterministic way (on the contrary, smart contracts' behaviours are deterministic). The model of scl is a transition system that enables symbolic analysis of properties – see Sect. 3. In particular, transitions retain two informations: one is a standard label, say μ, highlighting the action performed, the other one, say ψ, is a formula that records the choices and the guards of conditionals. The two labels play different roles in our analysis technique.

Given the model of a scl program, in Sect. 4 we define an objective function as a map from labels μ to integer expressions. For example, such function may return 1 if the label has a given type, or it may return some expression on the symbolic names occurring in the label. In general we are interested in determining computations that maximize or minimize the sum of the values of an objective function on their labels and in selecting strategies that allow users to behave correspondingly. Once this is done, we analyze whether tuning up and down the symbolic names may generate more profit or reduce loss for one interacting party. To this aim, we select a sensible state S and the corresponding transition system rooted at S (we assume there is no cycle and that the transition system is finite). By means of the labels μ and ψ of the transitions, we define a first order logic formula, called the *characteristic formula*, that summarizes the transition system describing concisely the values of the objective function for every possible run.

When the model is Presburger (a decidable fragment of arithmetics where formulas contains only integer numbers, equality, strict inequality, addition and multiplication by a constant), the characteristic formula belongs to an extension of Presburger arithmetics that can be decided via quantifier elimination.

The formula without quantifiers allows us to reason about strategies that bring to goals with higher values (e.g. maximize the profit) for each actor by solving arithmetic constraints. The general cases of infinite, acyclic models are addressed in our technique by analyzing finite unfoldings.

We are currently terminating the implementation in OCaml of a tool that, given a set of contracts, an initial state and an objective function, automatically extracts the open model, computes the characteristic formula and applies quantifier elimination over it. This elimination step also checks whether the formula is satisfiable, i.e. it detects the reachable final states and computes the set of values of the objective function that can be observed in runs that lead to them. These sets are represented as linear mappings over domains that are union of polytopes, i.e. solutions of a systems of linear inequations in normal form. The inequations constrain the choices that users can take according to those of other users or to external inputs to the system. Maximizing linear functions over linear inequations is mathematically trivial.

We conclude in Sect. 5 by discussing future research directions.

Related Works. In the past few years formal methods have been largely used to analyze smart contracts with the aim of verifying the security of potentially dangerous compositions with untrusted codes. One of the most cited motivation has been the famous `TheDAO` attack [15] that stole several million dollars during a crowdfunding procedure and caused an hard fork in the Ethereum blockchain.

An initial contribution is [2], which proposes an analysis framework based on a compilation of Solidity to F*, a functional language aimed at program verification with a powerful type and effect system. Using F* types, they are able to trace Ethers (the Ethereum cryptocurrency) and discover critical patterns in smart contracts. A different technique has been followed by [10] and [11], sticking to symbolic execution. Similarly to our technique, they use symbolic values for inputs and study symbolic computations by mean of the formula that accumulates the constraints on the inputs. This formula is different from our characteristic formula in Sect. 4. In particular, while our formula describes *every possible computation* and we use constraints on symbols to determine values that maximize some quantity, in [10] and [11], they are interested in discovering critical patterns of a *single computation*.

In the same line of verifying and validating smart contracts, the contribution [3] combines formal methods and game theory to analyze protocols that also involve players (human users) with different/competing gaming strategies. The technique is the following: game theory is used to analyze the behaviour of the players in the protocol, then the resulting strategies are modelled in a probabilistic system for automated validation. Our approach is somehow the opposite: we define the overall system (or part of it) in a formal model and derive the strategies by analyzing the model. In this paper, we stick to a discrete model (the choice operator in users' behaviours is not probabilistic), leaving to future research the extension to stochastic models.

Another contribution that is close to our one is [4]. In this case, the authors define a simplified language for smart contracts that is loop-free. Then they provide an automatic translation into stateful concurrent games and analyze these games by means of interval abstraction that is demonstrated to be sound. The technique is very powerful and of practical relevance, considering that models of concurrent games are very large. Unlike to this work, our modelling technique is based on process algebra and our analysis relies on Presburger arithmetics formulae. The evaluation of the practical relevance of our technique is postponed to future research.

2   The Calculus of Smart Contracts

In this section we define a core language of programs featuring a minimal set of smart contract primitives, such as method invocations, field updates, conditional behaviour, recursion and failures.

We use a countable set of *variables*, ranged over by x, y, z, a countable set of *smart contract names*, ranged over by a, b, c, and a countable set of *user names*, ranged over by id, id', id''. Smart contract names and user names are generically addressed by α, α', ... and we assume they are partitioned into disjoint sets such that names of a same set belong to *a same class* and those in different sets belong to *different classes*. The property that a name α belongs to a class C is expressed by $\alpha \in$ C.

Classes C have the form $C : (\overline{F}, \overline{M})$ where $\overline{F}$ is a sequence of *field definitions* T f, $\overline{M}$ is a sequence of *method definitions* T m$(\overline{T\,x})\{\ s_m\ \}$ with $\overline{T\,x}$ and s_m respectively being the *formal parameters* and the *body* of m. In the whole paper, we assume that sequences of declarations $\overline{T\,x}$ and method declarations $\overline{M}$ do not contain duplicate names. *Types* T are either naturals *Nat* or names α. Hereafter we write $\overline{k}$ for possibly empty, finite sequences $k_1, \ldots, k_n$ of various entities.

The syntax of statements, rhs-expressions and expressions is given in Fig. 1. A statement s may be either a return of an expression, or a field update (plus a continuation), or a conditional or the nondeterministic choice $s + s'$. We assume that bodies of smart contract methods (*i*) do not have nondeterministic choice (they are deterministic) and (*ii*) do not have expressions with fail, except for return fail.

A rhs-expression z may be either an expression e or a *synchronous* method invocation. An expression e may be either a standard expression or fail. In e op e', op is a standard operation on naturals. We assume that method bodies of users also have the expression isfailed(e) that returns 1 if the value of e is fail, 0 otherwise.

The semantics of scl statements is defined by a transition relation

$$\alpha : s, \ell \xmapsto[\psi]{\mu} s', \ell'$$

where s and s', with an abuse of notation, are *runtime statements*, ℓ and ℓ' are *memories*, e.g. maps from field names to values v, μ is either empty or $v.\mathtt{m}(\overline{v'})$,

Syntax:

$$
\begin{array}{llll}
s & ::= & \text{return } e \quad | \quad \text{this.f} = z; s \quad | \quad \text{if } e \text{ then } s \text{ else } s \quad | \quad s + s & \text{(statements)} \\
z & ::= & e \quad | \quad e.\mathtt{m}(\bar{e}) & \text{(rhs-expressions)} \\
e & ::= & naturals \quad | \quad x \quad | \quad \alpha \quad | \quad \text{fail} \quad | \quad \text{this} \quad | \quad \text{this.f} \quad | \quad e \text{ op } e & \text{(expressions)}
\end{array}
$$

States and runtime statements:

$$
\begin{array}{llll}
\ell & ::= & [\cdots, \mathtt{f} \mapsto v, \cdots] & \text{(memories)} \\
v & ::= & naturals \quad | \quad \alpha \quad | \quad \text{fail} & \text{(values)} \\
s & ::= & \cdots \quad | \quad 0 \quad | \quad id \quad | \quad id[v] \quad | \quad \alpha.\mathtt{f} = \bullet; s \quad | \quad s; s \quad | \quad s +^x s & \text{(runtime statements)}
\end{array}
$$

runtime statement transition $\xmapsto[\psi]{\mu}$ (μ may be empty or α; ψ is a formula):

[UPD]
$$
\frac{[\![e]\!]_{\alpha,\ell} = v}{\alpha : \alpha.\mathtt{f} = e; s, \ell \xmapsto[\text{true}]{} s, \ell[\mathtt{f} \mapsto v]}
$$

[METH]
$$
\frac{[\![e]\!]_{\alpha,\ell} = v \quad [\![\overline{e'}]\!]_{\alpha,\ell} = \overline{v'} \quad \text{fail} \notin v, \overline{v'}}{v \in C \quad \mathtt{m}(\overline{x}) = s_\mathtt{m} \in C \quad s'' = s_\mathtt{m}\{^{\overline{v'},v}/_{\overline{x},\text{this}}\}}{\alpha : \alpha.\mathtt{f} = e.\mathtt{m}(\overline{e'}); s, \ell \xmapsto[\text{true}]{v.\mathtt{m}(\overline{v'})} s''; \alpha.\mathtt{f} = \bullet; s, \ell}
$$

[METH-FAIL]
$$
\frac{[\![e]\!]_{id,\ell} = v \quad [\![\overline{e'}]\!]_{id,\ell} = \overline{v'} \quad \text{fail} \in v, \overline{v'}}{id : id.\mathtt{f} = e.\mathtt{m}(\overline{e'}); s, \ell \xmapsto[\text{true}]{} s, \ell[\mathtt{f} \mapsto \text{fail}]}
$$

[RETURN]
$$
\frac{[\![e]\!]_{\alpha,\ell} = v}{\alpha : \text{return } e; s, \ell \xmapsto[\text{true}]{} s[v], \ell}
$$

[IF-TRUE]
$$
\frac{[\![e]\!]_{\alpha,\ell} \neq 0}{\alpha : \text{if } e \text{ then } s \text{ else } s'; s'', \ell \xmapsto[\text{true}]{} s; s'', \ell}
$$

[IF-FALSE]
$$
\frac{[\![e]\!]_{\alpha,\ell} = 0}{\alpha : \text{if } e \text{ then } s \text{ else } s'; s'', \ell \xmapsto[\text{true}]{} s'; s'', \ell}
$$

[FIX]
$$
\frac{x \text{ fresh}}{id : (s_1 + s_2); s, \ell \xmapsto[\text{true}]{} (s_1 +^x s_2); s, \ell}
$$

[CHOICE]
$$
\frac{i \in \{1, 2\}}{id : (s_1 +^x s_2); s, \ell \xmapsto[x=i]{} s_i; s, \ell}
$$

Fig. 1. Syntax and runtime statement semantics of scl.

and ψ is a formula. The transition means that executing s in an actor α with a memory ℓ amounts to produce an action μ and a formula ψ and executing s' in ℓ'. Actions μ are commitments to the context, formulas ψ are essential for our analysis in the next sections.

Runtime statements, as reported in Fig. 1, extend statements with 0 representing termination, id recording the user that initiated the transaction, $id[v]$ returning a value to the user id, $\alpha.\mathtt{f} = \bullet; s$ representing a continuation waiting for a value that will replace the symbol $\bullet$, with $s; s'$ denoting the sequential composition, and $s +^x s'$, an alternative form of $s + s'$ that retains the fresh variable to be used for recording the choice (this information is necessary in the analysis of Sect. 4). Sequential composition is considered associative.

The following auxiliary functions are used in the semantic rules:

- $\ell[\mathtt{f} \mapsto v]$ is the *memory update*, namely $(\ell[\mathtt{f} \mapsto v])(\mathtt{f}) = v$ and $(\ell[\mathtt{f} \mapsto v])(\mathtt{g}) = \ell(\mathtt{g})$, when $\mathtt{g} \neq \mathtt{f}$.

– $s[v]$ is the *delivery of a value v to a runtime statement s*, namely

$$s[v] \stackrel{\text{def}}{=} \begin{cases} \alpha.\mathtt{f} = v; s' & \text{if } s = \alpha.\mathtt{f} = \bullet; s' & \text{and } v \neq \mathsf{fail} \\ id.\mathtt{f} = \mathsf{fail}; s' & \text{if } s = id.\mathtt{f} = \bullet; s' & \text{and } v = \mathsf{fail} \\ id[\mathsf{fail}] & \text{if } s = a.\mathtt{f} = \bullet; s'; id & \text{and } v = \mathsf{fail} \\ id[v] & \text{if } s = id \end{cases}$$

It is worth to observe that $(\alpha.\mathtt{f} = \bullet; s')[\mathsf{fail}]$ behaves in different ways according to α being a user or a smart contract. In the first case the field of the user is updated with fail – which is possible for users, in the second case the whole statement fails and the failure is reported to the user that triggered the whole transaction.

– $[\![e]\!]_{\alpha,\ell}$ is a partial function that returns the value of e. The value of fields of α is retrieved in the memory ℓ of α: $[\![\alpha.\mathtt{f}]\!]_{\alpha,\ell} = \ell(\mathtt{f})$. The function is undefined if e tries to use fields of an actor $\neq \alpha$. We omit the definition of $[\![e]\!]_{\alpha,\ell}$ when e is an operation, but we require that it must be fail when one of the arguments is fail. $[\![\overline{e}]\!]_{\alpha,\ell}$ returns the tuple of values of $\overline{e}$.

Let us comment some semantic rules in Fig. 1. Rule [UPD] defines the semantics of a field update: the expression e is evaluated in an actor α with a memory ℓ; the resulting memory binds the value to the field $\mathtt{f}$. Rule [METH] defines method invocations $\alpha.\mathtt{f} = e.\mathtt{m}(\overline{e'}); s$ when the evaluation of e and $\overline{e'}$ does not return a failure. In this case, the method dispatch is performed by using the value v of the carrier (because every name belongs to a class) and the statement to evaluate becomes the instance of the body of $\mathtt{m}$, followed by the update $\alpha.\mathtt{f} = \bullet$, where $\bullet$ represents a place-holder, and the continuation s. The transition is labelled $\xrightarrow[\text{true}]{v.\mathtt{m}(\overline{v'})}$ meaning that we are invoking the method $\mathtt{m}$ of actor v with actual parameters $\overline{v'}$. Rule [METH-FAIL] addresses failures in the evaluation of expressions of a method invocation; in this case the invocation is not performed and the field is updated with fail. Rule [RETURN] defines the semantics of $\mathsf{return}\ e$. There are two types of return continuations s: one is $\alpha.\mathtt{f} = \bullet; s'$ – see rule [METH], the other one is id (this will be clear in the semantics of $\mathtt{scl}$ programs). Additionally, the semantics depends on whether α is a smart contract or a user, and on whether the value v is a failure or not. To manage all these cases we use the auxiliary function $s[v]$. The semantics of conditionals is standard. On the contrary, the semantics of nondeterminism is not standard and deserves few comments. First of all, nondeterminism may only occur in user codes, therefore the actor here is id. Then, we need to keep track of the nondeterministic choices in order to study the behaviour of smart contract programs. To this aim we use a fresh variable x each time a choice is about to be performed and $(s_1 + s_2); s$ transits into an intermediate statement $(s_1 +^x s_2); s$. In turn this statement becomes either $s_1; s$ or $s_2; s$ and the choice is recorded by letting $x = 1$ or $x = 2$ in the formula labelling the transition, respectively.

States:

$$S ::= \quad s \quad | \quad a(\ell \cdot \ell') \quad | \quad id(\ell, s) \quad | \quad S \,|\, S \qquad\qquad \text{(states)}$$

Auxiliary functions $commit(\cdot)$ and $backtk(\cdot)$ (the two functions are homomorphic with respect to $|$):

$$commit(s) = s \qquad commit(a(\ell \cdot \ell')) = a(\ell \cdot \ell) \qquad commit(id(\ell, s)) = id(\ell, s)$$
$$backtk(s) = s \qquad backtk(a(\ell \cdot \ell')) = a(\ell' \cdot \ell') \qquad backtk(id(\ell, s)) = id(\ell, s)$$

State transition $\xrightarrow[\psi]{\mu}$ (μ may be empty, α, $\checkmark$ or fail; ψ is a formula):

[SC-MOVE]
$$\frac{a : s, \ell \xmapsto[\psi]{} s', \ell'}{a(\ell \cdot \ell'') \,|\, s \xrightarrow[\psi]{} a(\ell' \cdot \ell'') \,|\, s'}$$

[ID-MOVE]
$$\frac{id : s, \ell \xmapsto[\psi]{} s', \ell'}{id(\ell, s) \xrightarrow[\psi]{} id(\ell', s')}$$

[INVK]
$$\frac{a : s, \ell \xmapsto[\psi]{a'.\mathtt{m}(\overline{v})} s', \ell \quad a \neq a'}{a(\ell \cdot \ell') \,|\, a'(\ell'' \cdot \ell''') \,|\, s \xrightarrow[\psi]{} a(\ell \cdot \ell') \,|\, a'(\ell'' \cdot \ell''') \,|\, s'}$$

[INVK-SELF]
$$\frac{a : s, \ell \xmapsto[\psi]{a.\mathtt{m}(\overline{v})} s', \ell}{a(\ell \cdot \ell') \,|\, s \xrightarrow[\psi]{} a(\ell \cdot \ell') \,|\, s'}$$

[INVK-SC]
$$\frac{id : s, \ell \xmapsto[\psi]{a.\mathtt{m}(\overline{v})} s''; id.\mathtt{f} = \bullet; s', \ell \quad \bullet \notin s''}{id(\ell, s) \,|\, a(\ell' \cdot \ell') \,|\, 0 \xrightarrow[\psi]{} id(\ell, id.\mathtt{f} = \bullet; s') \,|\, a(\ell' \cdot \ell') \,|\, s''; id}$$

[INVK-ID-SELF]
$$\frac{id : s, \ell \xmapsto[\psi]{id.\mathtt{m}(\overline{v})} s', \ell}{id(\ell, s) \xrightarrow[\psi]{} id(\ell, s')}$$

[END-OK]
$$\frac{v \neq \text{fail}}{id(\ell, s) \,|\, id[v] \xrightarrow[\text{true}]{\checkmark} id(\ell, s[v]) \,|\, 0}$$

[END-FAIL]
$$id(\ell, s) \,|\, id[\text{fail}] \xrightarrow[\text{true}]{\text{fail}} id(\ell, s[\text{fail}]) \,|\, 0$$

[CMT]
$$\frac{S \xrightarrow[\psi]{\checkmark} S'}{S'' \,|\, S \xrightarrow[\psi]{\checkmark} commit(S'') \,|\, S'}$$

[BKT]
$$\frac{S \xrightarrow[\psi]{\text{fail}} S'}{S'' \,|\, S \xrightarrow[\psi]{\text{fail}} backtk(S'') \,|\, S'}$$

[TAU]
$$\frac{S \xrightarrow[\psi]{} S'}{S'' \,|\, S \xrightarrow[\psi]{} S'' \,|\, S'}$$

Fig. 2. Semantics of scl.

2.1 Semantics of scl programs

A *smart contract program* is a pair $(\mathcal{D}, S)$, where $\mathcal{D}$ is a *finite set* of *class definitions* and S is *state*. States, as defined in Fig. 2, are *parallel composition* of actors $a(\ell \cdot \ell')$, called *smart contracts*, or actors $id(\ell, s)$, called *users*, and *exactly one* runtime statement, called *blockchain-statement*. Smart contracts have *pairs of memories* $\ell \cdot \ell'$ where ℓ is the *current memory* and ℓ' is the *last committed memory*. In case of commits, the current memory ℓ becomes the last committed memory; in case of failures, the system will backtrack by restoring ℓ'. In a state, names a and id are unique. As usual, parallel composition in states is associative and commutative.

The semantics of a smart contract program is defined by means of transition relation $S \xrightarrow[\psi]{\mu} S'$, where μ may be either empty or $\checkmark$ or fail, and ψ is a formula. The class declarations are kept implicit in the transition relation. The reader may find the formal definition of $\xrightarrow[\psi]{\mu}$ in Fig. 2.

States may evolve in two ways: either by a transition of the blockchain-statement or by a transition of a user.

The blockchain-statement may evolve because of an empty-labelled statement transition – rule [SC-MOVE] – or because of a method invocations of a smart contract – see rules [INVK] and [INVK-SELF]. In this last case, the state must contain the smart contract whose method is invoked in the label of the transition. Users have a behaviour, which is modelled by a runtime statement, and evolve *concurrently* either with empty-labelled transitions – rule [ID-MOVE] – or with self-invocations – rule [INVK-ID] (therefore a user cannot invoke another user, *e.g.* user interactions are always mediated by a smart contract). When the blockchain-statement is 0, a user may invoke a smart contract's method – rule [INVK-SC]. This is the only way to start a *blockchain transaction* and, in this case, in order to return the result to the caller, method's body is suffixed with user's name. The transaction terminates either successfully returning a not-fail value to the user that triggered it – rule [END-OK] – or with a failure – rule [END-FAIL]. In the first case, the smart contracts that were involved in the transaction are committed – rule [CMT], e.g. their current local memory is saved; in the second case the smart contracts backtrack – rule [BKT] – e.g. their current memory is deleted and the current one becomes the last memory that has been committed. Backtrack and commit are defined by the auxiliary functions $backtk(\cdot)$ and $commit(\cdot)$ in Fig. 2.

We conclude by noticing that blockchain-statements are executed *sequentially* and in a *deterministic way* (because they originated in smart contracts' methods). On the contrary, users' method are performed *concurrently* and are *nondeterministic* (because the operator + may occur in their code).

Example 1. We use a simple example to illustrate the technicalities we have introduced. The example is about garbage collection and defines the interactions between a citizen and a smart bin. In particular, a citizen gets rid of the garbage in two ways: either throwing the garbage bags into a smart bin or dumping it (littering the street, for instance). The throwing in the bin is performed by invoking a method "throw"; this invocation returns a natural value that corresponds to a cash prize for having behaved well. If the garbage bag is dumped, the prize is 0. Every two garbage bags, the cash owned by the citizen is deposited in his bank account (in order to reduce his overall garbage taxes). The classes of the citizen and of the smart bin are displayed in Fig. 3 (notice that the citizen is a user, while the bin is a smart contract). For simplicity, the management of failures has been removed by the codes of Fig. 3. The smart bin class has a method throw whose behaviour depends on the value of the field h. When h is 0, two bags can be taken: the field h is set to 1 and a prize k is returned to the citizen, subtracting it from the field a that represents the money hold by the bin. When the second bag arrives, a value k' is returned to the citizen (notice that k may be different from k'), after having re-charged the field a and asked to the truck to empty the bin, re-setting h to 0.

Let us discuss a possible state and its transitions. Let $man \in$ Citizen, $bin \in$ Garbage_bin, $bank \in$ Bank and $truck \in$ Truck. We assume that Bank

```
Citizen = (
   Nat v1, v2, tmp ;
   Nat behaviour(Id bin, Id bank) =
         this.v1 = bin.throw() ; ( this.v2 = bin.throw() ; CONT
                                        + this.v2 = 0 ; CONT )
         + this.v1 = 0 ; ( this.v2 = bin.throw() ; CONT
                                + this.v2 = 0 ; CONT )
      where CONT = this.tmp = bank.deposit(v1+v2); this.v1 = 0; this.v2 = 0;
                   this.tmp = this.behaviour(bin,bank); return this.tmp
)

Garbage_bin = (
   Nat h, a, tmp ;
   Nat throw() =
         if (this.h == 0) then this.h = 1 ; this.a = this.a - k ; return k
         else this.a = this.a + bank.withdraw(k + k'); this.h = 0 ;
              this.tmp = truck.empty(); this.a = this.a - k'; return k'
)
```

Fig. 3. The citizen and garbage bin classes

has methods deposit and withdraw (with the obvious meanings); Truck has a method empty that empties the bin and returns 0. Let also

$$\ell_m = [v_1 \mapsto 0, v_2 \mapsto 0, tmp \mapsto 0]$$
$$\ell_b = [h \mapsto 0, a \mapsto k' + k, tmp \mapsto 0]$$
$$s = man.tmp = man.behaviour(bin, bank); \text{return } 0$$
$$S = man(\ell_m, s) \mid bin(\ell_b \cdot \ell_b) \mid bank(\ell \cdot \ell) \mid truck(\ell' \cdot \ell') \mid 0$$

We have

$$S \xrightarrow{\text{true}} man(\ell_m, s') \mid bin(\ell_b \cdot \ell_b) \mid bank(\ell \cdot \ell) \mid truck(\ell' \cdot \ell') \mid 0$$

where $s' = s_{bh}; man.tmp = \bullet; \text{return } 0$ and s_{bh} is the body of behaviour with the instantiation $\{^{bin,bank,man}/_{bin,bank,this}\}$. In this state, s_{bh} may evolve either by invoking $bin.throw()$ (throwing the garbage into the bin) or by updating v_1 to 0 (illegal dumping of garbage). Let us discuss the first alternative, which is more interesting. Therefore, let $s'' = s'_{bh}; man.tmp = \bullet; \text{return } 0$, where

$$s'_{bh} = man.v1 = \bullet; (man.v2 = bin.throw(); CONT + man.v2 = 0; CONT)$$

Then we have the following transitions (x_1 and x_2 are two fresh variables for tracing the choices that has been done):

$$man(\ell_m, s') \mid bin(\ell_b \cdot \ell_b) \mid bank(\ell \cdot \ell) \mid truck(\ell' \cdot \ell') \mid 0$$
$$\xrightarrow{\text{true}\,x_1=1} man(\ell_m, s'_{bh}) \mid bin(\ell_b \cdot \ell_b) \mid bank(\ell \cdot \ell) \mid truck(\ell' \cdot \ell') \mid s_{thw}; man$$
$$\xrightarrow{\text{true}}^4 man(\ell_m, s'_{bh}) \mid bin(\ell'_b \cdot \ell_b) \mid bank(\ell \cdot \ell) \mid truck(\ell' \cdot \ell') \mid man[k]$$
$$\xrightarrow{\text{true}}^{\checkmark} man(\ell'_m, s'_{bh}\{^k/_\bullet\}) \mid bin(\ell'_b \cdot \ell'_b) \mid bank(\ell \cdot \ell) \mid truck(\ell' \cdot \ell') \mid 0$$
$$\xrightarrow{\text{true}\,x_2=1} man(\ell'_m, s''_{bh}) \mid bin(\ell'_b \cdot \ell'_b) \mid bank(\ell \cdot \ell) \mid truck(\ell' \cdot \ell') \mid s_{thw}; man$$

where s_{thw} is the instance of the body of throw with the name bin for this; $\ell'_m = \ell_m[v_1 \mapsto k], \ell'_b = \ell_b[h \mapsto 1, a \mapsto k']$ and $s''_{bh} = man.v2 = \bullet; CONT$. The continuation is omitted.

3 The Open Semantics and the Analysis Model

A decentralized application is never a closed system: smart contract's methods can always be invoked not only by users and the smart contracts designed to interact with them, but also by unknown actors. Therefore, to study properties of our systems, we need to analyse open configurations. In particular, we need to reason on invocations without any knowledge of the actual parameters of the caller. A standard solution of this problem is to use *symbolic variables* – see Fig. 4, i.e. extending values with (unbound) variables and admitting that operators return terms, such as $x + 1$, in addition to integers and actor names. Therefore the evaluation function $[\![e]\!]_{\alpha,\ell}$ may now return terms with symbolic variables and it follows that actor's fields may also record terms with symbolic variables.

The extensions of runtime statements transitions in Fig. 1 and of state transitions in Fig. 2 are given in Fig. 4. As regards runtime statements, the rules [IF-TRUE] and [IF-FALSE] are replaced by [IF-OPEN-TRUE] and [IF-OPEN-FALSE] where the formulas of transitions report whether the guard is true ($\neq 0$) or false ($= 0$). These formulas and those of the rule [CHOICE] will enable the analysis of smart contract systems in Sect. 4.

As regards the open state transition, we extend the rules of Fig. 2 with those for invoking a method of a unspecified smart contract – rules [INVK-OPEN] and [INVK-OPEN-ID]. We discuss the former, the latter one is similar. The function $\bullet \notin s''$ returns true if $\bullet$ does not occur in the runtime statement s'' (which is always the case when a method body is instantiated). This expedient is used to select in $s'' ; a.\mathtt{f} = \bullet ; s', a, \ell$ the prefix representing the instance of method's body and to drop it because we don't want to analyze behaviours of unspecified actors. Henceforth, the rule delivers to the continuation either a symbolic variable or fail, therefore covering every possible output of the invocation.

Rule [INPUT-OPEN-SC] defines the invocation of a smart contract method by a hypothetical user. In this case, actual parameters are all fresh symbolic variables and the instance of method body is suffixed by the name of the hypothetical user. According to the returned value is fail or not, we will have a backtrack – rule [END-FAIL-OPEN] – or a commit – rule [END-OPEN], respectively.

The open transition system in Fig. 4 defines a *model* that is a tuple $(\mathcal{S}, \mathsf{S}_0, \mathcal{T})$, where $\mathcal{S}$ is a non-empty set of *states*, $\mathsf{S}_0 \in \mathcal{S}$ is the initial state, and $\mathcal{T} \subseteq \mathcal{S} \times \mathcal{S} \times \Theta \times \Psi$ is the set of labelled transitions. The set Θ is the collection of labels $\{\varepsilon, \mathsf{fail}, \checkmark, v = a'.\mathtt{m}(\overline{v}), id : \overline{z}\}$ (ε represents the empty label) while Ψ is a set of formulae. As usual $\langle \mathsf{S}_1, \mathsf{S}_2, \mu, \psi \rangle \in \mathcal{T}$ is abbreviated into $\mathsf{S}_1 \xrightarrow[\psi]{\mu} \mathsf{S}_2$.

Actually, in Sect. 4 we use a slightly different model than the foregoing one, that we call *analysis model*. In the forthcoming analysis we need to deal with the constant fail. To this aim, in order to remain in Presburger arithmetics, we decided to encode fail by extending the *Nat* type to *Integers*. Henceforth fail is encoded by -1 and we use a function $|\psi|$ replacing every occurrence of fail with -1 and turning every actor name into a (global) integer variable. We also extend

Symbolic values:

$$v ::= \quad \dots \quad | \quad x \quad | \quad v \text{ op } v \qquad\qquad \text{(symbolic values)}$$

Open runtime statements transition $\xmapsto[\psi]{\mu}$:

[IF-OPEN-TRUE]
$$\frac{[\![e]\!]_{\alpha,\ell} = v}{\alpha : \text{if } e \text{ then } s \text{ else } s';s'',\ell \xmapsto[v \neq 0]{} s;s'',\ell}$$

[IF-OPEN-FALSE]
$$\frac{[\![e]\!]_{\alpha,\ell} = v}{\alpha : \text{if } e \text{ then } s \text{ else } s';s'',\ell \xmapsto[v = 0]{} s';s'',\ell}$$

Open state transition $\xrightarrow[\psi]{\mu}$ (μ may be empty, $\checkmark$, fail, $a.\mathtt{m}(\overline{v})$, or $id : \overline{z}$; ψ is a formula):

[INVK-OPEN]
$$\frac{a : s,\ell \xmapsto[\text{true}]{a'.\mathtt{m}(\overline{v'})} s'';a.\mathtt{f} = \bullet;s',\ell \quad \bullet \notin s'' \quad v \text{ either } x \text{ fresh or fail}}{S \mid a(\ell \cdot \ell') \mid s \xrightarrow[a' \notin S]{v = a'.\mathtt{m}(\overline{v'})} S \mid a(\ell \cdot \ell') \mid (a.\mathtt{f} = \bullet;s')[v]}$$

[INVK-OPEN-ID]
$$\frac{id : s,\ell \xmapsto[\text{true}]{a.\mathtt{m}(\overline{v'})} s'';id.\mathtt{f} = \bullet;s',\ell \quad \bullet \notin s'' \quad v \text{ either } x \text{ fresh or fail}}{S \mid id(\ell,s) \xrightarrow[a \notin S]{v = a.\mathtt{m}(\overline{v'})} S \mid id(\ell,(id.\mathtt{f} = \bullet;s')[v])}$$

[INPUT-OPEN-SC]
$$\frac{id, \overline{z} \text{ fresh} \quad a \in C \quad \mathtt{m}(\overline{x}) = s_{\mathtt{m}} \in C \quad s'' = s_{\mathtt{m}}\{\overline{z},a/\overline{x},\text{this}\}}{S \mid a(\ell \cdot \ell) \mid 0 \xrightarrow[id \notin S]{id:\overline{z}} S \mid a(\ell \cdot \ell) \mid s'';id}$$

[END-OPEN]
$$\frac{v \neq \text{fail}}{S \mid id[v] \xrightarrow[id \notin S]{\checkmark} commit(S) \mid 0}$$

[END-FAIL-OPEN]
$$S \mid id[\text{fail}] \xrightarrow[id \notin S]{\text{fail}} backtk(S) \mid 0$$

Fig. 4. The open semantics of scl.

labels Θ with a new label, written (x), which is meant to expose in the label the fixing of the variable x by rule [FIX] of Fig. 1. In particular, in the analysis model

- if $S \xrightarrow[\psi]{\mu} S'$ follows from the open semantics *without using the rule* [FIX] then the analysis model has $S \xrightarrow[|\psi|]{\mu} S'$;
- if $S \xrightarrow[\psi]{} S'$ follows from the open semantics *using the rule* [FIX] and x is the fresh variable that has been introduced then the analysis model has $S \xrightarrow[|\psi|]{(x)} S'$.

An (analysis) model is *finite* if the set of states S is finite; it is a *Presburger* model if the set of conditions Ψ and the actual parameters used in Θ range respectively over Presburger formulas and Presburger expressions. We recall that Presburger arithmetics is the decidable subset of classical first order logic over integer numbers where the only predicates allowed are equality and (strict) inequality and the only function symbols are addition between integer expressions and multiplication of an integer expression by a constant.

Example 2. In Fig. 5 we illustrate the analysis model of a citizen and a garbage bin discussed in Example 1. In order to have a more compact picture, we have collapsed empty-labelled transitions. We have also used a simple hack to have

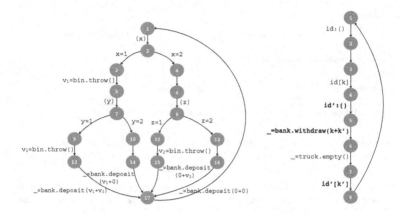

Fig. 5. The models of the citizen and the bin

finite models: we have added an empty labelled transition from state 17 to state 1, even if they are not exactly equal as systems states. This is because the stack of the citizen grows at every call since we do not optimize tail recursion in the transition systems of Fig. 2. However, our analyzer always performs these optimizations. We also remark that the two models are also Presburger models.

Due to lack of space, Fig. 5 does not report the interactions between the citizen, the garbage bin and other actors. The complete model has a large number of states because all possible interactions. In particular, every time the citizen wants to throw out her garbage, she can either succeed immediately—and in that case an empty labelled move is performed by the system via the [INVK-SC] rule—or she can be pre-empted by an unknown *id* via the [INPUT-OPEN-SC] rule.

4   Observables and Strategies

A user can behave in different ways and obtain different results because of the choice operator + that may occur in its code. In this section we study users' behaviours and how choices influence results in a sensible way.

Definition 1. *Let* (S, S_0, T) *be a* scl *analysis model. An* objective function ω *maps labels* μ *of transitions* $S \xrightarrow[\psi]{\mu} S'$ *in* T *to some integer expression. Given a computation* $S_1 \xrightarrow[\psi_1]{\mu_1} \cdots \xrightarrow[\psi_n]{\mu_n} S_{n+1}$, *its* ω-*observation is* $\sum_{1 \leq i \leq n} \omega(\mu_i)$.

In Example 1, a citizen is interested into maximizing the amount of cashback that is saved in the bank, i.e. its objective function called ω_C, is defined as follows

$$\omega_C(\mu) = \begin{cases} v_1 + v_2 & \text{if } \mu = \_ = \text{bank.deposit}(v_1 + v_2) \\ 0 & \text{otherwise} \end{cases}$$

We notice that the result of an objective function may be *a term containing symbolic names*. (As a consequence our analysis will enable programmers to design smart contracts with instances of symbolic names that support "optimal strategies" – see below.) Contrary to citizens, the city hall is interested on minimizing the amount of garbage dumped or, equivalently, to maximize the amount of garbage thrown in the bins. Thus its objective function ω_H is defined as follows

$$\omega_H(\mu) = \begin{cases} 1 & \text{if } \mu = \_ = \texttt{bin.throw()} \\ 0 & \text{otherwise} \end{cases}$$

A *strategy* is a function that determines the transition to perform in states where the next statement to execute is a choice. Since these decisions are taken by users, which only have a *partial understanding* of the state (every user has full visibility of its own state and of smart contracts' states, they cannot access the internal state of other users), in general, a user can only devise "sub-optimal" strategies. A strategy is *optimal* with respect to an objective function ω, if, for any other strategy, all the possible future computations (which follow by the behaviour of the other users involved) cannot yield a higher ω-observation. Users that, at any choice point, try to maximize some *objective function* are called *rational*. In the rest of the section we are interested into rational users.

In general we cannot expect the existence of optimal strategies, nor we can expect that a strategy that is optimal for a given objective function is also optimal for another objective function. For example, if we just analyze the model of our citizen in isolation (see Fig. 5), we can only deduce the following facts about the pair of objective functions $\langle \omega_C, \omega_H \rangle$, i.e. the first element observes the cash-back (according to the citizen objective function) and the second one the number of calls to $\texttt{throw()}$ (according to the city hall objective function):

1. the strategy that dumps the garbage twice at each execution 1–17 yields the pair $\langle 0, 0 \rangle$;
2. the two strategies that dump the garbage once yield the pairs $\langle v_1, 1 \rangle$ and $\langle v_2, 1 \rangle$ respectively, for some v_1, v_2;
3. the strategy that never dumps the garbage yield the pair $\langle v_1 + v_2, 2 \rangle$, for some v_1, v_2.

Note that v_1 and v_2 are not fixed: a garbage bin may return different values at every invocation of $\texttt{throw()}$, depending on its own internal logic and on the interaction with other actors. From the point of view of the city hall, the optimal strategy for the citizen is clearly the last one. From the point of view of the citizen, instead, there is no optimal strategy: it depends on the behaviour of the garbage bin that is unknown since we are analyzing the citizen in isolation.

Here is where smart contracts enter into the picture. A smart contract is used to regulate interaction between (human) users. In many real world examples, the smart contract is designed so that the system obtained composing humans with contracts has two relevant properties: (*i*) every user has an optimal strategy and (*ii*) the optimal users' strategies also maximizes the objective function of the smart contract programmer. In Example 1, this second function is exactly ω_H, that is the programmer aims at minimizing the garbage dumped by citizens. If we combine the citizen and the smart contract and we analyze again the model obtained, we realize that the garbage bin sometimes pays back k coins and sometimes k' coins. In particular, the strategy of point 1 always yield $\langle 0, 0 \rangle$, both strategies of point 2 sometimes yield $\langle k, 1 \rangle$ and sometimes $\langle k', 1 \rangle$, while the strategy of point 3 can yield any pair of observations among $\langle k+k, 2 \rangle$, $\langle k+k', 2 \rangle$, $\langle k'+k, 2 \rangle$, $\langle k'+k', 2 \rangle$. It follows that the strategy of point 1 is clearly not optimal for the citizen, but the remaining three are incomparable because, for example, getting a k' from one strategy frequently can be better than getting a $k+k$ from another strategy.

Our analysis, however, suggests a simple solution to the programmer: if the programmer chooses $k = k' > 0$, then the four strategies now yield the pairs $\langle 0, 0 \rangle, \langle k, 1 \rangle, \langle k, 1 \rangle, \langle 2k, 2 \rangle$. In this case, the last strategy is optimal both for the citizen and for the city hall. The same result can be obtained picking any value for k and k' such that $0 < k < 2k' < 4k$, so that getting two cashbacks is always better than getting just one of them.

In the rest of the section, the analysis models will be *acyclic* and *finite*, namely models such that the transition relation has always finite maximal computations. These models can be obtained by unfolding cyclic models up to a certain depth. This makes sense in the context of smart contracts where the executions are always bound in the number of steps by some quantity called *gas* that is bought by the caller (a user) with the virtual currency of the blockchain [6]. It also makes sense in examples like Example 1 where the model is one big cycle; therefore it is sufficient to maximize the objective function over just one iteration of the loop.

4.1   Automatic Analysis

We use an automatic technique to verify whether an analysis model retains optimal strategies for some objective function or whether maximizing some objective function – e.g. the cash-back to the citizen – implies the maximization of other objective functions – e.g. the amount of garbage thrown into smart bins. Given an objective function, our technique derives a first order logic formula specifying every possible observation with respect to unknown symbolic inputs and to the internal choices of every agent.

Let $\mathcal{Q}$ be the following map from labels to a possibly empty sequence of quantifiers:

$$\mathcal{Q}((x)) = \exists x \qquad\qquad \mathcal{Q}(x = a.\mathtt{m}(\overline{v})) = \forall x$$
$$\mathcal{Q}(id : \overline{z}) = \forall id \forall \overline{z} \qquad\qquad \mathcal{Q}(\mu) = \varepsilon \qquad \text{(otherwise)}$$

Let also $\mathcal{M} = (\mathcal{S}, \mathsf{S}_0, \mathcal{T})$ be finite and acyclic and ω be an objective function. The *characteristic formula* $(\!|\, \mathsf{S}_0 \,|\!)_\omega^{\mathcal{M}}$ is the first-order logic formula defined as follows

– when there is at least one transition $S \xrightarrow[\psi]{\mu} S' \in \mathcal{T}$:

$$(S)_{\omega}^{\mathcal{M}} = \bigvee_{S \xrightarrow[\psi]{\mu} S' \in \mathcal{T}} \mathcal{Q}(\mu)\left(\psi \wedge \mathcal{O}(S, \{\omega(\mu)\}) \wedge (S')_{\omega}^{\mathcal{M}} \right) \quad ;$$

– when there is no μ, ψ, S' such that $S \xrightarrow[\psi]{\mu} S' \in \mathcal{T}$ (S is final):

$$(S)_{\omega}^{\mathcal{M}} = \top$$

where $\top$ is the proposition "true".

The binary predicate $\mathcal{O}(S, \mathcal{A})$ in the characteristic formula is to be read as follows: there exists a computation originating from S that eventually leaves the state S observing one element of the set $\mathcal{A}$. For example, $\mathcal{O}(13, \{v_1 + v_2\})$ means that there will be a transition from state 13 where the user observes $v_1 + v_2$; $\mathcal{O}(15, \{2\}) \vee (\mathcal{O}(12, \{v_1, v_2\})$ means that either state 15 will be reached and left observing 2, or the state 12 will be reached and left observing either v_1 or v_2.

In order to ease the reading, we simplify the characteristic formula as follows:

– $G \wedge \mathcal{O}(S, \{0\})$ is simplified to G because observing 0 is useless for maximizing an objective function;
– $G \wedge \top$ is simplified to G;
– $\forall x.G$ is simplified to G when x does not occur in G (similarly for $\exists$).

After these simplifications, the characteristic formula for the objective function ω_C of the citizen (we remove the empty-labelled transition from state 17 to state 1 in Fig. 5) is:

$$(1)_{\omega_C}^{\mathcal{M}} = \exists x \Big[x = 1 \wedge \forall v_1 \exists y \left((y = 1 \wedge \forall v_2 \, \mathcal{O}(13, \{v_1 + v_2\})) \vee (y = 2 \wedge \mathcal{O}(14, \{v_1 + 0\})) \right)$$
$$\vee \ x = 2 \wedge \exists z \left(z = 1 \wedge \forall v_2 \, \mathcal{O}(15, \{0 + v_2\})) \vee (z = 2 \wedge \mathcal{O}(16, \{0 + 0\})) \right) \Big] \quad (1)$$

The characteristic formula for the objective function ω_H of the city hall instead is:

$$(1)_{\omega_H}^{\mathcal{M}} = \exists x \Big[x = 1 \wedge \left(\mathcal{O}(3, \{1\}) \wedge \exists y((y = 1 \wedge \mathcal{O}(9, \{1\})) \vee y = 2) \right)$$
$$\vee \ x = 2 \wedge \exists z \left((z = 1 \wedge \mathcal{O}(11, \{1\})) \vee z = 2 \right) \Big] \quad (2)$$

4.2 Quantifier Elimination

When the analysis model is Presburger, the characteristic formula belongs to the extension of Presburger arithmetics with the observation predicate $\mathcal{O}(S, \mathcal{A})$. It turns out that this fragment of first order logic can be decided via quantifier elimination [13]: at every step the formula is rewritten so that each innermost quantifier is existential, and then that quantified formula is replaced with a logically equivalent one where the existentially bound variable no longer occurs.

As a special bonus, the sets $\mathcal{A}$ of observation predicates can be rewritten in the elimination step in such a way that at the end we can recover from the quantifier free formula a set of polytopes that describe the value of all possible variables in every observable state that can be reached, together with the observation performed in that state. It is then easy to compare different strategies observing the value taken by the objective function when its input ranges over the polytope.

The quantifier elimination algorithm starts rewriting an innermost quantified subformula into the normal form

$$\exists x.\bar{l} \leq kx \wedge kx \leq \bar{u} \wedge \bigwedge_i \natural_i \mathcal{O}(\mathsf{S}_i, \mathcal{A}_i)$$

where $x \notin \bar{l}, \bar{u}$ and $\natural F$ stands for either F or $\neg F$. Then it replaces the formula with its logically equivalent one

$$(\bigwedge_{l_i \in \bar{l}} \bigwedge_{u_j \in \bar{u}} l_i \leq u_j) \wedge \bigwedge_i \natural_i \mathcal{O}(\mathsf{S}_i, \{a \in \mathcal{A}_i \mid \bar{l} \leq kx \wedge kx \leq \bar{u}\})$$

Afterwards the algorithm loops on another innermost quantifier until no quantifiers are left. Special care is required to avoid simplifying $\top \vee F$ into $\top$ and $\bot \wedge F$ into $\bot$ to avoid loosing the polytopes recoverable from F.

Example 3. We illustrate the quantifier elimination technique on the characteristic formula (1). In the following, the underlined formulas are the next ones to be simplified. For the sake of readability, we shorten expressions as $0 + 0$ into 0 and $v + 0$ into v.

$$\langle 1 \rangle^{\mathcal{M}}_{\omega_C} = \exists x \Big[x = 1 \wedge \forall v_1 \exists y \, ((y = 1 \wedge \forall v_2 \, \mathcal{O}(13, \{v_1 + v_2\})) \vee (y = 2 \wedge \mathcal{O}(14, \{v_1\}))) $$
$$\vee \, x = 2 \wedge \exists z (z = 1 \wedge \forall v_2 \, \mathcal{O}(15, \{v_2\})) \vee (z = 2 \wedge \mathcal{O}(16, \{0\})) \Big]$$

$$\Longleftrightarrow \exists x \Big[x = 1 \wedge \forall v_1 \exists y \, ((y = 1 \wedge \underline{\neg \exists v_2 \, \neg \mathcal{O}(13, \{v_1 + v_2\})}) \vee (y = 2 \wedge \mathcal{O}(14, \{v_1\}))) $$
$$\vee \, x = 2 \wedge \exists z (z = 1 \wedge \underline{\neg \exists v_2 \, \neg \mathcal{O}(15, \{v_2\})}) \vee (z = 2 \wedge \mathcal{O}(16, \{0\})) \Big]$$

$$\Longleftrightarrow \exists x \Big[x = 1 \wedge \forall v_1 \exists y \, ((y = 1 \wedge \neg\neg\mathcal{O}(13, \{v_1 + v_2\})) \vee (y = 2 \wedge \mathcal{O}(14, \{v_1\}))) $$
$$\vee \, x = 2 \wedge \exists z (z = 1 \wedge \neg\neg\mathcal{O}(15, \{v_2\})) \vee (z = 2 \wedge \mathcal{O}(16, \{0\})) \Big]$$

$$\Longleftrightarrow \exists x \Big[x = 1 \wedge \forall v_1 (\underline{\exists y(y = 1 \wedge \mathcal{O}(13, \{v_1 + v_2\}))} \vee \underline{\exists y(y = 2 \wedge \mathcal{O}(14, \{v_1\}))}) $$
$$\vee \, x = 2 \wedge (\underline{\exists z(z = 1 \wedge \mathcal{O}(15, \{v_2\}))} \vee \underline{\exists z(z = 2 \wedge \mathcal{O}(16, \{0\}))}) \Big]$$

$$\Longleftrightarrow \exists x \Big[x = 1 \wedge \forall v_1 (\mathcal{O}(13, \{v_1 + v_2 \mid y = 1\}) \vee \mathcal{O}(14, \{v_1 \mid y = 2\}))) $$
$$\vee \, x = 2 \wedge (\mathcal{O}(15, \{v_2 \mid z = 1\}) \vee \mathcal{O}(16, \{0 \mid z = 2\})) \Big]$$

$$\Longleftrightarrow \exists x \Big[x = 1 \wedge \underline{\neg \exists v_1 (\neg \mathcal{O}(13, \{v_1 + v_2 \mid y = 1\}) \wedge \neg \mathcal{O}(14, \{v_1 \mid y = 2\}))} $$
$$\vee \, x = 2 \wedge (\mathcal{O}(15, \{v_2 \mid z = 1\}) \vee \mathcal{O}(16, \{0 \mid z = 2\})) \Big]$$

$$\Longleftrightarrow \exists x \Big[x = 1 \wedge (\mathcal{O}(13, \{v_1 + v_2 \mid y = 1\}) \vee \mathcal{O}(14, \{v_1 \mid y = 2\})) $$
$$\vee \, x = 2 \wedge (\mathcal{O}(15, \{v_2 \mid z = 1\}) \vee \mathcal{O}(16, \{0 \mid z = 2\})) \Big]$$

$$\Longleftrightarrow \exists x \Big[x = 1 \wedge \mathcal{O}(13, \{v_1 + v_2 \mid y = 1\}) \vee x = 1 \wedge \mathcal{O}(14, \{v_1 \mid y = 2\}) $$
$$\vee \, x = 2 \wedge \mathcal{O}(15, \{v_2 \mid z = 1\}) \vee x = 2 \wedge \mathcal{O}(16, \{0 \mid z = 2\}) \Big]$$

$$\Longleftrightarrow \exists x \underline{\big[x = 1 \wedge \mathcal{O}(13, \{v_1 + v_2 \mid y = 1\})\big]} \vee \exists x \underline{\big[x = 1 \wedge \mathcal{O}(14, \{v_1 \mid y = 2\})\big]} $$
$$\vee \, \exists x \underline{\big[x = 2 \wedge \mathcal{O}(15, \{v_2 \mid z = 1\})\big]} \vee \exists x \underline{\big[x = 2 \wedge \mathcal{O}(16, \{0 \mid z = 2\})\big]}$$

$$\Longleftrightarrow \mathcal{O}(13, \{v_1 + v_2 \mid x = 1 \wedge y = 1\}) \vee \mathcal{O}(14, \{v_1 \mid x = 1 \wedge y = 2\}) $$
$$\vee \, \mathcal{O}(15, \{v_2 \mid x = 2 \wedge z = 1\}) \vee \mathcal{O}(16, \{0 \mid x = 2 \wedge z = 2\})$$

Applying the above technique to the Eq. (2), we derive

$$\Big(\mathcal{O}(3, \{1 \mid x = 1\}) \wedge \mathcal{O}(9, \{1 \mid x = 1 \wedge y = 1\})\Big) \vee \mathcal{O}(11, \{1 \mid x = 2 \wedge z = 1\})$$

We notice that, in the case of this last formula, the best strategy to maximize ω_H is to choose $x = 1 \wedge y = 1$ that yields the observation $1 + 1 = 2$. More precisely, the strategy consists in picking the branch 1 of the rule [CHOICE] in the state $\ldots +^x \ldots$ and the branch 1 in the state $\ldots +^y \ldots$. With an abuse of notation, we will indicate strategies as conjunctions $\bigwedge_{i \in 1..n} x_i = k_i$.

Let us discuss strategies for ω_C. According to the formula

$$\mathcal{O}(13, \{v_1 + v_2 \mid x = 1 \wedge y = 1\}) \vee \mathcal{O}(14, \{v_1 + 0 \mid x = 1 \wedge y = 2\})$$
$$\vee\, \mathcal{O}(15, \{0 + v_2 \mid x = 2 \wedge z = 1\}) \vee \mathcal{O}(16, \{0 + 0 \mid x = 2 \wedge z = 2\})$$

there is no best strategy to maximize ω_C because, for example, by choosing $x = 1 \wedge y = 1$, one can observe any value in the set $\{v_1 + v_2\}$. In fact, putting the citizen in parallel with the garbage bin, the formal parameters v_1 and v_2 can only be instantiated with either k or k', according to the interleaving of the moves of the citizen with the other actors. In particular, running the analysis again on the larger model – due to the interleaving, we obtain the characteristic formula:

$$\mathcal{O}(\{k + k \mid x = 1 \wedge y = 1\}) \vee \mathcal{O}(\{k + k' \mid x = 1 \wedge y = 1\})$$
$$\vee\quad \mathcal{O}(\{k' + k \mid x = 1 \wedge y = 1\}) \vee \mathcal{O}(\{k' + k' \mid x = 1 \wedge y = 1\})$$
$$\vee\quad \mathcal{O}(\{k \mid x = 1 \wedge y = 2\}) \vee \mathcal{O}(\{k' \mid x = 1 \wedge y = 2\})$$
$$\vee\quad \mathcal{O}(\{k \mid x = 2 \wedge z = 1\}) \vee \mathcal{O}(\{k' \mid x = 2 \wedge z = 1\})$$
$$\vee\quad \mathcal{O}(\{0 \mid x = 2 \wedge z = 2\})$$

In this case, there is still no optimal choice because, for example, by taking $x = 1 \wedge y = 1$ one may observe $k + k$, which may be smaller than k' that is observed for $x = 1 \wedge y = 2$. As already discussed, it is sufficient for the implementor to pick $0 < k < 2k' < 4k$ to force the existence of a best strategy which is $x = 1 \wedge y = 1$ and that coincides with the best strategy from the city hall point of view, as expected.

Remark 1. The standard formal specification languages to verify and specify properties of transition systems are temporal logics [12]. Actually one may use tools that are based on these logics, such as [1], to automatically analyze systems based on smart contracts. In fact, our characteristic formula is actually a compilation of linear-time temporal logics with Presburger constraints, which is decidable [5]. We have preferred the current presentation because it is the one we use in our prototype implementation.

4.3   Implementation

We are terminating the implementation in OCaml of a tool that, given a set of actors, an initial state and an objective function, automatically extracts the analysis model, computes the characteristic formula and applies quantifier elimination over it.

Initially we hoped to be able to reuse off-the-shelf implementations of Presburger quantifier elimination by dropping the $\mathcal{O}$ predicate and recovering the polytopes from the tools. But the tools we analyzed are unable to spit out the polytopes. In fact, because of the double-exponential complexity of quantifier elimination over the number of alternations of quantifiers, the tools avoid quantifier elimination and rather use model checking or reduction to finite state automata. However, these two techniques can only enumerate the points in the polytope, without providing a closed description of it [8,9]. Therefore we decided to implement quantifier elimination straight away. We need to evaluate whether our quantifier elimination is is doable in practice on characteristic formulae generated from realistic examples of smart contracts. This is left as future work, once the whole implementation is completed. We will also study the application of other techniques, like temporal logic, to analyse the formal calculus and the models introduced in the paper. To ease these analyses, we will write transpilers from our smart calculus language to existing languages, initially targeting both Solidity and Liquidity.

5   Conclusions

In this paper we have introduced a unified calculus for modelling smart contracts and users, which are the primary actors of decentralized applications. These applications run on blockchain systems and handle and transfer assets of considerable value. We have therefore studied how to regulate by means of smart contracts the interaction between (rational) users that systematically try to maximize their revenue or to minimize losses. This is achieved by expressing the system behaviour as a formula in Presburger arithmetics and solving arithmetic constraints. Our technique is amenable to automated verification and we are currently completing an OCaml implementation.

The analysis of smart contracts for deriving strategies and distilling the most meaningful ones opens unexpected connections between (micro) economy and computer science that deserves further investigations. While this direction of research has been already pointed out in other contributions (see *e.g.* [3]), we believe that there is much work still to be done.

As regards our calculus, several extensions must be considered. First of all, the types must be extended with simple dynamic data types, such as arrays and maps. Then, if we want to model faithfully the (human) users, we need to take into account probabilities because users are not always 100% rational; they may be irrational with some percentage.

Dedication. Cosimo is proud to dedicate this paper to Stefania Gnesi and to the unforgettable Friday afternoons spent together with Alessandro Fantechi. Stefania and Alessandro have been Cosimo's Master Thesis advisors and they first led him to concurrent systems, formal methods and temporal logics. Thank you Stefania!

References

1. Asirelli, P., ter Beek, M.H., Fantechi, A., Gnesi, S.: A model-checking tool for families of services. In: Bruni, R., Dingel, J. (eds.) FMOODS/FORTE -2011. LNCS, vol. 6722, pp. 44–58. Springer, Heidelberg (2011). https://doi.org/10.1007/978-3-642-21461-5_3

2. Bhargavan, K., et al.: Formal verification of smart contracts: short paper. In: Proceedings of Programming Languages and Analysis for Security, pp. 91–96. ACM (2016)

3. Bigi, G., Bracciali, A., Meacci, G., Tuosto, E.: Validation of decentralised smart contracts through game theory and formal methods. In: Bodei, C., Ferrari, G.-L., Priami, C. (eds.) Programming Languages with Applications to Biology and Security. LNCS, vol. 9465, pp. 142–161. Springer, Cham (2015). https://doi.org/10.1007/978-3-319-25527-9_11

4. Chatterjee, K., Goharshady, A.K., Velner, Y.: Quantitative analysis of smart contracts. In: Ahmed, A. (ed.) ESOP 2018. LNCS, vol. 10801, pp. 739–767. Springer, Cham (2018). https://doi.org/10.1007/978-3-319-89884-1_26

5. Demri, S.: Linear-time temporal logics with presburger constraints: an overview. J. Appl. Non-Class. Logics **16**(3–4), 311–348 (2006)

6. Ethereum Foundation. Ethereum's white paper (2014). https://github.com/ethereum/wiki/wiki/White-Paper

7. Ethereum Foundation. Solidity 0.4.24 documentation (2019). https://solidity.readthedocs.io/en/develop/

8. Ganesh, V., Berezin, S., Dill, D.L.: Deciding presburger arithmetic by model checking and comparisons with other methods. In: Aagaard, M.D., O'Leary, J.W. (eds.) FMCAD 2002. LNCS, vol. 2517, pp. 171–186. Springer, Heidelberg (2002). https://doi.org/10.1007/3-540-36126-X_11

9. Haase, C.: A survival guide to presburger arithmetic. ACM SIGLOG News **5**(3), 67–82 (2018)

10. Luu, L., Chu, D.H., Olickel, H., Saxena, P., Hobor, A.: Making smart contracts smarter. In: Proceedings of the Conference on Computer and Communications Security, pp. 254–269. ACM (2016)

11. Mueller, B.: Smashing Ethereum smart contracts for fun and real profit. HITB SECCONF Amsterdam (2018)

12. Pnueli, A.: The temporal logic of programs. In: Proceedings of Symposium on Foundations of Computer Science. IEEE Computer Society, pp. 46–57 (1977)

13. Pope, J.: Formalizing constructive quantifier elimination in Agda. In: Proceedings of MSFP@FSCD 2018 of EPTCS, vol. 275, pp. 2–17 (2018)

14. OCamlPro SAS. Welcome to Liquidity's documentation! (2019). http://www.liquidity-lang.org/doc/

15. Siegel, D.: Understanding the DAO attack (2016). Accessed 13 Jun 2018

Hunting Superfluous Locks
with Model Checking

Viet-Anh Nguyen[1], Wendelin Serwe[2], Radu Mateescu[2(✉)], and Eric Jenn[1]

[1] IRT Saint Exupéry, Toulouse, France
[2] Univ. Grenoble Alpes, Inria, CNRS, Grenoble INP, LIG, 38000 Grenoble, France
radu.mateescu@inria.fr

Abstract. Parallelization of existing sequential programs to increase their performance and exploit recent multi and many-core architectures is a challenging but inevitable effort. One increasingly popular parallelization approach is based on OpenMP, which enables the designer to annotate a sequential program with constructs specifying the parallel execution of code blocks. These constructs are then interpreted by the OpenMP compiler and runtime, which assigns blocks to threads running on a parallel architecture. Although this scheme is very flexible and not (very) intrusive, it does not prevent the occurrence of synchronization errors (e.g., deadlocks) or data races on shared variables. In this paper, we propose an iterative method to assist the OpenMP parallelization by using formal methods and verification. In each iteration, potential data races are identified by applying to the OpenMP program a lockset analysis, which computes the set of shared variables that potentially need to be protected by locks. To avoid the insertion of superfluous locks, an abstract, action-based formal model of the OpenMP program is extracted and analyzed using the ACTL on-the-fly model checker of the CADP formal verification toolbox. We describe the method, compare it with existing work, and illustrate its practical use.

1 Introduction

Nowadays, to take full advantage of modern hardware architectures (multi-core and many-core processors, Systems-on-Chip, etc.), it is necessary to parallelize applications, even in constrained environments, such as avionics. Designing correct parallel programs on shared-memory architectures is a difficult task facing classical synchronization issues, such as the presence of data races (concurrent accesses to shared variables that make the program nondeterministic [20]) or deadlocks, both of which are unacceptable for critical systems. These difficulties occur not only in the design of new parallel programs, but also in the parallelization of existing sequential programs, which have been optimized during years and for which it is too costly to redevelop parallel versions from scratch.

An increasingly popular approach to parallelize sequential code is based on OpenMP [33], which does not require to modify the code but simply annotate it

---

Grenoble INP—Institute of Engineering Univ. Grenoble Alpes.

M. H. ter Beek et al. (Eds.): Gnesi Festschrift, LNCS 11865, pp. 416–432, 2019.
https://doi.org/10.1007/978-3-030-30985-5_24

with parallelization constructs expressing a variety of mechanisms (creating parallel regions executed by teams of threads, inserting locks on variables and array elements, introducing synchronizations, etc.). The underlying compiler and execution framework are in charge of implementing these constructs, building and executing the parallel program on a given architecture. Unfortunately, OpenMP is not equipped with a formal semantics suitable for reasoning about OpenMP programs and ensuring the correctness of annotation-based parallelization: [33, Section 1.1] explicitly states that "OpenMP-compliant implementations are not required to check for data dependencies, data conflicts, race conditions, or deadlocks, any of which may occur in conforming programs."

A naive way to eliminate data races in a parallel program is to protect all shared variables by locks that serialize the accesses of parallel threads to these variables. Although safe, this approach may introduce deadlocks, and also increase the overhead, negatively impacting the performance of the program. Even more importantly, the approach may induce a too sequential execution of the program and thus not (fully) exploit the benefits of parallelization. In this paper, we refine this naive lock-based approach and propose an iterative method to prevent data races in safety-critical parallel applications. The method combines a simple lockset analysis [36] to detect all the shared variables potentially unprotected by locks (which may produce false positives about variables that actually do not need to be protected) and a model checking analysis to reduce the number of false positives and consequently avoid introducing superfluous locks.

Lockset analysis is based on the application of a "locking discipline", by considering that a race condition may occur if a shared variable is not protected by an appropriate lock. Lockset based race detectors are easy to implement and never produce false negatives, i.e., they detect all potential data races, which is essential for safety-critical applications. However, these detectors are pessimistic, since data races can be prevented not only by using locks, but also by performing accesses to shared variables sequentially.

We exhibit such sequentiality using model checking, by extracting from the parallel program a formal model capturing (an abstraction of) the concurrency and data dependencies, and detecting the presence of concurrent accesses to shared variables using temporal properties in ACTL (*Action Computation Tree Logic*) [8, 9]. The precision of the model has no impact on the soundness of the method (since the lockset analysis has already produced a data race free, albeit not optimal, parallel program), but only on the efficiency of the parallel code (a better model precision will yield a more accurate analysis and hence a more drastic elimination of superfluous locks). We instantiated this method on top of the CADP (Construction and Analysis of Distributed Processes)[1] [14] verification toolbox and illustrated it for the design of data race free OpenMP applications.

Stefania's work on defining action-based temporal logics and various extensions thereof, as well as on designing efficient on-the-fly verification algorithms, was a source of inspiration in this field. The implementation of ACTL used in this paper relies on the translation from ACTL to the modal μ-calculus ($L\mu$)

---

[1] http://cadp.inria.fr.

proposed by Stefania and colleagues [10]. For checking ACTL formulas, we used the on-the-fly model checker EVALUATOR [29] of CADP, which handles formulas of MCL, an extension of alternation-free $L\mu$ with data and generalized Büchi automata. Although it relies on different techniques based on the local resolution of Boolean equation systems [27], EVALUATOR is similar in spirit to the on-the-fly model checkers FMC [16] and UMC [5] developed by Stefania and colleagues, which handle formulas of μACTL (ACTL extended with fixed point operators) and UCTL (μACTL extended with state-based and data-aware operators), respectively.

Also, Stefania's contributions on ACTL characteristic formulas [12] and the adequacy of action-based logics with bisimulations [11] paved the way towards an $L\mu$ fragment adequate with divergence-sensitive branching bisimulation [30]. Recently, this $L\mu$ fragment, which subsumes μACTL\X (μACTL without the next time operator) was extended with strong modalities and equipped with an improved compositional verification technique [24] applicable to the ACTL formulas we use for detecting concurrent accesses to shared variables.

The paper is organized as follows. Section 2 gives a brief overview of OpenMP and data races. Section 3 presents our parallelization workflow and its practical implementation using CADP. Section 4 reviews existing work on data race prevention. Finally, Sect. 5 gives some concluding remarks and directions for future work.

2   OpenMP

OpenMP [33][2] is an API (Application Programming Interface) for developing portable parallel programs using a shared memory communication paradigm in the C, C++, and Fortran programming languages. The OpenMP API consists of directives to extend the base languages with portable parallel programming constructs (to be implemented by an OpenMP-compliant compiler) and functions and environment variables (to be implemented by a corresponding run-time library). In the C/C++ languages, OpenMP directives are pragmas of the form of `#pragma omp` .... Directives and calls to library routines are grouped under the generic designation of *constructs*. OpenMP supports both parallel and sequential execution, the latter being achieved by simply ignoring the OpenMP constructs.[3]

The execution model of OpenMP follows a fork-join discipline. Initially, an OpenMP program begins with a single *thread* of execution. Whenever a thread encounters an OpenMP `parallel` construct, the thread creates a *team* of threads (containing at least itself) and becomes the *master thread* of the team. The code executed by each of these threads depends on the code inside the `parallel` construct. These threads then execute independently and synchronize

---

[2] http://www.openmp.org.

[3] However, OpenMP does neither require nor guarantee that parallel and sequential executions produce the same results; also, executing the same program with a different number of threads may yield different results [33, Section 1.3].

(using an implicit barrier) on termination; only the master thread continues afterwards. OpenMP supports nested parallelism: each thread of a team can itself create a new team, when it encounters a `parallel` construct. Hence, several teams may exist simultaneously.

Initially designed for the parallelization of regular loops, OpenMP supports since version 3.0 also the notion of *task*. In OpenMP, a task is a pair of a piece of code together with a specific piece of data. Tasks can be generated explicitly or implicitly, and are to be executed by the threads. As an example, the `for` construct implicitly creates a task for each iteration of the associated `for`-loop. The `single` construct implicitly creates a task for its associated code, so that this code is executed exactly once; other threads encountering the construct wait for its termination (using an implicit barrier). A task can be suspended (and resumed later) only on so-called *task scheduling points*, e.g., when creating new task(s) or when waiting on a barrier. OpenMP provides constructs to express further constraints on task creation and execution, such as the fact that a task can only be executed if another task has completed.

All OpenMP threads have access to the same shared memory. Each thread may read or write any shared variables, and there is no constraint as to when those operations are allowed to occur. The memory model of OpenMP is relaxed-consistency: each thread has a *temporary view* of the shared memory; this temporary view is not required to be consistent with the memory at all times. Each thread has also access to a local, private memory, to which other threads have no access.

OpenMP provides synchronization constructs (locks, barriers, etc.), variable attributes defining data sharing (private, shared, etc.), a flush operation (enforcing the consistency of the temporary views with the shared memory), and data-dependencies between tasks (enforcing the execution of a task computing some value before the execution of a task using this value).

In OpenMP, parallelization is user-directed, i.e., the programmer explicitly uses the OpenMP constructs to specify how to parallelize the execution of the program. Hence, OpenMP relies on the programmer to ensure the correctness of the program [33, Section 1.1], e.g., to ensure the absence of memory management errors, such as data races. However, this is a heavy responsibility for the programmer, given the inherent complexity of parallelization, the rich set of constructs, and the fact the creation and ordering of tasks might depend on information only available at runtime. Consequently, any assistance to the programmer is more than welcome.

A first approach to assist programmers is to make a list of common pitfalls and to derive a set of recommended best practices and coding guidelines [38]. These common mistakes can be classified into two categories: errors (leading to an incorrect behavior) and performance issues (leading to inefficient programs). For instance, using the clause `default (none)` implies that data-sharing attributes of all variables in all parallel regions of the OpenMP program must be explicitly specified. Although following carefully chosen coding guidelines may ensure correctness, it might be difficult to apply these guidelines to an existing sequential code and obtain a parallel version with acceptable performance.

A second approach is the development of analysis tools that detect errors. However, due to the expressive power of the OpenMP constructs and in particular the fact that the parallel execution might depend on data values, developing such analysis tools is extremely challenging. As for the first approach, limiting the scope of the tools to a subset of OpenMP constructs is not always acceptable in an industrial context (the constructs have been included for good reasons). Similarly, applying coarse data abstractions increases the rate of false positives/negatives and reduces the practical usefulness of the analysis.

In the following section, we present a method to assist the programmer to ensure the absence of data races. To illustrate this method, we use the following simple example, which computes the sum of the squares of the elements of an array a, counting the last element (a[4]) twice. Figure 1 shows the OpenMP code.[4] The construct `#pragma omp parallel` (line 5) creates a team of threads to execute the block from lines 6–15 in parallel; the number of threads in the team is determined at runtime, depending on the available hardware. The construct `#pragma omp for schedule` (`static, 1`) (line 7) indicates that the body of the for-loop should be statically splitted in as many tasks as there are iterations (i.e., 5). Obviously, there is a data race on the update of variable sum in the for-loop (line 11). However, there is no data race for the accesses to the array a and variable sum between the body of the for-loop and assignment at line 14, because the assignment is executed after the termination of all iterations of the for-loop (i.e., there is an implicit barrier at the end of the `#pragma omp for` construct), and the assignment is executed by a single thread (this is ensured by the `single` construct at line 13).

3   Parallelization Workflow

Figure 2 depicts the suggested workflow for the parallelization of a sequential application, guaranteeing the absence of data races by enforcing a locking discipline and avoiding superfluous locks by means of model checking. This iterative flow comprises several activities in each iteration:

1. Lockset analysis is used to build the variable-set *SUV* (*Set of Unprotected Variables*), which might present the risk of a data race. It is sufficient to use the simplest version of lockset analysis presented in [36], which raises an alarm if any access to a shared variable is not protected by a lock.
2. A formal model expressed in the LNT language [15] is built to capture all the possible control flows of OpenMP threads and their synchronizations. The process of building the LNT model is presented in the next section.
3. The verification tools provided by CADP are used to identify the "sequentiality constraints" that prevent some data race conditions to occur. The set of unprotected variables is updated accordingly.

---

[4] The meaning of "work unit" (in the comments) can be found in Sect. 3.2.

```
1   int a[5] = {2, 3, 4, 5, 6};
2   int main()
3   {
4       int i, sum = 0; // work unit WU0
5       #pragma omp parallel
6       {
7           #pragma omp for schedule (static, 1)
8           for (i = 0; i < 5; i++)
9           { // work units WU1 to WU5
10              a[i] = a[i] * a[i];
11              sum += a[i];
12          }
13          #pragma omp single
14          sum += a[4]; // work unit WU6
15      }
16      return 0;
17  }
```

Fig. 1. Minimalist OpenMP example

4. The refined list of unprotected variables is given to the programmer, who can add new locks in the program to protect them.

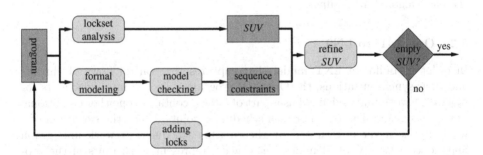

Fig. 2. Parallelization workflow

Considering that the programmers may make a mistake when adding locks to the program, the verification process is repeated until the list of unprotected variables is empty. At the end, we ensure that the program is free from data races. These steps are detailed in the following.

3.1 Lockset Algorithm

Lockset analysis [36] is a technique for dynamic detection of possible data races. The technique has been successfully implemented in the Eraser tool. Rather than checking the absence of data races, lockset analysis checks whether a program adheres to a *locking discipline*, which requires that each access to a shared variable is protected by at least one lock. Notice that the respect of this locking discipline guarantees absence of data races, because all accesses to a shared variable are mutually exclusive.

The original definition of the simplest possible version of the lockset algorithm [36, Section 2] is the following. "For each shared variable v, the algorithm maintains the set $C(v)$ of candidate locks for v. This set contains those locks that have protected v for the computation so far. That is, a lock l is in $C(v)$ if, in the computation up to that point, every thread that has accessed v was holding l at the moment of the access. When a new variable v is initialized, its candidate set $C(v)$ is considered to hold all possible locks. When the variable is accessed, the algorithm updates $C(v)$ with the intersection of $C(v)$ and the set of locks held by the current thread. This process, called lockset refinement, ensures that any lock that consistently protects v is contained in $C(v)$. If some lock l consistently protects v, it will remain in $C(v)$ as $C(v)$ is refined. If $C(v)$ becomes empty this indicates that there is no lock that consistently protects v."

Under the hypothesis that the set of locks held by a thread for each point of the program is deterministic, a single run of the lockset algorithm is sufficient. Otherwise, for instance if the operations on locks are data-dependent or vary in different branches of conditional statements, several runs might be necessary.

The basic lockset algorithm can be refined [36] to reduce the number of false alarms, for instance to take into account that read accesses need not to be protected if there is no concurrent write access. For the purpose of this paper, the basic algorithm is sufficient.

3.2   OpenMP to LNT

In order to build an LNT model that captures the control flows of threads and their synchronizations, the OpenMP program is broken into *work units* (or blocks). A work unit is defined as a part of a task, containing neither conditional branches synchronizations, nor task scheduling points. Thus, the execution of a work unit is never interrupted by the runtime scheduler. A work unit graph may contain two types of nodes: *basic nodes* represent work units of the program, and *synchronization nodes* represent synchronizations between threads enforced by OpenMP constructs (i.e., `#pragma omp critical`, `omp_set_lock()`, `omp_unset_lock()`, ...).

An edge between a pair of nodes represents the execution order. For a pair of basic nodes, this edge reflects the order of the corresponding work units, which is imposed by the control flow. For a pair of a basic node and a synchronization node, the edge reflects that the work unit denoted by the basic node starts (respectively, ends) with a synchronization construct corresponding to the synchronization node. The work unit graph can be obtained by static analysis of the code, akin to the construction of a control flow graph in an optimizing compiler.

Figure 3 represents a work unit graph of the program given in Fig. 1. This work unit graph contains no synchronization nodes, but the one shown later in

Fig. 5 contains basic nodes (depicted as circles) and synchronization nodes (lock and unlock nodes, depicted as rectangles with rounded corners). Inspection of the OpenMP source code (Fig. 1) yields the following information about variables accessed by the various work units. All work units access (read/write) the variable sum. All work units but WU0 access (read/write) the array a; however, they access separate elements—the only exception being a[4], which is read and written by WU5 and read by WU6. Thus, there might be a data race for variables a[4] and sum.

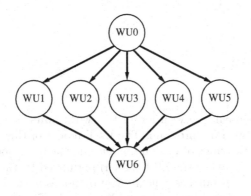

Fig. 3. Work unit graph for the program of Fig. 1

To analyze the work unit graph using model checking, we first transform it into an LNT model by applying the following rules:

- Basic nodes are modeled as LNT processes
- Lock/unlock nodes are modeled as synchronizations on gates ACQUIRE/RELEASE representing acquire/release actions on the lock; two further actions INIT and DESTROY denote the creation and deletion of the lock
- Barrier nodes are modeled as multiway rendezvous on dedicated LNT synchronization gates
- Edges are modeled as LNT sequential composition
- Branch conditions are modeled as nondeterministic choice using the select operator

For example, Table 1 shows the LNT code for the work unit graph of Fig. 3.

3.3 Sequentiality Detection

A data race may occur on a shared variable x if at least two work units WUi and WUj accessing x can execute concurrently at some moment. If the two work units always execute in a deterministic order, they cannot cause a data race on x, meaning that it is not necessary to protect x by a lock.

Table 1. LNT code for work unit graph of Fig. 3

```
module OMP is
   process MAIN [WU0, WU1, WU2, WU3, WU4, WU5, WU6: none] is
      WU0;
      par
            WU1
      || WU2
      || WU3
      || WU4
      || WU5
      end par;
      WU6
   end process
end module
```

To detect the sequential execution of two work units, we exploit the work unit graph of the OpenMP program. The LNT model of this graph represents all the possible interleavings of work units (encoded as basic nodes in the graph, and simply as gate names in the LNT model) permitted by the OpenMP parallelization constructs (encoded as synchronization nodes in the graph and as gate names or implicit synchronizations in the LNT model). The behavior of the LNT model is represented by an LTS, in which every state corresponds to a global state of the work unit graph (i.e., an abstract state of the OpenMP program), each action denotes the execution of a basic node or a synchronization node, and each transition indicates that the program can move from one state to another by performing a certain action.

In terms of this LTS, the sequential execution of two basic nodes corresponding to work units WUi and WUj can be ensured by checking that, in every state, it is not possible to execute both basic nodes immediately. This property can be expressed in ACTL [8] as follows:

$$\neg EF_{true}(EX_{WUi}true \wedge EX_{WUj}true)$$

The formula expresses the absence of a transition sequence leading (from the initial state of the LTS) to a state having an outgoing transition labeled by WUi and an outgoing transition labeled by WUj.

For the LNT model of work unit graph shown on Table 1, the above formula holds for all pairs of work units $(WU0, WUi)$ and $(WUi, WU6)$ with $1 \leq i \leq 5$, and fails for all pairs of work units (WUi, WUj) with $1 \leq i, j \leq 5$ and $i \neq j$. This reflects the structure of the work unit graph (WU0 is executed before WU1, ..., WU5, which are executed before WU6) and indicates the possibility of data races on the shared variables accessed by work units WU1, ..., WU5, which therefore must be protected by locks.

3.4   Inserting Locks

To protect the access to sum in the for-loop, the programmer declares its body as critical. The resulting code is shown on Fig. 4, the corresponding work unit graph on Fig. 5 (the principal difference with Fig. 3 being the addition of Lock-/Unlock nodes), and the corresponding LNT code in Table 2. The principal difference between Tables 1 and 2 is that the execution of the work units WU1, WU2, WU3, WU4, and WU5 is protected by a lock (represented by process LOCK), which has to be acquired before the execution of the work unit, and released afterwards: these steps are grouped into to process PROTECTED_WU (used similarly to a procedure). Process LOCK executes as an additional process. It has a local variable FREE indicating the status of the lock, and ensures that the lock can only acquired when it is free and that only the process holding the lock can release it. Gates INIT (respectively, DESTROY) are used to start (respectively, terminate) the execution of the lock.

Rerunning lockset analysis on the modified program, the accesses to a and sum in work unit 6 are still not protected by a lock, but model checking shows sequentiality of work units 1 to 5 with work unit 6, and thus the absence of a data race without the need of adding any further lock.

4   Related Work

Much effort has been spent on detecting data races in parallel programs. These efforts can be classified into dynamic and static approaches [4].

Dynamic techniques rely on observations of the running program. Such techniques have been implemented in several tools for race detection in OpenMP programs. Happens-before analysis monitors accesses to shared variables. If an access to a shared variable is logically concurrent with any previous conflicting access, the tool will raise an alarm; a pair of concurrent accesses to the same variable is conflicting if and only if at least one of them is a write. This technique leads to no false positives (i.e., each detected issue is indeed a data race), but might produce false negatives, because its precision depends on the definition of logically concurrent accesses, which is often expensive to compute. The happens-before technique has been implemented for instance in RaceStand [23].

Closer related to our suggested method are techniques based on lockset analysis, which we also use in our flow. The lockset analysis [36] (see also Sect. 3.1) aims at enforcing a locking discipline, rather than checking for absence of data races in general. Tools based on lockset analysis raise an alarm when some access to a shared variable is not protected by an appropriate lock. Lockset based race detectors are safe (i.e., they do not produce false negatives), but too pessimistic because locking is not the only way to provide safe synchronization. Thus, the Eraser tool [36] implements various improvements of the simple lockset algorithm to reduce the number of false positives, taking into account frequent programming patterns. Our workflow has a similar goal, but rather than trying to improve the algorithm, we use model checking to filter the results.

```
int a[5] = {2, 3, 4, 5, 6};
int main()
{
    int i, sum = 0; // work unit WU0
    #pragma omp parallel
    {
        #pragma omp for schedule (static, 1)
        for (i = 0; i < 5; i++)
        { // work units WU1 to WU5
            #pragma omp critical
            {
                a[i] = a[i] * a[i];
                sum += a[i];
            }
        }
        #pragma omp single
        sum += a[4]; // work unit WU6
    }
    return 0;
}
```

Fig. 4. Corrected OpenMP code for Fig. 1 (added `#pragma omp critical` inside the `for`-loop)

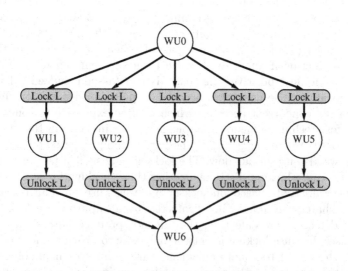

Fig. 5. Work unit graph for the program of Fig. 4

Table 2. LNT code for work unit graph of Fig. 5

```
module OMP2 is
   channel LOCK_CHANNEL is (Nat) end channel
   process LOCK [INIT, DESTROY: none,
                 ACQUIRE, RELEASE: LOCK_CHANNEL] is
      var FREE: Bool, TID: Nat in
         INIT;
         FREE := true; -- initially the lock is free
         TID := 1;     -- to make LNT2LOTOS happy
         loop L in
            select
               only if FREE then ACQUIRE (?TID) end if
            []
               only if not (FREE) then RELEASE (TID) end if
            []
               DESTROY; break L
            end select;
            FREE := not (FREE)
         end loop
      end var
   end process
   process PROTECTED_WU [WU: none,
                         ACQUIRE, RELEASE: LOCK_CHANNEL]
                        (id: Nat) is
      ACQUIRE (id); -- acquire the lock
      WU;           -- work
      RELEASE (id)  -- release the lock
   end process
   process MAIN [WU0, WU1, WU2, WU3, WU4, WU5, WU6,
                 INIT, DESTROY: none,
                 ACQUIRE, RELEASE: LOCK_CHANNEL] is
      par INIT, ACQUIRE, RELEASE, DESTROY in
         WU0;
         INIT;
         par
            PROTECTED_WU [WU1, ACQUIRE, RELEASE] (1)
         || PROTECTED_WU [WU2, ACQUIRE, RELEASE] (2)
         || PROTECTED_WU [WU3, ACQUIRE, RELEASE] (3)
         || PROTECTED_WU [WU4, ACQUIRE, RELEASE] (4)
         || PROTECTED_WU [WU5, ACQUIRE, RELEASE] (5)
         end par;
         DESTROY;
         WU6
      ||
         LOCK [INIT, DESTROY, ACQUIRE, RELEASE]
      end par
   end process
end module
```

This has the advantage of taking into account dependencies, without any prior knowledge about the kind of dependency.

To improve precision, some tools combine several approaches. Adaptive Dynamic Analysis Tool (ADAT) [22] selects, for a given program, suitable race detection techniques, based on their scalability and their efficiency in term of thread labeling, access filtering and access detecting. Intel® Thread Checker [35] emulates the sequential version of the application and uses it to derive the happens-before relation. The tool checks the data dependency of accesses to shared variables (whenever an OpenMP directive is detected) by using sequentially traced information, and reports the accesses as races if their dependency satisfies an anti (write-after-read), flow (read-after-write), and output data dependency (write-after-write). Oracle® Developer Studio Thread Analyzer [34] is based on similar techniques and yields comparable results as Thread Checker [18].

Static analysis tools do not require to run the program. To reduce the complexity of the analysis, some approaches limit their scope to subsets of OpenMP. For instance, the race avoidance tool [37] is limited to OpenMP programs using only the `#pragma omp parallel for` construct. ompVerify [3] detects data races using a polyhedral model (used to describe execution order of statement instance, and the relation of statement instances to the memory cells where they are read or write). The tool covers a class of program fragments called Affine Control Loops.

OpenMP Analysis ToolKit (OAT) [26] uses an SMT (Satisfiability Modulo Theories) solver based symbolic analysis to detect data races. In the tool, every parallel code region of an OpenMP program is encoded into a first-order logic formula, which is then solved by the SMT solver. The solution reported by the SMT solver is interpreted to point out errors and generate a feasible execution trace that reveals the errors. Nonconcurrency analysis [25] statically detects whether two statements in an OpenMP program will not be executed concurrently by different threads in a team. The RacerD tool [6,17] of the Infer static analyser[5] for concurrent Java code aims at easily usable and understandable bug reports. Thus RacerD favors the absence of false positives over the guarantee of the absence of data races.

Model checking is another static analysis technique, based on the analysis of the reachable state space derived from a *model* of the program. In the context of parallel programs, this state space is in general huge, because it has to take into account every possible execution scenario. Thus, usually it is necessary to apply property-preserving abstractions to reduce the state space to a tractable size, but still preserve the control-flow and operations on shared variables. The more concrete the model, the more precise the results reported by the model checker, but the more resources are required. Hence, the principal challenge of model checking based approaches is to find the right abstraction level, with just the right balance between precision and analysis complexity. This challenge can be somehow circumvented by not using the model-checker for the verification of the core property, but to supplement another analysis technique, for instance

---

[5] https://fbinfer.com/.

to construct a more precise happens-before relation [32] or to refine the set of variables that need a lock as in our approach.

In order to further enhance the accuracy and the scalability of data race analysis, some approaches employ static analysis to provide guided information for the dynamic race detectors. For example, ARCHER [2] first identifies data race-free code regions (i.e., which do not contain data dependencies) with a static analysis, and then instruments only the remaining, potentially unsafe regions, for data race detection. Another approach is the combination of a thread labeling scheme (to maintain the logical concurrency of thread segments) with the happens-before technique (to analyze the happens-before relations to detect conflicting accesses to every shared memory location) [19,21]. The ThreadSafe [1] tool (for Java code) applies the principles of the lockset algorithm in the setting of a static analysis: locksets are computed for abstract summaries of methods. A generic and formal OpenMP epoch model, which describes memory events of all OpenMP threads that occur between two synchronization events, has been used as basis for determining the happens-before relations, which are then applied for detecting data races [7].

5 Conclusion

We proposed an iterative method to ensure the absence of data races in parallel programs using a combination of lockset analysis (to identify unprotected shared variables) and ACTL model checking (to detect superfluous locks). Although simple, our method is modular, separating the concerns of parallelization and verification on a formal model of the program. This enables to balance the precision of the model with the quality of the resulting data race free parallel program: a more detailed model will increase accuracy in detecting superfluous locks, but also require more computing resources to analyze it by model checking. We illustrated the method on the parallelization of programs using OpenMP, by proposing an intermediate representation of the concurrent blocks and their synchronizations as a work unit graph, which is transformed into an LNT model.

The proposed method could be applied for parallel programs in other languages as well, provided that a suitable translation to LNT is available (e.g., AADL2LNT [31]). Once an abstract LNT model of the parallel program is available, it can be used not only for checking sequentiality constraints and deadlocks as in our analysis flow, but also other properties, both qualitative (safety, liveness, fairness) and quantitative ones [28]. The method can be further refined by tackling an industrial case-study involving parallelization using OpenMP. For model checking large work unit graphs, the compositional verification techniques for ACTL provided by CADP [13,30] (and notably the recent combined bisimulation technique [24], suitable for the ACTL sequentiality detection formulas given in Sect. 3.3), can be experimented to find appropriate composition strategies. Also, alternative ways of translating an OpenMP application into an LNT program can be investigated, with various degrees of abstraction.

Acknowledgements. This work has been supported by the CAPHCA (*Critical Applications on Predictable High-Performance Computing Architectures*) project funded by the PIA programme of the French government.

References

1. Atkey, R., Sannella, D.: ThreadSafe: static analysis for Java concurrency. In: Electronic Communications of the EASST 72 (2015). https://doi.org/10.14279/tuj. eceasst.72.1025
2. Atzeni, S., et al.: ARCHER: effectively spotting data races in large OpenMP applications. In: 2016 IEEE International Parallel and Distributed Processing Symposium (IPDPS), pp. 53–62, May 2016. https://doi.org/10.1109/IPDPS.2016.68
3. Basupalli, V., et al.: ompVerify: polyhedral analysis for the OpenMP programmer. In: Chapman, B.M., Gropp, W.D., Kumaran, K., Müller, M.S. (eds.) IWOMP 2011. LNCS, vol. 6665, pp. 37–53. Springer, Heidelberg (2011). https://doi.org/10. 1007/978-3-642-21487-5_4. https://hal.inria.fr/hal-00752626
4. Beckman, N.E.: A survey of methods for preventing race conditions (2006)
5. ter Beek, M.H., Fantechi, A., Gnesi, S., Mazzanti, F.: A state/event-based model-checking approach for the analysis of abstract system properties. Sci. Comput. Program. **76**(2), 119–135 (2011). https://doi.org/10.1016/j.scico.2010.07.002
6. Blackshear, S., Gorogiannis, N., O'Hearn, P.W., Sergey, I.: RacerD: compositional static race detection. Proc. ACM Program. Lang. **2**(OOPSLA), 1441–14428 (2018). https://doi.org/10.1145/3276514. http://doi.acm.org/10.1145/3276514
7. Cramer, T., Schwitanski, S., Münchhalfen, F., Terboven, C., Müller, M.S.: An OpenMP epoch model for correctness checking. In: 2016 45th International Conference on Parallel Processing Workshops (ICPPW), pp. 299–308, August 2016. https://doi.org/10.1109/ICPPW.2016.51
8. De Nicola, R., Fantechi, A., Gnesi, S., Ristori, G.: An action-based framework for verifying logical and behavioural properties of concurrent systems. Comput. Netw. ISDN Syst. **25**(7), 761–778 (1993). https://doi.org/10.1016/0169-7552(93)90047-8
9. De Nicola, R., Vaandrager, F.: Action versus state based logics for transition systems. In: Guessarian, I. (ed.) LITP 1990. LNCS, vol. 469, pp. 407–419. Springer, Heidelberg (1990). https://doi.org/10.1007/3-540-53479-2_17
10. Fantechi, A., Gnesi, S., Ristori, G.: From ACTL to mu-calculus. In: Proceedings of the ERCIM Workshop on Theory and Practice in Verification, Pisa, Italy, pp. 3–10, January 1992
11. Fantechi, A., Gnesi, S., Ristori, G.: Model checking for action-based logics. Formal Methods Syst. Des. **4**(2), 187–203 (1994). https://doi.org/10.1007/BF01384084
12. Fantechi, A., Gnesi, S., Ristori, G.: Modelling transition systems within an action based logic. Technical report, IEI-CNR, Pisa (1996)
13. Garavel, H., Lang, F., Mateescu, R.: Compositional verification of asynchronous concurrent systems using CADP. Acta Informatica **52**(4), 337–392 (2015)
14. Garavel, H., Lang, F., Mateescu, R., Serwe, W.: CADP 2011: a toolbox for the construction and analysis of distributed processes. Springer Int. J. Softw. Tools Technol. Transf. (STTT) **15**(2), 89–107 (2013)
15. Garavel, H., Lang, F., Serwe, W.: From LOTOS to LNT. In: Katoen, J.-P., Langerak, R., Rensink, A. (eds.) ModelEd, TestEd, TrustEd. LNCS, vol. 10500, pp. 3–26. Springer, Cham (2017). https://doi.org/10.1007/978-3-319-68270-9_1

16. Gnesi, S., Mazzanti, F.: On the fly verification of network of automata. In: Arabnia, H.R. (ed.) Proceedings of the International Conference on Parallel and Distributed Processing Techniques and Applications, PDPTA 1999, Las Vegas, Nevada, USA, pp. 1040–1046. CSREA Press, June–July 1999

17. Gorogiannis, N., O'Hearn, P.W., Sergey, I.: A true positives theorem for a static race detector. Proc. ACM Program. Lang. 3(POPL), 57:1–57:29 (2019). https://doi.org/10.1145/3290370

18. Ha, O.-K., Kim, Y.-J., Kang, M.-H., Jun, Y.-K.: Empirical comparison of race detection tools for OpenMP programs. In: Ślęzak, D., Kim, T., Yau, S.S., Gervasi, O., Kang, B.-H. (eds.) GDC 2009. CCIS, vol. 63, pp. 108–116. Springer, Heidelberg (2009). https://doi.org/10.1007/978-3-642-10549-4_13

19. Ha, O.K., Kuh, I.B., Tchamgoue, G.M., Jun, Y.K.: On-the-fly detection of data races in OpenMP programs. In: Proceedings of the 2012 Workshop on Parallel and Distributed Systems: Testing, Analysis, and Debugging, PADTAD 2012, pp. 1–10. ACM (2012). https://doi.org/10.1145/2338967.2336808

20. Henzinger, T.A., Jhala, R., Majumdar, R.: Race checking by context inference. In: Pugh, W., Chambers, C. (eds.) Proceedings of the ACM SIGPLAN Conference on Programming Language Design and Implementation, PLDI 2004, Washington, D.C., USA, pp. 1–13. ACM, June 2004. https://doi.org/10.1145/996841.996844

21. Kang, M.-H., Ha, O.-K., Jun, S.-W., Jun, Y.-K.: A tool for detecting first races in OpenMP programs. In: Malyshkin, V. (ed.) PaCT 2009. LNCS, vol. 5698, pp. 299–303. Springer, Heidelberg (2009). https://doi.org/10.1007/978-3-642-03275-2_29

22. Kim, Y., Song, S., Jun, Y.: ADAT: an adaptable dynamic analysis tool for race detection in OpenMP programs. In: 2011 IEEE Ninth International Symposium on Parallel and Distributed Processing with Applications, pp. 304–310, May 2011. https://doi.org/10.1109/ISPA.2011.49

23. Kim, Y.-J., Park, M.-Y., Park, S.-H., Jun, Y.-K.: A practical tool for detecting races in OpenMP programs. In: Malyshkin, V. (ed.) PaCT 2005. LNCS, vol. 3606, pp. 321–330. Springer, Heidelberg (2005). https://doi.org/10.1007/11535294_28

24. Lang, F., Mateescu, R., Mazzanti, F.: Compositional verification of concurrent systems by combining bisimulations. In: ter Beek, M.H. et al. (eds.) FM 2019. LNCS, vol. 11800, pp. 196–213. Springer, Cham (2019)

25. Lin, Y.: Static nonconcurrency analysis of OpenMP programs. In: Mueller, M.S., Chapman, B.M., de Supinski, B.R., Malony, A.D., Voss, M. (eds.) IWOMP 2005. LNCS, vol. 4315, pp. 36–50. Springer, Heidelberg (2008). https://doi.org/10.1007/978-3-540-68555-5_4. http://dl.acm.org/citation.cfm?id=1892830.1892835

26. Ma, H., Diersen, S.R., Wang, L., Liao, C., Quinlan, D., Yang, Z.: Symbolic analysis of concurrency errors in OpenMP programs. In: 2013 42nd International Conference on Parallel Processing, pp. 510–516, October 2013. https://doi.org/10.1109/ICPP.2013.63

27. Mateescu, R.: CAESAR_SOLVE: a generic library for on-the-fly resolution of alternation-free boolean equation systems. Springer Int. J. Softw. Tools Technol. Transf. (STTT) 8(1), 37–56 (2006). Full Version Available as INRIA Research Report RR-5948, July 2006

28. Mateescu, R., Serwe, W.: Model checking and performance evaluation with CADP illustrated on shared-memory mutual exclusion protocols. Sci. Comput. Program. 78(7), 843–861 (2013)

29. Mateescu, R., Thivolle, D.: A model checking language for concurrent value-passing systems. In: Cuellar, J., Maibaum, T., Sere, K. (eds.) FM 2008. LNCS,

vol. 5014, pp. 148–164. Springer, Heidelberg (2008). https://doi.org/10.1007/978-3-540-68237-0_12

30. Mateescu, R., Wijs, A.: Property-dependent reductions adequate with divergence-sensitive branching bisimilarity. Sci. Comput. Program. **96**(3), 354–376 (2014)

31. Mkaouar, H., Zalila, B., Hugues, J., Jmaiel, M.: From AADL model to LNT specification. In: de la Puente, J.A., Vardanega, T. (eds.) Ada-Europe 2015. LNCS, vol. 9111, pp. 146–161. Springer, Cham (2015). https://doi.org/10.1007/978-3-319-19584-1_10

32. Nakade, R., Mercer, E., Aldous, P., McCarthy, J.: Model-checking task parallel programs for data-race. In: Dutle, A., Muñoz, C., Narkawicz, A. (eds.) NFM 2018. LNCS, vol. 10811, pp. 367–382. Springer, Cham (2018). https://doi.org/10.1007/978-3-319-77935-5_25

33. OpenMP Architecture Review Board: OpenMP Application Programming Interface, November 2018. https://www.openmp.org/wp-content/uploads/OpenMP-API-Specification-5.0.pdf

34. Oracle Studio 12.6: Thread Analyzer User's Guide, June 2017. https://docs.oracle.com/cd/E77782_01/html/E77800/index.html

35. Petersen, P., Shah, S.: OpenMP support in the Intel® Thread Checker. In: Voss, M.J. (ed.) WOMPAT 2003. LNCS, vol. 2716, pp. 1–12. Springer, Heidelberg (2003). https://doi.org/10.1007/3-540-45009-2_1

36. Savage, S., Burrows, M., Nelson, G., Sobalvarro, P., Anderson, T.: Eraser: a dynamic data race detector for multithreaded programs. ACM Trans. Comput. Syst. **15**(4), 391–411 (1997). https://doi.org/10.1145/265924.265927

37. Shah, D.: Analysis of an OpenMP program for race detection. Master's thesis, San Jose State University (2009)

38. Süß, M., Leopold, C.: Common mistakes in OpenMP and how to avoid them: a collection of best practices. In: Mueller, M.S., Chapman, B.M., de Supinski, B.R., Malony, A.D., Voss, M. (eds.) IWOMP 2005. LNCS, vol. 4315, pp. 312–323. Springer, Heidelberg (2008). https://doi.org/10.1007/978-3-540-68555-5_26. http://dl.acm.org/citation.cfm?id=1892830.1892863

Formal Verification of Railway Timetables
- Using the UPPAAL Model Checker

Anne E. Haxthausen[✉] and Kristian Hede

DTU Compute, Technical University of Denmark, Kongens Lyngby, Denmark
aeha@dtu.dk, krhede@gmail.com

Abstract. This paper considers the challenge of validating railway time-tables and investigates how formal methods can be used for that. The paper presents a re-configurable, formal model which can be configured with a timetable for a railway network, properties of that network, and various timetabling parameters (such as station and line capacities, headways, and minimum running times) constraining the allowed train behaviour. The formal model describes the system behaviour of trains driving according to the given railway timetable. Model checking can then be used to check that driving according to the timetable does not lead to illegal system states. The method has successfully been applied to a real world case study: a time table for 12 trains at Nærumbanen in Denmark.

Keywords: Formal methods · Model checking · UPPAAL · Railways · Timetables

1 Introduction

This paper considers the challenge of validating time tables in the railway domain.

Background. As timetables specify how the trains should run in the railway network, they have a great influence on the railway operations. Therefore, for any railway operator, it is of very high priority that the timetables are feasible as well as robust against delays. However, the process of creating train timetables [6] is very complicated and goes through many steps taking various wishes, requirements and scheduling constraints into account. Traditionally, time tables are created in a stepwise manner, where schedules are manually adjusted until all constraints are met.[1] When a timetable has been created in this way, it should be verified that it is feasible and satisfies all the many stated requirements and scheduling constraints. For instance, it should be checked that at any time the number of trains waiting at a station does not exceed the station

---

[1] Research in optimisation models and techniques for generating optimal timetables have been done [6], but these are very rarely used by the railway operators.

© Springer Nature Switzerland AG 2019
M. H. ter Beek et al. (Eds.): Gnesi Festschrift, LNCS 11865, pp. 433–448, 2019.
https://doi.org/10.1007/978-3-030-30985-5_25

capacity and that the minimal headways between trains are satisfied. Tools for automated checking of all such requirements are highly needed. Today there are some timetabling tools [10] like RailSys and TPS on the market which can be used for managing timetables and estimating the effect of train delays. The tools typically have functionality for displaying time tables graphically (showing the planned train positions as a function of time). In order to verify a timetable, one can inspect such graphs and manually check whether the requirements are fulfilled. Although this is very useful, it would be desirable to have a tool that could automatically check all requirements.

Contribution. In this paper we propose a fully automated method for verifying timetables. This method is formal and based on model checking. The idea is as follows: To check a timetable for a given railway network, one should create a real-time model simulating how trains move around in the network, from station to station over time, according to the timetable. During the simulation, a number of required properties of timetables should be checked. If any of these fail, the system should go into an error state. Then one can model check that all trains reach their final destination without ending in an error state. We have explored this idea using UPPAAL [3], which is an integrated tool environment for modelling, validation and verification of real-time systems modelled as networks of timed automata. We choose to use UPPAAL as our system is a real-time system and the UPPAAL symbolic model checker has shown to very be effective. The UPPAAL model is re-configurable: It can be configured with a timetable and a railway network description including various scheduling parameters (such as station and line capacities, headways, and minimum running times) constraining the allowed train behaviour. The verification method has successfully been applied to a real world case study: a time table for 12 trains at Nærumbanen Local Railway in Denmark.

To our best knowledge it is a novelty to verify railway timetables by model checking.

Related Work. Over the last decade formal methods have been widely used for developing railway systems, cf., the surveys given in [2,5]. According to these surveys, formal methods have mostly been applied to railway interlocking systems[2] (as e.g. in [1,7,8,11,12]) and other control system components, but less for railway operations, where formal methods have primarily been used for capacity analyses (as e.g. in [4]).

Paper Overview. First, in Sects. 2 and 3, short, informal introductions to the UPPAAL modelling language and to the domain of railway timetables are given, respectively. Then Sect. 4 presents a formal UPPAAL model of trains driving according to a given railway time table, whereupon, in Sect. 5, it is described

---

[2] An interlocking system is a signalling system component responsible for the safe routing of trains through a railway network.

how the verification of model instances is done. Finally, Sect. 6 gives a conclusion and states ideas for future work.

2   The UPPAAL Modelling Language

This section gives an ultra short, informal introduction to the major UPPAAL modelling language constructs used in this paper. The reader is assumed familiar with the theory of timed automata. For more details, especially on semantics of the concurrency construct, the reader should consult [3].

In UPPAAL a system is modelled as a network of parallel timed automata (called processes) which are finite-state machines extended with time in the form of real-valued clocks which progress synchronously and with data variables of simple data types (bounded integers, arrays, etc.).

The specification of a system model consists of (1) templates for timed automata, (2) declarations of clocks, data variables, constants, channels, and functions which can be used in the templates, and (3) a system declaration which is a parallel composition of processes which are instances of the templates. The processes can communicate asynchronously via shared variables or synchronously via channels.

A timed automaton consists of locations and edges.

In the UPPAAL graphical representation of timed automata, locations are shown as circles and may have a name shown in red colour. The *initial* location is shown by double circles. A location may be *committed* (shown as a circle with a C inside). If a process is in a committed location, the time must not pass and the next system transition must involve an edge from a committed location. A location may be labelled with an *invariant* (shown in purple colour) which is a Boolean expression over variables and clocks. The process can stay in that location and let the time pass as long as the invariant is satisfied, but when the invariant becomes false, it must leave the location.

In the graphical representation, edges are shown as arrows. An edge may be labelled with (1) a guard (shown in green colour) which is a Boolean expression over variables and clocks determining when the edge is enabled and can be fired, (2) updates of variables and clocks (shown in blue colour) that should be executed when the edge is fired, and (3) synchronisations of the form $c?$ or $c!$ over a channel c (shown in light blue colour). (An edge labelled with $c!$ in one process may synchronise with an edge labelled with $c?$ in another process provided that both edges are enabled.)

3   Domain Description

This section presents the definitions of basic terms of timetabling, as used in this paper, and requirements to timetables.

3.1   Basic Concepts and Terms

Railway Networks. A *railway network* consists of *stations* and *open lines* between stations. A *station* can be a passenger station where people embark and disembark trains, or a technical station where e.g. trains can overtake each other. An *open line* is a collection of tracks between two stations. In this paper it is assumed that each open line is either a *single track* or is a *double track* (has two tracks).[3] For double track lines it is assumed that there is one track dedicated to each driving direction.

Railway Timetables. A *railway timetable* for a given railway network is a collection of individual *train timetables/schedules* for train journeys in the network. Each train timetable has a unique (train) identifier and a list of stations at which the train should stop, along with the arrival and departure times at those stops.

A train is said to *drive according to its timetable*, if it arrives at and departs from the stations in its timetable at the stated arrival and departure times.

Parameters in Timetabling. The requirements to timetables are expressed in terms of a number of *scheduling parameters* described below. These depend among others on the track layout, train properties, and signalling system properties. It is out of the scope to explain how these parameters are determined - for an explanation of that, see e.g. [9]. Often some time supplements are added to/included in the minimum times mentioned below to make the timetable robust against small train delays.

The *capacity* of a station is the maximal number of trains that are allowed to be at the station at the same time. (In this paper, for simplicity, we will assume that if a station has capacity n, then it consists of n parallel tracks, each track having capacity for one train. Furthermore, we will assume that each station track is connected to each open line track.) The *minimum dwell time* of a train at a station is the minimum time it must wait at the station, such that there is time to open and close doors and let people enter and exit the train.

The *capacity* of an open line is the maximal number of trains that are allowed to be on each of its tracks at the same time. An open line also has a *minimum running time*, i.e. the time it must at least take for a train to drive between the two stations connected by the open line. Furthermore, an open line has a *minimum headway*, i.e. the minimum time that must pass between two following trains both entering the same track or both leaving the same track. Stations can also have different kinds of minimum headways between two trains entering/leaving the stations (depending on the signalling system). In this paper we just illustrate how this can be done for a minimum headway between two trains entering the station.

---

[3] In Denmark this is the case for most railway networks, with only very few exceptions.

3.2   Requirements

For a timetable to be *valid*, a number of requirements must hold when the trains drive according to the timetables. Below we state examples of typical requirements, but these might differ for different railways.

no overtaking: Trains must not overtake another train on the same track of an open line (as this is physically not possible and would prevent the plan from being executable.)

no opposing trains: Single track open lines must not be utilised in both directions simultaneously (as that would lead to deadlocks preventing the plan from being executable.)

open line running times: Trains must satisfy the minimum running times of the open lines.

open line capacities: The capacity of open lines must never be exceeded.

open line headways: The headway times of open lines must be respected.

station dwell times: Trains must satisfy the dwell times at the stations.

station capacities: The capacity of stations must never be exceeded.

station headways: The headway times of stations must be respected.

It is seen how the two first requirements concern internal inconsistencies in a given timetable (in this case conflicting train schedules)[4], while the remaining ones concern the timetabling parameters identified above.

4   UPPAAL Model

This section presents the UPPAAL model created for verifying timetables. The model can be found here: http://www2.compute.dtu.dk/~aeha/RobustRailS/ data/timetabling/uppaal-models/. The model has been designed to be re-configurable, so that it can be re-used for a whole class of railway networks and timetables, without having to change the templates of the model, but only constant data representing the railway network and the timetables.

4.1   Overview

The model consists of the following three parts:

1. Global declarations of (1) the configuration data (constants) defining a railway network layout and timetabling parameters and a timetable for that network, (2) clocks, (3) variables, (4) types, and (5) functions.
2. Two templates: **Train** and **Initialiser**. A process instance of the **Train** template represents a single train, running according to one of the timetables in the global declarations. The **Initialiser** template is used to initialise the system.
3. The system declaration, which creates a single **Initialiser** process and a **Train** process for each of the trains in the timetable.

The following sections describe these parts, except the types and functions.

---

[4] Note that the interlocking system has the responsibility to ensure that collisions would not happen in such cases.

4.2   Railway Network Data

The railway network data (describing the network layout and the timetabling parameters) are represented by a collection of constants as shown in Listing 1.1, where the constants are configured for the network of *Nærumbanen* in Denmark which has 9 stations connected one by one by single track open lines. The first constants give the number of stations, the number of open lines, and the station ids. The `stationTable` is an array with one entry for each station giving the capacity (`capacity`) and minimum headway (`HWT`) for that station. The `openLineTable` is an array with one entry for each open line (represented as a pair of the two stations it is connecting) stating the kind of line (`false` means single track and `true` means double track) and giving the minimum running time (`MRT`), the capacity (`capacity`), and the minimum headway (`HWT`) for that open line.

```
const int STATIONS  = 9; //number of stations
const int OPENLINES = 8; //number of open lines

//station ids for station numbers 0 .. STATIONS-1:
const int remisen = 0;
...
const int narum = 8;

const StationTableEntry stationTable[STATIONS] =
{{remisen, 6, 1},
{jagersborg, 2, 1},
{norgaardsvej, 1, 1},
{lyngbylokal, 1, 1},
{fuglevad, 2, 1},
{brede, 1, 1},
{orholm, 2, 1},
{ravnholm, 1, 1},
{narum, 2, 1}};

const OpenLineTableEntry openLineTable[OPENLINES] =
{{{remisen,jagersborg},false,2,1,1},
{{jagersborg,norgaardsvej},false,1,1,1},
{{norgaardsvej,lyngbylokal},false,1,1,1},
{{lyngbylokal,fuglevad},false,1,1,1},
{{fuglevad,brede},false,2,1,1},
{{brede,orholm},false,2,1,1},
{{orholm,ravnholm},false,1,1,1},
{{ravnholm,narum},false,2,1,1}};
```

Listing 1.1. Example of network data for *Nærumbanen*.

4.3   Timetable Data

The railway timetable is represented by a collection of constants as shown in Listing 1.2, where the constants are configured for an extract of the timetable of

Nærumbanen in Denmark. stops is an array of timetables – one for each train, and each timetable is an array of stop entries. Each stop entry gives the station id (StationID), the arrival time (AT), the departure time (DT), and the minimum dwell time[5] (DWT) for a stop. For the shown train timetables the minimum dwell time has been chosen to be zero for stations where the trains need not to stop.

```
const int TRAINS = 2; //number of trains in the timetable
const int TRAINSTOPS[TRAINS] = {8,9}; //number of stops for
                                      each train time table
const int MAXLENGTH = 9; //max number of stops for any train

/* timetable for each train */
const StopEntry stops[TRAINS][MAXLENGTH] = {
//timetable for train 0
{{jagersborg,26,30,1},
{norgaardsvej,31,31,0},
{lyngbylokal,33,33,0},
{fuglevad,35,35,0},
{brede,37,37,0},
{orholm,39,40,1},
{ravnholm,41,41,0},
{narum,43,47,1},
{-1,-1,-1,-1}},
//timetable for train 1
{{remisen,0,34,0},
{jagersborg,36,40,1},
{norgaardsvej,41,41,0},
{lyngbylokal,43,43,0},
{fuglevad,45,45,0},
{brede,47,47,0},
{orholm,49,50,1},
{ravnholm,51,51,0},
{narum,53,57,1}}};
```

Listing 1.2. Example of a timetable for Nærumbanen.

4.4   Clocks

To express time constraints in the model, a number of clocks are introduced in addition to the system clock time:

```
clock TrainClock[TRAINS];
clock openLineLastEntered[OPENLINES][2];
clock openLineLastExit[OPENLINES][2];
clock stationLastEntered[STATIONS];
```

For each train id, TrainClock[id] is used to record how long time the train has been in its current location. For each open line number o (which is an index in the

---

[5] To allow for different minimum dwell times at the same station for different trains, this scheduling parameter has been placed here and not in stationTable.

openLineTable) and driving direction $d \in 0 \, .. \, 1$, openLineLastEntered[o][d] and openLineLastExit[o][d] records the time elapsed since a train last time entered o and exited o in direction d, respectively. Direction 0 is used for the direction towards the first station found in the open line entry openLinetable[o], and direction 1 is used for the other direction. For each station id s, stationLastEntered[s] records the time elapsed since a train last time entered s.

4.5   Variables

A number of variables are introduced:

```
int currentStop[TRAINS];
int[0, TRAINS] trainsAtStation[STATIONS];
int[0, TRAINS] trainsAtOpenLine[OPENLINES][2];
queueEntry queue[OPENLINES][2][TRAINS];
```

For each train id t, currentStop[t] stores the station id of the station at which the train is currently waiting or towards which it is currently moving (when it is on an open line). For each station s, trainsAtStation[s] stores the number of trains currently waiting at s. For each open line number o and direction $d \in 0 \, .. \, 1$, trainsAtOpenLine[o][d] stores the number of trains currently driving on o in direction d. For each open line number o and direction d, queue[o][d] is a queue (an array) of entries for trains currently present on o in direction d. Each entry contains the id of a train and the time it is planned to leave the open line. The trains appear in the order they entered o, with the head in queue[o][d][0].

4.6   The Initialiser Template

The Initialiser template is shown in Fig. 1. The initial location is committed making the outgoing edge of that location, the first to be fired in the system - without any delay. This edge invokes a function to initialise global variables and clocks.

Fig. 1. The Initialiser template.

4.7   The Train Template

The Train template has a single parameter, id, which can be instantiated with the identifier of a train from the timetable. The resulting train process simulates the behaviour of the train driving perfectly according to its timetable

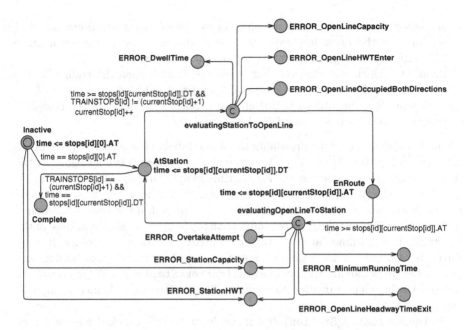

Fig. 2. The `Train` Template only showing state invariants and edge labels expressing conditions ensuring that the train drives according to its time table.

in `stops[id]` without any deviations. During the simulation, the timetable is checked to satisfy the requirements stated in Sect. 3.2.

Figure 2 shows the template with all its locations and edges, but for readability only with those state invariants and edge labels that enforce the train to drive according to its time table. Later, the remaining edge labels will be explained.

As it can be seen, a train has the following locations:

- `Inactive` which is the initial location.
- `AtStation` which reflects that at the current time the train is waiting at a station according to the timetable.
- `EnRoute` which reflects that at the current time the train is driving on the open line between two consecutive stations in its timetable.
- `evaluatingStationToOpenLine` which is a committed, intermediate location between `AtStation` and `EnRoute`. It is an auxiliary location (not existing in a real system) which is only used for checking that neither leaving the current station nor entering the next open line would break a requirement.
- `evaluatingOpenLineToStation` which is a committed, intermediate location between `EnRoute` and `AtStation`. It is an auxiliary location (not existing in a real system) which is only used for checking that neither leaving the current open line nor entering the next station would break a requirement.

– An error location for each possible error (breaking a requirement). For instance, if the open line capacity is exceeded at time t, the error state ERROR_OpenLineCapacity will be reached at that time.
– Complete which is a location that is reached if and when the train has successfully run through its whole timetable and reached its destination without any errors have been detected. If all trains reach this location, the complete railway timetable has successfully been validated.

Figure 2 shows those state invariants and edge labels that enforce the train to drive according to its time table: A train starts in the Inactive location. At the start time of its timetable (i.e. the arrival time stops[id][0].AT of its first stop) it will enter the AtStation location modelling that it is at the first stop of its timetable. Whenever the AtStation location is entered, if the train has reached its final stop (TRAINSTOPS[id] == currentStop[id] + 1) and final time of the timetable, it will immediately go to the Complete location. Otherwise, it must leave the AtStation location and enter the evaluatingStationToOpenLine location at its departure time stops[id][currentStop[id]].DT for its current station. During that transition the currentStop[id] counter is incremented by one.

In the evaluatingStationToOpenLine location it is checked whether some requirements are broken. If that is the case, the system goes into an error location, and otherwise it goes to the EnRoute location.

Similarly, whenever the train is in the EnRoute location (i.e. is driving on the open line towards the next station in its route), it must leave the location and enter the evaluatingOpenLineToStation location at the arrival time stops[id][currentStop[id]].AT for the train's next station.

In the evaluatingOpenLineToStation location it is checked whether some requirements are broken. If that is the case, the system goes into an error location, and otherwise it goes to the AtStation location.

Figure 3 shows the full model with all edge labels included. The additional guards and variable/clock updates are used to express the checks for the requirements stated in Sect. 3.2. On each edge from the evaluatingStationToOpenLine and evaluatingOpenLineToStation locations to an error state for a certain kind of error, there is a guard expressing that this error is found. The guard of the edge from the evaluatingStationToOpenLine/evaluatingOpenLineToStation location to the EnRoute/AtStation location is a conjunction of the negated error conditions in the guards of each of the edges leading to an error location from the evaluatingStationToOpenLine/evaluatingOpenLineToStation location. The guards are expressed in terms of the clocks and variables declared in Sects. 4.4 and 4.5. These clocks and variables are updated when a train is entering a station or an open line.

Below we will give an overall idea of how the updates and checks for the various requirements are done.[6]

---

[6] There is no space to show and explain the many auxiliary functions used in the edge labels to implement that.

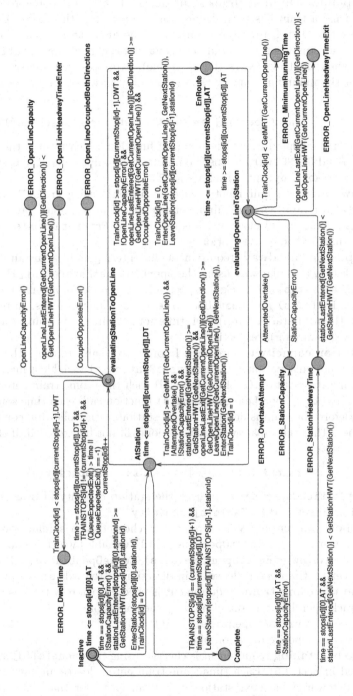

Fig. 3. The complete Train template.

The **openline running times** requirement: In order to be able to measure how long time a train has been driving on an open line, the `TrainClock[id]` clock is reset to 0 each time the train enters the `EnRoute` location. Then, the following condition, when evaluated in the `evaluatingOpenLineToStation` location (i.e. when the train leaves the open line), expresses that the train has at least spent the minimum running time of the current open line in the `EnRoute` location:

$$\texttt{TrainClock[id]} \; \texttt{>=} \; \texttt{GetMRT(GetCurrentOpenLine())}$$

where `GetCurrentOpenLine` is an auxiliary function which returns the current open line o and `GetMRT(o)` returns the minimum running time of o as stated in the `openLineTable`: `openLineTable[o].MRT`.

The **dwell times** requirement is checked similarly using `TrainClock[id]`.

The **station headways** requirement is checked in a similar way using the `stationLastEntered[s]` clock which is reset (by an `EnterStation(s)` function call) each time a train enters station s.

The **open line headways** requirements for entering and leaving an open line o are checked in a similar way using the `openLineLastEntered[o][d]` and the `openLineLastExit[o][d]` clocks, respectively. These clocks are reset to 0 (by `EnterOpenLine(o, s)` and `LeaveOpenLine(o, s)` function calls, respectively, where s is the next station/stop) each time some train enters o and leaves o in direction d[7] (towards s), respectively.

The **station capacity** requirement: In order to be able to count the number of trains present on a station s, the `trainsAtStation[s]` variable is incremented by 1 (by an `EnterStation(s)` function call) each time some train enters s and is decremented by 1 (by a `LeaveStation(s)` function call) each time some train leaves s. Before the train is entering a new station s, the following condition is used to check that the capacity of that station will not be exceeded, if the train enters the station:

$$\texttt{trainsAtStation[s]} \; \texttt{<} \; \texttt{GetStationCapacity(s)}$$

where `GetStationCapacity(s)` returns the station capacity of s as stated in the `stationTable`: `stationTable[s].capacity`

The **open line capacity** requirement is checked in a similar way for an open line o using the `trainsAtOpenLine[o][d]` variables which are incremented/decremented (by an `EnterOpenLine(o, s)`/`LeaveOpenLine(o, s)` function call) each time a train enters/leaves o in direction d (towards s).

The **no opposing trains** requirement is checked before a train is entering a single track open line o in direction d by the condition

$$\texttt{trainsAtOpenLine[o][d']} = 0$$

where d' is the opposite direction of d.

The **no overtaking** requirement is checked using the `queue[o][d]` variables (introduced in Sect. 4.5). Each time some train enters/leaves an open line o in direction d towards the next station s, a train entry for that train (keeping

---

[7] d can be found from s as explained in Sect. 4.4.

its name and planed arrival time at next station) is pushed/popped to/from the queue in `queue[o][d]` (by an `EnterOpenLine(o, s)`/`LeaveOpenLine(o, s)` function call). When a train is leaving its current open line o in direction d, the following condition is used to check that the first train in the queue `queue[o][d]` is the train it-self which means that it has not overtaken any train:

$$\texttt{GetQueueFirstTrain(o, d) = id}$$

where `GetQueueFirstTrain(o, d)` returns the train id in `queue[o][d][0]`.

A Concurrency Issue: If one train t_1 enters an open line o at the same time t (according to the timetable) as another train t_2 leaves the same open line according to the timetable (both driving in the same direction d), the interleaving semantics of UPPAAL would lead to two different traces sequencing the two events: one in which t_1 enters first and t_2 leaves afterwards, and one in which the order is opposite. If we assume that there are no other trains on the line, the value of `trainsAtOpenLine[o][d]` will at time t in the first trace first be 2 and then 1, while in the other trace it will be 1 in both states. If the capacity of the line is 1, then the first trace will give rise to a false line capacity error. Therefore, we should ensure that only the second trace is considered. In order to ensure this, the following time constraint was added to the guard of the edge from the `AtStation` location to the `evaluatingStationToOpenLine` location:

$$\texttt{QueueExpectedExit() > time}$$

where `QueueExpectedExit()` returns the expected exit time of the train in the head of the queue in `queue[o][d]`: `queue[o][d][0].expectedExit`. This would mean, that a train can only enter the open line at time `time`, if the next train that will leave the same open line in the same direction will do that later on. Hence, for the example above, trace 1 would not anymore be possible.

Note that we do not have the same concurrency issue for stations, since if one train enters the station at the same time as another leaves it, there should be space for both of them at the same time, so both traces should be considered.

4.8 System Declaration

The system declaration

```
system Train, Initialiser;
```

creates a single `Initialiser` process and a `Train` process `Train(id)` for each train identifier id, id = 0, .. ,TRAIN-1.

5 Verification

This section explains how a railway timetable can be verified by model checking a system model instantiated with data for that timetable against some properties.

5.1   Properties

To verify that a railway timetable is valid, it should be checked that eventually all the trains have reached their destination as expressed by the property

A<> forall(i: t_id) Train(i).Complete

If this property is true, it in particular follows that no error states have been reached and therefore all the requirements stated in Sect. 3.2 are fulfilled for trains driving according to the timetable.

However, if the property fails, one can't from the property itself conclude what went wrong. In such a case, if one wishes to know which kind of errors were encountered and which trains did not reach their destination, one can instead check

A[] forall(i: t_id) not Train(i).$ERROR\_S$

for each error location $ERROR\_S$, and

Train(i).Inactive --> Train(i).Complete

and for each train i.

5.2   Verification Results

For an extended version of the model created in Sect. 3.2 for Nærumbanen (now with 12 trains), we used the symbolic model checker of UPPAAL to check the properties above. All properties were successfully verified as shown by green lamps in Fig. 4.

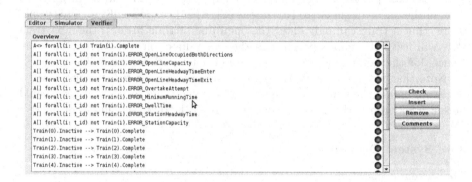

Fig. 4. Verification results for the timetable for Nærumbanen in Denmark. (Color figure online)

Verification[8] using the A<> forall(i: t_id) Train(i).Complete property took less than a second. The alternative (more informative) verification of all the detailed properties (for individual errors and individual trains) took 5–6 s.

---

[8] The experiments were done with an Intel(R) Core(TM) i5-5200U processor at 2.2 GHz with 12 GB RAM.

We also made examples with illegal timetables to test that the model checker would be able to catch the different kinds of errors. For instance, we changed the capacity of `orholm` station from 2 to 1, such that the station capacity would be exceeded when two trains should pass each other at the station.

Once an error has been detected, it is possible to identify how, where and when it occurred by choosing the 'Some' option of the Diagnostic Trace. Then the failing query should be chosen and verified by itself, resulting in a diagnostic trace, which will provide the entire diagnostic trace up until the state of the error.

6 Conclusion and Future Plans

This paper has shown how railway timetables can be formally verified to be feasible (executable) and satisfy a number of scheduling constraints. The UPPAAL model checker was used for that purpose. To our knowledge, it is the first time that model checking has been used for that. The approach is quite promising as it was applied successfully to a real-world case study for which the timetable for 12 trains on a railway with 9 stations was successfully verified in less than a second. In future work, it would be interesting to apply the method to larger examples.

It should be straight forward to extend the model to allow more than two tracks on open lines and take more details of station topologies into account (e.g. the number of platforms and which open line tracks they are connected to) and include scheduled track occupation information for trains in their timetables. Furthermore, it could be interesting to investigate how model checking could be used for investigating the effects of train delays.

We have also investigated how model checking can be used to generate timetables and we plan to describe those results in a future paper.

Acknowledgements. This paper is dedicated to Professor Stefania Gnesi on the occasion of her 65th birthday. The first author has had the great pleasure of meeting Stefania Gnesi at many occasions and would like to thank her for inspiration, discussions, and collaboration, especially in European Technical Working Group on Formal Methods in Railway Control.

The research was partially funded by the RobustRailS project (2012-17) granted by Innovation Fund Denmark under grant agreement 0603-00483B. The authors are grateful to the organisers of the Festschrift Symposium for giving the opportunity to prepare this paper. We would like to thank the anonymous reviewers for their comments, and we would like to thank Alex Landex for discussions and sharing of his deep knowledge about railway timetabling while he was employed as a researcher in railway operations at DTU Transport.

References

1. Banci, M., Fantechi, A., Gnesi, S.: Some experiences on formal specification of railway interlocking systems using statecharts. In: TRain Workshop at SEFM (2005)

2. Basile, D., et al.: On the industrial uptake of formal methods in the railway domain - a survey with stakeholders. In: Furia, C.A., Winter, K. (eds.) IFM 2018. LNCS, vol. 11023, pp. 20–29. Springer, Cham (2018). https://doi.org/10.1007/978-3-319-98938-9_2

3. Behrmann, G., David, A., Larsen, K.G.: A tutorial on UPPAAL. In: Bernardo, M., Corradini, F. (eds.) SFM-RT 2004. LNCS, vol. 3185, pp. 200–236. Springer, Heidelberg (2004). https://doi.org/10.1007/978-3-540-30080-9_7

4. Di Giandomenico, F., Fantechi, A., Gnesi, S., Itria, M.L.: Stochastic model-based analysis of railway operation to support traffic planning. In: Gorbenko, A., Romanovsky, A., Kharchenko, V. (eds.) SERENE 2013. LNCS, vol. 8166, pp. 184–198. Springer, Heidelberg (2013). https://doi.org/10.1007/978-3-642-40894-6_15

5. Fantechi, A.: Twenty-five years of formal methods and railways: what next? In: Counsell, S., Núñez, M. (eds.) SEFM 2013. LNCS, vol. 8368, pp. 167–183. Springer, Cham (2014). https://doi.org/10.1007/978-3-319-05032-4_13

6. Hansen, I.A., Pachl, J.: Railway timetable & traffic: analysis, modelling, simulation. Eurailpress (2008)

7. James, P., Moller, F., Nguyen, H.N., Roggenbach, M., Schneider, S., Treharne, H.: Techniques for modelling and verifying railway interlockings. Int. J. Softw. Tools Technol. Transf. 16(6), 685–711 (2014)

8. Khan, U., Ahmad, J., Saeed, T., Hayat, S.: Real time modeling of interlocking control system of Rawalpindi Cantt train yard. In: 2015 13th International Conference on Frontiers of Information Technology (FIT), pp. 347–352 (2015). https://doi.org/10.1109/FIT.2015.28

9. Landex, A., Kaas, A., Hansen, S.: Railway Operation. Technical report, Technical University of Denmark, Centre for Traffic and Transport (2006)

10. Schittenhelm, B., Landex, A.: Jernbanesimuleringsværktøjer i Danmark (Eng.: Railway Simulation Tools in Denmark). Aalborg Trafikdage (2008) (in Danish). www.trafikdage.dk/papers_2008/praesentationer/bernd_schittenhelm_158.pdf

11. Vu, L.H., Haxthausen, A.E., Peleska, J.: Formal modelling and verification of interlocking systems featuring sequential release. Sci. Comput. Program. 133, Part 2, 91–115 (2017). https://doi.org/10.1016/j.scico.2016.05.010. http://www.sciencedirect.com/science/article/pii/S0167642316300570

12. Winter, K.: Symbolic model checking for interlocking systems. In: Flammini, F. (ed.) Railway Safety, Reliability, and Security: Technologies and Systems Engineering. IGI Global (2012)

An Axiomatization of Strong Distribution Bisimulation for a Language with a Parallel Operator and Probabilistic Choice

Jan Friso Groote[iD] and Erik P. de Vink[(✉)][iD]

Department of Mathematics and Computer Science,
Eindhoven University of Technology, Eindhoven, The Netherlands
J.F.Groote@tue.nl, evink@win.tue.nl

Abstract. In the setting of a simple process language featuring non-deterministic choice and a parallel operator on the one hand and probabilistic choice on the other hand, we propose an axiomatization capturing strong distribution bisimulation. Contrary to other process equivalences for probabilistic process languages, in this paper distributions rather than states are the leading ingredients for building the semantics and the accompanying equational theory, for which we establish soundness and completeness.

1 Introduction

Probabilistic extensions of process algebraic languages have been studied since the 90s. A frequently reoccurring issue is the interplay of indeterminacy caused by non-determinism or stemming from probability. Process equivalences, seeking to identify processes for purposes of formal analysis, need to take this into account. A number of process equivalences for probabilistic process languages have been proposed, including strong probabilistic bisimulation as introduced in [27]. For logical characterizations of these process relations, equivalence of two processes coincides with the two processes satisfying exactly the same formulas of a particular logic, cf. [11,25,31] for example. For equational characterizations, equivalence of two processes exactly coincides with the two processes being provably equal with respect to the axioms of the equational theory at hand. See, e.g., [6,14,17].

In this paper we study an equational theory for a process language which includes non-deterministic choice and a parallel operator in the style of ACP [3,8] as well as probabilistic choice as in PCCS [27]. We present an operational semantics based on a two-sorted transition system, distinguishing non-deterministic processes and probabilistic processes, as is usual for the set-up with both types of indeterminacy. Following [32] we incorporate so-called combined transitions, meaning that for any two transitions with the same action label any convex combination of these two transitions is possible as well. The notion of process

© Springer Nature Switzerland AG 2019
M. H. ter Beek et al. (Eds.): Gnesi Festschrift, LNCS 11865, pp. 449–463, 2019.
https://doi.org/10.1007/978-3-030-30985-5_26

equivalence on the basis of which we identify processes is strong distribution bisimulation as proposed in [16]. In particular, this process equivalence is based on distributions rather than on single states, in line with our recent work on branching distribution bisimulation [22]. For our process language we introduce an equational theory which characterizes strong distribution bisimulation. Borrowing from [6], the equational theory quite naturally extends the axiomatizations of its non-deterministic sublanguage. We prove that our set of axioms is sound and complete indeed. Also for the proofs we manage to extend the established approach. The latter constitutes the main contribution of the paper.

Early work on complete axiomatizations for probabilistic process algebras includes [18]. However, it provides no treatment of a parallel operator. In [4] a parallel operator is included, but non-determinism is resolved in favor of probabilistic behavior. Completeness in [4,18] is established with respect to strong probabilistic bisimulation [27]. In [9], in a different vein, an axiom system is provided for a process algebra including a parallel operator in the setting of Markovian bisimulation. The paper [6] treats both strong and weak bisimulation, presenting equational theories for a process language with non-deterministic and probabilistic choice, in the alternating model [24] and in the non-alternating model [33]. The alternating model is also underpinning [1] where an axiomatization is given for (non-convex) probabilistic version of branching bisimulation. In [2] it is formally shown that branching bisimulation in the alternating model and in the non-alternating model differ. In [14] a complete axiomatization is given, with respect to both strong and weak probabilistic bisimulation, for a language that also covers recursion, extending [34] to include non-deterministic choice. In [15] the work of [14] is expanded further to deal with a CCS-style parallel operator. To the best of our knowledge, [15] is the only paper proposing a complete equational theory for a parallel operator in a semantical model that supports both non-deterministic and probabilistic behavior. Recursion is also incorporated in the process language of [17] (but no parallel operator). This paper focuses on infinitary semantics and weak probabilistic bisimulation. Also [17] provides a complete equational theory.

The remainder of this paper is organized as follows: After a short recollection of preliminaries in Sect. 2, we introduce in Sect. 3 the process language under study together with its transition system. We continue in Sect. 4 to define strong distribution bisimulation and establish that it is a congruence for the operators of our language. In Sect. 5 the equational theory is given and it is shown that it is sound and complete with respect to strong distribution bisimulation. Section 6 wraps up with concluding remarks.

2   Preliminaries

Let $Distr(X)$ be the set of distributions over the set X of finite support. A distribution $\mu \in Distr(X)$ can be represented as $\mu = \bigoplus_{i \in I} p_i * x_i$ when $\mu(x_i) = p_i$ for $i \in I$ and $\sum_{i \in I} p_i = 1$. We assume I to be a finite index set. In concrete cases, when no confusion arises, the separator $*$ is omitted from the notation.

For convenience later, we do not require $x_i \neq x_{i'}$ for $i \neq i'$ nor $p_i > 0$ for $i, i' \in I$. We use $\delta(x)$ to denote the Dirac distribution for $x \in X$. For $\mu, \nu \in Distr(X)$ and $r \in [0,1]$ we define $\mu \oplus_r \nu \in Distr(X)$ by $(\mu \oplus_r \nu)(x) = r \cdot \mu(x) + (1-r) \cdot \nu(x)$. By definition $\mu \oplus_0 \nu = \nu$ and $\mu \oplus_1 \nu = \mu$. For an index set I, $p_i \in [0,1]$ and $\mu_i \in Distr(X)$, we define $\bigoplus_{i \in I} p_i * \mu_i \in Distr(X)$ by $(\bigoplus_{i \in I} p_i * \mu_i)(x) = \sum_{i \in I} p_i \cdot \mu_i(x)$ for $x \in X$. For $\mu = \bigoplus_{i \in I} p_i * \mu_i$, $\nu = \bigoplus_{i \in I} p_i * \nu_i$, and $r \in [0,1]$ it holds that $\mu \oplus_r \nu = \bigoplus_{i \in I} \mu_i \oplus_r \nu_i$. For a relation $\mathcal{R}$ on $Distr(X)$ we define the convex closure $cc(\mathcal{R})$ by $cc(\mathcal{R}) = \{ \langle \bigoplus_{i \in I} p_i * \mu_i, \bigoplus_{i \in I} p_i * \nu_i \rangle \mid \mu_i \, \mathcal{R} \, \nu_i, \sum_{i \in I} p_i = 1 \}$.

3   A Process Language

We introduce a process language of non-deterministic processes featuring non-deterministic choice and a parallel operator, intertwined with probabilistic processes built on Dirac distributions and probabilistic choice. Since the axiomatization presented in Sect. 5 requires auxiliary operators $\parallel$ and $\mid$, called leftmerge and synchronization operator, we introduce an extended class of processes too.

Fix $\mathcal{A}$ to be a non-empty alphabet of actions. We use a to range over $\mathcal{A}$. We assume a so-called communication function $\gamma : \mathcal{A} \times \mathcal{A} \to \mathcal{A}$ to be given, that determines the result of two synchronizing actions. The function γ is both commutative and associative.

Definition 3.1 (syntax). The class $\mathcal{E}$ of non-deterministic processes over $\mathcal{A}$, with typical element E, and the class $\mathcal{P}$ of probabilistic processes over $\mathcal{A}$, with typical element P, are given by

$$E ::= \mathbf{0} \mid a \cdot P \mid E + E \mid E \| E$$
$$P ::= \Delta(E) \mid P \oplus_r P$$

where $r \in (0,1)$.

We see that a non-deterministic process is either the nil process $\mathbf{0}$, which performs no action, a prefixed probabilistic process $a \cdot P$, which performs the action a, a non-deterministic choice $E_1 + E_2$, which can behave both like E_1 and like E_2, or a parallel composition $E_1 \| E_2$, which interleaves or synchronizes actions from E_1 and E_2. In the latter case synchronization is governed by the communication function γ introduced above.

The subclasses $\mathcal{E}_0 \subseteq \mathcal{E}$ of basic non-deterministic processes and $\mathcal{P}_0 \subseteq \mathcal{P}$ of basic probabilistic processes consists of processes $E \in \mathcal{E}$ and $P \in \mathcal{P}$ such that the parallel operator $\|$ doesn't occur in E and P, respectively. The extended classes of non-deterministic processes $\mathcal{E}'$ and of probabilistic processes $\mathcal{P}'$ are obtained by adding (see Definition 3.2 below) the leftmerge operator $\parallel$ and the synchronization operator $\mid$ to the grammar of Definition 3.1.

Definition 3.2 (basic and extended processes).

(a) The subclasses $\mathcal{E}_0 \subseteq \mathcal{E}$ of basic non-deterministic processes and $\mathcal{P}_0 \subseteq \mathcal{P}$ of basic probabilistic processes are given by

$$E ::= \mathbf{0} \mid a \cdot P \mid E + E$$
$$P ::= \Delta(E) \mid P \oplus_r P$$

(b) The superclass $\mathcal{E}' \supseteq \mathcal{E}$ of extended non-deterministic processes and $\mathcal{P}' \supseteq \mathcal{P}$ of extended probabilistic processes are defined by the BNF

$$E ::= \mathbf{0} \mid a \cdot P \mid E + E \mid E \| E \mid E \lfloor\!\lfloor E \mid E \mid E$$
$$P ::= \Delta(E) \mid P \oplus_r P$$

The behavior of processes is defined using transition relations. We distinguish a transition relation $\rightarrow$ for non-deterministic processes and a relation $\mapsto$ for probabilistic processes. We blur the difference of probabilistic processes and distributions over non-deterministic processes by an implicit interpretation given by the relation $\mapsto$.

Definition 3.3 (transition relation).

(a) The transition relations $\rightarrow \subseteq \mathcal{E} \times \mathcal{A} \times Distr(\mathcal{E})$ and $\mapsto \subseteq \mathcal{P} \times Distr(\mathcal{E})$ are induced by

$$\frac{P \mapsto \mu}{a \cdot P \xrightarrow{a} \mu} \text{ (PREF)}$$

$$\frac{E_1 \xrightarrow{a} \mu_1}{E_1 + E_2 \xrightarrow{a} \mu_1} \text{ (ND-CHOICE 1)} \qquad \frac{E_2 \xrightarrow{a} \mu_2}{E_1 + E_2 \xrightarrow{a} \mu_2} \text{ (ND-CHOICE 2)}$$

$$\frac{E_1 \xrightarrow{a} \mu_1}{E_1 \| E_2 \xrightarrow{a} \mu_1 \| \Delta(E_2)} \text{ (PAR 1)} \qquad \frac{E_2 \xrightarrow{a} \mu_2}{E_1 \| E_2 \xrightarrow{a} \Delta(E_1) \| \mu_2} \text{ (PAR 2)}$$

$$\frac{E_1 \xrightarrow{a} \mu_1 \quad E_2 \xrightarrow{b} \mu_2}{E_1 \| E_2 \xrightarrow{c} \mu_1 \| \mu_2} \text{ if } \gamma(a,b) = c \text{ (PAR 3)}$$

$$\Delta(E) \mapsto \delta(E) \text{ (DIRAC)} \qquad \frac{P_1 \mapsto \mu_1 \quad P_2 \mapsto \mu_2}{P_1 \oplus_r P_2 \mapsto r * \mu_1 \oplus (1-r) * \mu_2} \text{ (P-CHOICE)}$$

(b) The combined transition relation $\rightarrow \subseteq Distr(\mathcal{E}) \times \mathcal{A} \times Distr(\mathcal{E})$ is such that $\mu \xrightarrow{a} \mu'$ whenever $\mu = \bigoplus_{i \in I} p_i * E_i$, $\mu' = \bigoplus_{i \in I} p_i * \mu'_i$, and $E_i \xrightarrow{a} \mu'_i$ for all $i \in I$.

The rules (PAR 1) to (PAR 3) above use the parallel operator in combination with distributions. For $\mu_1, \mu_2 \in Distr(\mathcal{E})$ the distribution $(\mu_1 \| \mu_2) \in Distr(\mathcal{E})$ is such that $(\mu_1 \| \mu_2)(E) = \mu_1(E_1) \cdot \mu_2(E_2)$ if $E \equiv E_1 \| E_2$ and $(\mu_1 \| \mu_2)(E) = 0$ if E is not a parallel composition. See e.g. [26,28] for similar use of this construction. Note the use of the communication function γ in rule (PAR 3).

The combined transition relation on $Distr(\mathcal{E})$ allows one to split a distribution μ into $\mu_1 \oplus_r \mu_2$ and to consider transitions of μ_1 and μ_2 for a specific action a independently and combining the resulting distributions. See Example 4.5 in the next section.

Also for the classes of extended processes we provide transition relations.

Definition 3.4 (extended transition relation).

(a) The transition relations $\rightarrow \, \subseteq \mathcal{E}' \times \mathcal{A} \times Distr(\mathcal{E}')$ and $\mapsto \, \subseteq \mathcal{P}' \times Distr(\mathcal{E}')$ are induced by the transition rules PREF, ND-CHOICE 1,2, PAR 1,2,3, DIRAC, and P-CHOICE together with the transition rules

$$\frac{E_1 \xrightarrow{a} \mu_1}{E_1 \,\|\, E_2 \xrightarrow{a} \mu_1 \,\|\, \Delta(E_2)} \text{ (LEFT)} \qquad \frac{E_1 \xrightarrow{a} \mu_1 \quad E_2 \xrightarrow{b} \mu_2}{E_1 | E_2 \xrightarrow{c} \mu_1 \,\|\, \mu_2} \text{ if } \gamma(a,b) = c \text{ (SYNC)}$$

(b) The combined transition relation $\rightarrow \, \subseteq Distr(\mathcal{E}') \times \mathcal{A} \times Distr(\mathcal{E}')$ is such that $\mu \xrightarrow{a} \mu'$ whenever $\mu = \bigoplus_{i \in I} p_i * E_i$, $\mu' = \bigoplus_{i \in I} p_i * \mu_i'$, and $E_i \xrightarrow{a} \mu_i'$ for all $i \in I$.

The machinery of Definition 3.4 is similar to that of Definition 3.3. The additional rules (LEFT) and (SYNC) capture that in a leftmerge $E_1 \,\|\, E_2$ only the component E_1 is responsible for determining a possible transition, while for the synchronization operator the synchronization of transitions of both components is required. The former corresponds to rule (PAR 1), the latter corresponds to rule (PAR 3).

4   Strong Distribution Bisimulation

In this section the notion of process equivalence of strong distribution bisimulation is presented. Strong distribution bisimulation has been advocated a.o. in [12,16,25], called bisimulation, strong probabilistic distribution bisimulation, and strong d-bisimulation, respectively.

Since strong distribution bisimulation deals with distributions rather than states, one has to take a proviso for subsumed behavior. For example, one wants to distinguish the deadlock process $\mathbf{0}$ and the process $(a \cdot \Delta(\mathbf{0})) \oplus_{1/2} (b \cdot \Delta(\mathbf{0}))$ although both processes do not provide a transition. We follow [25] by introducing the concept of a decomposable relation.

Definition 4.1 (decomposable relation).   A symmetric relation $\mathcal{R}$ on $Distr(\mathcal{E})$ is called *decomposable* iff for all $\mu, \nu \in Distr(\mathcal{E})$ such that $\mu \mathcal{R} \nu$ and $\mu = \bigoplus_{i \in I} p_i * \mu_i$ there are $\nu_i \in Distr(\mathcal{E})$, for $i \in I$, such that $\nu = \bigoplus_{i \in I} p_i * \nu_i$ and $\mu_i \mathcal{R} \nu_i$ for all $i \in I$.

A notion of a decomposable relation on $Distr(\mathcal{E}')$ is defined similarly. Clearly, an arbitrary union of decomposable relations is decomposable again.

The next result is a technical aid to go from comparing distributions to comparing states. It states that every strong distribution bisimulation can be obtained as the convex closure of a relation on states, cf. [13].

Lemma 4.2 Let $\mathcal{R}$ is a decomposable relation on $Distr(\mathcal{E})$. If $\mu \, \mathcal{R} \, \nu$, then there are an index set K and non-deterministic processes $E_k, F_k \in \mathcal{E}$ and probabilities r_k for each $k \in K$ such that

$$\mu = \bigoplus_{k \in K} r_k * E_k' \qquad \nu = \bigoplus_{k \in K} r_k * F_k' \qquad \Delta(E_k') \, \mathcal{R} \, \Delta(F_k') \text{ for all } k \in K$$

Proof. Suppose $\mu \, \mathcal{R} \, \nu$ and $\mu = \bigoplus_{i \in I} p_i * E_i$. By decomposability of $\mathcal{R}$ we can write $\nu = \bigoplus_{i \in I} p_i * \nu_i$ and have $\Delta(E_i) \, \mathcal{R} \, \nu_i$ for suitable $\nu_i \in Distr(\mathcal{E})$, for all $i \in I$. Say, $\nu_i = \bigoplus_{j \in J_i} q_{ij} * F_{ij}$. By decomposability of $\mathcal{R}$, we have $\Delta(E_i) = \bigoplus_{j \in J_i} q_{ij} * \Delta(E_i)$ and, more importantly, $\Delta(E_i) \, \mathcal{R} \, \Delta(F_{ij})$ for all $j \in J_i$.

Put $K = \{ (i,j) \mid i \in I, \, j \in J_i \}$. Put $E_k' = E_i$, $F_k' = F_{ij}$, and $r_k = p_i \cdot q_{ij}$ if $k = (i,j)$. Note, $E_k' \, \mathcal{R} \, F_k'$ for $k \in K$. Moreover, we have $\mu = \bigoplus_{i \in I} p_i * E_i = \bigoplus_{i \in I} \bigoplus_{j \in J_i} (p_i \cdot q_{ij}) * \Delta(E_i) = \bigoplus_{k \in K} r_k * E_k'$, and $\nu = \bigoplus_{i \in I} p_i * \nu_i = \bigoplus_{i \in I} p_i * (\bigoplus_{j \in J_i} q_{ij} * F_{ij}) = \bigoplus_{k \in K} r_k * F_k'$ as was to be shown.

The transition systems of Definitions 3.3 and 3.4 incorporate so-called combined transitions. In order to cater for this when dealing with bisimulation we rely on the fact that the convex closure of a decomposable relation is decomposable again.

Lemma 4.3. If a relation $\mathcal{R}$ on $Distr(\mathcal{E})$ is decomposable, then $\mathcal{R}_{cc}$ the convex closure of $\mathcal{R}$ given by

$$\mathcal{R}_{cc} = \{ \, (\bigoplus_{i \in I} p_i * \mu_i, \bigoplus_{i \in I} p_i * \nu_i) \mid \forall i \in I \colon \mu_i \, \mathcal{R} \, \nu_i \, \}$$

is decomposable as well.

Proof. Suppose $\mu = \bigoplus_{i \in I} p_i * \mu_i$, $\nu = \bigoplus_{i \in I} p_i * \nu_i$ where $\mu_i \, \mathcal{R} \, \nu_i$ for $i \in I$. By applying Lemma 4.2 for each pair μ_i, ν_i and combining the results we obtain $\mu = \bigoplus_{j \in J} q_j * E_j$ and $\nu = \bigoplus_{j \in J} q_j * F_j$ and $\Delta(E_j) \, \mathcal{R} \, \Delta(F_j)$ for a suitable index set J, processes $E_j, F_j \in \mathcal{E}$ and $q_j > 0$ for $j \in J$.

Now suppose $\mu = \bigoplus_{k \in K} r_k * \mu_k'$. Then we have $\mu_k' = \bigoplus_{j \in J} r_{jk} * E_j$ for suitable r_{jk} such that $\sum_{k \in K} r_{jk} \cdot r_k = q_j$. Put $\nu_k' = \bigoplus_{j \in J} r_{jk} * F_j$. Then we have $\mu_k' \, \mathcal{R}_{cc} \, \nu_k'$ since $\Delta(E_j) \, \mathcal{R} \, \Delta(F_j)$ for all $j \in J$. Moreover, $\nu = \bigoplus_{j \in J} q_j * F_j = \bigoplus_{j \in J} (\sum_{k \in K} r_{jk} \cdot r_k) * F_j = \bigoplus_{k \in K} r_k * (\bigoplus_{j \in J} r_{jk} * F_j) = \bigoplus_{k \in K} r_k * v_k'$. This proves $\mathcal{R}_{cc}$ to be decomposable. $\qquad \square$

We are now ready to define the notion of equivalence of processes.

Definition 4.4 (strong distribution bisimulation).

(a) A decomposable relation $\mathcal{R} \subseteq Distr(\mathcal{E}) \times Distr(\mathcal{E})$ is called a *strong distribution bisimulation*, iff for all $\mu, \nu \in Distr(\mathcal{E})$ such that $\mu \, \mathcal{R} \, \nu$ and $\mu \xrightarrow{a} \mu'$ for some $a \in \mathcal{A}$ and $\mu' \in Distr(\mathcal{E})$ then $\nu \xrightarrow{a} \nu'$ and $\mu' \, \mathcal{R} \, \nu'$ for some $\nu' \in Distr(\mathcal{E})$.

(b) Strong distribution bisimulation, denoted by $\leftrightarrow \subseteq Distr(\mathcal{E}) \times Distr(\mathcal{E})$, is defined as the largest strong distribution bisimulation on $Distr(\mathcal{E})$.

By the definition of a decomposable relation we have that a strong distribution bisimulation is symmetric. Also note that the relation $\leftrightarrows$ on $Distr(\mathcal{E})$ is well-defined. It extends to $Distr(\mathcal{E}')$ straightforwardly.

Example 4.5. Consider the two non-deterministic processes depicted in Fig. 1. We verify that the Dirac distributions μ and ν corresponding to these processes, i.e. $\mu = \delta(a \cdot (P \oplus_{1/2} Q) + a \cdot (P \oplus_{1/3} Q))$ for the process on the left and $\nu = \delta(a \cdot (P \oplus_{1/2} Q) + a \cdot (P \oplus_{5/12} Q) + a \cdot (P \oplus_{1/3} Q)))$ for the process on the right, are strongly distribution bisimilar.

Let $\mathcal{R}$ be the relation on $Distr(\mathcal{E})$ given by $\mathcal{R} = \{\langle \mu, \nu \rangle, \langle \nu, \mu \rangle\} \cup Id_{Distr(\mathcal{E})}$ with $Id_{Distr(\mathcal{E})}$ the identity relation $\{\langle \varrho, \varrho \rangle \mid \varrho \in Distr(\mathcal{E})\}$. We claim that $\mathcal{R}$ is a strong distribution bisimulation. It is straightforward to check that $\mathcal{R}$ is decomposable. To see that $\mathcal{R}$ satisfies the transfer condition of Definition 4.4 too, we let ϱ_P and ϱ_Q denote the distributions corresponding to the probabilistic processes P and Q, respectively, and consider the transition $\nu \xrightarrow{a} \varrho_P \oplus_{5/12} \varrho_Q$. Since $\mu = \frac{1}{2}\mu \oplus \frac{1}{2}\mu$ and both $\mu \xrightarrow{a} \varrho_P \oplus_{1/2} \varrho_Q$ and $\mu \xrightarrow{a} \varrho_P \oplus_{1/3} \varrho_Q$ we obtain from the operational semantics captured by Definition 3.3 $\mu \xrightarrow{a} (\varrho_P \oplus_{1/2} \varrho_Q) \oplus_{1/2} (\varrho_P \oplus_{1/3} \varrho_Q) = \varrho_P \oplus_{5/12} \varrho_Q$. Thus, the distribution μ exactly matches the transition $\nu \xrightarrow{a} \varrho_P \oplus_{5/12} \varrho_Q$ which is an explicit option of the non-deterministic process on the right of Fig. 1 but not of the other.

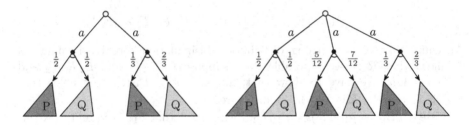

Fig. 1. Two bisimilar processes

Example 4.6. Consider the probabilistic processes P and Q given by

$$P = \Delta(a \cdot \Big(\Delta(b \cdot \Delta(\mathbf{0})) \oplus_{1/2} (\Delta(c \cdot \Delta(\mathbf{0})) \oplus_{1/2} \Delta(c \cdot (\Delta(\mathbf{0}) \oplus_{1/2} \Delta(\mathbf{0})))) \Big))$$
$$Q = \Delta(a \cdot \Big((\Delta(b \cdot \Delta(\mathbf{0} + \mathbf{0})) \oplus_{1/2} \Delta(b \cdot \Delta(\mathbf{0}))) \oplus_{1/2} \Delta(c \cdot (\Delta(\mathbf{0}) \oplus_{1/2} \Delta(\mathbf{0}))) \Big))$$

Then we have $P \xrightarrow{a} \mu$ and $Q \xrightarrow{a} \nu$ for distributions $\mu, \nu \in Distr(\mathcal{E})$ where

$$\mu = \tfrac{1}{2}\delta(b \cdot \Delta(\mathbf{0})) \oplus \tfrac{1}{4}\delta(c \cdot \Delta(\mathbf{0})) \oplus \tfrac{1}{4}\delta(c \cdot (\Delta(\mathbf{0}) \oplus_{1/2} \Delta(\mathbf{0})))$$
$$\nu = \tfrac{3}{8}\delta(b \cdot \Delta(\mathbf{0} + \mathbf{0})) \oplus \tfrac{1}{8}\delta(b \cdot \Delta(\mathbf{0})) \oplus \tfrac{1}{2}\delta(c \cdot \Delta(\mathbf{0}))$$

By decomposability, bisimulation relating μ and ν should also relate $\delta(b \cdot \Delta(\mathbf{0}))$ to $\delta(b \cdot \Delta(\mathbf{0} + \mathbf{0}))$ and $\delta(c \cdot (\Delta(\mathbf{0}) \oplus_{1/2} \Delta(\mathbf{0})))$ to $\delta(c \cdot \Delta(\mathbf{0}))$, which requires in turn that $\Delta(\mathbf{0})$ and $\Delta(\mathbf{0} + \mathbf{0})$) are related. Therefore, we define $\mathcal{R}$ to be the least binary relation on $Distr(\mathcal{E})$ which

(i) contains the pairs $\langle P, Q \rangle$, $\langle \mu, \nu \rangle$, $\langle \delta(0), \delta(0+0) \rangle$, $\langle \delta(b \cdot \Delta(0)), \delta(b \cdot \Delta(0+0)) \rangle$, and $\langle \delta(c \cdot (\Delta(0) \oplus_{1/2} \Delta(0))), \delta(c \cdot \Delta(0)) \rangle$

(ii) contains the diagonal $Id_{\mathcal{E}}$

(iii) is symmetric and convex closed.

It is straightforward to verify that $\mathcal{R}$ is a strong distribution bisimulation relation for P and Q. In particular, because of condition (iii) it is easy to see that $\mathcal{R}$ indeed relates μ_1 and ν_1 as well as μ_2 and ν_2 for the decompositions $\mu = \mu_1 \oplus_{1/2} \mu_2 = \delta(b \cdot \Delta(0)) \oplus_{1/2} (\frac{1}{2}\delta(c \cdot \Delta(0)) \oplus \frac{1}{2}\delta(c \cdot (\Delta(0) \oplus_{1/2} \Delta(0))))$ and $\nu = \nu_1 \oplus_{1/2} \nu_2 = (\frac{3}{4}\delta(b \cdot \Delta(0+0)) \oplus \frac{1}{4}\delta(b \cdot \Delta(0))) \oplus_{1/2} \delta(c \cdot \Delta(0))$.

The next result states that strong distribution bisimulation is a process equivalence indeed. The congruence property of $\leftrightarrows$ is essential for proving the soundness of the equational theory for strong distribution bisimulation that is introduced in the next section.

Theorem 4.7 (congruence). The relation $\leftrightarrows$ is an equivalence relation and a congruence on $\mathcal{E}$ and $\mathcal{P}$.

Proof. The proof of $\leftrightarrows$ being an equivalence relation is straightforward. For congruence we treat the case of the parallel operator.

Suppose $\mathcal{R}_1, \mathcal{R}_2$ are two strong distribution bisimulations. Put

$$\mathcal{R} = cc(\{ (\Delta(E_1 \| E_2), \Delta(F_1 \| F_2)) \mid E_1 \mathcal{R}_1 F_1, \ F_1 \mathcal{R}_2 F_2 \})$$

We claim that $\mathcal{R}$ is a strong distribution bisimulation too. By Lemma 4.3 it follows that $\mathcal{R}$ is decomposable. Now suppose $E_1 \mathcal{R}_1 F_1$ and $E_2 \mathcal{R}_2 F_2$ and $E_1 \| E_2 \xrightarrow{a} \mu$. We have to show that, for some $\nu \in Distr(\mathcal{E})$, it holds that $F_1 \| F_2 \xrightarrow{a} \nu$ and $\mu \mathcal{R} \nu$. We distinguish three cases.

Case (i), $E_1 \xrightarrow{a} \mu_1$ and $\mu = \mu_1 \| E_2$: Pick ν_1 such that $F_1 \xrightarrow{a} \nu_1$ and $\mu_1 \mathcal{R}_1 \nu_1$. Put $\nu = \nu_1 \| F_2$. Assume, with help of Lemma 4.2, $\mu_1 = \bigoplus_{i \in I} p_i * E_i'$, $\nu_1 = \bigoplus_{i \in I} p_i * F_i'$ and $\Delta(E_i') \mathcal{R}_1 \Delta(F_i')$ for $i \in I$. Since $\Delta(E_i') \mathcal{R}_1 \Delta(F_i')$ for $i \in I$ and $\Delta(E_2) \mathcal{R}_2 \Delta(F_2)$ it follows that $\Delta(E_i' \| E_2) \mathcal{R} \Delta(F_i' \| F_2)$. Since $\mu = \mu_1 \| E_2 = \bigoplus_{i \in I} p_i * (E_i' \| E_2)$ and $\nu = \nu_1 \| F_2 = \bigoplus_{i \in I} p_i * (F_i' \| F_2)$ we obtain $\mu \mathcal{R} \nu$.

Case (ii), $E_2 \xrightarrow{a} \mu_2$ and $\mu = E_1 \| \mu_2$: Symmetric to case (i).

Case (iii), $E_1 \xrightarrow{a_1} \mu_1$, $E_2 \xrightarrow{a_2} \mu_2$, $\mu = \mu_1 \| \mu_2$ and $\gamma(a_1, a_2) = a$: Suppose $\mu_1 = \bigoplus_{i \in I} p_i * E_i'$, $\mu_2 = \bigoplus_{j \in J} q_j * E_j''$. Since $\Delta(E_1) \mathcal{R}_1 \Delta(F_1)$ and $\Delta(E_2) \mathcal{R}_2 \Delta(F_2)$ we can find $\nu_1 = \bigoplus_{i \in I} p_i * F_i'$, $\nu_2 = \bigoplus_{j \in J} q_j * F_j''$ in $Distr(\mathcal{E})$ with $\Delta(E_i') \mathcal{R}_1 \Delta(F_i')$ for $i \in I$ and $\Delta(E_j'') \mathcal{R}_2 \Delta(F_j'')$ for $j \in J$. Note $\Delta(E_i' \| E_j'') \mathcal{R} \Delta(F_i' \| F_j'')$ for $i \in I$, $j \in J$. Moreover,

$$\mu = \mu_1 \| \mu_2 = \bigoplus_{i \in I} \bigoplus_{j \in J} (p_i \cdot q_j) * (E_i' \| E_j'')$$
$$\nu = \nu_1 \| \nu_2 = \bigoplus_{i \in I} \bigoplus_{j \in J} (p_i \cdot q_j) * (F_i' \| F_j'')$$

from which it follows that $\mu \mathcal{R} \nu$, as was to be shown. $\qquad \square$

5   A Complete Axiomatization

In Table 1 we present the equational theory AX that characterizes strong distribution bisimulation for non-deterministic and probabilistic processes. The axioms of AX are inspired by the axiomatization of [6] regarding probabilistic choice and that of [8] regarding the synchronization merge. As argued by Moller [30] the availability of the leftmerge $\|$ is essential for a finite axiomatization of the merge $\|$ itself. This explains why we introduced extended processes incorporating $\|$ and $|$ in Sect. 3.

Definition 5.1 (theory AX). The theory AX consists of the axioms listed in Table 1.

Table 1. Axioms for strong distribution bisimulation

A1	$E + F = F + E$
A2	$(E + F) + G = E + (F + G)$
A3	$E + E = E$
A4	$E + \mathbf{0} = E$
P1	$P \oplus_r Q = Q \oplus_{1-r} P$
P2	$P \oplus_r (Q \oplus_s R) = (P \oplus_{r'} Q) \oplus_{s'} R$
	where $r = r's'$ and $(1-r)(1-s) = 1-s'$
P3	$P \oplus_r P = P$
M	$E \| F = E \| F + F \| E + E | F$
L1	$\mathbf{0} \| F = \mathbf{0}$
L2	$(a \cdot P) \| F = a \cdot (P \| F)$
L3	$(E_1 + E_2) \| F = (E_1 \| F) + (E_2 \| F)$
S1a	$\mathbf{0} | F = \mathbf{0}$
S1b	$E | \mathbf{0} = \mathbf{0}$
S2	$(a \cdot P) | (b \cdot Q) = c \cdot (P \| Q)$ if $\gamma(a,b) = c$
S3	$(E_1 + E_2)	F = (E_1 | F) + (E_2 | F)$
S4	$E	(F_1 + F_2) = (E | F_1) + (E | F_2)$
C	$a \cdot P + a \cdot Q = a \cdot P + a \cdot (P \oplus_r Q) + a \cdot Q$

The axioms A1 to A4 are as usual. The axioms P1 and P2 express the commutativity and associativity of probabilistic choice, taking into account the probabilities involved. Axiom P3 allows for splitting of a probabilistic process.

The group of processes M, L1 to L3, and S1a to S4 capture the parallel operator $\|$ with the help of the auxiliary operators $\|$ and $|$. Axiom M is an interleaving rule: behavior of a parallel composition $E \| F$ of two processes E and F is either stemming from the process E expressed by $E \| F$, stemming from the process F expressed by $F \| E$, or stemming from the processes E and F synchronizing expresses by $E|F$.

In a leftmerge $E \mathbin{\|\!\|} F$, by definition, the first step must be taken by the component E. In the extended transition relation of Definition 3.4 only rule (LEFT) applies. This explains axioms L1 and L2. In L2 the expression $P \| F$ for $P \in \mathcal{P}$ and $F \in \mathcal{E}$ is defined by $\Delta(E) \| F = \Delta(E \| F)$ and $(P_1 \oplus_r P_2) \| F = (P_1 \| F) \oplus_r (P_2 \| F)$. Axiom L3 expresses that non-deterministic choice distributes over the leftmerge.

Similar considerations apply to axioms S1a to S4 capturing the synchronization operator $|$. Since $E|F$ requires a transition from both operands, deadlock results if either of them doesn't have such. Synchronization of an a-transition of E and a b-transition of F results in a transition labeled with $\gamma(a, b) \in \mathcal{A}$ as given by the communication function γ. Non-deterministic choice also distributes over the synchronization operator.

The final axiom C expresses combined behavior. If a non-deterministic process has an a-transition evolving into the probabilistic process P and has an a-transition evolving into the probabilistic process Q, then the non-deterministic process also admits an a-transition evolving into any convex combination of P and Q.

Before moving to completeness of AX for $\leftrightarrow$ we treat soundness of AX.

Theorem 5.2. The theory AX is sound with respect to strong distribution bisimulation for $\mathcal{E}'$ and $\mathcal{P}'$, i.e. for all $E, F \in \mathcal{E}$, if $AX \vdash E = F$ then $\Delta(E) \leftrightarrow \Delta(F)$ and for all $P, Q \in \mathcal{P}'$, if $AX \vdash P = Q$ then $P \leftrightarrow Q$.

Proof. In view of Theorem 4.7 it suffices to show that for each axiom of AX the left-hand side and right-hand side are strongly distribution bisimilar. We only cover the case of axiom M.

Pick $E', F' \in \mathcal{E}$ arbitrarily. Define

$$\mathcal{R} = \{\langle \Delta(E' \| F'), \Delta(E' \mathbin{\|\!\|} F' + F' \mathbin{\|\!\|} E' + E'|F') \rangle\} \cup$$
$$cc(\{ \langle \Delta(E \| F), \Delta(F \| E) \rangle \mid E, F \in \mathcal{E} \}) \cup Id_\Delta$$

where $Id_\Delta = \{ \langle \Delta(E), \Delta(E) \rangle \mid E \in \mathcal{E}' \}$. We have that $\mathcal{R}$ is decomposable, cf. Lemma 4.3.

To see that $E' \| F'$ and $E' \mathbin{\|\!\|} F') + F' \mathbin{\|\!\|} E' + E'|F'$ match each other, we distinguish six cases: (i) If $E' \| F' \xrightarrow{a} \mu \| F'$ because $E' \xrightarrow{a} \mu$, then $E' \mathbin{\|\!\|} F' \xrightarrow{a} \mu \| F'$ and $\mu \| F' \mathcal{R} \mu \| F'$.

(ii) If $E' \| F' \xrightarrow{a} E' \| \nu$ because $F' \xrightarrow{a} \nu$, then it holds that $F' \mathbin{\|\!\|} E' \xrightarrow{a} \nu \| F'$ and $E' \| \nu \mathcal{R} \nu \| E'$.

(iii) If $E' \| F' \xrightarrow{c} \mu \| \nu$ because $E' \xrightarrow{a} \mu$ and $F' \xrightarrow{b} \nu$ while $\gamma(a, b) = c$, then $E'|F' \xrightarrow{c} \mu \| \nu$ and $\mu \| \nu \mathcal{R} \mu \| \nu$.

(iv) If $E' \mathbin{\|\!\|} F' \xrightarrow{a} \mu \| F'$ because $E' \xrightarrow{a} \mu$, then $E' \| F' \xrightarrow{a} \mu \| F'$ and $\mu \| F' \mathcal{R} \mu \| F'$.

(v) If $F' \mathbin{\|\!\|} E' \xrightarrow{a} \nu \| E'$ because $F' \xrightarrow{a} \nu$, then it holds that $E' \| F' \xrightarrow{a} E' \| \nu$ and $E' \| \nu \mathcal{R} \nu \| E'$.

(vi) If $E'|F' \xrightarrow{c} \mu\|\nu$ because $E' \xrightarrow{a} \mu$ and $F' \xrightarrow{b} \nu$ while $\gamma(a,b) = c$, then $E'\|F' \xrightarrow{c} \mu\|\nu$ and $\mu\|\nu \mathcal{R} \mu\|\nu$.

It follows that $\mathcal{R}$ is a strong distribution bisimulation relating $\Delta(E'\|F')$ and $\Delta(E' \mathbin{\|\mkern-9mu\_} F' + F' \mathbin{\|\mkern-9mu\_} E' + E'|F')$, hence $\Delta(E'\|F') \leftrightarroweq \Delta(E' \mathbin{\|\mkern-9mu\_} F' + F' \mathbin{\|\mkern-9mu\_} E' + E'|F')$, which was sufficient to show.   □

In the proof of completeness of AX we make use of a complexity function c for our inductive argument. We want c to be such that for an axiom $E = F$ or $P = Q$ of AX the weight $c(E)$ or $c(P)$ of the left-hand side is strictly larger in weight than the right-hand side $c(F)$ or $c(Q)$. We will deploy sequences of natural numbers as weights.

Addition on $\mathbb{N}^*$ is defined as element-wise addition. More concretely: (i) $\varepsilon + v = v$, (ii) $u + \varepsilon = u$, (iii) $(n \cdot u) + (m \cdot v) = (n + m) \cdot (u + v)$, for $u, v \in \mathbb{N}^*$ and $n, m \in \mathbb{N}$. The ordering of $\mathbb{N}^*$ is the lexicographic order restricted to sequences of equal length. Thus $n_1 \cdot n_2 \cdots n_s < m_1 \cdot m_2 \cdots m_t$ iff $s = t$ and for some j, $1 \leqslant j \leqslant s$ it holds that $n_i = m_i$ for $1 \leqslant i < j$ and $n_j < m_j$. Since we only compare sequences of equal length, it holds that $<$ is a well-founded partial order on $\mathbb{N}^*$.

Definition 5.3 (Complexity function). The function $c : \mathcal{E}' \cup \mathcal{P}' \to \mathbb{N}^*$, assigning a complexity measure to processes, is defined as follows:

$$
\begin{aligned}
c(\mathbf{0}) &= 0 & c(E\|F) &= 4 + c(E) + c(F) \\
c(a \cdot P) &= 1 \cdot c(P) & c(E \mathbin{\|\mkern-9mu\_} F) &= 1 + c(E) + 0 \cdot c(F) \\
c(E + F) &= c(E) + c(F) & c(E|F) &= 1 + c(E) + c(F) \\
c(\Delta(E)) &= 0 \cdot c(E) & c(P \oplus_r Q) &= c(P) + c(Q)
\end{aligned}
$$

Please note, with $\mathbb{N}^*$ the '$\cdot$'-operator in the definition of c above denotes concatenation of strings. The complexity function c and the well-foundedness of $\mathbb{N}^*$ are exploited in the technical lemma below.

Lemma 5.4.

(a) For each extended non-deterministic process $E' \in \mathcal{E}'$ a basic non-deterministic process $E_0 \in \mathcal{E}_0$ exists such that $AX \vdash E' = E_0$.

(b) For each extended probabilistic process $P' \in \mathcal{P}'$ there is a basic probabilistic process $P_0 \in \mathcal{P}_0$ such that $AX \vdash P' = P_0$.

Proof. Suppose $AX \vdash C[E_1] = C[E_2]$ for a context $C[\cdot]$ and $E_1 = E_2$ an instance of the axiom X of AX with E_1 its LHS and E_2 its RHS. If the axiom X is M, L1-L3, or S1-S4, then it holds that $c(C[E_1]) > c(C[E_2])$. Otherwise, it holds that $c(C[E_1]) = c(C[E_2])$. Moreover, in all cases, it holds that the strings $c(C[E_1])$ and $c(C[E_2])$ are of equal length.

If a process $E \in \mathcal{E}'$ or $P \in \mathcal{P}'$ contains any of the operators $\|$, $\mathbin{\|\mkern-9mu\_}$ or $|$ then at least one of the axioms M, L1–L3, or S1a–S4 applies, matching its LHS to E or to P, respectively.

If a process $E \in \mathcal{E}'$ or $P \in \mathcal{P}'$ contains none of the operators $\|$, $\mathbin{\|\mkern-9mu\_}$ or $|$, thus $E \in \mathcal{E}_0$ or $P \in \mathcal{P}_0$, then $c(E) = 0^\ell$ or $c(P) = 0^\ell$ for suitable $\ell \in \mathbb{N}$. This is directly verified by structural induction on E and P: $c(\mathbf{0}) = 0 = 0^1$, $c(a \cdot P) = 0 \cdot c(P)$, $c(E + F) = c(E) + c(F)$, $c(\Delta(E)) = 0.c(E)$, $c(P + Q) = c(P) + c(Q)$. Note, a string 0^ℓ is a minimal element in $\mathbb{N}^*$ for the specific ordering on $\mathbb{N}^*$ introduced above.

It follows that successive elimination of the operators $\|$, $\|\!\!\|$ or $|$ from an extended non-deterministic process $E \in \mathcal{E}'$ by application of the axioms M, L1–L3, or S1–S4, with the LHS of the axiom matching the redex and the RHS yielding the reduct, is a terminating rewrite procedure, with a basic process $E_0 \in \mathcal{E}_0$ as its normal form. The same applies to an extended probabilistic process $P \in \mathcal{P}'$ yielding a basic probabilistic process $P_0 \in \mathcal{P}$. $\qquad \square$

In view of the lemma, relating two bisimilar processes with possible occurrences of $\|$ boils down to relating their basic counterparts. However, for this argument to be helpful, we need completeness of AX, or part of it, for bisimilar basic processes.

Theorem 5.5. The equational theory AX_0 consists of the axioms A1–A4, P1–P3, and C. Then it holds that AX_0 is sound and complete for strong distribution bisimulation for $\mathcal{P}_0$.

As claimed in [6] the proof of Theorem 5.5 is a variation of the standard proof method, cf. [29], and omitted here.

We are now ready to prove completeness of the proposed axiomatization.

Theorem 5.6. The equational theory AX is complete with respect to $\leftrightarrow$ for $\mathcal{P}$.

Proof. Suppose $P, Q \in \mathcal{P}$ such that $P \leftrightarrow Q$. Choose with help of Lemma 5.4 basic processes $P_0, Q_0 \in \mathcal{P}_0$ such that $AX \vdash P = P_0$ and $AX \vdash Q = Q_0$. Then also $P_0 \leftrightarrow Q_0$ by Theorem 4.7. By Theorem 5.5 we obtain $AX_0 \vdash P_0 = Q_0$. Since AX_0 is subsumed by AX it follows that $AX \vdash P = Q$. $\qquad \square$

We see that the extra complexity in proving Theorem 5.6 and subsequently our resort to the complexity measure c is caused by the mixture $P\|F$ of a probabilistic process and a non-deterministic process in the axiom L2 and the propagation of parallel composition in $P\|Q$ in the axiom S2. The general outline however is as established in [8, 29].

6   Concluding Remarks

We studied an elementary process language featuring non-deterministic choice and a parallel operator with synchronous communication on the one hand and probabilistic choice on the other hand. For this language we presented an axiomatization characterizing strong distribution bisimulation and proved soundness and completeness of the proposed set of axioms. The transition system of the language supports so-called combined transitions and treats distributions over non-deterministic processes as its building blocks. In order to support a finite equational theory the processes language was extended with a leftmerge operator and a synchronization operator.

Soundness of the equational theory with respect to strong distribution bisimulation involved, as usual, proving congruence and soundness of the axioms themselves. For completeness, because of the interplay of non-deterministic processes involving the parallel operator, via the leftmerge and synchronization merge, with probabilistic processes, some technical effort was required. The proof, however, stays in line with the standard approach known from the set-up without probabilities.

In [22] a sound and complete equational theory for branching distribution bisimulation, a weak variant of strong distribution bisimulation as treated in the present paper, for a similar process language is proposed. The language however doesn't include a parallel construct. One may expect that establishing a conservative extension of the theory AX, thus covering a parallel operator, that captures branching distribution bisimulation will require substantial effort. Not so much for the completeness proof itself, in view of Lemma 5.4, but because of the before-mentioned interplay of non-deterministic and probabilistic processes triggered by the parallel construct. This entanglement requires specific attention when verifying transitivity of the process equivalence at hand and of a congruence result for the parallel operator.

Future work aims at building a framework of a distribution-based notion of process equivalence that allows a complete equational theory, an efficient decision algorithm, and a logical characterization, both with respect to strong bisimulation as well as to a form of weak bisimulation. Especially the construction of a decision algorithm for branching distribution bisimulation attracts our attention. A decision algorithm for weak distribution bisimulation is proposed in [16]. A rather efficient algorithm for strong probabilistic bisimulation has been presented in [21], building on the the work of [5] and [35]. We hope to be able to extend the approach of [21] to cater for strong distribution bisimulation first.

In the long run we aim to build a probabilistic extension of the mCRL2 toolset [10] (also see www.mcrl2.org) of which a modest part has been realized as yet [23]. Possibly the completeness result presented in the current paper will provide a similar building block for our framework as the completeness result of [20], reworked in [19], does for ACTL, the action-based version of CTL, which is underpinning the KandISTI tool family [7] developed at CNR/ISTI.

Acknowledgement. JFG acknowledges the mutual inspiration of the development teams of mCRL2 and KandISTI. A nice example is the inclusion of the LTS minimization algorithm as provided in the mCRL2 toolset which has been incorporated in the KandISTI family members UMC and FMC. Also the attention for model checking of variability and software product lines with the mCRL2 toolset is such an example. EV acknowledges the warm hospitality of Stefania Gnesi and her research group at the CNR in Pisa at various occasions and the many *pasti accoglienti* shared together.

References

1. Andova, S., Baeten, J.C.M., Willemse, T.A.C.: A complete axiomatisation of branching bisimulation for probabilistic systems with an application in protocol verification. In: Baier, C., Hermanns, H. (eds.) CONCUR 2006. LNCS, vol. 4137, pp. 327–342. Springer, Heidelberg (2006). https://doi.org/10.1007/11817949_22
2. Andova, S., Willemse, T.A.C.: Branching bisimulation for probabilistic systems: characteristics and decidability. Theor. Comput. Sci. **356**, 325–355 (2006)
3. Baeten, J.C.M., Basten, T., Reniers, M.A.: Process Algebra: Equational Theories of Communicating Processes. Cambridge Tracts in Theoretical Computer Science, vol. 50. CUP, Cambridge (2010)
4. Baeten, J.C.M., Bergstra, J.A., Smolka, S.A.: Axiomatizing probabilistic processes: ACP with generative probabilities. Inf. Comput. **121**(2), 234–255 (1995)
5. Baier, C., Engelen, B., Majster-Cederbaum, M.E.: Deciding bisimilarity and similarity for probabilistic processes. J. Comput. Syst. Sci. **60**, 187–231 (2000)
6. Bandini, E., Segala, R.: Axiomatizations for probabilistic bisimulation. In: Orejas, F., Spirakis, P.G., van Leeuwen, J. (eds.) ICALP 2001. LNCS, vol. 2076, pp. 370–381. Springer, Heidelberg (2001). https://doi.org/10.1007/3-540-48224-5_31
7. ter Beek, M.H., Gnesi, S., Mazzanti, F.: From EU projects to a family of model checkers. In: De Nicola, R., Hennicker, R. (eds.) Software, Services, and Systems. LNCS, vol. 8950, pp. 312–328. Springer, Cham (2015). https://doi.org/10.1007/978-3-319-15545-6_20
8. Bergstra, J.A., Klop, J.W.: Process algebra for synchronous communication. Inf. Control **60**(1–3), 109–137 (1984)
9. Bernardo, M., Gorrieri, R.: Extended Markovian process algebra. In: Montanari, U., Sassone, V. (eds.) CONCUR 1996. LNCS, vol. 1119, pp. 315–330. Springer, Heidelberg (1996). https://doi.org/10.1007/3-540-61604-7_63
10. Bunte, O., et al.: The mCRL2 toolset for analysing concurrent systems. In: Vojnar, T., Zhang, L. (eds.) TACAS 2019. LNCS, vol. 11428, pp. 21–39. Springer, Cham (2019). https://doi.org/10.1007/978-3-030-17465-1_2
11. Crafa, S., Ranzato, F.: Logical characterizations of behavioral relations on transition systems of probability distributions. ACM Trans. Comput. Logic **16**(1), 2:1–2:24 (2014)
12. Deng, Y., Hennessy, M.: On the semantics of Markov automata. In: Aceto, L., Henzinger, M., Sgall, J. (eds.) ICALP 2011. LNCS, vol. 6756, pp. 307–318. Springer, Heidelberg (2011). https://doi.org/10.1007/978-3-642-22012-8_24
13. Deng, Y., Hennessy, M.: On the semantics of Markov automata. Inf. Comput. **222**, 139–168 (2013)
14. Deng, Y., Palamidessi, C.: Axiomatizations for probabilistic finite-state behaviors. Theor. Comput. Sci. **373**, 92–114 (2007)
15. Deng, Y., Palamidessi, C., Pang, J.: Compositional reasoning for probabilistic finite-state behaviors. In: Middeldorp, A., van Oostrom, V., van Raamsdonk, F., de Vrijer, R. (eds.) Processes, Terms and Cycles: Steps on the Road to Infinity. LNCS, vol. 3838, pp. 309–337. Springer, Heidelberg (2005). https://doi.org/10.1007/11601548_17
16. Eisentraut, C., Hermanns, H., Krämer, J., Turrini, A., Zhang, L.: Deciding bisimilarities on distributions. In: Joshi, K., Siegle, M., Stoelinga, M., D'Argenio, P.R. (eds.) QEST 2013. LNCS, vol. 8054, pp. 72–88. Springer, Heidelberg (2013). https://doi.org/10.1007/978-3-642-40196-1_6

17. Fischer, N., van Glabbeek, R.: Axiomatising infinitary probabilistic weak bisimilarity of finite-state behaviours. J. Log. Algebr. Methods Program. **102**, 64–102 (2019)
18. Giacalone, A., Jou, C.-C., Smolka, S.A.: Algebraic reasoning for probabilistic concurrent systems. In: Broy, M. (ed.) Proceedings of IFIP WG 2.2 & 2.3 Working Conference on Programming Concepts and Methods, pp. 443–458 (1990)
19. Gnesi, S., ter Beek, M.H.: From the archives of the formal methods and tools lab. In: Boreale, M., Corradini, F., Loreti, M., Pugliese, R. (eds.) Models, Languages, and Tools for Concurrent and Distributed Programming. LNCS, vol. 11665, pp. 219–235. Springer, Cham (2019). https://doi.org/10.1007/978-3-030-21485-2_13
20. Gnesi, S., Larosa, S.: A sound and complete axiom system for the logic ACTL. In: De Santis, A. (ed.) Proceedings of ICTCS 1995, Ravello, 9–11 November 1995, pp. 291–306 (1995)
21. Groote, J.F., Rivera Verduzco, H.J., de Vink, E.P.: An efficient algorithm to determine probabilistic bisimulation. Algorithms **11**(9), 131-1-22 (2018)
22. Groote, J.F., de Vink, E.P.: A complete axiomatization of branching bisimulation for a simple process language with probabilistic choice, Submitted
23. Groote, J.F., de Vink, E.P.: Problem solving using process algebra considered insightful. In: Katoen, J.-P., Langerak, R., Rensink, A. (eds.) ModelEd, TestEd, TrustEd. LNCS, vol. 10500, pp. 48–63. Springer, Cham (2017). https://doi.org/10.1007/978-3-319-68270-9_3
24. Hansson, H., Jonsson, B.: A calculus for communicating systems with time and probabilities. In: Proceedings of RTSS 1990, pp. 278–287. IEEE (1990)
25. Hennessy, M.: Exploring probabilistic bisimulations, part I. Formal Aspects Comput. **24**, 749–768 (2012)
26. Hillston, J.: A compositional approach to performance modelling. Ph.D thesis, University of Edinburgh (1994)
27. Larsen, K.G., Skou, A.: Bisimulation through probabilistic testing. Inf. Comput. **94**, 1–28 (1991)
28. Latella, D., Massink, M., de Vink, E.P.: Bisimulation of labelled state-to-function transition systems coalgebraically. Log. Methods Comput. Sci. **11**(4) (2015). https://doi.org/10.2168/LMCS-11(4:16)2015, https://lmcs.episciences.org/1617
29. Milner, R.: Communication and Concurrency. Prentice Hall, Englewood Cliffs (1989)
30. Moller, F.: The importance of the left merge operator in process algebras. In: Paterson, M.S. (ed.) ICALP 1990. LNCS, vol. 443, pp. 752–764. Springer, Heidelberg (1990). https://doi.org/10.1007/BFb0032072
31. Parma, A., Segala, R.: Logical characterizations of bisimulations for discrete probabilistic systems. In: Seidl, H. (ed.) FoSSaCS 2007. LNCS, vol. 4423, pp. 287–301. Springer, Heidelberg (2007). https://doi.org/10.1007/978-3-540-71389-0_21
32. Segala, R.: Modeling and Verification of Randomzied Distributed Real-Time Systems. Ph.D thesis, MIT (1995). Technical report MIT/LCS/TR-676
33. Segala, R., Lynch, N.: Probabilistic simulations for probabilistic processes. In: Jonsson, B., Parrow, J. (eds.) CONCUR 1994. LNCS, vol. 836, pp. 481–496. Springer, Heidelberg (1994). https://doi.org/10.1007/978-3-540-48654-1_35
34. Stark, E.W., Smolka, S.A.: A complete axiom system for finite-state probabilistic processes. In: Plotkin, G.D., Stirling, C., Tofte, M. (eds.) Proof, Language, and Interaction, Essays in Honour of Robin Milner, pp. 571–596. The MIT Press (2000)
35. Valmari, A.: Simple bisimilarity minimization in O(mlogn) time. Fundamenta Informaticae **105**(3), 319–339 (2010)

Applications

Enabling Auditing of Smart Contracts
Through Process Mining

Flavio Corradini, Fausto Marcantoni, Andrea Morichetta, Andrea Polini,
Barbara Re$^{(\boxtimes)}$, and Massimiliano Sampaolo

University of Camerino, Camerino, Italy
{flavio.corradini,fausto.marcantoni,andrea.morichetta,
andrea.polini,barbara.re,massimiliano.sampaolo}@unicam.it

Abstract. The auditing sector is acquiring a strong interest in the diffusion of blockchain technologies. Such technologies guarantee the persistence, and authenticity of transactions related to the execution of a contract, and then enable auditing activities. In particular, they make possible to check if observed sequences of transactions are in line with the possibly expected ones. In other words, auditing blockchain transactions allow users to check if the smart contract fits the expectation of the designers, that for instance could check if a given activity is performed or if it satisfies a given set of properties. In such a setting we propose a methodology that exploits process mining techniques to evaluate smart contracts, and to support the work of the auditor. Models resulting from the mining can be used to diagnose if the deployed application works as expected, and possibly to continuously improve them. We illustrate the use of our approach using a small, but real, case study.

Keywords: Blockchain · Smart contract · Process mining · Audit

1 Introduction

The adoption of blockchain-related technologies is spreading over many different contexts. When adopted in a new context [26] they generally have disruptive effects on traditional business, and they introduce novel ways of interactions (e.g., payment [19], agriculture [23] and others). Such transformations involve not only companies but also public authorities, that are currently recognising the potentialities of such technologies. The success of the "blockchain" is also confirmed by the significant interest of the community towards a technology able to guarantee trust natively using a faultless and robust validation system (e.g., in the last two years there have been 3.7 million Google searches for blockchain). The other key factor in the success of such a technology is tied to smart contracts. A smart contract is very much similar to a real physical contract which however takes the form of a digital artefact, and it can be used to establish business relations. These relations are enforced automatically via transactions as soon as the terms of the contract are fulfilled, and then the transactions are

© Springer Nature Switzerland AG 2019
M. H. ter Beek et al. (Eds.): Gnesi Festschrift, LNCS 11865, pp. 467–480, 2019.
https://doi.org/10.1007/978-3-030-30985-5_27

stored in the blockchain. The execution of a smart contract results in a set of activities that are carried out in a particular order. The order of execution of the activities describes the business logic of the contracts, and provide evidence to the interested partners about their completion.

Even though in a contract it is generally useful to define an order for the permitted actions, the smart contract specification does not provide mechanisms to enforce an order. It is then generally useful to define new methodologies for auditing the control flow of blockchain-based applications [13], and then to check if the actual execution of the contract functions conforms to the expected ones. Process mining is certainly a possible strategy to support auditors in such checks. Indeed, previous experiences show the possible benefits of process mining [2] in relation to auditing activities [4,20]. Such experiences underline the possibility to perform a better analysis of the process flow based on historical data as well as the possibility of auditing processes on-the-fly. Up to now, blockchain has the potential to impact the audit sector making particularly significant the application of process mining as a supporting technique.

In this paper, we illustrate the methodology, and we report the results we obtained in applying process mining for auditing smart contracts. In particular, we consider the list of transactions resulting from the execution of RotoHive, that is an online fantasy sport running weekly tournaments. The application has been implemented as a smart contract on the Ethreum blockchain, that provides a set of functions that a player can invoke to play in a tournament. In running process mining we apply three different algorithms: the Heuristics Miner [24], the Inductive Miner [21,22], and the Split Miner [10]. Fitness, precision and generalisation are measured to check the quality of the mining activity. The major benefits of our methodology are as follows.

- Reduce time and cost for auditing contracts usually done manually on a set of transactions randomly selected.
- Improve the effectiveness of auditing, since by looking at all the transactions, auditors will inevitably find more exceptions requiring follow-up.
- Make it easier to investigate deviations highlighting anomalies at run-time.

The rest of the paper is organised as follows. Section 2 provides an overview of blockchain technology and process mining. Sections 3 introduces the methodology we follow in our study, while Sect. 4 presents the case study we consider as well as recommendations resulting from the conducted analysis. Section 5 presents related works available in the literature. Finally, Sect. 6 closes the paper with some remarks and opportunities for future works.

2   Background

This section presents the relevant notions related to blockchain, with a particular focus on Ethereum, and process mining.

Blockchain and Ethereum. A blockchain is a distributed ledger composed by a linked list (cf. chain) of records called blocks [26]. Each block contains a limited number of transactions in its body, while the header includes, among other things, the hash of the current block and the hash of the previous block. New blocks are added to the chain at regular intervals of time by the so-called "miners". These are computational nodes related to the blockchain infrastructure that is needed to derive the hash of a block. The mining process and the use of consensus protocols permit us to verify the genuineness of the transactions included in each block. Finally, the replication of the chain in any node of the network guarantees decentralization and trustworthiness, without the need of a third party independent authority. The blockchain ideas have been initially proposed to support payment systems based on cryptocurrencies. In the last years, its adoption spread off in many different contexts, also about the inclusion of additional mechanisms, such as that of *smart contracts*. These can be considered as special programs which are executed over the blockchain infrastructure, whose nodes are now equipped, in some specific technologies such as Ethereum, with computational power. The execution of smart contracts produces transactions to be stored in the blockchain, thus ensuring trust among the parties.

Ethereum is a concrete implementation of the blockchain that includes support for the execution of smart contracts [33]. This is the technology we used in our approach. In Ethereum every node connected to the Ethereum network embeds an instance of the Ethereum Virtual Machine (EVM). The operations executed in the EVM, like storage of information or contract instructions have an associated economic cost defined in terms of *GAS*, which is the unit measuring the amount of computational effort needed for the execution of the operation. The execution cost has two main advantages: (i) it reduces the risk of malicious computational tasks, and (ii) it encourages mining activities by network participants and, hence, it permits to keep the overall system working. Indeed, miners are rewarded for each block they mine with a default amount of Ethers plus the sum of the transaction fees included in the block. Currently, the most prominent language to write smart contracts for Ethereum is *Solidity* (https://solidity.readthedocs.io/).

Process Mining. Process Mining is a discipline in between data mining and computational intelligence on the one hand, and process modeling and analysis on the other [2]. Process mining aims to extract non-trivial and useful information from event logs available in today's information systems for discovering, monitoring and improving real processes [3]. It is an evidence-based approach, and this ensures a closer correspondence between modeled and observed behavior because the evaluation and definition of the model are based on real process execution traces.

In process mining, we can distinguish different activities such as discovery and conformance. The first technique, **discovery**, produces a model from an event log without using any a priori information, and usually, the discovered model is a process model expressed in a formal notation. The second class is **conformance**; it allows users to compare a process model with an event log of the same process. This is a useful technique to check whether a process as inferred from the log corresponds to the expected model and vice versa.

The discovery activity is generally based on an algorithm able to produce a model from a log. Over the years several mining algorithms have been developed, each with its proper characteristics [9]. In this paper, we apply three of them, such as Heuristics Miner, Inductive Miner and Split Miner, and we shortly discuss the results we get.

- The **Data-aware Heuristic Miner (DHM)** is an algorithm for discovering process models where the behaviour is obscured in the event logs by noise, infrequent outliers or recording errors [24]. Data-aware Heuristic Miner uses the data attributes and dependency condition to distinguish infrequent paths from random noise by using classification techniques directly embedded in the discovery algorithm built upon the Heuristic Miner. The discovered models are, then, visualized as Causal Nets (C-Nets), a concise graphical notation with clear semantics, which includes information on split and join gateways.
- The **Inductive Miner** is an algorithm based on a divide-and-conquer approach [21,22]. Such an approach is applied to the log splitting it into sub-logs and then recursively applied to these sub logs until they contain only a single activity. In this way, the problem of discovering a process model for a log is broken down in discovering several sub-processes, one for each sub-log. The algorithm ensures to return a sound, fitting and block-structured process model in finite time.
- The **Split Miner** is an algorithm similar to the heuristic miner, however experiments showed that the algorithm is 2–6 times faster than other state-of-the-art methods [10]. The first step of the algorithm constructs the Directly-Follows Graph; then it detects self-loops and short-loops to discover concurrency relations between pairs of tasks. Whenever a likely concurrency relation between two tasks is discovered, the arcs between these two tasks are pruned from the Directly-Follows Graph resulting in a pruned Directly-Follows Graph. In the third step filtering is applied to the pruned Directly-Follows Graph to strike balanced fitness and precision, still maintaining low control-flow complexity. In the fourth step, split gateways are discovered for each task in the filtered pruned Directly-Follows Graph with more than one outgoing arc. This is followed by the discovery of join gateways that is the last step of the algorithm.

It is worth noticing that processes resulting from the mining are different in term of representation language. All of them can be traced back, up to some transformations, to BPMN [27] that is the target language we use in this paper being well-know and understandable to auditors.

To measure the quality of a discovered model in comparison to the event log that generated it several quality parameters have been defined [30]. Among the other we refer to:

- **Fitness**: permits to measure the extent to which the discovered model can accurately reproduce the cases recorded in the log;
- **Precision**: permits to measure how much additional behaviour is included in the model i.e. a poor precision means that a model admits much additional behaviour with respect to that reported in the log;

– **Generalization**: permits to measure how much the model just reproduce the behaviour reported in the log i.e. a low level of generalization means that the model cannot handle much more behavior with respect to the one reported in the log, maybe because not yet observed.

Overall the purpose of mining is to discover a model representative of the behaviour expressed by the event log and "to guess" additional behaviour. To generate a process model in line with reality, the algorithms should maintain a proper balance between overfitting and underfitting. The former property means that the generated model is too specific and only admits behaviour similar to that observed, while the latter property, however, presents a model too general which also accepts behaviours that are probably unrelated to the observed one.

3   Enabling the Auditing of Blockchain Contract

In this paper, we envisage a scenario based on process mining techniques to support auditing of processes "enacted" using smart contracts. In Fig. 1 we illustrate how the methodology we propose fits in the life-cycle of business transactions established through a smart contract. In particular, given a set of requirements on the transactions, a developer will define a smart contract (expressed in Solidity in our case), that will be successively deployed and executed over a blockchain infrastructure (EVM in our case). The execution of the contract will lead to a set of related transactions stored in the blockchain. At that point, it is important to check that, among other checks, the sequence of actions and interactions put in place by the contract participants are in line with what was expressed in the requirements. To enable such auditing activity we conceived and implemented the ABC (Auditing Blockchain Contracts) methodology that we will detail in the following. The methodology consists of four phases executed one after the other iteratively as represented in Fig. 2.

Smart Contract Transactions Retrieval. The first phase of the methodology consists in the selection of a smart contract to be audited from the blockchain. The proposed approach has some interest in case the contract embeds a complex behaviour in terms of ordering of the contract foreseen operations. In general, not all contracts implement complex behaviours, since they contain single functionality usually not correlated each others. In this work, we are interested in challenging contracts with a complex logic since we believe that auditing can give greater benefit in case of complex behaviour. In this work, we select two requirements to consider the contract auditable: (i) the number of recorded transactions should be higher of a given threshold calculated on the dimension of the contract (i.e., in our case we set such threshold to 100), and (ii) it should contain at least one user any links to multiple interactions on different methods of the contract to observe meaningful emergent behaviours. Indeed, if this were not the case, we would not have a concrete order on the operations of the contract. From a technical point of view, the described operations are pretty

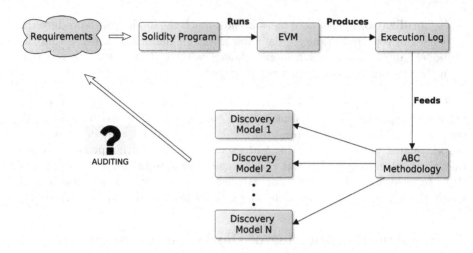

Fig. 1. ABC methodology context.

straightforward. We developed a simple application in C# integrating the Etherscan API, that permits to scan the blockchain looking for contracts according to pre-selected requirements, and it allows users to get the list of transactions in JSON format.

Transactions Clustering. The second phase of the methodology performs clustering activities on the retrieved blockchain transactions. The main challenge at this point is connected to the selection of the clustering criteria. Smart contracts do not integrate the notion of traces; each transaction represents something performed without any links with other transactions. To implement a significant correlation and to generate a set of traces we need to cluster transactions according to some logic.

In our approach, we solve the problem of creating traces grouping together transactions coming from the same sender. This means that a new trace is generated for each user. This trace contains the list of transactions exchanged between the user, and the contract ordered according to their timestamps. The main drawback of this clustering methodology refers to the possibility of correlating sequential operations just because they are executed one after the other, even if in reality they do not have any causal dependency.

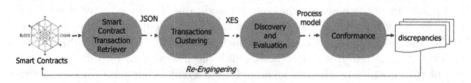

Fig. 2. ABC methodology.

From a technical perspective, in the clustering step we take the JSON file produced in the previous phase, and we generate an event log, which is then stored in a file in XES format [28].

Discovery and Evaluation. The third phase of the methodology performs a process mining discovery activity. In this work we have used three different discovery algorithms: the Heuristics Miner [24], the Inductive Miner [21,22], and the Split Miner [10]. We consider the Inductive Miner and the Split Miner thanks to its performance characteristics [9], and we also include the Heuristic Miner because it generally performs better with respect to quality criteria [12]. The used algorithms generate three different models that are compared using quality measures like fitness, precision and generalization [1]. Running three algorithms the auditor has the possibility to consider a wider spectrum of possible behaviours. Indeed the three resulting models collectively represent different and possible working scenarios. From a technical perspective, we take in input the log in the XES format and using the Apromore process mining tool[1] we discover the behavioural model emerging from the recorded transactions using Split Miner, while we use ProM[2] in the case of Heuristic and Inducting. Finally, ProM was used to compute quality measure.

Conformance. The last phase of the methodology analyses the models generated by the discovery phase, to find discrepancies concerning what is expected by the specified requirements. This is the most important phase of the auditing activity; furthermore, this analysis phase will lead to a successive contract re-engineering in case of unsatisfactory results. In the presented approach this activity does not include automatic support, yet. Nevertheless, it is clear that model checking techniques [15,16], to check interesting temporal properties, seem to be a perfect fit for such an activity. Clearly, in such a case it will be necessary to equip the auditor with user-friendly tools to define relevant properties out of the requirements list.

4   Process Mining in Blockchain: The RotoHive Case

In this section, we show the methodology in practice considering a real case study such as RotoHive[3]. More details on data used in the experiment as well as resulting model are available on-line[4].

4.1   RotoHive Overview

RotoHive is a fantasy sport running weekly tournaments. Every Tuesday a new tournament starts, and users are asked to rank National Football League (NFL)

---

[1] http://apromore.unicam.it.
[2] http://www.promtools.org.
[3] https://www.rotohive.com.
[4] http://pros.unicam.it/blockchainauditing/.

players by role based on projected performance for the week. RotoHive user submissions are then rated against real player performances. At the end of Monday night football matches, top performing RotoHive users are paid according to the rank of the selected players. This process repeats on Tuesday morning when the next weekly tournament begins. Roto can then be staked to user submissions to win a portion of a separate weekly Ethereum prize pool.

4.2   ABC Methodology in Practice

Considering **the smart contract transactions retrieve** activity, the RotoHive application was selected since it contains more than 3000 transactions[5] distributed over 4 months (from August to December 2018), and it includes several users. This characteristics make it a quite challenging scenario for experimenting with the proposed approach.

The **transactions were clustered** and formatted in a XES file considering the users interacting with the contract. Each trace is identified by a tag containing the address of the user, and a list of events performed by the user on the contract. Each event contains the name of the method called if it is completed and the corresponding timestamp. Listing 1.1 shows an excerpt of the XES file representing a trace performed by a user for the RotoHive *stake* method resulting in a transaction.

Listing 1.1. Log Excerpt.

```
1    <trace>
2        <string key= ''concept:name''  value=''0xd12c89fe9dccb84dd8fc2ba426dffe94169''/>
3            <event>
4            <string key= ''concept:name''  value=''stake''/>
5            <string key= ''lifecycle:transition''  value=''  complete''/>
6            <date key= ''time:timestamp''  value=''2018-10-12T04:39:00.000+02:00''/>
7            <string key= ''event''  value= ''stake''/>
8            </event>
9            .
10           .
11           .
12           <event> ... </event>
13   </trace>
```

The **process discovery** resulted in three models generated applying the Split Miner, Inductive Miner and the Heuristic Miner. The processes are depicted in Figs. 3, 4 and 5 respectively.

The three discovered models contain the same number of tasks, with two principal dominant behaviours, one representing the users playing the game and the other covering the behaviour of the administrator. The path representing the users contains just one task *stake* closed in a loop, indicating that a player can perform multiple stakes in each tournament. The path representing the administrator is composed of two initial tasks *constructor* (i.e., 0x60806040) and *settokencontract* indicating the first initialization of the game followed by the tasks representing the tournaments. In the tournament we have *createtournament* for the creation of a new tournament followed by the operation performed once the tournament is completed *releaseroto, rewardroto, destroyroto,* and *closetournament.*

---

[5] https://etherscan.io/address/0x0d19d264207a3afad4094f26b693ff5590361b0d.

Analysing the models we can state that the behaviour of each player is rather simple, and all the models reproduce a similar structure. Different is the case for the administrator part where the three models differ significantly for the tasks executed at the end of each tournament: *destroyroto, releaseroto, rewardroto,* and *closetournament*. The Split Miner, in Fig. 3, admits a first occurrence of the *rewardroto* task, and then the other tasks. In particular, *destroyroto* when executed occurs always after *releaseroto*. The Inductive Miner, in Fig. 4, admits to create the tournament and then two paths are possible. It can complete or execute *rewardroto* followed by two paths in parallel. The first includes the possibility to eventually execute several times *releaseroto*, while the other can execute *destroyroto* follow by *closetournament* tasks enclosed in a loop structure. This two paths are successively synchronised, and then the process ends. The Heuristic Miner, in Fig. 5, instead admits *createturnament* that is always followed by *rewardroto*. Than the three tasks *releaseroto, destroyroto* and *closeturnament* can be execute in sequence. Eventually *releaseroto* and *destroyroto* can be skipped.

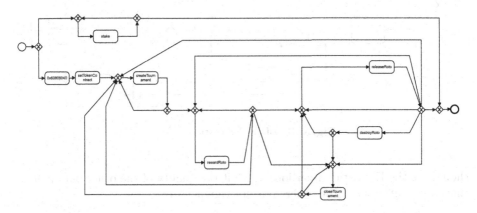

Fig. 3. RotoHive Split Miner.

To evaluate the quality of the mining algorithms applied to the RotoHive case study we considered fitness, precision, and generalisation in Table 1. Generally, we can observe that both fitness and generalization values are quite good for all 3 algorithms, while precision is more variable, and in general observed values are lower. Notably, having models with a value of fitness equal to one guarantees that all the traces in the log can be reproduced by it.

All three models represent quite well the application domain, so it is challenging to choose the best process mining algorithm to be used for audit applied to the blockchain domain. At this point, the evaluation is up to the auditor, who must consider all the models and their quality. If the auditors are interested in a model reflecting better the whole log our best solution is the Split Miner or Inductive Miner with the highest value of fitness, but with the drawback of low precision. If the auditors are more interested in highest value of precision they

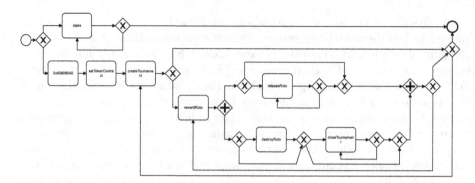

Fig. 4. RotoHive Inductive Miner.

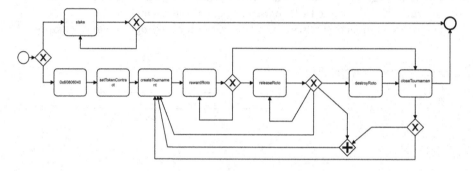

Fig. 5. RotoHive Heuristic Miner.

should use the Heuristic Miner loosing a bit the quality of the other parameters that are slightly below the others but not significantly.

4.3   Discussion

The used approach has lead to good results with sound models discovered, and pretty good quality parameters measured. The usage of more than one mining algorithm seems somehow desirable for auditing purpose. Indeed, the objective of the auditors is to identify any potential risk, and to make a careful assessment on what happened, but also on what could potentially happen. In this sense, we are working to make the presentation of potential risks easier.

Potentially the methodology used could also be useful to understand how a user interacts with a system, and to compare different behaviours with the expected one defined by requirements. Going even further in this direction we could understand the characteristics of certain users by analysing how they interacted on different systems. The designer after an accurate evaluation of the divergences can also decide to review the contract to force or avoid specific behaviour.

Table 1. RotoHive quality measures.

Algorithm	Fitness	Precision	Generalization
Split Miner	1	0.20486	0.99897
Inductive Miner	1	0.20389	0.99881
Heuristic Miner	0.92307692	0.5	0.99872

5   Related Work

In this section, we refer to the research available in the literature that inspired our work. We first discuss other papers proposing process mining techniques for audit, then we discuss solutions to enable secure and trustworthy auditing of logs.

Much effort has been devoted to the application of process mining techniques to auditing scenarios. Here in the following, we refer to those contributions supporting, as in the case of our approach, a semi-automatic strategy.

Dogana and Curbera [17] present a semi-automatic auditing approach in cases where there is no process execution engine. Ghose and Koliadis [18] present a broad auditing framework suitable to check the compliance status of a business process against given regulations. Zerbino et al. [34] propose a novel methodology for auditing information systems; they also discuss an application on the information exchange among port stakeholders. The authors provide operational guidance bridging the gaps of the current approaches for off-line information system auditing. Similarly to our approach the proposed methodology promotes the process reengineering, and for revising the boundaries in the process flow of the port community system. Accorsi and Stocker [5] use conformance checking for security auditing. They also discuss a case study employing a bank scenario and a real-life loan application process. Conformance checking is also introduced by Ramezani et al. [29]. In this paper the check considers the control flow and the normative requirements. Mayers et al. [25] use process mining and conformance checking analysis techniques to identify anomalous behaviour and cyber-attacks using industrial control systems data logs. Moreover, Arya et al. [7] use event logs collected in real time to run conformance on the operational process. The obtained results are also compared with simulated event logs to perform more accurate conformance checking. Different from our work none of the considered papers take into account blockchain transactions as a log for auditing those applications based on blockchain.

Finally, we considered solutions to enable secure and trustworthy auditing of logs. Among the others, we refer to Ahmad et al. [8], and Sutton and Samavi [31,32] discussing the possibility of the blockchain to enable privacy auditing. In particular, Ahmad et al. [8] present a scalable and tamper-proof system. Sutton and Samavi [32] provide a mechanism for log integrity and authenticity verification, by means of compliance checking queries. These papers underline the importance of performing the auditing in blockchain-related scenarios even though they do not propose any possible solutions for such an activity.

6 Conclusions and Future Work

The increasing adoption of blockchain technology disrupts traditional businesses, and it introduces a novel way to sign and run contracts. The combined use of blockchain technologies and process mining presents novel challenges and opportunities for auditing activities that can rely on trustworthy logs.

In this paper, we present the results we obtained in applying process mining for auditing Ethereum applications. In particular, we consider RotoHive's generated transactions. This is an on-line fantasy sport that runs weekly tournaments. The auditing activity has been performed using the discovered models and considering fitness, precision and generalization.

In the future, we plan to continue our programme to support auditors of blockchain-based applications effectively. Therefore we aim at enlarging the study running a more extensive validation, and considering a broad set of different blockchain-based applications that can be optimized via cost/reward method [6]. We also intend to deepen our research on the possible selection of one or more mining algorithm, and their suitability and checking its performance and effectiveness. Moreover, we would evolve the methodology with a prototype suitable to run auditing activity in a user-friendly manner. Finally, we would like to explore other analysis techniques for auditing, i.e. monitoring [11] and conformance [14].

Acknowledgement. It is really our pleasure to take part in Stefania's Festschrift. The cooperation with her and her group is somehow recent, nevertheless it has been very profitable, and inspiring both from the professional and human profile. In particular the cooperation has strengthened in relation to the Learn PAd European research project where both UNICAM and ISTI–CNR were partners. The work we present here can be somehow considered a germination of the research carried on together within Learn PAd. We thank Stefania for her friendship, and wish her all the best for the future.

References

1. Van der Aalst, W., Adriansyah, A., van Dongen, B.: Replaying history on process models for conformance checking and performance analysis. Wiley Interdisc. Rev. Data Min. Knowl. Disc. **2**(2), 182–192 (2012)
2. van der Aalst, W.M.P.: Process Mining - Data Science in Action, 2nd edn. Springer, Heidelberg (2016). https://doi.org/10.1007/978-3-662-49851-4
3. van der Aalst, W.M.P., et al.: Process mining manifesto. In: Daniel, F., Barkaoui, K., Dustdar, S. (eds.) BPM 2011. LNBIP, vol. 99, pp. 169–194. Springer, Heidelberg (2012). https://doi.org/10.1007/978-3-642-28108-2_19
4. van der Aalst, W.M.P., van Hee, K.M., van der Werf, J.M.E.M., Verdonk, M.: Auditing 2.0: using process mining to support tomorrow's auditor. IEEE Comput. **43**(3), 90–93 (2010)

5. Accorsi, R., Stocker, T.: On the exploitation of process mining for security audits: the conformance checking case. In: Symposium on Applied Computing, pp. 1709–1716. ACM (2012)
6. Aceto, L., Larsen, K.G., Morichetta, A., Tiezzi, F.: A cost/reward method for optimal infinite scheduling in mobile cloud computing. In: Braga, C., Ölveczky, P.C. (eds.) FACS 2015. LNCS, vol. 9539, pp. 66–85. Springer, Cham (2016). https://doi.org/10.1007/978-3-319-28934-2_4
7. Adriansyah, A., van Dongen, B.F., van der Aalst, W.M.P.: Towards robust conformance checking. In: zur Muehlen, M., Su, J. (eds.) BPM 2010. LNBIP, vol. 66, pp. 122–133. Springer, Heidelberg (2011). https://doi.org/10.1007/978-3-642-20511-8_11
8. Ahmad, A., Saad, M., Bassiouni, M., Mohaisen, A.: Towards blockchain-driven, secure and transparent audit logs. In: 15th EAI International Conference on Mobile and Ubiquitous Systems: Computing, Networking and Services, pp. 443–448. ACM (2018)
9. Augusto, A., et al.: Automated discovery of process models from event logs: review and benchmark. IEEE Trans. Knowl. Data Eng. **31**, 686–705(2018)
10. Augusto, A., Conforti, R., Dumas, M., Rosa, M.L.: Split Miner: discovering accurate and simple business process models from event logs. In: International Conference on Data Mining, pp. 1–10. IEEE (2017)
11. Bertolino, A., Marchetti, E., Morichetta, A.: Adequate monitoring of service compositions. In: 9th Joint Meeting of the European Software Engineering Conference and the ACM SIGSOFT Symposium on the Foundations of Software Engineering, pp. 59–69 (2013)
12. Buijs, J.C.A.M., van Dongen, B.F., van der Aalst, W.M.P.: On the role of fitness, precision, generalization and simplicity in process discovery. In: Meersman, R., et al. (eds.) OTM 2012. LNCS, vol. 7565, pp. 305–322. Springer, Heidelberg (2012). https://doi.org/10.1007/978-3-642-33606-5_19
13. Casino, F., Dasaklis, T.K., Patsakis, C.: A systematic literature review of blockchain-based applications: current status, classification and open issues. Telematics Inform. **36**, 55–81 (2019)
14. Corradini, F., Morichetta, A., Polini, A., Re, B., Tiezzi, F.: Collaboration vs. choreography conformance in BPMN 2.0: from theory to practice. In: 22nd International Enterprise Distributed Object Computing Conference, pp. 95–104. IEEE (2018)
15. Corradini, F., Fornari, F., Polini, A., Re, B., Tiezzi, F.: A formal approach to modeling and verification of business process collaborations. Sci. Comput. Program. **166**, 35–70 (2018)
16. Corradini, F., Fornari, F., Polini, A., Re, B., Tiezzi, F., Vandin, A.: BProVe: a formal verification framework for business process models. In: Proceedings of the 32nd IEEE/ACM International Conference on Automated Software Engineering, ASE 2017, Urbana, IL, USA, 30 October–03 November 2017, pp. 217–228 (2017)
17. Doganata, Y., Curbera, F.: Effect of using automated auditing tools on detecting compliance failures in unmanaged processes. In: Dayal, U., Eder, J., Koehler, J., Reijers, H.A. (eds.) BPM 2009. LNCS, vol. 5701, pp. 310–326. Springer, Heidelberg (2009). https://doi.org/10.1007/978-3-642-03848-8_21
18. Ghose, A., Koliadis, G.: Auditing business process compliance. In: Krämer, B.J., Lin, K.-J., Narasimhan, P. (eds.) ICSOC 2007. LNCS, vol. 4749, pp. 169–180. Springer, Heidelberg (2007). https://doi.org/10.1007/978-3-540-74974-5_14

19. Holotiuk, F., Pisani, F., Moormann, J.: The impact of blockchain technology on business models in the payments industry. In: Towards Thought Leadership in Digital Transformation: 13. Internationale Tagung Wirtschaftsinformatik, pp. 12–15 (2017)
20. Jans, M., Alles, M.G., Vasarhelyi, M.A.: The case for process mining in auditing: sources of value added and areas of application. Int. J. Accounting Inf. Syst. 14(1), 1–20 (2013)
21. Leemans, S.J.J., Fahland, D., van der Aalst, W.M.P.: Discovering block-structured process models from event logs containing infrequent behaviour. In: Lohmann, N., Song, M., Wohed, P. (eds.) BPM 2013. LNBIP, vol. 171, pp. 66–78. Springer, Cham (2014). https://doi.org/10.1007/978-3-319-06257-0_6
22. Leemans, S.J., Fahland, D., van der Aalst, W.M.: Discovering block-structured process models from event logs - a constructive approach. Petri Nets 7927, 311–329 (2013)
23. Leng, K., Bi, Y., Jing, L., Fu, H., Nieuwenhuyse, I.V.: Research on agricultural supply chain system with double chain architecture based on blockchain technology. Future Gener. Comp. Syst. 86, 641–649 (2018)
24. Mannhardt, F., de Leoni, M., Reijers, H.A., van der Aalst, W.M.P.: Data-driven process discovery - revealing conditional infrequent behavior from event logs. In: Dubois, E., Pohl, K. (eds.) CAiSE 2017. LNCS, vol. 10253, pp. 545–560. Springer, Cham (2017). https://doi.org/10.1007/978-3-319-59536-8_34
25. Myers, D., Suriadi, S., Rad, K., Foo, E.: Anomaly detection for industrial control systems using process mining. Comput. Secur. 78, 103–125 (2018)
26. Nakamoto, S., et al.: Bitcoin: A peer-to-peer electronic cash system (2008)
27. OMG: Business process model and notation (2011)
28. OMG: XES standard definition (2019)
29. Ramezani, E., Fahland, D., van der Aalst, W.M.P.: Where did i misbehave? diagnostic information in compliance checking. In: Barros, A., Gal, A., Kindler, E. (eds.) BPM 2012. LNCS, vol. 7481, pp. 262–278. Springer, Heidelberg (2012). https://doi.org/10.1007/978-3-642-32885-5_21
30. Rozinat, A., de Medeiros, A.K.A., Günther, C.W., Weijters, A.J.M.M., van der Aalst, W.M.P.: The need for a process mining evaluation framework in research and practice. In: ter Hofstede, A., Benatallah, B., Paik, H.-Y. (eds.) BPM 2007. LNCS, vol. 4928, pp. 84–89. Springer, Heidelberg (2008). https://doi.org/10.1007/978-3-540-78238-4_10
31. Samavi, R., Consens, M.P.: Publishing privacy logs to facilitate transparency and accountability. J. Web Semant. 50, 1–20 (2018)
32. Sutton, A., Samavi, R.: Blockchain enabled privacy audit logs. In: d'Amato, C., et al. (eds.) ISWC 2017. LNCS, vol. 10587, pp. 645–660. Springer, Cham (2017). https://doi.org/10.1007/978-3-319-68288-4_38
33. Wood, G.: Ethereum: A secure decentralised generalised transaction ledger. Technical report, Ethereum Project Yellow Paper 151 (2014)
34. Zerbino, P., Aloini, D., Dulmin, R., Mininno, V.: Process-mining-enabled audit of information systems: methodology and an application. Expert Syst. Appl. 110, 80–92 (2018)

A Refined Framework for Model-Based Assessment of Energy Consumption in the Railway Sector

Silvano Chiaradonna[1], Felicita Di Giandomenico[1], Giulio Masetti[1(✉)], and Davide Basile[1,2]

[1] Institute of Science and Technology "A. Faedo", 56124 Pisa, Italy
giulio.masetti@isti.cnr.it
[2] University of Florence, Florence, Italy

Abstract. Awareness and efforts to moderate energy consumption, desirable from both economical and environmental perspectives, are nowadays increasingly pursued. However, when critical sectors are addressed, energy saving should be cautiously tackled, so to not impair stringent dependability properties such contexts typically require. This is the case of the railway transportation system, which is the critical infrastructure this paper focuses on. For this system category, the attitude has been typically to neglect efficient usage of energy sources, motivated by avoiding to put dependability in danger. The new directives, both at national and international level, are going to change this way of thinking. Our study intends to be a useful support to careful energy consumption. In particular, a refined stochastic modeling framework is offered, tailored to the railroad switch heating system, through which analyses can be performed to understand the sophisticated dynamics between the system (both the cyber and physical components) and the surrounding weather conditions.

Keywords: Stochastic modeling · Rail road heating system · Reliability · Energy management

1 Introduction

Energy efficiency is increasingly a target at Country level, and directives are issued to take appropriate measures to use energy more efficiently at all stages of the energy chain, from production to final consumption. Both economical aspects and environmental impact are at the basis of such initiatives. At EU level, on 30 November 2016 the Commission proposed an update to the Energy Efficiency Directive, including a new 30% energy efficiency target for 2030, and measures to update the Directive to make sure the new target is met[1].

---

[1] https://ec.europa.eu/energy/en/topics/energy-efficiency.

© Springer Nature Switzerland AG 2019
M. H. ter Beek et al. (Eds.): Gnesi Festschrift, LNCS 11865, pp. 481–501, 2019.
https://doi.org/10.1007/978-3-030-30985-5_28

When dealing with critical sectors such as transportation infrastructures, the trend so far has been mainly to neglect energy saving, thus affording higher energy costs, being mostly concentrated on assuring dependability properties. However, the above mentioned initiatives are going to put the development of even dependability-critical systems under a new perspective, where energy consumption will gain more attention. In fact, while priority remains on dependability and resilience requirements, these need to be reconciled with other relevant requirements as well, among which the energy consumption. To assist the designer in devising appropriate energy management strategies, it is highly beneficial to develop supports able to analyze the behavior of such strategies, especially in critical situations such as in presence of failures. The contribution of this paper goes in this direction.

In more details, the paper focuses on the railway sector, and specifically on the rail road switch heating system [10, 21]. A rail road switch is a mechanism enabling trains to be guided from one track to another. It works with a pair of linked tapering rails, known as points. These points can be moved laterally into different positions, in order to direct a train into the straight path or the diverging path. Such switches are therefore critical components in the railway domain, since their correct operation highly impacts on the reliability of the railway transportation system. Among environmental conditions that may prevent the switches to work properly there are snow and ice, which are typical in many regions in winter time. In consequence, the mechanisms that enable a train to be directed can be blocked by an excessive amount of snow or ice. To overcome this issue, rail road switches heaters are used nowadays, so that the temperature of the rail road switches can be kept above freezing. The heaters may be powered by gas or electricity [10]. In this paper, we focus on electricity and develop an approach to model and evaluate the behavior of heating policies. In particular, resorting to a stochastic model-based approach, the switch heating system and control policies are modeled and properly analyzed, to assess the impact of major factors characterizing the system components and the environment (weather conditions) it operates in, as well as failure events, on indicators representative of the energy consumption.

This paper extends previous work [2–9] recently published by a subset of the authors in two main directions: (i) a more comprehensive architectural framework of the system under analysis is targeted, starting from current practice at the Italian railway system level; (ii) more sophisticated aspects are included in the modeling and evaluation effort, such as humidity and power line communications failure, which have an impact on both energy consuming and dependability/resilience but were neglected in previous studies. The result is a more accurate modeling and analysis framework, to support heating policies definition aiming at reaching the highest energy saving, while satisfying dependability/resilience related requirements. The framework is built following a modular and compositional approach to promote further extensions, some of which are already identified and discussed as future work.

The rest of the paper is structured as follows. Section 2 overviews related work, to better position the current contribution. The logical architecture of the rail road switch heating system and related stochastic process are presented in Sect. 3. Then, the modeling framework, through which energy consumption for the target system can be assessed, is the subject of Sect. 4. The case study and the scenarios considered to exemplify the usage of the developed modeling framework are introduced in Sect. 5, and obtained results are discussed. Finally, conclusions and future research lines are briefly outlined in Sect. 6. A list of acronyms and symbols used in this paper is given at the end.

We would like to underline that this work is strictly related with Stefania's research activities in recent years, as testified by the several publications on the topic included in the reference list of this paper. Stefania's competences in the railway domain are outstanding; therefore, discussing with her about these new directions to energy consumption awareness and containment was very interesting, fruitful and enjoyable!

2   Related Work

Formalisms such as hybrid automata [16], hybrid Petri nets [14], Stochastic Activity Networks (SANs) [22] have been proposed for modeling and evaluating energy-saving systems. Several tools have been proposed for their modeling, evaluation and verification, as for example Uppaal [17], Kronos [24], Möbius [12].

Previously, Stefania Gnesi et al. have analyzed the problem of energy optimization of rail-road switch heaters and the trade-off between energy consumption and reliability of the system. We briefly summarize the previous efforts in this specific domain. The adopted policy of energy consumption was an on/off strategy based on temperature thresholds (both for turning off and on the energy). The system has been initially modeled and analyzed using Möbius and SANs in [2–4,6]. It was supposed that heaters have different priorities in accessing the energy resources, and so the policy of energy consumption was tuned to adapt to the different priorities of the heaters as well as the different periods of a day (warmer and colder). The presented model was equipped with both a logical part representing the energy consumption policy and a physical part modeling the temperature behavior and the weather. In [9] the same system has been modeled and analyzed with Uppaal SMC and stochastic hybrid automata. Temporal logic was used instead of Markov Reward Models to model the measures of interest, that are the energy consumption and the probability of failure. The logic of the energy policy was verified in [7] against progress of interactions, to prevent deadlocks in the communications between the different components. The two formalizations were then compared in [5] to draw pros and cons of each of these approaches. Finally, in [8] the methodology was generalized so to automatically map an automata-based model representing a qualitative verified policy of energy consumption to a stochastic Petri net dialect equipped with stochastic behavior related to phenomena such as weather conditions, to perform quantitative evaluation.

In this paper we took different steps forward in analyzing the rail road switch heating problem. A more accurate physical model is proposed, which takes into account humidity and dew points as parameters affecting the probability of failure. Moreover, the communication layer is modeled as a power line. Different topologies are analyzed that affect the relation between failures of different heaters.

Analyzing the trade-off among dependability parameters and energy consumption is a rather new research field. Hence, there is not a uniform methodology to tackle this problem but rather several techniques and formalisms have been used. The chosen formalism comes paired with specific analysis techniques. Whilst we focus on modeling the system through SANs and evaluating the measures of interest through simulations, other families of Petri net models and state machine models have also been used in the literature, and other evaluation techniques such as quantitative (e.g. probabilistic, statistical) model checking are used.

We firstly review a set of contributions using Petri net dialects and simulations for evaluating the energy consumption. An example of combining stochastic simulation and model checking is in [19], where a tool chain comprising Uppaal and Möbius is used for the proactive schedule generation for manufacturing scenarios with resource competition, stochastic resources breakdowns, and earliness/tardiness penalties. We do not model competitions in accessing the energy resource: all switches must be heated. Hence, no strategy is synthesized for scheduling the access to the energy source. Hybrid Petri Nets [14] are used for modeling the survivability of a smart house in [15], that is the probability that a house with locally generated energy (photovoltaic) and a battery storage can continuously be powered in case of a grid failure. The authors consider a randomly chosen probability of failure and fixed thresholds. Whilst a threshold-based policy is also adopted in [15], we aim at building a more comprehensive modeling framework, able to account for dependencies among components/environmental aspects and a variety of failure events.

In addition to our energy consumption policy, other aspects have been considered in the literature. For example, in [25] a dynamic voltage and frequency scaling is also studied in the context of self-organizing systems for different fields of power system control [20]. The authors study how to balance the voltage and frequencies stability of the network to meet the demand of energy. Similarly to the previous papers, these parameters are linked to reliability and safety of the system. Dynamic voltage and frequency scaling were coupled with energy consumption policies in [1] to reduce the energy consumption in multiprocessor dataflow applications by means of analyses performed through Statistical Model Checking. Energy consumption policies reduce the energy consumption of processors while they are idle, and dynamic voltage and frequency scaling reduce the energy consumption by lowering the voltage and clock frequency. Adopting sophisticated policies regulating energy consumption is certainly a valuable direction, and our framework is open to accommodate such investigations in future studies. The effort so far has been primarily directed to build an evaluation framework rich enough to account for behavioral and structural aspects of the system at hand in the addressed railway context, as well as failure and weather dynamics, to set the basis for accurate analyses.

3   System Under Analysis: Logical Architecture and Stochastic Process

The system under analysis is logically structured in three parts, as shown in Fig. 1: (i) n railroad switch heaters $SH_1, \ldots, SH_n$, one for each switch, that heat the switches through electricity, (ii) the heater control system, that decides when to turn on or off the heaters as needed to prevent the congelation of the railway switches, and (iii) the weather conditions, i.e., the weather data, varying over time, used by the control subsystem to decide the control actions.

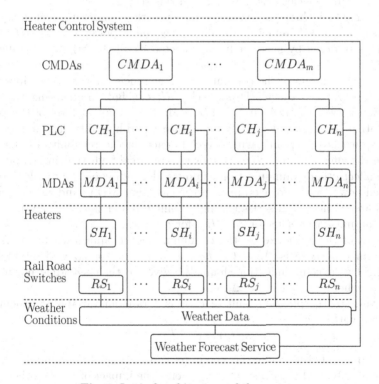

Fig. 1. Logical architecture of the system.

Each heater SH_i is installed close to the switch RS_i and is powered through power lines connected to the power system. Different heaters can be connected in series on the same power line. The state at time t of each heater SH_i is represented by the stochastic process $\{X_i(t)|t \geq 0\}$ defined by

$$X_i(t) = \begin{cases} 1 & \text{if } SH_i \text{ is } on \text{ at time } t, \\ 0 & \text{otherwise.} \end{cases} \tag{1}$$

A heater consumes electrical energy only when it is switched-on.

The heater control system is composed by the following logical components: (i) n Modules for Data Acquisition (MDAs) $MDA_1, \ldots, MDA_n$, one for each heater, partitioned in m different subsets, (ii) m Coordinator Modules for Data Acquisition (CMDAs) $CMDA_1, \ldots, CMDA_m$, one for each different subset in which the whole set of MDAs is partitioned, (iii) a Power-Line Communication (PLC), composed by n logical communication channels, $CH_1, \ldots, CH_n$, each one connecting a MDA with the associated CMDA.

CMDAs and MDAs are in charge of switching on or off the heaters, in accordance to heating policies described later in this section.

Each MDA_i includes a sensor to measure the temperature of RS_i, it is installed close to SH_i and is powered by the same power line as SH_i. Each $CMDA_j$ is powered by a power line connected to all the MDAs controlled by $CMDA_j$.

The physical layers of the communication channels are the power lines powering the MDAs and the CMDAs. Each CH_i can fail, interrupting the communication between MDA_i and $CMDA_i$, due to a fault at level of the power line. Weather conditions, especially temperature and humidity, may induce malfunctions on the power line, with direct impact on the reliability of the PLC based on the affected power line. Moreover, a physical fault that interrupts CH_i can also affect other communication channels, depending on the topology of the connected power lines. For example, in the case that MDAs and the associated CMDAs are connected in series through a single power line, the physical fault of CH_i can impact on some or all CH_h, for $h = i, i+1, \ldots, n$.

The list of the δ_i indexes of the communication channels where the failure of CH_i can propagate is $\Delta_i = \{h_1, h_2, \ldots, h_{\delta_i}\}$. The topology of interactions among the logical communication channels is given by the $n \times n$ adjacency matrix $T = [T_{i,j}]$, where $T_{i,j} = 1$ if $j \in \Delta_i$, else $T_{i,j} = 0$.

The time to the physical fault of CH_i is a random variable exponentially distributed with rate

$$\lambda_i(t_k) = c \cdot w^{H_i(t_k)} \tag{2}$$

where w represents the weight, i.e. the impact, over time of the humidity $H_i(t_k)$ on the fault rate, and the constant c represents the impact of all the other influencing aspects (including the characteristics of the power lines, e.g. the distance between MDAs and CMDAs, the air temperature and others) on the fault rate. The recovery time of CH_i is a random variable exponentially distributed with constant rate μ_i.

Concerning the weather aspects, to advance on previous studies also the humidity is accounted for in addition to the temperature, since they both contribute to the ice formation. Because of this particular emphasis on humidity, also the above expression of the CH_i failure rate explicitly accounts for it. In more detail, at each instant of time t_k, weather conditions are represented by a stochastic process composed by a $(2n + 3)$-tuple of random variables:

$$(T_0(t_k), H_0(t_k), T^{dew}(t_k), T_1(t_k), \ldots, T_n(t_k), H_1(t_k), \ldots, H_n(t_k),$$

where $t_k = t^w \cdot k, t^w \in \mathbb{R}_{>0}, k \in \mathbb{N}, T_i(t_k) \in [-50, 50]$ °C and $H_i(t_k) \in [0.01, 1]$. Thus, the random variables representing the weather conditions are piece-wise constants over time and change value every t^w units of time.

$T_0(t_k)$, $H_0(t_k)$ and $T^{dew}(t_k)$ are the temperature, the air relative humidity and the dew point, respectively, provided by the weather forecast service for the geographical area where the n railroad switches are installed. $T_i(t_k)$ and $H_i(t_k)$ with $i = 1, \cdots, n$ are the temperature and the air relative humidity, respectively, close to the switch RS_i heated by SH_i. The values of $T_i(t_k)$ and $H_i(t_k)$ can be different from those of $T_0(t_k)$ and $H_0(t_k)$, due to specific conditions at the position of RS_i (e.g., better/worse exposition to sun, or the presence of shadow, or others).

The measurement of the dew point is related to humidity. A higher dew point means that there is more moisture in the air. The dew point is defined as a function of $T_0(t_k)$ and $H_0(t_k)$, and can be computed following the Magnus-Tetens approximation as

$$T_{dew}(t_k) = \frac{b\,\alpha(t_k)}{a - \alpha(t_k)}, \text{ with } \alpha(t_k) = \frac{a\,T_0(t_k)}{b + T_0(t_k)} + \ln(H_0(t_k)), \qquad (3)$$

where $a = 17.27, b = 237.7$ °C [18, 23].

When the temperature is below the freezing point of water, i.e., $T^{dew}(t_k) \leq 0$ °C, the dew point is called the *frost point*, as frost is formed rather than dew. In this case, i.e., when $T_i(t_k) \leq T^{dew}(t_k) \leq 0$ °C, the moisture on RS_i turns into ice that can prevent the switch from working correctly.

It is assumed that if $T_i(t_k) \leq 0$ °C then $T_i(t_{k-1}) \leq 5$ °C, i.e., the temperature cannot drop from 5 °C to 0 °C in less than t^w time units. This is a realistic assumption for the weather conditions and for the value of $t^w = 10$ min considered in this paper.

The relative humidity $H_i(t_k)$ is a function of the local temperature $T_i(t_k)$ and the dew point $T^{dew}(t_k)$, according to the formulation

$$H_i(t_k) = e^{\left(\frac{a T^{dew}(t_k)}{b+T^{dew}(t_k)} - \frac{a T_i(t_k)}{b+T_i(t_k)}\right)}, \qquad (4)$$

where a and b assume the same values as in Eq. (3).

After introducing the logical structure of the reference system, the control actions performed by the heater control system are now detailed. At a higher level, the behavior is the following. At each instant of time t_k, each MDA_i transmits instantaneously to the associated $CMDA_j$ the value of the temperature obtained from its local sensor and receives instantaneously from $CMDA_j$ the command to turn on or off SH_i (if needed). This exchange occurs if the communication channel between MDA_i and $CMDA_j$ is working.

Otherwise, when the communication channel between MDA_i and $CMDA_j$ does not work, MDA_i turns on SH_i as soon as $T_i(t_k) \leq 5\,°\mathrm{C}$ and turns off SH_i as soon as $T_i(t_k) > 5\,°\mathrm{C}$. The previous assumption that the temperature cannot drop from a value greater than $5\,°\mathrm{C}$ to a value lower than or equal to $0\,°\mathrm{C}$ in less than t^w time units, prevents the switch RS_i from freezing in the interval between two consecutive instants of time t_{k-1} and t_k.

Going in more details, at each instant of time t_k, for each working communication channel CH_i, $CMDA_j$ associated to SH_i receives instantaneously from MDA_i the measured value of $T_i(t_k)$. Then, using the temperature and humidity values received from the weather forecast service at time t_k, $CMDA_j$ sends to MDA_i the following command:

- if $T_i(t_k) \leq T^{dew}(t_k)$ and $T_i(t_k) \leq 0\,°\mathrm{C}$, the command is to turn on SH_i;
- if $T_i(t_k) > T^{dew}(t_k)$ or $T_i(t_k) > 0\,°\mathrm{C}$, the command is to turn off SH_i.

Note that this last condition, used by $CMDA_j$ to turn off SH_i, could not prevent the railway switch RS_i from freezing when the values of $T_i(t_k)$ and $H_i(t_k)$ are different from those of $T_0(t_k)$ and $H_0(t_k)$, respectively. In fact, SH_i is turned off when SH_i is working, $T_i(t_k) > T^{dew}(t_k)$ and $T_i(t_k) < 0\,°\mathrm{C}$, but $T_i(t_k)$ could be lower than, or equal to, the dew point local to RS_i. In this case, RS_i freezes. In the weather profiles considered for this paper, the values of $T_i(t_k)$ and $H_i(t_k)$ are such that, although they differ from $T_0(t_k)$ and $H_0(t_k)$, respectively, the just described event cannot occur.

Another observation is that the values of $H_i(t_k)$, with $i = 1, \cdots, n$, are not exploited by the control system in taking decisions on the heating of the railway switches, since humidity sensors are currently not deployed close to switches (at least considering the Italian railway system, which inspired our study). However, we used humidity values at each CH_i, as defined by Eq. (4), to determine with higher accuracy the failure rate of each communication channel CH_i, according to Eq. (2).

In order to evaluate the impact of the failure of CH_i on the energy consumption, it is assumed that all the components other than CH_i do not fail, i.e., they work correctly.

Let P^{SH} be the electrical power required by each switched-on heater SH_i, i.e., when $X_i(t) = 1$. The electrical energy consumed in the interval of time $[0, t]$ by all the heaters is

$$E(t) = P^{SH} \sum_{i=1}^{n} J_i^{\mathrm{on}}(t)dt, \qquad (5)$$

where

$$J_i^{\mathrm{on}}(t) = \int_0^t X_i(t)\, dt$$

is the random variable representing the total time X_i is equal to 1, i.e., the total time SH_i is switched on, in the time interval $[0, t]$.

4 SAN Model

A stochastic model-based approach is adopted to analyze the rail road switch heating system. In particular, the logical architecture of the system under analysis is modeled and evaluated following the *DARep* compositional approach, as proposed in [11], by means of the tool Möbius [13]. The *DARep* approach is based on: (i) template stochastic models, each one representing a different generic component; (ii) dependency-aware State Variables (SVs), representing part of the state of a template model; (iii) a topology, associated to each dependency-aware SV; (iv) two functions *Index()* and *Deps()* that extend the template model; (v) the compositional operator $\mathcal{D}$.

An SV defined in a template model can be: (i) *local*, if each instance (replica) of the SV can be accessed only by the instance of the template model where it has been generated by $\mathcal{D}$, i.e., instances of the local SV cannot be shared among different instances of the template model, (ii) *common*, if it is shared among all the instances of templates, i.e., the operator $\mathcal{D}$ merges all the instances (replicas) of the SV into one unique SV, (iii) *dependency-aware*, if each instance of the SV can be accessed (shared) by different instances of template models, following the topology of dependencies associated to the SV. The topology associated to each dependency-aware SV defines which different instances of the SV are generated by $\mathcal{D}$ in each instance of the template model. The instances of a dependency-aware SV can be accessed in the template model only using the function *Deps()*. Moreover, the function *Deps()* can be used in the template model to access only to the instances of the dependency-aware SV defined by the topology for the current replica of the template. Thus, for example, *H->Deps()* and *H->Deps()* return the list of instances of the dependency-aware SV H or the h-th instance of the list (that is usually different from the h-th instance of H), respectively, as defined by the topology for each instance of the template model. The operator $\mathcal{D}$ generates automatically the instances, replicas with identity, of each template model. Moreover, it shares, i.e. merges into one SV, all the occurrences of an instance of dependency-aware SV in different instances of the template model. The function *Index()* can be used to access to the index of the current instance of the template model in order to obtain a parametric definition of the template model as a function of the index of the instance.

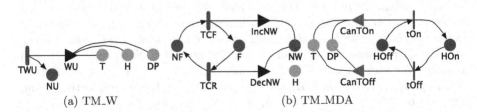

(a) TM_W   (b) TM_MDA

Fig. 2. SAN template model for weather conditions (a) and SAN template model for CH_i and MDA_i (b). (Color figure online)

Two atomic template models TM_W and TM_DMA, shown in Fig. 2, are defined using the SAN formalism [22], a stochastic extension of Petri nets, based on the following primitives: plain and extended places (blue and orange circles, respectively), timed and instantaneous activities (hollow and solid vertical bars, respectively), input and output gates (triangles pointing left or right, respectively). The SAN primitives are defined by expressions or statements of the programming language C++. Places and activities correspond to SV and actions, respectively. Plain places represent C++ short types, whereas extended places represent primitive C++ data types (like short, int, float, double) including also structures and arrays. Input gates control when an activity is enabled. Marking changes occur when an activity completes (fires), as defined by the input and output gates.

The overall system model is obtained generating and composing automatically through the $\mathcal{D}$ operator one instance TM_W_1 of the template model TM_W and n instances $TM\_DMA_1, \ldots, TM\_DMA_n$ of the template model TM_DMA. TM_W_1 represents the changes of the weather conditions at each instant of time t_k. Each instance TM_DMA_i represents the failure and repair of CH_i and the actions of MDA_i turning on and off SH_i at each instant of time t_k. In the template models, the function $Index()$ represents the generic index i of an instance of template. In the i-th instance of template $Index()$ returns the value of i.

The extended places T and H are dependency-aware SVs with n instances, $T_1, \ldots, T_n$ and $H_1, \ldots, H_n$, respectively. The instances T_i and H_i represent the current values of $T_i(t_k)$ and $H_i(t_k)$, respectively. The topology associated to T and H in TM_DMA is defined such that the instances T_i and H_i are only generated in TM_DMA_i, where $T->Deps(0) = T_i$ and $H->Deps(0) = H_i$. The topology associated to T and H in TM_W is defined such that in TM_W_1 are generated all the instances of T and H, such that $T->Deps(i) = T_i$ and $H->Deps(i) = H_i$, with $i = 1, \ldots, n$. The extended place DP is a common SV representing the current value of $T^{dew}(t_k)$ and is shared among all the instances of TM_W and TM_DMA.

In TM_W, the always enabled timed activity TWU represents the deterministic time t^w between two consecutive updates of the weather conditions data. The values of $T_i(t_k)$, $H_i(t_k)$ and $T^{dew}(t_k)$, in the interval of time $[0, t]$, are statically defined at compilation time in C++ constant arrays, one array for each different weather condition profile considered in the analysis, and can be accessed at time t_k using the index k. The local place NU (initialized to 0) has only one instance generated in TM_W_1, that represents the index k of t_k used to access to the current weather condition data. At each completion, TWU adds 1 token to NU and performs the code of the output gate WU. Such code consists in assigning the current values of $T_i(t_k)$ and $H_i(t_k)$, for $i = 1, \ldots, n$, to T_i (i.e., $T->Deps(i) = T_i(t_k)$) and H_i (i.e., $T->Deps(i) = T_i(t_k)$), respectively, and $T^{dew}(t_k)$ to DP, where $k = NU->Mark()$ (the marking of the place NU).

In TM_DMA, the timed activities TCF and TCR represent the exponentially distributed random time to the fault occurrence and to the recovery of the fault, respectively, in CH_i. The rate $\lambda_i(t_k)$ is defined by the C++

expression: $c*pow(w, SANDAREP::TM\_DMA::H->Deps(0)->Mark())$, being $SANDAREP::TM\_DMA::H->Deps(0) = H_i$ in the instance TM_DMA_i. TCF is enabled when there is 1 token in the local place NF (initialized with 1 token), i.e., when CH_i is not faulty. TCR is enabled when there is 1 token in the local place F (initialized with 0 token), i.e., when a fault occurred in CH_i.

The place NW is a dependency-aware SV with n instances $NW_1, \ldots, NW_n$, one for each TM_DMA_i. Each instance NW_i represents the dependency of the failure of CH_i on the faults occurred on other communication channels, depending on the topology $\mathcal{T}$ associated to NW. The value of NW_i is the current number of faulty communication channels the failure of CH_i depends on. The channel CH_i is working when $NW_i = 0$, otherwise it is failed when $NW_i > 0$. For each TM_DMA_i, a subset of δ_i instances of NW is automatically generated by $\mathcal{D}$, such that $NW->Deps(j) = NW_{h_j}$ with $h_j = \Delta_i[j]$, for $j = 1, \ldots, \delta_i$.

At each completion in the instance TM_DMA_i, TCF moves the token from NF to F and propagates the failure, by executing the C++ code of the output gate $IncNW$ that adds one token to each instance $NW->Deps(j)$ for $j = 1, \ldots, \delta_i$. At each completion in the instance TM_DMA_i, TCR moves the token from F to NF and removes the failures propagated from the just removed fault, executing the C++ code of the output gate $DecNW$ that remove one token from each instance $NW->Deps(j)$ for $j = 1, \ldots, \delta_i$.

The places HOn or $HOff$ are local SVs with n instances $HOn_1, \ldots, HOn_n$ and $HOff_1, \ldots, HOff_n$, respectively, one instance for each TM_DMA_i. Notice that the notation HOn and $HOff$, used for local SVs in the template model TM_DMA, corresponds to HOn_i and $HOff_i$, respectively, in the instance TM_DMA_i of the template model. The instances HOn_i and $HOff_i$ represent the state of the heater SH_i, that is *on* or *off* when there is one token in HOn_i or $HOff_i$, respectively. In each TM_DMA_i, the instantaneous activities tOn and $tOff$ represent the turning on and off, respectively, of SH_i.

tOn is enabled when $HOff->Mark() = 1$ (i.e., the heater is off) and one of the following conditions defined in the input gate $CanTOn$ is true:

- $SANDAREP::TM\_DMA::NW->Deps(0)->Mark() > 0$ (i.e., the channel is not working) and
  $SANDAREP::TM\_DMA::T ->Deps(0)->Mark() \le 5$ (i.e., $T_i(t_k) \le 5\,°C$), or
- $SANDAREP::TM\_DMA::NW->Deps(0)->Mark() = 0$ (i.e., the channel is working) and
  $SANDAREP::TM\_DMA:: T ->Deps(0)->Mark() \le SANDAREP::$
  $TM\_DMA:: DP->Deps(0)->Mark()$ (i.e., $T_i(t_k) \le T^{dew}(t_k)$) and
  $SANDAREP::TM\_DMA::T ->Deps(0)->Mark() \le 0$ (i.e., $T_i(t_k) \le 0$).

$tOff$ is enabled when $HOn->Mark() = 1$ (i.e., the heater is on) and one of the following conditions defined in the input gate $CanTOff$ is true:

- $SANDAREP::TM\_DMA::NW->Deps(0)->Mark() > 0$ (i.e., the channel is not working) and
  $SANDAREP::TM\_DMA::T ->Deps(0)->Mark() > 5$ (i.e., $T_i(t_k) > 5\,°C$), or

– $SANDAREP::TM\_DMA::NW{-}{>}Deps(0){-}{>}Mark() = 0$ (i.e., the channel is
  working) and
  "$SANDAREP::TM\_DMA::T {-}{>}Deps(0){-}{>}Mark()$ > $SANDAREP::$
  $TM\_DMA:: DP{-}{>}Deps(0){-}{>}Mark()$ (i.e., $T_i(t_k) > T^{dew}(t_k)$) or
  $SANDAREP::TM\_DMA::T {-}{>}Deps(0){-}{>}Mark() > 0$ (i.e., $T_i(t_k) > 0$)".

At each completion in the instance TM_DMA_i, tOn moves the token from
$HOff$ to HOn, turning on SH_i, whereas $tOff$ moves the token from HOn to
$HOff$, turning off SH_i.

5   Evaluation Results

The case study introduced to demonstrate the feasibility and utility of the proposed analysis approach is based on a real-world system, namely the *Lecco-
Maggianico* railway station in the North of Italy. In particular, it is composed
by $n = 19$ railroad switches, partitioned in two groups denoted as *North* and
South switches, with size 9 and 10, respectively, and controlled by $CMDA_1$ and
$CMDA_2$, also denoted as *north* CMDA and *south* CMDA, respectively, as shown
in Fig. 3.

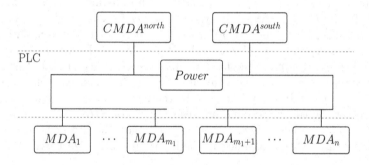

Fig. 3. Logical architecture of the PLC at Lecco-Maggianico railway station.

The focus of the analysis is on measuring the impact of the communication
channels behavior on the consumption of the electrical power needed to heat all
the railway switches in one day. To this purpose, the impact of different settings
for the PLC parameters c, w, and μ_i, together with the failure modes of each
SH_i (namely, either independent or correlated to the failure of one or more other
SH_k, according to a failure dependency topology) on $\mathbb{E}[Eday]$, the expected
value of the random variable E[day] as defined in Eq. (5), is evaluated during a
representative day. Different scenarios are considered, characterized by having a
subgroup of the parameters discussed in Sect. 3 at a fixed value and varying the
values of the other parameters, to conduct a sensitivity analysis. The measure
$\mathbb{E}[Eday]$ is obtained solving the model presented in Sect. 4 through simulation,
using the simulator of the Möbius tool and performing 10000 runs for each

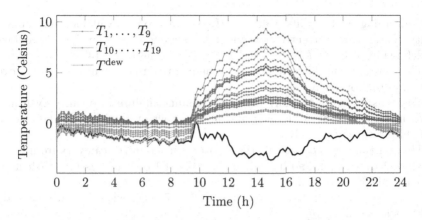

Fig. 4. Temperature $T_i(t)$ for the North region ($i = 1,\ldots,9$) and the South region ($i = 10,\ldots,19$) of *Lecco - Maggianico* railway station during December 21, 2018. The dew point $T^{\text{dew}}(t)$ is reported as a tick black line.

obtained result. When considered of particular relevance, also the Probability Density Function (PDF) of E^{day} is reported.

In detail, the parameters setting for the conducted evaluation is:

- Two configurations of the logical communication architecture to connect the CMDAs and the controlled MDAs through the electrical grid, shown in Fig. 3, are considered:
  - All the MDAs communicate directly with the CMDA they are associated to, implying that each CH_i fails independently from the others. We call this topology of interactions $\mathcal{T}^p$ as the failure-independent topology,
  - all the MDAs associated to the same CMDA are connected in series to a single electrical power line. In such configuration, the failure of CH_i propagates to all CH_h on the same power line, for $h \geq i$. We call this topology of interactions $\mathcal{T}^s$ as the failure-correlated topology.
- The values to assign to $H_0(t_k)$ and $T_0(t_k)$ are those of weather data collected by ARPA Lombardia[2] during December 21, 2018 for the city of Lecco, where $t_k = t^w \cdot k$ for $t^w = 10$ min and $k = 0,\ldots,143$.
- The dew point $T^{dew}(t_k)$ is then computed in terms of $H_0(t_k)$ and $T_0(t_k)$, as defined in Eq. (3), and depicted (thick line) in Fig. 4.
- Real values for $T_i(t_k)$ are not available, since it was not possible to get access to historical temperature data as detected by the sensors installed close to MDA_i. Therefore, they have been derived from $T_0(t_k)$ through a mathematical manipulation, with the objective to take into account the geographical exposition of switches in the analyzed railway station. Namely, temperatures at the *North* group of heaters are considered (in mean) lower than those at the *South* group of heaters.

---

[2] Agenzia Regionale per la Protezione dell'Ambiente (ARPA) of the Lombardia Italian region.

Concerning the humidity, values of $H_i(t_k)$ are also not available, since humidity sensors are currently not adopted. Therefore, their values have been defined in terms of $T^{dew}(t_k)$ and $T_i(t_k)$, according to Eq. (4).

- The constant c in the formula of the channel failure rate can vary from 1 over 5 days to 1 over 1 h.
- The constant w in the formula of the channel failure rate can vary from 1 to 10 (representing no impact and high impact of humidity on the channel failure rate, respectively).
- The constant μ_i, representing the recovery time of CH_i, can vary from 1 over 3 h to 1 over 5 min, and has a default value of 1 over 1 h, assumed whenever not explicitly specified.
- Each heater is supposed to consume $P^{SH} = 7.4$ kW when in state on, and 0 kW when in state off.

The performed analyses are grouped in three scenarios, where a subset of the above reported system characteristics (becoming parameters of the system model described in Sect. 4) are considered fixed and others are varied, to carry on sensitivity analysis. As already indicated, the emphasis of the evaluation is on the impact of the behavior of the communication network on power consumption, so the profiles for temperature and humidity are kept the same in all the scenarios (as in Figs. 4 and 5, respectively). In more details:

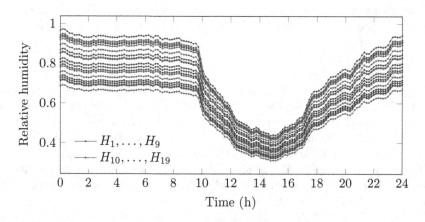

Fig. 5. Humidity $H_i(t)$ for the North region ($i = 1, \ldots, 9$) and the South region ($i = 10, \ldots, 19$) of *Lecco - Maggianico* railway station during December 21, 2018.

Scenario (**1**) this scenario considers the topology T^p, varying values for the parameters c and w, and fixed values for the other parameters;

Scenario (**2**) this scenario complements the previous one by considering the other channel failure model, i.e., the failure-correlated mode through the topology T^s, and adopting the same setting as in the previous study for the other parameters;

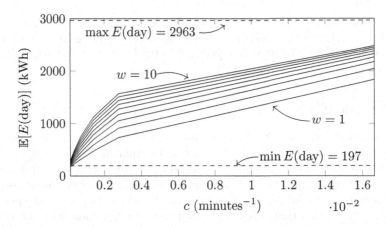

Fig. 6. Scenario 1: expected value of E[day] at increasing of c (from one every 5 days to one every hour), and varying w (from 1, i.e., no impact of H_i on λ_i, to 10). The failure-independent topology T^p is considered.

Scenario **(3)** the third scenario explores the impact of the recovery parameter μ_i in rather critical conditions for the other parameters as derived from the analysis in the previous two scenarios (namely, when the topology is T^s and c is equal to $3.47 \cdot 10^{-4}$ (minutes^{-1})).

The minimal and maximal energy that can be consumed during the day for the considered case study, corresponding to no channels failure and continuous channels failure, respectively, are statically computed and reported in Figs. 6, 7 and 9. The maximal energy is about one order of magnitude greater than the minimal energy, so choosing the right combination of parameters and topology can have a great impact on energy consumption, and then cost and environmental footprint. Notice that in Figs. 6, 7 and 9 the ordinates are in linear scale spanning from the minimal to maximal energy, whereas the abscissas are in linear scale for Figs. 6 and 7 and in logarithmic scale for Fig. 9, so it is possible to graphically compare results from different scenarios.

5.1   Scenario 1

In this scenario, the failure-independent topology T^p is considered and, fixing all the μ_i to their default value of one over 60 min, $\mathbb{E}[E(\text{day})]$ is evaluated at increasing values of c. As expected, keeping constant the relative humidity, a small c produces a small $\lambda_i(t_k)$, and then a large Mean Time Between Failures, whereas increasing c produces a small Mean Time Between Failures. Thus, at the increasing of c, $\mathbb{E}[E(\text{day})]$ increases, as shown in Fig. 6. As revealed by the sensitivity analysis, $\mathbb{E}[E(\text{day})]$ increases quite rapidly for c lower than $0.4 \cdot 10^{-2}$ (minutes^{-1}), still remaining under 2000 (kWh), and then increases slowly towards the maximal energy. Of particular relevance is then studying the impact of w on $\mathbb{E}[E(\text{day})]$. In Fig. 6, 10 curves, one for each w from 1 to 10, are depicted. For w equal to

1, relative humidity has no impact on $\lambda_i(t_k)$, because $1^{H_i(t_k)} = 1$, otherwise, for w equal to 10, if relative humidity is equal to 1 then $\lambda_i(t_k)$ is 10 times greater than c. As depicted in Fig. 6, for c equal to $0.4 \cdot 10^{-2}$ (minutes^{-1}), $\mathbb{E}[E(\text{day})]$ can double when switching w from 1 to 10.

5.2   Scenario 2

This scenario differs from Scenario 1 only for the topology. In fact, here the failure-correlated topology $\mathcal{T}^s$ is considered. Comparing Fig. 7 with Fig. 6, it is possible to appreciate the impact of correlations among channels failure. As expected, an high degree of correlation among channel failures produces values of E(day) that are in mean higher than those produced by the failure-independent topology. This means that, even with relatively small values of c, the energy consumed during one day can reach high values. For example, for c equal to $0.4 \cdot 10^{-2}$ (minutes^{-1}) and w greater than 2, the value of $\mathbb{E}[E(\text{day})]$ is already greater than 2000 (kWh).

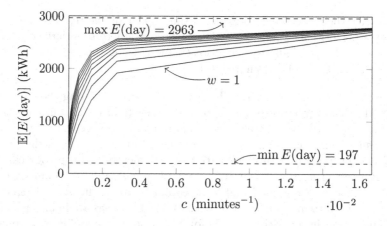

Fig. 7. Scenario 2: expected value of E(day) at increasing of c (from one every 5 days to one every hour), and varying w (from 1, i.e., no impact of H_i on λ_i, to 10). The failure-correlated topology $\mathcal{T}^s$ is considered.

For energy saving oriented analysis it is of particular importance to study not only the mean value of $E(\text{day})$ but also its Probability Distribution Function, because different choices of parameters can produce the same mean value but different distribution of $E(\text{day})$. Thus, in Fig. 8 the frequencies at which $E(\text{day})$ appears in the simulation are reported for three representative values of c and w. Scaling the values of the frequencies by a factor of 10000 it is possible to estimate the PDF of $E(\text{day})$.

5.3   Scenario 3

In this scenario a different perspective with respect to Scenarios 1 and 2 is considered. Here, the failure-correlated topology $\mathcal{T}^s$ is adopted, but the sensitivity analysis is performed with respect to μ_i and w, instead of c and w. At the increasing of μ_i, the Mean Time Between Failures decreases, and then $\mathbb{E}[E(\text{day})]$ decreases, as shown in Fig. 9, where the abscissas axis is in logarithmic scale. As expected, if μ_i is equal to 1 over 3 h then a channel failure can remain un-recovered for a long period of time, forcing all the MDA_i for $h = 1, \ldots, 9$ (North) or $h = 10, \ldots, 19$ (South) to follow the most energy consuming strategy of comparing $T_i(t_k)$ with $5\,°\text{C}$. In addition, for small values of μ_i, switching from

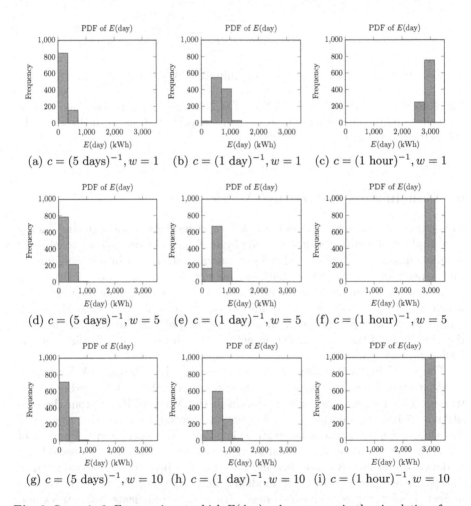

(a) $c = (5\text{ days})^{-1}, w = 1$ (b) $c = (1\text{ day})^{-1}, w = 1$ (c) $c = (1\text{ hour})^{-1}, w = 1$

(d) $c = (5\text{ days})^{-1}, w = 5$ (e) $c = (1\text{ day})^{-1}, w = 5$ (f) $c = (1\text{ hour})^{-1}, w = 5$

(g) $c = (5\text{ days})^{-1}, w = 10$ (h) $c = (1\text{ day})^{-1}, w = 10$ (i) $c = (1\text{ hour})^{-1}, w = 10$

Fig. 8. Scenario 2: Frequencies at which E(day) values appear in the simulation, from which the PDF of E(day) can be estimated, when c spans from one every 5 days to one every hour, and w spans from 1 to 10. Here, the failure-correlated topology $\mathcal{T}^s$ is considered.

$w = 1$ to $w = 10$ makes a great difference, whereas for greater values of μ_i the impact of w becomes less relevant.

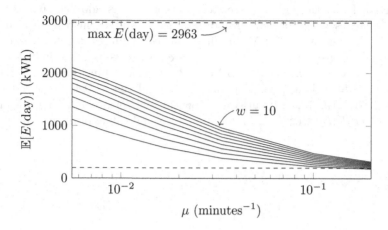

Fig. 9. Scenario 3: expected value of E(day) at increasing of μ_i, from one every 3 h to one every 5 min, and varying w from 1, i.e., no impact of H_i on λ_i, to 10. Here, the failure-correlated topology $\mathcal{T}^s$ is considered.

6   Conclusions and Future Work

This paper presented a stochastic model-based framework for assessing energy consumption of railroad switch heating systems. The developed approach, and obtained quantitative results, advance on previous studies by introducing important aspects of the weather conditions, namely the humidity and derived dew point, and more sophisticated failure models of the communication network, which have been shown to have an impact on the analysis outcomes. Moreover, a more structured picture of the heating control policies, physical structure of the switches and the communication network has been defined, inspired by the Italian railway system.

The feasibility and utility of the developed analysis framework have been demonstrated through a case study, which represents the switch heating infrastructure of a medium-size railway station in the North of Italy. From the sensitivity analysis to varying parameters values, representing relevant aspects of the communication network behavior, it is possible to understand the impact of different phenomena on the evaluated energy consumption; this is a useful basis to devise better energy-aware heating policies. The investigations conducted in this paper are partial, since the modeling and analysis framework introduced in Sect. 4 has the powerfulness to deal with more sophisticated structures and behaviors of the involved components (e.g., in terms of population size, failure models, heating policies, and others). Therefore, the agenda of future extensions includes several items, among which:

- generalize the correlation factor among channels failure to k out of n;
- relax the assumption of guaranteed reliability and identify heating policies leading to satisfactory trade-offs between reliability and energy consumption;
- address the analysis of bigger railway stations, with a variety of CMADs and communication topologies;
- develop and evaluate more sophisticated heating policies;
- introduce a more accurate representation of the heating physical model of the switch component (currently assumed to become warm instantaneously).

List of Main Acronyms and Symbols

CMDA Coordinator Module for Data Acquisition

MDA Module for Data Acquisition

PLC Power-Line Communication

SAN Stochastic Activity Network

SV State Variable

c constant parameter representing the impact of the characteristics of the power lines on the fault rate of CH_i

CH_i i-th communication channel

$CMDA_i$ i-th coordinator module for data acquisition

$\mathcal{D}$ $DARep$ operator

δ_i Number of communication channels where the failure of CH_i can propagate

Δ_i List of the indexes of the communication channels where the failure of CH_i can propagate

$E(t)$ Electrical energy consumed in the interval of time $[0, t]$ by all the heaters

$H_0(t_k)$ Relative humidity at time t_k provided by the weather forecast service

$H_i(t_k)$ Relative humidity at time t_k close to $SH_i, 1 \leq i \leq n$

$\lambda_i(t_k)$ Fault rate of CH_i at time t_k

m Number of CMDAS

MDA_i i-th module for data acquisition

μ_i Recovery rate of CH_i

n Number of rail-road switch heaters

P^{SH} Electrical power required by a switched-on heater

RS_i i-th rail-road switch, heated by SH_i

SH_i i-th rail-road switch, heated

$\mathcal{T}$ Topology of interactions among communication channels

$\mathcal{T}^p$ Failure-independent topology of interactions among communication channels, when each CH_i fails independently from the others

$\mathcal{T}^s$ failure-correlated topology of interactions among communication channels, when the failure of CH_i propagates to all CH_h connected in series on the same power line, for $h \geq i$

$T^{dew}(t_k)$ Dew point at time t_k provided by the weather forecast service

$T_0(t_k)$ Temperature at time t_k provided by the weather forecast service

$T_i(t_k)$ Temperature of SH_i at time t_k, $1 \leq i \leq n$

w Constant parameter representing the impact of the characteristics of the power lines on the fault rate of CH_i

$X_i(t)$ Switched-on or switched-off state at time t of SH_i

References

1. Ahmad, W., van de Pol, J.: Synthesizing energy-optimal controllers for multiprocessor dataflow applications with UPPAAL STRATEGO. In: Margaria, T., Steffen, B. (eds.) ISoLA 2016. LNCS, vol. 9952, pp. 94–113. Springer, Cham (2016). https://doi.org/10.1007/978-3-319-47166-2_7

2. Basile, D., Chiaradonna, S., Di Giandomenico, F., Gnesi, S.: A stochastic model-based approach to analyse reliable energy-saving rail road switch heating systems. JRTPM **6**, 163–181 (2016)

3. Basile, D., Chiaradonna, S., Di Giandomenico, F., Gnesi, S., Mazzanti, F.: Stochastic model-based analysis of energy consumption in a rail road switch heating system. In: Fantechi, A., Pelliccione, P. (eds.) SERENE 2015. LNCS, vol. 9274, pp. 82–98. Springer, Cham (2015). https://doi.org/10.1007/978-3-319-23129-7_7

4. Basile, D., Di Giandomenico, F., Gnesi, S.: Model-based evaluation of energy saving systems. In: Kharchenko, V., Kondratenko, Y., Kacprzyk, J. (eds.) Green IT Engineering: Concepts, Models, Complex Systems Architectures. SSDC, vol. 74, pp. 187–208. Springer, Cham (2017). https://doi.org/10.1007/978-3-319-44162-7_10

5. Basile, D., Di Giandomenico, F., Gnesi, S.: On quantitative assessment of reliability and energy consumption indicators in railway systems. In: Kharchenko, V., Kondratenko, Y., Kacprzyk, J. (eds.) Green IT Engineering: Social, Business and Industrial Applications. SSDC, vol. 171, pp. 423–447. Springer, Cham (2019). https://doi.org/10.1007/978-3-030-00253-4_18

6. Basile, D., Di Giandomenico, F., Gnesi, S.: Tuning energy consumption strategies in the railway domain: a model-based approach. In: Margaria, T., Steffen, B. (eds.) ISoLA 2016, Part II. LNCS, vol. 9953, pp. 315–330. Springer, Cham (2016). https://doi.org/10.1007/978-3-319-47169-3_23

7. Basile, D., Giandomenico, F.D., Gnesi, S.: Enhancing models correctness through formal verification: a case study from the railway domain. In: Proceedings of the 5th International Conference on Model-Driven Engineering and Software Development, MODELSWARD 2017, Porto, 19–21 February 2017, pp. 679–686 (2017)

8. Basile, D., Di Giandomenico, F., Gnesi, S.: A refinement approach to analyse critical cyber-physical systems. In: Cerone, A., Roveri, M. (eds.) SEFM 2017. LNCS, vol. 10729, pp. 267–283. Springer, Cham (2018). https://doi.org/10.1007/978-3-319-74781-1_19

9. Basile, D., Giandomenico, F.D., Gnesi, S.: Statistical model checking of an energy-saving cyber-physical system in the railway domain. In: The 32nd ACM Symposium on Applied Computing, SAC 2017, Marrakech, pp. 1356–1363 (2017)

10. Brodowski, D., Komosa, K.: A railroad switch and a method of melting snow and ice in railroad switches (2013). https://data.epo.org/publication-server/rest/v1.0/publication-dates/20131225/patents/EP2677079NWA1/document.html

11. Chiaradonna, S., Di Giandomenico, F., Masetti, G.: A stochastic modeling approach for an efficient dependability evaluation of large systems with non-anonymous interconnected components. In: The 28th International Symposium on Software Reliability Engineering (ISSRE 2017), Toulouse, pp. 46–55. IEEE. October 2017

12. Clark, G., et al.: The Möbius modeling tool. In: PNPM, pp. 241–250 (2001)

13. Courtney, T., Gaonkar, S., Keefe, K., Rozier, E.W.D., Sanders, W.H.: Möbius 2.3: an extensible tool for dependability, security, and performance evaluation of large and complex system models. In: 39th Annual IEEE/IFIP International Conference on Dependable Systems and Networks (DSN 2009), Estoril, pp. 353–358 (2009)

14. David, R., Alla, H.: On hybrid Petri nets. DEDS **11**(1–2), 9–40 (2001)

15. Ghasemieh, H., Haverkort, B.R., Jongerden, M.R., Remke, A.: Energy resilience modeling for smart houses. In: 45th Annual IEEE/IFIP, DSN 2015, pp. 275–286. IEEE Computer Society (2015)
16. Henzinger, T.A.: The theory of hybrid automata. In: LICS 1996, pp. 278–292. IEEE Computer Society (1996)
17. Larsen, K.G., Pettersson, P., Yi, W.: UPPAAL in a nutshell. JSTTT **1**, 123–133 (1997)
18. Lawrence, M.G.: The relationship between relative humidity and the dewpoint temperature in moist air: a simple conversion and applications. Bull. Am. Meteorol. Soc. **86**(2), 225–234 (2005)
19. Mader, A., Bohnenkamp, H., Usenko, Y.S., Jansen, D.N., Hurink, J., Hermanns, H.: Synthesis and stochastic assessment of cost-optimal schedules. Int. J. Softw. Tools Technol. Transfer (STTT) **12**(5), 305–317 (2009). http://doc.utwente.nl/69344/
20. Müller, S.C., Häger, U., Rehtanz, C., Wedde, H.F.: Application of self-organizing systems in power systems control. In: Dieste, O., Jedlitschka, A., Juristo, N. (eds.) PROFES 2012. LNCS, vol. 7343, pp. 320–334. Springer, Heidelberg (2012). https://doi.org/10.1007/978-3-642-31063-8_25
21. http://www.railsco.com/~electric_switch_heater_controls.htm. Accessed June 2016
22. Sanders, W.H., Meyer, J.F.: Stochastic activity networks: formal definitions and concepts. In: Brinksma, E., Hermanns, H., Katoen, J.-P. (eds.) EEF School 2000. LNCS, vol. 2090, pp. 315–343. Springer, Heidelberg (2001). https://doi.org/10.1007/3-540-44667-2_9
23. Tetens, O.: Uber einige meteorologische begriffe. Zeitschrift fur Geophysik **6**, 297–309 (1930)
24. Yovine, S.: KRONOS: a verification tool for real-time systems. Int. J. Softw. Tools Technol. Transfer **1**, 123–133 (1997)
25. Zhu, D., Melhem, R., Mossé, D.: The effects of energy management on reliability in real-time embedded systems. In: International Conference on Computer Aided Design (ICCAD), pp. 35–40, November 2004

Modelling of Railway Signalling System Requirements by Controlled Natural Languages: A Case Study

Gabriele Lenzini[1]([✉]) and Marinella Petrocchi[2,3]

[1] Interdisciplinary Center for Security Reliability and Trust (SnT),
University of Luxembourg, Luxembourg, Luxembourg
gabriele.lenzini@uni.lu
[2] Istituto di Informatica e Telematica, Consiglio Nazionale delle Ricerche (IIT-CNR),
Pisa, Italy
marinella.petrocchi@iit.cnr.it
[3] IMT Scuola Alti Studi Lucca, Lucca, Italy

Abstract. The railway sector has been a source of inspiration for generations of researchers challenged to develop models and tools to analyze safety and reliability. Threats were coming mainly from within, due to occasionally faults in hardware components. With the advent of smart trains, the railway industry is venturing into cybersecurity and the railway sector will become more and more compelled to protect assets from threats against information & communication technology. We discuss this revolution at large, while speculating that instruments developed for security requirements engineering can then come in support of in the railway sector. And we explore the use of one of them: the Controlled Natural Language for Data Sharing Agreement (CNL4DSA). We use it to formalize a few exemplifying signal management system requirements. Since CNL4DSA enables the automatic generation of enforceable access control policies, our exercise is preparatory to implementing the security-by design principle in railway signalling management engineering.

Keywords: System modelling · Analysis and enforcement ·
Railway systems · CNL4DSA · Moving block railway signalling

1 Modern Railways Systems and Cyber-Security

The railway system industry responsible for command and control systems, traffic, and operations is experiencing a radical change. In the last two decades it has

Lenzini is supported by Luxembourg National Research Fund (FNR) CORE project C16/IS/11333956 "DAPRECO: DAta Protection REgulation COmpliance"; Petrocchi is supported by the TOFFEe Integrated Activity Project funded by IMT Scuola Alti Studi Lucca.

M. H. ter Beek et al. (Eds.): Gnesi Festschrift, LNCS 11865, pp. 502–518, 2019.
https://doi.org/10.1007/978-3-030-30985-5_29

been shifting from relying on almost exclusive proprietary technology to relying on solutions based on information & communication technologies originally designed for more open-market sectors.

The shift is motivated by the need to ensure that the railway industry can rapidly adapt to forthcoming technological innovations and to future requests of integration and interoperability. Modern trains are expected to be "intelligent", critical assets in the development of smart public transport systems where trains and other means of transportation will work together to realize the full potential of emerging technologies in the functioning of smart cities.

Several EU projects, such as, Roll2Rail[1], In2Rail[2], and Shift2Rail[3], have highlighted the potentials of a data-enhanced railway infrastructure, where real-time rail data coming from intra-train, train-to-train, and/or train-to-ground communications is processed to ensure optimal control, keep schedules, and reduce consumption. Rail digital information comes also in forms of inputs for IP-connected signalling systems, as well as infotainment to provide better services to travellers. This communication revolution is pushing railway industry towards a future where the safety of train operations will depend on networked devices with access and control capabilities.

Not that safety will become less important: the railway industry has always been very attentive to safety and it will continue to be so. But with the adoption of information & communication technologies, railway safety-critical components, for long threatened mainly by hardware and software failures[4], no longer will be designed to be only fault-tolerant, thus only safeguarded by hardware/software redundancy; they will also be designed to be resilient against malicious attacks, protected by solutions proper of security engineering such as authentication protocols, access control enforcement points, and intrusion detection and attack containment systems. In a more general sense, safety gets intertwined with security.

Therefore, the railway industry has become attentive to matters of cybersecurity. Today, railway industry is concerned about disruption of railway services, about criminal damage to the information and communication infrastructure, and about terrorist cyber-attacks. As well, it is worried about loss of commercial sensitive information, reputation damage, and failure to comply with the data protection regulations such as the GDPR.

As a result, cybersecurity for railway systems is enjoying a great deal of attention. The already mentioned EU projects "∗2Rail" vouch for it, while others, like the EU CYRail[5], address specifically detection, assessment, and mitigation of safety and security threats in railway infrastructures. Cybersecurity is also in

---

[1] www.roll2rail.eu.

[2] www.in2rail.eu.

[3] www.shift2rail.eu.

[4] Not that it matters in the argument we are here developing, but one of the authors recalls to have worked in his early PhD to the validation of a safety-critical hardware system for the management of medium-large railway networks against the occurrence of Byzantine faults [18].

[5] www.cyrail.eu.

the agenda of the European Union Agency for Railways (formerly European Railway Agency - ERA), the agency charged to develop European-wide common approaches to safety and security; not surprisingly, it is also subject of interest for the European Union Agency for Network and Information Security (ENISA), which on June 2019 has become the EU Cybersecurity Agency. In January 2019, ENISA organized the first Transport Cybersecurity Conference[6]. A few years before, in 2015, it edited a report on good practices and recommendations for cybersecurity in intelligent public transport [14], suggesting the adoption of security standards and security best practices and principles such that of security-by-design. Later, in 2017 and 2018, CYRail published two reports giving recommendations and discussing a list of safety and security requirements for the railways industry [11,12].

1.1   Railways and Tools for Security Requirement Engineering

Despite the plethora of initiatives to provide guidelines and recommendations for railway cybersecurity, the documents of reference for the implementation of secure-by-design systems in the railway industry are largely the same as those used in cybersecurity in general, for instance the ISO/IEC 27001-2 standards or the NIST Cybersecurity Framework. Others domain-specific documents of reference are those released by the ERA, for instance the Technical Specifications for Interoperability (TSIs), which "defines the technical and operational standards which must be met by each subsystem or part of subsystem in order to meet the essential requirements and ensure the interoperability of the railway system of the European Union"[7].

However, railway cybersecurity is not the same as ICT cybersecurity. The complexity of the security issues in an European-wide train control system requires at least a specific understanding of the domain and, we believe, ad-hoc solutions. And to realize appropriate domain-specific defences and counter-measures, engineers have to identify, read, understand, and interpret relevant documents, regulations, and provisions. Eventually, they have to elicit clearly defined requirements and implement them. These are renowned and challenging tasks. Requirements are often written in natural language and their correct interpretation and implementation into systems, for instance as policies in access control mechanisms, is threaten by vagueness and ambiguity (e.g., see [15,16]).

We do not expect such problems being different in the railway sector than in other sectors, but because cybersecurity for railway system is a relative young discipline, there may be lack of evidence that security requirements engineering tools that have been used successfully in other sectors (e.g., in the banking sector) can work in railway as well.

Here, we are interested to test whether one of such tools, the *Controlled Natural Languages* (CNLs) (see Sect. 2), can be of benefit for the specification of railway requirements. CNLs are instruments that help write requirements,

---

[6] https://www.enisa.europa.eu/events/first-transport-cyber-security-conference/.

[7] www.era.europa.eu/activities/technical-specifications-interoperability_en.

still without departing from the natural language playground which remains pivotal for humans to express themselves and communicate ideas. But differently from natural languages, CNLs use a controlled grammar, a precise semantics, and the possibility to process statements automatically. For instance, from requirements written in *Controlled Natural Language for Data Sharing Agreement* (CNL4DSA), the CNL we consider in this paper, it is possible to generate access control policies and enforcement points.

As a case study, we take five requirements defined for real railway signalling systems. They are among the main pillars to guarantee sustainable transportation. Precisely, they are about the "ERTMS L3 moving block", one of the next generation railway signalling systems currently under trial deployment that promises to increase capacity on railway tracks, reduce costs, and improve reliability. L3 moving block technology is fully radio-based: instead of sidetrack blocks on the rail track, it uses special equipment within the train to continuously supply the train position to a remote control centre, the Radio Block Center (RBC), from which it receives inputs. If communication is lost because of a train radio failure or because the radio network has become defective due to interference or attacks, the message fail to be delivered and the train is stopped with no easy means of recovery.

We translate the five ERTMS L3 moving block requirements from their expression in natural language into the CNL4DSA. This particular CNL was originally developed to formally model legal contract regulating data sharing [9,25], but then extended to model requirements in other sectors as well. Thus, we hypothesise, it fits our motivation of being of help in expressing railway security-related requirements. The translation is evaluated with respect to key properties defined in the so-called PENS (*Precision, Expressiveness, Naturalness, Simplicity*) classification scheme [21]. In addition, we consider one more property, *Policy Enforcement*.

The characterisation of CNL4DSA, with respect to that set of properties, will allow railway engineers to judge the pertinence of such formalisms to automatically process the terms and conditions regulating the next generation railway signalling systems.

Outline. The rest of the paper is structured as follows. Section 2 briefly presents control natural languages and the CNL4DSA. Section 3 describes the key properties of the PENS evaluation scheme. Section 4 introduces our case study and the translation of part of its rules into CNL4DSA. Section 5 presents an assessment of the considered translations and of the CNL4DSA. Outlines directions for future work and conclusions are discussed in Sect. 6.

2   Controlled Natural Languages

Controlled Natural Languages, hereafter CNLs, are a subset of natural languages, specifically conceived to make machine processing simpler. A CNL is, in essence, a developed language that is based on natural language, but it is more restrictive in terms of lexicon, syntax, semantics, while at the same time retaining most of its natural properties [21]. CNLs have a more contrived representation, in terms of grammar and vocabulary, and they thus reduce the ambiguity and complexity of a complete language [28]. CNLs have been proved to be effective in mitigating linguistic ambiguity challenges, as they can easily be translated into a formal language such as first-order logic or different version of description logic, automatically and mostly deterministically [28]. Noticeably, a branch of CNLs conceived for expressing data privacy regulations are formal *per se*, being born with an associated formal syntax and semantics, see, *e.g.* [25]. In general, these languages can conveniently express the kind of information that occurs in, *e.g.*, software specifications, formal ontologies, business rules, legal and medical regulations.

One interesting feature of CNLs is that they usually maintain a readability that is not so different from that of pure natural languages. This makes them more easy to write and understand by people than pure formal languages. Furthermore, they are precisely defined subsets of natural languages and they can be translated into rigorous target languages and, then, used for automated reasoning [28]. For example, the Attempto Controlled English (ACE) [17] has been designed with an expressive knowledge representation that is easy to learn, read and write for domain experts; RABBIT was developed for ontologies authoring with the help of domain experts [20], Sydney OWL Syntax (SOS) [10] was designed as high-level interface language for OWL [29] and developed for domain specialists for knowledge representation, authoring ontologies and knowledge processing mapping to OWL. The variety of CNLs attributes suggests that it is difficult to identify their general properties. CNLs are defined for different areas (*e.g.*, academia and industry), and for different fields (*e.g.*, computer science, mathematics, engineering, linguistics, etc), and even if CNLs usually share common properties some resemble natural languages, others programming languages or logic-based formalisms, others are complex and their syntax and semantics are not easy to define and/or understand [21].

2.1   CNL4DSA

Controlled Natural language (CNL) for Data Sharing Agreement (DSA) has been introduced with the purpose to reduce the barrier of adoption of DSA in terms of privacy as well as to ensure DSA mapping to formal languages that allow the automatic verification of the agreement [25]. A data sharing agreement is essentially a contract between two or more parties to agree on some terms and conditions with respect to data sharing and usage. This language can also support the enforcement of privacy and security of electronic data exchange. CNL4DSA allows simple, yet formal, specifications of different classes of privacy policies, as listed below:

- **authorizations**, expressing the permission for subjects to perform actions on objects (*e.g.*, data), under specific contextual conditions;

- **prohibitions**, referring to prohibit the fact that a subject performs actions on an object (*e.g.*, on a set of data), under specific contextual conditions;
- **obligations**, defining that subjects are obliged to perform actions on objects, under specific contextual conditions.

Central to CNL4DSA is the notion of *fragment*, *i.e.*, a tuple $f = \langle s, a, o \rangle$, where s is the subject, a is the action, o is the object. A fragment simply says that 'subject s performs action a on object o'. By adding the *can/must/cannot* constructs to the basic fragment, a fragment becomes an authorisation, an obligation, or a prohibition. Such *composite fragments* are by the following BNF-like syntax:

$$F := \mathbf{NIL} \mid mod\ f \mid F;\ F \mid \mathbf{IF}\ C\ \mathbf{THEN}\ F \mid \mathbf{AFTER}\ f\ \mathbf{THEN}\ F$$

where:

- **NIL** is the null policy;
- *mod* ranges over $\{\mathbf{CAN}, \mathbf{MUST}, \mathbf{CANNOT}\}$ and models different type of policies and respectively, *authorization*, *obligation*, and *prohibition* policies;
- *mod f* is the atomic authorization/obligation/prohibition fragment that expresses that $f\ (= \langle s, a, o \rangle)$ is allowed/obliged/denied. Its informal meaning is that subject s can/must/cannot perform action a on object o.
- $F; F$ is a list of composite fragments.
- **IF** C **THEN** F expresses the logical implication between a composite context C (see later) and a composite fragment: if C holds, then F is permitted.
- **AFTER** f **THEN** F is a temporal sequence of fragments. Informally, after f has happened, then the composite fragment F is permitted.

Fragments are evaluated within a *context*. In CNL4DSA, a context c is evaluated as a boolean value (true/false) and it asserts properties of subjects and objects, in terms, *e.g.*, of users' roles, data categories, time, and geographical location. Simple examples of contexts are 'subject hasRole Facebook_admin', or 'object hasCategory user_post'. The constructs linking subjects and objects to their values, like hasRole and hasCategory in the above examples, are called *predicates*. To describe complex policies, contexts can be combined using the boolean connectors *and*, *or*, and *not*. Specifically, *composite contexts* are defined as follows:

$$C := c \mid C\ \mathbf{AND}\ C \mid C\ \mathbf{OR}\ C \mid \mathbf{NOT}\ c$$

2.2 CNL4DSA-Based Toolkit

Although born as a language to describe data sharing policies, CNL4DSA has been proved suitable for expressing other kind of requirements, such as software product lines specifications, *e.g.*, see [19]. The language is not domain-specific, since it has not a fixed vocabulary associated. Hence, it can be applied to various use cases, as, *e.g.*, social networking [31], e-health [24] and emergency management [22] scenarios.

The strength of this language is that, over the years, a series of tools have been developed around it, each of which serves a precise purpose within the life cycle of a rule. Below, we describe each of these tools, and the role covered by CNL4DSA.

A textual rule, either written in CNL4DSA or in natural language, is managed by a CNL4DSA-based toolkit, originally proposed in [27] and successively renewed. Initially comprising a CNL4DSA Authoring Tool, a CNL4DSA Policy Analyser, and a CNL4DSA Mapper Tool, the toolkit has recently been enriched with a translator from natural language rules to CNL4DSA rules, the NL2CNL translation tool [31].

- NL2CNL Translator: a user with no expertise of CNLs can edit rules in natural language (e.g., in English); with a minimal user's effort, the translator outputs the rules in CNL4DSA;
- CNL4DSA Authoring Tool: an author with expertise in CNLs can edit rules directly in CNL4DSA. The rules are constrained by CNL4DSA constructs (see Sect. 2) and the terms in the rules come from specific vocabularies (ontologies);
- CNL4DSA Analyser: it analyses a set of CNL4DSA rules, detecting potential conflicts among them. In case a conflict is detected, a conflict solver strategy based on prioritisation of rules is put in place to correctly enforce the right rules;
- CNL4DSA Mapper: it translates the CNL4DSA rules into an enforceable language. The mapping process takes as input the analysed CNL4DSA rules, translates them in a XACML-like language [26], and combines all the rules in line with the predefined conflict solver strategies. The outcome of this tool is an enforceable policy. Such policy will be evaluated at each request to use the objects specified in the policy itself.

A CNL4DSA Lifecycle Manager orchestrates all the previous components[8]. When a user logs into the Lifecycle Manager, this enacts her specific functions, according to the user's role (e.g., end-user, policy maker, legal user, as defined in [4]). Thus, users interact with the toolkit via the Lifecycle Manager.

Overall, CNL4DSA richness and flexibility, both in terms of describing specifications from different domains and of being equipped with different specifications processing tools, go into the direction to achieve an integrated framework for the specification and analysis of safety, security and trust in complex and dynamic scenarios, as demanded in [23].

3   The PENS Classification Scheme

A standard classification scheme is a good approach for controlled natural languages analysis, to determine whether a language fulfils certain characteristics.

---

[8] The integration of the NL2CNL Translator is under development.

The PENS scheme [21] was defined following the intuition that CNLs place themselves in between natural and formal languages. In general, CNLs are quite structured and constrained (thus, closer to pure formal languages). Still, their syntax is close to natural terms.

Furthermore, to establish a general, but, at the same time, restricted classification, the PENS scheme considers English as a natural language and propositional logic as a formal language.

Also, to develop a base classification scheme, it was important to put the properties under a few dimensions, to avoid as much as possible dependence between each other [21]. The PENS classification scheme considers only four properties *Precision, Expressiveness, Naturalness, Simplicity*, to condense under those hats the highest number of possible characteristics. For example, attributes like ambiguity in text, formal definition of language, and capability to transform the language into a propositional logic can be merged under the Precision dimension. Natural writing, and natural feeling and understanding of the language can be put under the Naturalness dimension. Instead, Simplicity measures the (non)complexity of the language. Expressiveness of a language is a measure of the variety of lexical and grammatical constructions it allows (irrespective of the reader).

In the following, we will consider such four properties as the standard base for our evaluation, plus one more property *Policy enforcement*, which is discussed later in this section.

Each of the PENS dimensions are measured through five classes, ranging over the interval $1, \ldots, 5$. Each of the five classes presents a one-dimensional area between the two extremes, i.e., English at one end and propositional logic on the other one. The decision to assign a language to one of the five classes, for each dimension, is left arbitrary. Considering Simplicity and Precision, English is at the bottom, i.e., S^1 and P^1, while propositional logic is at the top, S^5 and P^5. Conversely, for Expressiveness and Naturalness, English is at the top: E^5 and N^5 while propositional logic is at the bottom: E^1 and N^1. We remand the reader to [21] for all details about the PENS scheme.

The five classes for each dimension are described in a broadened scope and cover a wide range of CNLs. Therefore, to make a simple but effective evaluation, we select only one class for each dimension (usually, a class in the middle).

Precision. Precision is referred as the degree to which the meaning of a text can be directly understood and recovered from its textual form in a particular language, i.e., the sequence of linguistic symbols [21]. The ambiguity in the meaning, predictability, and formality of the definition can be combined with precision. Formal logic languages are highly precise because the meaning of the text is strictly defined based on the possible sequences of the symbols of the language, as compared to natural languages which are, according to the property definition, imprecise and ambiguous.

The precision classes are defined as: Imprecise languages, Less imprecise languages, Reliably interpretable languages, Deterministically interpretable languages, Languages with fixed semantics. We select *'Deterministically Interpretable Languages'* as the reference class: this class includes languages that are completely formal at the *syntactic* level. Texts in this language can be deterministically translated into a logical representation that define the meaning of sentences. However, any sensitive deduction may require additional background axioms, external or heuristic resources [21].

Expressiveness. Expressiveness is related to the range of propositions that a language is capable of expressing. For example, language 'Y' is more expressive than language 'Z' if 'Y' can describe all that 'Z' can, but 'Z' can not do the same w.r.t. 'Y'. This relationship does not necessarily induce a total order. For example, given two languages, it might be that none of them is more expressive than the other one. This makes it hard, or even unfeasible, to objectively rank in a linear order a set of languages, in terms of expressiveness [21].

PENS considers the following characteristics of expressiveness:

a universal quantification over individual s, i.e., the presence in the language syntax of the logical predicate ∀, 'given any' or 'for all'.
b relations of arity greater than one, i.e., languages which functions/predicates taking as input more than one argument.
c general rule structures, e.g., if-then-else conditions.
d negation (failure or strong negation).
e second-order (extension of first order logic) universal quantification over concepts and relations [30].

By considering the above characteristics, it is possible to categorize languages according to five different classes of expressiveness: inexpressive languages, languages with low expressiveness, languages with medium expressiveness, languages with high expressiveness and languages with maximal expressiveness.

In this paper, we concentrate on *'Languages with Medium Expressiveness (LwME)'*, i.e., languages with all the characteristics of expressiveness as above, except second-order universal quantification.

Naturalness. The dimension of naturalness defines how a language is 'natural', in terms of reading and understanding from the user standpoint. Linguistic properties such as modification of grammar, comprehensibility, and natural reading and writing can be considered elements of naturalness. CNLs retain most of the natural properties of native languages, so that native language users can, quite effortlessly, understand texts without the need of language experts.

The five naturalness classes are as follows: unnatural languages, languages with dominant unnatural elements, languages with dominant natural elements, languages with natural sentences, languages with natural texts. This study considers *'Languages with Dominant Natural Elements (LwDNE)'* as point of reference. With these types of languages, natural elements of languages dominates unnatural elements and the overall grammar structure corresponds to grammar of natural language. However due to rest of natural elements or combination of unnatural elements, these languages can not be considered valid natural sentences. Natural language speakers can not easily recognizes the sentences statements and can not understand their essence without any guidance or instructions but still intuitively understand the language to a substantial degree [21].

Simplicity. This dimension considers how much simple (resp., complex) is to describe the language in an exact and comprehensive manner, covering syntax and semantics. These 'exact and comprehensive descriptions' should define all syntactic and semantic properties of the language using accepted grammar notations to define the syntax and accepted mathematical or logical notations to define the semantics.

With respect to the PENS classification scheme, the indicator of simplicity is the number of natural language pages needed to describe the language in an exact and comprehensive way, consisting in the definition of all the syntactic and semantic properties of the language. Page counting should be done considering a single-column format, with a maximum of 700 words per page. The language descriptions do not require to include vocabularies [21].

The five categories of simplicity are as follows: very complex languages, languages without exhaustive descriptions, languages with lengthy descriptions, languages with short descriptions and languages with very short descriptions. For our study, we consider *'Languages with Short Descriptions (LwSD)'* as the term of comparison: a language considered to be simple enough to be described in more than a single page but less than ten pages.

3.1   Policy Enforcement

A standard architecture for the application (technically, 'enforcement') of policies is as follows. Consider a generic subject 'S' that tries to perform some action on the object 'O'.

A module, called Policy Enforcement Point (PEP) temporarily blocks the subject's request. The PEP takes as input the values of some attributes of the subject 'S', of the object 'O', and of the external environment (for example, the role of the subject, the type of object, the date and time when the request is made). These values are sent by the PEP to the Policy Decision Point (PDP). The PDP is a decision-making module of the architecture used to establish whether or not to allow the subject to access the object. The decision is made by evaluating the policies regulating which actions can be performed on the object. The PDP evaluates the policies based on the attributes values, and grants or denies the request of S, accordingly. Finally, the PEP applies the PDP decision.

This sketched architecture is adopted by the most common and tested control systems, such as the one implemented in the authorization infrastructure associated with XACML [26].

We will thus consider a further property, Policy Enforcement, taking into accounts if the CNL under investigation is enforceable, or not. In other words, we will consider if it serves as input to standard tools for policy enforcement.

4 Translating Railway Requirements in CNS4DSA

The European Railway Traffic Management System (ERTMS) is a set of international standards for the interoperability, performance, reliability, and safety
of modern European rail transport [13]. 'It relies on the European Train Control
System (ETCS), an automatic train protection system that continuously super-
vises the train, ensuring to not exceed the safety speed and distance. The current
standards distinguish four levels (0–3) of operation of ETCS signalling systems,
depending largely on the role of trackside equipment and on the way information
is transmitted to and from trains' [2]. In particular, in the next generation Level
3 signalling systems, the train carries the Location Unit (LU) and OnBoard Unit
(OBU) components, while the Radio Block Center (RBC) is a trackside component. The LU receives the train's location from a Global Navigation Satellite
System (GNSS), sends this location, together with a messages ensuring of the
train integrity, to the OBU, which, in turn, sends the location to the RBC. Upon
receiving a train's location, the RBC sends a Message Authority (MA) to the
OBU (together with speed restrictions and route configurations), indicating the
space the train can safely travel based on the safety distance with preceding
trains. The RBC computes the MA by communicating with neighbouring RBCs
and by exploiting its knowledge of the positions of switches and other trains
(head and tail position) by communicating with a Route Management System
(RMS)[9].

4.1 ERTMS L3 Signalling System Security Requirements

Work in [2,3] extracts a series of requirements from the general description of
the next generation L3 signalling system. Here, we report (an excerpt of) such
requirements in natural language. Later, we translate them in CNL4DSA.

– **Temporal Requirements**

  R1: GNSS must send the train location to LU every 5 s.
  R2: If the train position cannot be received within the maximum time limit,
  the OBU must transit to degraded mode.
  R3: If the train integrity cannot be confirmed within the maximum time limit,
  OBU shall order the brake activation.

– **Alarm Triggering Requirements**

  R4: If the connection between the RBC and OBU is lost, OBU must trigger
  an alarm.
  R5: Once OBU receives an alarm, it must send it to RBC.

---

[9] The description of the L3 signalling system is kindly provided by the authors of [3].

R1–*R5* can be expressed in CNL4DSA. We observe that they all express an obligation, as they all express some mandatory requirement for the L3 signalling system. We name subjects 'subject' and objects 'object' followed by a number (*e.g.*, subject1, subject2), while we name actions with a phrase, in slanted style, that reminds their doing (hasCategory). Actions are used in infix (*e.g.*, subject1 Trigger objects1), with the exception of the action of *s* sending *o* to *s'*, which we write in a mixed prefix-infix form as *s* sendTo(*s'*, *o*).

R1: **IF** c1 **THEN MUST** f1

where c1 is a composite context and f1 is an atomic fragment, defined as follows:

- c1 = **IF** subject1 hasRole 'GNSS' **AND** subject2 hasRole 'LU' **AND** object1 hasCategory 'TrainPosition' **AND** object1 isProvidedBy subject1 **AND** object2 hasCategory 'ElapsedTime' **AND** object2 hasValue '5'.
- f1 = ⟨subject1, sendTo(subject2), object1⟩

where sendTo(*s'*) is the action of sending to *s'*.

R2: **IF** c1 **THEN MUST** f1

where c1 is a composite context and f1 is an atomic fragment, defined as follows:

- c1 = subject1 hasRole 'OBU' **AND** object1 hasCategory 'TrainPosition' **AND NOT** object1 isReceivedBy subject1 **AND** object2 hasCategory 'ElapsedTime' **AND** object2 hasValue 'maxtimelimit' **AND** object3 hasCategory 'mode' **AND** object3 hasValue 'Degraded'.
- f1 = ⟨subject1 ,Transit, object3⟩

R3: **IF** c1 **THEN MUST** f1

where c1 is a composite context and f1 is an atomic fragment, defined as follows:

- c1 = subject1 hasRole 'train' **AND** object1 hasRole 'Integrity' **AND** object1 isRelatedTo subject1 **AND NOT** object1 hasStatus 'Confirmed' **AND** object2 hasCategory 'ElapsedTime' **AND** object2 hasValue 'MaxTimeLimit' **AND** subject2 hasRole 'OBU' **AND** object3 hasCategory 'OrderToBrake'.
- f1 = ⟨subject2, SentTo(subject1), object3⟩

R4: **IF** c1 **THEN MUST** f1

where c1 is a composite context and f1 is an atomic fragment, defined as follows:

- c1 = subject1 hasRole 'RBC' **AND** subject2 hasRole 'OBU' **AND** object1 hasCategory 'Connection-RBC-OBU' **AND** object1 hasStatus 'Lost' **AND** object2 hasCategory 'Alarm'.
- f1 = ⟨subject2,Trigger,object2⟩

$R5:$ **IF** c1 **THEN MUST** f1

where c1 is a composite context and f1 is an atomic fragment, defined as follows:

- c1 = subject1 hasRole 'OBU' **AND** subject2 hasRole 'RBC' **AND** object1 hasCategory 'alarm' **AND** object1 isReceivedBy subject1 **AND** object2 hasCategory 'BrakeActivation'.
- f1 = ⟨subject1,Order,object2⟩

5   Evaluation

In order to assess whether our exercise of expressing cybersecurity requirements in CNL4DSA has the potentiality to lead to a better implementation of the requirements, as we claimed in the introduction, we evaluate to which degree our translation fulfils the evaluation criteria that we introduced in Sect. 3. The result of this evaluation depends in large part on the classification that the PENS scheme gives to CNL4DSA, in the sense we would not be able to conclude that our translation of the requirements satisfies, for instance, naturalness if CNL4DSA would not be enjoying that property in the first place.

Regarding *precision*, our translation in CNL4DSA is formal at syntactic level, thus it falls into the category of *Deterministically Interpretable Language*.

The CNL4DSA syntax does not include a universal quantification operator. It supports negation for predicates but not negation for actions [25]. Thus, it cannot be classified as a pure *Language with Medium Expressiveness*. However, it should be noticed that negation on actions can be handled through the **CANNOT** modality. Moreover, being CNL4DSA coupled with hierarchical vocabularies, it is possible to express fine-grained terms, representing specific subjects, actions, and objects, as well as coarse-grained terms, representing generic subjects, actions, and objects. This implies the capability to express policies valid for every possible subject, action, and object as our translation shows clearly.

In terms of *naturalness*, CNL4DSA can be classified as a *Language with Dominant Natural Elements*, because the translations show the domination of natural elements over unnatural elements and the overall grammar structure of this language correlates to natural language grammar. Our translations harder to read than the natural language, but we claim they can be intuitively understood by non experts. This claim, to be substantiated, requires experimental validation, an activity we consider for future work.

As for *simplicity*, the description of the language, in terms of explanations of its syntax and semantics, needs more than a single page but less then ten pages [9]. Therefore, it can be classified as a *Language with Short Descriptions*.

The most interesting property at least in the scope of this work is that CNL4DSA is amenable to automatic policy verification [8] and enforcement. This can be realized via the existing implementation of the automatic translation of CNL4DSA into the enforceable language UPOL *Usage control POLicy* that has been introduced in [5–7]). Thus, CNL4DSA indirectly enjoys, through an automatic translation, the property of *policy enforcement*. Although we did show it here, being out of scope in this work, it is possible to have the requirements automatically translated in to XACML enforceable policies.

6   Conclusions

Aware of the technological shift that drives modern railway system industry towards the adoption of cybersecurity solutions, we tested the use of controlled natural language in expressing five exemplifying requirements. The requirements, coming from a subset of real control rules about the "ERTMS L3 moving block", have been expressed in CNL4DSA, a controlled natural language, and evaluated for precision, expressiveness, naturalness, and simplicity.

The chosen requirements describe obligations in case of communication failure between the L3 moving block on-line unit (OBU), the train, and the Radio Block Center (RBC). One could argue that these are not purely cybersecurity requirements, and that this choice of ours is not appropriate for our goal to test the helpfulness of tools for security requirement engineering in the railway sector. We sustain that in the railway requirement engineering, security and safety requirements are usually entangled, since security issues often require a safety response. Thus, deciding whether a certain set of requirements concerns more security than safety, or the *vice versa*, may be argued differently by different experts. We are not interested in taking position. Rather, we are willing to see among the reasons for a L3 moving block's communication failure also signal jamming. In that case, a safe stop of the train is still the right response to avoid dramatic consequences, and this is unquestionably a safety reaction to a cybersecurity threat. And if jamming is a possible threat, then in a more cybersecurity perspective one could considered that signals can also be spoofed. In a spoofing attack one successfully masquerades itself as being another. If such an attack against train-to-ground communication is feasible, then safety will become dependent on signal integrity and authenticity. Thus, future L3 moving block requirements could also be about signal assurance levels, signal source authentication and signal integrity. In that case, having proved that tools from security requirement engineering are able to express already original ERTMS L3 moving block requirements will make the transition to integrate further cybersecurity requirements easier.

That said, our exercise shows that the user of a CNL output a specification that is formal, with a clear syntax and an unambiguous semantics. The language used, the CNL4DSA, features degrees of expressiveness (in terms of expressible logical operators and functions), presence of natural elements, and simplicity of its description. Moreover, it gives our translation a further desirable property: the possibility to generate inputs for a standard policy enforcement infrastructure à la XACML.

Despite our work alone is not sufficient to draw a general conclusion, we can at least say that our exercise to automatically translate railway signalling system requirements in CNL4DSA has been possible without problem. On the contrary, we appreciate CNL4DSA's closeness to a natural language, which helped readability, and its rigorous syntax and semantics, which was expressive enough to express the modalities in the chosen requirements. Besides, learning how to use CNL4DSA (one of the two author was not familiar with the formalism) required little effort. These are notable qualities in themselves, but there is one more that we should consider: CNL4DSA comes with a devoted toolkit for policy authoring, analysis and enforcement and this feature potentially enables at least within the scope of railway requirements in our use case, an implementation of the principle of security-by design.

A natural next step is to encode more requirements that express different modalities than obligation to test how far we succeed in producing comprehensible translations and in composing guidelines for a good practice in such a translation task. Future work is also designing a quantitative methodology to assess CNL4DSA's output for understandability by non experts in formal methods, which likely calls for user studies similar to what has been proposed in [1]. To preserve readability for non expert end-users may indeed become a challenge when trying to obtain formal requirements that are automatically machine-readable (*i.e.*, analyzable and enforceable).

Acknowledgement. This work has been written for the *Festschrift* in honor of Stefania Gnesi, head of the Formal Methods & Tools group of the Istituto di Scienza e Tecnologie dell'Informazione "A. Faedo" (ISTI) of the National Council of Research (CNR), in Pisa, Italy. Both authors wish to express their professional and personal gratitude to Stefania for the time spent together at the CNR in Pisa and for years of fruitful collaboration. Stefania has been our mentor but she is also a friend. Rephrasing what we took from a comic strip about Livorno, the seaside town where she lives, we could affectionately say: "È una livornese, una donna forte con un cuore di madre".

References

1. Bartolini, C., Lenzini, G., Santos, C.: An agile approach to validate a formal representation of the GDPR. In: New Frontiers in Artificial Intellingence. New Frontiers in Artificial Intelligence. Springer (2019, in press)
2. Basile, D., ter Beek, M.H., Ciancia, V.: Statistical model checking of a moving block railway signalling scenario with Uppaal SMC - experience and outlook. In: Leveraging Applications of Formal Methods, Verification and Validation. Verification - 8th International Symposium, ISoLA 2018, Limassol, Cyprus, 5–9 November 2018, Proceedings, Part II, pp. 372–391 (2018). https://doi.org/10.1007/978-3-030-03421-4_24
3. Basile, D., ter Beek, M.H., Ferrari, A., Legay, A.: Modelling and analysing ERTMS L3 moving block railway signalling with simulink and Uppaal SMC. In: Formal Methods for Industrial Critical Systems - 24th International Conference, FMICS 2019, Amsterdam, The Netherlands, 30–31 August 2019, Proceedings (2019). https://doi.org/10.1007/978-3-030-27008-7_1

4. Caimi, C., Gambardella, C., Manea, M., Petrocchi, M., Stella, D.: Legal and technical perspectives in data sharing agreements definition. In: Privacy Technologies and Policy - Third Annual Privacy Forum, APF 2015, Luxembourg, 7–8 October 2015, Revised Selected Papers, pp. 178–192 (2015). https://doi.org/10.1007/978-3-319-31456-3_10

5. Coco Cloud Consortium - Confidential and Compliant Clouds: Deliverable 4.2: First DSA management infrastructure (2015). http://www.coco-cloud.eu/deliverables

6. Coco Cloud Consortium - Confidential and Compliant Clouds: Deliverable 4.3: Final DSA management infrastructure (2016). http://www.coco-cloud.eu/deliverables

7. Coco Cloud Consortium - Confidential and Compliant Clouds: Deliverable 5.3: Final version of the enforcement infrastructure (2016). http://www.coco-cloud.eu/deliverables

8. Costantino, G., Martinelli, F., Matteucci, I., Petrocchi, M.: Analysis of data sharing agreements. In: Information Systems Security and Privacy, pp. 167–178 (2017)

9. Costantino, G., Martinelli, F., Matteucci, I., Petrocchi, M.: Efficient detection of conflicts in data sharing agreements. In: Mori, P., Furnell, S., Camp, O. (eds.) ICISSP 2017. CCIS, vol. 867, pp. 148–172. Springer, Cham (2018). https://doi.org/10.1007/978-3-319-93354-2_8

10. Cregan, A., Schwitter, R., Meyer, T., et al.: Sydney OWL syntax - towards a controlled natural language syntax for OWL 1.1. In: OWL: Experiences and Directions, vol. 258. CEURs Workshop Proceedings (2007)

11. CYRAIL: Safety and security requirements of rail transport system in multi-stakeholder environment. Technical report, EU, June 2017

12. CYRail: Recommendations on cybersecurity of rail signalling and communications systems. Technical report, CYRail, September 2018

13. EEIG ERTMS Users Group: ERTMS/ETCS RAMS Requirements Specification - Chapter 2 - RAM (1998). http://www.era.europa.eu/Document-Register/Documents/B1-02s1266-.pdf

14. ENISA: Cyber Security and Resilience of Intellingent Public Transport, Good Practices and Recommendations. Technical report, ENISA, December 2015

15. Ferrari, A., Lipari, G., Gnesi, S., Spagnolo, G.O.: Pragmatic ambiguity detection in natural language requirements. In: Proceedings of AIRE, pp. 1–8 (2014)

16. Ferrari, A., Spoletini, P., Gnesi, S.: Ambiguity cues in requirements elicitation interviews. In: Proceedings of RE, pp. 56–65 (2016)

17. Fuchs, N.E., Kaljurand, K., Kuhn, T.: Attempto controlled English for knowledge representation. In: Baroglio, C., Bonatti, P.A., Małuszyński, J., Marchiori, M., Polleres, A., Schaffert, S. (eds.) Reasoning Web. LNCS, vol. 5224, pp. 104–124. Springer, Heidelberg (2008). https://doi.org/10.1007/978-3-540-85658-0_3

18. Gnesi, S., Lenzini, G., Latella, D., Abbaneo, C., Amendola, A., Marmo, P.: An automatic SPIN validation of a safety critical railway control system. In: Proceedings of the International Conference on Dependable Systems and Networks (DSN 2000), 25–28 June 2000, New York, NY, USA, pp. 119–124 (2002)

19. Gnesi, S., Petrocchi, M.: Towards an executable algebra for product lines. In: 16th International Software Product Line Conference, SPLC 2012, Salvador, Brazil, 2–7 September 2012, vol. 2, pp. 66–73 (2012). https://doi.org/10.1145/2364412.2364424

20. Hart, G., Dolbear, C., Goodwin, J.: Lege Feliciter: using structured English to represent a topographic hydrology ontology. In: OWL: Experiences and Directions (2007)

21. Kuhn, T.: A survey and classification of controlled natural languages. Comput. Linguist. **40**(1), 121–170 (2014)
22. Martinelli, F., Matteucci, I., Petrocchi, M., Wiegand, L.: A formal support for collaborative data sharing. In: Multidisciplinary Research and Practice for Information Systems - IFIP WG 8.4, 8.9/TC 5 International Cross-Domain Conference and Workshop on Availability, Reliability, and Security, CD-ARES 2012, Prague, Czech Republic, 20–24 August 2012, Proceedings, pp. 547–561 (2012). https://doi.org/10.1007/978-3-642-32498-7_42
23. Martinelli, F., Petrocchi, M.: A uniform framework for security and trust modeling and analysis with crypto-CCS. Electr. Notes Theor. Comput. Sci. **186**, 85–99 (2007). https://doi.org/10.1016/j.entcs.2007.03.024
24. Matteucci, I., Mori, P., Petrocchi, M., Wiegand, L.: Controlled data sharing in E-health. In: Socio-Technical Aspects in Security and Trust (STAST), pp. 17–23. IEEE (2011)
25. Matteucci, I., Petrocchi, M., Sbodio, M.L.: CNL4DSA: a controlled natural language for data sharing agreements. In: Symposium on Applied Computing, pp. 616–620. ACM (2010)
26. OASIS XACML Technical Committee: eXtensible Access Control Markup Language (XACML) Version 3.0 (2013)
27. Ruiz, J.F., et al.: A lifecycle for data sharing agreements: how it works out. In: Schiffner, S., Serna, J., Ikonomou, D., Rannenberg, K. (eds.) APF 2016. LNCS, vol. 9857, pp. 3–20. Springer, Cham (2016). https://doi.org/10.1007/978-3-319-44760-5_1
28. Schwitter, R.: Controlled natural languages for knowledge representation. In: Proceedings of the 23rd International Conference on Computational Linguistics: Posters, pp. 1113–1121. Association for Computational Linguistics (2010)
29. Schwitter, R., Kaljurand, K., Cregan, A., Dolbear, C., Hart, G., et al.: A comparison of three controlled natural languages for OWL 1.1. In: OWL: Experiences and directions (2008)
30. Stanford Encyclopedia of Philosophy: Quantifiers and quantification (2018). https://plato.stanford.edu/entries/quantification/#SecOrdQua
31. Tanoli, I.K., Petrocchi, M., De Nicola, R.: Towards automatic translation of social network policies into controlled natural language. In: 12th International Conference on Research Challenges in Information Science, RCIS 2018, Nantes, France, 29–31 May 2018, pp. 1–12 (2018). https://doi.org/10.1109/RCIS.2018.8406683

Single-Step and Asymptotic Mutual Information in Bipartite Boolean Nets

Tommaso Bolognesi$^{(\boxtimes)}$

CNR–ISTI, Pisa, Italy
t.bolognesi@isti.cnr.it

Abstract. In this paper we contrast two fundamentally different ways to approach the analysis of transition system behaviours. Both methods refer to the (finite) global state transition graph; but while method A, familiar to software system designers and process algebraists, deals with execution paths of virtually unbounded length, typically starting from a precise initial state, method B, associated with *counterfactual* reasoning, looks at single-step evolutions starting from all conceivable system states.

Among various possible state transition models we pick *boolean nets* – a generalisation of cellular automata in which all nodes fire synchronously. Our nets shall be composed of parts P and Q that interact by *shared variables*. At first we adopt approach B and a simple information-theoretic measure – *mutual information* $M(y_P, y_Q)$ – for detecting the degree of coupling between the two components *after one transition step* from the uniform distribution of all global states. Then we consider an asymptotic version $M(y_P^*, y_Q^*)$ of mutual information, somehow mixing methods A and B, and illustrate a technique for obtaining accurate approximations of $M(y_P^*, y_Q^*)$ based on the attractors of the global graph.

Keywords: Boolean network · Mutual information ·
Counterfactual analysis · Integrated Information Theory ·
Transition system behaviour · Attractor

1 Introduction

This paper is dedicated to Stefania Gnesi. In spite of my long term permanence in the Formal Methods group of ISTI that, under her coordination, has reached results of internationally recognized excellence, Stefania and I have not had many opportunities of doing joint, cheek-by-jowl work, for reasons that I tend to attribute more to the meanderings of chance than to the (often prolonged) divergence of our specific research inclinations and goals.

If I had to mention today just one topic in the large area of Software Engineering in which I suspect we might have enjoyed working together, that topic would be Requirements Engineering (RE), especially in those aspects that con-

© Springer Nature Switzerland AG 2019
M. H. ter Beek et al. (Eds.): Gnesi Festschrift, LNCS 11865, pp. 519–530, 2019.
https://doi.org/10.1007/978-3-030-30985-5_30

nect to Natural Language Processing.[1] But it is, in many respects, too late to draft notes on a possible joint RE-paper!

In the present contribution I will instead focus on the most elementary and abstract mathematical structure that one encounters when engaging with Formal Methods for system specification and analysis – the omnipresent Global State Transition Graph – but will handle it in a rather peculiar way, at least when compared with the traditional analytical techniques familiar to our research group.

Once the global graph of a concurrent, distributed system is available, typical analytical objectives include reachability, deadlocks, livelocks, connected components, attractors, liveness or fairness properties, all of which involve – in practice or in principle – execution paths of virtually infinite length, starting from the specified initial state.

By following an alternative approach, one tries to obtain information about the system by considering paths of length one – just one transition – starting from any state, including those that are not reachable from the assumed initial state. Indeed, under this *counterfactual* reasoning, the notion of a *definite* initial state becomes irrelevant. Counterfactual thinking informs J. Pearl's *Do-Calculus of intervention* [8] and is at the core of Integrated Information Theory (IIT) [1,7], which studies massively parallel artificial/natural systems and aims at modelling and measuring phenomena associated with consciousness.

Crucial to IIT is the idea to partition a system (typically modelled as a boolean net) into parts that communicate with one another by sharing some variables – some nodes of the net. Roughly speaking, Integrated Information, denoted 'Φ', measures the added value provided by the composition/integration of the parts w.r.t. the plain sum of their contributions. (More precisely, Φ is a function of the current global state X of the system, and of some partition, say $\{P,Q\}$, and measures the *entropy* of the distribution $pre(X)$ of the predecessor states of X *relative to* the product $pre(X_P) \times pre(X_Q)$ of the analogous distributions referring to the state components X_P and X_Q and to the *independent behaviours* of system components P and Q. *Relative entropy* is also known as Kullback-Leibler divergence. The *independent behaviour* of the parts is achieved by cutting the communication channels between P and Q and replacing with noise the information that they would exchange under normal, *cooperative* behaviour. The interested reader may consider the simple examples in [1], Figs. 3 and 4.).

For this reason it seems attractive to export the tools of the theory to other areas beyond neurophysiology, e.g. for investigating communication mechanisms and processes in Software Engineering.

In this paper we initially retain the IIT approach of *one-step-from-all-states*, as opposed to *many-steps-from-one-state*, but without using Φ, a rather sophisticated concept which is still evolving as new versions of IIT are elaborated;

---

[1] Among other things, I am particularly grateful to Stefania for having offered me to replace her for several years in teaching Software Engineering at the Engineering Dept. of the University of Siena.

we shall instead use a more fundamental and familiar informational measure, namely mutual information M (which indeed plays a role also in the definition of Φ in IIT 2.0 [1]).

The paper is organised as follows.

In Sect. 2 we introduce the state transition model of *boolean nets* and the idea to partition them into parts P and Q that interact by shared variables, introducing also a measure of their structural (or syntactic) degree of coupling.

In Sect. 3 we recall the notion of *mutual information* between two (discrete) random variables, to be applied to the next states y_P and y_Q of the two bool net components, written $M(y_P, y_Q)$.

In Sect. 4 we plot values of $M(y_P, y_Q)$ for randomly generated, bipartite bool nets, as a function of the syntactic coupling degree between the two components.

In Sect. 5 we push the analysis of mutual information to bool net computations of virtually infinite length, and show how these asymptotic values can be obtained by using the attractors of the bool net global graph. This technique has been implemented in a freely downloadable interactive demonstration, which is briefly illustrated.

The main objective of the paper is to obtain some numerical characterisation of the behavioural (semantic) coupling between system parts P and Q that interact by shared variables, and of its dependence on the structural (syntactic) coupling, expressed by the number of variables that P and Q share.

2   Bipartite Boolean Nets

Boolean nets [6] are discrete sequential dynamical systems. An (n, k)-*boolean net* ('bool net' in the sequel) is a pair $(G(B, E), F)$ where:

- $G(B, E)$ is a directed graph with vertex set $B = \{b_1, \ldots, b_n\}$ and edge set E; each vertex $b_i \in B$ has exactly k incoming edges:[2] $b_{i,1} \to b_i, \ldots, b_{i,k} \to b_i$, so that $|E| = nk$.
- $F = \{f_1, \ldots f_n\}$ is a set of n boolean functions of k arguments, one for each vertex in B.

Each vertex $b_i \in B$ is a boolean variable controlled by boolean function $f_i(b_{i,1} \ldots b_{i,k})$, where the ordered k-tuple of arguments $(b_{i,1} \ldots b_{i,k})$ corresponds to the edges incident to b_i.[3]

A bool net *computation* is a sequence of *steps*, assumed to take place in *discrete time* – one step at each clock tick. Each step consists of the instantaneous and *synchronous* firing of all nodes, which means that the computation is *deterministic*. (The *asynchronous* execution mode in which one randomly chosen node is fired at each step yields *nondeterministic* computations, but we shall not deal with this alternative here.).

---

[2] This limitation on node in-degree is not essential; we adopt it only for convenience of implementation and notation.

[3] Note that the graph is not sufficient for correctly identifying the order of function arguments: this is disambiguated in F.

Bool net steps are computed by the *transition probability matrix* (*tpm*), in which entry $tpm(X, Y)$ expresses the conditional probability $p(Y|X)$ that the next state be Y, given current state X. The introduction of transition *probabilities*, which are derived from the (normalised) count of possible transitions, is a natural and necessary step for being able to apply formal informational measures.

We use lower case letters, e.g. x or y, to denote a state *variable* (e.g. the current or next state of a bool net), but also, with symbol overloading, their distributions; we use upper case letters, e.g. X or Y, to denote a specific state *value* (a specific bit-tuple). The *tpm* of an (n, k) bool net S has 2^n rows and 2^n columns, since 2^n is the number of possible states of S. Each row of the *tpm* must be a probability vector – its total must be 1; since (standard) bool nets are deterministic, each row is formed by 0's except for one entry with value 1.

Let $\bar{x}_S$ denote the uniform distribution of all 2^n possible states of an (n, k)-bool net S, and let *tpm* be the transition probability matrix of the net. Then, the next state distribution is:

$$y_S = \bar{x}_S.tpm \qquad (1)$$

where '.' denotes dot product.

Let us now split the node set B of boolean net S into parts P and Q and let α be the number of *P-Q bridges*, i.e. edges in E with one endpoint in P and one in Q. We take α to represent the coupling factor between P and Q. If $b_i \rightarrow b_j$ is a bridge from P to Q and the inputs to b_i are from P, then, at each step, Q reads a node of P which has been written, at the previous step, by P itself, implementing a form of *shared variable cooperation* between the two parts – an alternative to the *shared labelled transition* interaction mechanism commonly adopted in process algebra.

We shall use notation

$$P(n_P, k) < \alpha > Q(n_Q, k)$$

to indicate the number of nodes in P and Q, the fixed arity k of the involved boolean functions and the α coupling parameter, where $<\alpha>$ is reminiscent of process algebraic parallel composition operators. We shall also use abbreviations $P < \alpha > Q$ and PQ for denoting the same system, especially in subscripts.

3 Mutual Information Between y_P and y_Q

Two random variables y_1 and y_2 are *independent* if and only if their *mutual information* [5] is null: $M(y_1, y_2) = 0$.

Mutual information $M(y_1, y_2)$, a symmetric quantity representing the information provided on average by one variable about the other, is:

$$M(y_1, y_2) = \sum_{i,j} p_{y_1 y_2}(Y_i, Y_j) Log_2 \frac{p_{y_1 y_2}(Y_i, Y_j)}{p_{y_1}(Y_i) p_{y_2}(Y_j)}, \qquad (2)$$

where $p_{y_1 y_2}$ is the joint distribution of the two variables, while p_{y_1} and p_{y_2} are the respective marginal distributions.

It is customary to represent two random variables y_1 and y_2 as bubbles in a sort of Venn diagram, where the area of the bubble corresponds to the information provided by each variable. In that case, the mutual information that y_1 provides about y_2, and vice versa, corresponds to the area of the intersection of the two bubbles. When the variables are independent, their joint distribution $p_{y_1 y_2}$ is simply the product of their individual distributions p_{y_1} and p_{y_2}, which implies that the fraction in Eq. (2) assumes value 1, yielding $M(y_1, y_2) = 0$; pictorially, the two bubbles are disjoint.

Let x_{PQ} be a random variable ranging in the set $\{0, 1\}^n$ of n-tuples of bits, denoting the *current state* of an (n, k)-bool net $P<\alpha> Q$. Similarly, let y_{PQ} denote the *next state* of the bool net: $y_{PQ} = x_{PQ}.tpm$. Let then y_P and y_Q denote the two variables obtained by splitting y_{PQ} in its P and Q components.

As anticipated, with notational abuse we let x_{PQ}, y_{PQ}, x_P, x_Q, y_P and y_Q denote not only random variables, but also their probabilistic density functions (or their 'distributions') – the meaning being clear from the context.

If variable x_{PQ} is uniformly distributed, written $\bar{x}_{PQ}$, then its components x_P and x_Q are independent random variables, so that their mutual information is null: $M(x_P, x_Q) = 0$. Knowing x_P does not give any clue about the value of x_Q. On the other hand, when bool net $P<\alpha> Q$ performs *just one* transition, starting from $\bar{x}_{PQ}$, variables y_P and y_Q will in general be coupled, due to the interaction between the parts, yielding $M_{P<\alpha>Q}(y_P, y_Q) > 0$. In the sequel we shall sometimes drop the subscript from $M_{P<\alpha>Q}$. We are interested in observing this value and its dependence on α.

4   Experimental Results

In Fig. 1 we consider a family of bool nets of form $P(n, k)<\alpha>Q(n, k)$ with $n = 5$, $k = 3$ and α ranging from 0 to $\alpha_{max} = 2nk$. The maximum value of α is obtained when all $2nk$ edges of the net become bridges: in this case, the nodes of P only read those of Q and viceversa.

At first thought one might perhaps expect $M(y_P, y_Q)$ to grow monotonically with α: the tighter the structural P-Q coupling measured by α, the higher the mutual information between the local next states y_P and y_Q. As apparent from the plots, however, $M(y_P, y_Q)$ tends to assume a bell shape, with value 0 at both endpoints of the spectrum of α values.[4] Indeed, this fact can be easily established formally.

---

[4] The averaged plot in Fig. 1-right suffers from a slight asymmetry. We conjecture that this corresponds to an asymmetry in the bool-net construction procedure: in the initial bipartite net each node has incoming edges from k *distinct* from-nodes while in the creation of new edges that cross between P and Q this concern is dropped and multiple edges between the same two nodes may appear, with boolean functions possibly reading duplicated arguments. The validity of the subsequent propositions is not affected by this asymmetry.

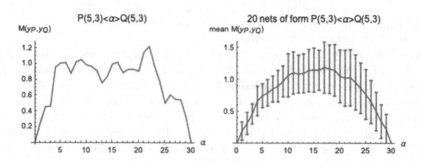

Fig. 1. Left: Mutual information $M_{P<\alpha>Q}(y_P, y_Q)$ between the P and Q components of the next state y_{PQ}, starting from a uniformly distributed state $\bar{x}_{PQ}$, of a randomly generated bool net of form $P(5,3)<\alpha>Q(5,3)$ as a function of α – the structural coupling factor of the net that counts the number of P-Q bridges. Right: Similar plot, obtained by averaging the mutual information over a set of 20 bool nets of the same form. Standard deviations are also shown.

Proposition 1. *Let $P(n_P, k)<\alpha>Q(n_Q, k)$ be a bool net with $n_P + n_Q$ nodes, as many k-ary bool functions, and α bridges between P and Q. Let y_P and y_Q denote the P and Q components of state y_{PQ} reached by the net in one transition, starting from the uniform distribution $\bar{x}_{PQ}$ of global states. If $\alpha = 0$, then $M(y_P, y_Q) = 0$.*

Proof. Since bool net computations are deterministic we can write transition $x_{PQ} \rightarrow y_{PQ}$ in functional form: $y_{PQ} = PQ(x_{PQ})$, where 'PQ' is the function that transforms one state into the next (in fact, this function is implemented by the *tpm* – see Eq. 1). Let us write state x_{PQ} as a concatenation $x_P.x_Q$ of local states. It is easy to see that if x_{PQ} is uniformly distributed, then its components x_P and x_Q are (uniformly distributed and) independent: $M(x_P, x_Q) = 0$. When $\alpha = 0$ there are no bridges between P and Q and the two components are completely separated. Thus the global transition can be decomposed into $y_P = P(x_P)$ and $y_Q = Q(x_Q)$. From the independence of x_P and x_Q, then, the independence of y_P and y_Q immediately follows: $M(y_P, y_Q) = 0$.   []

Proposition 2. *Let $P(n_P, k)<\alpha>Q(n_Q, k)$, x_P, x_Q, y_P and y_Q be as defined for Proposition 1. If $\alpha = \alpha_{max} = 2nk$, then $M(y_P, y_Q) = 0$.*

Proof. When $\alpha = \alpha_{max}$ all edges of $P(n_P, k)<\alpha>Q(n_Q, k)$ are bridges between P and Q. Thus, the global transition can be decomposed into $y_P = P(x_Q)$ and $y_Q = Q(x_P)$ (note the swap of indices w.r.t. Proposition 1). Again the independence of x_P and x_Q implies that of y_P and y_Q: $M_{P<\alpha_{max}>Q}(y_P, y_Q) = 0$.   []

The *one-step policy* adopted for the above analysis, involving just one transition $\bar{x}_{PQ} \rightarrow y_{PQ}$, is the same that inspires the already mentioned Integrated Information Theory (IIT) and, in particular, its central informational measure 'Φ' [1,7]. While the application of Φ to bool nets that interact by shared variables as well as by the process-algebraic mechanism of shared labelled transitions (see Sect. 6) will be the subject of a forthcoming paper, we are interested here in dropping the one-step restriction for pushing the analysis of mutual information to transition sequences of virtually infinite length, thus recovering in part an analytical style more familiar to process algebraists and system designers at large.

5 Asymptotic P-Q Mutual Information via Global Graph Attractors

Let

$$y_{PQ}^h = \bar{x}_{PQ}.tpm_{PQ}^h \tag{3}$$

be the next state distribution after h steps of bool net $P{<}\alpha{>}Q$, where tpm_{PQ}^h is the hth power of matrix tpm_{PQ}, $y_{PQ}^0 \equiv \bar{x}_{PQ}$ and $y_{PQ}^1 \equiv y_{PQ}$. Recall that the 'transitions' we handle here involve state distributions, not definite states.

As in the case of a single transition, we split y_{PQ}^h into its components y_P^h and y_Q^h and set to analyse $M_{P{<}\alpha{>}Q}(y_P^h, y_Q^h)$, with fixed α, as $h \to \infty$.

The sequence of global state distributions y_{PQ}^h is defined by the recurrence

$$y_{PQ}^0 = \bar{x}_{PQ} \tag{4}$$
$$y_{PQ}^{h+1} = y_{PQ}^h.tpm_{PQ}. \tag{5}$$

Consider, for simplicity, a bool net $P(2,2){<}\alpha{>}Q(2,2)$ with a total of 4 nodes and some unspecified coupling parameter α, and consider distribution y_{PQ}^h for a specific value of h. This distribution will be a probability vector with $2^4 = 16$ elements, whose values are represented by grey levels in Fig. 2-left. By splitting this vector into 4 segments of length 4 and stacking them on top of one another, we obtain precisely the *joint distribution* matrix $p_{y_P^h, y_Q^h}$ for random variables y_P^h and y_Q^h.

All we need for computing the mutual information between two random variables y_1 and y_2 is their joint distribution p_{y_1, y_2}, since the marginal distributions that appear in Eq. 2 are derived from it by adding up rows or columns. In fact, we could write $M(p_{y_1, y_2})$ in place of $M(y_1, y_2)$.

Hence, given the sequence of global state distributions y_{PQ}^h, we rearrange each element as illustrated in Fig. 2 and compute the associated mutual information, obtaining the sequence $M(y_P^h, y_Q^h)$.

Four such sequences are illustrated in Fig. 3. Depending on the structure of the bool net, the sequence of M values may stabilise or permanently enter an oscillatory phase. The red dotted lines in Fig. 3 provide a quite good approximation of the values of M in the long run, and are obtained by an attractor-based technique that we now illustrate.

Let GG denote the directed, global state transition graph of the (n, k)-bool net under study. GG has 2^n nodes – as many as the bit tuples of length n.

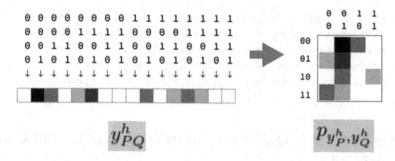

Fig. 2. Left: the y_{PQ}^h distribution assigns a probability, represented by a grey level, to each global state, represented as a quadruple of bits. Right: by stacking the 4 segments of length 4 from y_{PQ}^h we obtain the joint distribution matrix for the (coupled) variables y_P^h and y_Q^h.

The 16-node GG of a $(4,3)$-bool net is shown in Fig. 4. Each node of the graph represents a different state of the bool net, i.e. a quadruple of bits (only the node corresponding to $(0,0,0,0)$ is identified in the diagram).

The fact that bool net computations are deterministic has an impact on the general structure of GG. The graph may be formed by multiple weakly connected components (WCC) (the GG in Fig. 4 has three of them with, respectively, 10, 4 and 2 nodes). But each WCC has *exactly one attractor*, which can take the form of a cycle of nodes (two 4-node attractor cycles are found in the 10-node and 4-node WCC's) or a single node (one is found in the 2-node WCC). This general structure of each WCC is a direct consequence of the fact that the directed paths of GG cannot bifurcate.

For obtaining an intuitive idea about how distribution y_{PQ}^h develops from the initial distribution $\bar{x}_{PQ}$ as h progresses we can imagine 2^n 'agents', each initially placed on a different GG node, that simultaneously start moving synchronously along the directed paths of the graph. Assume we have m WCC's. Let $size(WWC(i))$ be the size of the i-th WCC, with $i = 1 \dots m$, and let $size(A(i))$ be the size of the attractor $A(i)$ of $WCC(i)$. Sooner or later each agent will be trapped in the attractor of the WWC where it was initially placed, and we will have $size(WWC(i))$ agents trapped in $A(i)$. All nodes that are not elements of an attractor will be deserted. For our approximation, we imagine these trapped agents to end up being *uniformly distributed* across the nodes of the attractor. In conclusion, for the approximate, asymptotic distribution y_{PQ}^* we can write:

$$
y_{PQ}^*(X) = \begin{cases} \gamma \dfrac{size(WWC(i))}{size(A(i))} & \text{if } X \in A(i) \\[2ex] 0 & \text{if } X \text{ is not in any attractor,} \end{cases} \tag{6}
$$

where γ is the normalisation factor that makes y_{PQ}^* a probability vector.

Once y_{PQ}^* is computed, the joint distribution matrix for variables y_P^* and y_Q^* is derived as illustrated in Fig. 2, and the associated value $M(y_P^*, y_Q^*)$ is

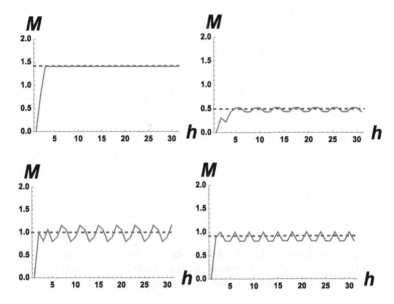

Fig. 3. Each of the four plots shows $M(y_P^h, y_Q^h)$ as a function of h, the number of computation steps, for a different bool net of form $P(2,2){<}\alpha{>}Q(2,2)$ (values of α are irrelevant here). The dotted red lines indicate the M values as computed by the approximation technique based on the attractors of the global state transition graph. (Color figure online)

obtained. The advantage of this technique is that it does not require to compute the sequence of distributions y_{PQ}^h (Eqs. 4 and 5); its accuracy is illustrated by the dotted lines of Fig. 3.

5.1 A Demonstration Tool

The attractor-based approximation technique described above has been implemented in Mathematica and is at the core of a freely downloadable Demonstration [3].

The tool interface is shown in Fig. 5. The upper portion of the panel offers selectors and cursors allowing the user to control various parameters:

- the number nn of bool net nodes – an even number, in light of the partition of the node set into parts P and Q of equal size;
- the arity k of the boolean functions associated to each node;
- the P-Q coupling factor – the number of bridges between P and Q, called α in the paper;
- the degree of visual separation ('P-Q unravel') between node sets P and Q, that facilitates the visualisation of bridges between them;
- the seed that triggers the random number generator that supports the construction of the net.

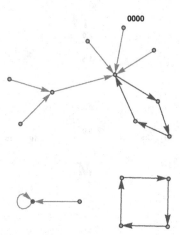

Fig. 4. The Global Graph of a $(4, 3)$-bool net, with three weakly connected components, each with one attractor. One of the attractors is a single node (in red). The other two attractors are cycles of four edges (in red). (Color figure online)

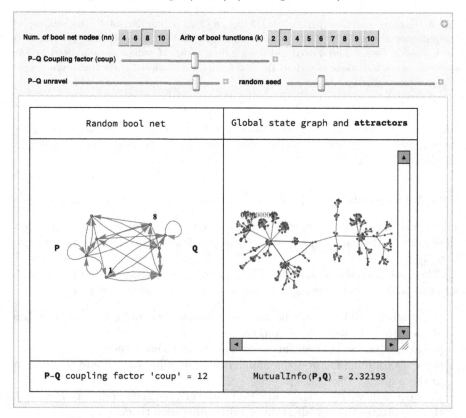

Fig. 5. The interface of Demonstration 'Mutual Information between Boolean Net Regions'.

The outputs are shown in the lower part of the panel. They include the bool net graph on the left and the global state graph GG on the right, with attractors highlighted in red. The lower-right field contains the value of approximate asymptotic mutual information, denoted $M(y_P^*, y_Q^*)$ in this paper.

6 Conclusions

We have investigated the degree of coupling that arises between the interconnected parts P and Q of a simple state transition model – boolean nets – as measured by the mutual information $M(y_P, y_Q)$ between their states, both after one step and after a large number of steps. This type of analysis requires one to view states as random variables, and transitions as relations between probabilistic distributions rather than definite states. With the 'one-step' analysis, we have elucidated the dependency between $M(y_P, y_Q)$ and the structural (syntactic) coupling between P and Q, as measured by the number α of bridge-edges between them. For the 'multi-step' analysis we have illustrated an accurate approximation technique that enables us to compute $M(y_P^*, y_Q^*)$ by simply exploiting the weakly connected components and the attractors of the deterministic, directed global state transition graph of the net. These features of the graph are readily computed by primitive functions of the *Mathematica* language.

This work can be seen as a preliminary step towards a more elaborate analysis of communication mechanisms within partitioned transition systems. We are not suggesting that information-theoretic measures such as entropy, mutual information, integrated information, and their variants, can *directly* support the design of communicating systems, at least as carried out in the area of Formal Methods for Software Engineering to which most contributions in the present volume refer. We do believe, however, that these measures, with their ability to treat *information* as a precisely measurable quantity, and to track information flows across space and time – from one process to another, from one partial or global state to the next – can provide a useful method (possibly, *the only method*) for assessing and comparing different communication paradigms on mathematically rigorous grounds.

Some of the possible developments are listed below.

- Beside the *shared-variable* communication mechanism, expressed here by notation $P<\alpha> Q$, one could study the process-algebraic, *shared-labelled-transition* mechanism, as expressed, e.g., by the LOTOS parallel composition operator $P|\beta|Q$ [4], where β is the set of communication labels, and compare the communication performance of the two paradigms in terms of quantities such as mutual information. (The idea to compose boolean networks by process-algebraic parallel composition is already explored, to a limited extent, in [2].).
- Beside the traditional, *synchronous* execution mode of boolean nets, one could consider an *asynchronous* mode in which at each step a single, randomly chosen node of the net fires, as it happens, for example, in traditional Petri nets. This mode of operation appears particularly appropriate when time

is assumed to be continuous, as opposed to discrete. The nondeterministic behaviours obtained in this way may enable further interesting comparisons with process algebraic systems.

- Beyond mutual information, one could characterise the degree of interaction/ integration between system parts by means of other, more sophisticated measures, as those adopted in IIT [1,7] – most notably integrated information 'Φ'.

References

1. Balduzzi, D., Tononi, G.: Integrated information in discrete dynamical systems: motivation and theoretical framework. PLoS Comput. Biol. **4**(6), e1000091 (2008)
2. Bolognesi, T.: LOTOS-like composition of Boolean nets and causal set construction. In: Katoen, J.-P., Langerak, R., Rensink, A. (eds.) ModelEd, TestEd, TrustEd - Essays Dedicated to Ed Brinksma on the Occasion of His 60th Birthday. LNCS, vol. 10500, pp. 27–47. Springer, Cham (2017). https://doi.org/10.1007/978-3-319-68270-9_2
3. Bolognesi, T.: Mutual information between Boolean net regions. The Wolfram Demonstrations Project (2018). https://demonstrations.wolfram.com/MutualInformationBetweenBooleanNetRegions/
4. Bolognesi, T., Brinksma, E.: Introduction to the ISO specification language LOTOS. Comput. Netw. ISDN Syst. **14**, 25–59 (1987)
5. Cover, T.M., Thomas, J.A.: Elements of Information Theory, 2nd edn. Wiley (2006)
6. Kauffman, S.A.: Homeostasis and differentiation in random genetic control networks. Nature **224**, 177–178 (1969)
7. Oizumi, M., Albantakis, L., Tononi, G.: From the Phenomenology to the mechanisms of consciousness: integrated information theory 3.0. PLoS Comput. Biol. **10**(5), e1003588 (2014)
8. Pearl, J.: Causality: Models, Reasoning and Inference, vol. 29. Cambridge University Press, Cambridge (2000)

Application of Model Checking to Fault Tolerance Analysis

Cinzia Bernardeschi$^{(\boxtimes)}$ (iD) and Andrea Domenici (iD)

Department of Information Engineering, University of Pisa, Pisa, Italy
{cinzia.bernardeschi,andrea.domenici}@ing.unipi.it

Abstract. A basic concept in modeling fault tolerant systems is that anticipated faults, being obviously outside of our control, may or may not occur. A fault tolerant system design can be proved to correctly behave under a given fault hypothesis, by proving the observational equivalence between the system design specification and the fault-free system specification. Additionally, model checking of a temporal logic formula which gives an abstract notion of correct behavior can be applied to verify the correctness of the design. Another activity that must be considered in fault tolerance is the issue of fault detection, since the existence of undetectable faults makes the system more vulnerable. The usage of model checking and temporal logic gives opportunities to better analyze the system behavior in presence of faults and to identify undetectable faults.

Keywords: Formal methods · Fault modeling · Fault tolerance

1 Introduction

Process algebras are a standard tool for the specification of concurrent systems. In order to specify a process and to prove its correctness, it is useful to decide which properties of the model are relevant and which ones can be ignored. Following [24], the semantics of processes is given in terms of labeled transition systems, which can describe their behavior in details, including their internal computations. It is common to define equivalences over labeled transition systems to verify if a process is a correct *implementation* of a *specification* process.

A widely used equivalence is *weak bisimulation,* or *observational* equivalence, first introduced by Milner [24], based on the idea that only the externally observable actions of a system are relevant in its interaction with the environment: Two systems are then observationally equivalent whenever no observation can distinguish them.

Model checking [12] is an alternative verification technique, in which the system is modeled using a process algebra or an automaton-based formalism and its correctness properties are expressed as temporal logic formulae [23].

Work partially supported by the Italian Ministry of Education and Research (MIUR) in the framework of the CrossLab project (Departments of Excellence).

M. H. ter Beek et al. (Eds.): Gnesi Festschrift, LNCS 11865, pp. 531–547, 2019.
https://doi.org/10.1007/978-3-030-30985-5_31

Then these formulae are automatically checked on the specification of the system. Proofs are carried out by exhaustive search of the transition system of the model.

In fault-tolerance analysis, the main goal is verifying that a system works correctly in the presence of a given set of *anticipated faults*. In absence of implementation techniques to detect, confine and recover from erroneous states, a system exhibits *failing behaviors* that deviate from the specified *normal*, or *correct*, behaviors. Different kinds of faults cause different kinds of failing behaviors, or *failure modes*, and the constraints on how faults are expected to occur in the system are expressed in the *fault hypothesis*. Given a set of anticipated faults, under a particular failure mode, a system is fault-tolerant with respect to the occurrence of faults as stated by the fault hypothesis if and only if the occurrence of such faults does not inhibit the system's ability to correctly satisfy its specification.

With the process-algebraic approach, checking for fault-tolerance is accomplished by defining a specification process that models the normal, or correct, behaviors, and an implementation process that models the possible behaviors in the presence of faults. The system is considered fault-tolerant with respect to the anticipated faults if the two processes are observationally equivalent.

This paper first discusses an issue related to the application of observational equivalence to fault-tolerance verification, then it reports results on the application of model-checking to the challenging problem of fault untestability in *Field Programmable Gate Array* (FPGA) devices.

As reported in [20], one problem of using bisimulation equivalence for fault tolerance is that proving fault tolerance towards a given set of faults does not imply fault tolerance towards a subset of those faults. A typical example is that of compensating faults such as the loss and creation of messages in a communication channel. Fault actions are modeled as alternatives to the correct ones, but according to the standard process algebra semantics, when the correct actions are not enabled the system is forced to execute the fault actions. In these situations, faults are no longer random events independent of the system logic. Moreover, one fault may compensate the effects of another fault. We may note, however, that the equivalence-based analysis in [20] is not sufficient to reveal some useful information in case of occurrence of faults, such as infinite loops. In this paper we use model checking to verify the system liveness under different conditions.

Single Event Upsets (SEU) faults are a main concern in the development of aerospace applications based on FPGAs [17]. Such applications operate in an environment exposed to cosmic radiations that increase the likelihood of hardware faults. Radiation-hardened devices are expensive, so it is convenient to use on-line testing and on-the-fly reconfiguration to cope with radiation-induced faults. Given the large number of possible faults, it is important to identify undetectable faults and to optimize the test set in order to reduce execution time and energy consumption for on-line testing. Finding untestable faults is therefore an important contribution to this purpose. The problem of fault untestability has been dealt with by modeling FPGA applications as state machines and using model checking to prove if the fault is untestable or not. In this paper, our previous work on FPGAs fault untestability is presented and related to the concept of system's fault tolerance.

The paper is structured as follows: Sect. 2 reports related work, Sect. 3 discusses the use of process algebras, observational equivalence, and model checking in the analysis of the alternating bit protocol with multiple faults, Sect. 4 describes the application of model checking to the problem of fault untestability of FPGAs, and Sect. 5 concludes the paper.

2   Related Work

A growing corpus of works on formal modeling and verification of fault tolerant systems has been produced, in particular concerning the application of process algebras and model checking. This section presents a small sample of the literature.

Partial model checking and μ-calculus are advocated by Gnesi et al. [16] to frame the problem of fault-tolerance verification within a general μ-calculus validation problem.

Francalanza and Hennessy [15] extend the Dπ language [18] to develop a behavioral theory of distributed programs in the presence of failures, using bisimulation equivalence to compare systems.

A formal framework for the specification and verification of fault tolerant system designs was presented in [9]. The work was focused on the possibility of using automatic verification tools, exemplifying the use of tools working on a particular process algebra and automata-based semantics (CCS/MEIJE and networks of automata [11]) and the temporal logic ACTL [13].

The specification and verification of the GUARDS Inter-consistency mechanism is reported in [7,8]. This fault-tolerance mechanism was developed within the European project GUARDS (Generic Upgradable Architecture for Real-time Dependable Systems [26]) as a component of an architecture for embedded safety-critical systems. The validation approach is based on model checking technique and exploits the verification methodology supported by the JACK environment [10].

A method for the verification of fault-tolerant distributed systems was presented by Jones and Pike [22], based on calendar automata [14] to model systems, and introducing the technique of *symbolic fault injection*. The SAL (*Symbolic Analysis Laboratory*) model checker [25] is used for verification.

The Promela modeling language and the SPIN model checker [19] are used by John et al. [21] to present an approach to model *threshold-guarded* distributed algorithms.

The present work is positioned on a line of research aiming at the application of automatic tools to fault analysis and assessment of fault tolerance. More specifically, Sect. 3 deals on the difficulty of correctly modeling the behavior of systems affected by multiple types of faults, while Sect. 4 shows how model checking can be used successfully to refine the search for faults in hardware devices.

3 Fault Tolerance for Systems with Multiple Faults

Assume specifications given using process algebras [24]. A system consists of a set of communicating processes; each process executes input and output actions, and synchronizes with other processes. Moreover, a special action τ denotes an unobservable action and model internal process actions or internal communications. The semantics of process algebras are Labeled Transition Systems (LTSs) which describe the behavior of a process in terms of states, and labeled transitions, which relate states.

To abstract unobservable moves during observation, the weak transition relation $\overset{a}{\Rightarrow}$ is used. We have: $\forall a \in Act$, $\overset{a}{\Rightarrow} = (\overset{\tau}{\rightarrow})^{\star} \overset{a}{\rightarrow} (\overset{\tau}{\rightarrow})^{\star}$, where $\star$ means zero or any number of times.

Observational equivalence ($\approx$ in the following) is then defined upon the $\overset{a}{\Rightarrow}$ relation.

Definition 1. *Given an LTS $\mathcal{A} = (X, x^0, Act \cup \{\tau\}, \rightarrow)$, a weak bisimulation equivalence over X is a maximal binary symmetric relation S such that, for any $x, y \in X$, we have xSy if and only if: $\forall a \in Act \cup \{\tau\}$,*
1. $x \overset{a}{\Rightarrow} x' \rightarrow (\exists y', y \overset{a}{\Rightarrow} y' \wedge x'Sy')$
2. $y \overset{a}{\Rightarrow} y' \rightarrow (\exists x', x \overset{a}{\Rightarrow} x' \wedge x'Sy')$

Two states x and y are considered as observational equivalent if and only if x and y must be able to perform equal sequences of actions evolving to equal (up to S) states. The relation between states of a transition system can be easily extended to a relation between two distinct transition systems.

Definition 2. *Given two processes R and Q, they are called* observational equivalent *if and only if a weak bisimulation S exists which relates the initial states of the LTSs which describe their behavior and we write $R \approx Q$.*

When observational equivalence is used to assess fault tolerance of a system with respect to a given set of anticipated faults, the issue of *fault monotonicity* must be considered. Simply stated, an equivalence criterion is fault monotonic if and only if fault tolerance of an implementation with respect to a set Φ of anticipated faults implies fault tolerance with respect to any subset Φ' of Φ.

Janowski [20] has shown that bisimulation is in general not fault-monotonic, using the alternating bit protocol as an example.

The purpose of the protocol is ensuring reliable communication over a medium which may loose messages. A possible implementation of the protocol (Fig. 2), similar to the one discussed in [20], consists of four processes: the Sender, the Receiver, and two communication channels: one for the delivery of the message, and another for the acknowledgment of message reception.

Sender and Receiver use the value of one bit to identify a message, so that the identifier bit of each message is the complement of the preceding message's bit; a new message is not sent until the sender receives acknowledgment of the current message. Since the channels can loose messages, both the Sender and the Receiver resend the same message or, respectively, acknowledgment repeatedly until the acknowledgment is received.

In the rest of this section, we show that the protocol tolerates a set of faults consisting in creation or omission of messages. The protocol tolerates also the subset consisting only in omission faults, but it does not tolerate the subset consisting only in creation faults.

We first consider an implementation Sys_{oc} of the protocol affected by the set $\Phi_{oc} = \{\text{omission}, \text{creation}\}$ of anticipated faults, i.e., we assume that the channels may drop messages or acknowledgments and also emit spurious ones, represented in CCS as in the following, where S_0 and R_1 are the Sender and Receiver, respectively, A_{oc} is the delivery channel, and B_{oc} the acknowledgment one:

$$S_0 = in.S_0'$$
$$S_0' = \overline{a_0}.S_0' + d_1.S_0' + d_0.S_1$$
$$S_1 = in.S_1'$$
$$S_1' = \overline{a_1}.S_1' + d_0.S_1' + d_1.S_0$$

$$A_{oc} = a_0.A_{oc0}' + a_1.A_{oc1}' + \overline{b_0}.A_{oc} + \overline{b_1}.A_{oc}$$
$$A_{oc0}' = \overline{b_0}.A_{oc} + \tau.A_{oc}$$
$$A_{oc1}' = \overline{b_1}.A_{oc} + \tau.A_{oc}$$

$$B_{oc} = c_0.B_{oc0}' + c_1.B_{oc1}' + \overline{d_0}.B_{oc} + \overline{d_1}.B_{oc}$$
$$B_{oc0}' = \overline{d_0}.B_{oc} + \tau.B_{oc}$$
$$B_{oc1}' = \overline{d_1}.B_{oc} + \tau.B_{oc}$$

$$R_1 = b_0.R_0' + b_1.R_1 + \overline{c_1}.R_1$$
$$R_0' = \overline{out}.R_0$$
$$R_0 = b_1.R_1' + b_0.R_0 + \overline{c_0}.R_0$$
$$R_1' = \overline{out}.R_1$$

$$L = \{a_0, a_1, b_0, b_1, c_0, c_1, d_0, d_1\}$$

$$Sys = (S_0|A_{oc}|B_{oc}|R_1)\backslash L.$$

The above system is represented in Fig. 1 as a network of communicating automata. Upon an in action at the system's external interface, the Sender sends the message to the Receiver through channel A_{oc} (A in the figure) by synchronizing on action a_0 or a_1 depending on the current value of the alternating bit (the first message is identified as 0). Upon receiving the message, the Receiver executes $\overline{out}$, meaning that the message is available at the interface. Next, the Receiver sends the acknowledgment by synchronizing with channel B_{oc} (B in the figure) on action c_0 or c_1 according to the value of the identifier bit of the received message.

Omission of messages or acknowledgments is represented by the τ actions in the processes for the channels, which can take a channel from state A'_{oc0} or A'_{oc1} (B'_{oc0} or B'_{oc1}) to A_{oc} (B_{oc}) without executing the corresponding synchronization action.

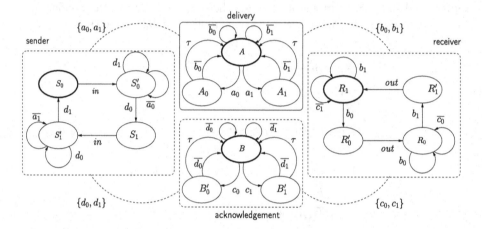

Fig. 1. Alternating bit protocol with omission or creation of messages or acknowledgments.

Creation is modeled by the additional transitions in state A_{oc} (B_{oc}), which execute a synchronization without changing state.

Fault tolerance of Sys_{oc} can be proved by checking that it is observationally equivalent to a process P (defined below) specifying the intended behavior, namely, the alternation of in and out actions:

$$Sys_{oc} = (S_0|A_{oc}|B_{oc}|R_1)\backslash L$$
$$P = in.\overline{out}.P$$
$$P \approx Sys_{oc}$$

The example shows tolerance to the creation and omission of messages of the protocol, in a context in which faults can freely occur.

Let us now consider a system Sys_o affected only by omission faults, i.e., $\Phi_o = \{omission\}$ is the set of anticipated faults. The CCS description of this system differs from the previous one in the channel processes, as shown in Fig. 2 and in the following code:

$$A = a_0.A_0' + a_1.A_1'$$
$$A_0' = \overline{b_0}.A + \tau.A$$
$$A_1' = \overline{b_1}.A + \tau.A$$

$$B = c_0.B_0' + c_1.B_1'$$
$$B_0' = \overline{d_0}.B + \tau.B$$
$$B_1' = \overline{d_1}.B + \tau.B$$

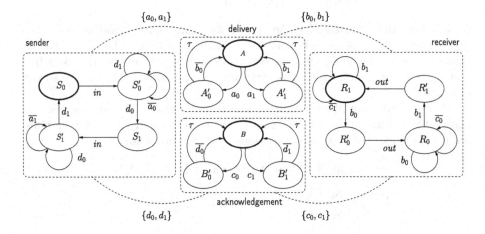

Fig. 2. Alternating bit protocol with omission.

The system can be proved to be observationally equivalent to process P.

$$Sys_o = (S_0|A_o|B_o|R_1) \backslash L$$
$$P = in.\overline{out}.P$$
$$P \approx Sys_o$$

If instead we consider a system Sys_c with channels that can misbehave only by creating messages or acknowledgments and not by dropping them, we would expect the implementation to be still fault tolerant, given that in this case the set $\Phi_c = \{\text{creation}\}$ of anticipated faults is a proper subset of Φ_{oc}. In this case, we have:

$$A_c = a_0.A'_{c0} + a_1.A'_1 + \overline{b_1}.A_c + \overline{b_0}.A_c$$
$$A'_{c0} = \overline{b_0}.A_c$$
$$A'_{c1} = \overline{b_1}.A_c$$

$$B_c = c_0.B'_{c0} + c_1.B'_{c1} + \overline{d_1}.B_c + \overline{d_0}.B_c$$
$$B'_{c0} = \overline{d_0}.B_c$$
$$B'_{c1} = \overline{d_1}.B_c$$

$$Sys_c = (S_0|A_c|B_c|R_1)\backslash L.$$

It is immediate to show that Sys_c is not observationally equivalent to P, thus proving that bisimulation is in general not fault-monotonic. Therefore, proving that a system with more faults is observationally equivalent to the fault-free system does not guarantee that observational equivalence holds for any subset of faults.

However, we may observe that in this case creation faults are modeled as observable actions on the same footing as the correct behavior. It may be more natural to model them as internal actions as shown below for Φ_c:

$$AA_c = a_0.AA'_0 + a_1.AA'_1 + \tau.\overline{b_1}.AA_c + \tau.\overline{b_0}.AA_c$$
$$AA'_0 = \overline{b_0}.AA_c$$
$$AA'_1 = \overline{b_1}.AA_c$$

$$BB_c = c_0.BB'_{c0} + c_1.BB'_{c1} + \tau.\overline{d_1}.BB_c + \tau.\overline{d_0}.BB_c$$
$$BB'_{c0} = \overline{d_0}.BB_c$$
$$BB'_{c1} = \overline{d_1}.BB_c.$$

The case for Φ_{oc} is handled similarly.

In this case, observational equivalence is not satisfied in either case: creation faults only, and omission and creation faults.

In addition, observational equivalence between the behavior of the fault free system and that of the system affected by faults does not reveal some useful information in case of occurrence of faults. For example, infinite loops of τ actions could not be detected. It is then advisable to introduce model checking of temporal logic formulae to complement the techniques based on bi-simulation.

First, checking temporal logic properties of a specification by model checking allows the specification to be validated. For example, we can use μ-calculus to express the property that action $\overline{out}$ will eventually be executed (a minimal sanity check), with the formula

$$\alpha \triangleq \mu.Z(<-> tt \wedge [-out]Z).$$

Model checking shows that α holds unsurprisingly for P, but it does not hold for any of the implementations considered above. This is caused by the fact that channels may drop messages or acknowledgments indefinitely by executing τ actions.

The failure to prove property α shows that there exists a path in which out is not executed. This is caused by cycles in which messages can be created and lost. And what we can see is that such property is false also on the original version of the protocol, with omission only. This because the specification of the protocol allows the Sender (Receiver) to re-send or loose the same message an unbounded number of times.

Other properties of the fault tolerant system can be proved by model checking if actions modeling faults are made explicit. In this case we can prove for example, that the system satisfies property α in case of one omission fault. What can be done is to state an assumption on fault occurrences, and prove tolerance in that specific case.

In real system modeling, this approach reduces the state space explosion problem. From the specification point of view, explicit actions modeling faults and a new process, the fault hypothesis process, which synchronizes with the system and states the possible occurrences of faults, are introduced in the specification.

4   Untestability of Faults: SEUs in SRAM-Based FPGAs

Fault tolerance relies both on fault masking and fault detection. In the latter activity, also the issue of fault detectability must be considered, since the existence of undetectable faults makes the system more vulnerable.

SRAM-based FPGAs are programmable devices made of logic blocks interconnected by switch elements called *switch boxes*, in a structure shown in a very simplified and scaled-down way by Fig. 3. A logic block contains a small number of memory elements and combinatorial logic. The latter is implemented with configurable *look-up tables* (LUT), which behave logically as associative memories mapping each combination of inputs to the corresponding value of a given Boolean function. Figure 4(a) is a logical representation, as a Karnaugh map, of a LUT configured to implement the disjunction of its four inputs.

A switch box is a matrix of switches called *Programmable Interconnect Points* (PIPs) [27], which route signals by connecting pairs of wires. An example of switch-box is shown in Fig. 5(a), where P_i and P_j are PIPs; P_i is programmed to connect the input wire A to the output wire B. Similarly, P_j is programmed to connect the input wire C to the output wire D. The connection between two wires, such as A to B, is called a *routing segment*.

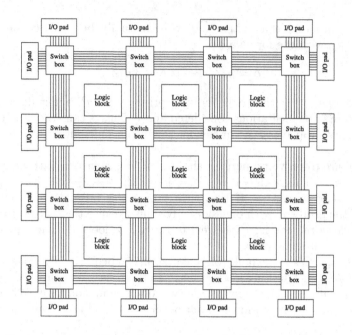

Fig. 3. Structure of an FPGA.

Programming an SRAM-FPGA device consists in downloading a configuration code, called a bitstream, into its configuration memory. The bitstream determines the functionality of each LUT and the configuration of the PIPs. The bitstream is generated by a tool from a high-level hardware design language (e.g., Verilog or VHDL). As an intermediate step, the Verilog/VHDL description is synthesized into a *logic netlist* showing the logical interconnections of FPGA components, such as LUTs and memory elements. Figure 6 shows a simplified logic netlist for a system composed of three 2-input LUTs, one D flip-flop, a clock generator, two input buffers (i.e., signal amplifiers), and one output buffer. The LUTs implement two AND and one OR gate.

In a further step, the logic netlist is transformed into a *place-and-routed netlist* including information on the physical placement of the components and on the configuration of the switch boxes.

Both LUTs and switch boxes are affected by various types of faults, including *Single Event Upsets* (SEU), caused by radiations, especially in aerospace applications [2]. SEUs affecting a LUT change its logic function, whereas those affecting a switch box modify the interconnection topology among logic blocks.

An example of a faulty LUT is shown in Fig. 4(b), where the dashed box represents a SEU that flips a bit from 1 to 0, so that the LUT maps the input vector (1111) to the output 0. However, the output of the faulty LUT differs from the one of the fault-free LUT only for that specific input. That fault is activated only when the input associated with the faulty configuration bit is applied to the LUT.

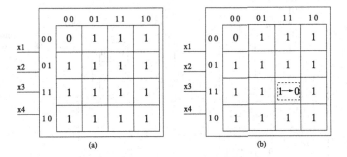

Fig. 4. A LUT and the effect of a SEU.

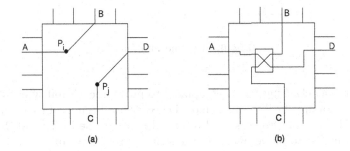

Fig. 5. (a) A switch-box; (b) effect of bridge fault.

A SEU in the configuration memory of PIPs may cause several types of topological modifications [28] that manifest themselves as logical faults on the output wires of the affected switch box [1], namely: *stuck-at-0* (*stuck-at-1*), when a wire is stuck at the 0 (1) logic value; *bridge*, when the values of two wires are exchanged; *wired-AND* (*wired-OR*), when the value of an output wire is the AND (OR) of the values of two input wires; and *wired-MIX*, when the values of two output wires B and D are mixed so that they keep their correct values if the values of the respective input wires are equal, otherwise they take the complementary values. Figure 5(b) shows the effects of a logical bridge fault.

When FPGAs are used in safety-critical applications, on-line testing is one of the methods that can be applied at run-time to detect SEUs, and possibly reconfigure the FPGA. Testing relies on a pre-computed set of test patterns, and it is important to optimize this set with respect to the contrasting goals of maximum fault coverage and minimum execution time and resource usage. One way of optimizing the test set is finding offline the faults that can be excluded from the set because they are undetectable, i.e., they are either unexcitable or masked. A fault is *unexcitable* if the combination of input values that could activate it will never be fed to the affected component. A fault is *masked* if it cannot propagate wrong values to the external pins of the device.

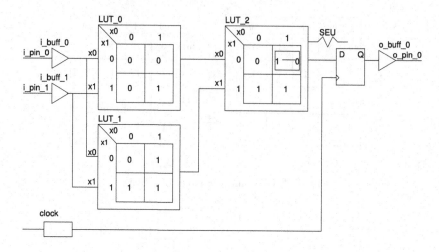

Fig. 6. SEU unexcitability.

In [6], model checking has been applied to prove unexcitability of SEUs and the counter-example facility of the model checker has been used to generate test patterns. The logic netlist was used to model faults in the LUTs and the route-and-placed netlist to model faults in the switch boxes. For faults in a LUT, the logic function of the faulty LUT was generated; for faults in the interconnect, their logical effects were modeled. The routing faults and their effects were computed using an external tool, E^2STAR [6], that operates on the place-and-routed netlist.

The behavioral model of the FPGA application is built in the Symbolic Analysis Laboratory (SAL) framework [25], and the unexcitability property is expressed as an LTL logic formula that checks whether the configuration activating the fault can be generated, starting from any possible input sequence of the FPGA.

The SAL input language describes a system (*context*) as the parallel composition of *modules*, each representing a state machine defined by its input, local, and output variables, by definitions equating variable values to functions of other variables, and by transitions equating the *next* values of variables (denoted by primes) to functions of the current state.

The SAL code for the netlist shown in Fig. 6 is reported in Fig. 7. In this case, only one module is sufficient. The behavior of LUTs and buffers is described by definitions:

- the behavior of LUTs is described by the corresponding logic functions;
- the behavior of an input buffer is described as an assignment between a local variable, modeling the buffer, and an input variable, modeling the associated input pin;
- similarly, two local variables are used for output buffers, one modeling the buffer and the other modeling the output pin.

```
netlist : CONTEXT =
BEGIN
    circuit: MODULE =
    BEGIN
        INPUT i_pin_0: BOOLEAN;          INPUT i_pin_1: BOOLEAN;
        OUTPUT o_pin_0: BOOLEAN;
        LOCAL i_buff_0: BOOLEAN;         LOCAL i_buff_1: BOOLEAN;
        LOCAL LUT_0: BOOLEAN;            LOCAL LUT_1: BOOLEAN;
        LOCAL LUT_2: BOOLEAN;
        LOCAL d_ff_0: BOOLEAN;           LOCAL O_buff_0: BOOLEAN;
    DEFINITION
        i_buff_0 = i_pin_0;              i_buff_1 = i_pin_0;
        LUT_0 = (i_buff_0 AND i_buff_1); LUT_1 = (i_buff_0 OR i_buff_1);
        LUT_2 = (i_LUT_0 OR LUT_1);
        o_buff_0 = d_ff_0;               o_pin_0 = o_buff_0;
    INITIALIZATION
        d_ff_0 = FALSE;
    TRANSITION
        d_ff_0' = LUT_2;
    END;
END
```

Fig. 7. SAL specification.

Flip-flops are described by transitions, that are executed at each clock cycle.

If a fault f in an n-input LUT affects a location corresponding to the input vector $i_f = (v_0, v_1, \ldots v_{n-1})$ (e.g., $i_f = (10)$ in LUT_2 of Fig. 6), fault f is unexcitable if the configuration i_f can never occur in the context C modeling the whole system [4], therefore the property of unexcitability in LTL has the general form

$$C \vdash \mathbf{G}(\neg(x_0 = v_0 \wedge x_1 = v_1 \wedge \cdots \wedge x_n = v_{n-1})).$$

The unexcitability property for the SEU in the configuration bit of LUT_2 associated with input (10) is then

```
unex_LUT_2_10: THEOREM
    circuit |- G(NOT(LUT_0 = TRUE AND LUT_1 = FALSE));
```

The theorem holds, since this fault can never be excited, because it is not possible that the output of LUT_1 is 0 while the output of LUT_0 is 1 (Fig. 6), because LUT_1 implements the OR function, and LUT_0 implements the AND of the same input signals. Similarly, the formula for the SEU in the configuration bit of LUT_0 associated with input 11 is the following:

```
unex_LUT_0_11: THEOREM
    circuit |- G(NOT(i_buff_0 = TRUE AND i_buff_1 = TRUE));
```

Table 1. Unexcitability formulae for routing faults.

s-a-0 on P_i	$C \vdash \mathbf{G}(\neg(\hat{A}))$
s-a-1 on P_i	$C \vdash \mathbf{G}(\neg(\neg\hat{A}))$
bridge between P_i and P_j	$C \vdash \mathbf{G}(\neg(\hat{A} \neq \hat{C}))$
Wired-AND between P_i and P_j	$C \vdash \mathbf{G}(\neg((\hat{A} \neq (\hat{A} \wedge \hat{C})) \vee (\hat{C} \neq (\hat{A} \wedge \hat{C}))))$
Wired-OR between P_i and P_j	$C \vdash \mathbf{G}(\neg((\hat{A} \neq (\hat{A} \vee \hat{C})) \vee (\hat{C} \neq (\hat{A} \vee \hat{C}))))$
Wired-MIX between P_i and P_j	$C \vdash \mathbf{G}(\neg((\hat{A} \neq \hat{C}) \wedge (\neg\hat{A} \vee \hat{C})))$

This theorem does not hold, and a trivial counter-example is shown:

```
Counter_example: (i_pin_0 = true, i_pin_1 =true)
```

The formulae for routing faults in the switch box of Fig. 6, referring to the logical netlist, are shown in Table 1, where $\hat{A}$ and $\hat{C}$ are the values of A and C (true if equals to 1, false otherwise) [5]. A Stuck-at 0 (1) on P_i is unexcitable if the signal on A is always 0 (1). A Bridge between P_i and P_j is unexcitable if the value of A always equals the value of C. A Wired-AND between P_i and P_j is unexcitable if the value of A always equals $A \wedge C$ and the value of C always equals $A \wedge C$. A Wired-OR between P_i and P_j is unexcitable if the value of A always equals $A \vee C$ and the value of C always equals $A \vee C$. A Wired-MIX between P_i and P_j is unexcitable if (i) the value of A always equals the output of C or (ii) the value of A is 1 and the value of C is 0, or vice versa. The unexcitability theorem associated with the Bridge fault in Fig. 5 is:

```
unex: THEOREM circuit |- G(NOT(B=D));
```

Experimental results [6] show that a substantial number of SEU faults are not excitable. Knowing which faults are unexcitable reduces significantly the time needed for test pattern generation and testing. In the same framework, untestability of faults, that includes both unexcitability and fault masking, is analyzed. Masked faults are found by comparing the values at the output pins of the fault-free system to the values at the output pins of the faulty system at each clock cycle, considering the full end-to-end paths from input to output. The counter-example gives information on the test vector that must be applied at every input to test the fault. The ability of model checkers to produce counter-examples has been used in our framework to generate test patterns for testable faults, optimized with a genetic algorithm [3].

5   Conclusions

This work reports on applications of model checking to different issues related to fault tolerance. In particular, the problem of assessing fault tolerance in systems with multiple faults modeled with process algebras has been discussed, and a method to analyze untestability of hardware faults has been presented. Model checking has been shown as useful complement to methods based on weak-bisimulation equivalence. Model checking on state-machine based models has been shown experimentally to be an effective tool to improve the performance of on-line testing for systems affected by radiation faults.

During the development of this work, the issue has arisen of expressing faults and failure modes in a state-based formalism instead of an action-based one. This issue opens interesting perspectives for future work.

Acknowledgments. Working with Stefania has been both a challenge and a pleasure. Her rigorous approach, knowledge, experience and insight, together with her collaborative attitude and general friendliness have been a source of inspiration and motivation not only behind the work done together, but also in other research fields.

References

1. Battezzati, N., Sterpone, L., Violante, M.: Reconfigurable Field Programmable Gate Arrays for Mission-Critical Application. Springer, New York (2011). https://doi.org/10.1007/978-1-4419-7595-9

2. Baumann, R.C.: Radiation-induced soft errors in advanced semiconductor technologies. IEEE Trans. Device Mater. Reliab. **5**(3), 305–316 (2005). https://doi.org/10.1109/TDMR.2005.853449

3. Bernardeschi, C., Cassano, L., Cimino, M.G., Domenici, A.: GABES: a genetic algorithm based environment for SEU testing in SRAM-FPGAs. J. Syst. Architect. **59**(10, Part D), 1383–1254 (2013). https://doi.org/10.1016/j.sysarc.2013.10.006, http://www.sciencedirect.com/science/article/pii/S1383762113001975

4. Bernardeschi, C., Cassano, L., Domenici, A.: SEU-X: a SEU un-excitability prover for SRAM-FPGAs. In: 18th IEEE International On-Line Testing Symposium, IOLTS 2012, pp. 25–30 (2012)

5. Bernardeschi, C., Cassano, L., Domenici, A., Sterpone, L.: Unexcitability analysis of SEus affecting the routing structure of SRAM-based FPGAs. In: Great Lakes Symposium on VLSI 2013 (part of ECRC), GLSVLSI 2013, Paris, 2–4 May 2013, pp. 7–12 (2013)

6. Bernardeschi, C., Cassano, L., Domenici, A., Sterpone, L.: UA^{2}TPG: an untestability analyzer and test pattern generator for SEUs in the configuration memory of SRAM-based FPGAs. Integration **55**, 85–97 (2016). https://doi.org/10.1016/j.vlsi.2016.03.004

7. Bernardeschi, C., Fantechi, A., Gnesi, S.: Formal validation of the GUARDS inter-consistency mechanism. In: Felici, M., Kanoun, K. (eds.) SAFECOMP 1999. LNCS, vol. 1698, pp. 420–430. Springer, Heidelberg (1999). https://doi.org/10.1007/3-540-48249-0_36

8. Bernardeschi, C., Fantechi, A., Gnesi, S.: Formal validation of fault-tolerance mechanisms inside GUARDS. Reliab. Eng. Syst. Saf. **71**(3), 261–270 (2001). https://doi.org/10.1016/S0951-8320(00)00078-8

9. Bernardeschi, C., Fantechi, A., Simoncini, L.: Formally verifying fault tolerant system designs. Comput. J. **43**(3), 191–205 (2000). https://doi.org/10.1093/comjnl/43.3.191

10. Bouali, A., Gnesi, S., Larosa, S.: The integration project for the JACK environment. Technical report CS-R9443, Centrum voor Wiskunde en Informatica, Amsterdam, The Netherlands (1994)

11. Boudol, G.: Notes on algebraic calculi of processes. In: Apt, K. (ed.) Logics and Models of Concurrent Systems. NATO ASI Series (Series F: Computer and Systems Sciences), vol. 13, pp. 261–303. Springer, Heidelberg (1985). https://doi.org/10.1007/978-3-642-82453-1_9

12. Clarke, E.M., Emerson, E.A., Sistla, A.P.: Automatic verification of finite-state concurrent systems using temporal logic specifications. ACM Trans. Program. Lang. Syst. **8**(2), 244–263 (1986). https://doi.org/10.1145/5397.5399

13. De Nicola, R., Fantechi, A., Gnesi, S., Ristori, G.: An action based framework for verifying logical and behavioural properties of concurrent systems. In: Larsen, K.G., Skou, A. (eds.) CAV 1991. LNCS, vol. 575, pp. 37–47. Springer, Heidelberg (1992). https://doi.org/10.1007/3-540-55179-4_5

14. Dutertre, B., Sorea, M.: Modeling and verification of a fault-tolerant real-time startup protocol using calendar automata. In: Lakhnech, Y., Yovine, S. (eds.) FORMATS/FTRTFT -2004. LNCS, vol. 3253, pp. 199–214. Springer, Heidelberg (2004). https://doi.org/10.1007/978-3-540-30206-3_15

15. Francalanza, A., Hennessy, M.: A theory of system behaviour in the presence of node and link failures. In: Abadi, M., de Alfaro, L. (eds.) CONCUR 2005. LNCS, vol. 3653, pp. 368–382. Springer, Heidelberg (2005). https://doi.org/10.1007/11539452_29

16. Gnesi, S., Lenzini, G., Martinelli, F.: Logical specification and analysis of fault tolerant systems through partial model checking. Electron. Notes Theor. Comput. Sci. **118**, 57–70 (2005). https://doi.org/10.1016/j.entcs.2004.09.032

17. Graham, P., Caffrey, M., Zimmerman, J., Sundararajan, P., Johnson, E.: Consequences and categories of SRAM FPGA configuration SEUs. In: In Proceedings of the International Conference on Military and Aerospace Programmable Logic Devices (MAPLD 2003 (2003)

18. Hennessy, M., Riely, J.: Resource access control in systems of mobile agents. Inf. Comput. **173**(1), 82–120 (2002). https://doi.org/10.1006/inco.2001.3089

19. Holzmann, G.J.: The model checker SPIN. IEEE Trans. Softw. Eng. **23**(5), 279–295 (1997). https://doi.org/10.1109/32.588521

20. Janowski, T.: On bisimulation, fault-monotonicity and provable fault-tolerance. In: Johnson, M. (ed.) AMAST 1997. LNCS, vol. 1349, pp. 292–306. Springer, Heidelberg (1997). https://doi.org/10.1007/BFb0000478

21. John, A., Konnov, I., Schmid, U., Veith, H., Widder, J.: Towards modeling and model checking fault-tolerant distributed algorithms. In: Bartocci, E., Ramakrishnan, C.R. (eds.) SPIN 2013. LNCS, vol. 7976, pp. 209–226. Springer, Heidelberg (2013). https://doi.org/10.1007/978-3-642-39176-7_14

22. Jones, B.F., Pike, L.: Modular model-checking of a byzantine fault-tolerant protocol. In: Barrett, C., Davies, M., Kahsai, T. (eds.) NFM 2017. LNCS, vol. 10227, pp. 163–177. Springer, Cham (2017). https://doi.org/10.1007/978-3-319-57288-8_12

23. Manna, Z., Pnueli, A.: The Temporal Logic of Reactive and Concurrent Systems - Specification. Springer, Heidelberg (1992). https://doi.org/10.1007/978-1-4612-0931-7

24. Milner, R.: Communication and Concurrency. Prentice-Hall Inc, Upper Saddle River (1989)

25. de Moura, L., et al.: SAL 2. In: Alur, R., Peled, D.A. (eds.) CAV 2004. LNCS, vol. 3114, pp. 496–500. Springer, Heidelberg (2004). https://doi.org/10.1007/978-3-540-27813-9_45

26. Powell, D., et al.: GUARDS: a generic upgradable architecture for real-time dependable systems. IEEE Trans. Parallel Distrib. Syst. **10**(6), 580–599 (1999). https://doi.org/10.1109/71.774908
27. Rodriguez-Andina, J., Moure, M., Valdes, M.: Features, design tools, and application domains of FPGAs. IEEE Trans. Industr. Electron. **54**(4), 1810–1823 (2007). https://doi.org/10.1109/TIE.2007.898279
28. Sterpone, L., et al.: Experimental validation of a tool for predicting the effects of soft errors in SRAM-based FPGAs. IEEE Trans. Nucl. Sci. **54**(6), 2576–2583 (2007). https://doi.org/10.1109/TNS.2007.910122

How Formal Methods Can Contribute to 5G Networks

María-del-Mar Gallardo, Francisco Luque-Schempp, Pedro Merino-Gómez[✉],
and Laura Panizo

Universidad de Málaga, Andalucia Tech, Málaga, Spain
{gallardo,fls,pedro,laurapanizo}@lcc.uma.es

Abstract. Communication networks have been one of the main drivers
of formal methods since the 70's. The dominant role of software in the
new 5G mobile communication networks will once again foster a relevant application area for formal models and techniques like model checking, model-based testing or runtime verification. This chapter introduces
some of these novel application areas, specifically for Software Defined
Networks (SDN) and Network Function Virtualization (NFV). Our proposals focus on automated methods to create formal models that satisfy
a given set of requirements for SDN and NFV.

Keywords: 5G networks · Software Defined Networks ·
Network Function Virtualization · New Internet Protocols ·
Model checking · Model-based testing

1 Introduction

Formal method techniques and tools have been very close to protocol engineering
since the 70's, when the first errors in communication protocols were detected
with reachability analysis over their models in finite state machines [31]. In the
80's and 90's, standardization bodies in information and communication technologies, like ISO and ITU, recognized the benefits of formal modelling and automatic verification with languages like LOTOS, ESTELLE, SDL and, later, the
sequence charts in UML. The paper by Bochmann et al. [3] is a good summary of
the history of Protocol Engineering in those decades. Another relevant milestone
at the beginning of the 21st century is the ACM System Award to SPIN, a tool
originally designed to support protocol design and validation [14,15]. However,
in recent years, the applications of formal methods for communication networks
seem to be less significant. In this position paper, we argue that 5G mobile
communication networks could once again reinforce the role of communication
networks and protocols as a relevant application domain for formal methods.

This work is partially supported by the projects EuWireless and 5GENESIS. These
projects have received funding from the European Union's Horizon 2020 research and
innovation programme under grant agreements No. 777517 and No. 815178, respectively.

M. H. ter Beek et al. (Eds.): Gnesi Festschrift, LNCS 11865, pp. 548–571, 2019.
https://doi.org/10.1007/978-3-030-30985-5_32

Mobile communication networks are evolving towards new paradigms in which softwarization is one of the key aspects. In particular, one of the most important features of 5G networks is the shift of vendor-locked networks to cloud-based systems to dynamically adapt the network to the changing user needs. To achieve these objectives, 5G networks implement the so-called *network slice*, which is similar to a private network tailored to run a service with specific *Key Performance Indicators* (KPI). For instance, a critical service, such as telesurgery, imposes hard constraints on packet latency (under 5 ms) in order to control a surgeon robot over a cellular network. Other services, such as high-resolution content delivery, require high downlink or uplink speed. In 5G networks, each kind of service will run on a different network slice that satisfies its performance and quality of service requirements, but all these network slices will be deployed over the same underlying infrastructure.

The implementation of the network slices will be feasible mainly thanks to two technologies: Software-Defined Networks (SDN) and Network Function Virtualization (NFV). SDN makes the key components in the network, the switches and routers, programmable and that way a single program can control aspects like traffic priorities, firewall capabilities or forwarding rules from a single point. NFV removes the vendor-locked network elements and provides a cloud-like method to deploy software versions of these components on demand.

The increasing presence and complexity of software in 5G networks will introduce new risks related to reliability and security, and will make it more difficult to predict the behavior of the whole system in case of an accident or on-purpose malfunctioning of some parts of the network. Continuous monitoring and other techniques from network operators will be more complex, but they will be useful at production time. Like in other application domains, formal methods could provide tremendous benefits by helping to design, deploy and operate such a complex system with analysis before the deployment of the network. Recently, some authors have been using different formal methods to ensure the correct deployment and configuration of SDNs [1,2,4,5,17,18,20,21]. One of the first works is the NICE [4] tool, that combines symbolic model checking and different search strategies to find errors, for instance, host reachability problems or undesirable packet lost. Compared to a general purpose model checking tool, NICE can directly analyze the code of the software governing the network. Although NFV technology is more recent, there are also proposals [22,28,34] to integrate Verification and Validation processes in the NFV deployment cycle, as well as not only to find functional bugs in the network but also to ensure the performance requirements [29,30], which is a very important issue in 5G networks. Most of these works are not connected to testbeds where some realistic experimentation can be combined with the models and the automatic analysis.

In the chapter, we propose the use of formal methods focusing on two aspects. First, modelling the SDN component of the network and checking that there are model instances satisfying a set of requirements, and second, the use of model-based testing and runtime verification to help in the placement and reconfiguration of Virtual Network Functions (VNFs) deployments. Both applications can be allocated in the area of automated synthesis of formal models, and in the wider context of Formal Methods for Industrial Critical Systems (FMICS). The term FMICS and the FMICS Working Group[1] is the main link between the first authors of the paper and Stefania Gnesi. Stefania was one of the founders and chair of FMICS WG and we have collaborated with her in the organization of the annual FMICS workshops and special publications. A relevant collaborative work co-led by Stefania is the book Formal Methods for Industrial Critical Systems: A Survey of Applications [11]. Actually, the SDN and VFV technologies addressed in this chapter are the evolution of the active networks paradigm that we presented as a chapter in Stefania's book in 2013 [10].

The paper is organized as follows. Section 2 introduces the 5G architecture and the relevant concept of network slicing. Section 3 provides a description of the SDN technology and our proposal to use the formal language Alloy [16] as the modelling language to support the synthesis of valid models from a given set of requirements. In Sect. 4, we present Network Function Virtualization as support technology of network slicing, and we propose combining model-based testing and runtime verification to solve the problem of placement and reconfiguration of VNFs in the network. Finally, in Sects. 5 and 6 we review the related work and provide some conclusions.

2   Background on 5G Networks

2.1   Architecture of the Network

One of the objectives of 5G networks is to support network operators to rapidly and flexibly deploy new services in order to meet customers' and verticals' needs. In this context, verticals refers to industrial sectors such as transport, media or manufacturing, whose digitalization and innovation relies on services with specific and different requirements. The 5G network architecture [9] aims to address these challenges using SDN and NFV as technical enablers. Figure 1 shows an overview of the network architecture. As can be seen, it is built on the three main domains that are also present in the previous 4G technology: radio access network (composed of the user equipment and the gNB access nodes), the transport network (a logical connection thanks to switches, aggregation points and communication links) and the core network. The main differences with respect to 4G networks are the technologies in each domain and the deployment of the services as part of the network (AF component in the figure). In the radio part, the new standard is called 5G NR (5G new radio) and offers features like lower latency and higher capacity than 4G networks. In the core network, the functionality is implemented with a number of software modules and interfaces following the standards to create a 5G core. It is expected that these 5G core VNFs will be deployed as VNFs in a central cloud. In the transport network, the switches are replaced with programmable OpenFlow switches, and the whole network is defined with apps running on top of the SDN controller.

---

[1] http://fmics.inria.fr/.

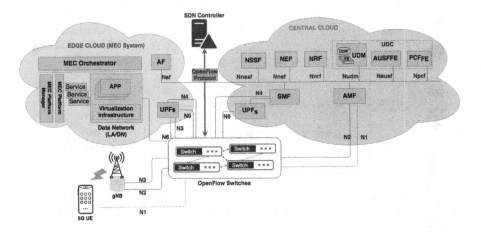

Fig. 1. 5G architecture

From the service provider perspective, the main novelty is the integration of the software to implement the service as part of the network thanks to the deployment of their own VNFs jointly with the 5G core VNFs and other network-oriented VNFs (e.g. caches and firewalls) in the same cloud. *Multi-access Edge Computing* (MEC) technology appears in order to have a computing platform within the RAN and in close proximity of users. MEC provides features like low latency, high bandwidth and proximity; sometimes MEC are called *Point of Presence* (PoP), which resources are shared by multiple VNFs (virtual machines installed on top). Thanks to the MEC location at the mobile edge, routing data that previously had to be sent to the core of the network can be eliminated and achieve a very low latency.

2.2 Slices for Verticals

Network slicing allows *Mobile Network Operators* (MNOs) to manage multiple virtual networks using a common shared physical infrastructure. These virtual networks enable a virtual partition of the RAN (Radio Access Network), the core network and the switching and aggregation network. Roughly speaking, Fig. 1 represents one slice, and a second slice could be created by assigning part of the RAN resources and adding more VNFs in the Edge cloud and the Central cloud to provide functionalities of 5G core and services. Each virtual network is created to provide a specific service with specific requirements that usually fit three profiles:

- **enhanced Mobile Broadband** (eMBB). It has the purpose of addressing the traffic demand that increases on a daily basis due to the number of users and new applications with increasingly demanding traffic requirements. Use cases related to multi-media content and data that are a very high throughput requirement (e.g. augmented reality or 4k video streaming).

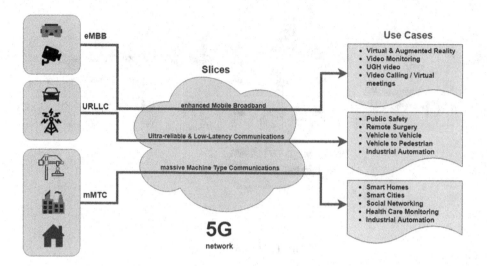

Fig. 2. 5G usage scenarios

- **Ultra Reliable Low Latency Communications** (URLLC). It is oriented to low latency and high reliability transmissions, usually with low packet size. Use cases related to critical applications (e.g. remote surgery or connected cars).
- **massive Machine Type Communications** (mMTC). It is oriented to a very large number of connected devices, usually with a low data transmission and non-delay sensitive data. Use cases related to the Internet of Things, where devices are required to have a long battery life (e.g. smart meters or sensor networks).

Figure 2 shows some usage scenarios where virtual networks mentioned above, known as *Network Slices*, help to provide a service that depends on use case requirements.

In the next sections, we present more details of the SDN and NFV technologies before describing the use of formal methods for both topics.

3   Software Defined Networks

3.1   The Technology

Software Defined Network [26,32] (SDN) is a new paradigm for deploying highly programmable and flexible communication networks. To this end, the control and data planes of the network are clearly separated. In addition, from the logical point of view, the control plane is a single entity that has a global view of the network at each time instant and can modify the data plane to achieve specific goals. Figure 3 shows the high-level architecture of a SDN:

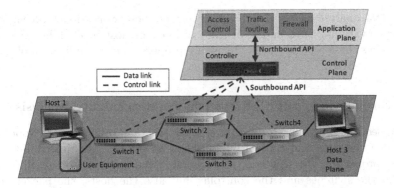

Fig. 3. Basic SDN architecture

- The **data plane** includes simple and programmable forwarding devices (switches) that route the traffic. To do this, each switch has a *routing table* with complex rules that specify the outgoing path for each input packet.
- The **control plane** comprises the controllers that carry out the configuration and management of the network. From the logical point of view, the control is centralized in an entity that has a global view of the network. However, the control plane can be implemented as a distributed set of controllers that communicate with each other using the east/westbound interfaces. The control plane offers interfaces to communicate with the other two layers. The southbound is used to control the data plane devices; for instance, to install the rules in the routing tables. There are different protocols that can be used in the southbound; currently the most popular is OpenFlow [23]. The northbound is used to communicate the controller with the applications. Usually, the controller provides its own API for applications. NOX [12] and POX [27] are two of the most used OpenFlow controllers.
- The **application plane** consists of a pool of applications that specify high-level management policies, such as routing, security or monitoring. SDN applications are dynamic in the sense that they can command the installation of new rules based on the state of the network

Thus, an SDN is a complex concurrent event-driven distributed system whose behavior is dynamically defined by the network applications. The separation of planes and the dependency on software introduces new challenges from the reliability point of view, such as the interaction of distributed controllers that must act as a single entity, or the dynamic update of the routing tables that lead to changes in the data plane topology. In addition, the adoption of SDN as an enabling technology of 5G networks introduces more challenging issues. For instance, 5G networks are characterized by the deployment of network slices for specific services or verticals. In this case, it is important to ensure not only the isolation of the slices but also to verify that these slices can support specific services with a predefined Quality of Service (QoS) and Quality of Experience (QoE). In the recent years, formal methods have used different approaches to model and analyze SDNs [2,4,17,21]. Most of these works focus on verifying network invariants, such as the absence of loops or host reachability. Section 5 summarizes these related works. Below, we propose a novel application of formal methods for SDN.

3.2   Formal Models of SDN Systems for Reachability Analysis

In this section, we propose an approach to generate valid network topologies (including the data and control plane) whose evolution over time fulfills some desired properties. To this end, we generate a meta-model of an SDN that includes the switches and the controller but also the hosts, the packets flowing through the data and control planes, and the logic behind the controller, that is, the SDN application.

To this end, we use ALLOY [16,24], a modelling and specification language and also a tool that generates model instances satisfying a set of requirements. ALLOY is a declarative language based on sets and set relations. In addition, it uses first order relational logic to describe properties and refine the models. Although, internally, the core of ALLOY tool uses a theorem prover, from the user perspective it is a completely automatic tool (similar to a model checker) that generates models that are correct w.r.t. the specification. All these characteristics make ALLOY suitable for modelling and analyzing structurally complex systems such as SDN, which can present complex and varying relations between the different network elements. The price to pay is that ALLOY models are bounded in size, i.e., it is not possible to analyze models of arbitrarily large size. Even though this is an important restriction, in practice, small models are usually sufficient to detect errors in the system design. In order to achieve our goal, we have to follow three steps. First, we have to implement the model of the static structure of a SDN; then, we have to define the dynamic behavior of the network elements; and finally, we must define the requirements and configuration of interest and run the ALLOY tool to generate valid SDN topologies. The rest of the section describes these steps in detail.

Modelling the Static Structure of an SDN

The static model of an SDN defines the elements of an SDN and the (static) relations between them. The model must abstract low-level details of an SDN so that ALLOY can run the analysis and return different topologies or configurations of the network. The set of actors constitutes the ALLOY metal-model, Fig. 4 shows a graphical description, and Fig. 5 shows the corresponding ALLOY code. The main actors are *hosts* and *switches* in the data plane, and the controllers in the control plane. These three elements are abstracted as network nodes that contain ports to connect them with other nodes using port-to-port (bidirectional) links. Although it is not explicitly reflected in the meta-model, each switch always has a specific link and a port that connects it with the controller. This connection is mainly used to configure the switches. The data transmitted between nodes are called *packets*. We define two types of packets: control packets include control plane information, such as new rules that must be installed in a specific switch,

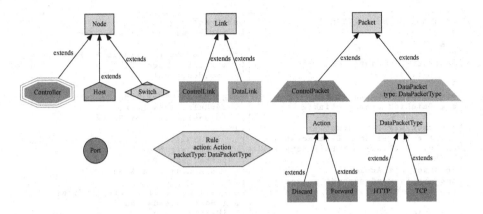

Fig. 4. Meta-model of the SDN model

or a request to know how to process a data packet. Data packets encapsulate information that must be transmitted from one host to another. Data packets also contain the source and destination hosts, their type, and their current position in the network.

Switches contain forwarding tables with *rules* that specify how to route data packets. In order to simplify the model, a rule includes the type of data packet (e.g. HTTP or FTP) and the input and output ports. The meaning of each rule is as follows: if a data packet of a particular type arrives at port *iPort*, it must be forwarded through port *oPort*. In addition, it is also possible to define rules that discard incoming data packets. When a switch has no rule to deal with a data packet, it sends a request to the controller in order to know how to process the packet. Finally, the controller can also send new rules to switches to update the routing tables.

Figure 5 shows how all these elements are defined using basic ALLOY constructors: *abstract signatures, signatures*, and *relations*. Signatures are sets whose elements are called *atoms*. Abstract signatures cannot have their own elements; they can only have them through their extensions. Relations are sets of tuples of the same arity. They are always defined in the context of a signature, which is the type of the first element of the tuples. For instance, the signature Rule has a relation iPort that relates each rule with the input port of the data packet. By default, the multiplicity of relations is one. In the example, each rule only has one iPort, but ALLOY's relations support other multiplicities such as lone (e.g. a Rule has at most one oPort), some (a Node is connected at least to another Node) and set (e.g. a Switch has zero or more Rule in its forwarding table).

ALLOY allows us to define both the static and dynamic behavior of an SDN. To this end, we include a special signature, called Time, whose atoms explicitly represent time instants. For example, we can specify that the iBuffer and oBuffer of a Host have zero or more DataPackets in each time instant.

At this point, ALLOY can generate model instances that are still far from been structurally correct. We need to add some constraints to the model, called

```
open util/ordering[Time]            abstract sig Packet{
sig Time{}                             position: Port lone -> Time
sig Port{}                          }
                                    sig DataPacket  extends Packet{
abstract sig Link{                     type: DataPacketT,
 p1,p2: Port                           src,dest:Host
}                                   }
sig CtrLink extends Link{}          sig CtrPacket extends Packet{
sig DataLink extends Link{}            newRule: lone Rule,
                                       request: lone DataPacket
abstract sig DataPacketT{}          }
one sig TCP extends DataPacketT{}
one sig HTTP extends DataPacketT{}  abstract sig Node{
                                       ports: some Port,
abstract sig Action{}                  connected: some Node
one sig Forward extends Action{}    }
one sig Discard extends Action{}    one sig Controller extends Node{}
                                    sig Host extends Node{
sig Rule{                              iBuffer: DataPacket set -> Time,
  packetType:DataPacketT,              oBuffer: DataPacket set -> Time
  iPort: Port,                      }
  action: Action,                   sig Switch extends Node{
  oPort : lone Port                    table: Rule set -> Time
}                                   }
```

Fig. 5. SDN signatures and relations in ALLOY

facts in ALLOY, to define, for instance, how the relations are constructed. In total, we have added 32 facts to the SDN model. Figure 6 shows some that define how links, ports and nodes are related.

Modelling the Dynamic Behavior of an SDN

The second step is to describe how the SDN evolves over time; for instance, how a DataPacket can be transmitted from the source to the destination Host, or how the forwarding table of a Switch is modified by the Controller. These actions, or system transitions, are specified in ALLOY with predicates. Each predicate has two input parameters t and t' that denote the time instant before and after executing the predicate, which are used to clearly state the pre- and post-conditions needed to execute the predicate, and the so-called *frame conditions* that establish the parts of the model that remain unchanged during the predicate execution. Figure 7 shows two predicates that define, respectively, how a Host sends and receives a DataPacket, and the definition of the frame conditions.

We can similarly specify the actions associated to the switches and the controller. For instance, we have defined predicates to describe how a switch forwards a data packet applying a rule installed in its forwarding table, or how a new rule is installed or updated when the controller sends a command to a switch. In addition, the actions of the controller can be more elaborate. We can describe not only how the controller receives a request from a switch but also the logic or decision making process associated to an SDN application.

Generating Valid Model Instances

The final step consists of using ALLOY analysis to generate correct model instances. These instances will differ in the network topology; that is, how the

```
fact {
//1-the ending ports of any link are different
 all l:Link| l.p1!=l.p2
//2- each port belongs to a node
 all p:Port| one node[p]
//3-each port belongs at most to a link
 all p:Port| lone link[p]
// 4- The ports of each link belong to different nodes
 all l:Link| node[l.p1]!=node[l.p2]
//5-connected is well defined
 all n:Node| n.connected = {m:Node-Controller| some l:Link|
     node[l.(p1+p2)] = n+m}
//6-Control links connect switches and Controller
 all l:Link| l in CtrLink implies one node[l.(p1+p2)] & Controller and
      one node[l.(p1+p2)] & Switch
//7-Data links connect two switches or a switch and a host
 all l:Link| l in DataLink implies some node[l.(p1+p2)] & Switch and
      Controller not in node[l.(p1+p2)]
//8-all controller links are control links
 nodeLinks[Controller] in CtrLink
//9-the controller has exactly a link to each switch
 all s:Switch| one nodeLinks[Controller] & nodeLinks[s]
}
```

Fig. 6. Examples of facts

```
pred sendPacket(t,t':Time, h:Host, pack:DataPacket){
  //pre
  some pack & h.oBuffer.t
  //post
  some p':remotePort[h.ports] | pack.position.t'=p'
  h.oBuffer.t' = h.oBuffer.t - pack
  //frame
  tablesUnmodifiedExc[none,t,t'] and packetsUnmodifiedExc[pack,t,t']
  oBuffersUnmodifiedExc[h,t,t'] and iBuffersUnmodifiedExc[none,t,t']
}
pred receivePacket(t,t':Time,h:Host,pack:DataPacket){
  //pre
  some (pack.position.t & h.ports)
  //post
  h.iBuffer.t' = h.iBuffer.t + pack
  pack.position.t'  = none
  //frame
  tablesUnmodifiedExc[none,t,t'] and packetsUnmodifiedExc[pack,t,t']
  oBuffersUnmodifiedExc[none,t,t'] and iBuffersUnmodifiedExc[h,t,t']
}
pred packetsUnmodifiedExc(pp:set Packet, t,t':Time){
   all pk:Packet-pp | pk.position.t = pk.position.t'
}
pred oBuffersUnmodifiedExc(hh:set Host, t,t':Time){
   all h:Host-hh | h.oBuffer.t = h.oBuffer.t'
}
pred iBuffersUnmodifiedExc(hh:set Host, t,t':Time){
   all h:Host-hh | h.iBuffer.t = h.iBuffer.t'
}
pred TablesUnmodifiedExc(ss: set Switch, t,t':Time){
    all s:Switch - ss | s.table.t = s.table.t'
}
```

Fig. 7. Predicates to send and receive data packets on hosts

network nodes are interconnected, and in their dynamic behaviors, for instance how packets flow through the network or how the switches' forwarding tables are updated. The ALLOY tool can run predicates and check assertions. In the first case, if the predicate is consistent, the tool generates model instances that satisfy the constraints (facts) and the predicate. In the second case, ALLOY looks for counterexamples that satisfy the model specification but not the assertion. In both cases, the ALLOY model is transformed into a set of boolean formulae that are analyzed using a SAT solver. Our objective is to produce valid SDN network topologies that can evolve over time taking into account the applications governing the SDN controller. The automatically generated network topologies and configurations can be used to test the SDN applications in real or simulated environments. To this end, we define a predicate that specifies the initial configuration of the SDN network, and the possible system transitions, which are given as non-deterministic calls to the predicates defining the dynamic behavior of the SDN. The non-deterministic choice is implemented using the disjunction logic and thus, for each time instant, only one system transition can be executed. Figure 8 shows a snapshot of a valid model instance in two different time instants (Time$0 and Time$5). To simplify the representation, we only show the data plane. Observe that in both time instants, the network topology is the same; that is, the interconnection of switches and host is the same, with the same links and ports. However, we observe changes in the relations that can evolve over time. For example, at Time$0 both data packets are in the oBuffer of Host1, while in Time$5 DataPacket1 has reached its destination and DataPacket0 is in an intermediate switch. At this point, the Switch1 does not have a rule in its table that can make the system evolve. In consequence, it has to send a request to the controller to ask how to forward the packet. The subsequent actions will depend on the SDN applications modelled.

Assertion checking in ALLOY is also useful to determine if the SDN applications are correct. For instance, if the SDN application has to discard all FTP packets transmitted from a specific host, we can check if all model instances satisfy this requirement. Otherwise, ALLOY will return a counterexample that will show why some packets are not correctly discarded.

4   Network Function Virtualization

4.1   The Technology

In 5G networks, the concept of NFV is especially important since it can entail a significant transformation for this network, reducing cost or increasing flexibility, although the most important change that NFV introduces is the possibility of providing different kinds of services and requirements on a common shared physical network through network slicing (see Sect. 2.2).

The reference architecture for NFV, represented in Fig. 9, has been proposed by ETSI in [6]. The deployment and reconfiguration of the VNFs in a cloud environment is an open challenge. This task is carried out by the Management and

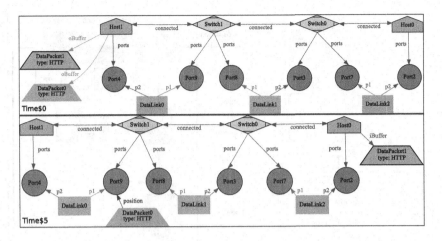

Fig. 8. Evolution over time of data packets

Orchestration entity (MANO). The left part of the figure is composed of *Operations Support System* (OSS)/*Business Support System* (BSS), *Element Manager* (EM) + VNF and by finally, *NFV Infrastructure* (NFVI) is composed of virtual/hardware computing, storage and network (the hardware supporting the Edge and Central clouds in Fig. 9). OSS/BSS are components that allow monitoring, controlling and managing different kinds of network services. EM provides network management of the virtualized and physical network elements. The VNF is an implementation of a network function that can be deployed on NFVI. The right part is composed of *Management and Orchestration* (MANO) layer, differentiating between *NFV Orchestration* (NFVO) + *VNF Manager* (VNFM) and *Virtualized Infrastructure Manager* (VIM). NFVO is responsible for orchestration and management of NFVI, software resources and realizing network services on NFVI. VNFM is responsible for control, management and monitorization of the VNF life cycle. It also controls EM. The VIM is the Virtualized Infrastructure Manager that, in most real deployments, is the well-known OpenStack software.

An Example. We illustrate the NFV architecture with an example. Figure 10 shows how a service is deployed in a network slice. We assume that the MNO offers a simple slice to deploy a video on demand service for mobile users. The slice includes network components, such as an instance of a 5G core, and some service-oriented VNFs, such as a video server and the cache function. The orchestrator (the MANO) addresses the following four phases to properly configure, deploy and terminate the service.

Phase 1: *Network Service Descriptor Processing.* The MANO "orchestrator" processes the information necessary to deploy a network slice oriented to a specific service (Netflix, in this case). This information includes the executable code of VNF (virtualized like a container, virtual machine, etc.) and the

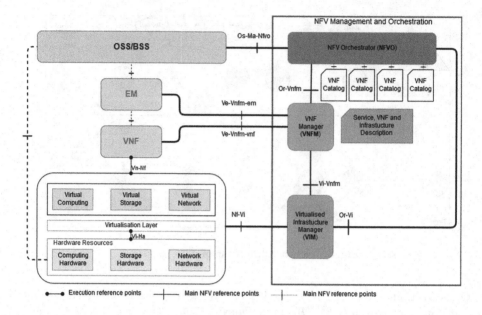

Fig. 9. ETSI MANO

descriptors of the different VNFs (VNFDs), which are defined by ETSI [7] as follows: "A VNFD is a deployment template which describes a VNF in terms of deployment and operational behavior requirements. It also contains connectivity, interface and virtualized resource requirements". Additionally, the VNF descriptor can include information about the quality of service expected by user (requirements) like the value of parameters such as delay, bandwidth, number of simultaneous users, etc. and auto-scaling properties. In cloud computing terminology, these requirements are called *Service Level Agreement* (SLAs) [6]. The fulfillment of SLAs is translated into the fulfillment of the expected quality by users (e.g. max delay between video frames and max response delay). In 5G network terminology, these quality indicators are usually referred to as *Key Performance Indicators* (KPIs) and, with less frequently, as *Quality Performance Indicators* (QPIs). The MANO also processes the *Network Service Descriptor* (NSD) [8] that consists of information used by the *NFV Orchestrator* to instantiate a *Network Service* constituted by one or more VNFs. Finally, *Network Slice Template* (NST) represents logical network function(s), resources linked to the services, and most importantly, the network capabilities that are required by services which, in fact, are closely related to *Service Level Agreement* (SLA), previously mentioned. In practice, all the descriptors are specified using description languages like TOSCA or YAML, which are widely used in cloud computing. All the information is processed to generate internal models of objects described in VNFD, NSD and NST which will be managed by the orchestrator in the next phase. Listings 1.1 and 1.2 show the code of the VNFD of a *Video on Demand* (VoD) VNF and the definition of the service type, respectively.

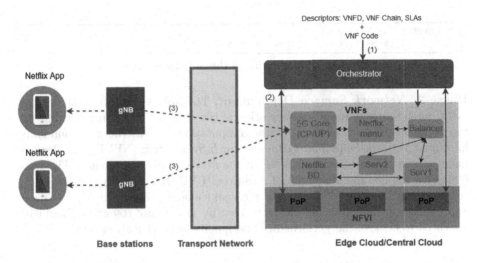

Fig. 10. Example of a slice for video on demand

```
vnfd-catalog:
    vnfd:
    -   connection-point:
        -   name: eth0
            type: VPORT
        ...
        description: ...
        mgmt-interface: ...
        name: slice_VoD_vnfd
        vdu:
        -   count: 1
            id: vdu1
            image: UbuntuVoD
            interface:
            -   external-connection-point-ref: eth0
                ...
                virtual-interface:
                ...
            monitoring-param:
                    -   id: metric_vdu1_cpu
                        nfvi-metric: cpu_utilization
            name: slice_VoD_vnfd-VM
            vm-flavor:
                memory-mb: 2048
                storage-gb: 100
                vcpu-count: 2
        monitoring-param:
        -   id: metric_vim_vnf1_cpu
            name: metric_vim_vnf1_cpu
            aggregation-type: AVERAGE
            vdu-monitoring-param:
                vdu-ref: vdu1
                vdu-monitoring-param-ref: metric_vdu1_cpu
        ...
```

Listing 1.1. Excerpt of a VNFD

```
-    SNSSAI-identifier:
         slice-service-type: eMBB/URLLC/mMTC
```

Listing 1.2. Definition of the slice service type

Phase 2: *Network Service Deployment.* The MANO performs the deployment, inter-connection and configuration of the chain of VNFs interacting with the points of presence of the operator computational infrastructure, commonly known as *Network Functions Virtualization Infrastructure* (NFVI). The deployment consists of locating each VNF at a suitable point of presence. The configuration implies the allocation of resources (CPU, RAM, disk) and the inter-connection with other VNFs and/or physical elements. Then, the MANO must apply some optimization algorithm to identify how many resources should be allocated to achieve the performance and quality of service given by the SLA.

Phase 3: *Network Service Execution and Re-configuration.* In this phase, the VNFs implementing the network and the service functionality are running, and the final service users start using the service uninterruptedly for days, weeks or months. Some examples of services are the distribution of high-resolution video (such as the popular service Netflix shown in Fig. 10), private communications for security forces, an augmented reality to offer sightseeing activities, remote control for critical infrastructures, etc. In this phase, the number of users and their location may vary, producing a changing network environment. Moreover, the network and computational resources can be modified due to the deployment or elimination of other services. The orchestrator must monitor that VNFs fulfill the SLAs so that users receive the expected quality (KPIs or QPIs). In addition, the orchestrator must re-locate or re-configure VNFs, if necessary.

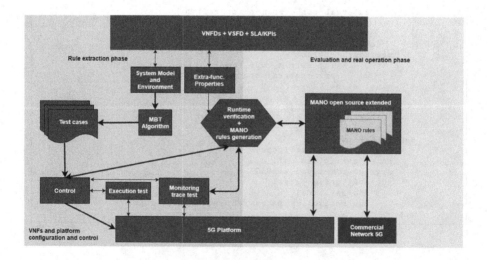

Fig. 11. Overall approach.

Currently, the algorithms that perform these tasks still admit a quite margin of improvement.

Phase 4: *Network Service Termination.* This phase is not represented in Fig. 10. It is devoted to the release of the resources previously allocated to the service, as well as the elimination of VNFs images. These actions are carried out when users are not expected to be connected for a long period of time, and thus, the elimination and subsequent creation of resources is possible.

4.2   Model Based Testing and Runtime Verification to Support Flexible Placement and Reconfiguration of VNFs

We now face the challenge of automatically generating useful information to help the orchestrator decide about the deployment, configuration and re-configuration of VNFs. To do this, it is necessary to use the description of the VNFs and the service level agreements for each service (SLA) to predict the suitable deployment that satisfies the SLA. This problem has been previously addressed with different estimation tools [25,29,30,34]. However, in these previous approaches, the main focus is the use of computational resources. They do not consider the impact of a realistic 5G network on the final QoS perceived by the users.

Our goal is to develop a novel learning method to specialize the orchestrator taking the whole end-to-end network into account; that is, considering the users and the communication component. We propose using different formal methods to generate and test the orchestrator decisions, making use of a realistic end-to-end 5G network to run the VNFs. In particular, we combine formal methods *model-based testing, model checking* and *runtime verification* to carry out a runtime analysis of extra-functional properties (related to time and resource utilization) which will be evaluated over event sequences which correspond to the executions of network service.

Figure 11 shows our approach to generate the so-called *book of rules* of a MANO in order to manage a specific service according to the requirements and performance specified in the SLA. The approach has two well differentiated phases. The first one is devoted to the extraction of the MANO rules using model-based testing and run-time verification techniques. The second phase focuses on the validation of the rules over an emulated 5G environment. Both phases have the VNF and service descriptors (VNFDs and VSFDs)as input, as well as the SLA. Both phases can be iterated several times in order to gradually refine the rules generated.

The first phase is shown on the left part of Fig. 11. The VNFDs and VSFDs are transformed into a model of the service combined with a non-deterministic model of the MANO that includes a wide variety of rules to be applied to each network scenario. With this model, we automatically generate test cases that show different management rules for different network scenarios. The VNFs pass these test cases in a controlled environment, a testing platform for 5G, where they can be monitored. We use runtime verification techniques to determine whether the service and the VNFs satisfy the SLA. To do this, SLAs are translated into a set of extra-functional properties (the runtime monitors) that evaluate whether the execution of each test case matches the desired SLA. The (non-)correct test cases help us to obtain new management rules for the MANO satisfying the extra-functional properties.

The objective of the second phase (shown on the right part of Fig. 11) is to validate the synthesized rules in a production environment. To this end, the rules are installed on a real MANO that manages and orchestrates the 5G testing platform (and that can even handle a commercial 5G network). Again, using the runtime verification engine, we can check the suitability of the synthesized rules during a normal operation of the service.

We propose running multiple iterations of the approach. In each iteration, we will refine the NFV and MANO models making use of the results of the previous iteration. These refined models can be used to extract new test cases that produce more precise rules. In the following section, we present some preliminary models of the NFVs and MANO.

4.3   Modeling the MANO

We assume that the MANO model consists of a number of MANO (sub-)models that execute concurrently. Each sub-model manages a unique service deployed on different points of presence (PoPs) to which users are connected. In consequence, in this section, we focus on the description of one of these sub-models. In the following text, to simplify the presentation, we simply call it MANO model.

The MANO model is a state machine that responds to events, provided by the infrastructure platform, executing functions to preserve the required SLA. Thus, the MANO and the infrastructure intensively communicate with each other over time. In addition, a complementary functionality of the MANO model is to periodically inspect the state of the infrastructure to carry out reconfiguration actions, if needed, even though no events are fired.

Figure 12 contains a prototype implementation of our proposal using Uppaal timed automata. State s0 is the initial state of the monitor. At this state, the automaton may receive events such as alarmCPU90 and newUser from the infrastructure through different synchronization channels. The first event occurs when the platform detects that some instance is reaching the 90% in the CPU usage. The second one is a notification that a new user has connected to the service. The monitor responds to the first event by transiting to state s2. During the transition, the identifier of the PoP which has provoked the alarm is recorded in variable eid. The monitor also searches for a new PoP, with more resources, that can hold a new instance of the service, if needed. From s2, the automaton can go to states s3, s4, s6 and NO_RESOURCES. This last state is an error which should never be reached. The rest of the states represent non-exclusive alternatives for the monitor: to increment the CPU resources in the PoP where the instance which fired the alarm is located, to deploy a new service instance and balance the users, to migrate the instance to a different PoP with enough CPU resources.

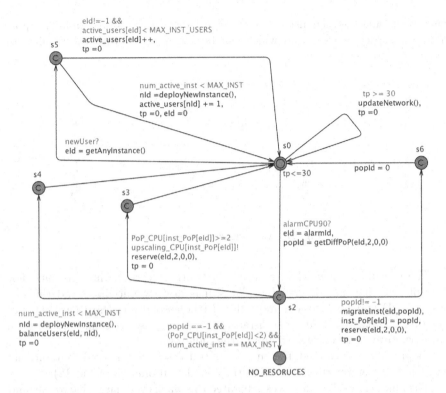

Fig. 12. Uppaal MANO model

Similarly, the monitor responds to the **newUser** event transiting to state **s5** and finding an instance which can hold it. From **s5**, the automaton can jump to the initial state through two different transitions: assigning the new user to an existing service instance or deploying a new service instance for the user. As in the previous case, if both transitions are enabled, the automaton may select any of them in a non-deterministic way.

Finally, observe that the automaton has a clock variable **tp** that is used to periodically check the state of the network and update it, if necessary. Currently, we use a bi-dimensional array with the network parameters of interest that contain the network state at three ordered previous time instants. This information may be used, for instance, to discover when a user may have disconnected to release its resources.

We have not included transitions that deal with alarms due to the RAM or HDD usage in the model of Fig. 12 to simplify the automaton. In addition, it is worth noting that the model is parametric w.r.t. a number of constants that have to be calibrated such as the thresholds to fire alarms, the maximum number of service instances and users (**MAX_INST**, **MAX_INST_USERS**) and so on.

The concurrent execution of the MANO model and the infrastructure produces a set of traces (sequence of infrastructure states) that constitute the test cases to be analyzed against the SLA. Figure 13 contains an example of a possible infrastructure execution which can be synchronized with the monitor of Fig. 12 to produce test cases.

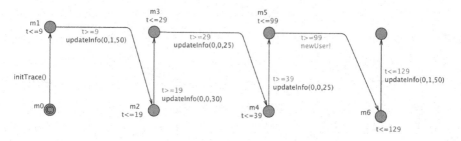

Fig. 13. An infrastructure execution

The execution shows changes in the network at certain time instants. For example, at time instant t=9 the platform is already initialized and the values of HDD and RAM usage are updated (the second and third parameter of function updateInfo). At time instant t=99, a new user is connected and the infrastructure sends event newUser to the monitor.

As previously described, the analysis of test cases may be used to iteratively improve the monitor rules (the transitions in the automaton of Fig. 12).

The number of different traces generated this way is very large due to the non-deterministic character of the monitor, and the range of values of the network variables. A way of pruning these traces is to use properties (described, for instance, in some temporal logic) to discard some non-interesting behaviors. For instance, we could add the TCTL property "A[](not monitor.s3)" to the monitor to generate test cases in which the monitor has carried out at least an upscaling_CPU task. The Uppaal model checker tries to check if no trace is eventually at state s3. The counterexamples for this property are precisely the test cases of interest wrt the property specified.

Table 1. Problems faced by SDN verification tools

Problems faced	Related work
Networks with multiple protocols	[17,20]
Networks with multiple SDN slices	[1,17,20]
Networks with multiple OpenFlow controllers/domains	[1]
Scalability	[4]
Unbounded space of input packets and control messages	[4,21]
Flow tables updating at runtime in switches	[2,5,18,21]
Interleaved processing of packets/events	[2,4,5,13,21]
Topology changes (robustness during an execution)	[2]

5   Related Work

The formal analysis of SDNs is a challenging task as they are distributed and open event-driven systems. Given the separation of data and control planes and the existence of a new application plane that provides the control intelligence, most works focus on analyzing SDN problems from the perspective of one of these planes, without considering the relation between them. In [19], we reviewed the state of the art of formal methods and tools to support SDN. Table 1 shows a list of problems addressed and related works. These proposals differ not only regarding the network plane and the problem faced, but they also use different formal methods, such as model checking [1,4,17,21], theorem proving [2,5,20], runtime analysis [18] or traditional network debugging [13].

The efficient management and orchestration of VNFs in the context of 5G networks is an interesting and challenging problem that can be addressed from different perspectives.

Currently, some proposals focus on predicting the performance behavior of VNF chains (services deployed interconnecting VNFs) deployed in the cloud without considering the role of the mobile network. However, the network and the service users are an important part of the environment that stimulates and interacts with the VNFs, and thus, they must be taken into account to predict the service performance in terms of extra-functional properties, Service Level Agreements (SLAs), Key Performance Indicators (KPIs) and Quality Performance Indicators (QPIs).

Peuster and Karl [29] proposed a methodology to characterize the performance of VNF and VNF chains prior to service deployment that can be part of a DevOps methodology. To this end, the authors execute the VNFs in different emulated network configurations and monitor how different performance parameters evolve. The paper includes an evaluation of a profiler prototype built on the emulation platform MeDICINE, which is based on an extension of Mininet that can execute production-ready VNFs (given as Dockers containers) in user-defined network topologies. The prototype can emulate the effect of the network and other services that compete for the resources. However, the emulation is limited by the capacity of the host machine that runs Mininet, which is far from emulating a real 5G network. The author states that the profile of the VNF can be used to improve the decisions carried out by the MANO, but there is no insight of how to transform the profile into MANO rules.

Gym [30] is other framework for VNF profiling. In this case, the VNF is tested under different resource configurations of the infrastructure, which is mainly composed of servers where the VNFs runs. However, the infrastructure lacks the components of a mobile network. The authors' objective is to use the framework to build testbeds for NFVs and services extending the framework with new components.

The characterization of VNFs performance has also been addressed from the analytical point of view. For instance, the tool Probius [25] aims to detect abnormal behaviors of NFVs due to performance uncertainties. Probius automatically generates all possible service chains with the given VNFs, collects and analyzes performance-related features of each chain, and analyzes performance problems through anomaly detection and graph-based behavior analysis, and is able to point out the reasons of the VNFs performance issues.

The project 5GTANGO [34] proposed a testing approach for VNFs based on TTCN-3 test cases that can be manually or automatically generated using model-based testing techniques. However, the authors do not discuss which entities are included in the model, or what requirements guide the test generation algorithms.

In [25,29,34], the VNFs, the services and the test cases run in an emulated infrastructure that cannot properly represent a 5G network.

Formal methods have been also used to verify VNFs and VNF chains against reachability and safety properties in order to determine whether services are interfering, are isolated, or are accessed by unauthorized users. In [28] and [33], the analysis of properties is based on SMT solvers, such as Z3, combined with static analysis and symbolic model checking. These approaches accept a logic formula as input and find the values (if any) that make the formula satisfiable. The main limitation of these approaches is the transformation of the VNF code into a model in the solver's input language. This task is not trivial and is error prone. To minimize this problem, in [22], a tool to automatically extract the VNF model from its code is proposed. The approach is limited to VNFs implemented using a set of Java libraries to facilitate the coding task.

6 Conclusions

The increasing presence of software in mobile communication networks, like 5G networks, requires the use of rigorous methods to ensure the correct behavior. The formal methods community can find here new challenges to demonstrate the applicability of well-known techniques for modelling and automatic analysis. We have introduced work in progress in the general topic of automated generation and specialization of formal models that can help the deployment of the SDN and NFV parts of the network. We use two different modelling languages because the objectives for each domain are different. The use of Alloy to model SDN overpasses the state space explosion problem of model checking when checking for valid network configurations. The use of SAT solvers in this context has been demonstrated with a middle size network; however we still need to confirm the feasibility of the approach with more complex configurations. The use of UPPAAL to model the NFV part is still a proof concept and more work will be done to produce experimental results. One future work is to analyze whether a single formal method could support the two domains considered in the 5G network. We are currently working on implementing some of these methods to be validated in realistic research networks in the context of the European H2020 research projects EuWireless and 5GENESIS.

References

1. Al-Shaer, E., Al-Haj, S.: FlowChecker: configuration analysis and verification of federated OpenFlow infrastructures. In: Proceedings of the 3rd ACM Workshop on Assurable and Usable Security Configuration, SafeConfig 2010, pp. 37–44. ACM, New York, October 2010. https://doi.org/10.1145/1866898.1866905
2. Ball, T., et al.: VeriCon: towards verifying controller programs in software-defined networks. SIGPLAN Not. **49**(6), 282–293 (2014). https://doi.org/10.1145/2666356.2594317
3. Bochmann, G., Rayner, D., West, C.H.: Some notes on the history of protocol engineering. Comput. Netw. **54**(18), 3197–3209 (2010). https://doi.org/10.1016/j.comnet.2010.05.019
4. Canini, M., Venzano, D., Perešíni, P., Kostić, D., Rexford, J.: A NICE way to test OpenFlow applications. In: Proceedings of the 9th USENIX Symposium on Networked Systems Design and Implementation (NSDI 2012), San Jose, CA, pp. 127–140. USENIX, April 2012
5. El-Hassany, A., Miserez, J., Bielik, P., Vanbever, L., Vechev, M.: SDNRacer: concurrency analysis for software-defined networks. SIGPLAN Not. **51**(6), 402–415 (2016). https://doi.org/10.1145/2980983.2908124
6. ETSI GS NFV: Network Functions Virtualization (NFV); Terminology for Main Concepts in NFV. Technical report ETSI GS NFV 003, European Telecommunications Standards Institute (ETSI), August 2018. v1.4.1
7. ETSI GS NFV-IFA: Network Functions Virtualization (NFV); Management and Orchestration; VNF Descriptor and Packaging Specification. Technical report ETSI GS NFV-IFA 011, European Telecommunications Standards Institute (ETSI), August 2018. v2.5.1
8. ETSI GS NFV-MAN: Network Functions Virtualization (NFV); Management and Orchestration. Technical report ETSI GS NFV-MAN 001, European Telecommunications Standards Institute (ETSI), December 2014. v1.1.1
9. ETSI TS 123 501: 5G; System Architecture for the 5G System. Technical report ETSI TS 123 501, European Telecommunications Standards Institute (ETSI), June 2018. v15.2.0
10. Gallardo, M.M., Martínez, J., Merino, P.: Applying formal methods to telecommunication services with active networks (2013)
11. Gnesi, S., Margaria, T.: Formal Methods for Industrial Critical Systems: A Survey of Applications, 1st edn. IEEE, Washington, D.C. (2013)
12. Gude, N., et al.: NOX: towards an operating system for networks. SIGCOMM Comput. Commun. Rev. **38**(3), 105–110 (2008). https://doi.org/10.1145/1384609.1384625. Tool https://github.com/noxrepo/nox
13. Handigol, N., Heller, B., Jeyakumar, V., Maziéres, D., McKeown, N.: Where is the debugger for my software-defined network? In: Proceedings of the 1st Workshop on Hot Topics in Software Defined Networks, HotSDN 2012, pp. 55–60. ACM, New York, August 2012. https://doi.org/10.1145/2342441.2342453
14. Holzmann, G.: The Spin Model Checker: Primer and Reference Manual, 1st edn. Addison-Wesley Professional, Boston (2003)
15. Holzmann, G.J.: Design and Validation of Computer Protocols. Prentice-Hall Inc., Upper Saddle River (1991)
16. Jackson, D.: Software Abstractions - Logic, Language, and Analysis. MIT Press (2006). http://mitpress.mit.edu/catalog/item/default.asp?ttype=2&tid=10928

17. Kazemian, P., Varghese, G., McKeown, N.: Header space analysis: static checking for networks. In: 9th USENIX Symposium on Networked Systems Design and Implementation (NSDI 2012), Lombard, IL, pp. 113–126. USENIX, April 2012
18. Khurshid, A., Zhou, W., Caesar, M., Godfrey, P.B.: VeriFlow: verifying network-wide invariants in real time. SIGCOMM Comput. Commun. Rev. 42(4), 467–472 (2012). https://doi.org/10.1145/2377677.2377766
19. Lavado, L., Panizo, L., Gallardo, M., Merino, P.: A characterisation of verification tools for software defined networks. J. Reliable Intell. Environ. 3(3), 189–207 (2017). https://doi.org/10.1007/s40860-017-0045-y
20. Mai, H., Khurshid, A., Agarwal, R., Caesar, M., Godfrey, P.B., King, S.T.: Debugging the data plane with anteater. SIGCOMM Comput. Commun. Rev. 41(4), 290–301 (2011). https://doi.org/10.1145/2043164.2018470
21. Majumdar, R., Tetali, S.D., Wang, Z.: Kuai: a model checker for software-defined networks. In: Formal Methods in Computer-Aided Design (FMCAD), Lausanne, Switzerland, pp. 163–170. IEEE, October 2014. https://doi.org/10.1109/FMCAD.2014.6987609
22. Marchetto, G., Sisto, R., Virgilio, M., Yusupov, J.: A framework for user-friendly verification-oriented VNF modeling. In: 2017 IEEE 41st Annual Computer Software and Applications Conference (COMPSAC), vol. 1, pp. 517–522, July 2017. https://doi.org/10.1109/COMPSAC.2017.16
23. McKeown, N., et al.: OpenFlow: enabling innovation in campus networks. SIGCOMM Comput. Commun. Rev. 38(2), 69–74 (2008). https://doi.org/10.1145/1355734.1355746
24. Milicevic, A., Near, J.P., Kang, E., Jackson, D.: Alloy*: a general-purpose higher-order relational constraint solver. Formal Methods Syst. Des. 1–32 (2017). https://doi.org/10.1007/s10703-016-0267-2
25. Nam, J., Seo, J., Shin, S.: Probius: automated approach for VNF and service chain analysis in software-defined NFV. In: Proceedings of the Symposium on SDN Research, SOSR 2018, pp. 14:1–14:13. ACM (2018). https://doi.org/10.1145/3185467.3185495
26. Nunes, B.A., Mendonca, M., Nguyen, X.N., Obraczka, K., Turletti, T.: A survey of software-defined networking: past, present, and future of programmable networks. IEEE Commun. Surv. Tutorials 16(3), 1617–1634 (2014). https://doi.org/10.1109/SURV.2014.012214.00180
27. Open Networking Lab: POX (Python Network Controller) Wiki (2013). https://openflow.stanford.edu/x/TYBr
28. Panda, A., Lahav, O., Argyraki, K.J., Sagiv, M., Shenker, S.: Verifying isolation properties in the presence of middleboxes. CoRR abs/1409.7687 (2014)
29. Peuster, M., Karl, H.: Understand your chains: towards performance profile-based network service management. In: 2016 Fifth European Workshop on Software-Defined Networks (EWSDN), pp. 7–12. IEEE Computer Society (2016). https://doi.org/10.1109/EWSDN.2016.9
30. Rosa, R.V., Bertoldo, C., Rothenberg, C.E.: Take your VNF to the gym: a testing framework for automated NFV performance benchmarking. IEEE Commun. Mag. 55(9), 110–117 (2017). https://doi.org/10.1109/MCOM.2017.1700127
31. Rudin, H., West, C.H., Zafiropulo, P.: Automated protocol validation: one chain of development. Comput. Netw. (1976) 2(4), 373–380 (1978)
32. Shenker, S., Casado, M., Koponen, T., McKeown, N., et al.: The future of networking, and the past of protocols. Open Netw. Summit 20 (2011)

33. Spinoso, S., Virgilio, M., John, W., Manzalini, A., Marchetto, G., Sisto, R.: Formal verification of virtual network function graphs in an SP-DevOps context. In: Dustdar, S., Leymann, F., Villari, M. (eds.) ESOCC 2015. LNCS, vol. 9306, pp. 253–262. Springer, Cham (2015). https://doi.org/10.1007/978-3-319-24072-5_18

34. Zhao, M., et al.: Verification and validation framework for 5G network services and apps. In: 2017 IEEE Conference on Network Function Virtualization and Software Defined Networks (NFV-SDN), pp. 321–326, November 2017. https://doi.org/10.1109/NFV-SDN.2017.8169878

Author Index

Printed in the United States
By Bookmasters